CW01022620

Is International Law International?

More Comments—

"Asking the disarming question of whether 'international law is international,' Anthea Roberts takes readers on an ingenious tour of the global flow of people and ideas in international law, the role of nationalism and transnational hierarchies in creating unequal and 'divisible colleges,' and the implications for foreign policy and for the future of international law. The book is built on painstaking research into the educational background of international law scholars, where they publish and in what languages, how international law casebooks and treatises differ both within the 'west' and from the materials in China and Russia. It is a stellar contribution to international law, the study of globalization and legal education, comparative law, international relations, and the sociology of legal knowledge."

Bryant Garth, Chancellor's Professor of Law and Co-Director, Center for Empirical Research on the Legal Profession, University of California, Irvine School of Law, United States

"Anthea Roberts has raised a fundamental issue that both international lawyers and decision-makers cannot afford to ignore in this era of shifting power. This issue is whether international law is 'international,' as people might have taken for granted for decades or centuries, and how the 'international' is likely to evolve with the rise of new great powers, like China. Her perspective is absolutely unique. Textbooks and casebooks, educational backgrounds, academic publications, and connections to practice—factors that have a significant influence on how international lawyers construct their understanding of the field but whose importance are often overlooked—are painstakingly collected, well-organized and cogently analyzed to support her arguments. What Roberts exhibits, through this book, is not only the strength of her academic insight but her ability to recognize and understand the perspectives of others."

Cai Congyan, Professor of international law of Xiamen University School of Law, China

"The results of Anthea Roberts's investigation sound an alarm for all stakeholders in the field of International Law: the author calls on all of us to recognize the necessity of tearing down the mask of 'internationality' from the discipline in its current state and paves the way for changes towards a truly international International Law. Thoughtful and inspiring."

Vera Rusinova, Professor of the Chair for Public and Private International Law, National Research University, The Higher School of Economics, Russia

"Roberts's groundbreaking study brings important and new insights into the sociology of the production of international law. It charts the regional and cultural islands that dot this supposedly cosmopolitan sea and provides a deep critique of the field's universalist aspirations/pretensions. It is essential reading for anyone interested in the international law project, whether working from the inside or as an external observer."

Paul Stephan, John C. Jeffries, Jr., Distinguished Professor of Law, University of Virginia School of Law, United States

"For a French international lawyer who by necessity has to work in (at least) two languages and navigate different cultural universes, there is no doubt that international law is indeed international, as a crucible of diverse legal cultures. Yet, as Anthea Roberts's (both intrepid and convincing) book demonstrates, in fact international law needs to be more international and less imperialist in the ways it is formed, practiced and conceptualized. From that perspective, Roberts's invigorating analysis of national approaches to international law provides a salutary reappraisal of the law of nations that will no doubt frame the field in the future."

Mathias Forteau, Professor of Public Law, University of Paris Ouest, Nanterre La Défense, France

"International law is full of myths. One of these is the global, universal character of the discipline that distances it from narrow national interests and mindsets. Anthea Roberts's book investigates this myth in depth and shows how, contrary to the self-depiction of much of the discipline, international legal scholarship differs heavily across countries, is shaped by national traditions and institutional structures, and often follows patterns of dominance in the international system. This is a major achievement that should lead us to ask major questions about international law in a different light. Perhaps the most pressing of these—is international law distinct from international politics, and how?—will now have to be tackled in a far more nuanced way. Thinking about international law will never be quite the same again."

Nico Krisch, Professor of International Law, the Graduate Institute Geneva, Switzerland

"Anthea Roberts's book has the potential of re-defining how we think about international law and its realities, both beyond and within the West. It shows us the field of international law in a new light and will open new directions for international legal research in the coming decades."

Lauri Mälksoo, Professor of International Law at the University of Tartu, Estonia, and the author of *Russian Approaches to International Law* (Oxford 2015)

Is International Law International?

Anthea Roberts

OXFORD
UNIVERSITY PRESS

OXFORD
UNIVERSITY PRESS

Oxford University Press is a department of the University of Oxford. It furthers the University's objective of excellence in research, scholarship, and education by publishing worldwide. Oxford is a registered trademark of Oxford University Press in the UK and certain other countries.

Published in the United States of America by Oxford University Press
198 Madison Avenue, New York, NY 10016, United States of America.

Library of Congress Cataloging-in-Publication Data
Names: Roberts, Anthea (Writer on international law), author.
Title: Is international law international? / Anthea Roberts.
Description: Oxford [UK] ; New York : Oxford University Press, 2017. | Includes bibliographical
   references and index.
Identifiers: LCCN 2017017662 | ISBN 9780190696412 ((hardback) : alk. paper)
Subjects: LCSH: International law.
Classification: LCC KZ3410 .R625 2017 | DDC 341—dc23
LC record available at https://lccn.loc.gov/2017017662

9 8 7 6 5 4 3 2 1

Printed by Edwards Brothers Malloy, United States of America

Note to Readers
This publication is designed to provide accurate and authoritative information in regard to the subject matter covered. It is based upon sources believed to be accurate and reliable and is intended to be current as of the time it was written. It is sold with the understanding that the publisher is not engaged in rendering legal, accounting, or other professional services. If legal advice or other expert assistance is required, the services of a competent professional person should be sought. Also, to confirm that the information has not been affected or changed by recent developments, traditional legal research techniques should be used, including checking primary sources where appropriate.

(Based on the Declaration of Principles jointly adopted by a Committee of the American Bar Association and a Committee of Publishers and Associations.)

Contents

List of Figures

List of Tables

Foreword

AT MEETINGS OF, say, the International Law Commission (ILC) or at annual sessions of the UN General Assembly's Sixth (legal) Committee, colleagues from all over the world often reminisce about their time as students at Yale or Columbia Law School, Harvard, perhaps Oxford, exchanging memories about Myres McDougal, Louis Henkin, Abram Chayes, Humphrey Waldock, or about when they were examined on Oppenheim's International Law or Schachter, Pugh, & Henkin's International Law. At conferences attended by international lawyers it is easy to testify to the thickness of the sociological reality of that "invisible college." Access to the college opens as soon as one is able to engage in small talk about the eccentricities of teachers or about the experiences of student life one shares with those already on the inside. The culture of international law has grown around a limited number of academic centers. It is really hard to enter the profession without an LLM or a doctorate from one of a handful of law schools in the Anglophone world, or maybe Paris, or at least without having taken a course at The Hague, or having spent some time at the Max Planck Institute in Heidelberg. No matter where one has been born, what school one has attended, access to the college is about being socialized into a professional vocabulary and a set of cultural mores conveyed through a well-known but narrow academic pathway.

No doubt the socialization is very useful. When legal advisers meet to coordinate positions before some conference, they regularly refer to the special ethos and camaraderie that enables them to cooperate independently of the state of the relations of their countries. Even as politicians quarrel, international lawyers address each other in collegial tones suggesting they share something beyond technical expertise; sometimes they express this in slightly grandiose themes about a "legal community" to which they feel accountable and which manifests itself when informal conversation unavoidably turns to the early days of one's career, or to the time at law school when one was examined in this or that doctrine that then seemed obscure and distant but now has become part of the professional acquis. What was it that made one choose this career and not the perhaps more lucrative one in corporate or tax law? One wanted to work for something "bigger"—peace and justice—and it was hardly a disadvantage that one got to travel around while doing this. Silent knowledge about the professional hard core is visible for example when countries make choices for their counsel in cases in the International Court of Justice or some arbitration tribunal. The team should always include some of the usual suspects from Oxford, Cambridge, Harvard, and Paris, men (indeed, still predominantly men) with experience in a large number of cases, seasoned members of the college, like the judges or arbitrators in front of whom they are expected to perform. These are professionals who can be encountered wherever the "international" happens—Geneva, New York, Brussels, and the odd conference in some more exotic capital. The market value of intimacy among members of the college is not hard to understand.

And yet, international law is taught at hundreds of law schools to thousands upon thousands of students most of whom will never have access, and may not even desire access, to that college. This may be owing to simple reasons of language. For those not trained in English or French (or possibly Spanish), the doors will remain closed. In countries where international law is taught as just another aspect of the domestic public law—such as US "foreign relations law"—the understanding of the field will remain parochial. As Anthea Roberts demonstrates in this wonderfully enlightening work, the "international" means different things in different places. And "international law," too, varies depending on the location from which it is examined, taught, or practiced. The book also demonstrates that the various understandings of the "international" do not form a harmonious pattern or, in United Nation's jargon, follow the principle of "equitable geographical distribution." Some understandings are weightier that others. Much of how "international law" is understood has come to depend on how those at Anglophone academic institutions think of it. On the other hand, countries such as Russia and France remain persistent objectors to that hegemony—to some extent at the cost of isolation from the professional center of the field. In many places, effort is made to combine hegemonic understandings with points of local interest and preference. Hence the incipient debate on "comparative international law"—then the need to focus on the varied ways in which international law is understood, taught, or practiced in different places.

What a welcome event the publication of this book is! None of us can hereafter teach international law quite in the way we used to, without paying attention to the questions "whose international law is it?" and "where has it come from?" What aspects of the world does it highlight, and what does it seem to ignore? Nor can we perhaps expect students or colleagues, or the public at large, to commit to the field quite as innocently as they may have done. It is the great merit of this work that it finally opens a view to study the understandings of "law" and "international law" that parade in various parts of the world, as well as the constitution of the "invisible college" that follows the hegemonic understanding. We now have the opportunity to view the "particular" that is usually hidden behind the field's universalist vocabulary. Roberts began this project by wanting to know "is international law international?" By engaging a group of collaborators to conduct an empirical study of international law training around the world, she is able to identify the centers that radiate their understandings of "law" everywhere, as well as those that persist in following their domestic lights, carrying out their conversations in their domestic context. She has examined questions such as: Where do "international" students go to learn international law? Where have their teachers been taught? How are textbooks written; what cases are usually referred to? What is the relationship between the international lawyers of a country, and its foreign policy elite? The result is not only a fascinating picture of the constitution of the hegemonic "international" but also a wider set of contrasts between different understandings of the field, techniques of teaching, and ideas of professional excellence.

The old academic debate on "universalism versus particularism" deals with a hugely important item—our ability to transcend our idiosyncrasies and backgrounds, our capacity to see the world "through the eyes of others." In a time of rising nationalism, xenophobia, and fear of "otherness," the importance of that theme has been accentuated. International lawyers have often adopted, expressly or not, the (liberal) view that they are in possession of a truly universal perspective of the "rule of law" in international affairs—a neutral, impartial representation of the world. That view has been questioned from historical, logical, and legal perspectives. Postcolonial scholarship has pointed to the way key notions of the field reflect European—or perhaps it is better to say "Western"—legal and political concepts and ideas and that many of its practices have been developed in the process of expanding or seeking to maintain Europe's predominance over the rest of the world. A philosophical critique has pointed to the impossibility of reaching a "view from nowhere": every truth is based on some set of propositions or techniques that are themselves particular and contestable. The ability to speak "truth" about the law is a type of power and different truth-regimes (like different legal regimes) are engaged in a constant struggle (for power) to be recognized as speaking that truth. And legal analyses have shown that the meaning and application of international legal doctrines, principles, concepts, and treaty provisions are dependent on interpretative priorities and presumptions that reflect larger—but specific and often contested—views and assumptions about the nature and objectives of international law.

Such perspectives challenge international law's "universalism." This painstaking and extremely valuable study by Anthea Roberts supports and highlights, indeed clinches, the view of international law as a product of specific academic and professional institutions situated predominantly in the developed West. Ideals of professional competence are hardly formed out of an equitable compromise between legal systems. Instead, like most things in the world, they are the result of the complex process of globalization of particular views and institutions, modeled after Western views and institutions, and resistance to such globalization. Does this then undermine international law in some way? Has a hidden secret now been revealed so that nothing more is left to do than turn off the lights at international law departments in law schools and foreign ministries? Of course not. Skepticism emerges from excessive ambition, it is the dark brother of utopia. No idea about government, no profession, or institutional practice emerges "from nowhere." Everything has a history and a background. To believe in universal truths in matters of law or government is to be in the grip of a baseless and ultimately dangerous illusion. A realistic pursuit of universality, the effort to see the world "through others' eyes," can only begin from a recognition of the limitedness of one's own vision. This need not mean that the sociology of knowledge should become the queen of the sciences (though its limited role in the law school is lamentable), only that for a good professional ("good" in the technical as well as the political sense—the two being inextricable) it is important to understand that what has made one such is the specific experience and education that one has received, and that they are the product of a world that is anything but "neutral, or impartial" or even "just."

As human beings, international lawyers access the world from particular standpoints. If the profession does have the ambition to transgress those standpoints, it must first become aware of them. This study helps its readers to do just that. It makes express the hidden knowledge of the best professionals, namely, that much teaching of international law remains intensely local, and that access to the most cherished "international" law jobs is open only through a certain path. But in showing us international law's "particularity" it also opens the way for dealing openly with that fact. "Comparative international law" need not be established as a special discipline—it is enough that there are courses within international law that compare the different (and similar) understandings of international law in different parts of the world. Comparison may easily end up suggesting that the internal coherence of the entities being compared is greater than it is, their boundaries higher and less porous that may actually be the case. Surely it is an absolutely central message of this book that there is work to be done so as to advance toward a world of cosmopolitan equality, universal rights, and global justice, objectives that the best professionals have always emphasized. Nothing here undermines that goal. But we now know that the work must begin "at home." International law did not descend from the sky to settle our conflicts or to provide a "neutral framework" for our debates. Its rules and institutions, ideas and symbols, its cultural and professional mores bear the history of a divided and unjust world. It would be a miracle if that burden were not borne also in the professional education that we carry and reproduce as part of what we do. But thanks to Roberts, we can no longer pretend to be in ignorance about that matter but can re-engage the best "universalist" practice available to us—namely, conversation with colleagues, with academic and funding institutions, in ministries and law schools regarding how to open access to the invisible college for those who previously could not even dream of such a possibility. No doubt there is a need to make the college eventually visible, to debate its biases and reform its ideals and its practices so that the "international" of the future would be less a reflection of past privilege than present needs. With this book, we now have the tools to begin that work.

Martti Koskenniemi
March 2017

Preface

DOMESTIC LEGAL SYSTEMS differ, yet lawyers often assume that international law is universal. But my experiences as an international lawyer who has studied, taught, and worked in three jurisdictions—Australia, the United Kingdom, and the United States—have made me conscious of national differences in approaches to international law, even among three Western, English-speaking, common law, liberal democratic states. This awareness led me to wonder how different international law might look from the perspective of those who study, teach, or apply it in non-Western, non-English-speaking, noncommon law, and/or nonliberal democratic states.

I was first struck by different national approaches when I began practicing at a US law firm in 2003. One of my first assignments was to write a brief about the Alien Tort Statute (ATS) for the US Supreme Court case *Sosa v. Alvarez-Machain*.[1] I was excited because I had heard that the ATS involved enforcement by US courts of customary international law, and enforcement is the Achilles heel of international law. I also knew that some US international lawyers were very proud of the ATS, seeing it as "a source of pride, a badge of honor."[2]

But there was a catch: I had never read an ATS case. That was absolutely normal for someone, like me, who had initially studied international law in the United Kingdom and Australia in the late 1990s, but was almost unthinkable for a US-trained

---

[1] Sosa v. Alvarez-Machain, 542 U.S. 692 (2004).
[2] Anne-Marie Burley, *The Alien Tort Statute and the Judiciary Act of 1789: A Badge of Honor*, 83 AM. J. INT'L L. 461, 464 (1989).

international lawyer at that time. Nonetheless, I felt little concern because it was all international law, after all.

As I read these cases, however, I felt some shock. We seemed to be using the same words and concepts, yet the analysis and conclusions felt unfamiliar. To my eye, the cases adopted a very strange approach to determining the existence of customary international law. They largely cited other US cases for propositions of international law, many of which seemed dubious to me. They involved a curious mix of international and domestic law on points like corporate liability and aiding and abetting liability. And basic steps— most notably determining whether international law permits domestic court jurisdiction over civil claims by foreigners, against foreigners, for acts occurring on foreign soil—were largely missing from the analysis.

What was I to say about these cases? "What did you think?" asked one of my colleagues. "This is like no international law I have ever seen," I reported back. My colleague looked shocked. "I thought you *knew* international law," he stammered. "I do," I replied, feeling strangely offended. "The problem isn't that I don't know international law. I *know* international law. *This isn't it!*"

What looked to my colleague (an American) like international law looked to me (a foreigner) like American law. To my eyes, the ATS was to international law what Tex-Mex was to Mexican cuisine: you could see the foreign influence, yet it seemed utterly Americanized. Was it international law, American law, or some hybrid of the two?

I had a similar dislocating experience when I arrived at Harvard Law School in 2011 to teach international law to a first-year class. Instead of the materials I had used at the London School of Economics, I prescribed a US cases and materials book called *International Law*. I had assumed that the content would be roughly the same, yet it was strikingly different in parts and seemed to have a strong focus on international law as interpreted and applied by US actors.

Even though I was the same teacher and was ostensibly teaching the same subject, my experience in that Harvard classroom felt radically different. Perhaps it was the greater domestic focus of the book or perhaps it just felt like a greater domestic focus because it was a different domestic setting. Perhaps it was that I was used to teaching international law to a broad mix of nationalities, whereas here I was teaching a class that was predominantly made up of a single nationality. Perhaps it was because that single nationality was American and the United States was the hegemon. Perhaps it was the students' generally skeptical and realist approach compared with the reverent and idealistic approach often exhibited by my students in the United Kingdom.

One difference I found striking was that my American students often assessed international law questions from a US perspective. Would this rule be good or bad for the United States? Should or would the United States comply? I could not recall my students in the United Kingdom adopting an analogous UK perspective. Nor was I aware of approaching international law from the perspective of what was in it for my home state of Australia or my adopted state of the United Kingdom. Did the difference evidence American exceptionalism? Did I approach international law from a denationalized perspective of the international community? Or did I implicitly approach it from the position of a nonhegemonic Western state, and which state that was did not really matter?

Whatever the reasons, I found myself having a comparative international law experience in that classroom where I did not realize how national the international law we sometimes teach is (in both materials and assumptions) until I found myself in another national setting. Dislocation was the key. By *dislocating* myself from my normal environment, I was able to experience international law from a different *location*. In doing so, I became conscious not only of the *located* way in which my students were approaching international law, but also the (differently) *located* way in which I had been approaching my field.

This sort of dislocation occurred again when I was appointed in 2012 as a non-American reporter for the *Restatement (Fourth) of the Foreign Relations Law of the United States*. I was tasked with working on the jurisdiction section, but there was a stumbling block. The *Restatement (Third) of the Foreign Relations Law of the United States* stated that international law recognized a three-part approach to jurisdiction, divided among jurisdiction to prescribe, jurisdiction to adjudicate, and jurisdiction to enforce. My US colleagues agreed. But in the United Kingdom and Australia I had learned that international law recognized a two-part approach, divided between jurisdiction to prescribe and jurisdiction to enforce. Which was the case?

To my eyes, much of what they called jurisdiction to adjudicate could simply be described as US constitutional law, not international law at all. What made things even more confusing was that my understanding of jurisdiction to prescribe and to enforce in my two-part scheme seemed to differ from my coreporters' understandings of the same terms in their three-part scheme. The textbooks and casebooks from our respective countries typically supported our respective understandings. When we looked at textbooks from other countries, including France, Germany, Russia, and China, we found some following the UK approach and others following the US approach.

This experience led to fundamental questions about the *Restatement* project. Were we trying to do a restatement of international law or of US approaches to international law? Who was to say what "international law" was? And what was the difference between international law and foreign relations law? Why did foreign relations law seem to be a big subject—one that people teach, write about, and produce casebooks on—in the United States, yet I could not think of anyone teaching or writing a textbook about this subject in the United Kingdom? Did it have something to do with the structure of government? Was it historical happenstance? Did it relate to the differential power of these states? Or was something else at play?

These questions made me recall a conversation in 2009 with a noted US international law/foreign relations law scholar. He proposed creating a Comparative Foreign Relations course with him teaching the US approach, me teaching the UK approach, and someone else teaching the German approach. That sounded fascinating, I said, but what exactly was foreign relations law and how did it differ from international law? Neither I nor anyone I knew in the United Kingdom taught a course called Foreign Relations Law, I explained. I vaguely recalled that F. A. Mann had written a book called *Foreign Affairs in the English Courts* in the 1980s, but I was not aware of any more recent treatment at that time.[3]

---

[3] For discussion of more recent developments in this area since 2009, see Chapter 5.I.B.

Defining foreign relations law and its relationship to international law is not an easy task, it turns out. A simple attempt at defining it led to dozens of e-mails and considerable disagreement among the *Restatement*'s reporters. We called a temporary truce after reaching exhaustion rather than agreement. In broad terms, it had something to do with how international law was interpreted and applied by the United States. It seemed particularly focused on how international law came into the US legal system and how authority with respect to these issues was allocated among the different arms of government. It also included issues such as when US courts could hear cases with foreign elements and recognize and enforce foreign judgments.

It was not as though there were no laws or cases on these issues in the United Kingdom; in fact, there were lots of them. Some of them, such as how international law comes into the UK system, formed a minor part of our international law courses. Others, such as the powers of different arms of government, might perhaps have come up in constitutional law classes, though I was not sure. Still others, such as jurisdiction to hear cases with foreign elements and recognition and enforcement of judgments came up in either public international law (when dealing with public and criminal laws) or private international law (when dealing with torts and contracts and the like). We just did not conceptualize the foreign relations law of the United Kingdom as a separate field. I wondered why this was so and how this difference might reflect or shape differences in the way international law was understood in different states.

When I wondered out loud whether the United Kingdom should develop a field called foreign relations law, a left-leaning US international lawyer quickly intervened to warn me against working on such a project. The turn from international law to foreign relations law was an inherently conservative move, he cautioned me; look at how it had developed in the United States. But was that true in the United States? I could think of liberal and conservative foreign relations lawyers, but did the liberals have a heavier load to lift? And, even if true for the United States, would that always be true of a movement to foreign relations law because it encouraged you to look at international law from a particular national perspective instead of from the perspective of the international community? Or did it depend on the nation in question?

I am grateful for having had these moments of dislocation because they helped open me to the possibility of comparative international law. Public international law is commonly studied as one subject in a first law degree alongside various topics of domestic law, like torts and property. Viewed in this way, whatever does not look domestic is assumed to be international. Usually, only when placed in an international context, such as competing in the international round of the Jessup Moot Court Competition or working for an international organization, or in another national context, such as studying or working in a foreign state, is one likely to become aware of national differences in approaches to international law. Instead of looking vertically (domestic to international), one is forced to look horizontally (domestic to foreign) and to consider how a foreign system might approach international law differently (foreign to international).

The key difference here is the movement from a *vertical* approach that considers domestic law and international law to a *triangular* approach that considers domestic law, international law, and foreign law. Just because something is not entirely domestic does not make it international since it might be a hybrid of the two that looks international to domestic audiences and domestic to international audiences. And one domestic approach to international law is not necessarily the same as another: international law traditions may be nationalized, so to speak. Looking sideways at foreign approaches to international law helps to clarify both points and to encourage us to reflect on how "international" our understanding of international law really is.

My first reaction to these experiences was to conclude that these Americans that I had encountered did not know international law: "You say that this is international law, but it is US foreign relations law. Or American international law. It is not really international law." This approach, it turns out, is not the best way to win friends and influence people.

My second reaction was more self-reflective. If the Americans thought something was international law but I did not, were they right or was I? Did I know international law, as I had previously thought? Or did I know British or Australian concepts of international law, without having realized the subconscious national lenses and filters that I had adopted in the process of learning and teaching it?

My third reaction was to wonder if none of us really knew international law because there was no "international law" to know. Our field is premised on coexistence and cooperation, but maybe we often simply talk past each other. This notion led to a crisis of confidence: just what had I been teaching all these years?

I am not alone in experiencing discomfort and disorientation upon coming face-to-face with international law pluralism. According to David Kennedy: "The professional experience of legal pluralism has two dimensions. First, encounter—encountering the other. Second, loss of confidence, destabilization. In the presence of legal pluralism, one is defeased of professional knowledge, certainty. Perhaps, one must acknowledge, the legal situation is, in fact, some *other way*."[4] My own roller-coaster ride clearly follows this pattern: dislocation, shock, and then doubt.

And so, with these experiences, my comparative international law journey had begun. But how could I start to capture what I had observed, moving beyond the level of anecdote to a point where I could find and analyze broader data to confirm, contradict, or nuance my impressions and convey them to people who had not shared the same experiences? How could I gain insights into other national approaches to international law from states with which I was unfamiliar? And what could a comparative international law approach tell international lawyers about how international law is conceptualized as a field and how universal or otherwise it might be?

These questions led me to consider the role that the globalization of law, legal education, and legal publishing might be playing in the construction of international law as a transnational field. Some fields seem inevitably international. For instance, we do not talk about German physics or American biology. Others are clearly nationally situated, like French literature and Chinese philosophy. But where does law fit in this spectrum?

---

[4] David Kennedy, *One, Two, Three, Many Legal Orders: Legal Pluralism and the Cosmopolitan Dream*, 3 N.Y.U. Rev. L. & Soc. Change 641, 642 (2007).

"Lawyers are professionally parochial. Comparative law is our effort to be cosmopolitan."[5] The same could be said of international law. Yet how successfully do we transcend our national boundaries? Do some national approaches end up having significantly more influence outside their borders than others? And are these patterns likely to shift in the next generation?

By focusing on the incoming influences, and outgoing spheres of influence, of international law academics in the five permanent members of the UN Security Council, and the way academics from these states construct and pass on understandings of the field in their textbooks, this book provides a window into the sociology of international law as a transnational legal field. By encouraging international lawyers to adopt a comparative international law approach, it aims at making international lawyers more aware of how their own understandings of and approaches to the field are shaped, as well as how these influences might be similar to or different from those of international lawyers from other states, regions, or geopolitical groupings. In trying to understand how others view international law, one is often able to see the field in a different light and to view one's biases and blind spots in sharper relief.[6] This process of trying to see international law through the eyes of others represents an important step toward encouraging greater understanding of diverse perspectives and facilitating enhanced communication and cooperation among those coming from different, and sometimes unlike-minded, states.

[5] JOHN HENRY MERRYMAN, THE LONELINESS OF THE COMPARATIVE LAWYER: AND OTHER ESSAYS IN FOREIGN AND COMPARATIVE LAW 10 (1999).

[6] Anne van Aaken, *Emerging from our Frames and Narratives: Understanding the World Through Altered Eyes*, EJIL: TALK! (Dec. 23, 2014).

Acknowledgments

MORE THAN ANY project I have ever undertaken, this project relied on conversations with, information provided by, and feedback from individuals from a wide variety of states.

Although I am sure to have missed some names, I want to acknowledge the following people for the insights they have given me into different academies and perspectives on international law: Timur Akchurin (Russia), Stéphanie Balme (France, China), Anu Bradford (United States), Congyan Cai (China), Wenting Cheng (China), Simon Chesterman (Australia, Singapore), Manjiao Chi (China), Sarah Cleveland (United States), Harlan Cohen (United States), Hanoch Dagan (Israel), Lori Damrosch (United States), Tom Dannenbaum (United Kingdom, United States), Jeff Dunoff (United States), Meredith Edelman (United States), Mathias Forteau (France), Henry Gao (China, Singapore), Gleider Hernández (United Kingdom), Rebecca Ingber (United States), Maria Issaeva (Russia), Aleksandra Ivlieva (Russia), Neha Jain (India, United Kingdom, Germany, United States), Anne Kent (China), Amy King (China), Karen Knop (Canada, Soviet Union), Martti Koskenniemi (Finland, United Kingdom, United States), Nico Krisch (Germany, United Kingdom, United States), Sudhir Krishnaswamy (India), Katerina Linos (United States), Lauri Mälksoo (Estonia, Russia), Chris McCrudden (Ireland, United Kingdom, United States), Robert McLaughlin (United States, Russia), Delphine Nougayrède (France, Russia), William Parlett (United States, Russia), Anne Peters (Germany, Switzerland), Katharina Pistor (Germany, United States), Antonios Platsas (Russia, United Kingdom), Sergio Puig (Mexico, United States), Bo Rutledge (United States), Irina Sakharova (Russia), Sergey Sayapin (Russia, Germany, Kazakhstan), Michael Schmitt (United States), Ryan Scoville

(United States), Alexandre Senegačnik (France), Greg Shaffer (United States, France), Mark Shulman (United States, China); V. M. Shumilov (Russia), Svitlana Starosvit (Ukraine, Russia), Paul Stephan (United States), Jinyuan Su (China), Bakhtiyar Tuzmukhamedov (Russia), Sergey Usoskin (Russia), Anne van Aaken (Germany, Switzerland), Grigory Vaypan (Russia), Mila Versteeg (the Netherlands, United States), Michael Waibel (Austria, United Kingdom), Baoshi Wang (China), Matt Waxman (United States), Binxin Zhang (China), and Luping Zhang (China).

I have been fortunate to have had assistance from a number of students who either completed law degrees in, or spoke the language of, the state that they researched, including: Anwar Mamdouh AlShammari (Saudi Arabia), Clava Brodsky (United States, Russian speaking), Rocio Jimena De la Puente (Argentina), Yang Du (China), Yamila Solange Etulain (Argentina), Sophia Harris (United Kingdom, French speaking), Zhao He (China), Hui-Ling Hung (Taiwan), Aleksandra Ivlieva (Russia), Qi Jiang (Australia), Meerim Kachkynbaeva (Kyrgyzstan, Russian speaking), Nicholas Alfonso Lawn (United Kingdom), Matthias Lippold (Germany), Jacob McGillivray (United States), Arthur Merle-Beral (France), Nominchimeg Odsuren (Mongolia, Russian speaking), Katherine Onyshko (United States), Hiroyuki Ota (Japan), Beham Markus Peter (Austria), Hansuya Reddy (South Africa), Carla Russo (Argentina), Yuki Sako (Japan), Fanny Sarnel (France), Alexandre Senegačnik (France), Asmita Singh (India), Harditya Suryawanto (Indonesia), Tsai-Ping (Sarah) Tang (Taiwan), Feifei Yu (China), Luping Zhang (China), Weijia (Vikki) Zhang (China), and Xuan Zhao (China). I also benefited from the help of Jesse Fleck in completing some additional coding on the International Court of Justice.

I owe a profound debt to Hilary Charlesworth, who has been a mentor from the time that she supervised my undergraduate honors thesis to the present when she engaged thoughtfully and critically with this project. I owe thanks to Anna Ascher, who edited my very first article and now my first book, as well as to Katelyn Cioffi and Junghyun Baek for their assistance with cite checking and Bluebooking the footnotes. I am grateful to Claire Merrill from Columbia Law School, Karina Pelling from the Australian National University, and Bernard Duggan, who helped in preparing my graphs and tables. I greatly appreciate the support my parents, Alan and Helen Roberts, have given me throughout my education. Most of all, I would like to thank my husband, Jesse Clarke, for countless discussions of these issues and my daughters, Ashley and Freya Roberts-Clarke, for providing a delightful distraction from them.

Abbreviations

ATS	Alien Tort Statute
Brexit	United Kingdom withdrawal from the European Union
BRIC	Brazil, Russia, India, China
BRICS	Brazil, Russia, India, China, South Africa
CCDCOE	Cooperative Cyber Defence Centre of Excellence
CPC	Communist Party of China
ECtHR	European Court of Human Rights
EEZ	Exclusive economic zone
EU	European Union
Fr.	France
FTAAP	Free Trade Area of the Asia-Pacific
GRULAC	Group of Latin American and Caribbean States
ICC	International Criminal Court
ICJ	International Court of Justice
ICTY	International Criminal Tribunal for the former Yugoslavia
ILA	International Law Association
ILC	International Law Commission
ISIS	Islamic State of Iraq and Syria
ITLOS	International Tribunal for the Law of the Sea
JSD	Doctor of Science of Laws
SJD	Doctor of Juridical Science
LLM	Master of Laws
MGIMO	Moscow State Institute of International Relations

NATO	North Atlantic Treaty Organization
NGO	Nongovernmental organization
NPOPSS	National Planning Office of Philosophy and Social Science (China)
NSSFC	National Social Science Fund of China
NUS	National University of Singapore
NYU	New York University
OECD	Organisation for Economic Co-operation and Development
PRC	People's Republic of China
R2P	Responsibility to protect
Rus.	Russia
RCEP	Regional Comprehensive Economic Partnership
SCO	Shanghai Cooperation Organization
TPP	Trans-Pacific Partnership Agreement
TTIP	Transatlantic Trade and Investment Partnership
TWAIL	Third World Approaches to International Law
UK	United Kingdom
UN	United Nations
UNCLOS	United Nations Convention on the Law of the Sea
UNESCO	United Nations Educational, Scientific and Cultural Organization
US	United States
USSR	Union of Soviet Socialist Republics
WEOG	Western European and Others Group
WTO	World Trade Organization
ZaöRV	Zeitschrift für ausländisches öffentliches Recht und Völkerrecht

1

The Divisible College of International Lawyers

WE ARE FAMILIAR with the question: Is international law law? I want to ask instead: Is international law international?

In some senses, this question sounds odd. International law is certainly international by definition: instead of being the law of any particular state, it is the law that applies in relations among states. It is frequently international by design. For instance, in terms of substantive law, the test for custom requires one to look for evidence of widespread and consistent state practice. Similarly, in terms of institutional design, the composition of the International Court of Justice is intended to ensure representation of the main forms of civilization and the principal legal systems of the world. And it is also international by aspiration. For example, many concepts that international lawyers celebrate rest on universalist ideologies, such as human rights and the rule of law.

Yet is international law international in reality? Not particularly, is my answer—at least, not in the way that it tends to be conceptualized by international law academics in different states and in the international law textbooks and casebooks that they use. This book is not about international law per se in the sense of studying the formal sources of international law, that is, treaties and custom. Instead, it explores how different national communities of international lawyers construct their understandings of international law in ways that belie the field's claim to universality and perpetuate certain forms of difference and dominance. It also calls attention to how some of these patterns are likely to be disrupted by changes, including shifts in geopolitical power. In doing so, this project encourages international lawyers to be more reflective about the particularities of their frameworks and perspectives, and more reflexive about how they engage with the field.

Is International Law International? Anthea Roberts.
© Anthea Roberts 2017. Published 2017 by Oxford University Press.

Instead of working from the premise that international law exists objectively some-where out there, this book assumes that, as an abstract concept, what counts as international law depends in part on how the actors concerned construct their understandings of the field and pass them on to the next generation.[1] In this sense, this project is constructivist in nature. International lawyers' vision of the field implicates many foundational issues, such as which areas are significant, which actors are important, which principles are fundamental, which sources are relevant, as well as which rules are settled and which are subject to change.[2] How lawyers construct their understanding of the law is relevant in all legal fields, but it is particularly noteworthy in international law for various reasons. International law does not have a central legislator. Even where they exist, multilateral treaties often lack a compulsory dispute settlement mechanism to resolve disagreements over their interpretation. Determining the existence and content of custom on the basis of general and consistent state practice and *opinio juris* is often more of an art than a science.

In examining the process by which international lawyers construct their understanding of international law, this book challenges the assumption that international lawyers work within a single field. When asked to reflect on the professional community of international lawyers, Oscar Schachter memorably called it an "invisible college" whose members were "dispersed throughout the world" yet "engaged in a continuous process of communication and collaboration."[3] Instead, I suggest that international lawyers may be better understood as constituting a "divisible college" whose members hail from different states and regions and often form separate, though sometimes overlapping, communities with their own understandings and approaches, as well as their own distinct influences and spheres of influence.[4]

In focusing on academics and textbooks, this study represents one strand in a broader, re-emerging subfield or set of approaches that I term "comparative international law," which examine cross-national similarities and differences in the way that international law is understood, interpreted, applied, and approached by actors in and from different states.[5] Comparative approaches are commonplace when dealing with national laws and domestic legal systems because it seems obvious that these might differ in interesting ways or that some approaches might be similar as a result of shared attributes such as language, colonial history, and legal family membership. But comparative approaches are employed less frequently when it comes to international law partly because the field's

---

[1] CARLO FOCARELLI, INTERNATIONAL LAW AS SOCIAL CONSTRUCT: THE STRUGGLE FOR GLOBAL JUSTICE 90 (2012).

[2] This focus on ideas also fits with the greater prominence that has been given in international relations literature since the 1990s to the role of ideas in shaping state identities and perceptions of global status. *See, e.g.,* Rosemary Foot, *Introduction* to CHINA ACROSS THE DIVIDE: THE DOMESTIC AND GLOBAL IN POLITICS AND SOCIETY 1, 1–2 (Rosemary Foot ed., 2013).

[3] Oscar Schachter, *The Invisible College of International Lawyers*, 72 NW. U. L. REV. 217, 217 (1977).

[4] As will be described in more detail below, there are many ways of dividing the divisible college, including along national lines, subject-matter lines, or with respect to connections to practice. *See* Chapter 2.I.B.

[5] *See* Chapter 2.I.A; *see also* COMPARATIVE INTERNATIONAL LAW (Anthea Roberts et al. eds., forthcoming 2017); Anthea Roberts et al., *Comparative International Law: Framing the Field*, 109 AM. J. INT'L L. 467 (2015).

universalist assumptions and aspirations can make comparativism seem both irrelevant and potentially dangerous.[6]

Nevertheless, to understand international law as a transnational legal field that encompasses multiple national traditions, international lawyers need to be aware of certain national or regional *differences* in approaches to international law, as well as the extent to which some of these approaches have come to *dominate* understandings of the "international" in a way that can make them appear, or allows them to be presented as, neutral and universal. Like processes of globalization more generally, the field of international law is defined by a dynamic interplay between the centripetal search for unity and universality and the centrifugal pull of national and regional differences.[7] The balance between these forces of convergence and divergence can also be *disrupted* by various changes, including technological innovation, changing domestic political preferences, and shifts in geopolitical power.

One way to understand these observations of difference, dominance, and disruption is through the reality and metaphor of language. International law aspires to be the world's Esperanto. Esperanto is a constructed international auxiliary language; it was created for mutual communication by speakers of different languages. It was intended to be an easy-to-learn, politically neutral means of expression that would transcend nationality and foster peace and international understanding among a variety of peoples. Esperanto was even proposed as the working language of the League of Nations after World War I.

Despite this ideal, international law is marked by tension between multiple languages and the increasing emergence of English as the lingua franca. The existence of multiple languages is analogous to the observation of national and regional differences. Instead of being a single community speaking a single language, albeit with different accents, international lawyers from different communities often speak different languages. People, materials, and ideas move more easily within linguistic communities than between such communities. And it is not always clear whether these communities are having the same debates, only in different languages, or whether their approaches differ in terms of their assumptions, arguments, conclusions, and world views.

Although these forces of divergence pull international lawyers apart, there are also forces of convergence that bring them together, but not ones that place all language-speakers on an equal footing. The language reality that parallels this observation of dominance is the increasing turn to English as the common tongue for international education, international conferences, international publications, international meetings, and international dispute resolution. English has gone from being one state's national language to the world's most common second language. One's access to the "international" often depends on whether one can understand, speak, and read this language,

[6] *See* Chapter 2.I.A.
[7] *See* Lauri Mälksoo, *International Legal Theory in Russia: A Civilizational Perspective, or Can Individuals Be Subjects of International Law?, in* THE OXFORD HANDBOOK ON THE THEORY OF INTERNATIONAL LAW 257 (Anne Orford & Florian Hoffmann eds., 2016).

which vests tremendous advantage in native English speakers, together with their concepts and approaches.

It was not always so. Greek served as the lingua franca during the Hellenistic period and was succeeded by Latin during the ascendancy of Rome and the Middle Ages. French was the language of European diplomacy from the seventeenth until the mid-twentieth century, whereas classical Chinese served as the diplomatic language of Far East Asia until the early twentieth century. The emergence of English as the modern common language owes much to the reach of the British Empire in the late nineteenth and early twentieth centuries and to the rise of the United States as the world's most powerful state following World War II. In this way, what counts as the lingua franca and the breadth of its reach may be subject to disruption based on a variety of factors, including technological innovation, such as the Internet; changes in domestic political preferences, such as openness to immigration; and changes in geopolitical power, such as the rise and fall of different regional and global hegemons.

This book examines these patterns of difference, dominance, and disruption with particular reference to how international law is constructed in different international law academies and textbooks in the five permanent members of the UN Security Council. Although they are not the only actors or materials to reflect and shape the field, academics and textbooks are important because the teachings of the most highly qualified publicists are a subsidiary source for determining international law; international law academics often take on significant roles in practice as, for instance, international judges and arbitrators, advocates before international tribunals, and advisers to governments; and these academics and textbooks play a key role in communicating understandings of the field to the next generation. They are also worth examining because they are visible, comparable, and understudied.[8]

The five permanent members of the Security Council—the People's Republic of China, the French Republic, the Russian Federation, the United Kingdom of Great Britain and Northern Ireland, and the United States of America—present an interesting set of case studies because they have historically been granted a privileged status within the international legal system with veto rights in the Security Council and de facto permanent seats on the International Court of Justice.[9] They include old great powers (like the United Kingdom and France) and new or re-emerging great powers (like China), as well as the two states that led the bipolar world during the Cold War (the Soviet Union/Russia and the United States). One of them thereafter emerged as the unipolar power (the United States) and the other recently has reasserted itself as a major power (Russia). The group also comprises a declining hegemon (the United States), a rising potential or regional hegemon (China), and two of the five states referred to as the BRICS (Russia and China).[10]

---

[8] For more explanation of this focus, see Chapter 2.II.

[9] For more explanation of this focus, see Chapter 2.III.

[10] The acronym BRIC originally referred to Brazil, Russia, India, and China, but it was later reframed as BRICS to include South Africa. See JIM O'NEIL, BUILDING BETTER GLOBAL ECONOMIC BRICs (Goldman Sachs Economic Paper No. 66, 2001); Why Is South Africa Included in the BRICS?, ECONOMIST, Mar. 29, 2013.

These states also differ along important axes, such as Western/non-Western, English-speaking/non-English-speaking, common law/civil law, and democratic/authoritarian lines.[11] Definitions of which states count as "Western" are inevitably controversial, and many states evidence a mix of Western and non-Western characteristics. For the purposes of this study, the term refers to states with membership or observer status in the Western Europe and Others Group at the United Nations, a geopolitical regional body whose "Other" component includes member and observer states in North America, as well as Israel, Australia, and New Zealand.[12] The United States, the United Kingdom, and France are treated as Western liberal democracies, and China and Russia as non-Western authoritarian states.[13] The growing tension between these two sets of states over a range of issues, including the law of the sea and cybersecurity, is one reason why these case studies are interesting.

This study is not comprehensive. I do not examine all of the actors and materials that play a role in the construction of international law, and one cannot assume that the patterns that hold true for academics and textbooks necessarily hold true more generally. The case studies do not include states in Africa, Latin America, or the Middle East, nor do I focus on the experiences and approaches of international lawyers from states that are less powerful and privileged than the permanent members. The project would be improved if other observers broadened it to look at more states, deepened it by delving into greater detail within particular states, and historicized it by examining continuities and change over time. Despite these limitations, this undertaking serves as a unique window into how different communities of international lawyers in five significant states construct themselves and their understandings of and approaches to the field.

In examining the extent to which international law is international in the academies and textbooks of these states, this book makes three arguments. First, international law academics are often subject to differences in their incoming influences and outgoing spheres of influence in ways that affect how they understand and approach international law. Second, actors, materials, and approaches from some states and regions have come to dominate certain transnational flows and forums in ways that make them disproportionately influential in constructing the "international"—a point that holds true for Western actors, materials, and approaches in general, and Anglo-American ones in particular. Third, existing understandings of the field are likely to be disrupted by factors such as changes in geopolitical power that will make it increasingly important for international lawyers to understand the perspectives and approaches of those coming from unlike-minded states.

---

[11] For further explanation of the choice of these states, see Chapter 2.III.

[12] For a list of which states form part of which regional grouping, see *United Nations Regional Groups of Member States*, U.N. DEP'T FOR GEN. ASSEMBLY AND CONFERENCE MGMT. (2015), http://www.un.org/depts/DGACM/RegionalGroups.shtml (last visited Feb. 26, 2017).

[13] *See* ECONOMIST INTELLIGENCE UNIT, DEMOCRACY INDEX 2015: DEMOCRACY IN AN AGE OF ANXIETY 4–8 tbl.2 (2016).

These three concepts—difference, dominance, and disruption—play a central role in this comparative international law study and will be explored in more detail in the rest of this chapter.

I. Difference

International lawyers from different states, regions, or geopolitical groupings often have distinct backgrounds, influences, opportunities, incentives, networks, and spheres of influence. Instead of constituting a single, uniform field, international law is an amalgamation of multiple, partially overlapping fields. Debates about fragmentation have focused on divisions within international law with respect to different subfields (like trade and human rights) and different international institutions (like the International Court of Justice and the International Tribunal for the former Yugoslavia). Comparative international law focuses attention on analogous divisions among international lawyers located in, coming from, or educated in different states, regions, or geopolitical groupings.

International lawyers typically exist at the intersection of two communities: a transnational community of international lawyers and a domestic community of national lawyers. When international lawyers are compared with their domestic peers, their international orientation often seems obvious. But comparing international lawyers from one state with their international peers in other states makes it possible to identify certain national differences as well. These differences affect how international lawyers in different states engage with the field, including which issues they treat as important, how they find and interpret international law, what assumptions they make, what questions they consider to be clear-cut or open to debate, and what arguments they view as persuasive. The approaches of international lawyers in China, for example, differ in significant ways from those of international lawyers in the United States.

Using a comparative international law approach to identify differences helps to challenge international lawyers' romantic understanding of themselves and their field as universal and cosmopolitan. Introducing a comparative element helps to disrupt this assumption by showing that other communities of international lawyers—often in different states or geopolitical regional groupings—approach international law in different ways. This knowledge encourages international lawyers to be more reflective about the limits to their understanding of and approach to the "international," and how much the way they have been socialized, the networks they have developed, and the sources on which they rely have led to or reinforced these limitations.

By ascertaining these differences, silos and disconnects within the field can be identified. The divisible college of international lawyers was aptly illustrated by the entirely different responses by Western international lawyers, on the one hand, and Russian international lawyers, on the other hand, to Crimea's annexation by, or reunification with, Russia in 2014.[14] These two groups spoke in different languages, assumed different

---

[14] *See* Chapter 5.II.A.

accounts of the facts, had different understandings of the content of international law, and reached diametrically opposed conclusions. The former condemned Russia's "illegal" annexation of Crimea, whereas the latter celebrated Crimea's "self-determination" and decision to reunite with the mother country. The members of each group often spoke internally to and referenced each other in self-reinforcing echo chambers, instead of communicating with the other group and seeking to bridge the divide between them.

Although not all lawyers from the same community are likely to approach international legal questions in an identical way, the contours of the "mainstream" debate in different communities can differ in significant ways. To understand how these national divisions come about, it is helpful to be aware of how these different communities are constituted. Russian international lawyers have frequently completed all of their legal education in Russia, primarily using Russian-language materials. They have their own international law textbooks, they publish the vast majority of their academic works in Russian journals and in the Russian language, and most of the authorities they cite are Russian. Even though they may enjoy more academic freedom in the post-Cold War period than during the Cold War, dissent can still be difficult, particularly since Russia began to take a resurgent stance on the international scene and on issues (like Crimea) that strike at core national interests. On the other side of the equation, few Western international lawyers speak Russian or study in Russia. Western international lawyers have their own textbooks, publish the vast majority of their articles in Western journals in languages such as English and French, and primarily cite other Western scholars. Both sets of lawyers are also likely influenced by the media on which they rely, and Russian and Western reporting on Crimea differed significantly. Not surprisingly, these communities of international lawyers find few points of commonality and connection, despite ostensibly operating in the same field.

A somewhat different picture emerges if one looks at the reactions of Chinese and Western international lawyers to the *South China Sea* arbitration by a tribunal constituted under the UN Convention on the Law of the Sea (UNCLOS) in 2016.[15] Chinese scholars were virtually unanimous in rejecting the tribunal's jurisdiction, though a handful dissented on whether the Chinese government had adopted the right approach in refusing to appear before the tribunal. Western international lawyers split on whether the UNCLOS tribunal was right to take jurisdiction, though they have tended to be critical of China's failure to participate and to reject China's claim that it is not bound by the arbitral decision. The divergent approaches between the Chinese and Western international lawyers reflect many differences in their processes of socialization, including in the way their respective governments and media portrayed the arbitration and the case's underlying merits. In comparison with the Crimean case, however, one striking difference is how many Chinese international lawyers are writing about the case in English-language outlets, permitting diverse perspectives to be considered within a single debate. The same point is not true in reverse for a variety of reasons.

---

[15] *See* Chapter 5.II.B.

The ability and motivation of Chinese international lawyers to bridge this divide owes much to their language skills, educational backgrounds, and incentive structures. It is common for high profile Chinese international lawyers to have completed a second or third law degree abroad, usually in a Western state, thereby building their language skills and transnational connections. They are given incentives to publish in foreign journals and in foreign languages. Their outwardly oriented advocacy aligned with the Chinese government's worldwide public relations campaign to popularize its viewpoint on the South China Sea. At the same time, the language abilities and incentive structures of Western scholars, along with explicit and implicit censorship by Chinese authorities, resulted in a more limited presentation of diverse viewpoints in domestic Chinese debates.

These examples reflect the more general reality that international lawyers in different states, regions, or geopolitical groups often form separate, though partially overlapping, communities, each with its own distinct socializing forces. That does not mean that all international lawyers within a state will have identical backgrounds and beliefs. For instance, this study highlights differences between the "Old Guard" of highly nationalistic Russian international law academics and a new wave of more transnationally oriented younger lawyers, many of whom do not join the academy. But, as seen above, international lawyers within a given state are often subject to similar influences, and these influences frequently differ across states. As a result, distinct communities of international lawyers frequently develop, with similar assumptions and approaches that often exist within, but not necessarily between, groups. For instance, American international lawyers may be more liberal or conservative, but they are often also distinctly American in some of their assumptions, preoccupations and approaches. This work focuses on some of the major patterns that distinguish international, lawyers in different states from one another. It also emphasizes that where significant intragroup dialogue occurs but extragroup dialogue is limited, self-reinforcing echo chambers can develop that give international lawyers from particular communities an inflated sense of the universality of their own approaches, while limiting opportunities for understanding and engagement among those holding diverse perspectives.

II. Dominance

International law does not exist only within states in a way that can be studied on a cross-national basis. The field is transnational in the sense that it is partly constituted by flows of people, materials, ideas, and approaches moving across borders. It is also sited in various transnational endeavors, like international organizations, international tribunals, international journals, and international blogs, where people from different national communities come together to produce, interpret, analyze, and apply international law. Yet if one asks how the "international" is constructed in these transnational flows and transnational sites, it turns out that they are shaped by certain forms of national and regional dominance that betray some of the field's claims to universality.

The ideal of international law suggests that it is constructed by drawing equally on people, materials, and ideas from all national and regional traditions. But in reality some national and regional actors, materials, and approaches have come to dominate much of the transnational field and international lawyers' understanding of the "international."[16] For instance, international lawyers who work in or appear before international courts and tribunals tend to be nationals of Western states in general, and of a handful of those states in particular, often the United Kingdom, the United States, and France.[17] Similarly, national case law that is cited in the decisions of international courts and tribunals, and imparted by international law textbooks, is often issued primarily in Western states, particularly the United States and the United Kingdom.[18]

The dominance of people, materials, and approaches from particular national and regional traditions within the field is consistent with the findings of sociologists of globalization, like Boaventura de Sousa Santos, who defines globalization as "the process by which a given local condition or entity succeeds in extending its reach over the globe and, by doing so, develops the capacity to designate a rival social condition or entity as local."[19] Ideas and materials from certain states that are successfully globalized by gaining acceptance throughout all or much of the world may be said to experience "globalized localism."[20] This process occurs on a horizontal level when ideas and materials move between states, and on a vertical level when certain national or regional approaches are adopted and applied at various transnational sites under the guise of being "international."

Although no state has a monopoly on defining international law, some powerful Western states function as international law exporters because they can successfully transport some of their national approaches to the international sphere in the name of "international law." By contrast, more peripheral states may experience "localized globalism," whereby local conditions are restructured in response to global influences.[21] These states function more like international law importers than exporters, though some hybridization of the international and domestic is typical.[22] Some states may also operate in between, having enough strength to withstand some of the forces of localized globalism but not enough to affect globalized localism. These states may lack the power to globalize their localisms altogether, though they may be influential in asserting their approach to international law within a particular region, geopolitical group, or linguistic community.

A good example of globalized localisms and patterns of dominance can be found in the language of international justice. Many international courts employ two working

[16] *See* Chapter 5.III.
[17] *See* Chapter 3.IV.
[18] *See* Chapter 4.IV.
[19] Boaventura de Sousa Santos, Toward a New Legal Common Sense: Law, Globalization, and Emancipation 178 (2d ed. 2002); *see also* Jane Jenson & Boaventura de Sousa Santos, *Introduction: Case Studies and Common Trends in Globalization, in* Globalizing Institutions: Case Studies in Regulations and Innovation 9, 11 (Jane Jenson & Boaventura de Sousa Santos eds., 2000).
[20] De Sousa Santos, *supra* note 19, at 179.
[21] *Id.*
[22] *See* Sally Engle Merry, Human Rights and Gender Violence: Translating International Law into Local Justice 19–21 (2006) (discussing "vernacularization" and "indigenization"); Sally Engle Merry, *Transnational Human Rights and Local Activism: Mapping the Middle*, 108 Am. Anthropologist 38, 39 (2006).

languages: English and French. This policy plays a significant role in determining which international lawyers are likely to be selected as judges, arbitrators, advocates, and staff. It privileges nationals of states whose national language is one or the other (for example, the United Kingdom, the United States, and France) and disadvantages nationals of states whose national language is neither one (for example, China and Russia). Language becomes an important filter for which nationals, and thus which national approaches, gain greater access to influencing the "international." Such access helps to explain why some international tribunals rely predominantly on English-language sources and, to a lesser extent, French-language sources in reaching their decisions.[23]

At the same time, many less formalized international forums are increasingly embracing English as the field's lingua franca. This trend can be seen in the prevalence of English in investment treaty arbitrations and awards, national and transnational journals and yearbooks of international law, and international law blogs. It can lead to the particular privileging of Anglo-American actors, materials, and approaches. As Carlo Focarelli has argued:

> Language is the key to the construction of reality, including the reality of international law. The fact that the *lingua franca* today is English implies that the English logic, worldview, and preferences are more likely to prevail and shape what "reality" is taken to mean. The dominance of the English language forces the international law debate into a specific mode of thought, which is far from being as universal as English itself apparently is, and reinforces the Western bias in its Anglo-American variant.[24]

Using a comparative international law approach to identify the existence of certain forms of *dominance* encourages international lawyers to think about the power dynamics that permit some national and regional approaches to transcend their borders and go global. Focusing on the origins of people, materials, and ideas in transnational flows and sites reveals how globalized localisms often skew toward Western approaches in general and Anglo-American approaches in particular. This perspective helps to illuminate criticisms of Western bias in the composition of international institutions and construction of international law. It also raises important questions about whether privileging a single language or a handful of languages does more to foster diversity in terms of which actors are benefited and which sources are relied upon.[25]

Identifying these patterns encourages international lawyers to take a more reflexive approach, to consider how they are positioned in relation to the "international" and how this posture might influence their perceptions of the field's universality and legitimacy. International lawyers work with a discourse that claims universality, but they are

---

[23] *See generally* Michael Bohlander, *Language, Culture, Legal Traditions, and International Criminal Justice*, 12 J. INT'L CRIM. JUST. 491 (2014); Michael Bohlander & Mark Findlay, *The Use of Domestic Sources as a Basis for International Criminal Law Principles*, 2 GLOB. COMMUNITY Y.B. INT'L L. & JURIS. 3 (2002).

[24] FOCARELLI, *supra* note 1, at 93.

[25] *See* Chapter 5.III.

likely to see that world through the prism of their location and thus understand international law differently depending on where they are situated. For lawyers in certain powerful Western states, international law often involves the export of domestic concepts, so they do not experience a strong disconnect between the local and the international. By contrast, international lawyers in other states are much more likely to be aware of this disconnect and to experience international law as a foreign, imported—and possibly illegitimate—construct.[26]

III. Disruption

Examining these observations of difference and dominance together, a comparative international law approach encourages international lawyers to think about the ways that international law, and their understandings of it, may be disrupted by a variety of factors, including technological innovation, changes in domestic political preferences, and shifts in geopolitical power.

Technological innovations, such as the creation of the Internet and the improvement of translation software, have the power to permit communication among people who speak different languages and come from far-flung parts of the world. These innovations, however, are often used by people primarily to connect with those with whom they already agree, which may reinforce particular narratives by creating echo chambers.[27] The movement of sources online has made it easier for international lawyers to access foreign materials, while improving translation software will enable more lawyers to understand such sources. Yet even though technology may assure greater access to diverse sources, it often also forms a conduit for already privileged sources to achieve even greater reach and influence throughout the world.

In terms of domestic political preferences, debates now occurring in many states about the relative merits of globalization and nationalism and recalibrations of the balance struck between the two may have an impact on some of the dynamics studied in this book. One example of these changes is likely to be shifts with respect to transnational flows of people. In the 1990s and early 2000s, the world witnessed a steady increase in people crossing borders in order to study or work in foreign states. These transnational flows raised the potential for breaking down some of the barriers between different national approaches, while also providing pathways for certain national approaches to exercise outsized influence beyond their borders. For instance, the attractiveness of elite US and UK universities as destinations for transnational legal education resulted in them having diverse student bodies and enabled them to extend the influence of their Anglo-American approaches to students coming from around the world. But the pushback against globalization in a series

---

[26] Arnulf Becker Lorca, Mestizo International Law: A Global Intellectual History 1842–1933, at 21–22 (2015).

[27] Christine Emba, *Confirmed: Echo Chambers Exist on Social Media. So What Do We Do About Them?*, Wash. Post, July 14, 2016; Walter Quattrociocchi, Antonio Scala, & Cass R. Sunstein, Echo Chambers on Facebook (June 13, 2016) (unpublished manuscript), https://ssrn.com/abstract=2795110.

of states reflects a recalibration in favor of nationalism that seems likely to restrict, at least to some extent, some of these transnational flows going forward. This may take the form of stricter immigration rules or reduced demand where anti-immigration sentiments make certain states less attractive destinations for foreign students.[28]

The writing of this book was completed in late 2016, before Donald J. Trump assumed the presidency of the United States and before the United Kingdom negotiated its exit from the European Union (Brexit). At the time of writing, it remains too early to tell how the United States will engage with the international legal system during Trump's presidency, what changes US foreign policy might bring about to the post-World War II international order, and whether US actions will result in increasing divisions within the West. It also remains to be seen whether and on what terms the United Kingdom leaves the European Union and what effects this might have, such as fracturing the United Kingdom or putting greater pressure on (or re-enlivening the commitment of other states to) the European project. Although it is too early to tell how these developments might change the international legal field in 2017 and beyond, it looks likely that 2016 will prove to be a watershed year in terms of these sorts of disruptions, particularly given the seismic shifts that have occurred in two states—the United States and the United Kingdom— that have been leading proponents of the post-World War II international order.

Upheavals both within the West and among various Western and non-Western powers appear imminent. Within the West, Trump has the potential to cause divisions over numerous issues, from his claimed belief in the utility of torturing terrorists to his doubts about the usefulness of the North Atlantic Treaty Organization to his denial of the existence of climate change. This has led to wariness from other Western leaders. For instance, Chancellor Angela Merkel of Germany responded to Trump's election with a reminder that "Germany and America are bound by their values," such as democracy, freedom, the respect for the law and the dignity of human beings, before providing the conditional endorsement that "On the basis of these values I offer the future president of the United States, Donald Trump, close cooperation."[29] Similarly, the Brexit negotiations have the potential to further fracture and sour relations between the United Kingdom and its European neighbors. This is important because a divided West is less powerful than a united one.

In terms of the Western/non-Western balance, US leadership in some areas, such as international economic law, now appears in doubt and may result in greater attention being paid to the practices of certain non-Western states, most notably China. For instance, while President Barack Obama urged the United States to ratify the Trans-Pacific Partnership Agreement (TPP) on the basis that "if we don't write the rules, China will,"[30] Trump broke with decades of US promotion of free trade by declaring the intention to withdraw from the TPP as soon as he assumed office.[31] As a result, increased

---

[28] *See* Chapter 6.

[29] Carol Giacomo, *Angela Merkel's Message to Trump*, N.Y. TIMES, Nov. 9, 2016.

[30] *See, e.g.*, Gerald F. Seib, *Obama Presses Case for Asia Trade Deal, Warns Failure Would Benefit China*, WALL ST. J., Apr. 27, 2015.

[31] *See* Donald J. Trump, A Message from President-Elect Donald J. Trump, YOUTUBE (Nov. 21, 2016), https://youtu.be/7xX_KaStFT8; *see also* Demetri Sevastopulo, *Trump Vows to Renounce Pacific Trade Deal on First Day in Office*, FIN. TIMES, Nov. 22, 2016.

attention is being focused on China's approach to global governance and various forms of regional economic governance in Asia, like the Regional Comprehensive Economic Partnership and the Free Trade Area of the Asia-Pacific.[32] This may well result in China becoming a stronger advocate for economic globalization than the United States or new alliances being formed, such as one between China and the European Union on the importance of addressing climate change.

Despite much uncertainty in the world, what does appear to be clear is that the locus of geopolitical power is shifting from unipolarity to greater multipolarity, and the era of Western-led international law appears to be giving way to an era of greater competition, and increased need for cooperation, among various Western and non-Western states.[33] After the relative hegemony of US and Western international law approaches in the post-Cold War period, the world is entering into what I refer to as a "competitive world order" in which divisions are becoming more apparent within the West and power is diffusing from West to East and from North to South.[34] In the coming decades, the international order is unlikely to be dominated by Western, liberal democratic states to the same extent as in recent decades. In this new phase, it will be increasingly important for international lawyers from different states and regions to understand the perspectives and approaches of those coming from unlike-minded states, as power will be disaggregated among a larger number of more diverse states.

Interest in comparative international law is likely to wax and wane with changes in geopolitical power. A generation ago, conferences were organized around Western and Soviet approaches to international law.[35] It made sense for international lawyers to focus on these competing approaches during the Cold War because the world was bipolar, consisting of two superpowers with radically different understandings of and approaches to international law. By contrast, little attention was paid in the 1990s and early 2000s to distinct national approaches to international law, let alone to the idea of comparative international law more generally. After the fall of the Berlin Wall and the emergence of the United States as a unipolar power,[36] theories about the End of History reflected and

---

[32] *See, e.g., Chile, Peru to Join China-led Trade Partnership*, BRICS POST, Nov. 21, 2016; Jason Scott & David Roman, *China Set to Push Asia Trade Deal Harder After Trump Win*, BLOOMBERG, Nov. 15, 2016; Janne Suokas, *Asia's Rival Trade Deals Explained: TPP, RCEP, FTAAP*, GB TIMES, Nov. 24, 2016; *TPP, RCEP, FTAAP: A User's Guide to Alphabet Soup of Trade Deals*, STRAITS TIMES, Nov. 20, 2016.

[33] *See, e.g.,* Ian Buruma, *The End of the Anglo-American Order*, N.Y. TIMES MAG., Nov. 29, 2016; Mercy A. Kuo, *The End of American World Order*, DIPLOMAT, Nov. 10, 2016.

[34] For more discussion of the factors leading to and evidencing this shift, see Chapter 4.IV.

[35] *See, e.g.,* LORI FISLER DAMROSCH ET AL., BEYOND CONFRONTATION: INTERNATIONAL LAW FOR THE POST-COLD WAR ERA (1995); INTERNATIONAL LAW AND THE INTERNATIONAL SYSTEM (William E. Butler ed., 1987); PERESTROIKA AND INTERNATIONAL LAW: CURRENT ANGLO-SOVIET APPROACHES TO INTERNATIONAL LAW (Anthony Carty & Gennady Danilenko eds., 1990) (essays by British and Soviet international lawyers); PAUL B. STEPHAN & BORIS M. KLIMENKO, INTERNATIONAL LAW AND INTERNATIONAL SECURITY: MILITARY AND POLITICAL DIMENSIONS: A U.S.-SOVIET DIALOGUE ON THE MILITARY AND POLITICAL DIMENSIONS (1991); William E. Butler, *Introduction* to PERESTROIKA AND INTERNATIONAL LAW 1, 4 (William E. Butler ed., 1990) (essays by British and Soviet international lawyers arising from the Anglo-Soviet Symposium on Public International Law).

[36] Charles Krauthammer, *The Unipolar Moment*, FOREIGN AFF., Sept. 18, 1990.

reinforced the sense that Western approaches had won out,[37] which resulted in a precip-
itous drop in interest in Russian approaches. The 1990s was a time of renewed optimism
in the West about the possibilities of universal international law and the transformative
potential of international organizations, such as the UN Security Council and international courts. It was also a time of ascendancy of a particularly Western, liberal vision of
international law.

Yet the distribution of geopolitical power has shifted once again.[38] From the bipolarity
of the Cold War to the unipolarity of the post-Cold War era, the world is now moving
into a competitive world order where power will increasingly be shared by a variety of
Western and non-Western states, heightening both competition and the need for coordination and cooperation by various states. In terms of economic power, the international
system has moved past dominance by Europe and the United States to greater multipolarity with the rise of major non-Western emerging economies (sometimes referred to as
the "rise of the rest").[39] In terms of security, many Western commentators have declared
that the "end of history has ended" and "geopolitics is back," focusing in particular on
increased regional assertiveness by Russia in Crimea and Georgia, and China in the
South and East China Seas.[40] Both individually and collectively, more states, including non-Western states, are making themselves heard on the world stage, such as by the
Group of Twenty's replacement of the Group of Seven and China's establishment of the
Asian Infrastructure Investment Bank. Meanwhile, the ability of Western states to act in
a unified and decisive way on the world state is being limited by the existence of wedge
issues, such as the Brexit negotiations and climate change, and domestic problems, such
as sluggish economies, popular discontent over increasing economic inequality, and rising political polarization.

Powerful states often seek to impose their own views of international law so that if the
international system contains multiple great powers, each may offer a distinct and competing version of the subject.[41] Whether and when their approaches result from different
national traditions, from different national interests, or from a combination of the two
is not easy to tell. But the diffusion of power between Western and non-Western states,
as well as increased divisions within the West, means that Western states will face more
checks and balances in advancing their strategic and normative agendas, whereas various

---

[37] FRANCIS FUKUYAMA, THE END OF HISTORY AND THE LAST MAN (1992); Francis Fukuyama, *The End of History?*, NAT'L INT., Summer 1989.

[38] *See generally* Chapter 6.

[39] *See, e.g.*, CHARLES A. KUPCHAN, NO ONE'S WORLD: THE WEST, THE RISING REST, AND THE COMING GLOBAL TURN (2012); William W. Burke-White, *Power Shifts in International Law: Structural Realignment and Substantive Pluralism*, 56 HARV. INT'L L.J. 1 (2015); Congyan Cai, *New Great Powers and International Law in the 21st Century*, 24 EUR. J. INT'L L. 755 (2013).

[40] *See, e.g.*, Walter Russell Mead, *The End of History Ends*, AM. INT., Dec. 2, 2013; Walter Russell Mead, *The Return of Geopolitics*, FOREIGN AFF., May/June 2014; Stewart Patrick & Isabella Bennett, *Geopolitics Is Back—And Global Governance Is Out*, NAT'L INT., May 12, 2015; John McLaughlin, *The Geopolitical Rules You Didn't Know About Are Under Siege*, OZY, Nov. 10, 2015.

[41] *See* Anu Bradford & Eric A. Posner, *Universal Exceptionalism in International Law*, 52 HARV. INT'L L.J. 1, 5–6, 12–13 (2011); Paul B. Stephan, *Symmetry and Selectivity: What Happens in International Law When the World Changes*, 10 CHI. J. INT'L L. 91, 107 (2009).

non-Western powers will be better equipped to promote their national traditions, interests, or narratives, either singly or collectively. This conflict and competition is likely to take place among many constellations of states that will vary across fields and issues, as evidenced by the different patterns appearing in subfields like the use of force and international human rights, trade law, and environmental law.

It may well be that the biggest challenges to the existing international order will come from the United States under the Trump presidency and from the more widespread pushback against globalization being witnessed in various Western states. These challenges have the potential to significantly destabilize the existing international world order, but they remain to be played out in 2017 and beyond and are thus not the focus of this book. Instead, I explore the challenges to the Western-led liberal international order that have been posed since around 2008 by China, as an emerging non-Western superpower, and Russia and China, as an evolving though loose coalition of non-Western, authoritarian great powers. This choice should not be taken to mean that China and Russia agree on their approaches to international law in all respects or that the challenges these two states are posing to the West are the only or most important challenges to the existing world order. Neither conclusion would be warranted. China and Russia are often more united in what they stand against—Western hegemony—than in what they stand for, as evidenced by their different approaches on key issues, such as international economic law and climate change. But challenges to the Western-led international order by non-Western states form a significant part of this comparative international law story and are thus worthy of attention.

In June 2016, Russia and China issued a joint declaration, the Promotion of International Law, setting out the principles that guide their approach to international law.[42] These principles, which reflect many of the themes and ideas that permeate their international law textbooks, privilege Westphalian notions of the importance of state sovereignty, sovereign equality, territorial integrity, and nonintervention over other norms such as human rights and democratic participation. These powers emphasize the centrality of states in shaping international law and constraining nonstate actors, rather than the reverse. They have a shared interest in regulating certain global commons, such as cyberspace, the seas, and outer space, so as to limit the freedom of more powerful states, like the United States. Although China and Russia differ in significant ways in their interests, capabilities, and approaches, they are acting both individually and collectively to challenge some of the Western, liberal approaches to international law that were championed by the United States and some of its allies during the post-Cold War period.[43]

---

[42] *See Russia's Position in Reinforcing the Legal Grounds of World Order*, MINISTRY OF FOREIGN AFFAIRS OF THE RUSS. FED'N, http://www.mid.ru/en/foreign_policy/position_word_order/-/asset_publisher/6S4RuXfeYlKr/content/id/2331698 (last visited Feb. 25, 2017).

[43] DAVID SHAMBAUGH, CHINA GOES GLOBAL: THE PARTIAL POWER 83 (2014) ("China and Russia . . . have forged a geostrategic axis and voting bloc in the UN Security Council. The heart of this axis is anti-Americanism and anti-interventionism. . . . Both share a strong opposition to coercion and the use of force in international affairs, and both cherish state sovereignty as the most basic principle of diplomacy.").

These differences are playing out in a variety of disputes within the international legal field. For instance, competition between the sanctity of state sovereignty and nonintervention, and the protection and promotion of human rights and democracy, has featured in debates about unilateral humanitarian intervention and the doctrine of the "responsibility to protect," especially in relation to China and Russia's decision to veto three Western-sponsored Security Council resolutions on Syria. Competition about how to strike a balance between treating the sea as a "global commons" subject to freedom of navigation and protecting the interests of coastal states is fueling clashes between China and the United States over the operation of military ships and aircraft within China's exclusive economic zone. And a growing divide has been emerging about how best to regulate the Internet and govern information security and cybersecurity. Russia and China advocate a sovereignty-based multilateral treaty that gives states strong national control over the Internet, whereas a variety of Western states, including the United States and the United Kingdom, favor a multistakeholder process that treats the Internet as a global commons where freedom of speech and the free flow of information are protected.

Western/non-Western cleavages do not exist on all issues. For instance, even though the United States has traditionally been the primary proponent of free trade, China has actively embraced trade and investment treaties and regularly makes use of the World Trade Organization's system of dispute resolution. Whether the United States continues to champion free trade in the same way going forward remains to be seen. The distance between the approaches of some of these states has also narrowed over time. For example, China's hostility to humanitarian intervention has lessened and become more nuanced in recent years, while Russia invoked the doctrine with respect to Crimea despite its earlier criticism of the concept. But to gain a better understanding of these different approaches, it is important for international lawyers to diversify their sources and networks with a view to improving their knowledge of how international legal norms and regimes appear from different perspectives and through different eyes. Whether or not differences of outlook are held genuinely or promoted strategically, lawyers ought to be aware of the diverse frameworks and narratives through which international law events are understood and arguments are made. In emphasizing the importance of understanding diverse positions, I am not advocating for or against particular approaches or claiming that all approaches are equal. Rather, understanding diverse perspectives will enable international lawyers to comprehend more fully the development of international law as a transnational field, both today and in the future.

In seeking to develop such understanding, international lawyers also need to be aware that some transnational flows are likely to be asymmetrical, leading to different patterns of diffusion and knowledge. For instance, elite Chinese international lawyers are far more likely to study in the United States than vice versa. Thus, US materials and approaches are more likely to be found in China than the reverse (the power of diffusion), but Chinese international law academics are more likely to exhibit broad comprehension of US perspectives on international law than the reverse (the power of knowledge). As China becomes an increasingly important international player, it will probably want to disseminate its approaches to international law more widely, while international lawyers in the

United States will need to deepen their knowledge of China's interests, interpretations, and approaches.

As the last point illustrates, patterns of difference and dominance are dynamic. The content and structure of international law typically lags behind changes in international power, and international law teaching typically lags behind changes in international law. The continued power of the United Kingdom and France in various international law fields owes much to their status as former great colonial powers, despite both having undergone significant declines in the past century. The same is bound to apply to the United States in the coming decades, as it remains singularly powerful in many areas—a first among equals, even if no longer a unipolar power. Yet the rise of non-Western powers in general, and China in particular, is likely to lead to changes in some of the Western-dominated international rules and institutions that have defined the field to date. This is even more so if some of the existing Western powers come to doubt these institutions or are unable to work together in a cooperative way. International law stands at an important inflection point. If international lawyers wish to equip themselves and their students with a grasp of how changing geopolitical power is likely to affect the form and substance of international law, they need to delve more deeply into the understandings of, and approaches to, international law of lawyers from a variety of unlike-minded states.[44] They also need to be sensitive to how the approaches to international law of particular states might vary over time, including in response to changes in domestic preferences and shifts in geopolitical power.

---

[44] YASUAKI ONUMA, A TRANSCIVILIZATIONAL PERSPECTIVE ON INTERNATIONAL LAW 32 (2010) (predicting that "a State-centric and Western-centric international society of the twentieth-century will become a multi-polar and multi-civilizational global society in the twenty-first-century. With this change, international law will change.").

2

Project Design

I. General Framework

A. COMPARATIVE INTERNATIONAL LAW

Domestic lawyers sometimes lump international and comparative law together as the "other" of domestic law; after all, it is all *foreign* law of sorts. By contrast, international and comparative lawyers often define their fields in opposition to each other. For instance, the *American Journal of International Law* does not generally publish manuscripts on "comparative or foreign law,"[1] whereas the *American Journal of Comparative Law* does not take those "purely about international law."[2] As a result, international and comparative law often run in parallel instead of intersecting; they sit next to each other but rarely converse.[3] There are many journals of international and comparative law, but no journals of comparative international law.

Comparative lawyers have traditionally had a blind spot when it comes to international law because of the assumption of universality. Harold Gutteridge explained that,

---

[1] *AJIL Submissions*, AM. SOC'Y INT'L L., http://www.asil.org/ajil-submissions (last visited Nov. 29, 2016).

[2] *What to Submit*, AM. J. COMP. L., http://comparativelaw.metapress.com/home/articles.mpx (last visited Nov. 4, 2014).

[3] *See* Mireille Delmas-Marty, *Comparative Law and International Law: Methods for Ordering Pluralism*, 3 U. TOKYO J. L. & POL. 43, 43 (2006) (the "two disciplines tend to ignore each other, isolated in their own specific languages, rites, dogma and clergy"); Colin B. Picker, *International Law's Mixed Heritage: A Common/Civil Law Jurisdiction*, 41 VAND. J. TRANSNAT'L L. 1083, 1086 (2008) ("most international law scholars are not comparatists" and "most comparatists study domestic legal systems, primarily their private law dimensions, and not the international legal system").

as regards international law, "the employment of the comparative method would at first sight appear to be excluded, because rules which are avowedly universal in character do not lend themselves to comparison."[4] Instead, the general practice has been to view comparative law and international law as separate fields, William Butler observed, rather than to deem "the former . . . a method as equally useful in comprehending the latter as in illuminating domestic legal systems."[5]

At the same time, international lawyers often resist emphasizing national or regional approaches because they are seen as potentially threatening to the field's universalist aspirations. In terms of assumptions, Hersch Lauterpacht described international law as "the only branch of law containing identical rules administered as such by the courts of all nations."[6] In terms of aspirations, Mathias Forteau expressed concern about a possible "catch-22: If one admits that there are different approaches to international law (i.e., a real comparative international law), is there still room for an '*international* law?'"[7] These anxieties frequently lead to minimizing rather than highlighting national or regional differences. As David Kennedy noted:

> One of the most puzzling aspects of international law is the intense desire within the profession to deny our common experience of professional pluralism—or to discuss it only over cocktails. As a result, there is no strong science of "comparative international law." We have intuitions, prejudices, impressions about one another, but we resist acknowledging, and studying, let alone embracing, our differences.[8]

Yet, if one moves around the globe to study, work, or attend conferences, it is hard not to be struck by the impression that international law seems "different in different places."[9] As Detlev Vagts, a US international lawyer, indicated: "Although international law is supposed to be universal . . . there are striking differences among national approaches to the subject."[10] B. S. Chimni, an Indian international lawyer, reflected that "location matters" when it comes to international law, "be it in terms of the issues that are addressed or the ways in which these are approached."[11] Likewise Xue Hanqin, the Chinese judge at the International Court of Justice (ICJ), insisted that international law should always be studied in its particular national context because, "[n]otwithstanding its universal character,

---

[4] H.C. Gutteridge, *Comparative Law and the Law of Nations, in* INTERNATIONAL LAW IN COMPARATIVE PERSPECTIVE 13 (William E. Butler ed., 1980).

[5] William E. Butler, *International Law and the Comparative Method, in id.* at 25, 27.

[6] Hersch Lauterpacht, *Decisions of Municipal Courts as a Source of International Law,* 1929 BRIT. Y.B. INT'L L. 65, 95.

[7] Mathias Forteau, *Comparative International Law Within, Not Against, International Law: Lessons from the International Law Commission,* 109 AM. J. INT'L L. 498, 499 (2015).

[8] David Kennedy, *One, Two, Three, Many Legal Orders: Legal Pluralism and the Cosmopolitan Dream,* 3 N.Y.U. REV. L. & SOC. CHANGE 641, 649 (2007).

[9] David Kennedy, *The Disciplines of International Law and Policy,* 12 LEIDEN J. INT'L L. 9, 17 (1999).

[10] Detlev Vagts, *American International Law: A Sonderweg?, in* WELTINNENRECHT: LIBER AMICORUM JOST DELBRÜCK 835, 835 (Klaus Dicke et al. eds., 2005).

[11] B.S. Chimni, *The World of TWAIL: Introduction to the Special Issue,* 3 TRADE L. & DEV. 14, 22 (2011).

international law in practice is nonetheless not identically interpreted and applied among States."[12]

If that is the case, why not examine these differences through a comparative lens? Studying international law in this way brings all of the usual advantages of comparativism: it increases knowledge of and understandings about different legal approaches; it enhances one's awareness of and ability to critique one's own approach; and it stimulates new ideas that might spark innovation.[13] But comparativism has special value in the international context because the field is meant to deal with common rules. When comparing domestic legal systems, it does not matter if one state does *x* and another state does *y*, because there is no assumption that all states are or should be doing the same thing. These differences are more profound with respect to international law, however, because it is a transnational field that aspires to develop common rules that facilitate inter-state coexistence and cooperation.

In adopting a comparative international law approach, three points are worth clarifying. First, when comparing national and regional approaches, it is helpful to look for evidence of differences and similarities in the way international law is understood, interpreted, applied, and approached. Comparative law in general is marked by searches for differences and similarities, and comparativists often acknowledge that whether one understands certain findings as evidence of differences or similarities may depend on the level of abstraction used.[14] Focusing only on differences may result in a false sense of the particular over the general, overplaying the field's diversity and underplaying its unity. It may also lead to failure to investigate the causes and consequences of similarities, such as whether certain national or regional approaches have become globalized localisms and, if so, how and with what effects?[15]

Second, differences in the way international law is understood, interpreted, applied, and approached can be examined without adopting a relativist stance that all positions are equal. A descriptive observation that certain international law values are not universal as a matter of origin, or universally accepted as a matter of sociological fact, does not necessitate a normative position that these values should not be recognized as universally applicable.[16] But such an observation does help to frame the argument. Rules can be justified on the basis of the process of their creation (for example, as selected through

---

[12] Xue Hanqin, Chinese Contemporary Perspectives on International Law: History, Culture and International Law 16 (2012).

[13] *See* Günter Frankenberg, *Critical Comparisons: Re-Thinking Comparative Law*, 26 Harv. Int'l L.J. 411 (1985); Kai Schadbach, *The Benefits of Comparative Law: A Continental European View*, 16 B.U. Int'l L.J. 331 (1998).

[14] Anthea Roberts et al., *Conceptualizing Comparative International Law*, in Comparative International Law (Anthea Roberts et al. eds., forthcoming 2017).

[15] On the concept of globalized localisms, see Boaventura de Sousa Santos, Toward a New Legal Common Sense: Law, Globalization, and Emancipation 178–79 (2d ed. 2002) and Chapter 1.II.

[16] Mathias Siems, Comparative Law 217 (2014) (discussing the "genetic fallacy" of assuming that because certain values have a Western origin, they cannot reflect universal principles); Franz von Benda-Beckmann, *Human Rights, Cultural Relativism and Legal Pluralism*, in The Power of Law in a Transnational World: Anthropological Enquiries 115, 120, 126 (Franz von Benda-Beckmann et al. eds., 2009) (distinguishing between normative and empirical claims about universality).

a representative and inclusive process) or their substantive content (for example, as embodying a universal value). One potential justification for international rules is that they were consented to by a widespread and representative group of states. If that turns out not to be the case, the onus shifts to those supporting the rule to justify it on other grounds, such as its substantive utility or morality.

Third, the adoption of a comparative approach to international law does not require one to take a position on the substance of international legal rules. How two or more states or groups of states differ over what is permissible under international law can be examined without taking a position on whether any of them are correct or whether the existence of such disagreement means that none of them are. Whether a given position reflects international law depends on many factors, such as the number of states that support it, how widespread and representative they are as a group, and whether they include specially affected states. This comparative international law study is more about identifying similarities and differences in approaches, and seeking to understand when and why these occur, than looking for "correct" legal answers about the content of international law.

As Lauri Mälksoo observed in his study of Russian approaches to international law, taking an intellectually honest look at national or regional approaches to international law is not the same as ideologically promoting them: rather, it means acknowledging in a pluralist—or realist—way that there may not be just one universal way of understanding and applying international law.[17] A comparative international law approach encourages international lawyers to be more self-aware and reflexive in their own engagement with the field by taking cognizance of which socializing factors and incentives influence their approaches to international law, how their national or regional approaches are positioned in relation to the "international" and how this vantage point might affect their understanding of the field's universality or legitimacy, and how things might look different from other perspectives.

In inviting international lawyers to adopt this approach, I recognize that actors with dominant or privileged positions within the field as it is are likely to resist the notion of comparative approaches to international law as not in tune with their interests. If one frames one's own approach as the universal international law approach, one can marginalize alternative approaches as illegitimate breaches of the rules rather than as legitimate contestations over the content of those rules. But even international lawyers or states that wish to promote a specific vision of international law as universal will find it useful to understand alternative perceptions, notably in light of shifting geopolitical power dynamics. For these states and lawyers, comparative international law might serve as an important backroom attempt to anticipate and be in a position to respond to the "other," even if they eschew comparativism and embrace universalism in public.[18]

---

[17] LAURI MÄLKSOO, RUSSIAN APPROACHES TO INTERNATIONAL LAW 17 (2015).

[18] As one former military international lawyer explained to me, this sort of research forms an important part of "getting inside your enemy's head" so that you can understand how they will perceive your moves and how they are likely to respond. One can engage in comparativism because one wishes to achieve a cosmopolitan perspective or because one wishes to protect a national interest.

Identifying similarities and differences in understandings and approaches is also not the end of the story. Even if one can identify differences, transnational forums often become places where different national approaches are mediated in distinctive ways. Understanding whether and how an international norm arises from national contestation forms part of understanding how international rules are created and changed. And this process is likely to vary in response to a variety of factors, such as the language used and geopolitical realities.

B. INTERNATIONAL LAW AS A TRANSNATIONAL LEGAL FIELD

This book is about the construction of international law as a transnational legal field, with a focus on the role of international law academics and textbooks. In analyzing this construction, I draw on theories about social fields by scholars like Pierre Bourdieu,[19] and their application to other transnational legal fields like international commercial arbitration by scholars such as Yves Dezalay and Bryant Garth.[20] I also draw on work about the sociology of legal globalization by scholars such as Bruce Carruthers, Terence Halliday, Pavel Osinsk, Boaventura de Sousa Santos, and William Twining.[21]

Although international lawyers are used to working with a discourse of universality, the way international lawyers understand the field may be different in different places. As Russian international lawyer Valerii Kuznetsov observes:

> We are often surprised when States understand and apply differently the same norm of international law. This surprise is a consequence, inter alia, of underestimating the phenomenon of legal consciousness, [that is,] differences in concepts of what international law is. . . . International law as an objective phenomenon does not necessarily coincide with our concepts of it, the more so since our concepts are often not the same.[22]

How international lawyers construct their understanding of the field assumes particular salience in international law because its nature as a transnational field without a

---

[19] PIERRE BOURDIEU & LOÏC J.D. WACQUANT, AN INVITATION TO REFLEXIVE SOCIOLOGY (1992); Pierre Bourdieu, *The Force of Law: Toward a Sociology of the Juridical Field*, 38 HASTINGS L.J. 805 (Richard Terdiman trans., 1987). *Cf.* Peter Haas, *Introduction: Epistemic Communities and International Policy Coordination*, 46 INT'L ORG. 1 (1992).

[20] *See, e.g.,* YVES DEZALAY & BRYANT GARTH, DEALING IN VIRTUE: INTERNATIONAL COMMERCIAL ARBITRATION AND THE CONSTRUCTION OF A TRANSNATIONAL LEGAL ORDER (1996). *Cf.* Mauricio García-Villegas, *A Comparison of Sociopolitical Legal Studies*, 12 ANN. REV. L. & SOC. SCI. 25 (2016).

[21] *See, e.g.,* DE SOUSA SANTOS, *supra* note 15; WILLIAM TWINING, GENERAL JURISPRUDENCE: UNDERSTANDING LAW FROM A GLOBAL PERSPECTIVE (2009); Bruce G. Carruthers & Terence C. Halliday, *Negotiating Globalization: Global Scripts and Intermediation in the Construction of Asian Insolvency Regimes*, 31 L. & SOC. INQUIRY 521 (2006); Terence C. Halliday & Pavel Osinsk, *Globalization of Law*, 32 ANN. REV. SOC. 447 (2006).

[22] Valerii I. Kuznetsov, *Concise Survey of Origin and Development of International Law: Russia and International Law*, *in* INTERNATIONAL LAW: A RUSSIAN INTRODUCTION 1, 3 (Valerii I. Kuznetsov & Bakhtiar R. Tuzmukhamedov eds., William E. Butler trans., 2009) [hereinafter INTERNATIONAL LAW].

centralized legislator and law enforcer means that concepts play a large role in its formation and application while differences in approach are often able to subsist.[23]

As a complex product of social construction, international law can be understood
through the sociological notion of fields developed by scholars like Bourdieu and Neil
Fligstein and Doug McAdam.[24] According to Bourdieu, a field is a social sphere made up
of objective relations between different agents who interact and compete. The position of
agents within a field is determined by the different forms of "capital" they possess, which
may include markers of prestige such as where they studied, where they work or have
worked, where they publish, what awards they have won, and to which learned societies
they belong. The amount of capital different agents possess determines their potential to
influence the functioning of the field.

A field's "habitus" provides agents within that field with a socially founded sense of
the "game" they are playing, but the rules of the game are never set and are always open
to challenge. Habitus helps to structure individuals' understandings of the field and
their "best" interests within it.[25] This notion helps to highlight the way actors' pursuit
of their best interests is conditioned by understandings within a given field of what is
best. Bourdieu's concepts of "doxa" and "opinion" denote a society's or field's taken-for-
granted, unquestioned truths, on the one hand, and the sphere of what may be openly
contested and discussed, on the other hand.[26]

Fields are dynamic spaces marked by forces of competition and change. Within a
field, agents and institutions constantly struggle, both within and over the rules of the
game.[27] Change within a field often occurs when incumbents, who are privileged because
of a certain set of rules and assumptions about capital, are challenged by newcomers,
who pioneer a novel version of the rules and a different set of assumptions about capital.
Examples include the rise of the Chicago School of Economics and the shift from the
European "grand old men" of international commercial arbitration to a younger set of
Anglo-American "arbitration technocrats."[28]

Scholars such as Dezalay and Garth have applied Bourdieu's insights to describe
dynamics in the emergence, operation, and change of transnational legal fields.[29] This
work calls attention to the role of legal experts, including academics and practitioners,
in building and legitimating markets for their expertise at the transnational level. Agents

---

[23] *Id.*

[24] *See* BOURDIEU & WACQUANT, *supra* note 19; NEIL FLIGSTEIN & DOUG MCADAM, A THEORY OF FIELDS
(2012); Bourdieu, *supra* note 19.

[25] PIERRE BOURDIEU, OUTLINE OF A THEORY OF PRACTICE 72–87 (1977).

[26] *Id.* at 164–70.

[27] BOURDIEU & WACQUANT, *supra* note 19, at 102.

[28] DEZALAY & GARTH, *supra* note 20, at 34–41; YVES DEZALAY & BRYANT G. GARTH, THE
INTERNATIONALIZATION OF PALACE WARS: LAWYERS, ECONOMISTS, AND THE CONTEST TO TRANSFORM
LATIN AMERICAN STATES 44–47 (2002) [hereinafter DEZALAY & GARTH, PALACE WARS].

[29] For a description of a range of work applying insights from Bourdieu to international legal fields, see Mikael
Rask Madsen, *Transnational Fields and Power Elites: Reassembling the International with Bourdieu and Practice
Theory, in* PERSPECTIVES FROM INTERNATIONAL POLITICAL SOCIOLOGY: TRANSVERSAL LINES IN
INTERNATIONAL RELATIONS (Tugba Basaran et al. eds., 2016).

often operate in both national and transnational fields. What counts as doxa, opinion, and capital may vary among different national communities, and may also vary between the national and international levels. The "national" plays an important role in constituting the "international" since typically agents are largely socialized in national settings, so that transnational forums frequently become spaces where different national models vie for influence.

International law is best understood as a transnational legal field made up of multiple, partially overlapping fields.[30] These underlying fields are helpfully analyzed by reference to three distinctions: between academia and practice, between national and transnational communities, and between different subject areas. Many of the questions that underlie this study concern the relationships between these fields. For instance, how do the fields of academia and practice relate in different states? Do the national and transnational academic fields have the same or different doxa and understandings of social capital? And which actors and materials tend to transcend their borders and give rise to transnational effects?

The academia/practice distinction captures the fact that some members of the divisible college of international lawyers are academics working at universities and others are practitioners working in a variety of contexts, including in states, international organizations, nongovernmental organizations (NGOs), and private firms. A hallmark of the invisible college is that many individuals cross over between these roles, some wearing multiple hats simultaneously. Still, as captured by the notion of the divisible college, the common types of crossover vary significantly among states and regions owing to differences in opportunities and incentive structures. As a result, international lawyers from different states and regions are also subject to different incoming influences and outgoing spheres of influence.

The transnational/national distinction captures the fact that international lawyers find themselves at the intersection of two communities: a transnational community of international lawyers and a national community of domestic lawyers. To understand international law as a transnational legal field, one must encompass both sets of communities and understand the relationship between them, which often varies across states. In some states, the accepted doxa and the valued forms of social capital will be closely aligned in the national and transnational communities. In other states, they will diverge significantly, so that the more an international lawyer seeks to conform to the doxa and social capital expectations of the national community, the less will they conform to those of the international community and vice versa.

For instance, in terms of social capital, if a national academy encourages its scholars to publish in national journals in the local language, the scholars' ties with their national community may be strengthened, but those with their transnational community loosened. By contrast, if the academy creates incentives for its scholars to publish in transnational journals in English, the opposite may occur. Likewise, because the line between

---

[30] Nico Krisch, *The Many Fields of International Law: A Conceptual Framework with a Case Study of German International Law*, *in* COMPARATIVE INTERNATIONAL LAW (Anthea Roberts et al. eds., forthcoming 2017).

doxa and opinion may vary markedly between different national and transnational communities, scholars may need to pitch their piece accordingly. One can easily imagine that what counts as opinion or doxa in the United States may be unlike what counts as such in Russia, and both might be unlike what counts as opinion or doxa in pleadings before the International Court of Justice or in submissions to the UN Human Rights Committee.

Although some international lawyers manage to devote equal time to both the transnational and the national levels, most focus their energies more on one than the other. Thus, some practitioners engage with international law primarily on the transnational level, for example, as advocates before international courts and tribunals or as lawyers for international organizations; others, primarily on the national level, for example, as advocates before national courts and tribunals. Each of these national and transnational communities may be understood as "nested" within broader communities whose doxa and forms of capital may prove highly influential for those international lawyers. For instance, international lawyers operating on the national level may be nested within a broader national community of lawyers, including noninternational law specialists like constitutional lawyers and national security lawyers. The doxa and forms of social capital valued by these broader communities may play an important role in setting the relevant standards for the groups of international lawyers nested within them. At the same time, they may hold little relevance for other international lawyers who operate primarily on the transnational level and who may be nested within a broader community of transnational practitioners with their own doxa and forms of social capital. The rules that define one national community may also not cross-apply to other national communities.

The transnational/national distinction does not apply as neatly to academia as to practice. The academy is generally organized along national lines, with different legal academies in different states. There is no equivalent of a transnational legal academy that, similarly to transnational legal practice and international organizations, exists above and beyond any state. Yet some actors and materials manifest greater transnational ambitions and influence than others. For instance, the best law schools in a state generally train the national legal elites of that state. But a growing number of students are now crossing borders to undertake legal studies in foreign states, often traveling to core Western states, particularly France, the United Kingdom, and the United States. Consequently, the top-tier universities in these states often play a disproportionate role in educating transnational legal elites, as well as national ones.

It is not easy to distinguish between international law journals that are national and those that are transnational. Although most entertain some transnational ambitions, they often differ over whether they are framed along national or transnational lines and the extent to which they can exert a transnational effect. Some publications are organized along national lines, such as the *German Yearbook of International Law* and the *Indian Journal of International Law*, whereas others are expressly transnational, such as the *European Journal of International Law* and the *Asian Journal of International Law*. But naming is not the end of the story because some "national" journals of international law may be aimed at, and very successful in achieving, a transnational audience. The *American Journal of International Law*, for example, characterizes itself as "indispensable for *all* professionals working in international law, economics, trade, and foreign affairs," and it is the most frequently cited international law journal in the world.[31]

Similar points could be made with respect to international law societies. Compare, for example, the Société française pour le droit international and the Asociación Argentina de derecho internacional, which are organized along national lines, with the African Society of International and Comparative Law, the European Society of International Law, and the International Law Association, which are organized along regional or transnational lines. Again, however, naming only tells part of the story because some "national" societies of international law are able to generate significant numbers of non-national members and meeting attendees. For instance, the American Society of International Law boasts nearly four thousand members from more than one hundred states, and its annual meetings attract international lawyers from around the world.[32] Yet the American nature of its membership and meeting attendees is still marked. For instance, the American society always holds its annual meeting in Washington, D.C., whereas the European society rotates among European states from year to year.

In addition to distinctions between academia and practice, and between transnational and national communities, the field of international law is also fragmented into subfields, including human rights law, trade law, and environmental law. These subfields are often partially governed by their own rules, institutions, and practices, and they may be subject to their own doxa and forms of capital. Some are marked by subject-specific transnational journals and societies, such as the *Journal of International Economic Law* and the Society of International Economic Law. Others enjoy a close association with certain international institutions or practitioners, such as the World Trade Organization (WTO) and human rights NGOs. Which subfields of international law are popular, and which are considered to form part of the mainstream of international law, may vary among states. And interdisciplinary connections may also vary among subjects, as exemplified by the strong ties between economists and international trade lawyers but the much weaker ties between economists and human rights lawyers.

Although this schema inevitably simplifies reality, it helps to clarify some of the multiple and sometimes overlapping fields that make up the transnational field of international law. The key points to take away are that many international law actors and materials sit at the intersection of the national and the transnational; some international lawyers and materials focus much more strongly on one community than the other; the two communities may be marked by different doxa and perceptions of social capital; and various incentives may encourage international lawyers to lean more in one direction than the other. In addition, the relationship between the national and the international will vary significantly among states, as actors and materials are more likely to enjoy transnational reach from some states (international law exporters) than those from other states (international law importers).

---

[31] *The American Journal of International Law (AJIL)*, Am. Soc'y Int'l L., https://www.asil.org/resources/american-journal-international-law (last visited Apr. 5, 2016) (emphasis added).

[32] *Overview*, Am. Soc'y Int'l L., https://www.asil.org/about/overview (last visited Apr. 5, 2016).

II. The Actors and Materials Studied

A. INTERNATIONAL LAW ACADEMICS

Dezalay and Garth have argued that faculties of law occupy central roles in the reproduction of knowledge, in governing elites, and in hierarchies of expertise.[33] Through their scholarship and practice, academics influence legal fields. Through their teaching and mentoring, academics influence students who end up shaping future legal fields as scholars and practitioners. Although academics wield leverage in all legal fields, "teachers and teachings" are especially prominent in the construction of international law for two reasons.[34]

First, the "teachings of the most highly qualified publicists of the various nations" are treated as subsidiary means for the determination of rules of international law.[35] Consequently, international law academics have considerable sway in interpreting and developing international law, particularly in new subfields (like international criminal law, economic law, and environmental law), when dealing with uncodified sources like customary international law, or when states are unable to reach agreement on how to move forward. The highly influential *Tallinn Manual* on cybersecurity represents a case in point.[36] Academic writings are often relied upon as evidence of international law by national courts, international courts, and states in diplomatic correspondence.[37]

The privileged status accorded to legal academics may partly reflect the influence of the civil law tradition on international law,[38] as well as the absence of a general legislature.[39] Although the judge may be understood to be the primary protagonist in the common law tradition, this honor is accorded to the teacher-scholar in the civil law tradition.[40] In some areas, the relative importance of academics may be declining, notably in fields

---

[33] DEZALAY & GARTH, PALACE WARS, *supra* note 28, at 5.

[34] *See* MANFRED LACHS, TEACHINGS AND TEACHING OF INTERNATIONAL LAW 163 (1976).

[35] Statute of the International Court of Justice, art. 38(1)(d), June 26, 1945, T.S. No. 993, 33 U.N.T.S. 993.

[36] TALLINN MANUAL ON THE INTERNATIONAL LAW APPLICABLE TO CYBER WARFARE (Michael N. Schmitt ed., 2013).

[37] *See generally* JAMES CRAWFORD, BROWNLIE'S PRINCIPLES OF PUBLIC INTERNATIONAL LAW 43 (2012); Alain Pellet, *Article 38*, *in* THE STATUTE OF THE INTERNATIONAL COURT OF JUSTICE: A COMMENTARY 868–70 (Andreas Zimmermann et al. eds., 2006); *Scholars in the Construction and Critique of International Law: Remarks of Bruno Simma*, 94 AM. SOC'Y INT'L L. PROC. 317, 319 (2000); Michael Wood, *Teachings of the Most Highly Qualified Publicists (Art. 38(1) ICJ Statute)*, MAX PLANCK ENCYCLOPEDIA OF PUB. INT'L L., para. 16 (2010).

[38] Michael Bohlander, *The Influence of Academic Research on the Jurisprudence of the International Criminal Tribunal for the Former Yugoslavia—A First Overview*, 2003 GLOB. COMMUNITY Y.B. INT'L L. & JURIS. 195; Colin B. Picker, *A Framework for Comparative Analyses of International Law and Its Institutions: Using the Example of the World Trade Organization*, *in* COMPARATIVE LAW AND HYBRID LEGAL SYSTEMS 117, 125–26 (Eleanor Cashin Ritaine et al. eds., 2010).

[39] *See* Robert Jennings, *International Lawyers and the Progressive Development of International Law*, *in* THEORY OF INTERNATIONAL LAW AT THE THRESHOLD OF THE 21ST CENTURY 413, 413 (Jerzy Makarczyk ed., 1996).

[40] JOHN HENRY MERRYMAN & ROGELIO PÉREZ-PERDOMO, THE CIVIL LAW TRADITION: AN INTRODUCTION TO THE LEGAL SYSTEMS OF EUROPE AND LATIN AMERICA 56–60 (3d ed. 2007).

where decisions by national and international courts and tribunals have proliferated.[41] But in other areas where states have been reluctant to articulate legal norms, or a standoff between different approaches exists, such as in cybersecurity, academic writings may play a crucial role.[42]

Second, academics are instrumental in shaping international law because they often engage in its practice as advisers to governments, counsel in disputes, judges and arbitrators, and members of expert bodies, such as the International Law Commission (ILC).[43] Historical examples abound,[44] but contemporary examples are also easy to come by, such as the crossover of international law academics who become the legal adviser of their state's foreign ministry.[45]

In terms of international judicial careers, a 2006 study by Daniel Terris, Cesare Romano, and Leigh Swigart of all sitting judges on international courts found that legal academia was the most significant feeder career.[46] Of the 215 judges identified, 85 had significant academic credentials (that is, they had been tenured or tenure-track professors), as compared with 70 who had served in national courts, 40 in international organizations, 20 in domestic governments, and 10 in private practice. Many past and present ICJ judges have spent substantial time in their careers as international law academics.[47]

---

[41] Sandesh Sivakumaran, *The Influence of Teachings of Publicists on the Development of International Law*, 66 INT'L & COMP. L.Q. 1 (2016).

[42] *See* Michael N. Schmitt & Sean Watts, *The Decline of International Humanitarian Law* Opinio Juris *and the Law of Cyber Warfare*, 50 TEX. INT'L L.J. 189, 191–92 (2015) (bemoaning the relative absence of states from the formulation of these rules).

[43] NEIL WALKER, INTIMATIONS OF GLOBAL LAW 38 (2014) (noting the phenomenon in international law that "some members of the transnational elite cohorts . . . move with relative ease between the worlds of legal or judicial practice and those of education and scholarship"); Lauri Mälksoo, *International Law in Russian Textbooks: What's in the Doctrinal Pluralism?*, 2 GÖTTINGEN J. INT'L L. 279, 281 (2009) (describing it as a "professional characteristic of the 'invisible college of international lawyers' that their more outstanding representatives usually have some sort of a role in, or proximity to, the formulation of their country's international legal positions").

[44] For instance, writing in the 1980s, Lachs gave numerous examples, including Dionisio Anzilotti (Italian: worked for Italian Ministry of Foreign Affairs, judge on the PCIJ); Paul Guggenheim (Swiss: adviser for the Swiss government, judge on the ICJ); Max Huber (Swiss: adviser for the Swiss government; judge, then president of the PCIJ); Manley O. Hudson (American: judge on the PCIJ, chairman of the ILC); Hersch Lauterpacht (British: member of the ILC, judge on the ICJ); A.D. McNair (British: judge, then president of the ICJ; president of the Eur. Ct. Hum. Rts.); Georges Scelle (French: member of the ILC). *See* MANFRED LACHS, THE TEACHER IN INTERNATIONAL LAW (TEACHINGS AND TEACHING) 97–130 (1982). Other examples include Eduardo Jiménez de Aréchaga (Uruguayan: member of the ILC; judge, then president of the ICJ); Fyodor Ivanovich Kozhevnikov (Soviet: member of the ILC, judge on the ICJ); Rein Müllerson (Soviet: adviser to the chairman of the Supreme Soviet of the USSR (Mikhail Gorbachev), member of the Hum. Rts. Comm., Estonia's first deputy foreign minister, then professor at King's College London); and Alfred Verdroß (Austrian: judge, Eur. Ct. Hum. Rts., member of the ILC).

[45] Examples include Daniel Bethlehem (Cambridge University; Legal Adviser for the UK Foreign & Commonwealth Office), Harold Koh (Yale Law School; Legal Adviser for the US State Department), and Martti Koskenniemi (University of Helsinki; Legal Adviser for the Finnish Ministry of Foreign Affairs).

[46] DANIEL TERRIS ET AL., THE INTERNATIONAL JUDGE: AN INTRODUCTION TO THE MEN AND WOMEN WHO DECIDE THE WORLD'S CASES 20 (2007).

[47] *Id.* For example, Ronny Abraham (France); Roberto Ago (Italy); Andrés Aguilar-Mawdsley (Venezuela); Ricardo Joaquín Alfaro (Panama); Alejandro Alvarez (Chile); Eduardo Jiménez de Aréchaga (Uruguay); Jules Basdevant

The same is true of WTO Appellate Body members[48] and some investment treaty arbitrators.[49]

As regards counsel before international courts and tribunals, Shashank Kumar and Cecily Rose conducted a study of all legal representatives who appeared in oral proceedings in contentious cases before the ICJ from 1999 to 2012.[50] Of these, 45 percent were academics, 34 percent were government lawyers, 10 percent were solo practitioners (for example, barristers), and 8 percent were from law firms.[51] When they narrowed their focus to lawyers who had appeared in two or more cases, whom they dubbed the "ICJ Bar," a majority of them were academics (59 percent), whereas the percentage of government lawyers was significantly reduced (16 percent).[52] As for the inner circle of 17 lawyers who had appeared four or more times, over 70 percent were academics.[53]

In terms of playing the role of expert, UN member states regularly elect academics to serve on the International Law Commission, a major contributor to the codification and progressive development of international law.[54] Many current and former ILC members were international law academics.[55] International law academics also frequently appear

---

(France); Richard R. Baxter (United States); Mohamed Bennouna (Morocco); Luigi Ferrari Bravo (Italy); Thomas Buergenthal (United States); James Crawford (Australia); Hardy Cross Dillard (United States); Taslim Olawale Elias (Nigeria); Isidro Fabela (Mexico); Giorgio Gaja (Italy); Sergei Alexandrovitch Golunsky (USSR); Gilbert Guillaume (France); Geza Herczegh (Hungary); Christopher Greenwood (United Kingdom); Rosalyn Higgins (United Kingdom); Robert Yewdall Jennings (United Kingdom); Kenneth Keith (New Zealand); Sergei Borisovitch Krylov (USSR); Guy Ladreit de Lacharrière (France); Arnold Duncan McNair (United Kingdom); Gaetano Morelli (Italy); Hisashi Owada (Japan); Raymond Ranjeva (Madagascar); John Erskine Read (Canada); Francisco Rezek (Brazil); Stephen M. Schwebel (United States); Bernardo Sepúlveda-Amor (Mexico); Shi Jiuyong (China); Bruno Simma (Germany); Peter Tomka (Slovakia); Antônio Augusto Cançado Trindade (Brazil); Vladlen Vereshchetin (Russia); Christopher Gregory Weeramantry (Sri Lanka); Xue Hanqin (China); and Abdulqawi Ahmed Yusuf (Somalia).

[48] See, e.g., Georges Michel Abi-Saab (Egypt); James Bacchus (United States); Luiz Olavo Baptista (Brazil); Peter Van den Bossche (Belgium); Seung Wha Chang (Korea); Claus-Dieter Ehlermann (Germany); Said El-Naggar (Egypt); Merit E. Janow (United States); Mitsuo Matsushita (Japan); Ricardo Ramírez-Hernández (Mexico); Giorgio Sacerdoti (Italy); Yasuhei Taniguchi (Japan); David Unterhalter (South Africa); and Yuejiao Zhang (China). On the significance of academics in shaping the WTO and international trade law, see generally Picker, *supra* note 38, at 117, 125–26.

[49] See, e.g., Georges Abi-Saab (Egypt); Lucius Caflisch (Switzerland); James Crawford (Australia); Gabrielle Kaufmann-Kohler (Switzerland); Vaughn Lowe (United Kingdom); Donald MacRae (Canada); Michael Reisman (United States); Giorgio Sacerdoti (Italy); Philippe Sands (United Kingdom); Bruno Simma (Germany); and Brigitte Stern (France).

[50] Shashank P. Kumar & Cecily Rose, *A Study of Lawyers Appearing Before the International Court of Justice, 1999–2012*, 25 EUR. J. INT'L L. 893 (2014).

[51] *Id.* at 908.

[52] *Id.* Within the ICJ bar, the percentage of solo practitioners was 16 percent and the percentage of lawyers from law firms was 10 percent. *Id.* at 909.

[53] These figures were collected and provided by Cecily Rose and Shashank P. Kumar, authors of *A Study of Lawyers Appearing Before the International Court of Justice, 1999–2012, supra* note 50 (on file with author).

[54] Statute of the International Law Commission, art. 1(1), G.A. Res. 174 (II), annex (Nov. 21, 1947).

[55] See, e.g., Roberto Ago (Italy); Gaetano Arangio-Ruiz (Italy); Milan Bartos (Yugoslavia); James Brierly (United Kingdom); Ian Brownlie (United Kingdom); Lucius Caflisch (Switzerland); James Crawford (Australia); John Dugard (South Africa); Abdullah El-Erian (Egypt); Mathias Forteau (France); J.P.A. Francois (the Netherlands); Giorgio Gaja (Italy); Manley O. Hudson (United States); Valery Kuznetsov (Russia); Ahmed Laraba (Algeria); Hersch Lauterpacht (United Kingdom); Igor Ivanovich Lukashuk (Russia); Stephen C. McCaffrey (United

as expert witnesses in international dispute settlement proceedings, such as investment treaty arbitrations.[56]

Of course, international law academics are not the only actors who contribute to the construction of the international legal field, nor are they the most important. International law is constructed by a multiplicity of actors, including judges on international and national courts, advocates before international and national tribunals, lawyers working for their governments, and lawyers working for international organizations and NGOs. International law is created by the dialogue and interaction between states (through their representatives), state-empowered bodies (like international courts and the ILC), and nonstate actors (like international law academics and those working for NGOs).

Nevertheless, one reason that academics are worth studying is that they are highly visible. Generally, online profiles of international law academics, including descriptions of their education, professional experience, and publications, can be easily found, unlike similar information about government lawyers or those working for international organizations or NGOs.[57] This information helps to construct a sense of the national and transnational influences and spheres of influence of different communities of international lawyers. For instance, do they tend to study law only in their home state (nationally) or also in another state (transnationally)? Do they typically engage in practice and, if so, is it more nationally or transnationally oriented? What language(s) do they usually publish in and does their work tend to appear in national or transnational journals?

One cannot assume that the patterns that hold true for international law academics necessarily hold true for all international lawyers based in or coming from those states. In some cases, they do. Thus, elite international lawyers in China, including academics, often complete at least one law degree in another state, most commonly in the West, whereas top-level international lawyers, including academics, in the United States and Russia rarely acquire any foreign legal education. But in other cases, the patterns for academics do not hold true for other international lawyers. For instance, many of the international

---

States); Donald McRae (Canada); Shinya Murase (Japan); Sean D. Murphy (United States); Georg Nolte (Germany); Ki Gab Park (Republic of Korea); Alain Pellet (France); Chris M. Peter (Tanzania); Robert Q. Quentin-Baxter (New Zealand); Georges Scelle (France); Stephen M. Schwebel (United States); Pavel Sturma (Czech Republic); Sompong Sucharitkul (Thailand); Dire D. Tladi (South Africa); Nikolai A. Ushakov (USSR); Francis Vallat (United Kingdom); Vladlen Vereshchetin (Russia); Humphrey Waldock (United Kingdom); Alexander Yankov (Bulgaria).

[56] *See, e.g.*, José Alvarez (United States); David Caron (United Kingdom); James Crawford (United Kingdom); Rudolf Dolzer (Germany); John Dugard (Leiden); Christopher Greenwood (United Kingdom); Rob Howse (United States); Benedict Kingsbury (United States); Martti Koskenniemi (Finland); Stephen McCaffrey (Canada); Georg Nolte (Germany); Alain Pellet (France); Michael Reisman (United States); Giorgio Sacerdoti (Italy); Christoph Schreuer (Austria); Ivan Shearer (Australia); Anne-Marie Slaughter (United States); M. Sornarajah (Singapore); Christian Tomuschat (Germany); Kenneth Vandevelde (United States); Nico Schrijver (the Netherlands). *See Expert Legal Opinions*, INVESTMENT TREATY ARB. L., http://www.italaw.com/browse/expert-legal-opinions (last visited Nov. 10, 2014).

[57] This sort of information is often available about international judges, but they represent a smaller pool and have been the subject of many other studies. *See, e.g.*, TERRIS ET AL., *supra* note 46; *iCourts*, DANISH NAT'L RES. FOUND. CTR. OF EXCELLENCE FOR INT'L COURTS, http://jura.ku.dk/icourts/ (last visited Feb. 26, 2017); *Our Research Topics*, PLURICOURTS: CTR. FOR STUDY OF LEGITIMATE ROLES OF JUDICIARY IN GLOB. ORDER, http://www.jus.uio.no/pluricourts/english/ (last visited Feb. 26, 2017).

law academics at the most highly ranked universities in the United Kingdom come from around the world, evidencing a high degree of national and educational diversity. The diversity of national origin is less likely to characterize international legal advisers in the UK Foreign and Commonwealth Office since one must be a UK national to apply.

B. INTERNATIONAL LAW TEXTBOOKS

International law textbooks, casebooks, and manuals, which I will often refer to collectively as "textbooks," can both reflect and shape different approaches to international law in different states. Comparing these books cross-nationally can give a sense of the way the field is conceptualized and taught in different states, which may encourage international lawyers to be conscious of similarities and differences in their perspectives, sources, and approaches.

International law textbooks are worth studying because they give a sense of how international law is understood by the current generation of international lawyers (output) and communicated to the next generation (input) within a given state. They are used by students who are new to the field and, at least in some states, they are also relied upon as a resource by practicing international lawyers.[58] International law textbooks are cited by international courts and governments, partly because they are not generally meant to be polemic but are typically understood as providing an account of what international law "is" rather than what the author thinks it "should be." These books thus figure importantly in framing how international lawyers understand and approach their field, though these forces often work unconsciously.

In his study of Latin American international law textbooks, Arnulf Becker Lorca explained that "textbooks express the professional common sense, the popular and tacit understanding about international law in the region, building up a national lore."[59] Writing about US casebooks, David Bederman reasoned that, as one of the public faces of the profession and as what will be the only real exposure of many students to international law methods, scholarship, and attitudes, "international law casebooks may be strikingly influential in forming the views and attitudes of practitioners and policymakers," and their content represents a repository of the "conventional wisdom" of the day.[60] Armand de Mestral made the same point about the leading French textbooks, which have long "constituted the accepted wisdom on the subject" for French readers.[61]

In introducing students to the field, international law textbooks impart the basic vocabulary and conceptual frameworks that the next generation of international lawyers

---

[58] This point appears to vary among states. For instance, while many of the UK international lawyers I spoke to viewed the UK textbooks as important sources for both students and practitioners, some of the Russian international lawyers viewed the Russian manuals as primarily written for students, not practitioners. E-mails on file with author.

[59] Arnulf Becker Lorca, *International Law in Latin America or Latin American International Law? Rise, Fall, and Retrieval of a Tradition of Legal Thinking and Political Imagination*, 47 HARV. INT'L L.J. 283, 287 (2006).

[60] David J. Bederman, Review Essay, *International Law Casebooks: Tradition, Revision, and Pedagogy*, 98 AM. J. INT'L L. 200, 200 (2004).

[61] Armand L. C. de Mestral, Book Review, 88 AM. J. INT'L L. 553, 553 (1994).

will bring to their practice and scholarship. These frameworks furnish guidance on what are seen as the core issues of international law, which issues are settled and which are controversial, what questions one should ask when confronted with international law problems, where to look for the sources of international law and how to value them, which arguments are plausible and which outcomes are likely, and even what counts as an "international law" problem in the first place. The subjects these books focus on and the materials they use communicate powerful messages to students about the field and form an important part of the process by which international lawyers are socialized into understanding their vocation.[62]

There are limits, of course, to relying on a study of textbooks. First, textbooks are not necessarily the only materials used to teach students, nor are they always fully covered, especially if the book is long and intended to be relatively comprehensive. Teachers may supplement these books with other materials, though this practice seems more common in some academies than others. For instance, various Chinese academics and students reported that they were typically taught from a single textbook without supplementary readings, whereas some Russian academics and students stated that textbooks were used for lectures, and supplementary materials were provided for tutorials or seminars.

Second, these books do not necessarily reflect how international law is practiced in the state concerned. In his study of Russian approaches to international law, Mälksoo explained that international law textbooks can provide a "useful shortcut to learn about the practice and views of the respective state."[63] Similarly, in his study of Turkish international law textbooks, Berdal Aral noted the interplay of legal doctrine, legal education, and foreign policy in Turkey, as the textbooks "reproduce[] and reinforce[] the dominant discourse on Turkish foreign policy."[64] Yet this pattern may prevail in some states but not others, as this study finds, for instance, with respect to Chinese international law textbooks that sometimes reflect, and sometimes entirely neglect, Chinese government positions.

Third, the type of book that is commonly used may differ among states, and different types may serve slightly different purposes, such as communicating accepted understandings of the law or sparking debate. Textbooks that are treatise-like are common in China, France, and the United Kingdom, books of cases and materials are common in the United States, and edited manuals that have a different author for each chapter but function as an integrated whole are common in Russia. Some aspects of the books may reflect specific pedagogical choices rather than specific approaches to international law.

International law textbooks are also not the only materials that contribute to the construction of the international legal field, nor are they the most important. International law is constructed by a multiplicity of materials, including primary sources, such as treaties

---

[62] Similar justifications have been given for comparing textbooks in areas such as corporate law and studying the role of nutshells in legal development. *See* Holger Spamann, *Contemporary Legal Transplants: Legal Families and the Diffusion of (Corporate) Law*, 2009 BYU L. REV. 1813, 1826 (2009); Alan Watson, *The Importance of "Nutshells,"* 42 AM. J. COMP. L. 1 (1994).

[63] Mälksoo, *supra* note 43, at 280.

[64] Berdal Aral, *An Inquiry into the Turkish "School" of International Law*, 16 EUR. J. INT'L L. 769, 770, 785 (2005).

and various forms of state practice that contribute to the creation of custom, and subsidiary means of determining the law, such as international and national judicial decisions. Textbooks, however, constitute a visible and comparable measure for conducting cross-national studies—visible, unlike many other national work products, such as confidential government memos; and comparable, unlike some other national sources, such as domestic court decisions, which may be rendered on any given issue by some but not all states.

Reading international law textbooks from another state allows one to see the field through different eyes. In William Butler's preface to a unique English-language translation of a Russian international law manual, he noted that it represents an alternative approach to teaching and thinking about international law and thus makes a welcome contribution to comparative approaches to international law.[65] In addition to considering state practice, including from unpublished sources, from Russia and other former Soviet states, the book "inevitably" projects "a Russian 'spin' on aspects of international law, conscious and unconscious, that permeates the entire enterprise," both because of informative differences in Russian "legal style" and because Russians "see the world differently from western colleagues in some respects."[66]

Although cross-national comparative textbook studies are relatively uncommon in international law,[67] analogous studies have proved popular in history.[68] Scholars have examined whether history textbooks in different states present the same picture of international events or one that is tilted to promote national identity or state interests. For instance, Daniel Sneider argued that textbooks in China and South Korea skew the portrayal of events involving Japan in order to promote patriotic feelings, and Erica Hashiba's linguistic analysis showed that both American and Japanese textbooks strive to portray a history of World War II that is favorable to their own country.[69] These studies are analogous to inquiries into national differences in the presentation of international law.

Historians have also scrutinized the content and organization of global or world history books to identify slants or dominant narratives.[70] Michelle Commeyras and Donna Alvermann maintained that world history books typically focus on European history and

---

[65] William E. Butler, *Preface to the English Edition, in* INTERNATIONAL LAW, *supra* note 22, at xix, xxiii.

[66] *Id.*

[67] For exceptions, see, for example, Becker Lorca, *supra* note 59 (comparing international law textbooks in Latin America); Anthony Carty, *A Colloquium on International Law Textbooks in England, France and Germany: Introduction,* 11 EUR. J. INT'L L. 615 (2000).

[68] *See, e.g.,* DANA LINDAMAN & KYLE ROY WARD, HISTORY LESSONS: HOW TEXTBOOKS FROM AROUND THE WORLD PORTRAY U.S. HISTORY (2006).

[69] HISTORY TEXTBOOKS AND THE WARS IN ASIA: DIVIDED MEMORIES (Gi-Wook Shin & Daniel C. Sneider eds., 2011); Erica J. Hashiba, *The Representation of World War II: A Comparison of Japanese and American Textbook Discourse,* 19 INTERCULTURAL COMM. STUD. 149 (2010); *see also* Grant K. Goodman et al., *The Japan/United States Textbook Study Project: Perceptions in the Textbooks of Each Country About the History of the Other,* 16 HIST. TEACHER 541 (1983); Tomoko Hamada, *Constructing a National Memory: A Comparative Analysis of Middle-School History Textbooks from Japan and the PRC,* 21 AM. ASIAN REV. 109 (2003); Kathleen Woods Masalski, *Examining the Japanese History Textbook Controversies,* JAPAN DIG., Nov. 2001.

[70] On the idea of global history, see CONCEPTUALIZING GLOBAL HISTORY (Bruce Mazlish & Ralph Buultjens eds., 1993); PATRICK MANNING, NAVIGATING WORLD HISTORY: HISTORIANS CREATE A GLOBAL PAST (2003); DAVID REYNOLDS, ONE WORLD DIVISIBLE: A GLOBAL HISTORY SINCE 1945 (2000); Peer Vries, *Editorial: Global History,* 20 J. GLOB. HIST. 5 (2009). On some of the controversy surrounding world

accord non-Western cultures an inferior status whose destinies are shaped by Western states.[71] For his part, Daniel Segal concluded that world history often principally consists of pasting some East Asian history onto a predominantly Western narrative.[72] These inquiries are analogous to studies that seek patterns of dominance within the content and sources of international law textbooks.

Although some might instinctively assume that there is only one history or one international law, studies of diverse national textbook traditions help to check and challenge those assumptions because they foreground the way that the "international" is often constructed and approached differently in different national environments. International law textbooks, like history textbooks, create narratives that both reflect and reinforce specific understandings about how the world or a given field has developed and what role a given state has played in that process. In somes cases, as with the Asian history textbook wars, they may also reflect different nationalist stances in interstate disputes.[73] This proclivity is evident in the treatment by history textbooks of different East Asian states of sovereignty over and the names of many islands in the South China Sea.[74]

Cross-national comparisons of textbooks are also interesting because they offer a way of examining which materials and sources transcend their state's national borders. In some states, international law textbooks are written by domestic authors for the national market. In other states, no national textbooks or casebooks on international law are produced, and they must instead be imported from elsewhere. Identifying which states function as exporters and importers, and in relation to which other states, helps to illustrate patterns of movement of international law materials from one state to another. Cross-country comparisons about which outside sources, such as national court decisions of one state, are referred to in textbooks written in other states also illustrate some of the hierarchical dynamics and asymmetrical flows of materials and ideas that shape the construction of international law as a transnational legal field.

III. The States and Universities Studied

This study looks primarily, though not exclusively, at international law academics at elite universities in, and textbooks from, the five permanent members of the Security Council. As with any case selection, this choice of both states and stratum reveals certain important elements about the field while obscuring others.

---

history courses, see Peter Stearns, *World History: Curriculum and Controversy*, WORLD HIST. CONNECTED, July 2006.

[71] Michelle Commeyras & Donna E. Alvermann, *Messages That High School World History Textbooks Convey*, 85 SOC. STUD. 268 (1994).

[72] Daniel Segal, *"Western Civ" and the Staging of History in American Higher Education*, 106 AM. HIST. REV. 770 (2000).

[73] *Teaching History, Textbook Cases, Chapter 10: In Which Democracies Join in East Asia's History Wars*, ECONOMIST, July 5, 2014.

[74] *Id.*

A. THE PERMANENT MEMBERS OF THE SECURITY COUNCIL

The five permanent members of the Security Council make for revealing case studies for a variety of reasons. Since 1945, the international legal system has granted these states a privileged role in the international legal system, with permanent membership and veto rights in the Security Council as well as an informal permanent seat on the International Court of Justice. As a result, the views of these states are critical to the resolution of many international law issues, such as whether to authorize a certain use of force and whether to admit a state as a member of the United Nations.

In addition to these institutional markers, economic and military might are significant elements in understanding a state's power.[75] The permanent members are all major economic powers, representing five of the top fifteen states in the world ranked by gross domestic product in nominal terms: the United States (No. 1), China (No. 2), the United Kingdom (No. 5), France (No. 6), and Russia (No. 14).[76] In terms of gross domestic product in purchasing power parity terms, they rank as China (No. 1), the United States (No. 2), Russia (No. 6), the United Kingdom (No. 9), and France (No. 10).[77] In terms of military spending, they represent five of the top seven spenders: the United States (No. 1), China (No. 2), Russia (No. 4), the United Kingdom (No. 5), and France (No. 7).[78]

Given the focus of this study on academics and textbooks, it is also worth noting that these states figure prominently in the global flow of students. Higher education represents a significant aspect of soft power,[79] which is the "ability to affect others through the co-optive means of framing the agenda, persuading, and eliciting positive attraction in order to obtain preferred outcomes."[80] According to the United Nations Educational, Social and Cultural Organization, the ten largest importers of foreign students at the tertiary level as of 2014 were the United States (with 19 percent of the global total), the United Kingdom (10 percent), Australia (6 percent), France (6 percent), Germany (5 percent), Russia (3 percent), Japan (3 percent), Canada (3 percent), China (2 percent), and Italy (2 percent).[81]

---

[75] JOSEPH S. NYE, JR., THE FUTURE OF POWER 6, 25, 51 (2012); see also KENNETH E. BOULDING, THREE FACES OF POWER (1989).

[76] INTERNATIONAL MONETARY FUND, REPORT FOR SELECTED COUNTRIES AND SUBJECTS, WORLD ECONOMIC OUTLOOK (2016); World Bank, GDP (current US$), WORLD DEVELOPMENT INDICATORS, http://data.worldbank.org/indicator/NY.GDP.MKTP.CD (last visited Feb. 25, 2017).

[77] World Bank, Gross domestic product 2015, PPP, WORLD DEVELOPMENT INDICATORS, http://data.worldbank. org/indicator/NY.GDP.PCAP.PP.CD (last visited Feb. 25, 2017).

[78] STOCKHOLM INT'L PEACE RES. INST., TRENDS IN WORLD MILITARY EXPENDITURE, 2015 (2016); INT'L INST. FOR STRATEGIC STUD., THE MILITARY BALANCE 2015 (2016).

[79] Joseph Nye, Soft Power and Higher Education, FORUM FOR THE FUTURE OF HIGHER EDUC. 11, 13–14 (2005), https://net.educause.edu/ir/library/pdf/FFP0502S.pdf; Joseph Nye, Soft Power and Higher Education, in THE INTERNET AND THE UNIVERSITY: FORUM 2004, 33, 41–43 (2005), https://net.educause.edu/ir/library/ pdf/ffpiu043.pdf; see also Haim Sandberg, Legal Colonialism: Americanization of Legal Education in Israel, 10 GLOB. JURIST art. 6 (2010); ExEdUK and Wild ReSearch, Education and British Soft Power—The Unexplored Connection, http://exeduk.com/wp-content/uploads/Education-and-British-Soft-Power-the-unexplored-connection.pdf.

[80] NYE, supra note 75, at 21. See generally id. at 81–109.

[81] Net Flow of Internationally Mobile Students, UNESCO INST. FOR STATISTICS, http://uis.unesco.org/indicator/ edu-mobility-indic-menf (last visited Dec. 27, 2016).

When foreign students come to study in a host state, the experience can help to famil-
iarize them with the values and views of that state, stimulating the development of both
goodwill and international networks.[82] For instance, education formed an important
plank of the report of the UK government's Select Committee on Soft Power and the
United Kingdom's Influence, which noted that international students typically develop
an awareness of and respect for UK norms and values, and that most alumni remain pos-
itively oriented toward the nation and retain professional and personal links there after
they leave.[83] Educational migration can also serve as an effective pathway for the trans-
mission of ideas and sources from one state to another, particularly as many students
return home after studying abroad.

Although all of these states have been granted a privileged status within the international legal system, they differ along meaningful axes, including Western/non-Western,
English-speaking/non-English-speaking, common law/civil law, and liberal democratic/
authoritarian.[84] There is evidence of growing friction between these Western democratic
and non-Western authoritarian powers and, in particular, between the United States and
both China and Russia, on a range of issues, including Crimea, the South China Sea, and
cybersecurity. Divisions also exist within these groupings, such as the divide between
France, on the one hand, and the United Kingdom and the United States, on the other,
on the legality of the 2003 Iraq war. These similarities and differences, together with certain rising tensions, make it interesting and instructive to compare the influences and
spheres of influence of the international law academics in these states, as well as the content and structure of their international law textbooks. Nevertheless, focusing on the five
permanent members of the Security Council obscures certain factors.

First, this focus necessarily results in one overlooking significant regions of the world
and approaches to law. The five permanent members include no states in Latin America
or Africa, so they do not reflect a good geographic cross-section of states, nor do they
include representatives from all of the UN geopolitical regional groupings. There are
no representatives from the Middle East or of certain recognized legal families, such as

---

[82] ASS'N OF INT'L EDUCATORS, IN AMERICA'S INTEREST: WELCOMING INTERNATIONAL STUDENTS 5 (2003)
("The millions of people who have studied in the United States over the years constitute a remarkable reservoir
of goodwill for our country, perhaps our most undervalued foreign policy asset."); Secretary Colin L. Powell,
Statement on International Education Week 2001 (Aug. 7, 2001), http://2001-2009.state.gov/secretary/former/
powell/remarks/2001/4462.htm ("We are proud that the high quality of American colleges and universities
attracts students and scholars from around the world. These individuals enrich our communities with their academic abilities and cultural diversity, and they return home with an increased understanding and often a lasting
affection for the United States. I can think of no more valuable asset to our country than the friendship of future
world leaders who have been educated here."); Charlotte Beers, Under Secretary for Public Diplomacy and Public
Affairs, U.S. Public Diplomacy in the Arab and Muslim Worlds (May 7, 2002), http://2001-2009.state.gov/r/
us/10424.htm (educational exchanges are the "bread-and-butter" of public diplomacy: "Considering that some
50 percent of the leaders of the International Coalition were once exchange visitors, this has got to be the best
buy in the government.").
[83] SELECT COMM. ON SOFT POWER AND THE UK'S INFLUENCE, PERSUASION AND POWER IN THE MODERN
WORLD, 2013–14, H.L. 150, ¶¶ 200–03 (U.K.), http://www.publications.parliament.uk/pa/ld201314/ldselect/
ldsoftpower/150/150.pdf.
[84] For details, see the introductory section of Chapter 1.

Islamic law.[85] These last points have broad relevance since many international law disputes have arisen in the Middle East and some argue that world politics involves a clash of civilizations, including between the West and Islam.[86] This choice of states also limits my consideration of the role of language in international law largely to the languages of these five states, which means that I focus less attention on other languages, such as Spanish and German.

Second, this focus on the permanent members results in more attention to "old" great powers than "new" great powers. Permanent membership of the UN Security Council has much to do with which states won and were powerful after World War II. Since then, however, the losing states of Japan and Germany have recovered their economic clout in the world. In addition, various non-Western states have increasingly grown in economic power. These include, but are not limited to, the other members of the BRICS (Brazil, India, and South Africa), as well as the so-called MINT states (Mexico, Indonesia, Nigeria, and Turkey).[87] The increasing economic influence of these states is also starting to be transformed into greater political power, particularly with the creation of new institutional structures, like the Group of Twenty and the BRICS.[88]

Third, the limited sample set means that some combinations of attributes are not adequately considered, while others are hard to disaggregate. A notable example is that China and Russia are the only non-Western states considered, but they are not representative of all non-Western states. For instance, Russia and China are authoritarian states, whereas many non-Western states are democratic, such as the other members of the BRICS.[89] If a difference is found between the approach of China/Russia and the US/UK/France, it may well result from divergence in the authoritarian/democratic axis rather than the non-Western/Western axis, or it could result from other factors altogether.

Fourth, this study focuses primarily on actors and materials from more powerful states rather than on those from less powerful states, and thus does not highlight certain important core-periphery dynamics. Although the United Kingdom and France differ in terms of language and legal systems, they are similar in the sense of having been great colonial powers that exported their legal systems to a variety of colonies, now independent states, throughout the world. A state's experience of and approach to international law may vary depending on factors such as whether it was a former colonizer or a former colony, and whether it is situated closer to the core or the periphery. In the same way, Russia's experience of international law is likely to differ from that of a state in Russia's "near abroad" (the other former Soviet states).

---

[85] See, e.g., KONRAD ZWEIGERT & HEIN KÖTZ, AN INTRODUCTION TO COMPARATIVE LAW (1987) (distinguishing among Romanistic, Germanic, Nordic, common law, Socialist, Far East, Islamic, and Hindu law).

[86] See, e.g., SAMUEL P. HUNTINGTON, THE CLASH OF CIVILIZATIONS AND THE REMAKING OF WORLD ORDER (2011).

[87] See The Mint Countries: Next Economic Giants?, BBC NEWS, Jan. 6, 2014.

[88] See Chapter 6.I.A.

[89] See ECONOMIST INTELLIGENCE UNIT, DEMOCRACY INDEX 2015: DEMOCRACY IN AN AGE OF ANXIETY 4–8 tbl.2 (2016) (listing Brazil, India, and South Africa as flawed democracies).

China represents an anomalous case in this regard because it is the only member of the UN Security Council that has dual identities as a great power and a developing state.[90] China is a great power given factors such as the size and global significance of its economy. Yet its enormous population means that it is not a wealthy state when judged on a per capita basis and its tremendous economic success has been of relatively recent origin. Accordingly, one would expect China to exhibit some of the characteristics of less powerful states in certain core-periphery relationships, particularly when one is looking at certain historical patterns and transnational educational flows. As its power and wealth grow, however, one would predict that China would increasingly identify as a great power that is returning, to some extent, to its former glory as the Middle Kingdom.

All of these limitations are important. In some cases, this study is able to supply some information on these points. For instance, some of the core-periphery dynamics and pathways that emerge from former colonial relationships surface when looking at the destinations and directionality of global student flows and the diffusion of textbooks. But, in many cases, these gaps highlight the need to broaden this study by including other states in the future.

B. FOCUS ON ACADEMICS AT ELITE UNIVERSITIES

To identify a reasonably sized, yet manageable, group of international law academics to profile, I selected the top five "elite" law schools in the five permanent members and then identified tenured and tenure-track international law academics at those law schools as of the end of 2013. In recent years, there has been a clear rise in popular sentiment against those identified as "the elite."[91] Nonetheless, I adopted this focus on elite institutions for several reasons.

The first set of reasons was practical. Focusing on a limited number of law schools in each state made a cross-national study manageable. Some states have many more law schools than are included in the study, including the United States and China with over one hundred each. To determine whether the patterns that characterize international law academics at top-ranked schools hold true for all schools within those states, a larger-scale comparison would need to be undertaken. I identified the most select schools within these states on the basis of rankings, where these were available, and discussions with academics from those states, where rankings were not available. Rankings of law schools in general were easier to come by for most states than those of international law as a field or international law academics.

---

[90] Rosemary Foot, *Introduction* to CHINA ACROSS THE DIVIDE: THE DOMESTIC AND GLOBAL IN POLITICS AND SOCIETY 1, 5 (Rosemary Foot ed., 2013); Courtney J. Fung, *What Explains China's Deployment to UN Peacekeeping Operations?*, 16 INT'L REL. ASIA-PACIFIC 409, 411 (2016); Wu Xinbo, *Four Contradictions in Constraining China's Foreign Policy Behavior, in* CHINESE FOREIGN POLICY: PRAGMATISM AND STRATEGIC BEHAVIOR 58, 58–59 (Suisheng Zhao ed., 2016).

[91] For a discussion of this, see, for example, Nick Clegg & Jonathan Haidt, The Rise of Populism and the Backlash Against the Elites, YOUTUBE (Nov. 21, 2016), https://youtu.be/6gZ5UD1hFM4.

The second set of reasons had to do with the stratification of legal education within states. International law often plays a more significant role at more prestigious institutions within a given state than less prestigious ones.[92] International law is sometimes presented as a luxury good, that is, as a subject that a highly ranked law school can more easily pay to have people teach than as a necessity that all law schools must teach. Students at top-tier law schools in different countries are also probably the most likely to become candidates for international or transnational work in their subsequent employment. They are more likely to be exposed to experiences like working at their state's foreign ministry or the United Nations, or for large international law firms in major cities rather than regional offices with a stronger local or domestic focus.[93]

The third set of reasons stemmed from the stratification of legal education among states. A 2006 study of all sitting judges on international courts found that many of those judges had studied at a handful of elite law schools in a small number of states.[94] Out of 205 sitting judges, 39 earned degrees from UK universities and 29 from US universities, including Cambridge (14), the University of London (11), Oxford (8), Columbia (7), Harvard (7), Yale (3), and New York University (NYU) (3).[95] In France, these institutions included the University of Paris (11).[96] In states that were previously in the Soviet sphere, many of the judges had studied at universities in Moscow.[97] The authors concluded that "a significant part of the international judiciary studied largely with the same professors and in many cases even the same textbooks."[98] The present study concerns these sorts of professors and textbooks.

The fourth set of reasons turned on identifying markers of social capital and understanding the importance of international law within a particular state's educational hierarchy. The profiles of international law academics in the most highly ranked schools yield evidence of what different academies privilege in their assessment of academic candidates, which in turn affects what sort of markers of social capital are encouraged and rewarded. For instance, do elite law schools in a particular state value domestic law degrees or foreign ones? Do they reward publishing in national or transnational journals? Do they value national or international practice? In addition, do all of the most prestigious schools evidence a strong focus on international law or is it possible for law schools in some states to be high ranking without an international focus?

---

[92] Christophe Jamin & William van Caenegem, *The Internationalisation of Legal Education: General Report for the Vienna Congress of the International Academy of Comparative Law, 20–26 July 2014*, in THE INTERNATIONALISATION OF LEGAL EDUCATION 3, 21 (Christophe Jamin & William van Caenegem eds., 2016).

[93] *Id.* at 8–9 (noting stratification of practice with only the top end of the profession strongly valuing foreign and international legal knowledge).

[94] TERRIS ET AL., *supra* note 46, at 17–18.

[95] *Id.* at 18; *see also* GLEIDER I. HERNÁNDEZ, THE INTERNATIONAL COURT OF JUSTICE AND THE JUDICIAL FUNCTION 133–34 (2014).

[96] TERRIS ET AL., *supra* note 46. The study treated the University of Paris and the University of London as single institutions, even though both have split into separate schools at various points.

[97] The pattern in Russia is slightly more complicated than this study suggests given the breakup of the Soviet Union into separate states. Historically, many Soviet and Russian international court judges studied at a handful of schools in the Soviet Union and Russia, including the Institute of International Law at Kiev University, the Moscow State Institute of International Relations (MGIMO), Saint Petersburg State University, and Kazan Federal University.

[98] TERRIS ET AL., *supra* note 46, at 18.

For the United Kingdom and the United States, I identified this highly ranked group by looking at various rating exercises, which led me to select the following UK institutions: the University of Cambridge Faculty of Law; the Dickson Poon School of Law, King's College; the London School of Economics; the University of Oxford Faculty of Law; and the University College London Faculty of Law;[99] and US counterparts: the University of Chicago Law School, Columbia Law School, Harvard Law School, Stanford Law School, and Yale Law School.[100] Although the top four UK universities appeared on every list, they varied on whether they included King's College or another law school in the top five. I selected King's because it was listed in the top five UK law schools on an international ranking.[101] NYU typically ranked sixth among domestic US law schools, but, as it often does better on international rankings[102] and on rankings focused on international law,[103] I separately coded its academics to draw some comparisons.[104]

In France, formal rankings are considered abhorrent, so I had to rely on information from a range of French legal academics. The law schools of the University of Paris I Panthéon Sorbonne and Paris II Assas are historically considered the top two and are perceived as such by academics and students. Nevertheless, others are competitive in individual specialties, which makes a real difference at the master's level, where most international law studies take place. I selected two additional schools that were valued for their strength in international law (Paris Ouest University Nanterre La Défense and Paul Cézanne University Aix-Marseilles), as well as one further institution that has been creating a stir in the French legal scene for taking a much more internationalized and interdisciplinary approach to legal education (the Paris Institute of Political Studies (Sciences Po) Law School).

For China and Russia, after examining the available rankings and consulting local academics and practitioners, I selected the following institutions in China: China University of Political Science and Law, Peking University Law School, Renmin University of China Law School, Tsinghua University School of Law, and Wuhan University School of Law;[105]

---

[99] *See University Guide 2015: League Table for Law*, Guardian, June 3, 2014 (2014 rankings); *QS World University Rankings by Subject 2014—Law*, Top Univs., https://www.topuniversities.com/university-rankings/university-subject-rankings/2016/law-legal-studies (2014 rankings) (last visited Sept. 22, 2016); *University Subject Tables: Law*, Complete Univ. Guide, http://www.thecompleteuniversityguide.co.uk/league-tables/rankings?s=law (2014 rankings) (last visited Sept. 22, 2016).

[100] *See The 2014 U.S. News Law School Rankings*, Above the Law, http://abovethelaw.com/2013/03/the-2014-u-s-news-law-school-rankings/ (2014 rankings) (last visited Sept. 22, 2016); *Best Law Schools*, U.S. News & World Rep., http://grad-schools.usnews.rankingsandreviews.com/best-graduate-schools/top-law-schools/law-rankings (2016 rankings) (last visited Sept. 22, 2016).

[101] *QS World University Rankings by Subject 2014—Law*, *supra* note 99.

[102] *Id.*

[103] *See Best Law Schools, supra* note 100.

[104] *See* Chapter 5.1.A.

[105] For Chinese rankings, see *Ten Most Famous Universities for Law Study in China*, AT0086, http://news.at0086.com/China-university/Top-10-Famous-Universities-for-Law-Study-in-China.html; *Top 10 China Universities for Law Study*, AT0086, http://www.at0086.net/news/Top-10-China-Universities-for-Law-Study.html (both last visited Sept. 22, 2016). *See also* 中国大学法学排行榜 [Chinese University Law Rankings], http://edu.people.com.cn/GB/116076/17669394.html; *Chinese Law Schools: A Ranking (Sort of)*, Chinese Law Prof

and in Russia: Lomonosov Moscow State University Faculty of Law, St. Petersburg State University Faculty of Law, Kutafin Moscow State Law University, Moscow State Institute of International Relations of the Ministry of Foreign Affairs of the Russian Federation (MGIMO), and the National Research University Higher School of Economics Faculty of Law.[106]

I used these law schools' websites to identify tenured and tenure-track academics who specialized in (1) public international law; (2) subfields of public international law, such as international human rights, international trade, international investment, international environment, and international criminal law; and (3) some fields that concern the relationship between public international law and domestic law, such as foreign relations law and national security. This task was not always easy, as some states and universities classify "international law" in distinct ways. For instance, in China, "international law" is an umbrella concept that covers public international law, private international law, and international economic law. Thus, various subfields identified above were spread between the Chinese subcategories of public international law and international economic law. For a full list of the academics included in this study with more detail about how they were selected, see Appendix A.

There are limits, of course, to this approach. The top law schools in a particular state do not necessarily employ the top international law academics in that state. Indeed, in the United States, where rankings are available both generally and by specialty, considerable divergence is found between the top five law schools according to general rankings and the top five ranked according to international law as a specialty.[107] In China, the Schools of Law of Beijing Normal and Xiamen Universities are particularly strong in international law, but neither makes the top five list overall. Likewise, in Russia, the top five law schools on general measures do not include the Peoples' Friendship University of Russia, which is famous for its international orientation and student body,[108] or Kazan Federal University, which was one of the three renowned international law faculties in the Union

---

BLOG, http://lawprofessors.typepad.com/china_law_prof_blog/2013/02/chinese-law-schools-a-ranking-sort-of.html (2012 rankings) (both last visited Sept. 22, 2016).

[106] For various Russian rankings, see Рейтинги российских юридических вузов (2010–2011 гг.) [Ratings of Russian Legal Higher Education Institutes (2010–2011)], LARGO MGMT. GRP. (Sept. 28, 2011), http://largo.ru/blog/legal/post/reytingi_rossiyskikh_yuridicheskikh_vuzov_2010_2011_gg_-136. See also MÄLKSOO, supra note 17, at 86 (identifying the leading academic institutions in the field of international law).

[107] Compare, for instance, the top five law schools based on general rankings, Best Law Schools, U.S. NEWS & WORLD REP., http://grad-schools.usnews.rankingsandreviews.com/best-graduate-schools/top-law-schools/law-rankings?int=e5dbob (2017 rankings) (Yale, Harvard, Stanford, Columbia, Chicago), with the top five law schools based on rankings in international law, International Law, U.S. NEWS & WORLD REP., http://grad-schools.usnews.rankingsandreviews.com/best-graduate-schools/top-law-schools/international-law-rankings (2017 Rankings) (NYU, Columbia, Harvard, Georgetown, American University) (both last visited Feb. 26, 2016).

[108] About RUDN University, RUDN UNIV., http://www.rudn.ru/en/?pagec=3 (last visited Sept. 22, 2016) ("It is the only university in the world every year uniting students from 145–150 countries.... More than 77 thousand graduates of the University work in 170 countries, among them more than 5500 holders of PhD and Doctorate degrees. Specialists are prepared in 62 majors and lines of study. More than 29 thousand graduate and postgraduate students from 140 countries are currently studying at the university. They represent more than 450 nations and nationalities of the world.").

of Soviet Socialist Republics (USSR), alongside those of the Universities of Moscow and Kiev.[109]

The top law schools in a state will also not necessarily train that state's diplomats and international legal advisers. In the Western states in the study, the elite law schools are often important feeders into all areas of international law practice, including the foreign service. In China, by contrast, diplomats often train at the China Foreign Affairs University, known as the "Cradle of Chinese Diplomats," which operates under the guidance of the Ministry of Foreign Affairs and does not make the top-five-ranked law schools.[110] Many Chinese diplomats also studied at universities specializing in foreign languages, whereas many Ministry of Commerce officials studied at the University of International Business and Economics.[111] In Russia, the two primary feeders for diplomats are MGIMO, which is in the study, and the Diplomatic Academy of the Ministry of Foreign Affairs of the Russian Federation, which is not, although the legal department of the Ministry of Foreign Affairs typically hires from MGIMO and Moscow State University, both of which are in the study.[112]

Despite these limitations, profiling the international law academics in the elite law schools of these states yields revealing information about the divisible college of international lawyers, including how nationally or transnationally oriented these academics are in terms of their education, teaching, publishing, and professional activities, as well as the direction and focus of their transnational orientation.

IV. Important Concepts and Factors

A. NATIONALIZING, DENATIONALIZING, AND WESTERNIZING INFLUENCES

In looking for patterns of difference, dominance, and disruption, this book considers evidence of various forms of nationalizing, denationalizing, and westernizing influences that have marked the field to date and that might be subject to various forms of disruption in the future. Nationalizing and denationalizing influences concern the tension between the national and the transnational, while westernizing influences concern the nature of the transnational.

The concept of "nationalizing influences" captures the extent to which the academies and textbooks from different states tend to focus on national actors, materials, and forums in their construction of international law. For the academies, this tendency would be evidenced by factors such as whether most of the international law academics studied

---

[109] *See Homepage*, KAZAN FED. UNIV., http://kpfu.ru/eng (last visited Sept. 22, 2016).

[110] *See Homepage*, CHINA FOREIGN AFF. UNIV., http://www.csc.edu.cn/studyinchina/universitydetailen.aspx?collegeId=168 (last visited Sept. 22, 2016).

[111] *See Homepage*, UNIV. INT'L BUS. & ECON., http://www.uibe.cn/app/eng/ (China) (last visited Sept. 22, 2016).

[112] *See Diplomatic Academy of the Ministry of Foreign Affairs of the Russian Federation*, WIKIPEDIA, http://en.wikipedia.org/wiki/Diplomatic_Academy_of_the_Ministry_of_Foreign_Affairs_of_the_Russian_Federation (last modified June 21, 2016, 1:49 PM); *Homepage*, MGIMO UNIV., http://english.mgimo.ru/ (last visited Sept. 22, 2016); *Moscow State Institute of International Relations*, WIKIPEDIA, http://en.wikipedia.org/wiki/Moscow_State_Institute_of_International_Relations (last modified Jan. 30, 2017, 10:05 PM).

law only in that state, whether they published primarily in journals from that state, and whether the forms of practice they engaged in tended to be nationally based, such as working for a domestic judge or their home government. For textbooks, this tendency would be evidenced by factors such as whether the books tended to privilege the perspective and practice of their state, for example, by primarily relying on that state's domestic case law and executive practice, and chiefly citing that state's academics.

By contrast, the notion of "denationalizing influences" captures the extent to which the academies and textbooks from different states tend to focus on foreign and transnational actors, materials, and forums in their construction of the field. For the academies, this tendency would be evidenced by factors such as whether most of the international law academics studied law in more than one state, whether they published primarily or significantly in foreign and transnational journals, and whether the forms of practice they engaged in tended to be on the transnational level, such as working for an international organization or appearing as counsel before an international court. For textbooks, this tendency would be evidenced by factors such as whether the books were inclined to downplay the perspective and practice of their state, for example, by primarily relying on case law from foreign and international courts, and chiefly citing foreign state practice and foreign academics.

The concept of "westernizing influences" captures the extent to which some denationalizing influences end up involving a Western orientation. For example, did academics who studied law in two or more states move from one Western state to another Western state, or from a non-Western state to a Western one? If they published in transnational journals, were these primarily edited by Western scholars? If they worked at an international organization or appeared before an international court, were most of their colleagues from Western states? With respect to textbooks, to the extent that international law textbooks incorporated foreign practice and perspectives, did they focus primarily on those of Western states? To the extent they cited foreign academics, were these primarily from Western states?

One should also not confuse these nationalizing, denationalizing, and westernizing influences with either motivations or effects. International lawyers may be motivated to study abroad to enrich their understanding of the world or because doing so would help them secure a higher-paid job at home. Similarly, a state might encourage its lawyers to acquire certain denationalizing and westernizing educational experiences as a strategy for protecting national interests. For instance, the Chinese government has adopted policies aimed at encouraging the development of lawyers with knowledge of international law and experience gained in Western legal systems, but its goals are expressly nationalistic: "the priority is to cultivate international law professionals who have knowledge of international laws and can participate in international affairs in order to protect national interests."[113]

---

113 教育部, 中央政法委员会关于实施卓越法律人才教育培养计划的若干意见 [Several Opinions of the Ministry of Education and the Central Politics and Law Commission of the Communist Party of China on Implementing the Plan for Educating and Training Outstanding Legal Talents], XINHUA (Ministry of Educ., Dec. 23, 2011).

B. CORE, PERIPHERY, AND SEMIPERIPHERAL STATES

This study uses the phrases core, periphery, and semiperiphery to describe certain characteristics of different states and core-periphery dynamics to describe certain relationships between states. Although somewhat inspired by the development of these terms in world-systems theory,[114] this study does not use these terms in a narrow, technical sense. Broadly speaking, core states tend to be more powerful economically, militarily, and politically than peripheral states. Semiperipheral states fall between these extremes, either because they hold intermediate power on these three measures or because they are strong on some but weak on others.

Core-periphery status is dynamic and evolves over time in light of changing economic and geopolitical realities. For instance, in the nineteenth and twentieth centuries, states like the United Kingdom, France, Portugal, the Netherlands, and Spain were regarded as core states because they were strong colonial powers. But after decolonization and various shifts in power, Portugal, the Netherlands, and Spain slipped into semiperipheral status, at the same time as the United Kingdom and France retained their core status, though their relative status as great powers is widely recognized as having declined in recent decades.

This book uses the core-periphery dynamic in describing the relationship between colonial powers and their former colonies, which still plays out in contexts such as the transnational flow of students and the export and import of textbooks. Thus, France maintains a core-periphery relationship with many of its former colonies in Africa and Asia, as does the United Kingdom with its former colonies like Australia, Canada, and India. Whether the latter states are classed as semiperipheral or peripheral, the main point of invoking the dynamic here is to pinpoint their relationship with their core state rather than the exact category in which they belong.

Another way this book uses the core-periphery concept is in distinguishing between more and less powerful Western, liberal democratic states. Although Australia, Canada, the United Kingdom, and the United States are all Western, liberal, and democratic, the latter two clearly wield more power on a variety of measures than the former two. Similarly, within Western Europe, France and Germany command much more power than many other states, such as Belgium and Austria. On some measures, all of these states would be considered "core" states given their levels of economic development. Nevertheless, this book refers to some of these less powerful Western states as "semiperipheral" states to capture this power differential.

The core-periphery terminology does not apply neatly to the BRICS, particularly as the economic and political power of many of these states has altered considerably in the past few decades. For this reason, this book does not tend to categorize these states as core, peripheral, or semiperipheral or invoke the core-periphery dynamic regarding them, with two main exceptions: first, these states are generally treated as moving from a more peripheral status to a more core-like status within the international system; and, second,

[114] *See generally* Immanuel Wallerstein, *World-Systems Analysis, in* ENCYCLOPEDIA OF LIFE SUPPORT SYSTEMS— WORLD SYSTEM HISTORY (George Modelski ed., 2004).

the history or current status of some of these states is sometimes viewed in specific core-periphery terms, such as the core-periphery relationship of the United Kingdom and India based on their history of colonial rule and the core-periphery relationship of Russia with other former Soviet states.

C. THE RELEVANCE OF LANGUAGE

Language is an important factor in understanding the construction of international law as a transnational legal field. Wittgenstein famously stated, "The limits of my language are the limits of my world."[115] Language drives how international lawyers approach their field and interact with each other. It shapes where they study, what job prospects they have, what they can read and write, which sources and concepts they are familiar with, and which networks they develop.[116] Common languages facilitate communication, whereas linguistic barriers separate communities. A lawyer's command of a language often goes hand in hand with socialization in a given legal culture, such as French and German with the civil law and English with the common law.

Not all languages are equal on the international level. Some are strong numerically in terms of the number of native speakers or first- and second-language speakers (for example, Mandarin, English, Spanish, Arabic, and Hindi).[117] Others are strong in terms of their geographical spread. A "national" language is one that is spoken primarily within a single state, such as Japanese and Thai. A "regional" language is dominant in multiple states within a specific part of the world, such as Russian in the former Soviet sphere. An "international" language is spoken in diverse parts of the world, like English, French, and Spanish, which were all exported through colonial power. English is particularly important in the former British colonies, as is French in francophone Africa, and Spanish in Latin America.

Some languages have been accorded a privileged place within the international system de jure, whereas others have assumed a dominant role de facto. In terms of de jure privilege, six languages have been recognized as official languages at the United Nations: Arabic, Chinese, English, French, Russian, and Spanish. All of these languages are used in UN meetings and all official UN documents are written in them. Of these languages, two have been especially "privileged" in international organizations: English and French. They are the working languages of the UN Secretariat, a variety of international organizations (for example, the Organisation for Economic Co-operation and Development), and many international courts and tribunals (for example, the ICJ, the International

---

[115] LUDWIG WITTGENSTEIN, TRACTATUS LOGICO-PHILOSOPHICUS, § 5.6 (1922) ("Die Grenzen meiner Sprache bedeuten die Grenzen meiner Welt").

[116] See generally GUY DEUTSCHER, THROUGH THE LANGUAGE GLASS: WHY THE WORLD LOOKS DIFFERENT IN OTHER LANGUAGES (2011).

[117] See List of Languages by Number of Native Speakers, WIKIPEDIA, https://en.wikipedia.org/wiki/List_of_languages_by_number_of_native_speakers (last modified Feb. 23, 2017, 8:17 AM); List of Languages by Total Number of Speakers, WIKIPEDIA, https://en.wikipedia.org/wiki/List_of_languages_by_total_number_of_speakers (last modified Feb. 23, 2017).

Criminal Court, the International Criminal Tribunal for the former Yugoslavia, and the International Tribunal for the Law of the Sea).

In terms of de facto dominance, although French was formerly the leading language of diplomacy, English has increasingly become the lingua franca of international law, business, and education, predominating in international negotiations, contracting, institutions, dispute resolution, publishing, and education.[118] English plays a striking role in law firms engaged in transnational legal services; all but three of the top one hundred such firms as measured by total revenue are headquartered in English-speaking states, primarily the United States and the United Kingdom.[119]

Whether an international lawyer's language is (or languages are) national, regional, or international, or privileged or dominant, is key to whether that lawyer can communicate across borders and, if so, with whom. These factors also govern his or her ability to access and engage with various transnational forums, such as international organizations and transnational journals. The differential advantage that attends different languages also influences incentives to learn multiple languages. The network effects created by the dominance of English in the transnational realm are self-perpetuating, as the more English speakers there are, the more attractive it becomes for others to learn English, and so on.[120] Consequently, incentives for non-native English speakers at least to become bilingual increase, whereas native English speakers are more likely to remain monolingual.

V. Three Points of Method

Three additional points of method are worth making at this stage.

A. FACTORS THAT REFLECT AND REINFORCE PARTICULAR APPROACHES

This project aims at identifying a constellation of factors that I believe reflect and reinforce similarities and differences in how international lawyers in different states understand and approach international law. From the methods adopted, I cannot prove whether one factor is best understood as a cause or a consequence of another. I am not a social scientist and, although I have collected and analyzed data, the reader will not find sophisticated regression analyses or statistical modeling intended to try to isolate variables or prove causation.

There are two reasons for this approach. First, some of the cross-national differences that emerge from this comparative international law study are so striking on the basis of the raw data that I believe that one can get away with using simple tools and visual

---

[118] *See, e.g.*, David Crystal, English as a Global Language (2d ed. 2003); Nicholas Ostler, The Last Lingua Franca: The Rise and Fall of World Languages (2011); Barbara Seidlhofer, *English as a Lingua Franca*, 59 ELT J. 339 (2005).

[119] *2014 Global 100: Top-Grossing Law Firms in the World*, Am. Law., Sept. 19, 2014.

[120] Bryan H. Druzin, *Buying Commercial Law: Choice of Forum, Choice of Law, and Network Effect*, 18 Tul. J. Int'l & Comp. L. 1, 18 (2009).

displays to portray these differences. My goal is to create a framework of analysis that can be used as a platform for others to delve more deeply into some of the particulars, including through large multistate studies and in-depth individual country case studies, to confirm, correct, or add nuance to the story that I tell.

Second, I believe that many of the factors identified both reflect and reinforce particular approaches to international law in a way that is mutually constitutive and self-reinforcing. Although I spend little time trying to parse differences between these factors or to examine ways of testing the existence and direction of causality, I invite others to build on this work by seeking to isolate and test individual variables to determine whether and, if so, to what extent they reflect and/or reinforce specific approaches to international law.

Every one of the measures looked at in this book has limitations and tells only part of the story. Textbooks may instruct us about how international law is understood and taught, but teachers may supplement these books or use only a selection from them. One can identify certain common professional experiences of academics, such as full-time work for governments or appearances before international courts, but academics might work for governments on a confidential basis or appear in nonpublic arbitrations. Looking at where legal academics obtained their law degrees can tell one something about educational diversity within those states, but it does not capture certain other transnational experiences, like foreign exchange or study abroad programs. That is why it is important to understand the various elements examined as different pieces of a puzzle in which the aspects are individually open to criticism but collectively paint a more compelling portrait.

B. IDENTIFYING AND SEEKING TO OVERCOME ONE'S OWN LIMITATIONS

As with anyone attempting to do a comparative international law exercise, I am inevitably situated and limited by my own experiences and parochialism. I was born and grew up in Australia, though I now have dual British/Australian citizenship. I spent fourteen years living and working in the United States and the United Kingdom, primarily in New York and London. I am only fluent in speaking English. I studied French in high school and have taken a number of French courses during my working life, but I have never developed any real proficiency in it. I have studied and worked full time only in Western, common law states (Australia, the United Kingdom, and the United States), other than a few months in Paris and The Hague. Some people have queried whether I should disclose these facts, but being aware of and open about one's limitations is a crucial part of this sort of analysis.

Given my own limitations, I have approached my analysis in a variety of ways. I began by engaging in discussions with academics and international law specialists from the states concerned to get a sense of the academy and field, especially with respect to which universities to focus on and which textbooks to profile. I hired a series of research assistants to help me collect information on these states, prioritizing international students who were studying for or had received LLMs in the United States (where I was teaching when I began this project) but who had undertaken their first law degrees in the other states within the project. In the case of Russia, I relied in some cases on students who had language skills and/or were from former Soviet states, like Ukraine and Mongolia, though I also engaged Russian LLM students as researchers.

As the information on these states began to come in, I developed a network of individuals from them with whom I discussed the results so that I could better understand the patterns that were emerging, as well as their possible causes and consequences. Some of these individuals were academics and practitioners, whereas others were former students of mine at the London School of Economics, Harvard, and Columbia who came from these states.[121] Many of these individuals pointed to additional sources for me to consider. My research assistants provided summaries and translations of the sources on which I rely in this book. I also read widely within the English-language literature on these states and from these states.

C. STUDYING THE PRESENT RATHER THAN CHANGES OVER TIME

This study takes a snapshot in time. It focuses on international law as it is conceptualized and taught in different academies in the mid-2010s, not twenty or forty years ago or even more distantly in the past. Although I believe that a historical treatment would be useful, I adopted this approach because it reflected the scope of the project that I felt able to undertake.

Although comparative international law is rarely discussed in current debates, it emerges in historical work that examines Latin American and American approaches to international law;[122] Third World Approaches to International Law that deal with the expansion of European international law through colonization;[123] French, German, and UK approaches to international law before World War II;[124] and Soviet and Western approaches to international law during the Cold War.[125] This book examines similarities and differences that exist today, but it does not consider how these patterns may have changed over time. Such a study often requires a single-country focus—as exemplified by Mälksoo's work on Russian approaches to international law and Mark Janis's work on American approaches to international law[126]—which I felt unable to maintain while adopting a comparative focus across five states.

---

[121] *See* Acknowledgments, *supra* pp. xxiii–xxiv.

[122] *See, e.g.,* ARNULF BECKER LORCA, MESTIZO INTERNATIONAL LAW: A GLOBAL INTELLECTUAL HISTORY 1842–1933 (2015); Harlen Grant Cohen, *The American Challenge to International Law: A Tentative Framework for Debate*, 28 YALE J. INT'L L. 551 (2003).

[123] *See, e.g.,* ANTONY ANGHIE, IMPERIALISM, SOVEREIGNTY AND THE MAKING OF INTERNATIONAL LAW (2005); BALAKRISHNAN RAJAGOPAL, INTERNATIONAL LAW FROM BELOW (2003); B.S. Chimni, *Third World Approaches to International Law: A Manifesto*, 8 INT'L COMMUNITY L. REV. 3 (2006); David P. Fidler, *Revolt Against or from Within the West? TWAIL, the Developing World, and the Future Direction of International Law*, 2 CHINESE J. INT'L L. 29 (2003); James Thuo Gathii, *Rejoinder: Twailing International Law*, 98 MICH. L. REV. 2066, 2067 (2000); Makau Mutua, *What Is TWAIL?*, 94 AM. SOC'Y INT'L L. PROC. 31 (2000).

[124] *See generally* MARTTI KOSKENNIEMI, THE GENTLE CIVILIZER OF NATIONS: THE RISE AND FALL OF INTERNATIONAL LAW 1870–1960 (2001).

[125] Boris N. Mamlyuk & Ugo Mattei, *Comparative International Law*, 36 BROOK. J. INT'L L. 385 (2011).

[126] *See* MARK WESTON JANIS, AMERICA AND THE LAW OF NATIONS 1776–1939 (2010); MÄLKSOO, *supra* note 17.

Some of the patterns that can be observed today have indeed changed and may be subject to future disruption. For instance, the profile of US international law academics has been transformed in the last few decades. After World War II, many of the prominent international law academics in the United States were refugees from Europe who frequently spoke a few languages. Most of these scholars had died by the late 1990s and early 2000s. In their place, the US international lawyers who came to prominence were largely homegrown, often spoke no foreign languages, and in large part concentrated more on foreign relations law and national security law than international law. International law academics at the most prestigious UK law schools in the past were often British, whereas today many hail from around the globe. Whether the openness and attractiveness of the UK legal academy will diminish as a result of Brexit remains to be seen, but is entirely possible.

As standard textbooks and academic profiles continue to change, a time assessment of the features identified in these pages would be a useful addition to this study. Still, I leave that project to others to pursue. Given current changes in this newly emerging competitive world order, which is also marked by significant shifts in sentiments regarding the relative merits of globalism and nationalism, it would be interesting to examine these themes in ten or twenty years to see which patterns held and which changed. It may well be that this book not only considers a snapshot in time, but also captures the end of an era. For instance, will the election of Trump in the United States lead to greater fracturing within and among Western states, a turning away from liberalism, and a reversal of many of the pillars of the post-World War II international system that were set up, in large part, by the United States and its Western allies? Will Brexit lead to or hasten the decline of the existence or power of the United Kingdom? How will the European Union respond? Will China take the opportunity to step up as a new or renewed great power and, if so, what will that entail for it both domestically and internationally? How will relations between Russia and the United States, Europe and China develop? And how might these changes impact upon the profiles of international law academics, the content of their textbooks, and the ways in which international law is understood and approached in these states? These are important questions, but those topics must await another day.

3

Comparing International Law Academics

WRITING IN 1977, Oscar Schachter famously described the professional community of international lawyers as an "invisible college of international lawyers."[1] In his words, "That professional community, though dispersed throughout the world and engaged in diverse occupations, constitutes a kind of invisible college dedicated to a common intellectual enterprise. As in the case of other disciplines, its members are engaged in a continuous process of communication and collaboration."[2] Evidence of this worldwide process of communication and collaboration could be found in "the journals and yearbooks of international law, in the transnational movement of professors and students, and in the numerous conferences, seminars and colloquia held in all parts of the globe."[3]

Schachter was quick to note that this process of communication was "by no means confined to the realm of scholarship."[4] International bodies and conferences were largely composed of jurists who maintained intellectual contact with the scholarly side of the profession. In addition, the invisible college extended into the sphere of government, as scholars frequently worked in or for their governments in ways that resulted in a "pénétration pacifique" of ideas from the academy into official channels.[5] It would be unrealistic, Schachter cautioned, to think of this as a one-way penetration. Instead: "Individuals

---

[1] Oscar Schachter, *The Invisible College of International Lawyers*, 72 Nw. U. L. Rev. 217, 217 (1977).
[2] *Id.*
[3] *Id.*
[4] *Id.*
[5] *Id.*

Is International Law International? Anthea Roberts.
© Anthea Roberts 2017. Published 2017 by Oxford University Press.

who move from one role to another are unlikely to remain uninfluenced by the ideas and considerations which impinge on them in their different capacities. The mingling of the scholarly and the official affects both categories, and often creates tension as individuals move from one role to another or perceive themselves as acting in the dual capacity of objective scientist and government advocate."[6]

International lawyers and academics have long been taken with this description of their professional community, but how accurate is it? I suggest that it might be better to understand the transnational field of international law as comprising a divisible college of international lawyers. International law academics in different states often have distinct profiles based on where they studied, whom they teach, which languages they use, what and where they publish, and how they engage with practice. Rather than a single community, the field consists of separate, though overlapping, communities, often demonstrating distinct approaches, reference points, hierarchies, areas of expertise, and spheres of influence.

This chapter identifies and explores some of the nationalizing, denationalizing, and westernizing influences that reflect and reinforce the divisible college of international lawyers, focusing in particular on (1) the transnational flow of students, (2) the educational profiles of international law academics, (3) the publication placements of international law academics, and (4) common connections between international law academia and practice in different states.

I. The Global Flow of Students and Ideas

Education plays a crucial role in shaping individuals' approaches and networks (incoming influences) and represents a meaningful form of soft power through which academics in some states are able to diffuse ideas and materials across borders (outgoing spheres of influence). Indeed, one element of the invisible college of international lawyers that Schachter pointed to is the "transnational movement of . . . students."[7] But what are the patterns that shape whether individuals from certain states are likely to cross borders to undertake tertiary studies and, if so, where they go? And how might these patterns influence the construction of international law as a transnational legal field?

No comprehensive data are available on the transnational flow of law students, let alone on students who cross borders to study international law. But the UN Educational, Scientific and Cultural Organization (UNESCO) has compiled reasonably comprehensive data about cross-border flows of tertiary students in general, and has data about the cross border flow of law students into around 35 states, mainly from the Organisation for Economic Co-operation and Development (OECD). Some information can also be gleaned from university websites and newspapers about transnational movements of

<hr>

[6] *Id.* at 218.
[7] *Id.* at 217.

students studying international law. On the basis of these data, it seems that, broadly, the global flow of students and ideas to date has been shaped by two asymmetrical dynamics.

First, students are more likely to move from peripheral and semiperipheral states toward core states, and from non-Western states to Western ones, than the other way around. The symbolic capital associated with undertaking further legal education differs markedly among states because enhanced status is generally associated with movement toward the core rather than away from it. Thus, when it comes to the transnational movement of students studying law, some states function primarily as sender states and others as host states.

Second, the transnational flow of ideas and materials is asymmetrical in the opposite direction: legal concepts and materials, like textbooks and case law, are more likely to move from core states to peripheral and semiperipheral ones, and from Western states to non-Western ones, than vice versa. This asymmetrical diffusion results from the hierarchical nature of student-teacher relationships—where diffusion works better from teacher to student, and from student to student, than from student to teacher—and from the tendency of foreign students who study law to return home to teach or practice rather than stay where they undertook foreign study.

Within these broad patterns, students often move within groupings of states that are bound together by a common language, colonial history, and membership in the same legal family. Consequently, multiple core-periphery relationships have emerged with an Anglophone core, a Francophone core, a Russophone core, and so forth, constituting different networks of students and professors and distinct pathways for the diffusion of legal concepts and materials. At the same time, many students are drawn toward studying at elite universities in English-speaking states, most notably the United Kingdom and the United States. Thus, the height of these apexes differs, as the joint Anglophone core attracts more students than the Francophone core, which in turn attracts more students than the Russophone core.

These dynamics affect which persons will probably study law in more than one state, where they are apt to go, what networks they develop, and which approaches and materials they are prone to bring home in ways that are likely to reflect and reinforce certain nationalizing, denationalizing, or westernizing influences within the field. These patterns are also subject to various forms of disruption arising from factors such as changes in domestic political preferences and shifts in geopolitical power.

A. CROSS-BORDER FLOWS OF TERTIARY STUDENTS IN GENERAL

UNESCO collects data on all "internationally mobile students" who have crossed a national border to complete a tertiary degree, showing where they come from and where they go to study.[8] The UNESCO data suggest that the globalization of tertiary education

---

[8] The website uses the term "internationally mobile students" to refer to "students who have [physically] crossed a national or territorial border for the purpose of education and are now enrolled outside their country of origin." *See* Glossary, UNESCO Inst. for Statistics, http://uis.unesco.org/en/glossary (last visited Dec. 26, 2016). Internationally mobile students are a subgroup of "foreign students," a category that includes all noncitizen

is a significant and growing business. For example, the number of internationally mobile students has almost doubled in the last decade, growing from 2 million students in 2000 to over 4 million in 2012. This figure represents 1.8 percent of all tertiary enrolments or two in one hundred students globally.[9]

Marked disparities are seen when it comes to which states are primarily exporting states and which are primarily importing states. Table 1 portrays the top ten states that import or export foreign students as of 2012, which was the date on which the most current information was available when this study began.[10] The top ten importing states are the United States, the United Kingdom, France, Australia, Germany, the Russian Federation, Japan, Canada, China, and Italy. The top ten exporting states are China, India, South Korea, Germany, Saudi Arabia, France, the United States, Malaysia, Vietnam, and Iran. The table gives an overview of these states, including their population size, their total number of outgoing and incoming international students, their percentage of the global total of outgoing and incoming international students, and their top five destination and source countries for outgoing and incoming students.

In absolute terms, China is the largest exporter of students; Chinese nationals form the most numerous group of incoming foreign students in seven of the top 10 importing states. The United States is the largest importer of foreign students, being the most common destination for foreign students from nine of the top 10 exporting states. Yet when one factors in population size, South Korea and Australia emerge as outlier exporters and importers of foreign students, respectively, in proportional terms. Korean students are almost five times more likely to study abroad than their Chinese counterparts, and Australia admits almost five times as many students as the United States on a per capita basis.

Several important patterns emerge from these data that are both consistent with, and help to explain, some of the findings that appear later in this study. First, student flows are hierarchical: In 2012, five Western states hosted nearly half of the world's internationally mobile students: the United States, the United Kingdom, France, Australia, and Germany. By contrast, non-Western states made up seven of the top ten sender states. Three Western states also appeared on the top ten sender list (Germany, France, and the United States), but most of their students go to other Western states.

Australia and South Africa represent good examples of these core/periphery and Western/non-Western dynamics because they are regional educational hubs that evidence a clear disparity between where their students come from (mainly non-Western states) and where their students go (mainly Western states) (see Figures 1 and 2 for Australia,

---

students in the country, including those who have permanent residency. *Id.* These data cover only students who pursue a higher education degree or diploma outside their country of origin, excluding students who are under short-term, for-credit study and exchange programs that last less than a full academic year. *Id.*

[9] *See* Net Flow of Internationally Mobile Students, *id.*, http://uis.unesco.org/indicator/edu-mobility-indic-menf (last visited Dec. 27, 2016).

[10] *See id.* (figures on the website as of May 2014). The figures for outgoing and ingoing students are based on student flows in 2012 unless information about that year was unavailable at the time the chart was created, in which case the closest prior year was used (e.g., for Canada and Malaysia, the figure is from 2011). The figures for population size were based on the "List of countries and dependencies by population accurate" as of May 2014. *Id.*

TABLE I

Top 10 Importer and Exporter States of International Students

Country	Population (millions)	Outgoing Int'l Students	Incoming Int'l Students	Total Int'l Global Students—Outgoing	Total Int'l Global Students—Incoming	Top 5 Destination Countries	Top 5 Source Countries
Australia	23.6	10,968	249,588	0.3%	7.1%	US, New Zealand, UK, Germany, France	China, Malaysia, India, Vietnam, Nepal
Canada	35.5	45,509	120,960	1.3%	3.4%	US, UK, Australia, France, Ireland	China, France, India, US, South Korea
China	1,367	694,365	88,979	19.8%	2.5%	US, Japan, Australia, UK, South Korea	No data
France	66	62,416	271,399	1.8%	7.7%	UK, Canada, US, Switzerland, Belgium	Morocco, China, Algeria, Tunisia, Senegal
Germany	80.8	117,576	206,986	3.4%	5.9%	Austria, Netherlands, UK, Switzerland, US	China, Turkey, Russia, Austria, Norway
India	1,260.2	189,472	31,475	5.4%	0.9%	US, UK, Australia, Canada, United Arab Emirates	Nepal, Bhutan, Iran, Malaysia, Afghanistan
Iran	77.8	51,549	4,512	1.5%	0.1%	Malaysia, US, UK, United Arab Emirates, Italy	Afghanistan, Iraq, Syria, Lebanon, Pakistan
Italy	60.8	51,236	77,732	1.5%	2.2%	UK, Austria, France, Germany, US	Albania, China, Romania, Greece, Iran

(*Continued*)

TABLE 1 (Continued)

Country	Population (millions)	Outgoing Int'l Students	Incoming Int'l Students	Total Int'l Global Students— Outgoing	Total Int'l Global Students— Incoming	Top 5 Destination Countries	Top 5 Source Countries
Japan	127	33,751	150,617	1.0%	4.3%	US, UK, Australia, France, Germany	China, South Korea, Vietnam, Thailand, Malaysia
South Korea	50.4	123,674	59,472	3.5%	1.7%	US, Japan, Australia, UK, Canada	China, Mongolia, Vietnam, US, Japan
Malaysia	30.3	55,579	63,625	1.6%	1.8%	Australia, UK, US, Russia, Indonesia	Iran, Indonesia, China, Nigeria, Yemen
Russia	146.1	51,171	173,627	1.5%	4.9%	Germany, US, France, UK, Ukraine	Belarus, Kazakhstan, Ukraine, Azerbaijan, Uzbekistan
Saudi Arabia	30.8	62,535	46,566	1.8%	1.3%	US, UK, Australia, Jordan, Canada	Yemen, Syria, Egypt, Pakistan, Palestine
United Kingdom	64.1	27,968	427,686	0.8%	12.2%	US, France, Ireland, Malaysia, Germany	China, India, Nigeria, Germany, Ireland
United States	318.8	58,133	740,482	1.7%	21.1%	UK, Canada, Germany, France, Australia	China, India, South Korea, Saudi Arabia, Canada
Vietnam	89.7	53,802	3,996	1.5%	0.1%	US, Australia, France, Japan, UK	Lao PDR, Cambodia, China, South Korea, Mongolia

Source: UNESCO Inst. for Statistics, Net Flow of Internationally Mobile Students (figures on the website as of May 2014).

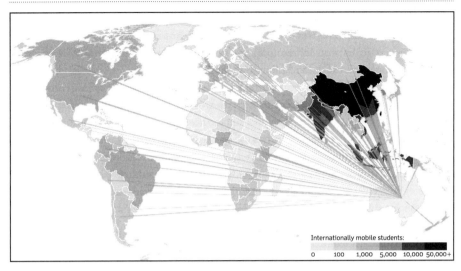

FIGURE 1 Australian Inbound Flow of International Students

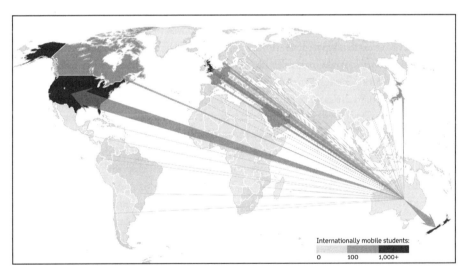

FIGURE 2 Australian Outbound Flow of International Students

and Figures 3 and 4 for South Africa, on the next page). Australia's top sender states are China, Malaysia, India, Nepal, and Vietnam, whereas the top destinations for Australian students are the United States, New Zealand, and the United Kingdom. Likewise, the principal sender states for South Africa are Zimbabwe, Namibia, Lesotho, Swaziland, and Botswana, whereas the top destinations for South African students are the United States, the United Kingdom, and Australia.

Second, language and legal families figure prominently in shaping student flows. The data show the significance of native languages in the global flow of students. A large percentage of international students traveling from Francophone states in Africa and Asia,

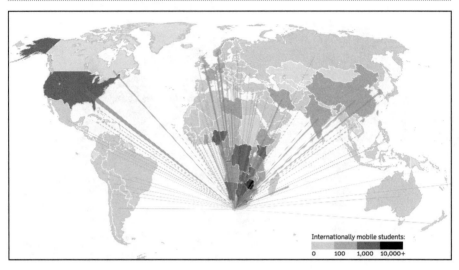

FIGURE 3 South African Inbound Flow of International Students

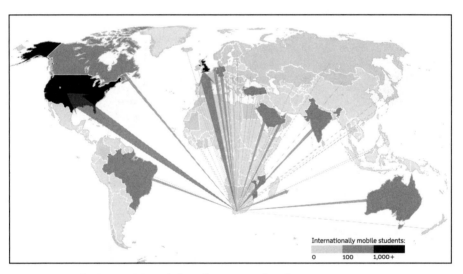

FIGURE 4 South African Outbound Flow of International Students

including Morocco, Algeria, Mali, and Vietnam, go to France to study. The highest number of German students go to Austria, and vice versa. US students go primarily to the United Kingdom, and UK students go primarily to the United States. Students from Angola head to Portugal and Brazil. Students from Belarus, Kazakhstan, Kyrgyzstan, Tajikistan, Ukraine, and Uzbekistan choose Russia first.

Student flows are often concentrated within legal families and, in particular, along excolonial pathways. On the basis of regression analysis of UNESCO statistics from previous years, Holger Spamann found that more than twice as many students from any state studying abroad select a state of the same legal family rather than a state in a different legal family.[11] When the attraction of host countries was held fixed, students from former colonies were twenty-five times more likely to study in a university of their former colonial power than elsewhere.[12] These influences are evident in the pattern of attendance of students from Nigeria (a common law, former UK colony) and Mauritania (a civil law, former French colony) (Figures 5 and 6 below).

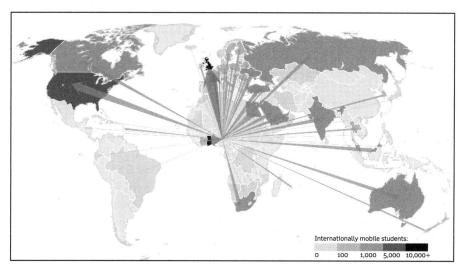

FIGURE 5 Nigerian Outbound Flow of International Students

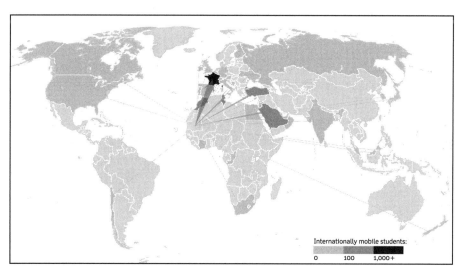

FIGURE 6 Mauritanian Outbound Flow of International Students

---

[11] Holger Spamann, *Contemporary Legal Transplants: Legal Families and the Diffusion of (Corporate) Law*, 2009 BYU L. Rev. 1813, 1851.

[12] *Id.*

Despite the influence of native languages and legal families, the educational institutions of core English-speaking states exhibit an especially far-reaching pull. English represents the closest thing to an educational lingua franca. Three of the top four importers of foreign students are English-speaking, common law states (the United States, the United Kingdom, and Australia), and together they host 35 percent of international students worldwide. Many students from non-English-speaking, noncommon law states study in these states. English-language programs are also becoming more common in non-English-speaking states, like China, Germany, the Netherlands, and Switzerland, which are seeking to attract foreign students.

Third, changes in the magnitude and orientation of student flows often track changes in the political and social orientation of sending and receiving states and in the broader geopolitical context. These changes can be illustrated by the student flows toward the Soviet Union (USSR) and Russia in pre- and post-Soviet times. According to UNESCO, the USSR accounted for 6 percent of the world's total of international students in 1970[13] and climbed to 11 percent by 1991.[14] These numbers include students from other Communist states, like Vietnam and Mongolia, but exclude internal student moves from regions that are now separate states, like Estonia and Kazakhstan. After the USSR collapsed in late 1991, Russia's share of worldwide student flows shrank dramatically, down to 2 percent in 2000, before starting to grow again to 5 percent by 2012, though the number dropped once more in 2013.[15]

Country-by-country outflows show a similar story but also highlight how student flows may vary among states. For instance, Lithuania was a constituent of the Soviet Union but declared its independence in March 1990. Following the dissolution of the USSR, outbound student flow from Lithuania to Russia decreased steeply from 60 percent in 1993 to 7 percent in 2011.[16] Meanwhile, various Western states experienced a dramatic increase in student flows, including the United Kingdom from 1 percent in 1993 to 37 percent in 2011.[17] By contrast, Belarus, also a former member of the Soviet Union, has retained much closer ties with Russia. Although the outbound student flow from Belarus to Russia also decreased, the change has been nowhere near as great, dropping from 94 percent in 1993 to 77 percent in 2011.[18] Russian is an official language in Belarus but not Lithuania, and Lithuania has joined the European Union but Belarus has not.

---

[13] 1983 UNESCO Statistical Y.B. at 3-430–32.

[14] 1995 UNESCO Statistical Y.B. at 3-395–97.

[15] *See* Inbound Internationally Mobile Students by Continent of Origin, UNESCO Inst. for Statistics, http://data.uis.unesco.org/Index.aspx?queryid=169 (last visited Dec. 27, 2016) [hereinafter Inbound Internationally Mobile Students].

[16] 1995 UNESCO Statistical Y.B., *supra* note 14, at 3-423; *see also* Outbound Internationally Mobile Students by Host Region, UNESCO Inst. for Statistics, http://data.uis.unesco.org/Index.aspx?queryid=172 (last visited Dec. 27, 2016) [hereinafter Outbound Internationally Mobile Students].

[17] 1995 UNESCO Statistical Y.B., *supra* note 14, at 3-420; *see also* Inbound Internationally Mobile Students, *supra* note 15.

[18] Outbound Internationally Mobile Students, *supra* note 16.

Taken together, these trends demonstrate that there are multiple cores and peripheries—an Anglophone core, a Francophone core, a Russophone core, and so forth. Each core state has its own semiperipheral or peripheral states, though the apex of each core differs in height. The United Kingdom has always been particularly influential in teaching elites from English-speaking, Commonwealth, and former Commonwealth states. France forms an apex for studies within the Francophone world and for students from civil law states. Russia forms an apex for studies within Russophone Eurasian states, though the relationship is changing for states like Ukraine. All in all, fewer students travel to Russia to study than to France, which in turn is fewer than those traveling to the United Kingdom and the United States to study.

B. THE GLOBALIZATION OF LEGAL EDUCATION

One cannot assume that the patterns that characterize transnational flows of students in general will necessarily apply to cross-border flows of law students in particular, let alone to those who study international law. For instance, although many Chinese students study abroad, this practice is more pronounced in some fields, like economics, finance, engineering, and computer science, than others, like law and literature, owing to factors such as the relative centrality of language skills in different fields and variations in post-study employment prospects in host states. Even when Chinese students cross borders to study law, many of them focus on corporate and commercial law, rather than international law, as these subjects are more useful in helping them secure prestigious law firm jobs if they return to China.[19]

Despite the lack of full data about transnational flows of law students, the following may be surmised on the basis of the available information. First, it would be reasonable to assume that the general data on student flows considerably underestimates the role of native languages and shared legal families in the global flow of law students. Unlike many subjects, such as medicine, economics, finance, engineering, and computer science, law is still very local or national in its orientation or, at a minimum, legal knowledge tends to be very specific to legal families.[20] Success in legal studies also relies strongly on language skills.[21] This hypothesis is supported by breakdowns of postgraduate students at Harvard Law School.[22] Thus, we should expect to see multiple core/periphery relationships in legal education based on language and legal families.

---

[19] One Chinese scholar who had completed an LLM at New York University explained that the students there shared a "little joke" about different branches in the LLM program: "Australians are studying international arbitration; Europeans are studying international human rights; Chinese are studying corporate law; Indians are studying tax law; Americans do not even care to take an LLM." E-mail on file with author.

[20] Sida Liu, *The Legal Profession as a Social Process: A Theory on Lawyers and Globalization*, 38 L. & Soc. Inquiry 670, 678–79 (2013).

[21] *Cf.* Carole Silver, *States Side Story: Career Paths of International LL.M. Students, or "I Like to Be in America,"* 80 Fordham L. Rev. 2383, 2404–05 (2012).

[22] For instance, Harvard Law School's LLM program from 2005 to 2009 included forty-eight students from the United Kingdom (population 59 million) and thirty-one from Australia (population 6 million) compared with only thirty from Germany (population 83 million), twenty-six from France (population 60 million), and nineteen from Brazil (population 178 million). Spamann, *supra* note 11, at 1851.

This suggestion conforms to descriptions of the first two waves of globalization of legal thought.[23] During the first wave, states like England, France, and the Netherlands spread their national versions of law directly to their colonies, while the Great Powers also forced the opening up of noncolonial states like China and Japan to Western law as a precondition for engaging in trade.[24] The second wave "followed the channels established by the first," as law students from the former colonies traveled to their "respective 'metropoles'" to study.[25] Legal ideas therefore flowed along colonial and language lines, first through direct transplantation and later through education.

Second, it would be reasonable to expect broad movement toward core, English-speaking states, most notably the United States and the United Kingdom, in view of the general importance of these states as educational destinations, the emergence of English as the educational and business global lingua franca, and the dominance of US and UK firms in the market of "global" law firms.[26] Carole Silver has undertaken the most extensive studies on this topic in the United States, primarily focusing on the growing size and significance of US Master of Laws (LLM) programs.[27] More than 110 US law schools now offer LLM programs, which cater almost entirely to foreign students,[28] and some schools are finding that their JD programs are beginning to attract higher numbers of foreign students.[29] The Institute of International Education (IIE) reports that the number of international students studying law in the United States grew from 3,464 in 1995–96 to 9,995 in 2012–13.[30]

UNESCO has also collected data on international students studying law in around 35 states for the period 2008–12,[31] which are reproduced in Table 2 and followed by a bar chart in Figure 7 of the most popular of these states for foreign students studying law.

---

[23] *See generally* Duncan Kennedy, *Three Globalizations of Law and Legal Thought: 1850–2000*, in THE NEW LAW AND ECONOMIC DEVELOPMENT: A CRITICAL APPRAISAL 19 (David Trubek & Alvaro Santos eds., 2006).

[24] *Id.* at 28.

[25] *Id.* at 46. *See also* YVES DEZALAY & BRYANT G. GARTH, THE INTERNATIONALIZATION OF PALACE WARS: LAWYERS, ECONOMISTS, AND THE CONTEST TO TRANSFORM LATIN AMERICAN STATES 6 (2002); ARNULF BECKER LORCA, MESTIZO INTERNATIONAL LAW: A GLOBAL INTELLECTUAL HISTORY 1842–1933, at 52–54 (2015).

[26] Christophe Jamin & William van Caenegem, *The Internationalisation of Legal Education: General Report for the Vienna Congress of the International Academy of Comparative Law, 20–26 July 2014*, in THE INTERNATIONALISATION OF LEGAL EDUCATION 3, 9 (Christophe Jamin & William van Caenegem eds., 2016) (several national reporters noted the major role played by big Anglo-American law firms in promoting the internationalization of legal education).

[27] *See, e.g.*, Carole Silver, *The Variable Value of U.S. Legal Education in the Global Legal Services Market*, 24 GEO J. LEGAL ETHICS 1 (2011); Carole Silver, *Internationalizing Legal Education: A Report on the Education of Transnational Lawyers*, 14 CARDOZO J. INT'L & COMP. L. 143 (2006) [hereinafter Silver, *Internationalizing U.S. Legal Education*]; Carole Silver, *Winners and Losers in the Globalization of Legal Services: Situating the Market for Foreign Lawyers*, 45 VA. J. INT'L L. 897 (2005); Carole Silver, *The Case of the Foreign Lawyer: Internationalizing the U.S. Legal Profession*, 25 FORDHAM INT'L L.J. 1039 (2002).

[28] Silver, *supra* note 21, at 2387 n.10.

[29] Silver, *Internationalizing U.S. Legal Education, supra* note 27, at 174.

[30] Inst. Int'l Educ., Open Doors Report on International Education Exchange 1948–2000, at 52, 64–65, 102–03 (2009) (tables of Foreign Students by Field of Study); *id.* 2013, at 69 (2013) (students studying "Legal Professions and Studies").

[31] Chiao-Ling Chen, UNESCO (data set) (on file with author).

TABLE 2

Foreign and International Students Studying Law in Select States

Country	Def'n of Int'l Student[a]	2008	2009	2010	2011	2012	Average
France	F	20,005	20,505	21,300	22,040	21,636	21,097
United Kingdom	N	16,504	18,006	18,961	19,826	20,729	18,805
United States	N	6,464	6,766	7,014	7,268	7,584	7,019
Germany	N	6,318	6,497	6,544	N/A	5,615	6,243
Australia	N	2,979	3,418	3,704	3,606	3,628	3,467
Austria	N	2,770	3,184	3,952	4,090	3,286	3,456
Italy	F	1,811	1,538	1,133	4,088	4,238	2,561
Switzerland	N	1,635	1,712	1,817	1,931	1,953	1,809
Greece	F	N/A	N/A	N/A	1,379	N/A	1,379
Czech Republic	F	999	1,081	1,154	1,026	896	1,031
Malaysia		N/A	1,112	884	705	N/A	900
Portugal	N	787	661	822	N/A	1,279	887
Belgium	N	761	390	1,081	1,030	1,048	862
New Zealand	N	998	902	855	768	768	858
Netherlands	N	871	470	743	N/A	N/A	694
Turkey	F	512	496	530	678	934	630
Canada	N	515	546	609	696	N/A	591
Slovak Republic	N	264	432	581	806	816	579
Romania		N/A	N/A	511	488	536	511
Poland	F	N/A	287	N/A	428	433	382
South Korea	F	N/A	N/A	N/A	N/A	380	380
Sweden	N	354	370	358	381	333	359
Lithuania		303	300	310	353	359	325
Norway	N	306	363	282	308	322	316
Hungary	N	284	329	314	314	301	308
Luxembourg		215	N/A	312	N/A	N/A	263
Bulgaria		211	234	231	211	220	221
Chile	N	314	N/A	252	35	61	165
Estonia	N	129	135	133	N/A	148	136
Slovenia	N	32	410	33	38	39	110
Latvia		127	105	81	89	106	101

(*Continued*)

TABLE 2 (Continued)

Country	Def'n of Int'l Student[a]	2008	2009	2010	2011	2012	Average
Denmark	N	28	41	84	99	107	71
Cyprus		8	22	19	38	201	57
Finland	N	50	43	42	42	70	49
Israel		N/A	N/A	33	63	N/A	48
Iceland	N	29	44	51	57	N/A	45
Malta		71	62	N/A	13	12	39

[a] N = nonresident students, F = foreign students. The data cover international students enrolled in full-degree programs. Where the data were not provided, this column is left blank.

Source: Chiao-Ling Chen, UNESCO (data set) (on file with author).

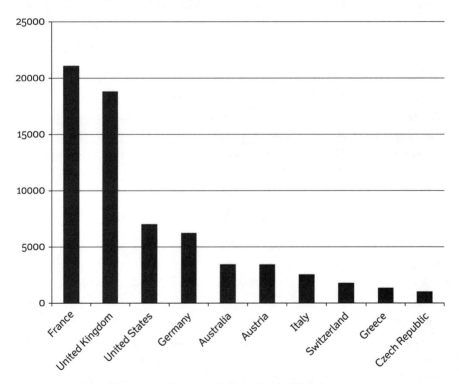

FIGURE 7 Foreign and International Students Studying Law in Select States

These data are somewhat problematic because some states, like France, reported statistics for "foreign" students studying law (that is, including foreign nationals who are permanent residents), whereas other states, like the United States and the United Kingdom, reported on "international" students (that is, excluding students who are nationals or permanent residents). The number of foreign students is likely to be higher than the number of international students, which skews the statistics in favor of France.

Nonetheless, the limited available data reveal a clear Anglophone core, based primarily on the United Kingdom and the United States, and a Francophone core. France and the United Kingdom benefit from two crosscurrents in global student flows. First, both are ex-colonial powers that exported their legal system and language to numerous states. Thus, more than half of all foreign students studying in France were from Francophone Africa. Although France did not colonize states in Latin America, the civil codes that were exported there by Spain and Portugal were derived from the French and German codes, so that students from Latin America often travel to France and Germany for further study.

Second, France and the United Kingdom are both located in Europe, where crossborder flows of students are notably high because of schemes like the Erasmus program. (It remains to be seen how Brexit, the UK withdrawal from the European Union, might change these patterns since university applications from Europe to the United Kingdom are already down given uncertainty over funding.[32]) Around 17 percent of the EU students who go to France study law.[33] Whereas the United Kingdom benefits from the worldwide movement toward English as the lingua franca, France retains its special appeal to European students from civil law systems. French is also the working language of major European institutions, like the European Court of Justice, contributing to its attractiveness as a destination for EU students. According to Campus France statistics, about twenty-five to twenty-six thousand international students have studied "Law or Political Science" in France in each year in recent years, which accounts for around 8.5 percent of all foreign university students in the country.[34]

The United States is often assumed to be the leading destination for legal studies, in terms of both numbers and prestige. For instance, Mathilde Cohen has explained that "[t]op students tend to study abroad for their Master's degrees. Common-law jurisdictions, particularly the United States, are the most popular destination."[35] "The dominance of US legal education in training legal talent for the global economy is one of the most notable developments in recent decades," Sida Liu has argued.[36] David Clark supported his assertion that "American legal education . . . has the highest prestige of any legal education in the world" by pointing to the "large number of foreign lawyers who enroll for further education in the United States, more than those who study in any other foreign country."[37]

---

[32] *See* Sally Weale, *UK University Applications from EU Down by 9%, Says Ucas*, GUARDIAN, Oct. 27, 2016.

[33] FRENCH CONTACT POINT OF THE EUR. MIGRATION NETWORK, IMMIGRATION OF INTERNATIONAL STUDENTS TO FRANCE 53 (2012).

[34] International Students in France, Inst. of Int'l Educ., http://www.iie.org/Services/Project-Atlas/France/International-Students-In-France#.WHv5MFN97cs (last visited Jan. 15, 2017) (statistics for 2014–15 and 2015–16); La mobilité en France, L'essentiel des chiffres clés No. 7 (Campus France, Paris, Fr.), June 2013, at 7 (statistics for 2011–12); La mobilité en France, *id.* No. 9, Sept. 2014, at 7 (statistics for 2013–14); La mobilité en France, *id.* No. 10 Jan. 2016, at 7 (statistics for 2014–15); Chiffres clés France, Les chiffres clés (Campus France, Paris, Fr.), Dec. 2016, at 11 (statistics for 2015–16).

[35] Mathilde Cohen, *On the Linguistic Design of Multinational Courts: The French Capture*, 14 INT'L J. CONST. L. 498, 508 (2016).

[36] Liu, *supra* note 20, at 686.

[37] David S. Clark, *American Law Schools in the Age of Globalization: A Comparative Perspective*, 61 RUTGERS L. REV. 1037, 1061 (2009).

US law schools may be the most prestigious according to international rankings, but UNESCO's law-specific data indicate that the number of foreign law students studying in the United States (an average of 7,019 per year from 2008 to 2012) is apparently a good deal lower than the average for France (21,097 per year) and the United Kingdom (18,805 per year), and only slightly higher than for Germany (6,243 per year). In the United States, international students studying law make up 1 percent of the total number of international students,[38] compared with 5 percent in the United Kingdom and 8 percent in France. Many factors may contribute to this result. In France, anyone with a high school degree may study law at the public universities; the universities cannot be selective as is routine in the United States and the United Kingdom. In addition, university education in France costs virtually nothing, compared with high fees for all students in the United States and for international students in the United Kingdom. US fees are often prohibitive for students from many other parts of the world. Although the United States does not appear to be leading the provision of legal education to foreign students in quantitative terms, the quality of foreign students studying in US law schools is high. The number of foreign students US law schools admit will likely increase, including into their JD programs, particularly given declining domestic applications.[39]

Although law students frequently move toward the core to study, most end up returning home to work.[40] In the United States, "stay rates" seem to be considerably lower for law than for fields like science and engineering.[41] The number of foreign-educated lawyers taking the New York bar examination has increased, even though only a fraction of these lawyers intend to stay and practice in the United States and an even smaller percentage end up staying. In 1995, 1,283 foreign-educated lawyers took the bar exam, accounting for 12.8 percent of the total test takers.[42] By 2013, the number had risen to 4,602 foreign-educated lawyers, totaling 29 percent of all takers.[43] In some states, such as China, qualifying for the New York bar functions as a signal of excellence and may be a

---

[38] A comparison with other disciplines is interesting. In 2012–13, 1.5 percent of foreign students studying in the United States studied law, behind 23.9 percent (biological and biomedical engineering), 14.6 percent (engineering), 14.6 percent (health sciences), 12 percent (physical sciences), 4.4 percent (social sciences and history), 3.9 percent (business and management), 3.8 percent (agriculture), 3.4 percent (computer and information sciences), 2.4 percent (foreign languages and literature), 2.3 percent (mathematics), and 2.1 percent (education). Inst. of Int'l Educ., Open Doors Report 2013, *supra* note 30, at 94 (Table of Major Field of Specialization of International Scholars, 2002/03–2012/13).

[39] US law schools are currently facing a crisis given a drastic drop in the number of law school applications. As fewer Americans apply for JDs, many law schools may seek to retain tuition dollars by admitting more foreign JD and LLM students. *See* Clark, *supra* note 37, at 1050–51; Christopher Edley, *Fiat Flux: Evolving Purposes and Ideals of the Great American Public Law School*, 100 CAL. L. REV. 313, 329 (2012); Lauren Robel, Association of American Law Schools Presidential Address 2012, in 1 AALS News 1 (2012); Ethan Bronner, *Law School's Applications Fall as Costs Rise and Jobs Are Cut*, N.Y. TIMES, Jan. 30, 2013.

[40] *See* Liu, *supra* note 20, at 685–86; Michael D. Goldhaber, *They Rule the World: One-Year LL.M. Programs at U.S. Law Schools Are on the Rise Again, Attracting Fledgling Power Brokers from Around the World*, AM. LAW., Sept. 14, 2005.

[41] *See* Silver, *supra* note 21, at 2396–98, 2433; *see also* Silver, *Winners and Losers in the Globalization of Legal Services*, *supra* note 27, at 899.

[42] 1995 Statistics, Bar Examiner, May 1996, at 23, 27.

[43] 2013 Statistics, *id.*, Mar. 2014, at 6, 11.

prerequisite for employment by international law firms or major multinational companies. In the United Kingdom, completing a UK LLM is not sufficient to entitle students to be admitted to practice. In France, even though many foreign students come to study law, very few go on to successful careers at the French bar or in the French academy. They are impeded partly by the need for impeccable language skills in the law, as well as by a lack of local networks that are often useful in facilitating legal careers. But many foreign students still value a UK or French legal degree for making them competitive in their home market or for enabling them to access other markets, such as Chinese students who seek to work for Chinese companies in Anglophone or Francophone African states.

C. IMPLICATIONS FOR THE DIVISIBLE COLLEGE

What implications might follow from these global and law-specific student flows for the construction of international law as a transnational legal field? First, the core/periphery and Western/non-Western dynamics affect which persons are likely to study law in one state only (nationalizing influence) or more than one state (denationalizing influence) and where they are apt to go (westernizing influence).

Those who start their education in core states may be unlikely to study law in other states in ways that denationalize their approach to law or diversify their perspective by making them cross a geopolitical, language, or legal family divide. Such students typically receive few incentives to travel to the semiperiphery or periphery to complete further legal study because doing so is not associated with enhanced symbolic capital and heightened career prospects. Accordingly, if stepping outside one's national context to view international law from a different vantage point is a formative part of being an international lawyer and understanding diverse approaches to the field,[44] lawyers from these states may be the least likely to gain these sorts of denationalizing experiences. On the other hand, these lawyers are more likely to experience diversity within the classroom if they study at one of the universities with a significant number of foreign students.

By contrast, students from semiperipheral or peripheral states are less likely to experience a diversity of student nationalities within their home classrooms. But elite students from these states have greater incentives than those from core states to study law in more than one state because obtaining foreign law degrees is typically associated with increased social capital in the form of higher levels of prestige and enhanced job prospects.[45] They are thus more likely to experience the denationalizing influences that come with such transnational study. Of course, since not all students will have the means to study abroad, this opportunity might be more open to students with private funds or scholarship opportunities.

---

[44] Peter Murray & Jens Drolshammer, *The Education and Training of a New International Lawyer*, 2 EUR. J.L. REFORM 505, 517 (2000) (arguing that "the international lawyer needs to have a sense of 'globality', to be able to step outside the boundaries of his/her own jurisdiction and consider international transactions, relationships and disputes from a global rather than national perspective").

[45] Silver, *supra* note 21, at 2386–87.

Achieving the potential status increase associated with foreign study typically requires that these students travel toward the core rather than laterally or away from it. The general direction of travel means that the degree of diversification these students undergo from studying abroad will depend in part on the state in which they began their legal training. Australian students have incentives to study abroad and thus denationalize, but they flock to the United Kingdom and the United States, so that on the whole they do not noticeably diversify by crossing a geopolitical, language, or legal family divide. Students from China, in contrast, are likely to study in places like the United States and the United Kingdom (because of the movement toward English and the common law) or France and Germany (because the Chinese legal code draws significantly on the Japanese one, which is based on the German civil code), meaning that they are apt to denationalize and diversify on geopolitical, language, and sometimes legal family grounds.

The direction of these movements may confirm or introduce a westernizing influence. Students from Western states who seek further legal training typically go to other Western states, which confirms or reinforces their Western orientation. Students from non-Western states who seek further law degrees often go to Western states, which introduces a Western orientation. Still, these students will not necessarily accept everything they learn in Western environments. For instance, some scholars noted that the Chinese government encouraged its lawyers to study abroad in Western states precisely so that these lawyers would be well equipped to understand Western approaches and schooled in the techniques that might enable China to beat some of these Western states at their own game. There are also exceptions to the movement toward Western states, such as movement from one non-Western state to another non-Western state, like students who transfer from a Russophone semiperipheral state to study in Russia itself or from China to study in Japan. But, in terms of overall trends, law students engaging in transnational study generally progress toward the core and toward the West, while Western students do not commonly leave the West.

Second, the asymmetric nature of these student flows means that legal academics at elite schools in core states are prone to be highly influential in constituting the transnational field of international law. Elite schools have proved to have great impact on domestic legal markets. For example, a study on the American legal academy found that far more US legal academics had obtained their law degrees from Harvard or Yale than from any other school and thus these two institutions were able to "infect" the broader academy with their intellectual ideas through the placement of their students as academics in other schools.[46] These student flows suggest that a similar phenomenon occurs in international law, though on a global scale, as international law academics and practitioners often complete part of their legal education at a handful of elite law schools in a small number of core states.[47]

---

[46] Daniel Katz et al., *Reproduction of Hierarchy? A Social Network Analysis of the American Law Professoriate*, 61 J. LEGAL EDUC. 76, 84 (2011).

[47] WILLIAM TWINING, GENERAL JURISPRUDENCE: UNDERSTANDING LAW FROM A GLOBAL PERSPECTIVE 282–83 (2009) (listing jurists as agents of diffusion).

This phenomenon has also been observed with respect to international judges. A 2006 study of all sitting international judges found that many had studied at a handful of elite schools, particularly in the United Kingdom, the United States, and France.[48] The media have highlighted the role played by elite schools in relatively few states in the creation of the international law field.[49] The importance of credentialing in core, typically Western, states has also been observed in other transnational legal fields, such as arbitration. In international commercial arbitration, Yves Dezalay and Bryant Garth have noted that the crucial difference between successful Third World arbitrators and their First World counterparts is that national stature is not enough.[50] An arbitrator from the periphery must find ways of gaining access to and credibility with the center, such as by completing graduate studies at elite universities in core states. Similarly, Sergio Puig found that most elite investment treaty arbitrators are Western, but that the backgrounds of frequently appointed non-Western arbitrators confirm the importance of obtaining a law degree from elite UK, US, or French schools.[51]

Third, the asymmetric student flows are likely to contribute to the asymmetric diffusion of legal ideas and materials. As noted, although law students frequently move toward the core to study, most end up going home to work.[52] These reverse flows are meaningful because where people study and the ideas and sources they are exposed to often affect their subsequent choices in scholarship and practice.[53]

Noted examples of such influence can be cited, such as the "Chicago Boys" from Chile who studied economics at the University of Chicago before returning home to introduce their neoliberal learning into President Augusto Pinochet's government.[54] Similar observations have been made in domestic contexts. For instance, one explanation given for why US lawyers advising businesses about selecting a state of incorporation usually choose either Delaware or their home state is that they typically know little about the laws of

---

[48] Daniel Terris et al., The International Judge: An Introduction to the Men and Women Who Decide the World's Cases 17–18 (2007); *see also* Gleider I. Hernández, The International Court of Justice and the Judicial Function 133–34 (2014); Gleider I. Hernández, *Impartiality and Bias at the International Court of Justice*, 1 Cambridge J. Int'l L. & Just. 183, 192 n.41 (2012). For more information, see Chapter 2.III.B.

[49] For instance, according to an article by Christopher Schuetze in the *New York Times*, although the field of public international law is gradually spreading globally, a handful of universities in the United States and Europe hold disproportionate sway when it comes to training the international law elite. *See* Christopher F. Schuetze, *A Bigger World of International Law*, N.Y. Times, Oct. 6, 2014. The article described a handful of universities in England and the United States as leading the way, citing reasons such as stellar brands; wealthy endowments; renowned faculties; and ready access to fellowships, internships, and development opportunities. These universities also create benchmarking standards as their degrees are easier for others to evaluate than degrees from thousands of universities across the world. *Id.*

[50] Yves Dezalay & Bryant Garth, Dealing in Virtue: International Commercial Arbitration and the Construction of a Transnational Legal Order 25–26 (1996).

[51] Sergio Puig, *Social Capital in the Arbitration Market*, 25 Eur. J. Int'l L. 387, 405 (2014).

[52] *See* Liu, *supra* note 20, at 685–86; Goldhaber, *supra* note 40.

[53] *See* Twining, *supra* note 47, at 280.

[54] *See* Dezalay & Garth, *supra* note 25, at 44–47; *see generally* Juan Gabriel Valdés, Pinochet's Economists: The Chicago School in Chile (1995).

other states.[55] Most US law schools teach only the law of their home state and Delaware corporate law, whereas elite law schools usually focus on Delaware law rather than the law of the state where they are based, and casebooks tend to contain more Delaware cases than cases from any other state.[56]

Diffusion studies show that legal ideas and materials typically move in the opposite direction to transnational student flows. In corporate law, for example, Spamann has found that diffusion of legal materials, including statutes, case law, and textbooks, occurs mainly within legal family trees and along ex-colonial lines.[57] Students moved primarily within legal families and from peripheral and semiperipheral states (former colonies) to core states (former colonial masters). By contrast, legal sources moved in the opposite direction. The textbooks of core states contained few references to legal materials from other legal systems. The textbooks of peripheral and semiperipheral countries contained numerous references to foreign case law, which came predominantly from core countries and especially from those within the same legal family.

The effect of interstate educational hierarchies on the transnational flow of ideas is often reinforced by the interpersonal hierarchy established by the teacher-student relationship. The diffusion of ideas works best in a downward direction, traveling from teacher to student. The teacher stands in front of the classroom and shares his or her views with the students. The teacher sets the intellectual agenda by prescribing the textbook and readings that are to be discussed. Students come to learn and are also tested on their understanding by the teacher, which gives students an incentive to try to understand what the teacher wants the students to know and what the teacher thinks about the materials.

Diffusion also works relatively well in a horizontal direction, from student to student. Students may listen to each other in the classroom and interact outside the classroom, creating a network of peer contacts.[58] Studies of technological diffusion found that peer-to-peer interactions are particularly useful in encouraging someone to adopt new ideas.[59] But there may be limits to the transfer of ideas in this way. Various studies have suggested that international students typically forge bonds with other international students, rather than with domestic students, particularly when they are de facto segregated into different

---

[55] *See* William J. Carney et al., *Lawyers, Ignorance, and the Dominance of Delaware Corporate Law*, 2 HARV. BUS. L. REV. 123, 129–30 (2012); Robert Daines, *The Incorporation Choices of IPO Firms*, 77 N.Y.U. L. REV. 1559, 1581 (2002); Roberta Romano, *Law as a Product: Some Pieces of the Incorporation Puzzle*, 1 J. L. ECON. & ORG. 225, 273 (1985).

[56] For explanations based on other factors, such as the importance of precedent and the corporate law expertise of Delaware courts, see generally Ehud Kamar, *A Regulatory Competition Theory of Indeterminacy in Corporate Law*, 98 COLUM. L. REV. 1908 (1998); *see also* Bernard S. Black, *Is Corporate Law Trivial?: A Political and Economic Analysis*, 84 NW. U. L. REV. 542 (1990); John Coates, *Managing Disputes Through Contract: Evidence from M&A*, 2 HARV. BUS. L. REV. 295 (2012); Melvin Aron Eisenberg, *The Structure of Corporation Law*, 89 *id.* 1461 (1989); Jill E. Fisch, *The Peculiar Role of the Delaware Courts in the Competition for Corporate Charters*, 68 U. CIN. L. REV. 1061 (1999); Sarath Sanga, *Choice of Law: An Empirical Analysis*, 11 J. EMPIRICAL LEGAL STUD. 894 (2014).

[57] Spamann, *supra* note 11, at 1876.

[58] Silver, *supra* note 21, at 2406.

[59] *See, e.g.*, JAMES S. COLEMAN ET AL., MEDICAL INNOVATION: DIFFUSION OF A MEDICAL DRUG AMONG DOCTORS (1966); EVERETT M. ROGERS, DIFFUSION OF INNOVATIONS 68 (4th ed. 1995).

programs.[60] For instance, Silver's work on US law schools suggests that a strong divide separates the JD students (who are primarily American) and the LLM students (who are primarily foreign).[61] Thus, diffusion of ideas may often work better within each group than between groups.[62]

Diffusion of ideas is likely to work less well in an upward direction, from student to teacher. In some states, such as China, France, and Russia, law professors primarily lecture without engaging in class discussion or encouraging questions.[63] This scenario offers little opportunity for student-to-teacher transfers of ideas. In other states, such as the United States, professors often involve their students in a Socratic dialogue, allowing for more room for two-way communication and reciprocal learning. Even there, however, a student will typically hear his or her professor speak far more than a professor will hear a given student speak. And professors have fewer incentives to try to get inside the heads of their students, as they are the ones that set the exams that students take, rather than the other way around.

Upward diffusion is possible, notably when dealing with LLM and Doctor of Philosophy (PhD) students or in small and interactive classroom settings. Nevertheless, downward and lateral diffusion are likely to be more common. This observation means that, in terms of the diffusion of ideas, where a state's students go to study is frequently a more important indicator of where individuals from that state will look to find ideas than where their foreign students come from. If Taiwanese judges study law in Germany, they are more likely to end up citing German precedents than German judges or law professors are to cite Taiwanese precedents on account of having had Taiwanese students in their classrooms. What one learns in a foreign environment as a student may well leave a deeper impression on one's intellectual makeup than what one learns as a teacher by having foreign students in the classroom.

---

[60] *See, e.g.,* Ioannis Itsoukalas, *The Double Life of Erasmus Students, in* STUDENTS, STAFF AND ACADEMIC MOBILITY IN HIGHER EDUCATION 131 (Mike Byram & Fred Dervin eds., 2008); Ruth Fincher & Kate Shaw, *The Unintended Segregation of Transnational Students in Central Melbourne*, 41 ENV'T & PLAN. 1884 (2009); Johanna Waters & Rachel Brooks, *"Vive la Différence?": The "International" Experiences of UK Students Overseas*, 17 POPULATION, SPACE & PLACE 567, 574 (2011).

[61] Silver, *Internationalizing U.S. Legal Education, supra* note 27, at 168–70; Silver, *supra* note 21, at 2407. Experiences may also differ between US law schools. Some law schools put JDs and LLMs in separate classes or place them on different curves within the same class. Others put them in the same classes and on the same curve, while others go further and have programs to facilitate interaction, such as a buddy JD/LLM system. *See, e.g.,* LL.M Program Description, B.C. L., https://www.bc.edu/bc-web/schools/law/admission-aid/llm-program.html (last visited Dec. 27, 2016).

[62] This seems to be particularly prevalent when domestic and international students are typically enrolled in different programs, like the JD or Bachelor of Laws and LLM or PhD programs. Where domestic and international students are combined within a single degree, the opportunities for them to mix, share insights, and develop networks with each other are greatly increased. For instance, some UK legal academics commented that they saw a much larger disconnect between undergraduate and graduate law students than between domestic and foreign law students who were in the same programs. (E-mail on file with author).

[63] On the traditional method of teaching international law in China, see WU QIZHI (吴启智), 国际法教学与人才培养的现状分析与建议—基于师生调查问卷形成的分析报告 [International Law Teaching and Training—Analysis and Suggestions Based on a Survey Study of Students and Teachers] (2016), http://mp.weixin.qq.com/; *see also* Lingyun Gao, Note, *What Makes a Lawyer in China? The Chinese Legal Education System After China's Entry into the WTO*, 10 WILLAMETTE J. INT'L L. & DISP. RESOL. 197, 224 (2002).

The asymmetric movement of students and lawyers means that the diffusion of legal ideas and materials is more likely to proceed from core to peripheral states, and from Western to non-Western states, than the other way around. These dynamics also help to explain how localisms from core states may come to be globalized and to define what is understood by "global" approaches. For instance, Liu observed that increasing numbers of international law students have entered UK and US law schools to receive "global" legal education,[64] and John Flood explained that many young lawyers from around the world now find it essential to obtain an LLM degree at a major UK or US law school so as to be "conversant with global legal techniques."[65] In this way, the national approaches of some states are able to assert disproportionate influence in defining the "international."

II. Comparing Educational Profiles

Professors at elite law schools in core states often teach quite internationalized student bodies, but how many of these instructors are internationalized in terms of their own legal education? And how might their own educational diversity or lack of it influence the approaches and networks of international law scholars in the states concerned?

Schachter pointed to the "transnational movement of professors" as one factor evidencing the invisible college of international lawyers.[66] In a report on the internationalization of legal education, the proportion of academics who had received degrees from other jurisdictions was viewed as a primary indicator of internationalization.[67] Yet when it comes to foreign legal education of international law academics, this sort of transnational movement is much more prevalent in some states than others. Educational migration also tends to follow predictable patterns that reflect and reinforce certain nationalizing, denationalizing, and westernizing influences that shape international law as a transnational legal field.

A. TRACKING EDUCATIONAL DIVERSITY

Some law professors have studied law in two or more states, whereas others have only studied law in a single state. I refer to the first set of professors as exhibiting "educational diversity," because they are subject to some denationalizing educational influences, even if these are only limited. At least to date, educational diversity has originated in two main ways. First, future professors study law in their home country and then complete graduate legal education in another state before returning home to teach. I refer to this as

---

[64] Liu, *supra* note 20, at 678.

[65] John Flood, *Lawyers as Sanctifiers: The Role of Elite Law Firms in International Business Transactions*, 14 IND. J. GLOBAL LEGAL STUD. 35, 54 (2007); *see also* John Flood, *Legal Education, Globalization, and the New Imperialism, in* THE LAW SCHOOL—GLOBAL ISSUES, LOCAL QUESTIONS 127, 140–44 (Fiona Cownie ed., 1999); Silver, *The Case of the Foreign Lawyer, supra* note 27, at 1040; Goldhaber, *supra* note 40.

[66] Schachter, *supra* note 1, at 217.

[67] Jamin & van Caenegem, *supra* note 26, at 7.

"outbound diversity" because it stems from outward travel by domestic lawyers. Second, future professors study law in their home country and then complete graduate legal education in a second state before going on to teach law in that second state or a third state. I refer to this as "inbound diversity" because it stems from the entry of foreign lawyers into a specific legal academy.

Table 3 shows the results for the international law academics from the elite universities of the five permanent members of the Security Council plus Australia with respect to educational diversity and inbound diversity. (As described in Appendix A, I added five elite law schools from Australia in order to look for certain core-periphery dynamics between the United Kingdom and its ex-colony, Australia.) The first column provides the percentage of international law academics that hold law degrees from more than one state (educational diversity). The second column reflects the percentage of international law academics who received their first law degree in a state other than the state where they are teaching (inbound diversity). At least to date, the location of academics' first law degrees has typically been a relatively good indicator of their nationality; having received a first law degree from a foreign state often signals that academics are not now or were not originally nationals of the place where they are teaching.

These figures confirm that the international law professors in some of the states studied, such as Russia and France, were highly nationalized in terms of their educational profiles. The vast majority had completed all of their legal education in Russia and France, respectively, so that their networks and perspectives were relatively nationalized. In other states, such as Australia and the United Kingdom, most of the international law academics at the elite schools had completed law degrees in two or more states. This educational diversity probably created a denationalizing influence on their approaches and networks, at least to some extent. The US and Chinese legal academies fell somewhere in between.

How educational diversity occurs also sheds some light on core/periphery dynamics: does it come about primarily from the return home of local lawyers who studied abroad (outbound diversity) or from the entry into the teaching market of foreign

TABLE 3

Educational Diversity of Academics in the Study

Country	Educational Diversity: Percentage of academics with law degrees from more than one state	Inbound Diversity: Percentage of academics with a first law degree from another state
Australia	73	20
China	41	4
France	7	5
Russia	8	0[a]
UK	77	74
USA	32	32

[a] I treated degrees from the USSR as being degrees from Russia, even if they were obtained in places that now form other ex-Soviet states, like Ukraine.

lawyers who originally trained elsewhere (inbound diversity)? In keeping with the patterns identified in global student flows, the educational diversity exhibited in core states like the United States and the United Kingdom primarily results from inbound diversity, whereas the educational diversity exhibited in China and Australia comes primarily from outbound diversity. The United Kingdom is an outlier with respect to its extremely high rate of inbound diversity.

B. EXPLAINING EDUCATIONAL DIVERSITY

Whether legal elites in a given state tend to study law abroad and, if so, where they go largely depends on perceptions of social capital in those states. Aspiring legal academics will have an incentive to study law in multiple states if foreign qualifications are valued by the academy that they are seeking to enter. In terms of the direction of these flows, status increases typically correspond with moves toward states with more highly ranked educational institutions, which often means core, Western states. These dynamics are likely to produce distinct nationalizing, denationalizing, and westernizing influences in different international law academies.

1. Lack of Educational Diversity: Russia and France

The international law academies in both Russia and France exhibited low levels of educational diversity. In Russia, all of the academics had earned two or three law degrees and almost all of them had obtained all of those degrees in Russia. In less than a handful of cases, an academic had completed a first law degree in Russia, followed by a foreign LLM (in the United Kingdom or Germany), and followed by a PhD in Russia. This lack of educational diversity is not surprising for academics who trained during the Soviet era when it was often not possible to study abroad. But no drastic movement in this regard appears to apply to the younger generations of international law professors appointed to these universities. This reality partly reflects how recently Russia opened up to the world after the collapse of the Soviet Union in 1991 and how long systemic changes require to take hold. It may also reflect the fact that younger lawyers who study abroad do not end up returning to join the Russian international law academy. In addition, none of the Russian international lawyers had completed their first law degree outside of Russia.

Discussions with Russian academics indicate that implicit hierarchies and language constraints mostly explain the low levels of foreign study to date. Russian students could study in other Russian-speaking states but, as Russia would consider itself to be at the core of this language and the constellation of post-Soviet states, these students have little incentive to do so. This outcome fits with patterns from the general student flows where students from other Russian-speaking states (like Belarus, Kazakhstan, Kyrgyzstan, Tajikistan, Ukraine, and other countries in the Commonwealth of Independent States) are much more inclined to study in Russia than the reverse. As for studying in a foreign language, since most domestic universities teach only in Russian, they do not prepare students well for studying abroad. In response to federal regulations, Russian law schools require all students to complete one language course.[68] Most students study English, German, or French, with English being the most popular. But this language instruction tends to consist of single courses rather than integrated study in other courses or the curriculum in general. Only a handful of Russian law schools teach courses in English.[69] There are few opportunities to practice foreign languages because most of the teaching materials are in Russian, few foreign academics teach in Russia, and many of the foreign students are Russian speakers from former Soviet states.

Two other factors are also at play. First, even though it has been twenty years since the end of the Cold War, the isolation of Russia from the West means that the senior generation has few links with international lawyers in Western states, which has made it more difficult to create pathways of connection for the younger generation. Second, in terms of academic incentives, although a foreign master's degree is readily understood within the Russian university framework, it is not clear what a foreign PhD or JSD (Doctor of Juridical Science) equates to in Russian credentials, which matters because an academic must hold a doctorate that is recognized in Russia in order to supervise PhD students in Russian universities. After the master's, Russian scholars usually seek a candidate of sciences degree, which involves writing a significant thesis. To become a full professor, a doctor of sciences degree is often (though not always) required. Russian doctorates are typically awarded at a much more senior stage than when a Western scholar would usually be awarded a PhD or JSD, so the two are not clearly equivalent. This disparity creates a disincentive for studying abroad at the PhD level, as the qualification is not readily understood within the Russian system in the absence of an Agreement on Mutual Recognition of Academic Degrees.

Movements are afoot to change the relative isolation of Russian students from global higher education. Two in particular are worth highlighting. First, in 1993, the government announced a national scholarship scheme to support talented students and postgraduate students wishing to study abroad, which has gained in popularity over time.[70]

---

[68] The standard says in paragraph 5.1 that a graduate must have necessary skills for professional communication in a foreign language, and in paragraph 6.3, that the program of study should include the mandatory coursework in "Foreign language in the field of jurisprudence[.]" Приказ Министерства образования и науки Российской Федерации об утверждении и внедрении в действие федерального государственного образовательного стандарта высшего профессионального образования по направлению подготовки 030900 Юриспруденция ("бакалавр") [Order of the Ministry of Education and Science of the Russian Federation on Enforcing Federal Educational Standard of Higher Professional Education in the Field of Jurisprudence (qualification (degree) "bachelor")] Бюллетень нормативных актов федеральных органов исполнительной власти [Bulletin of Legal Acts of Federal Executive Authorities] 2010, No. 26 (this Order will lose its force in September 2017 because of adoption of new federal standards by Order No. 1501, 2016).

[69] These include the Higher School of Economics, MGIMO, the Peoples' Friendship University, the Russian Foreign Trade Academy, and Saint Petersburg State University.

[70] *See* Распоряжение Президента Российской Федерации о стипендиях Российской Федерации [Directive of the President of the Russian Federation on Scholarships of the President of the Russian Federation], Собрание актов Президента и Правительства Российской Федерации [Collection of Acts of the President and Government of the Russian Federation] 1993, No. 37, p. 3451; *see also* Приказ Министерства образования и науки Российской Федерации о стипендиях направляемых на обучение за рубеж в 2016/2017 учебном году [Order of the Ministry of Education and Science of the Russian Federation on Scholarship Holders of the President of the Russian Federation for Education Abroad in 2016–17 Academic Year], approved by the Deputy Minister of the Ministry of Education and Science of the Russian Federation, June 1, 2016, No. 653, http://gzgu.ru/doc/in-student/2015/653.pdf (last visited Jan. 19, 2017).

Other schemes to encourage foreign higher education have been introduced, though many do not cover legal studies.[71] Second, international mooting competitions like the Jessup Moot Court Competition are becoming popular in Russia, leading to a new generation of Russian international law students whose members are familiar with non-Russian sources of international law, especially English textbooks like those written by Ian Brownlie, Malcolm Shaw, and Lassa Oppenheim and case law of international tribunals.[72]

These developments are essential to creating a more globally integrated body of well-trained, more denationalized legal professionals. Yet few of these individuals return to Russia and, when they do, they often work in law firms or nongovernmental organizations rather than joining the Russian legal academy. After all, Russian academia pays poorly and some young Russians complain that the existing international law academy is insular. According to one young Russian international lawyer who studied abroad, some members of the current generation are becoming more denationalized, but the Old Guard retains control at the universities:

> The scene at universities is still dominated by old guards, professors conditioned by the Soviet system. They serve as heads of departments and as such have significant influence over hiring decisions (both professors and PhD students) and curricula for international law courses. They serve as editors of textbooks co-written by professors of the department. They ensure that much of the Soviet legacy remains in the textbooks. . . .[73]

It may be, then, that denationalizing influences are growing in the younger generation, but these will inevitably need time to seep into the broader culture and the process may be still slower in the academy.

In France, all of the academics had received two or, more commonly, three law degrees and most of these degrees were French. Only a few had earned a first law degree in France, followed by an LLM in the United States, followed by a PhD in France. One had pursued a doctor of juridical science (SJD) in the United States. As with Russia, language barriers and implied hierarchies appear to play an explanatory role. Not only is it easier for most French scholars to study in French than in other languages, but also France would consider itself to be at the apex of the French-language and French-speaking civil law states, negating any substantial incentive to engage in further study at universities in Francophone Africa or Asia or elsewhere in French-speaking Europe. In addition,

---

[71] *See, e.g.*, Указ Президента Российской Федерации От 28 Декабря 2013 Г. No. 967 «О Мерах По Укреплению Кадрового Потенциала Российской Федерации» [Presidential Decree of the Russian Federation on Measures to Strengthen the Professional Potential of the Russian Federation], Собрание законодательства Российской Федерации [Russian Collection of Legislation] 2013, No. 52 (Vol. II), p. 7147 (not covering law or international relations).

[72] *See generally* Maria Issaeva, *Twelfth Anniversary of Russia's Participation in the Jessup Competition: A View from Behind the Curtain*, 3 Международное правосудие [Int'l Justice] (2013).

[73] E-mail on file with author.

French academics who study in the United Kingdom and the United States must deal with the language difference and shift from a civil law system to a common law one, which is difficult and makes the experience potentially less relevant in their local market. Accordingly, even though French students in general (not necessarily law students) seem to study abroad at a high rate, that does not appear to hold true for French international law professors.[74]

Recruitment processes are also part of the picture. No differentiation is made between the process for hiring academics in French law and hiring academics who specialize in international law. The selection committee is all French and, to be hired at an entry-level position, a would-be professor must have completed a PhD in law in France and demonstrate proficiency in French. These requirements generally have the effect of ruling out academics not trained exclusively or primarily in France and creating an incentive to privilege domestic rather than foreign educational experiences.

The main exception to this nationalized French approach is offered by the newer-style Sciences Po Law School (Sciences Po), one of the graduate schools of the Paris Institute of Political Studies, which has made a splash within the French academy. Christophe Jamin, its dean, explained that the idea was to break from the traditional French mold by being more interdisciplinary and internationalized.[75] Sciences Po embraces social science perspectives instead of spurning them in the name of doctrinalism and the autonomy of law. It employs some foreign professors and others with foreign training; it admits an extremely international student body; it teaches an increasing number of classes in English; and its students generally spend at least one year studying abroad. Several professors in the study who received foreign LLMs or PhDs/JSDs (doctors of the science of law) now hold positions at Sciences Po.[76]

2. Intermediate Educational Diversity: China and the United States

In China, 41 percent of the international law academics received at least one law degree outside the country, which typically resulted from outbound rather than inbound diversity (that is, scholars completing an LLB in China followed by an LLM or PhD outside

---

[74] Some academics noted that some French legal scholars go to study in Quebec where they have the advantage of learning in French about a mixed civil and common law system. E-mail on file with author. However, this pathway was not well trodden within the group of academics examined in this study. Similarly, when it comes to EU law, it may be that some French law professors choose to study in other states with well-respected EU law programs, such as Italy and Belgium, but French law professors tend to teach either international law or European law, so the profile of such academics was not checked for the purposes of this research.

[75] CHRISTOPHE JAMIN, LA CUISINE DU DROIT 263–67 (2012).

[76] The law school also relies much more heavily on professors who come from practice than the leading French law schools, reportedly having twenty full-time faculty to two hundred adjunct practitioners. Sciences Po also has a number of foreign professors who teach in English and French. *See Où en est l'enseignement du droit?*, FR. CULTURE RADIO (Sept. 25, 2014), http://www.franceculture.fr/emission-esprit-de-justice-ou-en-est-l-enseignement-du-droit-2014-09-25 (discussion between Olivier Beaud, Université Panthéon-Assas (Paris 2), and Christophe Jamin, Sciences Po, on the state of legal education in France and its future direction).

China).[77] Similar observations about educational diversity have been made about the training of most personnel at the Ministry of Foreign Affairs[78] and some elite Chinese law firms.[79] Foreign legal education seems to be most prevalent within the younger generation, suggesting that educational diversity is increasing over time. Of the academics who studied abroad, their educational destinations included Australia, Canada, Germany, Japan, South Korea, Switzerland, the United Kingdom, and the United States. Therefore, these academics not only experienced denationalizing influences, but also typically diversified by crossing geopolitical, language, and sometimes legal family divides in their foreign study.

Many factors help to explain these trends. The Chinese government actively encourages its nationals to study or spend time abroad by, for instance, offering scholarships or providing funding to help pay for the costs associated with studying or visiting educational institutions in other states. Another important factor facilitating this educational diversity is that many Chinese students know foreign languages, particularly English, and many Chinese universities bring in foreign professors to teach courses in foreign languages, mainly English. Implicit hierarchies also play a role. Instead of privileging domestic legal training, Chinese universities prize international experience, principally in the form of higher degrees (like LLMs, PhDs, JSDs, and SJDs) from elite schools in core Western states; they often treat such degrees as a stronger marker of quality and expertise than local ones. The educational diversity of China's top legal scholars is also paving the way for the appointment of a growing number of Chinese legal scholars, in both international law and other specialties, to law schools in a variety of states throughout the world.[80]

Modern legal education in China remains of relatively recent origin, which helps to explain the tendency to look to and privilege foreign legal education. This tendency results in part from the lasting effects of the Cultural Revolution (1966–76), which destroyed the former Chinese legal system. From 4,144 law students and 857 graduating law students in China in 1965, the numbers dropped to 410 law students and 49 graduating law students in 1976.[81] It was not until the late 1970s that Chinese universities began to recruit students by a national entrance examination. Since then, the number of law schools and law students has multiplied, rising sixfold in the last fifteen years alone.[82] By

[77] This pattern is consistent with observations about Chinese international lawyers and academics. See He Qinhua (何华), 中国近代国际法学的诞生与成长 [The Birth and Growth of International Law in Modern China], 4 法学家 [Jurist] 49 (2004).

[78] DAVID SHAMBAUGH, CHINA GOES GLOBAL: THE PARTIAL POWER 67 (2014).

[79] According to one Chinese scholar, some of the top Chinese law firms are now reportedly requiring Chinese students to have completed an LLM at Oxbridge or a top-fourteen US law school in order to be hired. E-mail on file with author.

[80] See, for example, Phil Chan (Macquarie University), Henry Gao (Singapore Management University), Wenhua Shan (University of New South Wales), Julia Ya Qin (Wayne State University), Jiangyu Wang (National University of Singapore), Dongsheng Zang (University of Washington), and Angela Huyue Zhang (King's College).

[81] See Wang Weiguo, A Brief Introduction to the Legal Education in China, Presented at the Conference of Legal Educators (May 24, 2000). For example, in 1957, only 385 graduated from politics and law programs. See Nat'l Bureau of Statistics of China, 1983 Statistical Y.B. of China at 521–22.

[82] Carl F. Minzner, The Rise and Fall of Chinese Legal Education, 36 FORDHAM INT'L L.J. 335, 336 (2013); see also Zuo Haicong, Legal Education in China: Present and Future, 34 OKLA. CITY U. L. REV. 51, 57 (2009).

2006, China could boast over six hundred law schools and over three hundred thousand law students.[83]

Foreign education in general, and the study of international and transnational law in particular, are encouraged by the government in the interest of better equipping its lawyers to protect China's national interests. For instance, in December 2011, the PRC Ministry of Education and Central Politics and the Law Commission released the Central Politics and Law Commission Opinion on the Implication of the Program for Legal Elite Education, which states the following five aims:

(1) Cultivate legal elites with different specialties: the emphasis of the Program is to cultivate legal professionals who are proficient in different areas of practice. *In order to make a breakthrough, the priority is to cultivate international law professionals who have knowledge of international laws and can participate in international affairs in order to protect national interests.*

(2) Innovate new training system for legal elites: to explore a training system with the cooperation of foreign law schools. For example, to promote the exchanges of teachers and students, mutual recognition of credits and mutual/joint granting of degrees between domestic and foreign law schools.

(3) Strengthen the socialist concept of legal education.

(4) Enhance the teaching of actual practice of law: to develop courses on legal methods, to increase case study teaching methods, and to organize moot courts and clinics.

(5) Improve the law faculty: to encourage law professors to pursue further study and research abroad, so as to continue their professional development and to enhance their teaching skills. In addition, to invite foreign law professors and high-level professionals to China to engage in teaching and research works.[84]

To achieve these goals, the government declared the intention to establish roughly twenty educational institutions specializing in international and transnational law and to set up a foundation to support study abroad by law school students and legal academics.[85] According to a 2016 study, international law is now taught at more than six hundred Chinese universities, and nearly twenty universities and research institutes may grant doctoral degrees in international law.[86]

In the United States, the vast majority of law professors obtain an undergraduate degree in a nonlegal subject and then a graduate degree in law. Some complete a master's

---

[83] Charles F. Irish, *Reflections on the Evolution of Law and Legal Education in China and Vietnam*, 25 Wis. Int'l L.J. 243, 251 (2007); Minzner, *supra* note 82, at 350.

[84] 教育部, 中央政法委员会关于实施卓越法律人才教育培养计划的若干意见 [Several Opinions of the Ministry of Education and the Central Politics and Law Commission of the Communist Party of China on Implementing the Plan for Educating and Training Outstanding Legal Talents], Xinhua (Ministry of Educ., Dec. 23, 2011) (emphasis added).

[85] *Id.*

[86] Wu Qizhi, *supra* note 63.

degree or PhD in another subject, mostly in the United States but often in the United Kingdom. Yet they rarely complete a second law degree at all, like a PhD in law or a JSD/ SJD, let alone doing so outside the United States, partly because of language difficulties and implied hierarchies. Limited foreign language skills prevent most US legal academics from studying in places like France and Germany. Within the English-speaking world, they find little incentive to study law abroad in states like Australia owing to implied hierarchies. Even though the greatest educational movement from the United States is to the United Kingdom, most elite US universities view themselves as superior to the elite UK universities. As the United States sits at the core, little prestige is associated with seeking educational degrees outside the country, with the possible exception of Oxford and Cambridge.[87]

Two law-specific factors are also at play. The fact that US academics complete nonlegal degrees in the United Kingdom, but not legal ones, partly reflects the timing of foreign study and the perception of US legal scholars that the enterprise they are engaged in is different from that of their foreign peers. Most of the US legal academics who studied abroad did so between graduating from college and attending law school in the United States. This route is standard for those on prestigious scholarships, such as the Rhodes and Marshall awards. As a result, these academics are much more inclined to pursue masters and PhD programs in nonlaw subjects, such as economics and international relations, than to embark on legal degrees. Legal realism also took hold in the United States in a way that has made the US legal academy deeply skeptical about the value of legal reasoning.[88] One consequence is that US legal academics typically dismiss European legal training and scholarship as doctrinal and formalist in comparison with the more realist and interdisciplinary approach they celebrate in their native legal training and scholarship.

Almost no US law academics who acquire their first law degree in the United States seek an additional law degree, let alone one in a foreign state. Some market factors help to drive this result. In the United States, unlike many states, law is a postgraduate degree so that US law students have fewer incentives to undertake additional legal study in another state. PhDs are becoming more common in nonlegal subjects, like economics, history, and sociology, but not in law.[89] This development reflects the value that the US legal academic market places on becoming interdisciplinary over becoming internationalized. Increasingly, aspiring US law professors are spending one or two years as a visiting assistant professor at a domestic law school before entering the US market. This route may function as a partial substitute for further legal study, but there are clear rewards to be gained by penetrating the domestic networks that help secure an entry-level teaching position in the United States.

---

[87] Jamin & van Caenegem, *supra* note 26, at 7 (noting that foreign legal education is particularly prevalent within common law countries, with the exception of the United States).

[88] *See generally* Richard A. Posner, *The Decline of Law as an Autonomous Discipline*, 100 HARV. L. REV. 761 (1987).

[89] *But see* PhD Program, Yale Law School, https://www.law.yale.edu/studying-law-yale/degree-programs/graduate-programs/phd-program (last visited Dec. 31, 2016).

This nationalized educational profile describes the majority trend in US law schools, where 68 percent of the academics in this study evidenced no educational diversity, but a minority trend has emerged in the last few decades at some of the elite schools, though it is not clear that this trend applies to US law schools more generally. Some 32 percent of the US international law academics at the elite schools in this study received their first law degree outside the United States, often before completing a second or third law degree in the United States or elsewhere. As a result, almost all of the diversity of education in the US law academy appears to come from inbound rather than outbound diversity, which reflects the United States' status as a core state. Some US professors seek to internationalize their perspective later in their legal careers through experiences such as being a senior Fulbright Scholar in a foreign country. But the well-trodden educational pathways to a US tenure track job are almost exclusively domestic, especially when dealing with legal education.

3. Significant Educational Diversity: The United Kingdom and Australia

In the United Kingdom and Australia, almost all of the academics held two or three law degrees and the vast majority received those degrees from at least two countries (77 percent in the United Kingdom and 73 percent in Australia). This finding accords with a recent study of the internationalization of legal education that concludes that the UK legal academy is one of the most internationalized in the world.[90] Still, while both states score highly in terms of diversity of legal education, they present very different models of denationalization. The United Kingdom evidences strong inbound diversity, whereas Australia evidences strong outbound diversity. This dichotomy reflects core-periphery dynamics.

In terms of inbound diversity, 74 percent of the UK international law academics in the study received their first law degree outside the United Kingdom. Thus, most of these UK international law academics are likely to be (or, at least, are likely to have been) foreign nationals. A considerable number of these foreign-trained academics came from Australia, but they also hailed from Austria, Canada, Germany, Greece, Ireland, Italy, Latvia, the Netherlands, Nigeria, the United States, and Zambia. Many received their LLMs in the United Kingdom, but others received them in Australia, Canada, Germany, the Netherlands, South Africa, Switzerland, the United States, and Zambia. Most of them received their PhDs in the United Kingdom, but PhDs or the equivalents were also awarded by Australia, Austria, France, Germany, Italy, Switzerland, and the United States. These findings reflect the tremendous—and highly unusual—educational diversity of the UK legal academy.[91]

---

[90] Antonios E. Platsas & David Marrani, *On the Evolving and Dynamic Nature of UK Legal Education, in* THE INTERNATIONALISATION OF LEGAL EDUCATION 299, 299–300 (Christophe Jamin & William van Caenegem eds., 2016).

[91] *Id.* at 304 (noting that there are considerable numbers of legal academics with foreign training contributing to the development of a scholarship in the United Kingdom, including some cases where a very large proportion of academics in a specific faculty of law have been trained outside the United Kingdom and have come to work in the UK academy).

The United Kingdom therefore represents an exception to the general asymmetric patterns of core states, which feature highly internationalized student bodies but relatively nationalized faculties. It is unclear what has made the UK legal academy so open to hiring foreign-trained academics. As the head of the Commonwealth legal empire, the UK law profession has developed strong connections with lawyers in many states throughout the world, and a significant amount of educational and professional movement has always taken place within the Commonwealth. European integration, which has seen the movement of lawyers and law students within Europe, adds to this phenomenon. Whether as a cause or an effect, UK law firms have traditionally hired large numbers of foreign-trained lawyers, particularly at midlevel positions. But the internationalization of the UK legal academy also seems to be driven by certain financial pressures and opportunities.

In terms of financial pressures, since academics are not well paid in the United Kingdom, gifted UK nationals have few incentives to enter the academy. To remain globally competitive, UK universities have responded by opening up the recruitment process to international applicants. As UK universities are some of the best-ranked in the world, foreign-trained academics are motivated to work at elite UK law schools. Moreover, because the UK academic recruitment process is both competitive and internationally open, some of the best British-trained international law academics end up at very good regional schools rather than the most elite schools. The United Kingdom has also been a magnet for internationally minded legal academics from other states that have traditionally been more domestically oriented, like Germany.

In terms of financial opportunities, UK universities admit a high percentage of foreign law students, particularly in their lucrative LLM programs. UK universities charge one fee for domestic and EU students and another, much higher, fee for international students. For instance, in 2012–13, an MPhil in law at Oxford University cost £4,100 for domestic and EU students and £14,845 for international students.[92] This differential makes international students attractive to UK universities as a major source of revenue. International and transnational offerings are popular with LLMs thanks to their transportable nature, which has enabled UK universities to hire more academics with these backgrounds and for these academics to assume a relatively central role in the law schools. The UK situation contrasts with the US market where a large proportion of the international students complete the LLM degree in order to take the New York bar, and those who have not completed a first law degree in a common law jurisdiction are required to study many US subjects, which are usually taught by US-trained professors.

For their part, Australian international law academics typically received their first law degree from Australia, which is on the Western semiperiphery, and then moved toward core countries, most commonly the United Kingdom and the United States, to complete their second and third law degrees. Around 80 percent of Australian international law

---

[92] *See* Tuition Fees from 2012/13 Onwards, Univ. Oxford, http://www.ox.ac.uk/students/fees-funding/fees/rates (last visited Dec. 27, 2016). This is unlike the US model where high fees, often around US$50,000, are charged to domestic and international students alike.

academics received their first law degree in Australia, which leaves 20 percent who were originally educated in foreign states. Those who originally studied law outside Australia attended schools in Brazil, Canada, Germany, Japan, New Zealand, the United Kingdom, and the United States. Around 73 percent of the academics received law degrees in two or more states, the most common pattern being for the academic to have completed the first law degree in Australia, followed by an LLM and/or a PhD in a foreign state. The high rate of outbound educational diversity has a lot to do with the position of Australia on the semiperiphery, which encourages its academics to look outward and to value the external. Australia is also a relatively affluent state with many available scholarship schemes for foreign study, mostly in the United Kingdom and, to a lesser extent, the United States.

The Australian international lawyers in this study tended to flock to like-minded or relatively similar states when pursuing LLMs and PhDs. The perspective of these international lawyers is likely to be denationalized to some extent by virtue of having studied abroad, but it is still probably westernized and not subject to the diversifying influence of crossing a geopolitical, linguistic, or legal family divide. Australian international law academics thus commonly experience semiperipheral-to-core diversification, but otherwise are not highly diversified. The relative consistency of their educational migratory patterns also suggests that the Australian legal academy is less radically diversified than the UK legal academy.

C. IMPLICATIONS FOR THE DIVISIBLE COLLEGE

How might the existence or not of educational diversity in international law professors, and whether or not this diversity comes about primarily from inbound or outbound diversity, affect the construction of the divisible college of international lawyers?

First, the lack or existence of educational diversity may have a nationalizing or denationalizing effect. If academics have studied law only in the place where they teach, the experience is likely to have a nationalizing effect. They may be more likely to have learned international law with an emphasis on the domestic case law and practices of that state (though, as demonstrated in chapter 4, this may vary among states), to have been exposed to the views of international law academics from that state, and to have developed national networks. There is a greater probability that they were a national of that state and that they learned in an environment where they were surrounded by other nationals of that state. They may be less apt to have had the sorts of dislocating experiences that would make them aware of their own national assumptions, lenses, and biases when approaching international law.

By contrast, if academics have studied law in multiple countries, this experience may have a denationalizing effect. These academics are more likely to have studied domestic case law and practices in relation to international law of more than one state, to have been exposed to academic work from different states, and to have developed transnational, rather than just national, networks. There is a greater chance that they will have been a national minority within the classroom or encountered students or teachers from diverse states with distinct national perspectives. All of these dislocating experiences may tend to make them aware of their own and others' national assumptions, lenses, and biases when approaching international law, providing them with a firsthand experience of the comparative international law phenomenon.

Anne Peters, a German international law scholar, has written about the espousal by international legal scholars of positions that can be linked to prior education in their domestic legal system and that serve the national interest, which she refers to as "epistemic nationalism."[93] She does not argue that scholars should completely detach themselves from their education and cultural context, which she concludes would be impossible and unnecessary, but that they should make a conscious effort to internalize the perspectives of their "others."[94] One way to become aware of one's national biases, and to see the world through the eyes of others, is to study international law in more than one state.

Nationalizing and denationalizing effects may have more impact at the wholesale than the retail level. Academics who have individually had a wholly national experience of learning international law may still become quite internationalized if they work in an academy that is largely composed of academics that come from or have studied in multiple states. But the nationalizing effect is likely to be intensified when the international law community in a state is predominantly made up of academics that have studied law only in that state, as is the case in Russia and France. There seems to be a greater probability that these communities will produce relatively self-contained dialogues about international law and thereby reinforce the divisible college of international lawyers.

This sort of self-contained community is exemplified by Russia. Lauri Mälksoo has observed that international law scholars in Russia are often first and foremost *Russian* international law scholars in the sense that they tend to be "linguistically and network-wise relatively distinct and separated from international law scholars in the West."[95] Russian international law scholars form a separate epistemological community that is tied together by a common language, history, and geography, resulting in a fairly "self-contained" international law dialogue with roots in the Soviet government's isolationist attitudes that created a parallel world to the West. This reality was stark in Russian debates about Crimea following its 2014 annexation by, or reunification with, Russia.[96]

Second, the lack or existence of educational diversity may affect the sources and approaches that scholars use when identifying and analyzing international law. In comparative law, diversity of legal education is linked with greater comfort in dealing with foreign legal materials in general, and in encouraging recourse to legal materials from the state where the foreign study took place in particular. For instance, Justice Gérard La Forest of the Canadian Supreme Court has noted a "definite link" between the use of US precedents by his colleagues on the court and the training of those justices in the United

---

[93] Anne Peters, *Die Zukunft der Völkerrechtswissenschaft: Wider den epistemischen Nationalismus* [The Future of Public International Law Scholarship: Against Epistemic Nationalism], 67 ZEITSCHRIFT FÜR AUSLÄNDISCHES ÖFFENTLICHES RECHT UND VÖLKERRECHT (ZaöRV) [Heidelberg J. Int'l L.] 721 (2007).

[94] *Id. See also* Christian Marxsen et al., *Introduction, Symposium: The Incorporation of Crimea by the Russian Federation in the Light of International Law*, 75 ZaöRV 3, 3 n.2 (2015).

[95] LAURI MÄLKSOO, RUSSIAN APPROACHES TO INTERNATIONAL LAW 87 (2015).

[96] *See* Chapter 5.II.A.

States.[97] Likewise, Justice Claire L'Heureux-Dubé of the same court has explained that judges, lawyers, and academics who go abroad for parts of their education naturally turn for inspiration and comparison to those jurisdictions whose ideas are already familiar to them.[98]

Beyond the level of anecdote, this link is beginning to be explored more systematically. For instance, David Law and Wen-Chen Chan have studied the connection between diversity of legal education and the willingness of justices on supreme or constitutional courts in various countries to draw on comparative law.[99] Law has demonstrated that whether the judges of the Japanese Supreme Court, the Korean Constitutional Court, the Taiwanese Constitutional Court, and the US Supreme Court are likely to draw on comparative law in deciding cases correlates with the commonness of foreign legal education in those systems, as indicated by the diversity of legal education of judges, law clerks, and constitutional law academics at elite schools in those states (see Table 4).[100]

Conversely, lack of educational migration may also produce tangible consequences. In discussing the parochialism of the US Supreme Court in its choice of authorities, Law and Chan reason that "American judges are not to be blamed if their own vision ends at the water's edge. They are simply products of the system that created them."[101] As long as US law school faculties do not place a premium on hiring scholars with foreign or comparative law expertise or training their own students in foreign law, today's US law clerks and tomorrow's US judges and law professors will neither seek nor possess foreign or comparative training. Law and Chan argue that the day that US law students prize a degree in comparative law or a foreign law degree as a stepping stone to a Supreme Court clerkship or a teaching position in a US law school is the day that judicial comparativism will become truly institutionalized.[102]

Specific emigrational patterns also have a palpable effect because lawyers and academics are more inclined to draw on materials from the foreign jurisdiction in which they trained. In Law and Chan's study of the Taiwanese Constitutional Court, they found a strong relationship between the educational backgrounds of the justices and the sources of foreign law that they cited. Judges with German law degrees accounted for 87 percent of citations to German precedents and 60 percent of the citations to German constitutional or statutory provisions. Judges with some US legal training were responsible for 62 percent of citations to American precedent.[103] These correlations are not difficult to explain: in Taiwan, as elsewhere, judges are more likely to cite what they know than what they do not know.[104]

---

[97] Gérard V. La Forest, *The Use of American Precedents in Canadian Courts*, 46 ME. L. REV. 211, 213 (1994).
[98] Claire L'Heureux-Dubé, *The Importance of Dialogue: Globalization and the International Impact of the Rehnquist Court*, 34 TULSA L.J. 15, 20 (1998).
[99] *See* David S. Law & Wen-Chen Chan, *The Limits of Global Judicial Dialogue*, 86 WASH. L. REV. 523, 571 (2011).
[100] David S. Law, *Judicial Comparativism and Judicial Diplomacy*, 163 U. PA. L. REV. 1, 42 (2015).
[101] Law & Chan, *supra* note 99, at 576.
[102] *Id.*
[103] Law, *supra* note 100, at 980. *See also* Law & Chan, *supra* note 99, at 558.
[104] Law, *supra* note 100, at 980.

TABLE 4

Diversity of Legal Education in Japan, South Korea, Taiwan, and the United States

	Japan	South Korea	Taiwan	United States
Foreign-trained justices	2/15 US: 2	4/9 US: 3 Germany: 1	11/15 Germany: 7 US: 4 Japan: 2 China: 1	None
Foreign law usage by parties and/or their attorneys	Low	Law firms tend to hire foreign law experts for cases that receive oral argument (i.e., high-profile cases)	Low	Low
Foreign-trained clerks	Roughly half, including at least one German-trained and one French-trained clerk	(1) Around 60% of clerks have foreign training (2) Additional researchers are hired specifically for their expertise in foreign law (3) Research Institute personnel all have foreign training	Most	None
Foreign-trained constitutional scholars at elite law schools	University of Tokyo: 1/4 (25%) Keio Law School: 2/4 (50%) Waseda Law School: 2/4 (50%)	Seoul National University: 6/6 (100%) Korea University: 5/6 (83%) Yonsei University: 5/5 (100%)	National Taiwan University: 8/8 (100%)	Harvard: 2/28 (7%) Stanford: 1/16 (6%) Yale: 2/19 (11%)

Source: David S. Law, *Judicial Comparativism and Judicial Diplomacy*, 163 U. PA. L. REV. 1, 42 (2015).

Similar observations have been made about the Americanization of legal education in Israel, which has been described as a modern form of "legal colonialism."[105] Many Israeli faculty members gain postgraduate education in American law schools and, as a result, have imported research and teaching practices, as well as theories, values, and case law, from US law schools to Israeli ones. This exposure affects Israeli legal scholarship: it tends to focus more on universal issues and less on local ones; the perceived value of doctrinal work is waning while the prestige of theoretical and interdisciplinary work is rising; the main language of legal academic discourse is English; and US content and materials are heavily featured. It also seems to extend beyond scholarship, influencing the way legal issues and cases are approached in Israeli society and courts.[106]

These patterns suggest that scholars who have studied law only in one state and work in a highly nationalized environment may be more likely to cite sources, such as case law and academic commentary, from that state. Because the Russian and French scholars have typically studied law only in Russia and France, they may tend to cite a high proportion of Russian and French materials, respectively. Similarly, because many US international law academics have studied law only in the United States, they may be predisposed to rely primarily on US cases, practice, and academic commentary. By contrast, because Chinese and Australian international law academics evidence a high degree of outbound educational diversity, these academics may be inclined to draw on materials and ideas from elsewhere, including first and foremost the states in which they studied.

The asymmetries of these educational movements mean that usually this sort of diffusion is primarily one-way rather than fully reciprocal. Chinese international law academics who have studied in the United States, the United Kingdom, and France are likely to be better placed to understand the perspectives of those states and to draw on materials and ideas from those states than the other way around. This circumstance may contribute to the field's Western orientation because it means that Western materials experience greater diffusion than non-Western materials and are more apt to constitute the field's common language. In the longer term, however, the lack of knowledge in Western international law academies about Chinese and other non-Western approaches and materials will become more problematic as China and other non-Western states grow in power.

Third, educational migration patterns might suggest some movement toward English common law approaches as a legal, global lingua franca. Although no large-scale data are available on this point, the educational backgrounds of many successful international lawyers suggest that students who originally studied law in a non-English-speaking civil law state and then acquire further legal training in an English-speaking common law state are more common than the reverse. Many students who engage in transnational legal study stay within their language and legal family. But, to the extent that some traverse

---

[105] Haim Sandberg, *Legal Colonialism—Americanization of Legal Education in Israel*, GLOB. JURIST, Mar. 2010, at 1, 2.

[106] *Id.* at 13–23 (giving examples of the influence of (1) *Brown v. Board of Education* on Israel policy with regard to allocation of land resources to minorities in a Jewish state; (2) American theories concerning indigenous people and distributive justice on the privatization of agricultural land in Israel; and (3) American theories of distributive justice and social responsibility on the attitude of the Israeli legal world to land expropriations).

these lines, they appear to favor somewhat asymmetric movement toward English-speaking common law states.[107] In some cases, students complete their first law degree in a common law state and then an LLM or PhD in schools like Leiden University in the Netherlands and the Graduate Institute of International and Development Studies in Geneva, but these institutions tend to be highly internationalized by virtue of their professors rather than steeped in civil law approaches.

These asymmetric patterns could be expected to affect what emerges as the lingua franca of international lawyers. For example, Colin Picker argues that international law evidences a mixed common law/civil law heritage but that the balance between the two influences has shifted over time. Whereas international law was originally much more like civil law, it has shifted in the last sixty years to become more like the common law.[108] In studying this drift in the context of the World Trade Organization (WTO), Picker identifies one explanatory factor as the large number of officials, practitioners, and scholars in the field who have pursued legal studies in common law states, including many civil-law-trained students who undertook postgraduate legal studies in common law systems.[109] Even when law students have not attended common law universities themselves, their lecturers and advisers will often have studied or spent considerable time at such universities.

In the nineteenth and early twentieth centuries, universities in civil law states played a far more prominent role in Western legal education and thought.[110] The emergence of English as the global lingua franca is a critical factor in developing and sustaining legal cultures and English is closely associated with the common law. Thus, Picker claims that the ever-increasing role of English in international law suggests that the influence of common law legal cultural characteristics will continue and possibly expand.[111] This process tends to be exacerbated by the linguistic insularity of most native English speakers.

Finally, states at the core of their language and legal family often evidence a clear asymmetry: for the most part, they are relatively internationalized in terms of their student bodies, but much more nationalized in terms of the education of their own professors. This pattern seems to be largely true of Russia, France, and, to a somewhat lesser extent, the United States. Such asymmetry means that they generally evidence a greater degree of international output than international input; these academics are well placed to diffuse some of their ideas to an international audience through their teacher-student

---

[107] Jamin & van Caenegem, *supra* note 26, at 7 (one reason for this may be language, another may be the relatively low number of LLMs offered by civil law universities).

[108] Colin B. Picker, *International Law's Mixed Heritage: A Common/Civil Law Jurisdiction*, 41 VAND. J. TRANS. L. 1083, 1104–06 (2008); Colin B. Picker, *Beyond the Usual Suspects: Application of the Mixed Jurisdiction Jurisprudence to International Law and Beyond*, 3 J. COMP. L. 160, 162 (2008).

[109] Colin B. Picker, *A Framework for Comparative Analyses of International Law and Its Institutions: Using the Example of the World Trade Organization*, in COMPARATIVE LAW AND HYBRID LEGAL SYSTEMS 117, 133–34 (Eleanor Cashin Ritaine et al. eds., 2010).

[110] COMPARATIVE LEGAL TRADITIONS: TEXTS, MATERIALS AND CASES ON WESTERN LAW 56–57 (Mary Ann Glendon et al., 3d ed. 2007); Clark, *supra* note 37, at 1060 n.165 (2009); Kennedy, *supra* note 23, at 24.

[111] Colin Picker, The Value of Comparative and Legal Cultural Analyses of International Economic Law 42–44 (May 13, 2012) (unpublished PhD thesis, University of New South Wales) (on file with UNSW Library).

relationships (output), but they are subject to relatively national influences in terms of determining their own approaches (input). This asymmetry is consequential because diffusion is more likely to occur in a downward and lateral direction than in an upward direction.[112]

The exception to this pattern is the United Kingdom, the only core state in the study to evidence double internationalization: a radically internationalized student body and international law academy. The international law academy is also internationalized through inbound diversity, with academics hailing from a wide range of other countries, including many non-English-speaking and civil law states. Double internationalization helps to make the UK legal academy a fertile place for the development of international law because it brings together international lawyers from a broad variety of states as both students and teachers. The common language of these professors and students is the "international" and "transnational" rather than the "national" because not even the professors have a national legal tradition in common.

The UK academy's double internationalization, coupled with the leading role of London in international law practice and its proximity to other centers of international law like The Hague, makes it well suited for an outsized influence on shaping the construction of international law as a transnational legal field. It becomes a true meeting place for the international—a melting pot of internationalization on both input and output levels. Of course, this diversity is not perfect. For example, the profile of inbound diversity shows that few international law academics at the elite schools come from non-Western states. Yet, compared with those in the other states in the study, UK international law academics may enjoy more internationally diverse professional networks, which could well encourage them to draw upon legal developments and sources from a much wider range of states than their peers in many other states. Nevertheless, these profiles and patterns are dynamic. Whether the unusual internationalization of the UK legal academy continues to the same degree following Brexit remains to be seen.[113] But, at least for now, the UK international law academy is extremely internationalized.

III. Comparing Publication Placements

International lawyers are simultaneously part of two communities: a transnational community of international lawyers from different states and a domestic community of lawyers, including but not limited to, international lawyers, in their own states. But who is—and whom do they view as—their primary audience? What factors drive their publication choices? And how might decisions about the language and forums in which they publish shape their audiences and spheres of influence?

There could be many ways to get a sense of the audiences of different international law academics. A Turkish academic who publishes a book about international law in Turkish

---

[112] *See* Chapter 3.I.C.
[113] *See* Chapter 6.

with a Turkish national press will almost inevitably be speaking primarily to a domestic rather than a transnational audience. By contrast, if the same scholar were to publish the book in English with a press with far-reaching global sales, like the Oxford University Press or the Cambridge University Press, that scholar might well be aiming for—and possibly achieving—a primary audience that is more transnational than domestic.

To explore the publication avenues that are open and attractive to academics in different states, I have chosen to look at where international law academics in the states studied publish their articles. When publishing articles, international lawyers face clear choices. What language do they write in? Do they select domestic, foreign, or transnational journals? Do they turn to generalist or specialist international law journals? These choices can be influenced by many factors, including linguistic abilities, which may open or close certain publishing options, and academic incentives, which may privilege particular types of outlets.

International legal academies differ significantly in their publication placements. The Russian scholars published almost all of their articles (over 98 percent) in Russian-based, Russian-language journals. The French and Chinese scholars placed a significant percentage of their articles (around 88 percent and 90 percent, respectively) in domestic journals that were typically native-language journals. The UK and US scholars overwhelmingly published in English-language journals, though US scholars favored domestic journals (around 80 percent), whereas UK scholars gave priority to transnational and foreign journals (around 65 percent).

A report on the internationalization of legal education pointed to publishing in foreign journals or another language as a key indicator of internationalization.[114] Nevertheless, publication strategies and outcomes clearly differ both between and within the English- and non-English-speaking academies of the states in this study. These publication choices are likely to affect the authors' primary audience in ways that reflect and reinforce certain influences that permeate the construction of international law as a transnational field.

A. TRACKING PUBLICATION PLACEMENTS

In evidencing the invisible college of international lawyers, Schachter pointed to the existence throughout the world of "journals and yearbooks of international law."[115] Yet not all journals are alike. To track publication placements, I distinguish among domestic, transnational, and foreign journals, and between generalist and specialist journals.

In many cases, journals are clearly associated with a particular state. They are often managed by a specific university or state and are guided by an editorial board composed largely of scholars or students based at that university or within that state. Examples include US journals (like the *Harvard Law Review* and the *Harvard International Law Journal*), French journals (like the *Journal du droit international* (*Journal of International Law*) and the *Revue générale de droit international public* (*General Review of Public International*

---

[114] Jamin & van Caenegem, *supra* note 26, at 7.
[115] Schachter, *supra* note 1, at 217.

Law)), and Russian journals (like the Московский журнал международного права (*Moscow Journal of International Law*) and the Российский юридический журнал (*Russian Law Journal*)). I count publication in a journal as "domestic" if the journal is associated with the same state as the one where the academic is employed, and "foreign" if it is associated with a different state.

An increasing number of journals are seeking to transcend national borders. These publications, which I refer to as "transnational," are sometimes identified by subject area, such as the *Journal of International Economic Law* and the *Journal of International Criminal Justice*, or region, such as the *European Journal of International Law* and the *Asian Journal of International Law*. Some have a regional name, but their editorial boards are primarily drawn from a single state, such as the *Revista latinoamericana de derecho internacional* (*Latin American Journal of International Law*), which is closely associated with Argentina.[116] Where it is unclear whether a journal should count as "transnational," I examined whether more than 50 percent of its editorial board came from multiple states (transnational) or a single state (domestic).

Journals may also be "generalist" or "specialist." For instance, the *Harvard Law Review* is a generalist US journal, whereas the *Harvard International Law Journal* is a specialist one that will take articles on US-focused topics (for example, Alien Tort Statute litigation) and non-US-focused ones (for example, the evolution of international investment treaties). Similarly, the *Modern Law Review* is a generalist UK journal, whereas the *International and Comparative Law Quarterly* is a specialist UK one. Depending on the journal concerned, generalist ones may generate a wider national audience of international and noninternational lawyers than specialist ones, whereas specialist ones may create a wider transnational audience primarily of international lawyers.

Many transnational international law journals are published in English by major Western publishing houses like Oxford University Press. The editorial boards of many of them are drawn exclusively or predominantly from Western states. When it comes to publishing in these transnational journals, the language criterion creates distinct advantages for scholars from English-speaking states over those from non-English-speaking ones. The Western nature of some of the editorial boards may also advantage Western scholars over non-Western ones. Under the circumstances, it may be useful to look for divergences in publication placements both between and within these differently situated groups.

It is hard to track publication placements with a high degree of accuracy. Some scholars place complete or relatively complete lists of their publications on their web profiles, whereas others offer only indicative lists or highlighted publications. In addition to searching online profiles, I also conducted searches on various databases (including Lexis, Westlaw, and CNKI (China Knowledge Resource Integrated Database)), but the results are not guaranteed to be complete. Some scholars move countries, which complicates the coding of domestic and foreign journals, particularly as the exact timing of the move

---

[116] *See* Acerca de LADI, Revista Latinoamericana de Derecho Internacional [Latin Am. J. Int'l L.], http://www.revistaladi.com.ar/acerca-de-ladi/ (last visited Dec. 27, 2016).

is sometimes unclear and there is an inevitable time lag between the writing of an article and its publication.[117]

In view of these limitations, one should not overstate the accuracy of the percentages used in this chapter. What is important, however, are the broader trends. Whether or not the precise level of publication of Russian international law scholars in domestic Russian-language journals is 95 percent or 98 percent, what matters is that the overwhelming majority of these publications are domestic, native-language publications. Likewise, whether UK international law academics publish 60 percent or 70 percent of their articles in foreign and transnational journals matters less than that they publish most of their articles in English-language nondomestic journals. The question is what these choices say about a scholar's probable audience, both intended and actual.

B. EXPLAINING PUBLICATION PLACEMENTS

Many factors influence where scholars publish their papers. In this section, two factors are explored that differ among international law academies—language abilities and academic incentives—first, with respect to the non-English-speaking states in the study, followed by the English-speaking ones.

In the Russian academy, the international law academics published around 98 percent of their articles in domestic journals that were almost always in the Russian language. The Russian Association of International Law's main periodical, the Российский ежегодник международного права (*Russian Yearbook of International Law*, formerly *Soviet Yearbook of International Law*) is published in Russian, as is the Московский журнал международного права (*Moscow Journal of International Law*, formerly *Soviet Journal of International Law*) and the Российский юридический журнал (*Russian Law Journal*).[118] Some English-language journals are published in Russia. For instance, in 2013, the *Russian Law Journal* was published for the first time, with the stated aim of "bring[ing] the Russian academic legal tradition closer to the international environment and mak[ing] Russian legal scholarship more accessible to other scholars and well-known worldwide."[119] As the editor in chief, Dmitry Maleshin, explained, the main problem with legal scholarship in Russia is its isolated nature, and an important step in

---

[117] I aimed at coding journals on the basis of where the academic was working at the time the article was published, allowing for a one-year delay between moving and publishing to account for the delay between writing and having a piece published. Thus, an article published in a domestic journal from State A would still be coded as domestic if it was published within one year of the academic's moving from State A to State B on the basis that it was probably written and accepted for publication while the scholar was based in State A even if it was published after the scholar moved to State B.

[118] *See* Московский журнал международного права [Moscow Journal of International Law], http://www.mjil.ru/ (last visited Dec. 26, 2016); Российский юридический журнал [Russian L.J.], http://www.ruzh.org/ (last visited Dec. 26, 2016). The first two journals listed require an English summary of the article in order to be published, whereas special issues of the *Russian Yearbook of International Law* that are based on papers presented at the Martens Reading Group in International Humanitarian Law are now bilingual.

[119] Russian L.J., http://www.russianlawjournal.org/ (last visited Oct. 17, 2016). This is an English-language journal with the same name as the Russian-language journal Российский юридический журнал, but they are different journals rather than one's being a translation of the other.

overcoming this isolation is to publish in English, the lingua franca of global legal schol-arship.[120] But these are fledgling endeavors, and most Russian journals, including those on international law, are published in Russian.

Linguistic and cultural barriers to publishing in foreign and transnational journals remain pervasive. Foreign language skills are often not integrated into legal teaching in Russian universities. As a result, many international law academics lack the capacity to write in foreign languages.[121] Even when they have foreign language skills, writing in their native tongue is much easier, and the end result will often be better as well. The effort-to-reward ratio is thus stacked in favor of native-language publications. In addition, as less than 5 percent of the Russian international law academics studied abroad, most are not educated in the ways and means of publishing in foreign and transnational journals, and they are not likely to have developed foreign contacts. They typically were not schooled in how to write and think in a way that would be well received by the editorial boards of foreign language journals, which are often dominated by Western or Western-trained academics or students. They probably know different international law authorities, have distinct starting assumptions, and exhibit different doxa.[122] Accordingly, even if they invest the time in writing in a foreign language, their piece may be unlikely to be accepted for publication in a foreign or transnational journal.

Clearly, this situation is dynamic and subject to counterforces. For instance, one of the Russian government's responses to the poor results Russian universities received in global rankings has been to encourage Russian scholars to publish in English and in transna-tional and foreign journals.[123] In 2012, the Russian Ministry of Education handed down a decree intended to "increase the proportion of publications by Russian researchers in world academic journals, indexed in the Web of Science, to 2.44% by 2015."[124] The new Russian Science Foundation, which is the Russian equivalent of the US National Science Foundation, sponsors two competitions for issuing grant money, at least one of which requires publishing articles in peer-reviewed journals indexed in the Web of Science and

---

[120] Dmitry Maleshin, *Chief Editor's Note on the Russian Legal Academia and Periodicals*, 3 RUSSIAN L.J. 5 (2015).

[121] As described above, see Chapter 3.II.B. Russian law schools require students to take a foreign language course, but foreign language materials and teaching typically are not integrated into the rest of the curriculum, so students have little opportunity to develop and practice these skills. There is more foreign language instruction at some institutions like MGIMO, the Higher School of Economics (Law), Friendship University, Kutafin University, St. Petersburg University (Law), and the Diplomatic Academy, but foreign language training and teaching in English remains much less extensive than in some other states, like China.

[122] *See* Chapter 2.I.B.

[123] In terms of other responses, Russian academics and government officials have been critical of global univer-sity rankings, suggesting that the poor performance of Russian universities reflects certain biases in the ranking metrics used. *See, e.g.*, Gleb Fedorov, *Why Are Russia's Universities Struggling in International Ratings?*, RUSSIA BEYOND THE HEADLINES, Oct. 14, 2014; Sophia Kishkovsky, *Russia Moves to Improve Its University Rankings*, N.Y. TIMES, Mar. 25, 2012. The Russian government has also reportedly been working on developing its own ranking scheme, though it has not yet been announced. *See Russia to Prepare International Higher Education Rankings by 2015*, SPUTNIK NEWS, May 27, 2014, http://sputniknews.com/russia/20140527/190164061/ Russia-to-Prepare-International-Higher-Education-Rankings-by.html.

[124] О мерах по реализации государственной политики в области образования и науки [Presidential Decree of the Russian Federation on Measures to Realize the Governmental Policy in the Area of Education and Science], Собрание законодательства Российской Федерации [Russian Collection of Legislation] 2012, No. 19, p. 2336.

Scopus databases (which are dominated by foreign and transnational journals); publishing in journals indexed in the Russian Science Citation Index is not sufficient.[125] Since 2013, universities have been required to ensure that a certain number of articles by their faculty are printed in Web of Science or Scopus journals if they wish to be eligible for federal grants.[126] And some universities, such as the Moscow State Institute of International Relations of the Ministry of Foreign Affairs (MGIMO) and the Higher School of Economics, offer cash bonuses to faculty members who publish articles in such journals.[127]

It is too early to tell whether these incentives will shift publishing patterns in the Russian academy. During the Soviet years, there was not only little pressure to publish in foreign and transnational journals but also little pressure to publish much at all. Many of the universities functioned primarily as teaching schools, and research was left to

---

[125] The first competition concerns applications for "Conducting advanced scientific research and exploratory investigations by research groups," for which applicants must have published at least three articles in peer-reviewed Russian or foreign academic journals that are indexed in the Russian Science Citation Index or the Web of Science and Scopus databases, which are mainly filled with English-language journals. *See* Конкурсная документация на проведение открытого публичного конкурса на получение грантов Российского научного фонда по приоритетному направлению деятельности Российского научного фонда «Проведен ие фундаментальных научных исследований и поисковых научных исследований отдельными научными группами» [Application Materials for the Open Competition for Receiving Grants from the Russian Science Foundation in the Program "Conducting Advanced Scientific Research and Exploratory Investigations by Research Groups"], Российский научный фонд [Russian Sci. Found.], Feb. 5, 2014, http://www.rscf.ru/sites/default/files/docfiles/konkursnaja_dokumentacija.pdf. The second competition concerns "Conducting Advanced Scientific Research and Exploratory Investigations by International Research Groups," for which applicants must have published at least five articles in peer-reviewed Russian or foreign academic journals that are indexed in the Web of Science and Scopus databases only. For the latter competition, publishing articles in the Russian Science Citation Index is not sufficient. *See* Конкурсная документация на проведение открытого публичного конкурса на получение грантов Российского научного фонда по приоритетному направлен ию деятельности Российского научного фонда «Проведение фундаментальных научных исследований и поисковых научных исследований международными научными группами» [Application Materials for the Open Competition for Receiving Grants from the Russian Science Foundation in the Program "Conducting Advanced Scientific Research and Exploratory Investigations by Research Groups"] Российский научный фонд [Russian Sci. Found.], Apr. 24, 2014, http://www.rscf.ru/sites/default/files/docfiles/Конкурсная%20документация_1.pdf.

[126] In 2013, the Ministry of Education issued another order aimed at increasing Russia's standing with respect to international publications. The order laid out the requirements universities need to meet in order to receive federal grants. Since the law was meant to increase the competitiveness of Russian universities, one of the stipulations introduces new publication requirements: "For every 100 staff members, the number of publications in peer-reviewed journals, which have been indexed in the Web of Science or Scopus databases, should not be less than five." *See* О перечне требований к отбору вузов для получения ими государственной поддержки в целях повышения их конкурентоспособности среди ведущих мировых научно-образовательных центров, [Order of the Ministry of Education and Science of the Russian Federation on the List of Requirements for Universities to Receive Federal Grants with the Aim of Increasing the Competitiveness of Russian Universities Among World Educational and Scientific Centers], Российская газета [RUSS. GAZ.], May 24, 2013, No. 110.

[127] *See, e.g.*, Интернационализация научной деятельности обретает материальную основу [The Internationalization of Scientific Activity Gets the Material Basis], MGIMO, http://www.mgimo.ru/news/university/document223805.phtml, and Список работников НИУ ВШЭ, которым установлена надбавка за статью в зарубежном рецензируемом журнале (3 уровень) в 2014–2016 гг [List of HSE Employees Who Got Allowance for an Article in a Foreign Peer-Reviewed Journal (3 Level) in 2014–2016], Higher Sch. of Economics, http://www.hse.ru/science/scifund/bonus_2014_3.

specialized research institutions, like the Institute of Legislation and Comparative Law and the Institute of State and Law of the Russian Academy of Sciences.[128] Of the academics listed in this study, a considerable number seem not to have appeared in print much—or sometimes at all—since they defended their dissertation (Russian scholars must have three publications to their credit to receive a PhD). Although Russia's poor showing on global university rankings has changed the incentive structures, Russian academia on the whole remains underfinanced, so that professors often lack time and resources, such as good libraries and money for research assistants, to complete high-quality research. Low university salaries impel many academics to hold down a second job, such as working as a lawyer or running a business, which then limits their ability to engage in research.[129] Moreover, even if Russian international law academics start to publish more articles in foreign and transnational journals, the overall publication statistics will remain highly nationalized for a long time.

In France, the French international law academics published approximately 88 percent of their articles in domestic French-language journals. Within this group, about 65 percent of the papers appeared in specialist international law journals (the opposite of the Russian papers, 65 percent of which appeared in domestic generalist journals). Major French international law journals include the *Journal du droit international*, the *Revue générale de droit international public*, and the *Annuaire français de droit international* (*French Yearbook of International Law*).[130] The French results partly stem from difficulties in publishing in foreign languages since law in France tends to be taught primarily, if not exclusively, in French. Yet academic incentives also contribute to shaping these choices.

Appearing in well-known French publications is much valued and readily understood by the broader French legal academy. When applying for an initial academic position, a candidate has been permitted since 2014 to submit a non-French publication provided that it is accompanied by a French translation.[131] Before that, the practice was to submit

---

[128] Inst. of Legislation and Comparative Law under the Gov't of the Russ. Federation, http://www.izak.ru/the-institute-of-legislation-and-comparative-law-under-the-government-of-the-russian-federation-162; Inst. of State and Law of the Russ. Acad. of Sci., http://www.igpran.ru/en.

[129] According to one Russian international lawyer:

> University professors (not tutors, full professors) earn on average 500–600 pounds or less a month (used to be worse in the 1990s). Many were forced to leave academia altogether to provide for their families. Others have to combine teaching with working as lawyer or running their businesses etc. There are two types of exceptions: martyrs and these who would not be able to find other employment. As the result, they have neither time nor energy to conduct any significant research or write high-quality articles. The concept of research assistants does not exist. The situation has been changing with grants from the state for certain research, but not significantly.

E-mail on file with author.

[130] Some French international law academics also published in foreign French-language publications, like the Belgian-based *Revue de droit international et de droit comparé* [Review of International and Comparative Law].

[131] Arrêté du 4 février 2014 fixant les modalités d'inscription en vue de pourvoir des emplois de professeur des universités dans les disciplines juridiques, politiques, économiques et de gestion pour le premier concours national d'agrégation de l'enseignement supérieur pour l'année 2014 [Decree of February 4, 2014 Laying Down Registration Arrangements in Order to Fill Position of University Professor in Legal, Political, Economic and Management Disciplines for the First National Competitive Examination of Aggregation in Higher Education

publications only in French. Even now, writing in English and translating into French would be a lot more work, and the results would probably not be ideal in any event. Civil law scholars from France and elsewhere often complain that the difference is not just one of language but also one of legal style. Rarely can an article be written in one language and just translated into another, as the composition and reasoning often differs between common law and civil law states.

The style of scholarship valued also diverges so that English-language publications will commonly not comply with French scholarly ideals, even if translated. French legal academic writing style is rich, more akin to literature than science. The writing in English-language publications is often criticized in France for being "standardized," meaning neutral and systematic, and lacking in literary merit or quality. The assumption is that the ideas expressed in that way are too simple or simplified to capture complexity and subtlety. The supposed risk to intellectual depth that arises from the poverty of the writing process is one reason given by French legal academics as to why they should not write or teach in English, and it explains why little value tends to attach to translations.

French legal scholarship often takes a form that does not necessarily translate well to or from English writing. Doctorates, for instance, are typically divided into two parts, which in turn are split into two subparts, which are then divided into two sub-subparts, even if this structure seems forced given the subject and argument.[132] (This rule is not followed as rigidly for articles.) French law academics generally have different philosophical and legal starting points from those of their English-speaking counterparts and engage with different literature and historical figures. French scholarship privileges a logical, deductive method and legal doctrinal analysis rather than engagement with nonlegal approaches, such as economics and sociology. Some English-language concepts (such as jurisdiction) are also not identical to the nearest French equivalent (like compétence), making translation again inadequate.

Academic incentives are not only key to landing a first position. In France, promotion to a better university post depends on impressing the domestic French academy; building one's domestic reputation is widely considered to be more important than building one's international reputation, even for international lawyers, which has the effect of privileging French and French-language publications. One French academic explained to me that this focus sometimes results in an inversely proportional relationship between internal and external reputations: "The more you focus on your international community, the less you are valued by your domestic community, and vice versa." Another said that the relationship was asymmetric: one could find prominent international lawyers in France who did not have strong reputations outside of France, but not vice versa.

Academic incentives can also move in the other direction. The Chinese international law academics published around 90 percent of their articles in Chinese journals that were usually native-language journals. Nevertheless, the academy creates incentives

---

of 2014], art. 7(1) ("When these documents are written in a foreign language, a translation in French will be attached.").

[132] JAMIN, *supra* note 75, at 70.

for scholars to publish in certain foreign and transnational journals. Promotions in the Chinese academy are tied to appearing in certain Chinese journals or in English-language journals listed in the Social Sciences Citation Index. These incentives apply to Chinese international law academics, but given the language difficulties involved, publishing in English-language journals is still very difficult, particularly for members of the older generation who tend to be less competent in English.

Although a handful of Chinese international law academics have written a substantial number of papers in transnational and foreign journals, most remain largely nationally bound. One reason is that the Chinese government partly assesses universities by setting numerical targets for the number of articles published, which creates incentives for academics to contribute many (often inferior) articles to national journals.[133] Writing such pieces in English would take too long, and they would probably not be accepted in any event. Nonetheless, the fact that Chinese international lawyers frequently study in English-speaking states and are given incentives to publish in English-speaking journals correlates with a higher percentage of foreign and transnational journal placements in comparison with their Russian peers.

In terms of English-speaking academies, US scholars publish the vast majority of their articles in US journals, whereas UK academics publish the majority of their articles in transnational and foreign journals like the *European Journal of International Law*, the *International Journal of Criminal Justice*, and the *Journal of International Economic Law*. This difference might partly arise from the fact that the *American Journal of International Law* is clearly associated with the United States, but the number of articles published in this journal made up such a small percentage of the overall figures that this association did not significantly influence the results. One explanation for the US statistics lies in the enormous number of journals in the US market since most law schools host multiple journals, usually including both a law review and a specialist international law journal. This proliferation is not found in the United Kingdom. Another explanation can be traced to academic incentives. In the United Kingdom, a premium is placed on publishing in peer-reviewed journals; they are often specialist journals, and many of them are transnational. By contrast, in the United States, a premium is placed on publishing in US law reviews and journals, often with a preference for generalist student-edited journals and, among them, with a preference for those published at the law school which ranks the highest on the US News & World Report.[134]

Within the domestic US journals, the US international law academics published roughly 60 percent in generalist or noninternational journals and 40 percent in specialist international journals. The incentive to privilege publishing in domestic law reviews

---

[133] Minzner, *supra* note 82, at 365 ("Pressure to hit designated numerical targets has helped fuel a widespread culture of academic corruption and junk research.") (quoting Ge Jianxiong, 学术腐败，不诚信和犯罪: 研究与思想, [Academic Corruption, Dishonesty, and Misdeeds: Research and Thoughts], *in* ANN. REPORT ON CHINA'S EDUCATION 123, 125 (Yang Dongping ed., 2010) ("Because existing evaluation systems unilaterally emphasize numbers of articles and length of manuscripts, researchers produce huge amounts of scholarly garbage.").

[134] *See 2017 Best Law Schools*, U.S. NEWS & WORLD REP., https://www.usnews.com/best-graduate-schools/top-law-schools (last visited Apr. 22, 2016).

over international specialist and peer-reviewed journals can be evidenced by looking at the rankings of US journals on sites like the Washington and Lee School of Law website. According to its combined score rating, the generalist law reviews of the elite law schools (like Harvard, Yale, and Stanford) dominate the list, whereas the most highly ranked specialist journal in any field—the *Harvard International Law Journal*—comes in at thirty-eighth, followed by the *Virginia Journal of International Law* at forty-fifth, the *Yale Journal of International Law* at sixty-fourth, and the *American Journal of International Law* at sixty-seventh.[135] The *American Journal*, which is one of the premier peer-reviewed journals in the field and one of the few US legal journals that is peer-reviewed, ranks just above the *Buffalo Law Review* and below a vast array of general law reviews of law schools that are not top ranked, such as Alabama, Ohio, Connecticut, and Emory.

Differences in style and substance can also make it difficult to place the same piece in US and non-US journals, so that quite often a choice must be made during the writing stage. US articles are generally much longer and more heavily footnoted than pieces that are accepted by non-US peer-reviewed journals. The submissions processes differ radically, as peer-reviewed journals often require exclusive submission, whereas the US student-edited journals usually permit multiple submissions and trading-up offers from lower-ranked journals to higher-ranked ones. Certain types of interdisciplinary work may also find a more natural home in US journals, such as law and economics approaches. But even interdisciplinary US international law academics explained that one of the main reasons for publishing in US journals was that those articles were more favorably recognized and valued by their generalist faculties.

US international law academics care so much about appealing to their noninternational law colleagues partly because of the way hiring occurs in the US market. To obtain an entry-level job or lateral move, academics ordinarily need to be approved by a vote of the entire faculty. Prospective applicants thus have an incentive to focus on work that is understandable and of interest to the faculty as a whole, not just to the international law specialists. The noninternational law academics not only determine how many international lawyers might be hired, but also are influential in determining who those international law academics will be. As generalist faculties privilege generalist journals, so do many US international law academics. The lack of symbolic capital associated with both foreign legal education and foreign legal publishing is also mutually reinforcing.[136] "And forget about publishing in a language other than English," one US legal academic explained, while another declared that publishing in a particular foreign, English-language journal would be the equivalent of "hiding the article under a rock" as far as her faculty was concerned.[137]

This hiring process contrasts with the approach taken in the United Kingdom where international law academics are normally selected by a committee in which the

---

[135] *See* Law Journals: Submissions and Ranking, 2008–2015, Wash. & Lee Sch. L., http://lawlib.wlu.edu/LJ/index.aspx (last visited Apr. 22, 2016).

[136] *See* Jamin & van Caenegem, *supra* note 26, at 7 (noting the relative absence of foreign legal education and foreign legal publishing in the United States and India).

[137] E-mails on file with author.

assessment by international lawyers is often compelling or decisive. The key to being hired and promoted is typically recognition by the academics' peer group of international lawyers, rather than their peer group of domestic legal academics comprised by the faculty at large. Certainly, prestige attaches to publication in generalist journals, such as the *Modern Law Review* and the *Oxford Journal of Legal Studies*, and there may be some pressure to publish in these journals, particularly for academics who work at the institutions in which they are based. But prestige also attaches to publication in top peer-reviewed journals in general, frequently with a preference for specialist international law journals, whether domestic, foreign, or transnational.

UK scholars are the outliers in the group studied when it comes to how much of their work they publish in foreign and transnational journals. While academic incentives play a part in influencing this publication strategy, this option is readily available to UK scholars given the prevalence of English-language international law journals, both foreign and transnational.[138] On the national level, many domestic journals and yearbooks on international law are only in English, even when published in non-English-speaking states (for example, the *Chinese Journal of International Law* and the *German Yearbook of International Law*). On the transnational level, many of the subject-specific and regional international law journals are only in English (for example, the *Journal of International Criminal Justice* and the *Asian Journal of International Law*).

The prevalence of English in international law publications means that UK international law academics have greater access to appearing in foreign and transnational journals than their Chinese, French, and Russian peers. That cannot be said of their US peers, but the difference between them lies more in academic incentives than language abilities. This difference may also relate to the diversity of UK international law academics, many of whom originally came from and studied outside the United Kingdom, which may carry over to their networks and perspectives when it comes to foreign and transnational publishing.

C. IMPLICATIONS FOR THE DIVISIBLE COLLEGE

Divergent publication placements can contribute to shaping the audiences and spheres of influence of different international law academies in ways that reflect and reinforce certain nationalizing, denationalizing, and westernizing influences characteristic of the divisible college of international lawyers.

First, language divides international lawyers. When international law academics publish in different languages, they often speak to distinct audiences. By publishing in local languages, international law scholars perform the important function of bringing international law home and communicating international ideas to domestic audiences, including noninternational law specialists. But, depending on the language involved, these choices can also severely limit the transnational audience of these scholars because language barriers are real.

---

[138] For further discussion, see Chapter 5.III.B and C.

Consider a Chinese international lawyer with the requisite linguistic skills to be able to choose between writing in Chinese and publishing in a Chinese journal or writing in English and publishing in a foreign or transnational journal. By doing the former, the academic will probably reach an almost exclusively domestic (Chinese) audience. The chance that the ideas will reach and influence a non-Chinese audience is minimal. By contrast, if the academic publishes in English in a foreign or transnational journal, the ideas will have a greater chance of reaching a transnational audience, but the scholar's domestic audience will be more circumscribed.

The audiences for different languages are not always demarcated along national lines and some languages have a greater transnational reach than others. A French international lawyer who publishes in a French-language domestic journal is likely to reach an audience of French international lawyers, as well as other international lawyers who speak French, including those from Francophone European, African, and Asian states. Similarly, the audience of a US international lawyer who publishes in an English-language domestic journal is apt to extend to other English-speaking international lawyers located outside the United States. This is particularly true for publishing in journals, like the *American Journal of International Law*, which have a large readership outside their home state.

The language of publication can make a real difference as to audience and uptake. For instance, a 2001 study found that the *Max Planck Encyclopedia of Public International Law* (a German-based publication written in English) had been cited 246 times in US journals, whereas the *Juris-Classeur de droit international* (a French-based publication written in French) had been cited only once.[139] In 2016, a search of these two sources in the International Law Review Articles of Lexis revealed 153 articles citing the former and 4 citing the latter.[140] The *Juris-Classeur* is undoubtedly cited more frequently in Francophone literature. But if the *Max Planck Encyclopedia* had been written in German, it is doubtful that it would have been as influential outside Germany as it has been. Indeed, it is now published by Oxford University Press and available online, and over 92 percent of its subscribers are not from Germany.[141]

Developing audiences across language lines is difficult considering the limits of multilingualism, as many people speak only one or a handful of languages and translations are not that common. Still, exceptions exist. For instance, the *Revista latinoamericana de derecho internacional*, which was launched in 2014, includes Spanish-language versions of famous articles originally published in other languages.[142] But, for the most part, the choice of which language to write in has a major effect on the makeup of the audiences of different international law academics, whether on national lines (for languages that are not widely spoken outside the state in question) or transnational lines

---

[139] Detlev F. Vagts, 95 AM. J. INT'L L. 726, 726 (2001) (book review).

[140] Search conducted Nov. 3, 2016. The equivalent search in Westlaw under International Law Reviews and Journals yielded ninety-nine articles citing the former and none citing the latter.

[141] *See* Max Planck Encyclopedia of Public International Law, Max Planck Inst. for Comp. Pub. L. & Int'l L., http:// www.mpil.de/en/pub/research/areas/public-international-law/max-planck-encyclopedia.cfm (last visited Oct. 27, 2016). I am grateful to Frauke Lachenmann of the Max Planck Foundation for International Peace and the Rule of Law for providing me with this figure (on file with author).

[142] *See* Acerca de LADI, *supra* note 116.

(for international languages that are spoken by linguistic communities existing across national lines).

Second, authorities and reference points often differ between language groups, which may result in relatively self-contained and self-referential debates that differ across national or linguistic communities. I am not aware of any study that has tracked citation patterns in different international law journals, but anecdotal evidence suggests a strong tendency to cite primarily from within a single language and sometimes from within a single state or region. For instance, Giorgio Sacerdoti, an Italian international lawyer, noted the "alarming development" that "[m]any authors use only sources in their own language. For example, citations in the American Journal of International Law are almost exclusively to articles that are written in English and predominantly to articles that are authored by American writers. For me, this reveals a certain parochial approach and provincialism."[143] Emmanuelle Jouannet, a French international lawyer, reflected that the same pattern would emerge if one were to examine the two leading French international law journals, the *Annuaire français de droit international* and the *Revue générale de droit international public*, with the exception of more frequent citations to European sources.[144]

English and French are the two leading languages of international law, yet academic cross-fertilization even between these languages remains limited. For instance, a comparison by one scholar of the 1980 volumes of the *American Journal of International Law* and the *Annuaire de droit international* showed that only 1.5 percent of the footnotes in the English-language journal were to French sources and only 7.3 percent of the footnotes in the French journal were to English-language sources.[145] Alain Pellet, a French international lawyer, objected to the lack of citations to French sources in the *American Journal of International Law*, stating:

> The most convincing explanation therefore seems to be, quite simply, that our American colleagues do not read French. But, as the same seems to be true for Spanish, German, Italian, Japanese and Russian, they certainly deprive themselves of the indispensable comparative dimension, and this also raises a more general and difficult "cultural" problem. "Self-confinement" might be the way empires collapse. . . .[146]

Because of these divisions, international law scholarship sometimes proceeds in relatively self-contained silos, as similar patterns of thought are perpetuated within, but not necessarily between, states or linguistic communities.[147]

---

[143] Panel Session, *Comparative Approaches to the Theory of International Law*, 80 Am. Soc'y Int'l L. Proc. 152, 174 (1986).

[144] Emmanuelle Jouannet, *French and American Perspectives on International Law: Legal Cultures and International Law*, 58 Me. L. Rev. 291, 324 (2006).

[145] Alain Pellet, *Correspondence*, 82 Am. J. Int'l L. 331 (1988).

[146] *Id.* at 332.

[147] Jouannet has noted that "[d]octrine has the tendency to reproduce itself within the same body of references on each side of the Atlantic and thus continue to perpetuate among the practitioners who read it the same patterns of thought." Jouannet, *supra* note 144, at 324.

When international law scholars primarily publish in domestic, native-language jour-nals, distinct national communities sometimes emerge that are characterized by their own hierarchies, preoccupations, and doxa. For instance, Mälksoo has observed that Russian scholars often give "special visibility" in their work to other Russian scholars instead of foreign authors.[148] One result is that the Russian international law commun-ity contains its own leading authorities on many issues who often have limited impact outside Russia. This inwardness contributes to the preoccupation of the Russian inter-national law community with debates that are largely nonissues in other international law academies, such as whether or not individuals can be subjects of international law.[149] According to Mälksoo:

> Schachter's image of "invisible college" has proven to be a very popular one. However, based on the Russian self-referential practice (which, however, Russians could object, is not very different from scholarly practices in the field of international law in the US), are international lawyers globally really all in the same college or temple? Perhaps instead there are a number of fragmented colleges, epistemic communi-ties, speaking each a different language or at least dialect of the same language, and thinking they are "predominant" while being relatively ignorant about the others? Each of such temples seems to have its own leading authorities and hierarchies and a result is that the way international law is talked about has different accents—or even content—in places like New York and Moscow.[150]

Maria Issaeva criticizes the "extremely isolated and self-referential system of the post-Soviet international law tradition of teaching," which manifests itself in a "requirement to cite the Russian doctrine in every scholarly work presented for defence in Russia."[151] Issaeva observes that the system openly disregards a thorough study of foreign inter-national legal scholarship and international jurisprudence, as evidenced by the lack of emphasis on these sources in most Russian textbooks and monographs.[152] The lim-ited English-language skills of many Russian international law academics reflects and reinforces the lack of interest in filling law libraries with foreign legal literature.[153] In Issaeva's view,

> [M]uch in the Russian doctrine of international law happens exclusively in the Russian language. However, . . . [c]an a person really have a grasp of international

---

[148] Lauri Mälksoo, *International Legal Theory in Russia: A Civilizational Perspective, or: Can Individuals Be Subjects of International Law?, in* THE OXFORD HANDBOOK ON THE THEORY OF INTERNATIONAL LAW 257, 272 (Florian Hoffmann & Anne Orford eds., 2016).

[149] For further discussion, see Chapter 4.I.C.

[150] Mälksoo, *supra* note 148, at 273.

[151] MARIA ISSAEVA, QUARTER OF A CENTURY ON FROM THE SOVIET ERA: REFLECTIONS ON RUSSIAN DOCTRINAL RESPONSES TO THE ANNEXATION OF CRIMEA (forthcoming 2017).

[152] *Id.*

[153] *Id.*

law today if s/he does not speak at least English? The libraries of most Russian law schools do not offer any of the major international legal databases, supposedly due to a lack of demand. As a result, both a Russian student in training and a Russian scholar doing research are limited to referring to Russian sources only. Hence those sources tend to remain self-referential by virtue of their own isolation and limit[ed] to Soviet and post-Soviet legal thought.[154]

As a result of these divisions, distinct groups of international lawyers may exhibit significantly different doxa. An example can be found in debates over Crimea's annexation by, or reunification with, Russia.[155] In the West, international law scholarship tended to treat the issue as an unlawful annexation of Crimea by Russia. In Russia, the international lawyers frequently analyzed the situation as a voluntary and lawful decision by Crimea to reunite with its mother country, Russia. The striking differences between debates in Russia and the West, along with the failure of the two groups to engage in a serious dialogue, led the *Heidelberg Journal of International Law* to take the unusual step of creating a symposium bringing together Russian and Western scholars to debate the issues. The editors stated:

> Tensions between Russia and all Western States have reached a level unknown since the end of the cold war. Moreover, the assessment of the events from an international law perspective mirrors the geo-political camps. Hardly any "Western" politician or scholar deems Russia's political course justifiable and justified under the precepts of international law. Inversely, from what we can perceive from the outside, Russian politicians and scholars seem confident to be able to properly justify the incorporation of Crimea within the framework of the existing international legal order. *The crisis is matched by the absence of a serious legal dialogue among international legal scholars of both camps.*[156]

Yet the differences between the Russian and Western approaches were so strong, and so entrenched, that even when these scholars interacted in the same forums, they seemed unable to bridge the gap.[157]

---

[154] *See* Maria Issaeva, *Does "Russian International Law" Have an International Academic Future?*, EJIL: *TALK!*, Sept. 21, 2015.

[155] For references and further discussion, see Chapter 5.II.A.

[156] Marxsen et al., *supra* note 94, at 3 (emphasis added).

[157] *Compare* Veronica Bilkova, *The Use of Force by the Russian Federation in Crimea*, 75 ZAöRV 27 (2015); Christian Marxsen, *Territorial Integrity in International Law: Its Concept and Implications for Crimea, id.* at 7; Oleksandr Merezhko, *Crimea's Annexation by Russia: Contradictions of the New Russian Doctrine of International Law, id.* at 167, *with* Anatoly Kapustin, *Crimea's Self-Determination in the Light of Contemporary International Law, id.* at 101; Alexander Salenko, *Legal Aspects of the Dissolution of the Soviet Union in 1991, id.* at 141; Vladislav Tolstykh, *Three Ideas of Self-Determination in International Law and the Reunification of Crimea with Russia, id.* at 119. *See also* Issaeva, *supra* note 154 ("a common trend discernible at various legal conferences was the complete breakdown in effective communication between speakers from Russian universities and those from other localities.").

Similar critiques about self-contained and self-referential debates have been leveled at US international law scholarship, including by Mälksoo and Pellet above. For instance, UK-based international lawyer Guglielmo Verdirame explained that the paucity of canonical references in US international law scholarship, together with the profusion of references to contemporary American scholarship, fuels the European perception that these contributions are part of an "inward-looking and largely self-referential debate," which he viewed as a shortcoming for any intellectual exchange, but specifically for one on international law.[158] These self-contained and self-referential debates may result in distinct understandings of "international law." Thus, US-based Naz Modirzadeh described the legal debates in the United States following the attacks of September 11, 2011, as "folk international law," which she defined as "a law-like discourse that relies on a confusing and soft admixture of [international humanitarian law], jus ad bellum, and [international human rights law] to frame operations that do not, ultimately, seem bound by international law—at least not by any conception of international law recognizable to international lawyers, especially those outside of the U.S."[159]

Third, even when writing in the same language, academics may target different national or transnational audiences, depending on their publication placements. Consider, for instance, the decision of a US scholar to publish in a domestic generalist US journal versus the decision of a UK scholar to publish in a transnational specialist international law journal. US international law articles that are pitched to a generalist US audience often include detailed background, whereas peer review pieces that are pitched to specialist international lawyers assume they have the relevant background knowledge. US pieces often give the impression that they are trying to justify the field's existence or importance to a skeptical generalist crowd, whereas peer review pieces can give the impression of preaching to the international law choir.[160] Student-run law reviews habitually encourage bold and hyperbolic claims; peer review journals tend to penalize over-claiming. These differences accumulate to produce distinct styles of scholarship.

But the differences can be substantive as well as stylistic. To be attractive to a generalist US audience, American international law scholarship often takes one of two turns. The first is an American substantive turn, which usually means focusing on foreign relations law or national security law rather than international law. In US journals, top billing frequently

---

[158] Guglielmo Verdirame, *"The Divided West": International Lawyers in Europe and America*, 18 Eur. J. Int'l L. 553, 563 (2007).

[159] Naz K. Modirzadeh, *Folk International Law: 9/11 Lawyering and the Transformation of the Law of Armed Conflict to Human Rights Policy and Human Rights Law to War Governance*, 5 Harv. Nat'l Security J. 225, 226, 229 (2014). I have made a similar point about much Alien Tort Statute case law and scholarship, which often looks international to US domestic lawyers and American to non-US international lawyers. *See* Anthea Roberts, *Comparative International Law? The Role of National Courts in International Law*, 60 Int'l & Comp. L.Q. 57, 77 (2011).

[160] *Cf.* Verdirame, *supra* note 158, at 554 (comparing Anne-Marie Slaughter's *New World Order* and Philippe Sands's *Lawless World*: "Slaughter assumes, probably correctly, that most of her American readers will be international law sceptics; Sands, in contrast, addresses a public and an intellectual community generally well-disposed towards international law, and open to the possibility of forms of legal and political organization above the nation-state.").

goes to international law pieces that concern how international law is incorporated into US law, the role of customary international law in US courts, international law and the US Constitution, the treaty power, the president's ability to wage war, or any topic related to the US use of force or threats to national security (particularly since 9/11). This proclivity creates a distinct scholarly incentive to nationalize, which is reinforced by the tendency to present draft papers in general faculty workshops. The second is to take an American methodological turn by employing techniques that are commonly used elsewhere in the US legal academy, such as economic analysis or empirical approaches, which may be appreciated by American colleagues who have little or no understanding of international law.

Both turns may limit the transnational audience of US international law scholars. For instance, US international law academic Detlev Vagts argued that the foreign relations turn "distinguishe[d] American scholarship and teaching on international law" but was "by and large of no interest to foreign scholars," had produced "no country to country dialogue," and disabled many US scholars from "participating in an international dialogue."[161] This deficiency may change with the emergence of new projects on comparative foreign relations law,[162] but foreign relations law is quite nationalized by its nature. National security law scholarship may be of interest to foreign scholars, particularly when it concerns US uses of force, but its frequent focus on protecting American interests may be jarring to foreign readers, while the assumptions and understandings of the law on which it is based will often strike non-US readers as peculiarly American. As for interdisciplinary scholarship, it is likely to be of interest to international law scholars in other states who are open to such approaches, and such scholarship is increasingly prevalent in transnational international law journals. But in legal academies that remain more doctrinally oriented, which is characteristic of many European academies, for instance, many of their scholars would not consider such pieces to be legal scholarship and would sometimes treat them as antithetical to legal scholarship.

Scholarly incentives to nationalize are not limited to the US academy. Germany serves as another example. As Swiss-based German international law academic Nico Krisch has explained, "academic careers in Germany are built on the back of achievements in national public law, not international law."[163] Because of the way German law faculties are structured, international law academics typically must also cover domestic constitutional or administrative law and European Union law.[164] Moreover, the ability to teach one or more of these other subjects is generally required of candidates for the main professorial chairs in international law since they are almost always joint positions in international and public law.[165] Not only are doctoral degrees and the postdoctoral

---

[161] Detlev F. Vagts, *American International Law: A Sonderweg?*, *in* WELTINNENRECHT: LIBER AMICORUM JOST DELBRÜCK 835, 839, 841, 847 (Klaus Dicke et al. eds., 2005).

[162] For developments, see Chapter 5.I.B.

[163] Nico Krisch, *The Many Fields of International Law: A Conceptual Framework with a Case Study of German International Law*, *in* COMPARATIVE INTERNATIONAL LAW (Anthea Roberts et al. eds., forthcoming 2017).

[164] *See also* Peters, *supra* note 93, at 771.

[165] One exception was a chair dedicated solely to (European and) international law in Munich, which was held by Austrian-trained international lawyer Bruno Simma, a dual Austrian/German national, but it was converted

habilitation ordinarily required to be from a German university, but also custom makes it virtually compulsory for only one to be in international law and the other to be in a domestic public law subject, like constitutional law, though often with a comparative or European focus.

One result of this structural orientation toward the domestic public law field is that German international lawyers tend not to be highly visible in English-speaking international law journals, such as the *American Journal of International Law* and *European Journal of International Law*. According to Krisch's study of articles over twenty pages long that were published between 2004 and 2013, only one article out of 111 in the *American Journal of International Law* had been written by a scholar based in Germany. In the *European Journal of International Law*, scholars from the United Kingdom had published more than three times the number of articles than German scholars. In the *International and Comparative Law Quarterly*, German pieces were outnumbered by those from scholars working in the Netherlands, despite Germany having a population between four and five times higher than the Netherlands. Krisch's results are reproduced below in Table 5.

This public law orientation also has a substantive impact on the German international law scholarship that reaches an international audience. For instance, a pronounced number of the scholars who argue in favor of the constitutionalization of international law were trained in or worked in the German legal academy. These include Mattias Kumm,

TABLE 5

Publications in Select International Law Journals from 2004–2013 by Scholars from Certain Countries

	Germany	United Kingdom	Netherlands	Total Articles
American Journal of	1	8	2	111
International Law	0.9%	7.2%	1.8%	
European Journal of	19	65.5	11.5	272
International Law	7.0%	24.1%	4.2%	
Leiden Journal of	18.83	42.5	55.9	223
International Law	8.4%	19.1%	25.1%	
International &	6	129.25	8.75	230
Comparative Law	2.6%	56.2%	3.8%	
Quarterly				
Totals	44.83	245.25	78.15	836
	5.4%	29.3%	9.3%	

Source: Nico Krisch, *The Many Fields of International Law: A Conceptual Framework with a Case Study of German International Law, in* COMPARATIVE INTERNATIONAL LAW (Anthea Roberts et al. eds., forthcoming 2017).

back into the typical "mixed" public law/international law chair after his departure in 2003. *See also* Krisch, *supra* note 163.

Andreas Paulus, Anne Peters, Bruno Simma, Christian Tomuschat, and Alfred Verdroß.[166] According to Jan Klabbers, there is not a country in the world where the UN Charter is so steadfastly and seriously regarded as a constitution for the international community as Germany.[167] The constitutionalization thesis by German international legal academics is a way of translating the experiences of Germany with its own constitution and with European law to the sphere of international law.[168]

Although scholarly incentives encourage many US and German international lawyers to nationalize, the opposite occurs in countries that privilege publishing in international peer-reviewed journals. In the United Kingdom, the main criterion for hiring and promotion is publication in the top peer-reviewed journals in the field. These could be national (like the *International and Comparative Law Quarterly* and the *British Year Book of International Law*) or foreign or transnational (like the *Leiden Journal of International Law* and the *Journal of International Dispute Settlement*). Because no significant premium is placed on publishing in national generalist journals, the incentive to nationalize by, say, taking a UK foreign-relations-law turn or trying to win over a UK generalist audience, does not appear in the same way.

Whereas the UK academy puts no particular premium on scholarship that is nationalized, others, like the Australian and Dutch academies, seem actively to encourage denationalization by emphasizing publication in foreign and transnational journals.[169] A powerful qualification for hiring and promotions in these states is an international reputation, which is easier to acquire for scholars of international law or some international or comparative aspect of domestic law. The incentives thus created for Australian

---

[166] *See* Andreas Paulus, Die internationale Gemeinschaft im Völkerrecht (2001); Alfred Verdross, Die Verfassung der Völkerrechtsgemeinschaft (1926); Mattias Kumm, *The Legitimacy of International Law: A Constitutionalist Framework of Analysis*, 15 Eur. J. Int'l L. 907 (2004); Bruno Simma, *From Bilateralism to Community Interest in International Law*, 250 Recueil des cours 217 (1994); Bruno Simma & Andreas L. Paulus, *The "International Community": Facing the Challenge of Globalization*, 9 Eur. J. Int'l L. 266 (1998); Christian Tomuschat, *International Law: Ensuring the Survival of Mankind on the Eve of a New Century*, 281 Recueil des cours 9 (1999); Christian Tomuschat, *Die internationale Gemeinschaft*, 33 Archiv des Völkerrechts 1 (1995); Mattias Kumm, *The Cosmopolitan Turn in Constitutionalism: On the Relationship between Constitutionalism in and beyond the State*, in Ruling the World? Constitutionalism, International Law, and Global Governance 258 (Jeffrey L. Dunoff & Joel P. Trachtman eds., 2009); Andreas Paulus, *The International Legal System as a Constitution*, in Ruling the World? Constitutionalism, International Law, and Global Governance 69 (Jeffrey L. Dunoff & Joel P. Trachtman eds., 2009); Anne Peters, *Are We Moving Towards Constitutionalization of the World Community?*, in Realizing Utopia—The Future of International Law 118 (Antonio Cassese ed., 2012). The "German" character of the debate can also be seen in the prominent position of constitutionalism in ten presentations in a lecture series hosted by the Max Planck Institute, The Future of International Law Scholarship in Germany. *See* Vorlesungsreihe, *Die Zukunft des Völkerrechtswissenschaft in Deutschland*, 67 ZaöRV 585 (2007).

[167] Jan Klabbers, *Ulla Hingst, Auswirkungen der Globalisierung auf das Recht der völkerrechtlichen Verträge*, 16 Leiden J. Int'l L. 201, 202–03 (2003) (book review).

[168] Andreas L. Paulus, *Zur Zukunft der Völkerrechtswissenschaft in Deutschland: Zwischen Konstitutionalisierung und Fragmentierung des Völkerrehcts* [On the Future of International Law in Germany], 67 ZaöRV 695, 701 (2007).

[169] Armin von Bogdandy, *National Legal Scholarship in the European Legal Area—A Manifesto*, 10 Int'l J. Const. L. 614, 620 (2012).

and Dutch academics to lean toward international and comparative law, and to publish outside their jurisdiction, in turn create incentives to denationalize.[170]

Nationalizing and denationalizing influences can also be subtle. US scholars frequently send their articles to twenty, thirty, or more US student-edited law reviews, but no foreign journals. In such cases, it is hard to guard against subconscious US biases and assumptions because all of the journals have one thing in common: they are American and the editorial teams are overwhelmingly American. Using US examples or assessing developments from a US perspective is likely to seem natural and in no need of justification, even when the subject matter is international law. Moreover, using these examples or adopting this perspective will probably enhance the chances for the submission to be accepted. The main exception to this is that many US scholars also submit to the *American Journal of International Law*, which evidences a mixed US and non-US editorial board, but it is the exception not the rule.

Compare this nationalizing approach to the process faced by academics trying to publish in international peer-reviewed journals. They might want to publish in the *American Journal of International Law*, or failing that, the *European Journal of International Law*, or failing that, *Leiden Journal of International Law* or the *Asian Journal of International Law*. In many cases, the editorial boards of these journals are made up of scholars located in many states, so that the peer review comments may challenge national biases and assumptions. Even absent this eventuality, the possibility that authors will have to send their articles to editorial boards in different states has a denationalizing effect because they cannot want to retailor their work each time it is submitted to a journal in a different country.

Transnational international law journals tend implicitly to encourage their authors to approach international law questions from the perspective of the "international community." But just as US journals may not problematize the American vantage point from which many of their articles are written, so transnational international law journals often fail to problematize their standpoint. Who constitutes the international community? Does it even exist? Is it a camouflaged way of referring to the interests of Western states? Is it a disguised way of referring to the interests of international lawyers themselves? Even if the international community exists, how can international lawyers know what its needs are? How can they be sure that they are working toward what is best for the international community, rather than what is best for the international law, cosmopolitan elite?

Those who write for a peer review audience of international lawyers tend to take for granted that "international law is good" and "more international law is better," and not to problematize the propensity of this audience to have a prointernational law bias, which may not be representative of the wider population. Jan Klabbers has characterized this mindset as the view that "everything international is wonderful precisely because it is

---

[170] Similar dynamics occur in other legal academies, such as China's (which rewards publishing in English-language legal journals that are part of the Social Sciences Citation Index) and Israel's (which privileges publishing in the US market, encouraging Israeli scholars to produce a disproportionate amount of international law and law and economics scholarship).

international,"[171] and Michael Waibel has explained that "[t]he prevalent view among international lawyers is that international law is a force for good, designed to keep arbitrariness by national governments in check, to moderate power struggles in international affairs, and to provide public goods. In this frame of mind, the more international law, the better."[172]

These tendencies lead some US international law academics, such as Kenneth Anderson, to caution that "'international law' in the hands of its experts and enthusiasts tends to march itself off a cliff, attuned only to its own song; it becomes ever more internally 'pure' but ever more disconnected from the world of international politics where, ultimately, it must live."[173] Having to pass through peer review may also make it harder for views that are critical of international law—or views that are critical in certain ways—to be published. For instance, some US scholars complained that critiques from international law's left, such as those by feminists or members of the Third World, often seemed to gain more acceptance within international law journals than critiques from the right, such as those by conservative new-sovereigntist Americans.

Fourth, because many of the transnational international law journals are published in English and by major Western publishing houses, certain communities of scholars, most notably Western, English-speaking, and often common law scholars, may play a disproportionate role in defining what counts as the "international" scholarly approach.

The editorial boards of many of the subject-specific transnational international law journals are dominated by Western international law academics. The editors in chief of the *Journal of International Economic Law* are located in the United States and Switzerland, and the editorial board comprises the following number of scholars and practitioners based in the following countries: the United States (18), the United Kingdom (5), Switzerland (5), Canada (3), Australia (2), Austria (2), Belgium (2), Japan (2), Germany (1), Korea (1), Mexico (1), the Netherlands (1), and Singapore (1).[174] Similarly, for the board of editors of the *Journal of International Criminal Justice*, the countries and figures are the United Kingdom (2), Switzerland (2), Italy (2), Germany (2), the Netherlands (2), the United States (1), Canada (1), and China (1).[175] And the editor in chief of the *Journal of International Dispute Settlement* is located in the United Kingdom; the countries and figures for the general editors and editorial board are the United Kingdom (9), Canada (3), Switzerland (3), the United States (3), Australia (2), Israel (2), France (1), and Singapore (1).[176]

No Russian scholars sit on these editorial boards. One Chinese scholar appears on the lists, and they contain no scholars based in Africa or South America and just a handful from Asia. The Western dominance on these editorial boards will in all likelihood result

---

[171] Jan Klabbers, *The Life and Times of the Law of International Organizations*, 70 NORD. J. INT'L L. 287, 288 (2001).

[172] Michael Waibel, *Demystifying the Art of Interpretation*, 22 EUR. J. INT'L L. 571, 573 (2011).

[173] *See* Kenneth Anderson, Commentary, *Michael Glennon on the "Incompleteness" of International Law Governing the Use of Force*, LAWFARE, May 13, 2013, https://www.lawfareblog.com/readings-michael-glennon-incompleteness-international-law-governing-use-force.

[174] Editorial Board, Int'l J. Econ. L., http://www.oxfordjournals.org/our_journals/jielaw/editorial_board.html (last visited Apr. 28, 2016).

[175] Editorial Board, J. Int'l Crim. Just., http://www.oxfordjournals.org/our_journals/jielaw/editorial_board.html (last visited Apr. 28, 2016).

[176] Editorial Board, J. Int'l Disp. Settlement, https://academic.oup.com/jicj/pages/Editorial_Board (last visited Apr. 28, 2016).

in the normalization of certain Western perspectives. Comparable Western dominance does not characterize the editorial boards of many of the regional international law journals, such as the *Asian Journal of International Law*[177] and the *African Journal of International Law*.[178] Both of these journals, however, are put out by UK publishers (Cambridge University Press and Edinburgh University Press, respectively) and at least the latter features a high proportion of UK-based academics on the editorial board.

Within the Western grouping, French scholars were not well represented on these transnational journals. The boards featured above include quite a few scholars from French-speaking states, like Switzerland and Belgium, yet only one from France. Whether French scholars are not invited to join these transnational editorial boards, or whether they decline such invitations, is not clear. One possibility is that a parallel world exists of French-language transnational journals whose editorial boards are made up of Francophone scholars from a diverse array of states. Yet, on the basis of discussions with French academics, I was unable to uncover French-language equivalents of these transnational journals, which suggests that even if there are some, they are certainly not the norm. To the extent that these observations hold true over time, English-speaking, Western scholars can be expected to figure disproportionately in defining what counts as "international" scholarship in these transnational forums, which may have the effect of normalizing certain Western, common law approaches to international law.

IV. Comparing Links Between Academia and Practice

International law academics often engage in the practice of international law as advisers to governments, counsel in disputes, judges and arbitrators, and members of bodies charged with developing and codifying international law, such as the International Law Commission. Through these experiences, their academic perspectives are likely to influence real world developments and vice versa. Indeed, central to Schachter's description of the invisible college of international lawyers were the significant connections between academia and practice and the two-way process of exchange that they enabled.[179]

Nevertheless, links to practice vary considerably among international law academies. In the United States, for instance, it is common for international law academics to have worked full-time for the US government and/or completed clerkships in domestic courts. These sorts of experiences are far less common in the UK and French legal academies, but numerous scholars from these states participate in international dispute resolution as both counsel and arbitrators. By contrast, neither Chinese nor Russian international law academics are well represented in international dispute resolution, and their respective connections to their own governments differ and have changed over time.

[177] *See* Asian Journal of International Law, Cambridge Univ., http://journals.cambridge.org/action/displayMore Info?jid=AJL&type=eb&sessionId=6726396C688A7F8CBC54606034AEB7AC.journals (last visited Apr. 28, 2016).
[178] *See* Editorial Board, African J. Int'l & Comp. L., http://www.euppublishing.com/loi/ajicl (last visited Apr. 28, 2016).
[179] *See* Schachter, *supra* note 1, at 217.

Diverse incentives and opportunities explain many of these patterns. States attach varying amounts of symbolic capital to different kinds of professional experiences. Some states value prospective academics that have completed PhDs in law or another field, whereas others value professional experiences, though they may prize specific experiences, such as judicial clerkships, or working for a law firm, a government, and international organizations. Once a scholar has entered the academy, states also differ over permissible professional experiences (for example, US law schools usually permit academics to take a two-year leave of absence to work in government) and opportunities likely to arise in professional networks (for example, senior UK academics may extend offers to junior colleagues to work together as counsel on an international dispute).

The dynamics that determine which professional experiences are possible and valued prior to entering the academy and afterward are typically set by larger forces within a state without regard to their impact on the international law field. Yet these differences can produce marked effects on the incoming influences on, and outgoing spheres of influence of, international law academics in different states in ways that often reflect and reinforce certain nationalizing, denationalizing, and westernizing influences.

A. TRACKING LINKS BETWEEN ACADEMIA AND PRACTICE

As there is no easy way to track connections between academia and practice, I adopted a threefold approach. First, I looked for evidence of professional experience listed on a scholar's academic or professional web page or curriculum vitae. In some states, like the United States, academics ordinarily provide considerable detail on their professional experience on their university profile pages. In other states, like the United Kingdom, the web pages of some scholars include their professional experience, while others provide that information on web pages of the law firms or barristers' chambers to which they are associated.

Second, I was able to work backward to some extent by looking at the prevalence of academics from different states within discrete areas of legal practice. Thus, academics who have served as counsel before the International Court of Justice (ICJ) can be identified by searching ICJ pleadings, for example. This approach can yield some information about which academies are active in certain types of legal practice, but it cannot prove how widespread that practice is within those academies.

Finally, I engaged in discussions with international law academics from the states studied to understand what forms of practice were common in those states and whether any recent shifts were occurring that might not be obvious from examining publicly available sources. I sought evidence of a variety of professional experiences, including full-time employment for a government (for example, for a state's foreign ministry), an international organization, a domestic court, and an international court or tribunal. I also looked for professional experiences that might be part-time, like appearing as an advocate in international law disputes before domestic or international courts and tribunals, serving as an arbitrator, and representing a state as a member of a diplomatic mission. Because these professional experiences might not be public in some cases, the information given here is inevitably incomplete.

B. EXPLAINING DIFFERENT CONNECTIONS BETWEEN ACADEMIA AND PRACTICE

In most of the academies studied, the percentage of international law scholars who had engaged in a particular form of practice was low. Instead of attempting to capture all of these nuances, this section concentrates on some of the broader trends about professional experiences that seemed widespread or highly valued in the academies studied.

1. The United States

The two most striking connections to practice within the US legal academy were the completion by many international law scholars of clerkships on US federal courts and/or full-time employment by the US government, often for the Department of State.

Clerking for a judge on a domestic court after graduation from law school is a time-honored US tradition and, depending on the reputation of the judge or the level of the court, one that affords significant symbolic capital. Graduating law students compete over clerkships with well-known judges or on well-respected courts, like the Court of Appeals of the District of Columbia or the Second and Ninth Circuits. Supreme Court clerkships are the most prized and applicants will have completed another domestic clerkship before a Supreme Court one. As a result, many US law academics at elite schools have two domestic clerkships under their belts, often one for a judge on a federal appellate court and another at the Supreme Court.

More than 40 percent of US international law academics in the study had worked for one or two domestic judges and more than 90 percent of these clerkships were on domestic US courts. It was unusual to find US international law academics with experience clerking on foreign courts or international tribunals. Such options are relatively new and are not widespread. Some US international lawyers had this experience a generation ago at the Iran–United States Claims Tribunal. For the most part, however, clerking at an international court became a possibility only after the proliferation of international tribunals in the late 1990s.

Some elite US law schools offer paid clerkships for students to work for a year at courts like the ICJ.[180] Few academics in the study had this experience, which may partly reflect the recent vintage of this opportunity and the paucity of available spots, as well as the diminished value of this experience in the US academy as compared with many domestic clerkships. US academics confirmed that, even for individuals aspiring to be international law scholars, a US Supreme Court clerkship would be far more valuable in securing an entry-level job than an ICJ clerkship. Domestic clerkships, like domestic law reviews, are a form of symbolic capital that generalist US faculties typically understand better and esteem more than international and foreign equivalents.

---

[180] *See, e.g.*, International Internship and Clerkship Opportunities, Colum. L. Sch., http://web.law.columbia.edu/international-programs/internships-and-clerkships/international-internship-and-clerkship-opportunities; International Clerkships, N.Y.U. L. Sch., http://www.law.nyu.edu/global/globalopportunities/icjclerkship-prog; International Fellowships, Yale L. Sch., https://www.law.yale.edu/studying-law-yale/areas-interest/international-law/international-fellowships (all last visited Oct. 17, 2016).

Almost half of the US international law academics in the study had worked full-time for a government, which was almost always the US government. In many cases, the person had this experience before becoming an academic. But some had engaged in government work during their academic careers, as US law professors generally may take a leave of absence for up to two years without losing their tenure. The movement of academics into and out of government is also facilitated by the changeover in government positions, notably at the higher levels, when a new US administration takes office.

The connection between the Office of the Legal Adviser ("L") at the US Department of State and the US international law academy was particularly strong. Michael Scharf and Paul Williams noted that L serves as a "training ground" for future professors of public international law and that L alumni, including the legal advisers, have authored more than one thousand articles and books.[181] Harold Koh, a former legal adviser who had also been a professor and dean at Yale Law School, described one of the faces of L as "Scholarly L" since many alumni have gone on to become international law professors and scholars.[182]

The list of US international law academics who were teaching at the time of writing and had previously worked for L includes José Alvarez, Richard Bilder, Andrea Bjorklund, Daniel Bodansky, Jacob Katz Cogan, Lori Fisler Damrosch, Kristina Daugirdas, Ashley Deeks, Mark Feldman, David Gantz, Monica Hakimi, Duncan Hollis, Michael Matheson, Timothy Meyer, Saira Mohamed, Sean Murphy, Bernard Oxman, Steven Ratner, Sabrina Safrin, Michael Scharf, Peter Spiro, Kenneth Vandevelde, and Allen Weiner. Many other State Department lawyers held at the time, or have gone on to hold, positions as adjunct or visiting lecturers or professors, including Michael Matheson and David Stewart.[183]

Another position in L is called counselor of international law, who is usually a mid-level or senior international lawyer drawn from the academy to spend one to two years working for the department. Past counselors from academia include Louis Sohn, Richard Baxter, John Norton Moore, Stephen Schwebel, Gordon Baldwin, Detlev Vagts, Stefan Riesenfeld, Fred Morrison, Harold Maier, Stephen McCaffrey, Malvina Halberstam, Robert Dalton, Philip C. Bobbitt, Theodor Meron, Curtis Bradley, Edward Swaine, Paul Stephan, John Harrison, Sarah Cleveland, and William Dodge.[184] Indeed, six of the eight academics who serve as reporters for the *Restatement (Fourth) of the Foreign Relations Law of the United States* previously worked for the US State Department, as did many of the project's counselors and advisers.[185]

---

[181] Michael P. Scharf & Paul R. Williams, Shaping Foreign Policy in Times of Crisis: The Role of International Law and The State Department Legal Adviser 18 (2010).

[182] Harold Hongju Koh, *The State Department Legal Adviser's Office: Eight Decades in Peace and War*, 100 Geo. L.J. 1747, 1749, 1753 (2012).

[183] *Id.* at 1776–78, app. 2.

[184] *Id.* at 1780–81, app. 4.

[185] These are Curtis Bradley, Sarah Cleveland, William Dodge, Paul Stephan, David Stewart, and Edward Swaine. *See* Restatement of the Law Fourth, The Foreign Relations Law of the United States: Participants, Am. L. Inst., https://www.ali.org/projects/show/foreign-relations-law-united-states/#_participants (last visited Oct. 27, 2016).

Other prominent international law academics have held posts elsewhere in the US government. Examples include Jack Goldsmith (Harvard), who served as assistant attorney general in the Office of Legal Counsel of the Department of Justice and special counsel to the Department of Defense;[186] Oona Hathaway (Yale), who served as special counsel to the General Counsel for National Security Law at the Department of Defense;[187] Anne-Marie Slaughter (Princeton), who served as director of policy planning for the Department of State;[188] and Matthew Waxman (Columbia), who served at the National Security Council, the Department of Defense, and the Department of State.[189]

Another connection between government service and the international law academy was the movement of former military, naval, air force, and coast guard officers into international law teaching, although lawyers with this background were not represented in the full-time faculty of the elite schools studied here.[190] In a handful of cases, a US-based international law academic had previously worked for a foreign government, such as Gabriella Blum (Harvard), who formerly served as a senior legal adviser in the International Law Department of the Military Advocate General's Corps in the Israel Defense Forces and a strategy adviser to the Israeli National Security Council.[191] But she was very much the exception, not the rule.

A fair number of the US international law academics had worked for American law firms, though there were apparently fewer such hires recently, as many of them held PhDs in other disciplines instead of experience in practice. Some of the US international law academics had engaged in dispute resolution in the form of signing or authoring amicus curiae briefs on international law issues in cases before domestic courts, like the US Supreme Court. Examples include *Sosa v. Alvarez-Machain, Hamdan v. Rumsfeld, Kiobel v. Royal Dutch Petroleum*, and *Bond v. United States*.[192] It was less common for them to appear as counsel for the litigants, though some had done so. A small number had extensive experience in international dispute resolution, such as Michael Reisman at Yale, who has been counsel, expert, and arbitrator in many international disputes,[193] but he was atypical.

---

[186] *See* Jack Goldsmith, Harv. L. Sch., http://hls.harvard.edu/faculty/directory/10320/Goldsmith (last visited Oct. 27, 2016).

[187] *See* Oona Hathaway, Yale L. Sch., https://www.law.yale.edu/oona-hathaway (last visited Oct. 27, 2016).

[188] *See* Anne Marie-Slaughter, Princeton Univ., http://scholar.princeton.edu/slaughter/home (last visited Oct. 27, 2016).

[189] *See* Matthew Waxman, Colum. L. Sch., http://web.law.columbia.edu/faculty/matthew-waxman (last visited Oct. 27, 2016).

[190] Examples include Craig Allen (University of Washington), Geoffrey Corn (South Texas College of Law Houston), Chris Jenks (SMU Dedman School of Law), John Dehn (Loyola University Chicago), Eric Jensen (Brigham Young University), James Kraska (US Naval War College), Raul Pedrozo (previously at the Naval War College), Michael Schmitt (US Naval War College), Rachel VanLandingham (Southwestern Law School), Sean Watts (Creighton University), and Thomas Wingfield (National Defense University). *See also* Chapter 6.II.C.

[191] *See* Gabriella Blum, Harv. L. Sch., http://hls.harvard.edu/faculty/directory/10089/Blum/ (last visited Oct. 27, 2016).

[192] Kiobel v. Royal Dutch Petroleum Co., 569 U.S. 12 (2013); Bond v. United States, 564 U.S. 211 (2011); Hamdan v. Rumsfeld, 548 U.S. 557 (2006); Sosa v. Alvarez-Machain, 542 U.S. 692 (2004).

[193] *See* W. Michael Reisman, Yale L. Sch., https://www.law.yale.edu/w-michael-reisman (last visited Oct. 27, 2016). Reisman's profile is closer to that of the older generation of US international lawyers, who have since passed or retired, than the younger generation of US international lawyers. *See* Chapter 2.V.C.

2. The United Kingdom and France

By contrast with the United States, academics in the UK and French legal academies rarely had significant experience clerking for domestic courts or working full-time for their own government. But an appreciable number of UK and French legal academics engaged in international dispute resolution practice.

In the United Kingdom, domestic clerkships are a relatively recent development and are not common. As a rule, elite UK universities do not have the resources to fund international clerkships for their students. Only around one in ten of the UK international law academics had worked full-time for a government, and many of them had worked for a government other than the UK government. Legal academics do not normally move into and out of the UK government, unlike the situation in the United States, whether in international law or otherwise. In addition, many UK international law academics came from outside the United Kingdom, so they may not have met the nationality requirements to join the UK Foreign and Commonwealth Office.

In France, domestic clerkships seem not to be an option and certainly were not a common credential for those wishing to join the academy. Few of the international law academics in France had experience working full-time for government, French or otherwise. Although French academics are usually civil servants in the sense that most of them work for state-run universities, the path to becoming an international law academic is typically wholly separate from the path to becoming a government lawyer for the Ministry of Foreign Affairs. There appears to be no revolving door between the two, although some academics apparently work informally or on a contract basis for the French government through consultancies or as advisers on specific projects or as advocates in individual cases.

What was common, however, was to find UK and French international law academics working in international dispute resolution. This sort of work also appeared to be prized in these academies, as many scholars aspired to undertake such work in the future even if they had not yet done so. In the United Kingdom, a significant number of the international law academics had joined chambers. For instance, Essex Court, 20 Essex Street, and Matrix Chambers list the following barristers and arbitrators as holding current or former UK academic positions: Daniel Bethlehem (ex-Cambridge), Alan Boyle (ex-Edinburgh), David Caron (King's College London), Christine Chinkin (London School of Economics), Zac Douglas (Geneva, ex-Cambridge and ex-University College London), Martin Hunter (ex-Nottingham), Vaughan Lowe (ex-Oxford), Philippe Sands (University College London), Dan Sarooshi (Oxford), Malcolm Shaw (Leicester/Cambridge), Stefan Talmon (Bonn, ex-Oxford), Guglielmo Verdirame (King's College London), and Philippa Webb (King's College London).[194]

In terms of the profile of this work, academics from both states were active in international dispute resolution by, for instance, appearing as counsel before the ICJ or as counsel or arbitrator in state-to-state or investor-state arbitrations. In the United Kingdom,

---

[194] *See* Essex Ct. Chambers, https://essexcourt.com/; 20 Essex Street Chambers, http://www.20essexst.com/; Matrix Chambers, https://www.matrixlaw.co.uk/ (last visited Oct. 27, 2016).

law professors also appeared as counsel for parties and amici in international law cases before domestic UK courts. For instance, in the case *Regina v. Bartle* and *Commissioner of Police ex parte Pinochet*, Brownlie appeared for Amnesty International and Christopher Greenwood appeared for the UK government.[195] In *Al-Jedda v. United Kingdom*, Greenwood appeared for the United Kingdom, Vaughan Lowe appeared for Al-Jedda, and James Crawford appeared for Liberty and JUSTICE.[196] Similar work by French international law academics before domestic French courts appeared to be less common.

UK and French international lawyers play a disproportionate role in some areas of legal practice, such as counsel in ICJ cases.[197] I coded all of the professors who appeared as counsel in contentious cases and advisory opinions before the Court that had been filed between 1994 and 2013. The Court hears cases involving a wide range of states, but the professors who often represent them were far less diverse. The dominant academies were all in Western states, with the UK and French being the clear leaders. Of the representations by professors, 22 percent came from the UK academy and 22 percent from the French academy, followed by Switzerland (7 percent), Belgium (7 percent), the United States (6 percent), Germany (6 percent), Italy (4 percent), and Spain (3 percent). Figure 8 shows all of the states from which professors had represented litigants in ten or more cases.

This finding largely confirms the results of two other studies completed on representations before the ICJ. The first, by Kurt Gaubatz and Matthew MacArthur, covered all representations before the ICJ between 1948 and 1998.[198] This study gathered data on forty-seven contentious cases, involving fifty states and 593 legal team members. The authors found that the community of litigators who practice before the International Court of Justice come from a very small set of Western states, leading them to conclude that international law is not as international as its name implies.[199]

The authors used OECD status as a proxy for whether states were Western or not. Western states tended to have a larger proportion of national representatives (that is, representatives from that state), whereas non-Western states tended to have a smaller proportion of national representatives. Of the fifty legal teams representing OECD states, forty-six were made up of more than 60 percent nationals. By contrast, of the forty-seven legal teams representing non-OECD states, only eighteen were made up of more than 60 percent of their nationals.[200] Of the 148 lawyers who served on foreign legal teams, only 4 percent were from non-OECD states.[201] Of all of these non-nationals, 77 percent came from just five states: France, the United States, the United Kingdom, Belgium, and Italy.[202]

---

[195] R. v. Bow St. Metro. Stipendiary Magistrate and Others, ex parte Pinochet Ugarte (No. 3) [2000] 1 AC 147.

[196] R. (on the application of Al-Jedda) (FC) v. Sec'y of State for Def. [2007] UKHL 58.

[197] Alain Pellet, *The Role of the International Lawyer in International Litigation*, *in* THE INTERNATIONAL LAWYER AS PRACTITIONER 147, 148 (Chanaka Wickremasinghe ed., 2000).

[198] Kurt Gaubatz & Matthew MacArthur, *How International Is "International" Law?*, 22 MICH. J. INT'L L. 239 (2001).

[199] *Id.* at 241.

[200] *Id.* at 251–52.

[201] *Id.* at 257.

[202] *Id.* at 258.

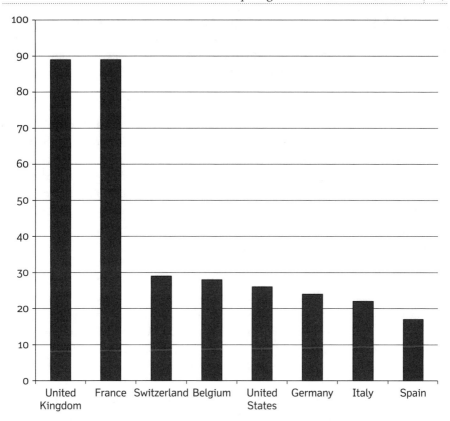

FIGURE 8 Number of ICJ Representations by Professors from Different States

These differences were magnified when speaking times were considered. Non-OECD states that hired foreign lawyers gave them a disproportionate share of the oral advocacy time. For example, Gilbert Gidel, Peru's French lawyer in the *Haya de la Torre* case, accounted for 79 percent of his team's oral argument. In the *Asylum* case, Peru's French lawyer Georges Scelle delivered 79 percent of his team's oral argument. In the *Northern Cameroons* case, 90 percent of Cameroon's oral argument was made by French international lawyer Prosper Weil. Earlier, Belgian international lawyer Henri Rolin made 87 percent of Iran's oral argument in the *Anglo-Iranian Oil Co.* case.[203] The Western preponderance of representation before the ICJ is thus more pronounced than is demonstrated by a simple counting of nationality.

The second study was completed by Shashank Kumar and Cecily Rose and focused on representations before the International Court of Justice from 1999 to 2012.[204] They found that the counsel before the Court during oral proceedings were overwhelmingly

[203] *Id.* at 256.
[204] Shashank P. Kumar & Cecily Rose, *A Study of Lawyers Appearing Before the International Court of Justice, 1999–2012*, 25 EUR. J. INT'L L. 893 (2014).

men from developed countries who were usually professors of public international law. Of the 205 lawyers who took part in these cases, 63 had appeared two or more times, and they accounted for 74 percent of the total speaking time during oral arguments. The authors referred to these lawyers as the "ICJ Bar."[205] UK- and French-based academics dominated the ICJ Bar.

Of all of the lawyers who appeared, 72 percent were nationals of OECD states and 28 percent were nationals of non-OECD states.[206] The disparity was more extreme in the ICJ Bar: 85 percent were nationals of OECD states and 15 percent were nationals of non-OECD states.[207] Strong differences also applied to speaking times. For legal teams from OECD states, 57 percent of the oral arguments were presented by nationals of the states concerned, whereas 43 percent were presented by non-nationals, 97 percent of whom came from other OECD states. For legal teams from non-OECD states, 15 percent of the speaking time was conducted by nationals and 85 percent by non-nationals, 97 percent of whom again came from OECD states.[208]

Although my study was limited to professors who appeared before the ICJ, Kumar and Rose studied all the advocates before the Court. This distinction led to some differences in results. For instance, Kumar and Rose found that the most commonly represented nationalities were US, French, and British. The inclusion of US lawyers in this list reflects the relatively high number of US government lawyers and US lawyers in private practice who participate in ICJ litigation,[209] even though far fewer US academics do so. One reason is that the State Department generally does not employ US academics to represent it before the International Court of Justice.

That UK- and French-based international law academics appear so frequently before the Court does not mean that these experiences are shared equally within these academies. Pellet has noted that a "quasi-monopoly" of around a dozen professors makes up the "invisible Bar" in The Hague and that they appear repeatedly before the Court regardless of the states in the case.[210] If the ICJ Bar were defined to include only lawyers who had appeared in four or more cases, it would comprise only 17 lawyers (8 percent of the total of 205 lawyers) who used 42 percent of the speaking time, among whom one academic (Pellet) accounted for 10 percent of all oral argument before the Court in the fourteen years studied.[211]

---

[205] *Id.* at 902.

[206] *Id.* at 904–05.

[207] *Id.* at 905.

[208] *Id.* at 902–03.

[209] This was particularly so for legal teams in cases involving the United States where the United States was primarily represented by US government lawyers and the opposing state often hired lawyers from US law firms to form part of their legal teams, e.g., LaGrand (*Germany v. United States*) and Avena (*Mexico v. United States*).

[210] Pellet, *supra* note 197, at 148; *see also* Keith Highet, *A Personal Memoir of Eduardo Jiménez de Aréchaga*, 88 AM. SOC'Y INT'L L. PROC. 577, 579 (1994) (describing the ICJ Bar as "those international lawyers who have practiced and continue to practice as oral advocates before the Court, who represent a variety of foreign states other than their own governments, who are well-known to the judges and Registrar of the Court, who know how things work out in practice, and who understand by experience the difficulties, pitfalls and tricks of the trade").

[211] These figures were collected and provided via e-mail by Shashank P. Kumar & Cecily Rose (on file with author).

Crawford and Pellet, UK-based and French international lawyers, respectively, exemplify this inner circle. Crawford, now an ICJ judge, appeared in at least twenty-six cases and advisory opinions representing Australia, Chile, Colombia, Costa Rica, Croatia, Georgia, Greece, Hungary, Iran, Libya, Liechtenstein, Malaysia, the Marshall Islands, the Federated States of Micronesia, Nauru, Nigeria, Palestine, Romania, Samoa, the Solomon Islands, Thailand, and the United Kingdom.[212] Pellet has appeared in at least sixteen cases representing Argentina, Benin, France, Greece, the Republic of Guinea, India, Indonesia, Iran, Japan, Liechtenstein, Peru, Romania, the Russian Federation, Singapore, Thailand, and Uganda.[213]

Several factors account for the dominance of UK and French international lawyers. English and French are the official languages of the Court.[214] Cases are heard in both languages and judgments are delivered in both languages, which gives an inescapable advantage to counsel who are native speakers of one of these languages and are bilingual or have a working knowledge of the other.[215] It is usually considered beneficial to draw members of the legal team from both common and civil law states, and geographical balance is often equated with having at least one UK and one French lawyer on the team![216] States that are former colonies often select lawyers who are nationals of the former colonial power; for instance, Francophone African states typically hire French international lawyers.

The strong connection between the UK and French legal academies and international dispute resolution is coming under pressure from the academic side. Thus, the top chairs in public international law at some elite UK law schools used to be filled by academic-practitioners, including Crawford, Lowe, and Greenwood. But their successors, Eyal Benvenisti, Catherine Redgwell, and Susan Marks, do not fit this mold, suggesting a shift in emphasis in hiring patterns. To the extent that this shift results in a lessening of the connection between academia and practice, one should expect to see a lessening of the two-way process of influence and exchange that this connection enables.

3. Russia

In Russia, a few younger lawyers now join the staffs of the Russian Constitutional Court and the Supreme Court, but such work is infrequent and is not a springboard to the academy. Some academics had experience working for the USSR or Russian government ministries, like the Russian Ministry of Foreign Affairs and the Russian Ministry of Economic Development. This experience, however, seemed less pervasive than in the

[212] *See* James Crawford, Wikipedia, https://en.wikipedia.org/wiki/James_Crawford_(jurist) (last modified July 6, 2016, 7:15 AM).
[213] *See* Curriculum Vitae—Fr, Allain Pellet, http://pellet.actu.com/wp-content/uploads/2016/07/16-07-13-CVFR.pdf (last visited Jan. 1, 2017).
[214] Statute of the International Court of Justice, art. 39(1), June 26, 1945, T.S. No. 993, 33 U.N.T.S. 993.
[215] Robert Jennings, *The Work of the International Bar*, in MAN's INHUMANITY TO MAN: ESSAYS ON INTERNATIONAL LAW IN HONOUR OF ANTONIO CASSESE 443, 446 (Lal Chand Vohrah et al. eds., 2003).
[216] Pellet, *supra* note 197, at 151.

United States. Moreover, several Russian international lawyers suggested that this crossover was more common during the Soviet Union than in Russia today. These connections may therefore represent more of a historical legacy than a replenishing reality.

Famous examples of international law academics who came from or engaged in government practice include Oleg Nikolaevich Khlestov, who was a professor of international law at the Diplomatic Academy after long service as director of the Treaty and Legal Department at the Soviet Ministry of Foreign Affairs;[217] Stanislav Chernichenko, who represented Russia on the UN Human Rights Commission, and was a member of the UN Sub-Commission on the Prevention of Discrimination and Protection of Minorities, a member of the Permanent Court of Arbitration, and vice president of the Russian Association of International Law, before becoming a professor at the Diplomatic Academy, where he coedited and coauthored a major textbook on international law;[218] and Mark Lvovich Entin, a professor of international and European law at MGIMO, who served as ambassador to Luxembourg, deputy permanent representative to the Council of Europe, first deputy director of the Directorate of European Cooperation of the Russian Ministry of Foreign Affairs, and the head of section of the Political Department of the Russian Ministry of Foreign Affairs.[219]

It is customary for international law academics from MGIMO to advise the Ministry of Foreign Affairs, for those from the Russian Academy of Foreign Trade to advise the Ministry for Economic Development, and for those from the NG Kuznetsov Naval Academy to advise the Russian Navy, as these universities are institutionally linked to these ministries.[220] For instance, many of the international law professors at the Russian Foreign Trade Academy have been active participants in the development of Soviet and Russian economic policies, such as Aleksandr Komarov, head of the Private International Law Department, who worked for the USSR Ministry of Foreign Trade's Law and Treaty Department, represented Russia at the UN Commission on International Trade Law, and is a member of the governing bodies of the International Institute for Unification of Private Law and the International Council for Commercial Arbitration.[221]

Numerous examples also exist of international law professors in Russia who hold important government positions moving on to appointment to international courts and tribunals (a large number hold their academic positions as second jobs). Examples include Bakhtiyar Tuzmukhamedov (Diplomatic Academy, judge at the International Criminal Tribunals for the former Yugoslavia and for Rwanda, and counselor to the

[217] See MÄLKSOO, *supra* note 95, at 80; Honorary Doctorates, Dipa Acad., http://www.dipacademy.ru/about/academy_today/honorary_doctorates/ (last visited Oct. 17, 2016).
[218] See Honorary Doctorates, *supra* note 217.
[219] See Entin Mark, MGIMO, http://mgimo.ru/files/2598/EntinMarkCV.doc (last visited Oct. 17, 2016).
[220] See Flot, http://flot.com/education/academies/vma (last visited Oct. 17, 2016); History, MGIMO, http://english.mgimo.ru/basic-facts/history; Russian Foreign Trade Acad., http://eng.vavt.ru (last visited Oct. 17, 2016).
[221] See CV: Alexander Sergeevich Komarov, Int'l Arb. Att'y Network, https://international-arbitration-attorney.com/wp-content/uploads/russianfederation.pdf; Prof. Alexander S. Komarov, Int'l Council for Com. Arb., http://www.arbitration-icca.org/about/governing-board/ADVISORY-MEMBERS/Alexander_Komarov.html (last visited Oct. 17, 2016).

Russian Constitutional Court);[222] Vladimir Golitsyn (Moscow State Institute of Foreign Relations, USSR Ministry of Foreign Affairs, Office of Legal Counsel at the United Nations, chief legal counsel of the delegation of the Russian Federation in two cases before the International Tribunal for the Law of the Sea (ITLOS), and now professor at Moscow State University and president of ITLOS);[223] and Vladlen Vereshchetin (Institute of State and Law of the Russian Academy of Sciences, deputy director and head of the International Law Department of the Institute of State and Law, and a member of the Soviet delegations to the UN Committee on the Peaceful Uses of Outer Space and its Legal Sub-committee, member of the International Law Commission, and judge of the International Court of Justice).[224]

Nevertheless, movement back and forth between government and academia in international law may be more of a historical legacy than an ongoing phenomenon. According to one Russian international lawyer:

[V]ery few people from the legal department of the Ministry of Foreign Affairs move to academia, especially now, they work from graduation to retirement at the Ministry or in cases of heads of legal offices move to the ICJ (Skotnikov, Gevorgyan) or other international institutions (e.g., [International Criminal Court] for Khodakov). There are few members of the old guard who used to work for MFA (Voronin, Khlestov), but they are the exception not the rule.[225]

Similar points were made by other Russian international lawyers.[226]

Russian international law academics also seem to be largely absent from the practice of international dispute resolution as advocates and experts, even when it comes to representing their own country.[227] In its first case before the International Court of Justice (*Georgia v. Russia*), Russia was represented by Pellet (a French academic), Andreas Zimmermann (a German academic), and Samuel Wordsworth (a UK barrister).[228] In the

---

[222] *See* Judge Bakhtiyar Tuzmukhamedov, Int'l Crim. Tribunal for the Former Yugoslavia, http://www.icty.org/x/file/About/Chambers/judges_bios_en/pj_tuzmukhamedov_Bio_en.pdf (last visited Oct. 17, 2016).

[223] *See* President Vladimir Vladimirovich Golitsyn, Int'l Tribunal for L. Sea, https://www.itlos.org/en/the-tribunal/members/president-vladimir-vladimirovich-golitsyn (last visited Oct. 17, 2016).

[224] *See* Judge Vladlen S. Vereshchetin, United Nations Audiovisual Libr., http://legal.un.org/avl/pdf/ls/Vereshchetin_bio.pdf and http://prabook.com/web/person-view.html?profileId=929997 (last visited Oct. 17, 2016).

[225] "From my personal experience there is a total divide between practice of international law and academia as it stands today. Very few professors combine their teaching with working for the MFA (or having worked with it recently). . . . The only MFA alumni in academia are very senior professors, who joined academia upon retirement and practiced most of the time during the Soviet Union time." E-mail on file with author.

[226] According to one Russian public international lawyer, such crossover might be true of MGIMO academics but would be atypical otherwise: "That being said, all leading Russian universities are state-funded, and these days this gives some people the ground to say they should not develop critical and independent judgments." E-mail on file with author.

[227] Issaeva, *supra* note 151.

[228] *See* Application of the International Convention on the Elimination of All Forms of Racial Discrimination (Geor. v. Russ.), Preliminary Objections, 2011 I.C.J. 70, 74–75 (Apr. 1).

cases against Russia in the European Court of Human Rights, the government does not normally make use of Russian international law academics. Similarly, in the Yukos international arbitration, Russia was represented by two US law firms.[229] This absence may be explained by the lack of familiarity with English of many of the prominent Russian international law academics and their immersion in Russian approaches that are unlikely to be influential before these courts and tribunals, as well as their dearth of experience studying or working abroad.[230]

4. China

China's international law academics maintain few connections with practice. Indeed, a 2016 study found that most Chinese international law academics believed that the biggest obstacle to teaching and research in international law in China was the lack of connections between academia and practice.[231] Still, though formal connections are hard to find, informal connections sometimes exist behind closed doors.

Clerkships are not ordinarily available in China. Chinese international law academics also seem to be largely absent from international dispute resolution, probably partly because China has hardly been involved in that arena. It has never been a party to an ICJ case. China has appeared once in the International Court of Justice in the case on Kosovo's declaration of independence, in which it was represented by Xue Hanqin, who is now a judge on the Court. China is a frequent litigant in the World Trade Organization (WTO), but as a rule it hires foreign and Chinese law firms to represent it in those cases.[232] China has had a couple of arbitrations filed against it under the auspices of the International Centre for Settlement of Investment Disputes, but one settled at a very early stage and another was dismissed at a preliminary stage. The Philippines brought an arbitration against China before ITLOS, but China rejected the tribunal's jurisdiction and refused to appear.

Historically, there has not been much movement back and forth by international law academics and government officials in China, although some scholars pointed to informal connections, such as invitations to some scholars to advise government ministers and leaders on certain international law issues.[233] In addition, some exceptions (i.e., academics who have taken on government roles and vice versa) also exist. For instance,

[229] *See* Yukos Universal Ltd. (Isle of Man) v. Russ., Case No. 2005-04/AA227 (Perm. Ct. Arb. 2014), http://www.pcacases.com/web/view/61 (last visited Oct. 17, 2016).

[230] *See* Issaeva, *supra* note 154.

[231] *See* WU QIZHI, *supra* note 63.

[232] Gregory Shaffer & Henry Gao, *From Paternalism to Partnership: The Development of WTO Law Capacity in China, in* THE CHINESE LEGAL PROFESSION IN THE AGE OF GLOBALIZATION: THE RISE OF THE CORPORATE LEGAL SECTOR AND ITS IMPACT ON LAWYERS AND SOCIETY (David Wilkins & Sida Liu eds., forthcoming).

[233] For instance, since 1994, a number of law professors, including four international law academics, have been invited to give lectures to the Political Bureau of the Chinese Communist Party on topics chosen by the Policy Research Office of the Central Committee of the Chinese Communist Party. In 2013, Gao Zhiguo gave a lecture on law of the sea issues. Gao received his initial education in China, followed by an LLM in the United States, a doctorate in Canada, and a postdoctorate in the United States. He is now director of China's Institute of

Cao Jianming, the former president and professor of international law of East China University of Politics and Law in Shanghai, was a renowned General Agreement on Tariffs and Trade/WTO expert. In 1994 and 1998, he was invited to give two lectures to the Political Bureau of the Central Committee of the Chinese Communist Party, which includes fewer than thirty members, including China's president and premier. Thereafter, Cao was appointed as a vice president of China's Supreme People's Court and later served as the procurator general of China's Supreme People's Procuratorate.[234] Another example is Wan E'xiang, a former professor of international law at Wuhan University School of Law, who was appointed as a vice president of the Supreme People's Court of China and vice chairperson of the Standing Committee of the Twelfth National People's Congress.[235] Going in the other direction, Yang Guohua was the deputy director general of the Department of Treaty and Law at China's Ministry of Commerce before becoming a law professor at Tsinghua University in 2014.[236]

Examples can also be found of Chinese government officials who are part-time or adjunct law professors or take on academic positions after they retire. Xue Hanqin, now an ICJ judge,[237] received her initial degrees in China before completing an LLM and JSD at Columbia Law School. She entered the Foreign Ministry of China in 1980 and served in numerous positions, including as deputy director general and then director general of the Department of Treaty and Law and later as legal counsel to the Ministry of Foreign Affairs. In addition to holding many international appointments, such as membership and then chair of the International Law Commission, she holds a position as professor at Wuhan University School of Law. Another example is Zhang Yuejiao, a former senior official with China's Ministry of Commerce who became a law professor at Tsinghua University and was appointed as a WTO Appellate Body member in 2008.[238]

Despite the earlier paucity of exchange between international law academics and those serving as international lawyers at the Ministry of Foreign Affairs and the Ministry of Commerce, this situation is slowly changing as China's engagement with the international system has increased.[239] Since around 2009, the Ministry of Commerce has employed two or three international law academics at a time on yearlong secondments. Part of the demand for this integration has come from the increased exposure of China

---

Maritime Affairs, a judge at International Tribunal of Law of Sea, and a professor at various Chinese universities. *See* Judge Zhiguo Gao, Int'l Tribunal for L. Sea, http://www.itlos.org/index.php?id=92 (last visited Nov. 29, 2016).

[234] *See* Cao Jianming, Wikipedia, https://en.wikipedia.org/wiki/Cao_Jianming (last modified Nov. 14, 2016, 12:13 PM).

[235] *See* Wan Exiang, Wikipedia, https://en.wikipedia.org/wiki/Wan_Exiang (last modified Mar. 13, 2016 5:11 AM).

[236] *See* Yang Guohua, Tsinghua Univ. Sch. L., http://www.tsinghua.edu.cn/publish/lawen/3503/index.html (last visited Oct. 17, 2016).

[237] *See* Current Members: Judge Xue Hanqin, Int'l Ct. Just., http://www.icj-cij.org/court/?p1=1&p2=2&p3=1&judge=170 (last visited Oct. 17, 2016).

[238] *See* Appellate Body Members, World Trade Org., https://www.wto.org/english/tratop_e/dispu_e/ab_members_bio_e.htm (last visited Oct. 17, 2016); Zhang Yuejiao, Tsinghua Univ. Sch. L., http://www.tsinghua.edu.cn/publish/lawen/3503/index.html (last visited Oct. 17, 2016).

[239] Much of the information in the following two paragraphs is based on conversations with Chinese international lawyers, some of whom had engaged in these secondments.

to international trade and investment disputes since its accession to the WTO in 2001 and its signature of investment treaties with strong arbitration clauses in recent decades. Many of these academics have worked on actual or threatened trade and investment disputes during their time at the ministry.[240]

The Ministry of Foreign Affairs has been slower to incorporate international law academics. Starting around 2011, it began employing three to five international law academics for three- or six-month secondments. Although this ministry deals with many controversial issues, such as the South China Sea disputes, it is not currently appearing before any international dispute resolution forums relating to these disputes. Instead of working on the front line of dispute resolution, these academics have usually been asked to conduct background research and to write memos on a range of issues before the Ministry.

These secondments are consistent with the approach adopted by the above-mentioned Central Politics and Law Commission Opinion on the Implication of the Program for Legal Elite Education, issued in December 2011.[241] One aim of this joint opinion has been to increase interchange between the Chinese government and Chinese law schools, including by calling for one thousand law professors to be rotated into the government for one- to two-year periods to obtain practical experience and for a significant number of government officials to be rotated into academic legal positions.[242]

C. IMPLICATIONS FOR THE DIVISIBLE COLLEGE

The prevalence of distinct sorts of professional experience in different international law academies is apt to produce variations in terms of the inward influences on, and outward spheres of influence of, those academics in ways that reflect and reinforce certain nationalizing, denationalizing, and westernizing trends within the field.

First, some forms of professional practice are likely to have a nationalizing influence, such as clerking for a judge on a domestic court, as is common for US international law academics. Clerking for a domestic judge may result in concentration on domestic legal issues as international law issues are usually encountered, if at all, through the lens of how they make their way into that domestic system. The focus would typically be on how international law is received in that state, and international law might well be subordinated to domestic law within this framework, as it certainly is within the United States. Clerking for a national court judge also means that these scholars are likely to have been surrounded by national peers and to have worked for a judge of the same nationality.[243]

---

[240] *See generally* Shaffer & Gao, *supra* note 232.

[241] Ministry of Education, *supra* note 84.

[242] *Id.* at 5; *see also* Minzner, *supra* note 82, at 373–74.

[243] By contrast, clerking for a judge on an international court or tribunal would be likely to have a denationalizing effect. The issues before the court would be likely to turn on how international law should be interpreted and applied on its own terms, not through a particular national filter. The focus would likely be on international law, or a particular subfield, like international criminal law, rather than on the interaction between international and national law. International law would be treated as superior to domestic law. Scholars undertaking this sort of professional experience would typically be surrounded by peers of various nationalities and might well work for a judge of a different nationality from their own.

These nationalizing experiences may help to explain why many US international law scholars deal largely with issues related to the reception of international law in the United States and foreign relations law more generally. This tendency is reinforced when they enter the US teaching market where they are often required to teach a domestic class in addition to international law, which also focuses them on domestic case law and domestic issues, such as the separation of powers under US constitutional theory and practice.

Second, other connections to practice are likely to have a denationalizing influence, such as appearing as an advocate before an international court or tribunal. When academics appear as advocates before domestic courts, they typically form a part of teams made up of other lawyers from that state, their task is to appeal to a bench composed of nationals from that state, and they must cast their arguments within a domestic legal framework. By contrast, in cases before international courts and tribunals, these academics typically appear as part of multinational teams, their task is to convince a multinational bench, and their arguments are principally crafted as a matter of international, rather than domestic, law. According to Pellet, a team pleading before the ICJ must address a bench with "very diverse legal 'sensitivities,'" which forces them to use a "legal language" that can be understood by fifteen to seventeen judges as different from one another as a British former professor and Queen's Counsel, a member of the French Conseil d'état, a former Soviet professor, a Chinese civil servant, and a Brazilian diplomat.[244] He concludes that this legal "melting pot" can be achieved only if the team is itself "legally diverse."[245] The international dispute resolution experience of UK and French international law academics may help to explain the focus of much of their scholarship on areas like ICJ judgments, investment treaty arbitration, and state responsibility.

Third, in some cases, the nationalizing or denationalizing effect of certain professional experiences will depend on the precise location and nature of the work and the baseline for comparison. Consider, for instance, whether the full-time employment by the US government of many US international law scholars should be counted as a nationalizing or denationalizing influence. On the one hand, this experience may be viewed as distinctly nationalizing. International lawyers who work for their own government are likely to be surrounded by their national peers. If they work in a domestic agency, like the US Department of Justice, they are less likely to come across international law issues and, even when they do, those issues are apt to be framed within a national context, such as a Supreme Court case, where international law is typically subordinate rather than supreme. If they work in a department with a more external function, such as the US Department of State, they will be more prone to interact with foreign colleagues, but they would be representing their home state, which may influence the way they frame international legal issues.

On the other hand, some of these experiences could also be viewed as denationalizing. Some US international law academics observed that they did not realize how much international law there was, or how seriously the United States and many other states took it,

---

[244] Pellet, *supra* note 197, at 152.
[245] *Id.*

until they worked for the State Department. These academics did not think they would have had the same denationalizing experience if they had worked for the Department of Justice. After all, the State Department interacts with foreign counterparts and is tasked with communicating their viewpoints to other US government departments. Accordingly, the State Department is often seen as "the most cosmopolitan" or "left-wing" of the major US government departments, and bureaucratic rivals sometimes view the department as having "gone native" in the international law community. As one academic who had formerly worked for the government explained to me: "The State Department views its mission as being to save the rest of the world from America."

This difference in perspective highlights the need to disaggregate different types of government experience and to consider the baseline from which these influences are judged. Some forms of government practice are going to be more nationalizing than others, as evidenced by comparisons between the Departments of Justice and State. Some forms of government experience sit on a nationalizing/denationalizing threshold where they may look denationalizing to domestic lawyers and nationalizing to foreign lawyers. One's benchmark for comparison also matters. If one is comparing two US academics with identical backgrounds except that one has worked for the State Department and the other has not, the denationalizing thesis assumes greater weight because the other influences are likely to be distinctly nationalizing. But when comparing US academics with UK academics, the same experience may be viewed as nationalizing because on the whole the UK academics start with a much more denationalized baseline.

Fourth, different forms of practice pave the way for distinct insights. Koh has stressed the importance for international law academics to engage seriously in practice, as otherwise it is like "talking about baseball without having ever played."[246] For the same reason, one Russian international lawyer lamented how little movement back and forth there now was between people working for the Russian government and people working in the Russian international law academy: "that's a pity because the academic world i[s] very much divorced from [the] practice of international law and the much stronger at least technically group of international lawyers at the MFA."[247] UK international lawyer Bethlehem, who engaged in considerable advocacy and advisory work as an academic, nonetheless reflected on how deeply his understanding of international law changed when he became the legal adviser of the UK Foreign and Commonwealth Office.[248] He was surprised by the "secret life of international law," that is, the volume and detail of international legal interactions between states that is invisible to those outside government.[249] He also reflected on how an inside view into the way a government works considerably changed his understanding of the relationship between international and national law. "As an international lawyer," Bethlehem contended, "the proposition is in our DNA that international law prevails over domestic law," because the notion of

[246] *See also* ASIL Presents Harold Koh, YouTube (Nov. 12, 2012), https://www.youtube.com/watch?v=COjHyHIpgwQ (American Society of International Law 2012 Midyear Meeting in Athens, Georgia).
[247] E-mail on file with author.
[248] Daniel Bethlehem, *The Secret Life of International Law*, 1 Cambridge J. Int'l & Comp. L. 23, 24 (2012).
[249] *Id.* at 24.

supremacy defines the relationship on the international plane and would be the approach taken by, for instance, the ICJ.[250] In practice, however, states are often more driven by domestic law considerations than international law ones, notably in areas like national security, which requires a more nuanced appreciation of how national law and international law interact.[251]

Fifth, different types of professional experiences also create their own potential for conflicts of interest. In discussing the phenomenon of *dédoublement fonctionnel*, Schachter noted that the mingling of scholarly and official roles creates tensions as individuals move from one role to another, leading to questions about whether they are acting in the capacity of objective scientist or government advocate.[252] The potential for academics to nationalize their scholarly agendas seems more likely to pervade academies where scholars frequently work for their governments and a high degree of symbolic capital is accorded to such work. This potential may disproportionately affect scholars who angle for a government position partway through their careers, rather than before their academic careers have begun, because it will often be harder for scholars who have been critical of their states to secure such jobs. Conflicts of interest may be posed in particular for academics who simultaneously write and practice. Crawford has noted that many international lawyers uncomfortably wear two hats as academic lawyers and professionals in active practice.[253] Although this experience contributes to the mutual exchange of ideas, it also raises questions about whether those who practice international law have given up their scholarly independence and become too caught up in pursuing the details of individual cases or the national interest.[254]

Sixth, the dominance of international lawyers, including international law academics, from Western states in various areas of international practice, like certain forms of international dispute resolution, reflects and reinforces certain westernizing influences within the field and may open avenues for certain national approaches to take an outsized part in defining the "international."[255] For instance, the docket of the International Court of Justice has become relatively diverse in the last few decades, with cases from all corners of the globe. Despite this geographical diversity, Robert Jennings has noted that "the judges can confidently expect to see mostly the same faces in the principal places on the benches of counsel, whatever the geographical or political provenance of the case," given the existence of an "informal international bar" made up of a "small club of the more familiar names."[256] More diverse approaches to international law that might come from the states before the Court are often channeled through Western (and, more specifically, UK and French) representation, giving academics from these states an opportunity to present

---

[250] *Id.* at 35.

[251] *Id.*

[252] Schachter, *supra* note 1, at 218.

[253] James Crawford, *International Law as Discipline and Profession*, 106 Am. Soc'y Int'l L. Proc. 471, 480 (2012).

[254] *Id.; see also* Gillian Triggs, *The Public International Lawyer and the Practice of International Law*, 2005 24 Australian Y.B. Int'l L. 201, 216.

[255] For more discussion of this phenomenon across a number of areas, see Chapter 5.III.C.

[256] Jennings, *supra* note 215, at 444.

their own national approaches to international law, which, if accepted by the Court, take on the form of "international" rather than "national" interpretations.

UK and French international lawyers may be understood as competing to establish the influence of the common law and civil law traditions on international tribunals like the ICJ. According to Jouannet, this competition involves a continuous "selling" of each national legal model so as to influence the establishment of international norms and institutions that reflect the principles of either the Anglo-Saxon tradition or the continental French tradition.[257] This process also reflects a struggle for influence in public international law between the two legal models, which can be seen in the formation of international criminal tribunals, the drafting of the decisions by international courts, and understandings of the appropriate role of international judges. The influence of lawyers and international law academics from different states and regional groupings must be analyzed on an area-by-area basis, as the patterns that hold true in ICJ litigation do not necessarily hold true in all other fields and institutions. Nevertheless, in various significant areas, the dominance of lawyers and academics from Western states in general, and from a handful of Western states in particular, represents an important mechanism through which Western approaches are translated into international approaches.

But do similar patterns of difference and dominance arise in international law textbooks? This question is addressed in Chapter 4.

---

[257] Jouannet, *supra* note 144, at 300.

4

Comparing International Law Textbooks and Casebooks

INTERNATIONAL LAW TEXTBOOKS and casebooks are interesting to study because they tell us something about how international law is understood, found, and interpreted by the current generation of international lawyers in a particular state and how these doxas are passed on to the next generation.[1] By providing the bread-and-butter materials that lawyers and law students first encounter in trying to understand the field, these books play an important socializing role in shaping understandings of which issues are core and form part of the field, which sources are important, which debates are controversial, which norms are settled, which rules are liable to change, and who and what the leading authorities are.[2]

This chapter compares the textbooks, casebooks, and manuals that are used to teach international law in different states (collectively usually referred to as textbooks).[3] One might intuitively assume that there is one international law. Yet, as with the divisible college of international lawyers, the reality is more variegated. I used a variety of methods to shed light onto how nationalized, denationalized, and westernized these books are in terms of their substance, sources, and approaches. This part sets out seven main observations distilled from this study, in each case drawing on examples of some of the similarities and differences in how these books presented and approached the field.

---

[1] For a discussion of the notion of doxa, see Chapter 2.I.B.

[2] For a justification for why it is useful to study these books, along with a discussion of the limits of what such a study can show, see Chapter 2.II.B.

[3] As explained in Chapter 2.II.B, Russian manuals typically comprise a series of chapters written by various authors that are integrated into a single volume that is edited by a senior academic. In this part, I refer to the contributions as being by the book's editor, rather than by the authors of individual chapters, so that readers may more easily follow which book is which.

Is International Law International? Anthea Roberts.

I. Preliminary Points of Method

A. IDENTIFYING TEXTBOOKS, CASEBOOKS, AND MANUALS

I collected information about commonly used international law textbooks in the five permanent members of the Security Council, current as of the end of 2013 when I began this study.[4] In addition, I also compiled information on such books from Argentina, Australia, Brazil, Cameroon, Germany, India, Japan, Senegal, and South Africa.[5] I was able to undertake some comparisons with respect to most of these books, such as of case citation patterns, but I undertook a deeper substantive review of the books only from the five states that form the primary case studies in this book. The full list of books that I selected for comparison is set out in Table 6.

One methodological challenge was to decide what it means to be a textbook of "international law." I confined the term to public international law, which I defined as including foundational topics, such as sources, statehood and state responsibility, and particular subfields, like human rights law, the use of force, and trade and investment law. This definition encompasses much of international economic law but excludes what is often called private international law or transnational law, that is, subjects such as choice of law and international commercial arbitration. This approach led to some disparities across states. For instance, although all of these topics are typically included in textbooks in the United States and the United Kingdom, in China it was common for separate textbooks to be published for public international law, private international law, and international economic law, and my approach captured information only on the first.

It was not possible to obtain reliable or complete information about the number of books sold or their relative market share in different states. Instead, in selecting these books, I relied on academics, academic publishers and students in these states to tell me which books were commonly prescribed for introductory international law courses. I aimed at choosing between two and four recent, generally used textbooks, casebooks, or manuals, although sometimes the most frequently used books were older, such as Wang Tieya's influential book in China, and other times textbooks and collections of cases were published separately, as was the case in Japan. In China and Russia, each elite law school usually uses a different manual, often authored or edited by academics based at that university. In such cases, I selected a sample of books from different schools. When it came to numerical comparisons of case law, I selected four books from each state at random, but otherwise drew on all of the books for the substantive comparisons.[6]

---

[4] In some cases, I relied upon 2013 reprints of older editions of textbooks, including the ones by Wang Tieya, Bai Guimei, & Zhu Lijiang, and Liang Xi, Wang Xianshu, & Zeng Lingliang (China).

[5] In a few cases, I relied upon older editions of these textbooks because they were the ones that I was able to access through my library, including the ones by Y.M. Kolosov & E.S. Krivchikova (Rus.), K.A. Bekyashev (Rus.), and John Dugard (South Africa).

[6] The case citation analyses of the Chinese and Russian books were based on the books by Wang Tieya; Bai Guimei & Zhu Lijiang; Liang Xi, Wang Xianshu, & Zeng Lingliang; and Liu Jiachen & Chen Zhizhong (China); and V.L. Tolstykh; G.V. Ignatenko & O.I. Tiunov; A.N. Vylegzhanin; and A.A. Kovalev & S.V. Chernichenko (Rus.).

TABLE 6

International Law Textbooks and Casebooks

Country	Authors/Editors	Name of Book	Year
Argentina	Guillermo R. Moncayo, Raúl E. Vinuesa, & Hortencia D. T. Gutierrez Posse	Derecho internacional público [Public International Law]	1990
Argentina	Manuel Diez De Velasco Vallejo	Instituciones de derecho internacional público [The Institutions of Public International Law]	2013
Australia	David J. Harris	Cases and Materials on International Law (7th ed. 2010) & Australian Supplement (2003)	2010/2003
Australia	Donald R. Rothwell, Stuart Kaye, Afshin Akhtarkhavari, & Ruth Davis	International Law: Cases and Materials with Australian Perspectives	2010
Australia	Gillian Triggs	International Law: Contemporary Principles and Practices (2d)	2011
Brazil	Celso D. de Albuquerque Mello	Curso de direito internacional público [Course in Public International Law] (Volume I and II)]	2008
Brazil	Hildebrando Accioly & G. E. do Nascimento e Silva	Manual de direito internacional público [Manual of Public International Law] (15th ed.)	2002
Cameroon	Pierre-Marie Dupuy & Yann Kerbrat	Droit international public [Public International Law] (11th ed.)	2012
Cameroon	Jean Combacau & Serge Sur	Droit international public [Public International Law] (10th ed.)	2012
Cameroon	Patrick Daillier, Mathias Forteau, & Alain Pellet	Droit international public [Public International Law] (8th ed.)	2009
Canada	Hugh M. Kindred & Phillip M. Saunders	International Law: Chiefly as Interpreted and Applied in Canada (7th ed.)	2006
Canada	John H. Currie, Craig Forcese, & Valerie Oosterveld	International Law: Doctrine, Practice, and Theory	2007

(Continued)

TABLE 6 (Continued)

Country	Authors/Editors	Name of Book	Year
Canada	J.-Maurice Arbour & Geneviève Parent	Droit international public [Public International Law] (8th ed.)	2012
Canada	Claude Emanuelli	Droit international public: Contribution à l'étude du droit international selon une perspective canadienne [Public International Law: Contribution to the Study of International Law According to a Canadian Perspective] (3d ed.)	2010
China	Wang Tieya (王铁崖)	国际法 [International Law]	1995
China	Liang Xi (梁西)	国际法 [International Law] (3d ed.)	2011
China	Bai Guimei & Zhu Lijiang (白桂梅 & 朱利江)	国际法 [International Law] (2d ed.)	2007
China	Liang Xi, Wang Xianshu, & Zeng Lingliang (梁西, 王献枢 & 曾令良)	国际法 [International Law] (3d ed.)	2011
China	Liu Jiachen & Chen Zhizhong (刘家琛 & 陈致中)	国际法案例 [International Law Casebook]	1998
France	Pierre-Marie Dupuy & Yann Kerbrat	Droit international public [Public International Law] (11th ed.)	2012
France	Jean Combacau & Serge Sur	Droit international public [Public International Law] (10th ed.)	2012
France	Patrick Daillier, Mathias Forteau, & Alain Pellet	Droit international public [Public International Law] (8th ed.)	2009
Germany	Andreas von Arnauld	Völkerrecht [International Law]	2012
Germany	Knut Ipsen	Völkerrecht [International Law]	2004
Germany	Wolfgang Vitzthum (ed.)	Völkerrecht [International Law] (5th ed.)	2010
India	Malcolm D. Evans (ed.)	International Law (3d ed.)	2010
India	David J. Harris	Cases and Materials on International Law (7th ed.)	2010

Japan	Takane Sugihara & Hironobu Sakai (eds.)	国際法基本判例 50 [50 Cases on International Law]	2010
Japan	Yoshirō Matsu, Shigeru Kozai, Kimio Yakushiji, Haruyuki Yamate, Norio Tanaka, & Shigeki Sakamoto (eds.)	判決国際法 [Cases on International Law] (2d ed.)	2006
Japan	Akira Kotera, Kōichi Morikawa, & Yumi Nishimura (eds.)	国際法判例百選 [100 Cases on International Law] (2d ed.)	2011
Japan	Akira Kotera, Yūji Iwasawa, & Akio Morita (eds.)	講義国際法 [Lectures on International Law] (2d ed.)	2010
Japan	Hironobu Sakai, Kōji Teraya, Yumi Nishimura, & Shōtaro Hamamoto	国際法 [International Law]	2011
Japan	Takane Sugihara	国際法学講義 [Lectures on International Law] (2d ed.)	2013
Japan	Mashiko Asada	国際法 [International Law]	2011
Russia	В. И. Толстых (V. L. Tolstykh)	Курс международного права [International Law Course]	2010
Russia	Г. В. Игнатенко и О.И. Тиунов (G. V. Ignatenko & O. I. Tiunov) (eds.)	Международное право [International Law]	2013
Russia	А. Н. Вылегжанин (A. N. Vylegzhanin) (ed.)	Международное право [International Law]	2012
Russia	Ю. М. Колосов и Э. С. Кривчикова (Y. M. Kolosov & E. S. Krivchikova) (eds.)	Международное право [International Law] (2d ed.)	2005
Russia	А. А. Ковалев и С. В. Черниченко (A. A. Kovalev & S. V. Chernichenko) (eds.)	Международное право [International Law] (3d ed.)	2008
Russia	Валерий Кузнецов и Бахтияр Тузмухамедов (Valerii I. Kuznetsov & Bakhtiar R. Tuzmukhamedov) (eds., William E. Butler ed. & trans.)	International Law: A Russian Introduction	2009

(Continued)

TABLE 6 (Continued)

Country	Authors/Editors	Name of Book	Year
Russia	К. А. Бекяшев (K. A. Bekyashev) (ed.)	Международное публичное право [Public International Law] (5th ed.)	2011
Russia	В. М. Шумилов (V. M. Shumilov) (ed.)	Международное право [International Law] (2d ed.)	2012
Senegal	Pierre-Marie Dupuy & Yann Kerbrat	Droit international public [Public International Law] (11th ed.)	2012
Senegal	Jean Combacau & Serge Sur	Droit international public [Public International Law] (10th ed.)	2012
Senegal	Patrick Daillier, Mathias Forteau, & Alain Pellet	Droit international public [Public International Law] (8th ed.)	2009
South Africa	John Dugard	International Law: A South African Perspective	1994
South Africa	David J. Harris	Cases and Materials on International Law (7th ed.)	2010
United Kingdom	James Crawford	Brownlie's Principles of Public International Law (8th ed.)	2012
United Kingdom	Malcolm D. Evans (ed.)	International Law (3d ed.)	2010
United Kingdom	David J. Harris	Cases and Materials on International Law (7th ed.)	2010
United Kingdom	Malcolm N. Shaw	International Law (6th ed.)	2008
United States	Barry E. Carter & Allen S. Weiner	International Law (6th ed.)	2011
United States	Lori Damrosch, Louis Henkin, Sean Murphy, & Hans Smit	International Law: Cases and Materials (5th ed.)	2009
United States	Jeffrey L. Dunoff, Steven R. Ratner, & David Wippman	International Law: Norms, Actors, Process: A Problem-Oriented Approach (3d ed.)	2010

B. THE NEED FOR MULTIPLE METRICS AND CASE STUDIES

Identifying similarities and differences between the books required the use of a variety of metrics and case studies. Criticisms can be leveled at any one measure or topic selected for comparison because every choice creates blind spots and yields only partial insights. The books differed in significant ways, both between and sometimes within states, so measures that were helpful in understanding some of the books provided little insight into others. Only by layering comparisons on top of each other did broader patterns start to emerge about the extent to which books from individual states could be considered to be nationalized, denationalized, or westernized, subject to the qualification that differences existed not just among, but also within, states.

A good example of the limits of relying on singular metrics is the analyses of the case law that is cited or extracted in the books. One metric that I employed in considering how nationalized or denationalized these books were was to sort the case law they cited into domestic cases (cases from the courts of the country in which the book was being used to teach students), international cases (cases from international courts or tribunals, including international arbitral tribunals and regional courts), and foreign cases (cases from domestic courts of a state other than the one in which the book was being used to teach students). To check for westernization, I also analyzed the foreign cases cited according to which states and UN geopolitical regional groups they came from.[7]

The problem with relying on this metric in isolation is that case law plays a much more important role in the way that international law is explicated in books from some states than from others. One might have expected to see a wide division between the common law states (the United Kingdom and the United States) and the civil law states (China, France, and Russia), with the former's citing case law much more extensively than the latter. In fact, as will be seen below, the Western states and the non-Western ones were more widely divided, with the former's citing case law much more extensively than the latter. The two factors also worked together, as the Western common law states relied the most heavily on case law, whereas the non-Western civil law states relied the least heavily on case law.

The US books and some of the UK books were casebooks that included many case extractions and citations. The French books and some of the other UK books were textbooks that often extensively cited and discussed case law. These books typically explained that the primary sources of international law were treaties and custom and that judicial decisions were simply a subsidiary means for the determination of international law. But in identifying the existence and content of custom, they routinely looked to domestic and international case law. The same was true when it came to the interpretation and application of treaties. International law was often presented through or with discussion of concrete controversies, including specific cases and judicial decisions.

---

[7] For a list of which states form part of which regional grouping, see United Nations Regional Groups of Member States, U.N. Dep't for Gen. Assembly and Conference Mgmt. (2015), http://www.un.org/depts/DGACM/RegionalGroups.shtml (last visited Feb. 26, 2017).

The Chinese and Russian textbooks, by contrast, seemed to be primarily devoted to setting out the theory of international law, rather than its practice. They not only referred to few cases but also cited few practical applications of the law at all. They largely taught international law without reference to cases or controversies rather than through discussion of cases and controversies.[8] This difference fits with Lauri Mälksoo's description of Russian international law textbooks as typically being "theoretical and philosophical in a scholastic way," basing the doctrine on deduction rather than induction, that is, on "'logical' arguments rather than analysis of cases and other empirical material."[9] It also accords with critiques of Chinese legal education as highly conceptual rather than practical, with an emphasis on explaining theory and concepts rather than applying that knowledge to concrete problems.[10]

On the whole, looking at the origin of the cited case law was more helpful in understanding the content and orientation of the French, UK, and US books than the Chinese and Russian ones. This analysis, however, still provided some interesting insights into the latter books. On the scarcity of case law in general, and domestic case law in particular, referred to in the Russian books, Mälksoo has asked: "how could there be many such cases when in Russia the judiciary only very recently became independent of the all-powerful executive, if it ever truly did?"[11] The answer seems to be that much of the case law referred to is related to Russia's experiences before joining the European Court of Human Rights, which includes domestic cases that sometimes involved resistance to that court's decisions. By contrast, none of the Chinese books cite a single domestic case, which is consistent with André Nollkaemper's conclusion in his study National Courts and the International Rule of Law that Chinese courts "play no role whatsoever" in applying (public) international law.[12]

This example illustrates why it is important to use a variety of metrics and case studies to identify similarities and differences between these books. Accordingly, in addition to case citation patterns, I examined what other sources were commonly relied upon in the books, such as treaties, General Assembly and Security Council resolutions, and academic commentary. For instance, the Chinese and Russian textbooks seemed to show much stronger reliance on treaties and General Assembly resolutions than on case law. One possible reason might be that these sources are typically translated into Chinese and

---

[8] In Russian universities, it is common for the lectures to be based on the textbook, but for seminars to be based on collections of cases that are compiled by either the university or the seminar teacher. According to one Russian international lawyer: "This is actually one way younger professors and arrogant PhD students can circumvent 'old guards' control over the content of textbooks." E-mail on file with author.

[9] LAURI MÄLKSOO, RUSSIAN APPROACHES TO INTERNATIONAL LAW 93 (2015).

[10] See Mao Ling, Clinical Legal Education and the Reform of the Higher Legal Education System in China, 30 FORDHAM INT'L L.J. 421, 426 (2007); Zhenmin Wang, Legal Education in Contemporary China, 36 INT'L LAW. 1203, 1208–09 (2002); Hou Xinyi, Modern Legal Education in China, 31 OKLA. CITY U. L. REV. 293, 297 (2006) (speech at Oklahoma City University School of Law on Aug. 25, 2005). This may be particularly true in international law as some scholars commented that it was easier for Chinese scholars to teach or write about theoretical or abstract issues because they were less likely to engender criticism than if they chose to deal with current political controversies, particularly ones involving China.

[11] MÄLKSOO, supra note 9, at 96.

[12] ANDRÉ NOLLKAEMPER, NATIONAL COURTS AND THE INTERNATIONAL RULE OF LAW 13 (2011).

Russian, unlike most foreign and international case law. Lack of available translations may also explain the relative emphasis in some of the Russian international law manuals on Russian domestic case law over international and foreign case law,[13] although the *Meždunarodnoe pravosudie* (*International Justice*) journal, established in 2011, is seeking to overcome the translation problem.[14]

Where possible, I also analyzed some of these sources for evidence of nationalizing, denationalizing, and westernizing patterns. For instance, in their classic introduction, John Henry Merryman and Rodrigo Pérez-Perdomo explain that civil law judges play a substantially more restricted and modest role than their common law counterparts, whereas the teacher-scholar is better understood as the real protagonist in the civil law tradition.[15] Accordingly, I examined which academics the books from the civil law states cited and where they came from. I asked questions such as: did the books privilege domestic authors or foreign ones? and, to the extent that they relied on foreign authors, where did these authors come from?

To get a sense of substantive differences, I looked at the books' tables of contents to see which topics they focused on and how much space they devoted to each issue to determine which subjects the authors presented as important.[16] I also compared the books' substantive treatment of issues where I was aware of divided state practice (like sovereign immunity), different ideologies (as occurs in the clash between state sovereignty and human rights or between nonintervention and unilateral humanitarian intervention), and distinct approaches (as occurs in jurisdiction). In some cases, I focused on issues reflecting divisions in state practice along Western/non-Western lines. In others, I examined issues reflecting divisions among the Western states.

To better understand and contextualize my findings, I examined literature on the way that textbooks, casebooks, and scholarly writings have developed in these states. This scrutiny helped show, for example, how these books have changed over time, often in response to broader changes in these states' political makeup (like the breakup of the

---

[13] According to one Russian international lawyer: "Russian textbooks mostly deal with cases involving Russia [but] this is not because people are completely not interested in other cases. Rather, cases against Russia are usually available [with a] Russian translation, while other cases are harder to find. UN documents are cited and studied more than EU documents for the same reason." E-mail on file with author. According to another: "The thinking is that the references should be predominantly to texts students will or may want to read. Given that c. 70% of students do not have sufficient command of English or French (or Chinese for that matter) to read sources in languages other than Russian the focus is on Russian sources." E-mail on file with author.

[14] According to the journal's website, "Russian translations of international judicial decisions, and interviews with influential representatives of international justice world are published in the journal" because it "aims at maintaining a fruitful and informative discussion of the international judicial institutions [*sic*] work, as the institutions are capable of making the contribution to the theory and practice of international law." About the Journal, Inst. L. & Pub. Pol'y, http://www.ilpp.ru/en/journal/mp/about (last visited Sept. 30, 2016). It is written in Russian specifically to reach a domestic audience given that "Russian is one of the most underused official languages of the United Nations." *See id.*

[15] John Henry Merryman & Rogelio Pérez-Perdomo, The Civil Law Tradition: An Introduction to the Legal Systems of Europe and Latin America 34–38, 56–60 (3d ed. 2007).

[16] Again, in some cases, this measure did not work perfectly across states. For instance, in Russia, it is common for textbooks to contain chapters on a large number of issues, and the practice seems generally to be that each chapter is roughly the same length.

Soviet Union) or geopolitical orientation (like the break of the People's Republic of China (PRC) from its alliance with the Soviet Union and its movement toward more active engagement with the international legal system following recognition of the PRC government). I also discussed my observations and analysis with academics and lawyers from these states, whose advice added nuance to my understanding and whose suggestion of additional materials gave me a more complete and accurate picture.

This study does not claim to have comprehensively compared and contrasted the books on all relevant measures. Some of the choices that I made, such as my focus on case law, were undoubtedly influenced by my own background and training as a Western common-law-trained lawyer. I concentrated on several substantive areas of general international law, like the use of force, jurisdiction, and immunity. But I did not cover many specialist areas, like human rights, the law of the sea, international environmental law, and trade and investment, where different patterns might emerge. I am also aware that academics in different states might take divergent approaches to which subject areas fall within "public international law" and which subjects might be considered generalist or specialist. However, although any individual measure is limited and open to critique, combining a variety of metrics and case studies made it possible to identify some broader similarities and differences among these books.

C. CHANGES OVER TIME IN CHINESE AND RUSSIAN TEXTBOOKS

Whether books adopt a more nationalized, denationalized, or westernized approach is likely to shift over time, often in response to broader changes in society. For instance, Martti Koskenniemi recounts the difference between Finland's leading international law textbook from a generation ago and today. In the 1970s, the standard textbook was Erik Castrén's *Suomen kansainvälinen oikeus* (*Finland's International Law*).[17] The book began with two brief chapters that covered general points about international law and sources before moving on to issues of particular significance for Finland, such as treaties with the Soviet Union and the Finnish Constitution's dualist approach to international law.

A generation later, a very different international law textbook had become standard in Finland. Law students now read Kari Hakapää's *Uusi kansainvälinen oikeus* (*New International Law*), with the "new" seeking to distance itself from the "old" world of before 1989.[18] As Koskenniemi notes, this book partakes of the wide European genre of textbooks that downplay a national perspective; they may make reference to domestic laws or emphasize disputes or events of national interest, but they carefully present most of the materials from the viewpoint of the "geographical and historical nowhere."[19] Implicitly, this approach seems to be taken as representing the perspective of the "international community."[20]

---

[17] Martti Koskenniemi, *The Case for Comparative International Law*, 2009 FINNISH Y.B. INT'L L. 1, 2.
[18] *Id.*
[19] *Id.*
[20] *Id.*

The changes that Koskenniemi describes in Finland's international law textbooks reflect broader shifts within Finland, as the state's geopolitical orientation changed from appeasing the Soviet Union during the Cold War to joining the European Union in 1995. Similar shifts in orientation surface in international law textbooks from other states that have undergone or are undergoing significant transitions, such as China and Russia. Although this study is largely a static portrait of international law textbooks and casebooks at a particular point in time, this part sketches some of the changes in orientation and doctrine of the Chinese and Russian books. As this part highlights, the study would benefit from further cross-temporal analysis given the likelihood of changes over time.

The first Western international law book that was introduced to China was Henry Wheaton's *Elements of International Law*, which was translated into Chinese by W. A. P. Martin and his Chinese associates in 1864.[21] During the first few decades of the twentieth century, the Chinese began to send students to study law in Japan, in recognition of Japan's well-developed international law tradition and the physical and linguistic proximity of the two states, and Japanese books and articles on international law were also translated into Chinese.[22] This influence began to decline in the 1920s after increasing numbers of Chinese international law scholars traveled to Europe and the United States to study.[23] For instance, China's first international law textbook was published in 1929 by Zhou Gengsheng, who was educated in Edinburgh and Paris and then taught at Peking and Wuhan Universities.[24]

After World War II, the Soviet Union became a significant influence on China's approach to international law.[25] In the 1950s and 1960s, Soviet experts in international law were invited to teach in China, their textbooks were translated and used in Chinese universities, and the Marxist theory of class struggle played a prominent role in studies of law, both domestic and international.[26] For example, Renmin University adopted

---

[21] Hungdah Chiu, *The Development of Chinese International Law Terms and the Problem of Their Translation into English*, 27 J. ASIAN STUD. 485, 486 (1968).

[22] *Id.* at 489; He Qinhua (何勤华), 中国近代国际法学的诞生与成长 [The Birth and Growth of Modern International Legal Studies in China], 4 法学家 [Jurist] 49 (2004); Pasha L. Hsieh, *The Discipline of International Law in Republican China and Contemporary Taiwan*, 14 WASH. U. GLOB. STUD. L. REV. 87, 93–94 (2015). For a list of Japanese translations, see RUNE SVARVERUD, INTERNATIONAL LAW AS WORLD ORDER IN LATE IMPERIAL CHINA: TRANSLATION, RECEPTION AND DISCOURSE 1847–1911, at 269–302 (2007).

[23] Hungdah Chiu, *supra* note 21, at 490.

[24] ARNULF BECKER LORCA, MESTIZO INTERNATIONAL LAW: A GLOBAL INTELLECTUAL HISTORY 1842–1933, at 117 (2015); Hsieh, *supra* note 22, at 95, 128; Chen Tiqiang, *The People's Republic of China and Public International Law*, 8 DALHOUSIE L.J. 3, 11 (1984); Liu Zhongmeng (刘中猛), 国际法之父周鲠生先生述略 [Father of International Law: A Brief Introduction to Mr. Zhou Gengsheng], 10 兰台世界 [Lantai World] (2010).

[25] ZHOU GENGSHENG (周鲠生), 国际法 [International Law] 155–57 (1981); He Qinhua (何勤华), 20世纪50年代后中国对苏联国际法的移植 [Transplantation of USSR International Law in China After 1950s], 2 金陵法律评论 [Jinling L. Rev.] 89 (2001). On the role of Soviet sources in Chinese law more generally, see Luke T. Lee, *Chinese Communist Law: Its Background and Development*, 60 MICH. L. REV. 439, 462–66 (1962).

[26] XUE HANQIN, CHINESE CONTEMPORARY PERSPECTIVES ON INTERNATIONAL LAW: HISTORY, CULTURE AND INTERNATIONAL LAW 25 (2012). For instance, *Stalin on the Basic Principles of Modern International Law* was translated into Chinese in 1950 and Lenin's *Theory of International Politics and International Law* was translated into Chinese in 1961. *See* He Qinhua, *supra* note 25, at 93–94.

a translation of *Contemporary Public International Law* by E. A. Korovin, and the University of International Relations and Beijing University used Korovin's *A Primer on International Law*.[27] Some Chinese international law terms were translated from the Soviet international law literature, including terms for proletarian internationalism and socialist international law.[28]

This close association with Soviet approaches began to wane in the 1970s. As He Qinhua describes, after the mid-1960s, China publicly severed its alliance with the Soviet Union and "began to walk independently on its own."[29] After the late 1970s, when China established cooperative relationships with the United States and other Western countries, regained its seat in the United Nations, and joined many international conventions, the PRC began to "create its own experience in the international law field, to get rid of the influence from the Soviet Union, and to gradually catch up with international trends."[30] Oppenheim's *International Law*, which was first translated into Chinese in 1955 and quickly gained considerable influence,[31] was translated anew by Wang Tieya and his associates in 1972 and has proved greatly influential in shaping the approaches of Chinese international law textbooks until today.

As for Russia, during the Cold War, the Soviet Union took a clear Soviet approach to international law that was adopted in the main textbooks. Since the end of the Cold War, however, an arms race among international law textbook authors has developed, with the publication by each chair holder in international law at the major universities of his or her own textbook. One result of this competition, coupled with the greater academic freedom in Russia that followed the dissolution of the Soviet Union, was the emergence of a variety of approaches to international law in textbooks. According to Mälksoo, writing in 2009, "there is no longer a monolithic, 'one and only state-approved' theory of international law" in Russia but, instead, doctrinal pluralism.[32]

This pluralism reflects how closely the author aligns himself or herself with previous Soviet approaches or Western-influenced approaches. Doctrinal choices seem to be no accident. As Mälksoo argues, they seem to correspond with a more conservative or more liberal vision of the world and the Russian Federation's role in it.[33] For historical, ideological, and political reasons, Russia is facing transition and debate about its approach to international law, and the current balancing point is neither fully Soviet nor fully Western.[34] As a result, some issues that are treated as well settled in Western textbooks are the subject of real disagreement among Russian textbooks, at least as of 2013.

---

[27] He Qinhua, *supra* note 25, at 93.

[28] Hungdah Chiu, *supra* note 21, at 493.

[29] He Qinhua, *supra* note 25, at 94.

[30] *Id.*

[31] Hungdah Chiu, *supra* note 21, at 493.

[32] Lauri Mälksoo, *International Law in Russian Textbooks: What's in the Doctrinal Pluralism?*, 2 GÖTTINGEN J. INT'L L. 279, 281 (2009).

[33] *Id.* at 282.

[34] Lauri Mälksoo, *International Legal Theory in Russia: A Civilizational Perspective, or: Can Individuals Be Subjects of International Law?, in* THE OXFORD HANDBOOK ON THE THEORY OF INTERNATIONAL LAW 257, 275 (Florian Hoffmann & Anne Orford eds., 2016).

One of the best examples of this doctrinal pluralism can be found in discussions about the status of the individual under international law. The Western books tend to tell a consistent story: it used to be that only states were subjects of international law, but it is now recognized that individuals may also be subjects of international law that are capable of holding rights and bearing obligations under that law. Just because individuals are now subjects of international law does not mean that they have all the same capacities as states, but that is not problematic because different subjects of international law may have distinct capacities. For instance, individuals may have been granted human rights, but they cannot enter into treaties.

By contrast, the status of the individual is one of the most divisive topics in Russian international law scholarship. For instance, the Bekyashev book (Rus.) states that individuals have become subjects of international law.[35] The Kuznetsov and Tuzmukhamedov book (Rus.) acknowledges that contemporary views are split on the issue, but notes that the argument that individuals are recognized as subjects of international law "would go beyond the framework of a doctrinal approach, encompassing the domain of norm-creation and judicial interpretation."[36] By contrast, the Kolosov and Krivchikova book (Rus.) and the Kovalev and Chernichenko book (Rus.) both state that the individual is not a subject of international law.[37] The latter two manuals are especially significant because they were written by authors from, and have been used at, the Moscow State Institute of International Relations (MGIMO) and the Diplomatic Academy, the leading institutions for training future diplomats in the Russian Federation.[38]

According to William Butler, the great amount of attention given to whether the individual is a subject of international law reflects Russian international lawyers' acute awareness that "the international system has changed and is changing to something beyond our experience."[39] Positions on this topic often seem to act as a proxy for a larger debate about whether Russia should follow the Western approach to human rights or should remain faithful to its Soviet state-centered approach. Scholars who argue that the individual enjoys the status of a subject of international law generally incline toward a more critical approach to Soviet history, whereas scholars who are reluctant to grant individuals such status tend to view the Soviet legacy in a less critical light and often conceptualize the world in an "us" (Russia) versus "them" (NATO, the West, the United States) framework.[40]

---

[35] For example, Bekyashev contrasts L.N. Shestakov's textbook, which "for the first time, acknowledges the individual as a subject of international law (albeit, only partially so)" with the stance taken in Kovalev and Chernichenko's textbook, which denies that the individual is a subject of international law. *See* Международное публичное право [International Public Law] 118–20 (K.A. Bekyashev (К.А. Бекяшев) ed., 5th ed. 2011).

[36] International Law: A Russian Introduction 63–68 (Valerii I. Kuznetsov & Bakhtiar R. Tuzmukhamedov (Валерий Кузнецов и Бахтияр Тузмухамедов) eds., William E. Butler ed. & trans., 2009); *see also id.* at 159.

[37] Международное право [International Law] 20, 107 (Y.M. Kolosov & E.S. Krivchikova (Ю.М. Колосов и Э.С. Кривчикова) eds., 2d ed. 2005); Международное право [International Law] 170 (A.A. Kovalev & S.V. Chernichenko (А.А. Ковалев и С.В. Черниченко) eds., 3d ed. 2008).

[38] Mälksoo, *supra* note 32, at 286.

[39] William E. Butler, *Preface to the English Edition, in* International Law, *supra* note 36, at xix, xxiv.

[40] Mälksoo, *supra* note 32, at 284.

To get a sense of the doctrinal pluralism, it is useful to compare two Russian textbooks in more detail. The first is the Kovalev and Chernichenko book (Rus.), which tends to be conservative and to hew relatively closely to the positions embraced by Soviet international law; it devotes just half a page to this question. The book begins by acknowledging the disagreement on the subject, distinguishing between a "widespread point of view" (presumably the Western viewpoint) and "domestic doctrine."[41] According to the former view, as subjects of international law, individuals may have direct access to international bodies as petitioners, plaintiffs, and defendants.[42] But domestic doctrine is of a different opinion: direct access to international bodies does not transform individuals into subjects of international law but shows only that governments have permitted individuals such access.[43]

By contrast, the Ignatenko and Tiunov book (Rus.), which is comparatively liberal and Western in its orientation, devotes seven pages to this issue. The book notes that, historically, individuals were objects but not subjects of international law, but it states that, over time, the individual has increasingly become a subject of international law. Today's situation is characterized by a marked change in the status of individuals under international law, which is accompanied by the consistent and evolutionary expansion of individuals' participation in international relations. Individual rights are now protected by the availability of domestic and international remedies, as evidenced by the *LaGrand* case in the International Court of Justice (ICJ) and investor-state arbitration.[44] International law also recognizes individual responsibilities under, for instance, international humanitarian law and international criminal law.[45] Acknowledging the individual as a subject of international law does not infringe on the position of the state as the main subject of international law, since the individual is allowed to engage in international relations only to the extent permitted by states. But the book concludes that it is no longer useful to ask whether the individual is a subject of international law given the sheer volume of rights and duties conferred on individuals and their ever-expanding participation in international legal relations.[46]

While Russian books as of 2013 evidenced doctrinal pluralism, it would be a mistake to think that the us-versus-them dynamic that pervaded the Cold War is necessarily a thing of the past, particularly in light of more recent events. Even as of 2013, different textbook approaches often reflected distinct conceptions about how Russia should relate to its "other," namely, Western states in general and the United States in particular. Many books remained infused with complaints against the United States, including that (1) the United States is aggressive and shows no regard for international law; (2) any regard that it does show for international law is hypocritical and based on double standards; and (3) the United States feels threatened by Russian success and is actively trying to contain or undermine Russia. The

---

[41] Kolosov & Krivchikova, *supra* note 37, at 170.

[42] *Id.*

[43] *Id.*

[44] Международное право [International Law] 114–15 (G.V. Ignatenko & O.I. Tiunov (Г.В. Игнатенко и О.И. Тюнов) eds., 2013).

[45] *Id.* at 118.

[46] *Id.* at 118–20.

antithesis of Russia and the United States is most pronounced when discussing the use of force, but it appears in many other contexts as well.

In terms of aggression, A. N. Vylegzhanin, who edited the textbook used at MGIMO, writes that NATO's mission since 1999 has been to "secure the interests of the West, and in particular the US, throughout the world and to affirm the power and supremacy of the Euro-Atlantic civilization in the international community."[47] Similarly, K. A. Bekyashev explains that "[n]otwithstanding the imperative nature of the principle forbidding the use or threat of force, several governments often, on the basis of a thought-up pretext, invade other countries, violating that country's sovereignty and territorial integrity."[48] After citing the US and UK 2003 invasion of Iraq as an example, Bekyashev quotes Vladimir Putin to the following effect: "Today we are witnessing an almost uncontained hyper use of force—military force—in international relations, force that is plunging the world into an abyss of permanent conflicts."[49] Similarly, V. M. Shumilov explains that, "[t]o justify its use of force, the US uses its foreign policy doctrine of 'preventive self-defense.'"[50] The doctrine of preventive self-defense, he claims, formulates the concept of "rogue States" and permits the United States to determine independently which states are "rogue."[51] He explains that, in 2003, the United States and the United Kingdom attacked Iraq, without permission from the UN Security Council, on the grounds of preventive self-defense.[52] "The American conception of 'preventive self-defense,'" Shumilov concludes, "is a doctrine of . . . 'everything is allowed in the name of national security.'"[53]

As for hypocrisy, some of the textbooks denounce the United States for its hypocritical use of human rights. On the one hand, the United States accuses other countries—namely, Russia—of violating the same human rights that it violates on a daily basis. This is the main claim of Shumilov in his discussion of the US response to the Russian law on nongovernmental organizations (NGOs) of 2005.[54] Shumilov never explains why the United States objected to the law, but instead seeks to undermine the US complaint by pointing to its hypocrisy on the basis that the FBI spies on America's own NGOs, "often on religious grounds."[55] On the other hand, the United States cloaks its own

---

[47] Международное право [International Law] 699 (A.N. Vylegzhanin (А.Н. Вылегжанин) ed., 2012).

[48] Bekyashev, *supra* note 35, at 125–26.

[49] *Id.* at 126.

[50] Международное право [International Law] 197 (V.M. Shumilov (В.М. Шумилов) ed., 2d ed. 2012).

[51] *Id.* at 198.

[52] *Id.*

[53] *Id.*

[54] In 2005, the Federal Assembly in Russia discussed changes to the law on noncommercial civil society, which would forbid nontransparent financing of organizations by foreign governments. In reply, the US Congress passed a resolution in December 2005, which requested that Russia not accept or rewrite the law because in its current version it was allegedly "incompatible" with Russia's membership in the "community of western democracies." A number of the provisions in Russia's NGO law, such as the onerous registration requirements and funding reports, were likely in violation of a number of international laws (e.g., European Convention on Human Rights' protection of freedom of expression (Article 10) and freedom of assembly and association (Article 11)).

[55] Shumilov, *supra* note 50, at 228 (Under the FBI's watch were "organizations for the fight against poverty, for the protection of animals, for the protection of the environment, Greenpeace, Catholic associations and Muslim organizations").

unlawful actions in human rights language. "The American administration," Kovalev and Chernichenko write in their Diplomatic Academy textbook, "seeks to justify its actions by arbitrarily interpreting norms of international law and sometimes misinterpreting them (e.g., preventive self-defense, so-called humanitarian intervention, meant to 'introduce' democracy into other countries)."[56] Similar complaints are made outside the human rights context. For instance, Shumilov criticizes the extraterritorial application of the US Sarbanes-Oxley Act as a "typical example of when law, ideology and morality are put into the service of one side's public interests, an example of hypocrisy and duplicity, which Western civilization-type states use to give themselves an edge in global competition."[57]

In terms of the United States' resenting and feeling threatened by Russia's success, Vylegzhanin states: "The high price of oil, which has allowed Russia to obtain crucial resources to modernize its military, and the new path of the Russian government to strengthen the Russian State clearly did not suit the U.S."[58] Apparently to hamper Russia's efforts, the United States resuscitated its old Cold War strategy and "renewed the arms race."[59] Referring to the US plan to build missile defense systems in Poland and the Czech Republic, Vylegzhanin asserts: "The propagandistic cover for this was the mythical nuclear threat from Iran and North Korea. In fact, there were at least two goals: to pull Russia into a new arms race and to reduce the Russian deterrent."[60]

Even though the level of academic freedom grew after the dissolution of the Soviet Union,[61] Russian academia is not entirely free and appears to have become less so over the course of this study. For instance, no international law academics in Russia "publicly declared the invasion and annexation of Crimea to be illegal under international law."[62] When noninternational law academics have spoken out, retribution has been swift. Thus, in March 2014, Andrey Zubov, a history professor at MGIMO, which is one of the feeder schools for the Russian Foreign Ministry, published an article criticizing Russia's policy toward Ukraine,[63] and comparing Russia's action in Crimea with Hitler's annexation of Austria.[64] Three days after the article appeared, Zubov was fired from his post at MGIMO.[65] MGIMO was forced to reinstate him on a technicality, but

---

[56] Kovalev & Chernichenko, *supra* note 37, at 20.

[57] Shumilov, *supra* note 50, at 123.

[58] Vylegzhanin, *supra* note 47, at 671.

[59] *Id.*

[60] *Id.* at 672.

[61] MÄLKSOO, *supra* note 9, at 82.

[62] *Id.* at 192.

[63] *See* Leonid Bershidsky, *Comparing Putin to Hitler Will Get You Fired*, BLOOMBERG VIEW, Mar. 25, 2014, http://www.bloombergview.com/articles/2014-03-25/comparing-putin-to-hitler-will-get-you-fired; Matthew Bodner, *Professor Says Sacked over Opinion Article*, MOSCOW TIMES, Mar. 5, 2014, http://www.themoscowtimes.com/news/article/professor-says-sacked-over-opinion-article-against-possible-ukraine-invasion/495616.html; Interview: In Crimea, Putin Has "Lost His Mind" (Radio Free Eur./Radio Liberty Mar. 3, 2014), http://www.rferl.org/content/interview-in-crimea-putin-has-lost-his-mind/25284114.html.

[64] Andrei Zubov (Андрей Зубов), Это уже было [This Has Already Happened], Ведомости [Statements], Mar. 1, 2014, http://www.vedomosti.ru/opinion/news/23467291/andrej-zubov-eto-uzhe-bylo.

[65] МГИМО уволило профессора "за критику действий государства" в связи с Украиной [MGIMO Fired a Professor "For His Criticisms of Government Policy" in Relations with Ukraine], Українська правда [Ukranian

the administration noted that reinstatement in no way changed the fact that Zubov had "violated the main principles of professional conduct."[66]

It remains to be seen whether these sorts of actions will create incentives for Russian international law scholars to publish more conservative or pro-Russian accounts of international law (which seems to be consistent with commentary on Crimea), or will cause them to denationalize their writings by commenting on international law in general without mentioning Russia's actions (which is the strategy sometimes adopted by Chinese textbook writers). The landscape of Russian books has certainly changed since the Soviet era, but only time will tell how these books might change in response to this new era if Russia continues to assert itself in Crimea and beyond.

II. The Nationalized/Denationalized Divide

The textbooks and casebooks from different states diverged on whether they took a more nationalized or denationalized approach to presenting international law. In some ways, this division replicates debates about how best to teach international law. Despite much agreement in the International Law Association's (ILA's) Committee on the Teaching of International Law, its final report describes one basic difference of approach: "whether the teaching of international law was or should be, in its broader orientation, 'internationalist' or 'municipalist/nationalist.'"[67] In other words, should international law be taught as it would be used by practitioners within their respective jurisdictions or as a field that is "nationally-unbounded"?[68]

Many measures could be looked at to determine whether a book adopts a more nationalized or denationalized approach. A more nationalized book might situate itself within a specific state's legal system; view international law issues from its own state's perspective; draw heavily on domestic sources, like case law, legislation, and executive practice, from its state; primarily cite or privilege the views of domestic academics; and focus on international cases or incidents involving its state. A more denationalized book might approach international law from a non-national perspective; draw primarily on international and foreign sources; cite foreign academics as equally or more authoritative than domestic academics; and focus on international cases and incidents that best illustrate general points, regardless of which states were involved.

Pravda], Mar. 24, 2014, http://www.pravda.com.ua/rus/news/2014/03/24/7020122 ("Let the inappropriate and offensive historical analogies and characterization lay [*sic*] on Zubov's conscience. The leadership of MGIMO considers it impossible for A.B. Zubov to continue working at the institute.").

[66] The Commission of the Presidential Council found that Zubov's dismissal was illegal. Federal Law No. 67-FZ states, "members of the election committee cannot be fired by the administration during the time of their service." Because Zubov was a member of the Precinct Election Commission in the 161st precinct of the Moscow City Election Commission, the federal law applied to him, and his termination was rescinded on April 11, 2014. *See* О Зубове А.Б. [About A.B. Zubov], MGIMO (МГИМО), Apr. 11, 2014, http://www.mgimo.ru/news/faculty/document250373.phtml.

[67] Int'l Law Ass'n, Hague Conf., Comm. on the Teaching of Int'l Law, Final Report 6 (2010).

[68] *Id.*

Of course, these choices are not clear-cut or binary. The above paragraph sketches two ideal types at either end of a spectrum. In reality, most books evidence a mix of nationalized and denationalized features, leaning in different directions on different measures. Nonetheless, as with debates about the teaching of international law, the books in different states often differ markedly on the extent to which they adopt a more nationalized or denationalized approach to presenting international law, though sometimes significant differences can be found within states.

A. IDENTIFYING HIGHLY NATIONALIZED TEXTBOOKS

When it comes to the sources that were relied upon, the US casebooks stood out for being highly nationalized compared with the others. They strongly emphasized domestic case law, US executive practice, US academics and publications, and international cases and controversies involving the United States. One way of illustrating this phenomenon is to identify all of the cases cited in the books from each state and then divide them among domestic cases, international cases, and foreign cases (see Table 7 and Figure 9 below). The US books are clear outliers on this measure, as they cite a significantly higher proportion of domestic case law than the books from any other state and are the only ones to cite domestic case law more frequently than international case law.

There may be many reasons why US casebooks cite domestic US case law so heavily. The courts of the United States produce a high volume of case law on international law because it is a large country, its culture is exceptionally litigious, and it maintains various domestic hooks that have attracted considerable international-law-related case law, such as the Alien Tort Statute and the treaty clause of the US Constitution. Unlike authors in some states where there may be little domestic case law, US casebook writers can draw from an abundance of publicly available and easily accessible domestic cases. Obviously, if a state has generated little or no domestic case law, or such case law has not been publicly reported, its textbook authors could not cite domestic decisions so

TABLE 7

Origin of All of the Cases Cited in the Textbooks

State	Number of Books	Number of Cases	Domestic	International	Foreign
China	4	159	0%	88%	12%
France	3	1784	28%	68%	3%
Russia	4	347	19%	78%	4%
United Kingdom	4	3956	20%	51%	29%
United States	3	1002	64%	31%	6%

Note: The figures shown are rounded to the nearest whole number, which can mean that they add up to slightly more or less than 100% for a given state.

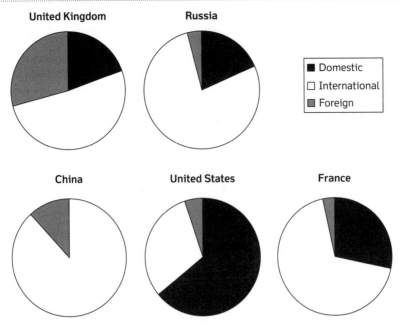

FIGURE 9   Percentage of Domestic, International, and Foreign Cases Cited in Textbooks

heavily. Nevertheless, in view of the large number of international and foreign decisions, the balance that US casebook writers strike represents a choice rather than a necessity.

What factors might drive this choice? One reason that US casebook writers might focus on US case law is that, since the United States is the most powerful state in the world, its case law is likely to be singularly influential in understanding the creation and enforcement of international law. Textbooks from many other states look to US practice, partly because of the prominence of the United States on the international stage. *Medellín v. Texas* is not just a case about a single state's approach to the enforcement of ICJ judgments—it is about the approach of the world's main or only superpower.[69] Just as feminists claim that "the personal is the political," so perhaps could US international lawyers claim that "the national is the international."

Another factor driving this choice may be a desire to justify the field's relevance to skeptics, of whom there are many in America. Although in its final report the ILA's Committee on the Teaching of International Law did not match positions taken with participants from particular states, this concern seemed to motivate some of those advocating more nationalist approaches. Some committee members argued that "national bias" was a duty of the teacher toward students preparing for practice and was necessary for the field's promotion: "if teachers can convince the 'powers-that-be' that a student needs international law to practice within his/her jurisdiction, the status of the subject

---

[69] *Medellín v. Texas*, 552 U.S. 491 (2008).

will be advanced."[70] This need to justify the field's existence—at all or as a type of law—may be more pronounced in some states than others. Relying on domestic case law may help to give the impression that international law really is law.

This divergence may also reflect and reinforce the stronger emphasis within the United States on foreign relations law in comparison with international law. A key difference between UK and US international law academics is that the UK ones often seem to orbit around the International Court of Justice, whereas the US ones often seem to orbit around the US Supreme Court. One can get a sense of this difference by looking at the relative emphasis placed on a variety of cases in UK and US textbooks and casebooks. For instance, the word-clouds in Figures 10 and 11 show all the cases referred to in a leading US casebook (Carter and Weiner)[71] and a leading UK textbook (Evans)[72] where the size of the word reflects the number of pages on which it is referenced in the index of cases.

Most of the main cases in the US book were decided by US courts, such as *Sosa v. Alvarez-Machain, Filartiga v. Pena-Irala, Dames & Moore v. Regan, Hamdan v. Rumsfeld, Samantar v. Yousuf,* and *Banco Nacional de Cuba v. Sabbatino,*[73] and most of these were ruled upon by the US Supreme Court. Many of these cases involve important issues in US foreign relations law, such as whether and when US courts have jurisdiction to hear claims based on customary international law or the power of the president to

FIGURE 10 Word Cloud of Cases in a US Casebook (Carter & Weiner)

[70] *Id.*

[71] BARRY E. CARTER & ALLEN S. WEINER, INTERNATIONAL LAW (6th ed. 2011).

[72] INTERNATIONAL LAW (Malcolm D. Evans ed., 3d ed. 2010).

[73] Samantar v. Yousuf, 560 U.S. 305 (2010); Hamdan v. Rumsfeld, 548 U.S. 557 (2006); Sosa v. Alvarez-Machain, 542 U.S. 692 (2004); Dames & Moore v. Regan, 453 U.S. 654 (1981); Banco Nacional de Cuba v. Sabbatino, 376 U.S. 398 (1964); Filartiga v. Pena-Irala, 630 F.2d 876 (2d Cir. 1980).

FIGURE II Word Cloud of Cases in a UK Textbook (Evans)

settle international claims on behalf of US nationals. The most prominent international case featured is *Nicaragua v. United States*, which not only involved the United States as a party but also implicated a critical issue of US foreign policy: its rejection of ICJ jurisdiction and its subsequent decision to withdraw its optional declaration recognizing the ICJ's general jurisdiction. Many of the cases were also based on the Alien Tort Statute, which has played a major role in US international law debates since the 1990s.

By contrast, almost all of the main cases in the UK book were decided by international courts, primarily the International Court of Justice, and do not implicate UK foreign relations issues. Most of the international cases did not involve the United Kingdom or UK nationals as a party, such as the *Nicaragua* case, *Armed Activities on the Territory of the Congo, North Sea Continental Shelf, Arrest Warrant of 11 April 2000*, and *Prosecutor v. Tadić*.[74] In some cases, the United Kingdom was a party or submitted pleadings, such as *Corfu Channel* and the *Nuclear Weapons* advisory opinion, but these did not seem to receive special emphasis. Very few domestic UK cases feature prominently in the UK word-cloud. The exceptions are *Pinochet* and, to a lesser extent, *Jones v. Saudi Arabia*;[75] the rest largely fade into the background as being of secondary importance.

Not all of the books in a single state necessarily have the same profile. While the Evans textbook (UK) is characteristic of the other UK books in its emphasis on international case law, particularly of the International Court of Justice, the Carter and Weiner casebook (US) is the most domestically oriented of all of the US books and, indeed, of the

---

[74] Armed Activities on the Territory of the Congo (Demo. Rep. Congo v. Ug.), 2005 I.C.J. 168 (Dec. 19); Arrest Warrant of 11 April 2000 (Dem. Rep. Congo v. Belg.), 2002 I.C.J. 3 (Feb. 14); Military and Paramilitary Activities in and Against Nicaragua (Nic. v. U.S.), 1986 I.C.J. 14 (June 27); North Sea Continental Shelf (Ger. v. Denmark), 1969 I.C.J. 3 (Feb. 20); and Prosecutor v. Tadić, Decision on the Defence Motion for Interlocutory Appeal on Jurisdiction, Case No. IT-94-1-AR72, 35 ILM 32 (1996).

[75] Jones v. Ministry of Interior for the Kingdom of Saudi Arabia and Others, [2007] AC 270; R. v. Bow St. Metro. Stipendiary Magistrate and Others, ex parte Pinochet Ugarte (No. 3) [2000] 1 AC 147.

entire study. A raw analysis of all of the cases listed in the Carter and Weiner table of authorities shows that 71 percent were domestic US cases. One might think that this figure simply reflects long string citations to many domestic cases rather than the balance of what was actually extracted. To check, I calculated the percentages of domestic, foreign, and international cases based on how many pages of each type of case law were extracted. When this weighted extraction approach was applied, far from decreasing, the percentage of domestic case law increased to 78 percent.

In the preface to the book, the authors acknowledge their US focus, stating:

> Although this casebook focuses on international law, it also aims at educating US lawyers. Consequently, it often considers international law from an American perspective, including substantial sections on the US Constitution and US laws that have an international impact. At the same time, because American lawyers must appreciate the different principles and possible strategies under foreign legal systems, materials from other legal systems are included to illustrate contrasting approaches.[76]

Yet in a review in the *American Journal of International Law* (AJIL) of an earlier edition of the book, US international lawyer David Bederman criticized it for being "strikingly parochial" in its selection of materials, stating that the authors seemed to "purposefully . . . reject a diversity of voices for international law."[77] Lamenting the heavy focus on US case law, Bederman noted that students using this book "will only occasionally be required to grapple with the difficult styles and divergent methodologies of international tribunals or of domestic courts from civil law jurisdictions."[78] The unmistakable message of this "selection bias," he concluded, is that "the only tribunals really competent to opine about international law—the only version of international law that actually matters to American lawyers—is that espoused by US courts."[79]

A similar point was made by Japanese international lawyer Yasuaki Onuma, who described his reaction upon first encountering the domestic focus of US international law casebooks when he was invited in the 1980s to give a paper on teaching international law at the American Society of International Law. In researching international law education in the United States, Onuma was "shocked" to realize that the major US international law casebooks were "incredibly egocentric, tacitly equating what is American with what is international or universal."[80] The books seemed like "coursebooks on US domestic law" rather than international law and, as a result, simply "lacked a notion that the United States is one of many sovereign States, which constitutes a fundamental basis for any study of international law."[81]

---

[76] Carter & Weiner, *supra* note 71, at xlii.

[77] David J. Bederman, *International Law Casebooks: Tradition, Revision, and Pedagogy*, 98 Am. J. Int'l L. 200, 206 (2004) (book review).

[78] *Id.*

[79] *Id.*

[80] Yasuaki Onuma, A Transcivilizational Perspective on International Law 184 (2010).

[81] *Id.* at 184–85.

Of course, there are two sides to this issue. On the one hand, the United States is one of many sovereign states and international law is based on the equality of states. On the other hand, the United States is the world's most powerful state, so that treating its practice as though it were simply that of any other state lacks realism. International law cannot be understood fully without understanding the United States because its practice is unusually influential in shaping the field. Yet international law also cannot be understood fully by focusing primarily on the United States because its experiences are not representative of those of the vast majority of other states.

One should not assume that references to or extractions of US case law are necessarily positive and uncritical. Casebooks extracting the *Medellín* case do not always treat it with pride, for instance. But primarily focusing on US materials risks creating the impression that US foreign relations law and international law are one and the same thing. James Crawford, formerly a professor of international law at Cambridge and now a judge on the International Court of Justice, has raised concern about this sort of conflation in the context of US international law scholarship more generally. According to Crawford:

> [M]uch that passes for the study of international law in the United States academy is at best the foreign relations law of the United States with ideological interpolations. But there is a cardinal difference between the foreign relations law of a state, even the United States, by definition specific to that state, and international law. The overwhelming impression on reading this body of scholarship . . . is one of isolationism. It is as if we heard the sound of one hand clapping; a conversation in which the United States is its own and only interlocutor. The theme song would be "It takes one to tango." International law is not to be reduced to a series of unilateral concessions by the United States.[82]

This focus on domestic materials and perspectives is consistent with broader observations about American exceptionalism and isolationism, including in the US educational system. For instance, in their review of US history textbooks, Dana Lindaman and Kyle Ward lamented that, while individuals in other states are exposed to a lot of information about the United States, "Americans, in sharp contrast, seem to know relatively little about other countries and cultures" owing to the "isolationist tendency" of the state's educational system.[83] Similarly, Mathias Reimann has described the biggest disadvantage of US legal training as the "tendency to inevitably (and often unconsciously) see American law at the center of the legal universe with all other legal cultures and systems being peripheral to it."[84] If US international law casebooks are anything to go by, this criticism appears to have some bite, as they often present what could be described as the international law of "me, myself, and I."

---

[82] James Crawford, *International Law as Discipline and Profession*, 106 AM. SOC'Y INT'L L. PROC. 471, 484 (2012).

[83] DANA LINDAMAN & KYLE ROY WARD, HISTORY LESSONS: HOW TEXTBOOKS FROM AROUND THE WORLD PORTRAY US HISTORY, at xviii (2006).

[84] Mathias Reimann, *The American Advantage in Global Lawyering*, 78 RABELS ZEITSCHRIFT FÜR AUSLÄN-DISCHES UND INTERNATIONALES PRIVATRECHT 1, 4 n.12 (2014).

B. IDENTIFYING HIGHLY DENATIONALIZED TEXTBOOKS

While the US casebooks stood out as highly nationalized, the textbooks of some states appeared to be highly denationalized, providing little or no information about their own state's practices or perspectives. Something is certainly lost if the main way international law is understood is through a state's own domestic case law and materials. But something is also lost when a state's international law textbooks and casebooks supply almost no focus on how that state interacts with the international legal system or how international law is incorporated into and approached within that state's domestic legal system. Far from the national being the international, here the national is lost or de-emphasized relative to the international.

This problem seems to be acute for certain semiperipheral and peripheral states where international law is frequently taught through the use of imported textbooks. Just as law might be transplanted through colonization or law and development movements, so may understandings of the law be transplanted through "legal colonization" in the form of imported textbooks. This section refers to an "imported" textbook as one that is written and published by an academic in State A and then imported for use in teaching international law in State B. These books represent overt legal transplants. A "local" textbook, by contrast, is written by authors in or from State B for use in State B. These books are home grown rather than transplanted.

As can be seen from Table 6 in Part I.A above, imported textbooks play an important role in teaching international law in a number of states. For instance, the two most commonly used international law textbooks in India, one of the two most commonly used books in South Africa, and one of the most commonly used books in Australia, all come from the United Kingdom. All of the most commonly used international law textbooks in Cameroon and Senegal come from France. One of the most commonly used books in Argentina comes from Spain. Textbooks often flow from core to semiperipheral and peripheral states, and along language and ex-colonial lines. Accordingly, students in peripheral and semiperipheral states often end up learning international law through books imported from their ex-colonizers.

In some states, like Australia and South Africa, these imported books sit alongside local books. In other states, like Cameroon and India, these imported books are the only or main books used in the teaching of international law. While local books can be more nationalized or denationalized, imported textbooks are almost always denationalized. They may be denationalized so as to cater to audiences in multiple states or this feature may be what made them attractive for such use. Or they may be denationalized because they feature and privilege the practice and perspectives of the state from which they come, rather than the state into which they are imported. Either way, students who study from these imported textbooks are likely to receive much less information about how their state interacts with the international legal system than those who study from nationalized local textbooks.

One way to illustrate this difference is to compare the proportion of domestic case law in these two different types of books in Australia, South Africa, and Argentina. The figures on the next page show diagrams comparing the share of domestic, international, and

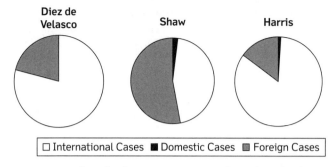

FIGURE 12 Cases in Imported Textbooks in Argentina, Australia, and South Africa

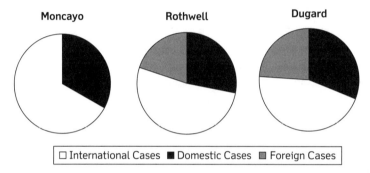

FIGURE 13 Cases in Local Textbooks in Argentina, Australia, and South Africa

foreign case law in books that are imported from that state's ex-colonial power (Figure 12) and in local books that feature domestic practices (Figure 13). The case law is coded on the basis of the perspective of the state in which the book is used. Thus, for a book that was written and published in the United Kingdom but imported for use in Australia, a UK case would count as foreign and an Australian case would count as domestic even though the reverse would be true when that book was used in the United Kingdom. These diagrams show how little domestic case law is included in imported textbooks when compared with more nationalized, local textbooks.

India constitutes a striking example of a large and important state that lacks a tradition of local international law textbooks. Indian students typically learn international law through UK textbooks. Their key texts do not include collections of Indian Supreme Court cases dealing with international law, even though that court has rendered numerous decisions concerning international law.[85] Nor do their books highlight Indian positions on key international law debates, such as the use of force or the legitimacy and consequences of expropriation. Nor do these books spend much time exploring India's

---

[85] Neha Jain, *The Democratizing Force of International Law: Human Rights Adjudication by the Indian Supreme Court, in* COMPARATIVE INTERNATIONAL LAW (Anthea Roberts et al. eds., forthcoming 2017).

particular experience of international law through the experience of colonization and the process of decolonization.[86] Although these textbooks might be supplemented by local materials in some courses, I am told that they seldom are. The failure to offer a contextualized and locally adapted approach risks making the subject feel removed and irrelevant to Indian students. It also makes it harder to locate relevant Indian practice when seeking to identify and interpret international law.

This external focus does not just concern textbooks. B. S. Chimni has explained that, after India achieved independence, "Indian international lawyers turned to the West to learn the language of international law."[87] Many of the most distinguished Indian international lawyers went to Yale Law School to pursue LLM or doctoral degrees.[88] This exposure tended to direct their attention to Cold War tensions, rather than Indian approaches to international law. This focus changed with the development of Third World Approaches to International Law (TWAIL), which aimed at re-examining international law from the perspective of the periphery. But a large proportion of the key TWAIL figures from India either spent much of their professional careers outside India (for example, Balakrishnan Rajagopal in the United States) or based themselves at the Centre for International Legal Studies at Jawaharlal Nehru University rather than at an Indian law school (for example, Chimni and R. P. Anand).

Chimni has noted the paradox that, "despite Indian scholarship playing a crucial role in the articulation of TWAIL, it has not been widely studied in Indian law schools."[89] One reason is what he describes as the "sorry state" of legal education in India, where law professors lack adequate libraries and research infrastructure; there are few Indian peer-reviewed journals and no tradition of legal scholarship; and the "colonial mind-set" assumes that work done in First World institutions is rigorous and of higher quality than work done locally, so that it is deemed sufficient merely to borrow from such work when the need arises.[90] The lack of Indian international law textbooks forms part of a broader problem of legal scholarship in India, but it means that international law is taught in a much more denationalized way than in places like South Africa where a local, more nationalized textbook is available.

For international law to seem relevant in particular local environments, teachers, and textbooks need to explore the interaction between the international and the domestic, and to consider the way "global" norms come to be adapted to particular localities. This point was made by a South African international law academic in explaining why she assigned John Dugard's *International Law: A South African Perspective* when teaching international law in South Africa. The problem with using imported UK textbooks, she

---

[86] On the significance of India's experience with colonization and decolonization for its approach to international law, see Simon Chesterman, *Asia's Ambivalence About International Law and Institutions: Past, Present and Futures*, 27 Eur. J. Int'l L. 945, 947–51 (2016).

[87] B.S. Chimni, *International Law Scholarship in Post-colonial India: Coping with Dualism*, 23 Leiden J. Int'l L. 23, 24 (2010).

[88] *Id.* (citing examples such as R.P. Anand, B.S. Murty, V.P. Nanda, K.V. Venkatraman, S.P. Sharma, and P.S. Rao).

[89] B.S. Chimni, *The World of TWAIL: Introduction to the Special Issue*, 3 Trade L. & Dev. 14, 14 (2011).

[90] *Id.* at 14–15.

noted, was that they did not link international law and South Africa. This linking was "crucial" because international law is "applied and brought to life in a national context." Teaching international law without including this national perspective was "very problematic from a practical point of view" and contributed to students' lack of a realistic sense of the impact or relevance of international law.[91]

A similar phenomenon is explored by anthropologists such as Arjun Appadurai, who analyzes the "indigenization" of globalized forms,[92] and Sally Engle Merry, who examines the "vernacularization" of international human rights by local actors.[93] As Merry has explained:

> As ideas from transnational sources travel to small communities, they are typically vernacularized, or adapted to local institutions and meanings. . . . Human rights language is similarly extracted from the universal and adapted to national and local communities. The term indigenization refers to shifts in meaning—particularly to the way new ideas are framed and presented in terms of existing cultural norms, values, and practices.[94]

Textbooks, or textbook supplements, with some local content can be used in both recording and furthering this process of indigenization and vernacularization, helping students to understand how international law is (or is not) brought home in their own domestic context. The interaction may vary among states and issue-areas, occurring along a spectrum from "replication," where international norms are largely reproduced in the local environment without significant changes, "hybridization," where imported concepts are merged with local ones, sometimes uneasily, and "rejection," where international ideas are rejected or subverted in a particular local environment.[95]

Books like Don Rothwell's *International Law: Cases and Materials with Australian Perspectives*, Dugard's *International Law: A South African Perspective*, and Hugh Kindred and Jean-Gabriel Castel's *International Law: Chiefly as Interpreted and Applied in Canada*, all explicitly engage with national approaches and materials in the context of presenting international law. The naming of these books reflects interesting core-periphery dynamics. The US casebooks are full of US cases, yet they are simply named "International Law" casebooks, not "International Law with US Cases" or, less charitably, "International Law: A Hegemon's Perspective." By contrast, these Australian, Canadian, and South African textbooks specifically note their national perspectives or emphasis, yet carry considerably lower percentages of domestic cases (28 percent,

---

[91] E-mail on file with author.

[92] Arjun Appadurai, Modernity at Large: Cultural Dimensions of Globalization (1996).

[93] Sally Engle Merry, Human Rights and Gender Violence: Translating International Law into Local Justice (2006).

[94] Sally Engle Merry, *Transnational Human Rights and Local Activism: Mapping the Middle*, 108 Am. Anthropologist 38, 39 (2006).

[95] *Id.* at 44.

27 percent, and 45 percent, respectively) than their US counterparts (64 percent). As Koskenniemi has noted:

> When one inhabits the centre, one feels no need to mark out one's place. One is "there" and everybody knows it. In the periphery, things look different. There it might well seem advisable to highlight one's exotic location, and to raise a different voice—or if not that different, nevertheless a voice from a different direction, a "fresh" voice.[96]

There may not be a sufficient market to justify writing and publishing local textbooks on international law in every state. But there could well be an adequate market to justify doing so on at least a regional basis. For instance, one could imagine the development of Asian or African international law textbooks that would introduce the international legal system but also consciously feature practices and perspectives from those regions, especially as certain Asian and African states have developed notable practice in relation to many areas of international law, including the law of the sea and international criminal law, respectively. Books with this sort of regional focus are starting to appear in certain subfields of international law,[97] but they seem yet to be developed on a generalist level.

III. Inconsistent Approaches

Of all of the books in the study, the Chinese textbooks demonstrated the most inconsistent mix of nationalized and denationalized characteristics. The books were all written in Chinese by Chinese scholars and published in China. But on many points, the books did not present China's views on and approaches to international law.[98] As one Chinese academic explained to me: "most international law academics in China believe that international law is a 'Bo Lai Pin' (舶来品, imported product)," whereas the way it is "taught in the United States and the United Kingdom is 'Zheng Zong' (正宗, authentic)."[99] Yet, on a handful of other issues, the Chinese books presented the official Chinese government line, often without giving any real sense of alternative viewpoints adopted by other states.

This two-speed approach seems in keeping with David Shambaugh's description of Chinese diplomacy as a mix of risk-averse and narrowly self-interested.[100] On most issues,

---

[96] Koskenniemi, *supra* note 17 at 1.

[97] *See, e.g.,* MAURICE KAMTO, DROIT DE L'ENVIRONNEMENT EN AFRIQUE [Environmental Law in Africa] (1996); TERESA TAN HSIEN-LI, THE ASEAN INTERGOVERNMENTAL COMMISSION ON HUMAN RIGHTS: INSTITUTIONALIZING HUMAN RIGHTS IN SOUTHEAST ASIA (2011).

[98] There are exceptions, of course, such as the famous international law textbook by Zhou Gengsheng, which was published in 1981 and frequently refers to Chinese practice, drawing on practice discussed in 中华人民共和国对外关系文件集 [Collection of External Relations Documents of the People's Republic of China]. *See* ZHOU, *supra* note 25; *see also* Hungdah Chiu, Book Review, 77 AM. J. INT'L L. 977, 978 (1983) (reviewing Zhou Gengsheng, *International Law*; Wang Tieya & Wei Min, *International Law*; Wang Tieya & Tian Ruxuan, *Selected Materials on International Law*).

[99] E-mail on file with author.

[100] DAVID SHAMBAUGH, CHINA GOES GLOBAL: THE PARTIAL POWER 9 (2014).

China takes a lowest-common-denominator approach, adopting the least controversial position and often waiting to see what other governments will do before revealing its position. It maintains a low profile and is extremely passive for a state of its size and importance, in line with Deng Xiaoping's famous dictum: "hide your strength, bide your time" (韬光养晦). On a handful of issues that concern China's narrow self-interest, however, Beijing is hypervigilant and diplomatically active. These include questions related to Taiwan, Tibet, Xinjiang, human rights, and China's maritime territorial claims.

All the same, just as the Russian books have changed during the last twenty years, so the Chinese ones may well be set to change in the next twenty years given China's increased assertiveness on the world stage.[101] In this regard, it is possible to witness the push and pull between certain denationalizing and nationalizing forces, although how the balance between them will settle remains to be seen.

A. A TWO-SPEED APPROACH IN CHINESE TEXTBOOKS

As noted above, none of the Chinese international law textbooks referred to a single domestic Chinese case dealing with international law. This absence might partly reflect the fact that the Chinese textbooks in general refer to very few cases. But, when they do refer to cases, they are invariably international or foreign. Domestic courts play a marginal role in interpreting and applying international law in China.[102] According to Congyan Cai, Chinese courts regularly apply international law in the private context, such as between individuals in cases involving the UN Convention on Contracts for the International Sale of Goods, but they are reluctant to apply it in more public cases, like those against the Chinese or other governments.[103] In China, there is a saying: "For a small case, law rules; for a mid-level case, influence rules; for a big case, politics rules." Perhaps public international law cases involving the Chinese or other governments are "big" by definition.

But the tendency to look outward rather than inward is not limited to case law. Consider, for instance, the issue of sovereign immunity. In the late nineteenth and early twentieth centuries, all states adopted the rule of absolute immunity, which means that foreign states were absolutely immune from the jurisdiction of national courts. In the early 1900s, several Western states started moving toward a restrictive approach whereby foreign states were immune for their governmental acts but not for their commercial acts. This movement started with a handful of states, including Belgium and Italy, and gained speed after World War II. In 1952, the US State Department issued the Tate letter, which indicated that the US government was switching to the restrictive approach, which was then codified in the Foreign Sovereign Immunities Act of 1976. In 1977, the UK Court of Appeal also adopted restrictive immunity. In 2004, the UN General Assembly adopted

---

[101] *See* Chapter 6.I.

[102] NOLLKAEMPER, *supra* note 12, at 55.

[103] Congyan Cai, *International Law in Chinese Courts During the Rise of China*, *in* COMPARATIVE INTERNATIONAL LAW, *supra* note 85.

the UN Convention on Jurisdictional Immunities of States and Their Property, which is based on the restrictive theory but has not yet received enough ratifications to enter into force.

Many states have since moved to adopting the restrictive approach to immunity, but China is not one of them. Nonetheless, most of the Chinese books do not refer to Chinese practice on sovereign immunity. The Bai and Zhu textbook (China) discusses the distinction between absolute and restrictive approaches to immunity purely by reference to international treaties, foreign statutes, and foreign case law.[104] It mentions no Chinese practice on the issue. The Liu and Chen casebook (China) summarizes five cases under the section on sovereign immunity, all of which are from the United States or the United Kingdom, and does not discuss the Chinese approach.[105] The Wang book (China) describes the difference between absolute and restrictive immunity, indicating that there is no clear rule either way.[106] It details how the courts of some states (for example, Belgium and Italy) began the movement toward a restrictive approach, enumerates domestic statutes of some states that have adopted restrictive immunity (for example, the United Kingdom and the United States), and cites the European Convention on State Immunity as a regional convention abandoning absolute immunity.[107] But it says nothing about China's approach.

A few books refer to Chinese practice, but only in a minimal way. For instance, the Liang, Wang, and Zeng textbook (China) observes that various states have transitioned from absolute to restrictive immunity before concluding that "Currently, most of the developed countries adopt the restrictive approach to immunity and . . . the number of developing countries that are shifting to adopt it is increasing as well."[108] As for China, the book states that

[o]n September 14, 2005, China officially signed the [UN] Convention and started the legislative process of transitioning to adopt restrictive immunity. Such practice suggests that the absolute immunity of states and their property is no longer a customary international law. However, as the Convention is still open for signature, and as a number of Latin American states are not willing to abandon the absolute approach, we cannot affirm that the restrictive approach already constitutes a customary international law.[109]

[104] BAI GUIMEI & ZHU LIJIANG (白桂梅 & 朱利江), 国际法 [International Law] 49–50 (2d ed. 2007).

[105] These were *The Schooner Exchange v. McFaddon* (an old US case endorsing the absolute approach); *The Parlement Belge* (a subsequent UK case implying a trend towards the restrictive approach); *The Arantzazu Mendi* (UK case endorsing immunity with respect to a governmental act); *The Philippine Admiral v. Wallem Shipping (Hong Kong) Ltd.* (UK case endorsing the restrictive approach); and *Trendtex Trading Corp. Ltd. v. Central Bank of Nigeria* (UK case endorsing the restrictive approach). *See* Liu JIACHEN & CHEN ZHIZHONG (刘家琛 & 陈致中), 国际法案例 [International Law Cases] 54–67 (1998).

[106] WANG TIEYA (王铁崖), 国际法 [International Law] 95 (1995).

[107] *Id.*

[108] LIANG XI, WANG XIANSHU, & ZENG LINGLIANG (梁西, 王献枢 & 曾令良), 国际法 [International Law] 88–89 (3d ed. 2011).

[109] *Id.* at 89.

None of the Chinese international law textbooks explain that Chinese courts have not exercised jurisdiction over sovereign states or that China has objected to the exercise of such jurisdiction over it by other national courts. For example, in cases against China in the United States and Hong Kong, the Chinese government has asserted absolute immunity.[110] In a 2010 case, the Court of Final Appeal of the Hong Kong Special Administrative Region clarified the Chinese approach as follows:

> The "consistent and principled position of China" in relation to state immunity is unequivocally stated in the OCMFA Letters referred to above. It is "that a state and its property shall, in foreign courts, enjoy absolute immunity, including absolute immunity from jurisdiction and from execution." There is no room for doubting that such is and has consistently been the policy of the State of the PRC.[111]

The court reached this conclusion on the basis of, inter alia, an official statement by the Chinese government explaining its signature of the 2004 UN Convention:

> China signed the Convention on 14 September 2005, to express China's support of the above coordination efforts made by the international community. However, until now China has not yet ratified the Convention, and the Convention itself has not yet entered into force. Therefore, the Convention has no binding force on China, and moreover it cannot be the basis of assessing China's principled position on relevant issues.
>
> []After signature of the Convention, the position of China in maintaining absolute immunity has not been changed, and has never applied or recognised the so-called principle or theory of "restrictive immunity."[112]

In the last paragraph, the government referenced an attached legal memorandum from the Chinese Embassy in Washington, D.C., to the US Department of State in relation to *Morris v. People's Republic of China*, in which it stated that "the Chinese side has declared a solemn position on sovereign immunity to the US side on many occasions."[113]

In her 2012 book *Chinese Contemporary Perspectives on International Law*, Xue Hanqin, the Chinese judge on the International Court of Justice, stresses that China has consistently maintained an absolute approach to immunity.[114] She notes that China

---

[110] *See, e.g.,* Voest-Alpine Trading USA Corp. v. Bank of China, 142 F.3d 887, 890–91 (5th Cir. 1998); Jackson v. China, 794 F.2d 1490, 1494 (11th Cir. 1986); Midland Inv. Co. v. Bank of Commc'ns, [1956] 40 H.K.L.R. 42, 45 (H.C.); Civil Air Transp. Inc. v. Chennault, [1950] 34 H.K.L.R. 358, 360–62 (H.C.).

[111] Dem. Rep. Congo v. FG Hemisphere Assocs. (Congo III), [2011] 14 H.K.C.F.A.R. 95, ¶ 224 (C.F.A.).

[112] *Id.* ¶ 202.

[113] Morris v. China, 478 F. Supp. 2d 561 (S.D.N.Y. 2007); FG Hemisphere Assocs. v. Dem. Rep. Congo (Congo II), [2010] 2 H.K.L.R.D. 66, ¶ 96 (C.A.) (quoting a Letter from the Office of the Comm'r of the Ministry of Foreign Affairs of China in the HKSAR, to the Constitutional and Mainland Affairs Bureau of the H.K. Gov't (May 21, 2009)). In terms of publicly available diplomatic statements, see also Foreign Broad. Info. Serv., People's Republic of China: Aide Memoire of the Ministry of Foreign Affairs, reprinted in 22 I.L.M. 75, 81 (1983).

[114] XUE HANQIN, *supra* note 26, at 85–89.

has enacted national legislative provisions that recognize the jurisdictional immunity of foreign states and certain persons entitled to immunity under international law and that Chinese courts have not exercised jurisdiction over acts of foreign states or enforced decisions involving public property of foreign states. In its foreign relations, China has been sued numerous times since the *Hukuang Railway Bonds* case in the US courts in the 1980s.[115] In those cases, China has repeatedly insisted that the absolute jurisdictional immunity of states in foreign courts remains a valid rule under international law based on the principle of sovereign equality and that there has not been enough state practice and opinio juris to change this customary international law rule. Similar points have been made by other academics.[116]

The focus on international and foreign practice over domestic practice is not unique to Chinese international law textbooks; rather, it is typical of many Chinese law courses and textbooks. The Cultural Revolution in the period 1966–76 destroyed the Chinese legal system: the Ministry of Justice was disbanded, laws were overthrown, lawyers had to find other, nonlegal jobs, and almost all law schools were closed.[117] It was not until the end of the 1970s that the Chinese legal system was revived, with the re-establishment of the Ministry of Justice and reopening of law schools. Since then, there has been a strong desire to look at models from other countries to learn about law and to think about how to build and reform the Chinese legal system. As a result, Chinese professors and textbooks often apply a comparative method and law school materials and classes are heavily influenced by similar courses taught in Western states.[118]

In international law, this tendency to focus on international and foreign practice rather than domestic practice may also partly result from the availability of materials, path dependence, and political considerations. China has not been a frequent participant in international dispute resolution, except in international trade law, and its courts have heard few domestic cases on international law, particularly cases that are reported and readily available. In terms of path dependence, one of the most well-known Chinese books on international law was written by Wang Tieya, who also translated Oppenheim's *International Law* and drew on its ideas in the formulation of his book. Wang's textbook does not include extensive discussions of Chinese state practice and many Chinese textbooks since then replicate the pattern.

In terms of political considerations, some Chinese international law academics explained that Chinese censorship has meant that most international law academics have opted to treat neutral, foreign practices rather than to engage with, characterize, or

---

[115] Jackson v. People's Republic of China, 550 F. Supp. 869 (11th Cir. 1982); Jackson v. People's Republic of China, 794 F.2d 1490 (11th Cir. 1986).

[116] *See, e.g.,* RODA MUSHKAT, ONE COUNTRY, TWO INTERNATIONAL LEGAL PERSONALITIES: THE CASE OF HONG KONG 66 (1997); Dahai Qi, *State Immunity, China and Its Shifting Position,* 7 CHINESE J. INT'L L. 307, 307 (2008); Jill A. Sgro, Comment, *China's Stance on Sovereign Immunity: A Critical Perspective on Jackson v. People's Republic of China,* 22 COLUM. J. TRANSNAT'L L. 101, 101 (1983).

[117] Carl F. Minzner, *The Rise and Fall of Chinese Legal Education,* 36 FORDHAM INT'L L.J. 334, 340–42 (2013).

[118] Ling, *supra* note 10, at 426–27; Minzner, *supra* note 117, at 350–51; Cheng Li, *The Rise of the Legal Profession in the Chinese Leadership,* CHINA LEADERSHIP MONITOR, Oct. 7, 2013.

potentially be seen as criticizing Chinese practices with respect to international law.[119] This censorship works directly: all Chinese textbooks and publications must be approved by the Ministry of Education or the State Administration of Press, Publication, Radio, Film, and Television, and approval may be denied if the books discuss sensitive issues or are seen to be critical of the state. But it also works indirectly through self-censorship: the possibility of censorship or of offending the government has meant that many academics have simply opted not to write about controversial issues in the first place. Thus, the books frequently avoid issues that are sensitive in China.

Immunity might be an example of such a sensitive topic. When I asked Chinese international law academics why Chinese practice is not cited on this topic, one answer I received was that China's position in the Hong Kong litigation (endorsing absolute immunity) was inconsistent with its signature of the UN Convention (accepting restrictive immunity). How was it possible to discuss these inconsistent approaches without appearing critical of the government? Better not to discuss them at all, I was told. But the result is that, at least for the books in this study, most students studying international law in China would not be given information about China's approach to this issue. Whether this situation will change over time, especially in light of the 2010 Hong Kong case, is anyone's guess.[120] But this case study helps to illustrate the lack of domestic focus in many areas of the Chinese international law textbooks.

Still, the Chinese books were not denationalized in all respects. On some issues of central importance to China, such as Taiwan and recognition of the PRC government as the rightful representative of China, the books present the official Chinese line without providing alternative perspectives. A good example is the books' treatment of the South China Sea disputes. Wang's book (China) starts out by citing Article 2 of the Law on the Territorial Sea and the Contiguous Zone (1992), which states: "The PRC's territorial land includes the mainland and its offshore islands, Taiwan and the various affiliated islands including Diaoyu Island, Penghu Islands, Dongsha Islands, Xisha Islands, Nansha (Spratly) Islands and other islands that belong to the People's Republic of China."[121] It then simply explains that China's government consistently and peacefully negotiates the territorial disputes over the Nansha Islands, is against the use of force, and recommends shelving disputes and carrying out joint development of disputed areas.[122]

This more nationalist approach tracks observations that have been made about Chinese international law scholarship concerning issues of central importance to China.[123] But it also creates a two-speed approach. Whereas the US books often implicitly send the

---

[119] On this point more generally, see SHAMBAUGH, *supra* note 100, at 15 ("Unlike the public policy culture in the West, Chinese scholars rarely advocate publicly that their government should do this or that, and they certainly do not explicitly criticize specific policies (to do so would be seditious).").

[120] Although this study was based on books that were current as of the end of 2013, a number of the Chinese books were 2013 reprints of 2011 editions, so they may have not been recent enough to include a 2010 case.

[121] Wang, *supra* note 106, at 200.

[122] *Id.* Another example is the Liang book (China), which states that China has had inarguable sovereignty over these islands since ancient times, and also noted that China has reached various delimitation agreements with some of its neighbors. LIANG XI (梁西), 国际法 [International Law] 166 (3d ed. 2011).

[123] *See* Chapter 5.II.B.

message that "international law is what we do," on many issues the Chinese books seem to suggest subliminally that "international law is what other states do." On a handful of issues, however, China asserts its interests and its ability to define reality, irrespective of the position of other states or international entities. On those issues, the books seem to assert that the matter is for China, not the international community, to decide.

B. FUTURE DIRECTIONS FOR CHINESE TEXTBOOKS

It will be interesting to watch how Chinese international law textbooks change as China grows in power and becomes increasingly engaged on the world stage. Two potential changes might be forecast, though they pull in opposite directions.

First, China's international law textbooks might become more westernized, at least in style, as has started to occur in its international trade law textbooks. In the lead-up to its joining the World Trade Organization (WTO), and in the years since, China invested heavily in building its international trade law expertise in government, academia, and the private sector. This effort has included developing capacity in litigation given the importance of, and China's increasing role in, WTO dispute settlement.[124] To broaden students' understanding of WTO rules, the Ministry of Commerce now organizes the China WTO Moot Court Competition with two of China's elite law schools, the China University of Politics and Law and the Southwest University of Political Science and Law. This competition, which was first held in 2012, is conducted in English and simulates WTO panel procedures with the aim of promoting the "training and selection of [China's] personnel for WTO negotiations and dispute settlement."[125]

One result of this focus on WTO dispute resolution has been that academics in China who teach WTO law have taken a leading role in introducing the case study method of teaching. As products of a civil law state, Chinese textbooks tend not to feature case law. Yet the WTO panels and Appellate Body have decided over three hundred cases, and China has been involved in around half of these as a party or third party. Understanding the jurisprudence that has emerged from these rulings is a crucial part of understanding the meaning and evolution of international trade law protections. This approach is also reinforced by the increasing number of Chinese legal academics studying international trade law in places like the United Kingdom and the United States. In the beginning, some professors translated WTO cases into Chinese.[126] More recently, some authors have begun including English excerpts of cases or writing entire casebooks in English,

---

[124] *See generally* Gregory Shaffer & Henry Gao, *From Paternalism to Partnership: The Development of WTO Law Capacity in China, in* THE CHINESE LEGAL PROFESSION IN THE AGE OF GLOBALIZATION: THE RISE OF THE CORPORATE LEGAL SECTOR AND ITS IMPACT ON LAWYERS AND SOCIETY (David Wilkins & Sida Liu eds., forthcoming 2017).

[125] *Id.*

[126] *See, e.g.,* GONG BAIHUA (龚柏华), WTO案例集 [WTO Cases] (2007); HAN LIYU (韩立余), 世界贸易组织案例分析 [WTO Case Analysis] (2002); ZHU LANYE (朱榄叶), 世界贸易组织国际贸易纠纷案例评析 [Cases Analysis of the WTO International Trade Disputes] (2008); *id.,* (2010); *id.,* (2013); *id.,* (2016).

such as Huang Dongli in his 2003 book *International Trade Law: Economic Theories, Law and Cases*, which is similar in style to American casebooks.

It remains to be seen whether similar developments will occur in public international law since Chinese universities tend to divide public international law, private international law, and international economic law into separate subject areas. In addition to its active participation in international trade litigation, China and its state-owned enterprises are beginning to become more active as disputing parties in international investment law. But China has not accepted the compulsory jurisdiction of the International Court of Justice or the International Criminal Court and, although China is a party to the UN Convention on the Law of the Sea, it strenuously objected to the jurisdiction of the arbitral tribunal in *Philippines v. China* and vowed not to comply with the award. That being said, the decision of the tribunal in that case has provoked enormous interest in China, along with reactions by many Chinese international law academics, so it is hard to imagine that this arbitration will not form part of international law courses going forward.

As Chinese legal academics increasingly study abroad, often in common law states, they are likely to gain greater familiarity with case law, which may influence the content of their materials.[127] In addition to the WTO moot, moot competitions are increasing in importance in China, including the Jessup Moot, the International Humanitarian Law Moot, and the Moot Court Competition of the International Criminal Court (ICC). The Jessup began in China in 2003, and many of its alumni have gone on to become law professors, government lawyers working for the Ministry of Foreign Affairs, and interns for or employees of international courts and tribunals or other international organizations and NGOs. This is an important development because these moot court participants typically compete in English, use English-language sources, and become adept at using common law approaches.[128] Some former moot court participants now teach classes in Chinese universities based on public international law cases.

Second, China's public international law textbooks might begin to draw more significantly on Chinese state practice in seeking to identify, interpret, and explain international law. This possibility finds some support in the October 2014 decision of the Central Committee of the Communist Party of China entitled "Decision Concerning Some Major Questions in Comprehensively Moving Forward with 'Governing the Country According to the Law.'"[129] This document provides that Marxist legal theories

---

[127] For instance, Bing Bing Jia, who completed a PhD at Oxford University under Ian Brownlie, has written a textbook that cites many cases. *See* JIA BING BING (贾兵兵), 国际公法:理论与实践 [Public International Law: Theory and Practice] (2009).

[128] *See* LIU DAN (刘丹), JESSUP模拟法庭结合国际法双语教学的探索与实践 [Exploration and Practice of Bilingual Teaching of JESSUP Moot Court in Combination with International Law], 5 云南大学学报法学版 [L. Edition J. Yunnan Univ.] 115 (2012); WEI YANRU (魏艳茹), 论Jessup国际法模拟法庭比赛对国际法本科教学的促进 [On the Promotion of International Law Teaching by the Jessup International Law Moot Court Competition], 3 黑龙江省政法管理干部学院学报 [J. Heilongjiang Admin. Cadre Inst. of Pol. & L.] 125 (2007).

[129] 中国共产党中央委员会 [Central Committee of the Communist Party of China], 中共中央关于全面推进依法治国若干重大问题的决定 [Decision Concerning Some Major Questions

and socialist rule-of-law theories with Chinese characteristics shall dominate legal education. As one step in achieving that goal, the Communist Party declared that "[u]niform core legal textbooks on a national level shall be written, edited and adopted, and shall be included and tested in the national bar examination" and that "[s]ocialist rule of law theories with Chinese characteristics shall be taught in class to cultivate legal talents who are familiar with and adhere to the socialist rule of law system with Chinese characteristics."[130]

It is too early to tell how this policy will play out. The Ministry of Education and the Ministry of Justice have previously sponsored textbooks under the "National Planned Textbooks" scheme, which includes international law textbooks like the famous one by Wang Tieya. Under the scheme, several international law textbooks were approved, and they are not noticeably more Chinese or pro-nationalist than others on the market. Under the Marxist scheme, by contrast, only one international law textbook is anticipated, and some Chinese academics have explained that its publication will mark one step in a series of efforts by China's Communist Party to become more directly involved in approving the content of university textbooks through its Department of Propaganda (中宣部), which is sometimes referred to as the Department of Public Relations.

In a 2014 speech, the minister for education confirmed the uniform textbook plan.[131] The minister stated that "the core textbooks shall reflect the latest achievement and rich practice of the rule of law with Chinese characteristics and the latest development within the discipline to the largest extent possible."[132] By way of example, a rule-of-law theory with Chinese characteristics must be elaborated in these uniform textbooks and shall be part of the essential knowledge required for the national bar examination.[133] He concluded: "Political orientation must be strengthened in the cultivation of legal talents to ensure that the universities properly employ the uniform core textbooks, the teachers properly teach the content therein and the students adequately study the content."[134]

The textbooks published under the Marxist program are meant to be privileged for use in universities, if not used exclusively: "Strong measures shall be taken to promote the adoption of such uniform core textbooks in higher education, including making them the textbooks for mandatory courses."[135] The textbook was due to be completed in late 2016 and go on sale in 2017. What its exact content will be and whether China's government will strictly require that this textbook be the only one used in law schools remain to be seen. But we could be at the start of a movement toward Chinese

in Comprehensively Moving Forward with "Governing the Country According to the Law"] (Oct. 23, 2014), http://news.xinhuanet.com/2014-10/28/c_1113015330.htm.
[130] Id.
[131] Yuan Guiren (袁贵仁), 创新法治人才培养机制 [Innovating the Training Mechanism of Rule of Law Talents], 中国教育新闻网 [China Educ. News Network], Nov. 14, 2014, http://www.jyb.cn/china/gnxw/201411/t20141114_604112.html ("Uniform core legal textbooks on a national level shall be written, edited and adopted, and shall be included and tested in the national bar examination.").
[132] Id.
[133] Id.
[134] Id.
[135] Id.

international law textbooks that are distinctly more nationalized than many of the ones now on the market.

These developments seem to accord with other measures that have been taken in China to strengthen the connection between government and the legal academy.[136] In addition to the increase in government-academic exchanges described above (Chapter 3.IV.B), a growing number of top Chinese Party political-legal authorities have delivered speeches and published editorials in state media warning of the ideological dangers posed by the infiltration of Western political, judicial, and legal concepts, which they view as resulting from increased international exchanges, accelerating globalization, and study in the West by many elite academics.[137] The growing efforts by the Chinese government to repoliticize and domesticate legal education mean that law school education bears watching as a "barometer of political change in China."[138] The content and orientation of China's international law textbooks may well evidence this change in temperature, especially as international law is typically viewed as more "political" in nature than many domestic law subjects.

IV. A Tendency to Look West

Although the books from different states varied in terms of how nationalized or denationalized they were, they were consistent on one point. When it came to looking at the practice of foreign states or the writings of foreign scholars, they tended to focus primarily on material from Western states in general, and core English-speaking Western states in particular. Two metrics used here illustrate this tendency: citation patterns to national case law and citation patterns to domestic and foreign academics. Whereas other sections often focus on differences between the books, this turn to the West represents an important similarity across many books.

The case law metric showed a more extreme tendency to look to the West in general and to US and UK practice in particular than if other metrics were adopted, like references to legislative or executive practice. Unlike cases, which are often collected in an index of cases, legislative and executive practice is harder to code because it was not typically tabulated. Even though I lacked the resources to code this practice exhaustively for the books, I was able to code it in quite a few areas, including jurisdiction, sovereign immunity, diplomatic immunity, international environmental law, use of force, statehood, human rights, and the law of the sea. As with the case citation patterns, the vast majority of foreign legislative and executive practice cited was Western, although citations to US and UK practice did not dominate as a duopoly in the same way as with the case law.

---

[136] Minzner, *supra* note 117, at 384–88.

[137] *Id.* at 369–70, 393–95; *see, e.g.,* Kou Guangping & Liu Dawei (寇广萍 & 刘大炜), 法学教育要契合我国的法治建设 [Legal Education Must Accord with National Construction of the Rule of Law], 法制日报 [Legal Daily] (Jan. 11, 2012), http://theory.people.com.cn/GB/16849963.html.

[138] Minzner, *supra* note 117, at 388.

US legislative and executive practice was by far the most heavily cited. UK practice was cited frequently, but references to it did not outstrip references to the practice of other core Western states, such as France and Germany, to the same extent as with case law. The patterns also varied according to subject area. The use of force, for instance, often brought the executive practice of the permanent members of the Security Council to the fore, bringing with it more frequent references to Russia and China, and there were also more references to the practice of other states that have frequently resorted to the use of force, such as Israel. Specific citation patterns are thus likely to vary somewhat depending on the type of practice considered and the subject area examined, though the general tendency to look primarily to the West, and particularly to the United States, was marked.

In some cases, this tendency meant that the textbooks of the Western states did not look much beyond Western practices and perspectives, which risked conveying a false sense of the universality of some of those approaches. In other cases, it meant that textbooks from the non-Western states looked to Western practice, in addition to or instead of their own domestic practice, without looking more broadly to the practice or perspectives of other non-Western states. Looking to the West is not necessarily the same thing as agreeing with the West. The Russian textbooks stood out for often juxtaposing native and Western approaches in an us-versus-them narrative, for instance. What looking to the West did signify, though, was that the practices and perspectives of certain Western states often played a disproportionate role in shaping understandings of the field.

A. LOOKING WEST IN CITATIONS TO NATIONAL COURT DECISIONS

Many international lawyers rely on national court decisions as a telling source of international law, either as evidence of state practice or as a subsidiary means of determining international law.[139] But this choice of metric often results in a primary focus on the practices of Western states in general and core English-speaking common law states in particular in a way that obscures or downplays the importance of non-Western, non-English-speaking, noncommon law states. This example reveals how one's choice of metric can influence the reality one sees, as some metrics are more likely to capture the practice of certain states than others.

To illustrate this phenomenon, consider the patterns that emerge if one breaks down all of the national court decisions (including domestic and foreign cases) referred to in these textbooks and casebooks according to the five geopolitical regional groups that states use to organize themselves at the United Nations. These groups are the African

---

[139] *See, e.g.*, Int'l Law Ass'n, Study Grp. on Principles on the Engagement of Domestic Courts with Int'l Law, Mapping the Engagement of Domestic Courts with International Law, Final Report (2016); NOLLKAEMPER, *supra* note 12; Antonios Tzanakopoulos, *Domestic Courts in International Law: The International Judicial Function of National Courts*, 34 LOY. L.A. INT'L & COMP. L. REV. 133 (2011); Anthea Roberts, *Comparative International Law? The Role of National Courts in Creating and Enforcing International Law*, 60 INT'L & COMP. L.Q. 57 (2011).

Group, which consists of fifty-four states; the Asia-Pacific Group, fifty-three states; the Eastern European Group, twenty-three states; the Latin American and Caribbean Group, thirty-three states; and the Western European and Others Group, twenty-nine states, including Canada, Australia, New Zealand, and Israel, together with the United States as an observer.

Instead of drawing on practices from a diverse array of states, these national court decisions were handed down primarily in Western states. The percentage of Western case law amounts to 29 percent of the Russian books, 75 percent of the Chinese, 95 percent of the British, 99 percent of the American, and 99.6 percent of the French (see Figure 14 below). To the extent that these books rely on national court decisions, they overwhelmingly chose Western case law, with the clear exception of Russia. Yet Russia is an outlier only because, of the national case law cited in the Russian books, a high percentage was issued by the domestic Russian courts rather than non-Western foreign courts. When it comes to foreign court citations, Russia, along with the other states, turns overwhelmingly toward Western case law at rates of 73 percent in Russia, 75 percent in China, 84 percent in the United States, 92 percent in the United Kingdom, and 99.6 percent in France.

When looking laterally at foreign case law, the textbooks and casebooks of these Western and non-Western states alike turn primarily to the case law of Western states, regardless of whether those states are geographically, linguistically, or culturally proximate to the state in which the book is being used. Within the West, foreign citations are often made primarily to the case law of two core English-speaking common law states: the United Kingdom and the United States. This result can be illustrated by breaking down

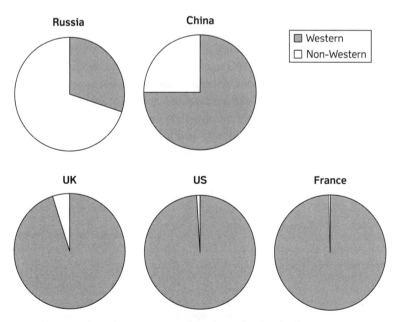

FIGURE 14 Western and non-Western National Cases Cited in Textbooks

all of the foreign cases cited according to national origin (Figure 15).[140] Looking sideways, US casebooks resort first to UK case law (55 percent), and UK books chiefly choose US case law (51 percent). The books from the other states also look first and foremost to US and UK cases—China (84 percent), France (62 percent), and Russia (46 percent); case law from no other state comes close.

Similar patterns characterize the foreign case law cited in the commonly used text-books and casebooks in a range of other states, subject to one important qualification. When books are imported from one state for use in another, such as the import of UK books into India, Spanish books into Argentina, and French books into Senegal and Cameroon, these books typically include a high percentage of domestic case law of the state from which they are imported. Thus, the French textbooks used in Senegal and Cameroon primarily select French decisions when looking at foreign decisions, and the Spanish textbook used in Argentina obviously cites mostly Spanish decisions. Subject to this exception, when looking to foreign case law, local books in a wide range of states turn primarily to US and UK case law, though common law countries feature UK case law to a greater extent than civil law countries. The figures of looking to US and UK case law were Australia (87 percent), Brazil (78 percent), Canada (79 percent), Germany (46 percent), India (83 percent), Japan (58 percent), and South Africa (90 percent).

There could be many explanations for these results. Western orientation might simply reflect the facts on the ground. It is not possible to determine how many international law cases are produced by different states, but it seems reasonable to suspect that Western liberal democratic states are responsible for the greatest number. Some states, like China, might engage in a lot of international law practice through their executives but little prac-tice through their national courts. But citations to foreign case law do not seem to be determined simply by the existence or number of judicial decisions in particular states. The domestic case law cited in textbooks of many states—including Russia, Japan, and South Africa—suggests that national decisions might have been rendered in other states without being picked up by books in still other states. Possible reasons for this omission include language, core-periphery dynamics, reasoning style, and availability.

In terms of language, foreign case citations refer overwhelmingly to decisions from English-speaking states, above all, the United States and the United Kingdom, as well as from states that publish some of their noteworthy international law decisions in English, such as Israel. This pattern is consistent with findings in comparative literature that sug-gest that if states want their decisions to be cited more frequently, they should publish them in multiple languages and especially in English.[141] Under the leadership of Aharon

---

[140] These statistics are based on determining the breakdown of citations to foreign decisions in each book and then combining the totals to get a combined picture for each state. If the same case was cited in all three books, it was recorded here three times in order to give a sense of the overall proportion of foreign cases cited across all of the books from a given state.

[141] Martin Gelter & Mathias Siems, *Networks, Dialogue or One-Way Traffic? An Empirical Analysis of Cross-Citations Between Ten of Europe's Highest Courts*, 8 UTRECHT L. REV. 88, 93 (2012); Martin Gelter & Mathias Siems, *Language, Legal Origins, and Culture Before the Courts: Cross-Citations Between Supreme Courts in Europe*, 21 SUP. CT. ECON. REV. 215, 269 (2013).

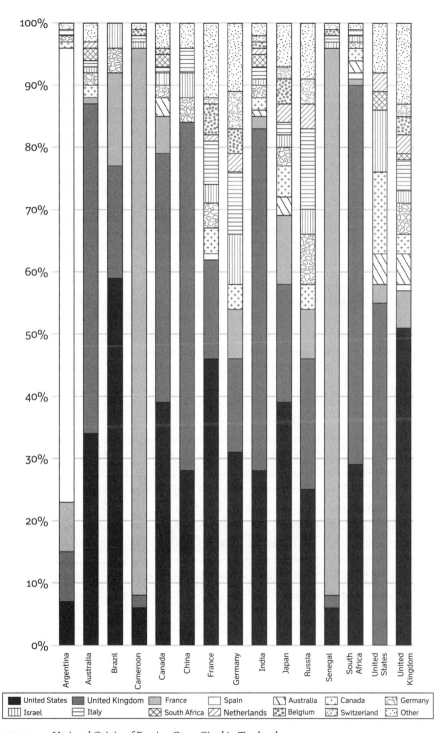

FIGURE 15 National Origin of Foreign Cases Cited in Textbooks

Barak, Israel's Supreme Court adopted this strategy, and these judgments are relatively well cited elsewhere, particularly in the US casebooks where Israeli judgments are the second most commonly cited foreign judgments after UK case law.

As for core-periphery dynamics, empirical studies of cross-citations between European courts find that small states are more likely to cite larger states than vice versa, and that states are more likely to cite within their legal system and language than between legal systems and languages.[142] For instance, Irish courts cite English courts more than the reverse, and Austrian courts cite German courts more than the other way around. This pattern might help to explain why, for example, Australian textbooks are more likely to cite UK and US case law than US and UK books are to cite Australian case law. But the prevalence of US and UK case law in the books of non-English-speaking civil law states suggests that foreign citation patterns in international law may be less bounded by language and legal family divides than in other areas of the law.

In terms of different styles of reasoning, in a study of cross-citation patterns between the high courts of ten European states, Gelter and Siems found that English and German cases tended to be highly cited, but French cases were not. They posited that French opinions are typically short and condensed in style, which makes them less useful and accessible to foreign courts than the longer and more discursive judgments of the English and German courts.[143] As common law courts often produce fully reasoned awards, these decisions might be more readily understood by international lawyers in foreign states than civil law judgments that lack fleshed-out explanations of the facts, law, and reasoning. The foreign case citation patterns above show that common law judgments are privileged over civil law ones, but do not show German decisions as privileged over French ones.

As regards availability, decisions of US and UK courts can usually be found on the Internet, which does not necessarily hold true for the decisions of all other states. To identify relevant foreign cases, international lawyers often rely on decisions that are collected and translated by sources like the International Law Reports (hosted by the Lauterpacht Centre at Cambridge University) and the International Law in Domestic Courts database (founded and coordinated by the University of Amsterdam and hosted by Oxford University Press).[144] When the domestic court decisions in these sources are divided according to national origin and geopolitical regional groupings, they are considerably more diverse than the textbooks and casebooks (see Figure 16). They still tend to feature more Western than non-Western case law (85 percent and 51 percent, respectively), but

---

[142] Gelter & Siems, Networks, *Dialogue or One-Way Traffic?, supra* note 141, at 98; Gelter & Siems, *Language, Legal Origins, and Culture, supra* note 141, at 245–53, 268.

[143] Gelter & Siems, *Language, Legal Origins, and Culture, supra* note 141, at 248; Gelter & Siems, *Networks, Dialogue or One-Way Traffic?, supra* note 141, at 93.

[144] The International Law Reports have been around since 1922, whereas the International Law in Domestic Courts database was launched only by 2007, and primarily focuses on cases decided since 2000. *See* International Law Reports, Lauterpacht Ctr. Int'l L., http://www.lcil.cam.ac.uk/publications/international-law-reports (last visited Nov. 21, 2014); Oxford Reports on International Law in Domestic Courts, Oxford Pub. Int'l L., http://opil.ouplaw.com/page/ILDC/oxford-reports-on-international-law-in-domestic-courts (last visited Nov. 21, 2014).

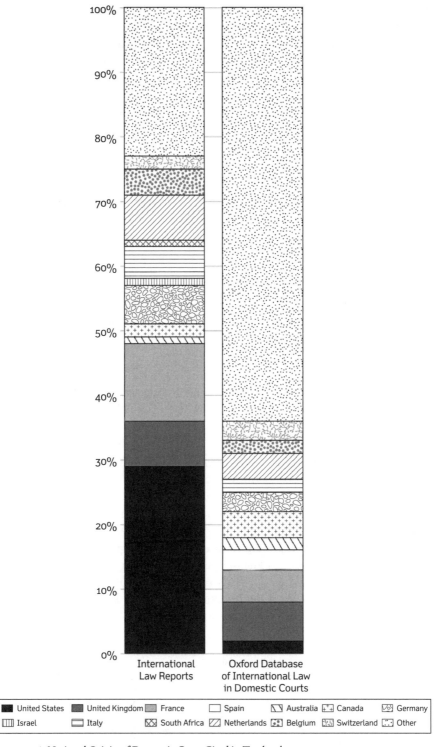

100%
90%
80%
70%
60%
50%
40%
30%
20%
10%
0%

International
Law Reports

Oxford Database
of International Law
in Domestic Courts

■ United States ■ United Kingdom France ☐ Spain Australia Canada Germany
Israel Italy South Africa Netherlands Belgium Switzerland Other

FIGURE 16 National Origin of Domestic Cases Cited in Textbooks

their emphasis on translating foreign judgments into English resulted in a lesser focus on US and UK cases (36 percent and 7 percent, respectively).

Whatever the causes of these patterns, the tendency to focus on Western case law in general, and US and UK case law in particular, has the effect of elevating the perceived importance of some states while obscuring or downplaying the apparent importance of others. It also means that international lawyers' understanding of state practice might not be representative of the approaches of a more diverse range of states because the metric that they use narrows and skews their field of vision.

B. LOOKING WEST IN CITATIONS TO ACADEMIC AUTHORITIES

According to Henry Merryman and Rodrigo Pérez-Perdomo, whereas the common law is the law of judges, the "civil law is a law of professors."[145] This element of the civil law tradition is credited as one of the reasons that teachings of the most highly qualified publicists are treated as a subsidiary source for determining international law alongside judicial decisions.[146] The lower importance that some states attribute to case law might help to explain the relative paucity of references to judicial decisions in the textbooks of certain states, most notably China and Russia. Thus, it might deepen this analysis to consider whether similar nationalizing, denationalizing, and westernizing patterns might be revealed by other metrics, such as citations to academic authorities, which may assume more influence in the legal traditions of those states.

Textbooks and casebooks differ over the extent to which they cite and privilege domestic and foreign authors. In general, Western English-language casebooks and textbooks overwhelmingly cite Western English-speaking authors. The US books predominantly cite US authors and publications, whereas the UK ones primarily cite Western English-language authorities, often from the United Kingdom and the United States, together with some French authors. The lack of diversity in these citations has been criticized. For instance, in the 1980s, Japanese international lawyer Onuma Yasuaki examined three leading US international law casebooks and found that the proportion of excerpted writings by US authors ranged from 75 percent to 98 percent—an outcome that he considered far from ideal.[147]

The French books typically refer primarily to French-speaking scholars (mainly from France) and secondarily to English-speaking scholars (generally from the United Kingdom and the United States); they make far fewer references to other European authors but on the whole these authors write in English or French. For example, the

---

[145] MERRYMAN & PÉREZ-PERDOMO, *supra* note 15, at 56.

[146] Statute of the International Court of Justice art. 38(1)(d), June 26, 1945, 59 Stat. 1031, 33 U.N.T.S. 993. *See generally* Michael Bohlander, *The Influence of Academic Research on the Jurisprudence of the International Criminal Tribunal for the Former Yugoslavia: A First Overview*, 2003 GLOB. COMMUNITY Y.B. INT'L L. & JURIS. 195; Colin B. Picker, *A Framework for Comparative Analyses of International Law and Its Institutions: Using the Example of the World Trade Organization*, *in* COMPARATIVE LAW AND HYBRID LEGAL SYSTEMS 117, 125–26 (Eleanor Cashin Ritaine et al. eds., 2010).

[147] ONUMA, *supra* note 80, at 184 n.105.

Daillier, Forteau, and Pellet book (Fr.) includes an indicative bibliography for particular subjects. The sections on sovereign immunity, state sovereignty, the ICJ Kosovo case, and jurisdiction contain references to about 125 French-speaking scholars (among whom are 90 French nationals), 50 English-speaking scholars, and 60 other foreign scholars, mostly from Italy, Germany, Spain, the Netherlands, and Austria, the majority of whose articles were published in English or French.[148]

Overall, the Western books refer to almost no non-Western scholars, whereas the Russian books include a handful of references to Western authors, and the Chinese books cite many such sources. But referring to foreign scholars and deferring to foreign scholars are different things. In his review of Latin American international law textbooks, Arnulf Becker Lorca found that some of the books created an implicit hierarchy, giving primary weight to the views of Western scholars and secondary weight to the views of local scholars.[149] A different pattern emerged in the Chinese and Russian international law textbooks, both from the Latin American textbooks and from each other.

Early Chinese international law textbooks referred primarily to Western authors rather than Chinese ones. For instance, as a review of Zhou's 1981 textbook explained:

> Each chapter . . . is annotated with references to works of all major American and European writers, including occasional references to Soviet and Japanese writers. The most frequently consulted writer is, of course, Oppenheim, and the most frequently cited journal is the American Journal of International Law. Ironically, there are no Chinese writers' views cited in the book.[150]

As the reviewer surmised, the dearth of citations to Chinese authors might be because, "at the time the author completed the manuscript, almost all Chinese international lawyers had been purged in the 1957 Anti-rightist Campaign or in the 1959 Anti-rightist Opportunism Campaign and it was simply too risky to cite their work in the manuscript."[151] The only Chinese writer cited was Wang Tieya and that was for his compilation of Chinese treaties before 1949 rather than for his scholarly writings.[152]

More recent Chinese international law textbooks frequently refer to Western and Chinese authors without generally privileging either one. For a full list of these references in three of the Chinese textbooks, see Appendix B. The foreign authors or publications

---

[148] Likewise, Dupuy & Kerbrat book (Fr.) contains twenty-seven references on the same topics, made up of nineteen references to French-speaking scholars (among whom seventeen are French nationals) and four references to English-speaking scholars (including one article that was published in French), and a handful of articles by foreign scholars that were typically not written in the scholar's native language. PIERRE-MARIE DUPUY & YANN KERBRAT, DROIT INTERNATIONAL PUBLIC [Public International Law] (11th ed. 2012).

[149] Arnulf Becker Lorca, *International Law in Latin America or Latin American International Law? Rise, Fall, and Retrieval of a Tradition of Legal Thinking and Political Imagination*, 47 HARV. INT'L L.J. 283, 288–89 (2006) ("[T]he main argument is presented through the works and ideas of the 'great' English, French, and German scholars," which is then "embellished with more precise content through comments provided by a 'second echelon' of scholarship, usually occupied by Spanish authors.").

[150] Hungdah Chiu, *supra* note 98, at 978.

[151] *Id.*

[152] *Id.*

referred to in these books come primarily from the United Kingdom, the United States, and Germany, as can be seen from the tables of the authors and materials cited in three of the Chinese international law textbooks. There are almost no citations of authors that are neither Chinese nor Western and many foreign citations are to Chinese translations of Western (often UK) texts. Indeed, some Chinese scholars listed the most significant Chinese translations of international law textbooks as:

- Ian Brownlie, *Principles of Public International Law*, translated by Zeng Linliang and others, Law Press, 2003 (UK book);
- Antonio Cassese, *International Law*, translated by Cai Congyan and others, Law Press, 2009 (Italian author but written in English and published by Oxford University Press);
- Robert Jennings & Arthur Watts, *Oppenheim's International Law*, 9th edition, translated by Wang Tieya and others, Encyclopedia of China Publishing House, 1995 (UK book);
- Hans Kelsen, *Principles of International Law*, translated by Wang Tieya, Huaxia Press, 1989 (Austrian author but based in the United States);
- Hersch Lauterpacht, *Oppenheim's International Law*, 8th edition, translated by Wang Tieya and others, The Commercial Press, 1971 (UK book);
- Malcolm N. Shaw, *International Law*, translated by Bai Guimei, Peking University Press, 2011 (UK book);
- Grigory Tunkin, *International Law*, translated by Shao Tianren, Law Press, 1988 (Russian book);
- Alfred Verdroß, *International Law*, translated by Li Haopei, The Commercial Press, 1981 (Austrian book); and
- Henry Wheaton, *Elements of International Law*, translated by W.A.P. Martin, Tsungli Yamen, 1864 (US book).[153]

By contrast, the Russian textbooks mainly cite domestic authors and contain only a handful of references to foreign authors. For a full list of these references in three of the Russian manuals, see Appendix B. In terms of Russian/Soviet authors, Igor Lukashuk, Chernichenko, Grigory Tunkin, and Friedrich Martens are staple references. Russian international law textbooks also frequently cite other Russian international law textbooks. The exception to this rule is a handful of references to foreign texts, most of which were translated into Russian or are in English. Of all the Russian books, the most commonly cited foreign authors are

---

[153] Other translations include: TIM HILLER, PRINCIPLES OF PUBLIC INTERNATIONAL LAW (Qu Bo trans., 2006) (UK book); FEDOR IVANOVICH KOZHEVNIKOV, INTERNATIONAL LAW (Liu Sha trans., 1985) (Russian book); NIKOLAOS POLITIS, LES NOUVELLES TENDANCES DU DROIT INTERNATIONAL [The New Aspects of International Law] (Yuan Jiang trans., 2004) (Greek author but written in French); BISWANATH SEN, A DIPLOMAT'S HANDBOOK OF INTERNATIONAL LAW AND PRACTICE (Zhou Xiaolin trans., 1987) (Indian author but written in English and originally published by Brill Academic Publishers); J.G. STARKE, AN INTRODUCTION TO INTERNATIONAL LAW (Zhao Weitian trans., 1984) (UK book). E-mails on file with the author.

Brownlie (UK: *Principles of International Law*), Shaw (UK: *International Law*), Oppenheim (UK: *International Law*), Cassese (Italian, but the book is written in English: *International Law*), and Eduardo Jiménez de Aréchaga (Uruguayan and former ICJ president: *El derecho internacional contemporáneo* (*Contemporary International Law*)).

In many cases, a specific edition of these foreign books was translated into Russian and that translation continues to be cited despite growing increasingly out of date. Thus, it is common to find references to the 1959 version of Verdroß's *Mezhdunarodnoe pravo*, the 1971 version of D. Anzilotti's *Kurs mezhdunarodnoga pravo*, the 1983 version of Jiménez de Aréchaga's *Sovremennoe mezhdunarodnoe pravo*, the 1949–50 version of Oppenheim's *Mezhdunarodnoe pravo*, and various versions of Brownlie's *Mezhdunarodnoe pravo*. One Russian scholar saw this practice as possibly accounting for why some Russian international law debates, such as on the status of the individual, seem like throwbacks to older Western debates:

> Russian international law discourse is not an original kind of discourse but, rather, appears to be a simplified, outdated version of the Western discourse. This feature is exemplified in academic texts. The field's scholarship is limited mostly to textbooks—there have been very few high-quality, well-written monographs published in post-Soviet times, as the "Old Guard" prefers to keep re-publishing the same textbooks originally authored as long as several decades ago.[154]

Although Western scholars had moved on from some of these issues, many of the ideas from the West that permeated Russian international law scholarship were transported by particular vehicles, like translated textbooks, and they often engendered time capsules in Russia with respect to the relevant international law approaches and debates. According to the same Russian international lawyer:

> Russian international law discourse is not autonomous. Legal architecture is internationalized. But the discourse is still a bad mirror image of the Western one. This image is particularly distorted due to the language barrier . . . [T]here are a handful of foreign books cited in Russian international law textbooks. The list includes Brownlie and Jimenez de Arechaga. There are a few random books in outdated editions. New sources enter the discourse slowly.[155]

During the Cold War, Soviet international law textbooks frequently compared the approaches of "otechestvennaya literatura" (meaning Russian authors) and "zapadnaya" (Western) or sometimes "zarubezhnaya" (foreign) literature on international law. During this period, the distinction between native and Western authors had a clear qualitative inflection, with "native" connoting trustworthy and "Western" connoting suspicious and erroneous. Even though the qualitative overtones were largely erased after the collapse

---

[154] E-mail on file with author.
[155] *Id.*

of the Soviet Union, this distinction still pervades Russian international law textbooks, as foreign and Russian authorities are clearly distinguished and the latter are often given special visibility.[156] Mälksoo characterizes this insistence on intellectual independence as a frequent hallmark of great powers: "Such states and academic cultures tend to be self-centric and self-referential; they subjectively feel that intellectually they have already got 'it all' and do not need to refer to or 'borrow' much from the others who, through their otherness, also happen to appear less trustworthy."[157]

In some instances, Russian and foreign scholars are cited as equally authoritative. For example, Shumilov's section on international economic law cites Mark Boguslavskii, G. E. Buvailik, Aleksandr Kovalev, Tunkin, Valerii Kuznetsov, and Nikolai Ushakov, among others, as relevant Russian sources, and Brownlie, Philip Jessup, and Wolfgang Friedmann, among others, as relevant foreign authors. Likewise, Tolstykh's chapter on jurisdiction refers to both Russian and foreign scholars, including Vaughan Lowe, Patrick Daillier, and Alain Pellet (foreign), and Ts. Berezovskii (Russian). In other circumstances, Western and Russian authors are juxtaposed with an implicit hierarchy that favors the Russian writers. Sometimes the distinctions seem technical. For instance, in "Western doctrine," the Kovalev and Chernichenko book (Rus.) explains, "the term 'reparation' is used in the broad sense as an umbrella term."[158] This notion stands in contrast to Russian doctrine, which, "in addition to reparation and restitution, also distinguishes between restoration and substitution."[159] On other occasions, the differences seem overtly political. For example, the same book notes that

[t]here is a widespread point of view in the Western doctrine, which has it that only intervention in the narrow sense of the threat or use of force is illegal, i.e., "dictatorial" intervention. . . . In Russian doctrine and practice, there is a different point of view, which holds that any intervention is forbidden. This includes attempts to raise a question with an international body if that question relates to the internal authority of a State.[160]

Whereas the Chinese and Russian books adopted different approaches in their treatment of domestic and foreign authors and doctrines, they are all similar in one respect: when they look to foreign scholars and doctrine, they overwhelmingly seek the

---

[156] Mälksoo, *supra* note 34, at 272.

[157] *Id.* This phenomenon may be stronger with respect to public international law than other legal areas, such as private international law. For instance, comparative legal scholarship has gained popularity in private international law, particularly given the reforms of the Russian Civil Code to bring it into line with European Union rules and to modernize it in light of successful experiences in other European civil code-based states. *See generally* Указ Президента Российской Федерации «О совершенствовании Гражданского Кодекса Российской Федерации» [Presidential Decree of the Russian Federation on Improvement of Civil Code of the Russian Federation], Собрание законодательства Российской Федерации [SZ RF] [Russian Collection of Legislation] 2008, No. 29, p. 3482.

[158] Kovalev & Chernichenko, *supra* note 37, at 240.

[159] *Id.*

[160] *Id.* at 52.

positions of Western authors and states. The textbook writers do not always agree with the Western approaches, but they feature them nonetheless. They did not seriously consider practices or writings from non-Western states, even from their own region or like-minded states. The resulting impression was that the non-Western books often look to the West, whereas the Western books often fail to look past the West.

V. A Lack of Diverse Comparativism

One of the problems about looking primarily to, or failing to look significantly past, domestic or Western case law and practice is that it can result in an inaccurate understanding of state practice and a false sense of universality. One way to guard against these problems is by adopting a more comparative approach to international law that captures domestic and foreign practice and gives due credit to divergent practices. On this measure, the UK textbooks are often more comparative and diverse in their content and orientation than the US casebooks and French textbooks, though they still tend to privilege practice from Western or common law states.

The French, UK, and US books all include considerable case citations and discussions, but the UK books refer to a much higher percentage of foreign cases than their French and US counterparts. In percentage terms, 29 percent of the opinions cited in the UK books were issued by foreign courts compared with 3 percent and 6 percent for the French and US books, respectively. The ratio of domestic cases to foreign cases constitutes a rough measure of how strongly books from a particular state feature that state's own experience with international law compared with other states' experience. The UK books feature domestic cases less than foreign cases by a ratio of 20:29, whereas the French and US books refer to domestic cases about ten times more often than foreign ones, by ratios of 64:6 and 28:3, respectively.

When looking externally at international and foreign cases, one can get a sense of how horizontal (comparative) or vertical (international) the approaches of these books are by examining the percentage of cases referred to that are foreign. A completely vertical approach would be 0 percent, as the book would consider international decisions but not foreign ones. A completely horizontal approach would be 100 percent, as the book would consider foreign decisions but not international ones. A book that equally cites both would be 50 percent. On this measure, France is largely international but not comparative with 6 percent, the United Kingdom is both international and comparative with 34 percent, and the United States falls in between with 17 percent. The US books largely focus on domestic case law, the French ones largely focus on domestic and international case law, and the UK books focus on all three.

There could be many explanations for the different levels of emphasis on foreign decisions. First, books from common law states might be inclined to draw more heavily on foreign case law than books from civil law states, and this effect might be particularly pronounced for books from Commonwealth states given their courts' and academics' long history of citing the courts of other Commonwealth states. This finding would conform with comparative studies in other areas of the law that have found that more borrowing occurs between common law states than civil law ones and that borrowing is especially strong among members of the Commonwealth.[161] By contrast, of all of the common law books analyzed in this study, the US books refer to the lowest percentage of foreign case law, which is consistent with the low levels of citations to foreign case law by US courts in general.[162]

Second, language differences may play a role in case selections. The French textbooks contain 69 percent international cases as against 3 percent foreign cases. French writers can easily cite international cases because French is one of the official languages of the United Nations, and it is one of two working languages of many international courts and tribunals, including the ICJ, the Permanent Court of International Justice, the ICC, the International Tribunal for the former Yugoslavia (ICTY), and the International Tribunal for the Law of the Sea. Full versions of the websites of the ICJ and the ICC appear in two languages only: English and French. Cases are heard in both languages, and judgments are typically handed down in both languages. However, in some other forms of international dispute resolution, like investment treaty arbitration, English awards are significantly more common.

One French international lawyer explained to me that the abundance of domestic French cases and international cases in French resulted in little need to examine foreign decisions. French textbooks could cite judgments from other Francophone countries, but since France is the core of the Francophone world, it is less likely to look outward to case law of states on the Francophone periphery and semiperiphery. The position is different for other non-English-speaking states like Germany and Japan. As the languages of losing powers in World War II, neither German nor Japanese was adopted as a working language of the United Nations or international courts and tribunals. The textbooks from these states must rely on foreign language judgments or translations regardless of whether the decisions are international or foreign, and their textbooks refer to a higher percentage of foreign decisions than the French books.[163]

Third, the relative dearth of references to foreign decisions in the US books compared with the UK books might partly stem from their nature as casebooks rather than textbooks. It is much easier to refer to foreign cases in passing, or to summarize and explain their facts and legal holdings, in a textbook than to extract their texts in a casebook, given the difficulties with translations and problems posed by different styles of judicial writing. Nevertheless, the use of casebooks does not explain why the US books often do not extract decisions from other English-speaking common law states whose judgments should be easier for US students to understand than translated civil law decisions. It also

---

[161] Holger Spamann, *Contemporary Legal Transplants: Legal Families and the Diffusion of (Corporate) Law*, 2009 BYU L. Rev. 1813, 1818, 1830–31 (2009).

[162] *See* David Zaring, *The Use of Foreign Decisions by Federal Courts: An Empirical Analysis*, 3 J. Empirical Legal Stud. 297, 326 (2006) (empirical study of surveys of sixty years of US federal court practice in citing opinions from of foreign high courts resulted in the conclusion that the "number of citations to foreign authority is minuscule compared to the citations to traditional domestic law, and it has not increased").

[163] The German textbooks included an average of 7 percent foreign cases, whereas the Japanese ones included an average of 12 percent foreign cases.

does not explain why these US books often do not refer at all or extensively to foreign practice in the notes and comments that follow case extractions.

Whatever the causes, by failing to be comparative, or by being comparative without being diverse, international law textbooks can project an inaccurate or insufficiently nuanced account of state practice and can give the mistaken impression that the featured approach is universally adopted or relatively uncontroversial. This problem is well illustrated by two examples: how certain US casebooks explain the principle of male captus, bene detentus (unlawful capture, lawful detention); and how many Western books describe the status of the doctrines of absolute and restrictive sovereign immunity.

A. TEXTBOOKS THAT LACK A COMPARATIVE APPROACH

Some US casebooks fail to take a comparative approach when explaining the male captus, bene detentus rule, whereas many UK textbooks take a comparative approach. For example, the Damrosch book (US) starts by posing the question: "If a state improperly seizes a person accused of a crime outside of its borders, may it nevertheless properly exercise judicial jurisdiction over this person in the United States?"[164] To enable students to answer this question, the book extracts sections of *United States v. Alvarez-Machain*, where the majority of the US Supreme Court found that US courts could exercise jurisdiction to adjudicate over an individual who had been abducted from Mexico and brought to the United States to stand trial, even though an extradition treaty was in force between the two states. The minority decried this decision on the basis that "most courts throughout the civilized world will be deeply disturbed by th[is] 'monstrous' decision."[165]

In the notes, the Damrosch book (US) states that "[t]he traditional rule of international law is that of 'male captus, bene detentus,' i.e., that a person who has been improperly seized may nevertheless properly be tried."[166] The book explains that this rule follows from the principle that "only the state in the territory of which the person was captured could complain."[167] But the book notes that US courts have exercised jurisdiction to adjudicate even when the offended state objects, such as in *Alvarez-Machain*.[168] It asks whether the Court should have considered if the violation of international law meant that US officials lacked the constitutional power to prosecute the person and, if so, whether the appropriate sanction should have been dismissal.[169] The book indicates that *Alvarez-Machain* "generated widespread international criticism" and asks whether an unratified treaty entered into by the United States and Mexico to prohibit the exercise of jurisdiction in such cases "reflect[ed] a rule of customary international law."[170]

---

[164] LORI FISLER DAMROSCH, LOUIS HENKIN, SEAN MURPHY, & HANS SMIT, INTERNATIONAL LAW 825 (5th ed. 2009) [hereinafter DAMROSCH ET AL.].

[165] *Id.* at 819–25.

[166] *Id.* at 825–26.

[167] *Id.* at 826.

[168] *Id.*

[169] *Id.*

[170] *Id.* at 826–27.

The Damrosch book (US) accurately states US law. It also makes assertions about international law rules and asks students for their view on the content of customary international law. But it refers to no practice from other states. The book observes that the *Alvarez-Machain* case generated international controversy but fails to provide any details. It cites no foreign case law on the subject. It provides no discussion of the division of foreign state practice on this issue or the significant shifts it has undergone in the last few decades. Instead, it extracts both *Alvarez-Machain*, which refers to several other US cases but no foreign cases, and the *Restatement (Third) of the Foreign Relations Law of the United States*. It also refers to some US journal articles and one US roundtable event.[171]

In comparison, the Harris book (UK) takes a much more international and comparative approach to the issue. After extracting sections of the Israeli *Eichmann* case, the book sets forth a note entitled "Illegally obtained custody."[172] The section begins with a discussion of the *Savarkar* case, an arbitration between France and the United Kingdom, before turning to the *Lawler Incident*, which involved a dispute between the United Kingdom and Spain.[173] After referencing a case note discussing a US-Canadian dispute, the book cites *Ex parte Elliot* from Israel as authority for the proposition that the Israeli courts were prepared to adjudicate claims against Eichmann despite his having been illegally abducted from Argentina.[174]

The Harris book (UK) notes that inconsistent decisions on this issue have been rendered but that the law has "now to an extent been clarified" by *Regina v. Horseferry Road Magistrates Court, ex parte Bennett*, which "reaches the opposite conclusion."[175] The book provides a short extract from the *Bennett* case, which held that where a person is illegally brought before a UK court in violation of an extradition treaty, and UK officials have been a knowing party in that process, the UK courts will refuse to hear the case.[176] The book asks whether the difference between *Eichmann* and *Bennett* could be justified on the basis that the former involved a crime against the state's security, whereas the latter involved an ordinary crime.[177] The book then indicates that approaches in other states vary, contrasting decisions by the New Zealand and South African courts that ruled against the exercise of jurisdiction in cases of abduction with the US *Alvarez-Machain* case, which permitted the exercise of jurisdiction even in the face of an extradition treaty.[178]

The Harris book (UK) takes a much more comparative approach to this issue than the Damrosch book (US), but it still tends to refer predominantly to decisions of other English-speaking common law courts. For instance, it does not refer to the practice of the

---

[171] *Id.* at 818–27. The only foreign source cited is a reference within the Alvarez-Machain dissent to the 1955 edition of Oppenheim, which itself did not address this issue and, in any event, predated the shifts in foreign state practice.

[172] DAVID J. HARRIS, CASES AND MATERIALS ON INTERNATIONAL LAW 247–50 (7th ed. 2010).

[173] *Id.* at 247–48.

[174] *Id.* at 248.

[175] *Id.*

[176] *Id.* at 249.

[177] *Id.*

[178] *Id.* at 249–50.

French and German courts.[179] Nor does it refer to relevant authorities from international courts and tribunals, such as the ICTY.[180] The UK book does not parse the extent to which national courts that have asserted discretion to decline to prosecute have done so as a matter of domestic or of international law. Nor does it address the fact that national courts seem less likely to apply the male captus, bene detentus rule when the injured state protests the violation of its sovereignty or officials from the prosecuting state are implicated in the unlawful abduction,[181] but more likely to apply it when the underlying crime is of universal concern.[182]

Although this discussion features one book from each state, similar points could be made of some of the other US and UK books.[183] For instance, the Carter and Weiner book (US) discusses this principle mainly through excerpts of the *Restatement (Third)* and the *Alvarez-Machain* case, along with some discussion of an Iranian statute and an Iranian civil damages action.[184] By contrast, the Crawford book (UK) states that abducting a suspect is clearly a breach of international law but, depending on the state in question, that illegality might not prevent the suspect from being tried.[185] The book then contrasts the US approach in *Alvarez-Machain* with the UK and South African approaches in *Bennett* and *Ebrahim*, respectively. It also notes that various European states used to accept jurisdiction in such cases, but that this practice had changed under the European Convention for the Protection of Human Rights and Fundamental Freedoms, citing a French case, a German case, and a pending case before the European Court of Human Rights.[186]

B. TEXTBOOKS THAT ARE COMPARATIVE BUT NOT NECESSARILY DIVERSE

An example of what might be missed by taking a comparative, but not necessarily diverse, approach to foreign practice can be found in the treatment of sovereign immunity by many of the Western international law textbooks.

---

[179] *See, e.g.*, Re Argoud, 45 I.L.R. 90 (Cass. crim. 1964) (Fr.); BVerfG, 2 BvR 1190/84, July 17, 1985 (Ger.); BGH Aug. 2, 1984, 2 StR 120/83 (Ger.).

[180] *See, e.g.*, Prosecutor v. Nikolić, Case No. IT-94-2-AR73, Appeals Chamber Decision on Interlocutory Appeal Concerning Legality of Arrest (June 5, 2003), http://www.icty.org/x/cases/dragan_nikolic/acdec/en/030605.pdf.

[181] *See, e.g.*, HARRIS, *supra* note 172, at 249 (State v. Ebrahim; R. v. Hartley).

[182] *See, e.g.*, Fédération National des Déportées et Internés Résistants et Patriots v. Barbie (The "Barbie" Trial), 78 I.L.R. 124 (Cass. crim. 1985) (Fr.); Attorney Gen. of Isr. v. Eichmann, 36 I.L.R. 277, 306 (CrimA 1962) (Isr.).

[183] This characterization is not true of the Dunoff book, which is much more comparative on this point than its US peers. It starts out by discussing a relevant ICTY case, before extracting some of the Eichmann case and the Alvarez-Machain case. It notes the strong international reaction to the Alvarez-Machain decision, citing international protests from China, Colombia, Costa Rica, Cuba, Denmark, Ecuador, Guatemala, Honduras, Jamaica, Malaysia, and Venezuela. The book examines reactions to the US decision in several multilateral forums, including the UN Working Group on Arbitrary Detention and an advisory opinion by the Inter-American Juridical Committee. It then looks at domestic court decisions in other states, citing or extracting sections from Bennett (UK), Levinge (Australia), Ebrahim (South Africa), Beahan (Zimbabwe), Ocalan (ECtHR), several ICTY decisions, and El-Masri (ECtHR). *See* JEFFREY L. DUNOFF ET AL., INTERNATIONAL LAW: NORMS, ACTORS, PROCESS: A PROBLEM-ORIENTED APPROACH 356–77 (3d ed. 2010).

[184] Carter & Weiner, *supra* note 71, at 700–05.

[185] JAMES CRAWFORD, BROWNLIE'S PRINCIPLES OF PUBLIC INTERNATIONAL LAW 483 (8th ed. 2012).

[186] *Id.*

A 2015 study of the movement from absolute to restrictive immunity suggested that about two-thirds of states now adopt the restrictive approach, but around one-third still embrace the absolute immunity rule based on pronouncements by their courts, legislatures, and executives.[187] Without seeking to support or challenge this study, this analysis surveys the Western international law textbooks and casebooks for the information they supply so as to enable scholars or students to test the veracity of this claim. The US and UK books describe the arc of the story as a transition from the adoption of absolute immunity by all states toward the adoption of restrictive immunity by many or most states. They cite evidence of this transition, including cases from the United States, the United Kingdom, Canada, France, and Germany, and statutes from Australia, the United States, and the United Kingdom. A handful of books also cite evidence from farther afield, including Argentina, South Africa, Pakistan, and Malaysia. This practice crosses Western/non-Western, civil/common law, and English-/non-English-speaking divides. But it is not diverse on another measure: all of these states now apply the restrictive approach to immunity.

Most of these books make little reference to the contrary position of absolute immunity or to how many states might still embrace it. Moreover, not all these states could be dismissed as minor powers with little impact on the creation of international law; they include, among others, China, India, and (at the time the casebooks and textbooks were written) Russia.[188] That is not to say that the books assert that there is consensus on the matter, but the amount of space given to the contrary state practice is limited. A state that accepts a restrictive approach to immunity is certainly likely to generate more case law on the subject than one that follows an absolute approach. But these textbooks and casebooks typically incorporate no citation to or extracts of primary materials from the executives, legislatures, or courts of the non-Western states that take an absolute approach. In addition, the veracity of the positions of these states is often called into question by the authors. As a result, contrary state practice is often de-emphasized or discredited.

For instance, the Carter and Weiner book (US) explains that, despite the historical importance of the theory of absolute immunity, "[n]ow existing in the United States, *and generally elsewhere*, is a limited scope for state immunity, often termed the 'restrictive' theory."[189] After spending sixty-five pages extracting the Tate letter of the US

---

[187] Pierre-Hugues Verdier & Erik Voeten, *How Does Customary International Law Change? The Case of State Immunity*, 50 INT'L STUD. Q. 209, 214 (2015).

[188] Russian legislation has since changed on this issue. On January 1, 2016, the Federal Law on Jurisdictional Immunity of a Foreign State and a Foreign State's Property in the Russian Federation entered into force. This legislation aimed at abolishing the old rule of absolute sovereign immunity, and to replace it with the restrictive approach to sovereign immunity subject to the condition of reciprocity. *See* Федеральный Закон Российской Федерации «О юрисдикционных иммунитетах иностранного государства и имущества иностранного г осударства в Российской Федерации» [Federal Law of the Russian Federation on Jurisdictional Immunities of a Foreign State and a Foreign State's Property in the Russian Federation], Собрание законодательства Российской Федерации [SZ RF] [Russian Collection of Legislation] 2015, No. 45, p. 6198. For a description in English, see Peter Roudik, Laws Lifting Sovereign Immunity: Russia, Libr. Cong., http://www.loc.gov/law/help/sovereign-immunity/russia.php (last updated Oct. 26, 2016).

[189] Carter & Weiner, *supra* note 71, at 535 (emphasis added).

Department of State, many US cases, and the US Foreign Sovereign Immunities Act, the section adds five pages under the rubric "The Current Status of Foreign Sovereign Immunity Outside the United States."[190] This section discusses the position of the United Kingdom, Germany, Italy, and France, and the European Convention on State Immunity, all of which embrace the restrictive approach. There is no discussion of the practice of Russia or India. As for China, it is allotted one paragraph out of seventy pages, with a citation to a book chapter by a US academic specialist on China to the effect that China "still purports to follow the absolute theory of immunity," but the book notes that "Chinese authorities . . . have reportedly been more willing recently to negotiate contractual provisions that waive the sovereign immunity of Chinese government entities in foreign courts or international arbitral arrangements."[191]

The Damrosch casebook (US) offers slightly more detail, stating: "While the clear trend today continues to be toward a more limited concept of immunities in international law and practice, [citing a conference paper by a US government lawyer], many countries still adhere to absolute immunity, including many in the developing world."[192] The book notes that the Soviet Union and its allies endorsed the absolute approach during the Cold War, but that "[n]ow that those formerly communist states have opted for a more market-oriented approach, they may be more inclined to the restrictive approach to sovereign immunity, though to date Russia remains an adherent to absolute immunity before its courts."[193] The book recounts that "China also *still purports* to embrace the absolute theory [citing the same book chapter by the same US professor as above]" and draws attention to an article by a Chinese scholar in the *Chinese Journal of International Law* for an "analysis that China may shift to the restrictive immunity doctrine."[194] This contrary practice receives only three paragraphs out of sixty-five pages, no underlying materials are extracted, and an implicit question mark is placed over it.

The Dunoff casebook (US) discusses sovereign immunity only from the perspective of US practice, without adverting to the possibility of divergent US and international approaches or the lack of an agreed-upon position under international law.[195]

By contrast, the Evans textbook (UK) gives a more nuanced account, noting that (1) many common law states apply the restrictive doctrine by means of legislation or case law, citing the United States, the United Kingdom, Australia, Canada, Malaysia, Pakistan, Singapore, and South Africa, as well as Malawi, Kenya, Ireland, New Zealand, Zimbabwe, and Nigeria; and (2) many civil law systems, for example, those of France and other Western or central European countries, have also adopted the restrictive approach, citing a study on the states belonging to the Council of Europe.[196] The book finds that, as to countries that have enacted no legislation and whose courts have heard no or few

---

[190] *Id.* at 599–604.

[191] *Id.* at 604.

[192] DAMROSCH ET AL., *supra* note 164, at 859.

[193] *Id.* at 859–60.

[194] *Id.* at 860 (emphasis added).

[195] DUNOFF ET AL., *supra* note 183, at 377–97.

[196] Evans, *supra* note 72, at 346–47.

proceedings, their position is "more difficult to ascertain" but that "some have indicated tentative signs of moving to a restrictive position."[197] Russian legislation made provision for reform of the absolute rule, but no such law had been enacted at the time the Evans book was published.[198] The book also notes that China had enacted a 2005 national law providing for judicial immunity from execution of central banks of foreign states, citing a Hong Kong case, and that "as a member of the WTO and signatory to other international conventions [China had] indicated a willingness to consent to applying a restrictive rule in its courts," citing a Chinese scholar.[199]

The Evans book (UK) then turns to the 2004 UN Convention on the Jurisdictional Immunities of States and Their Property, which adopts the restrictive approach to immunity. It explains that, as of March 2010, it had been signed by twenty-eight states, including China and Russia, and ratified by eight states.[200] The book reasons that "[a]rguably China and Russia as signatory States" are "obliged to refrain from acts which would defeat the object and purpose of the 2004 Convention" and hence would be "obliged to refrain from continuing activity to support an absolute rule contrary to the provisions of the 2004 convention."[201] But the book observes that the Convention will not enter into force until it has been ratified by thirty states, so that, for the time being, it remains necessary to ascertain the current law by construing the treaty's provisions by reference to the extent that they are supported by state practice.[202]

France has adopted the restrictive approach to immunity and the French books trace the same general arc as the above books, detail relevant French cases, and cite UK and US cases and legislation in support of the restrictive approach. They typically do not demonstrate any evidence of contrary approaches. For instance, the Combacau and Sur book (Fr.) notes that immunity is a subject of both international and domestic law, first detailing the international law rules on this subject (citing sources like the US and UK immunity statutes) and then examining French practice.[203] They state that the practice of restrictive immunity began in industrialized states with market economies but that the "more and more visible homogeneity of such national practices, even though not absolute, nonetheless enabled international customary rules to arise and its codification to be taken into consideration" in the drafting of the UN Convention.[204] They do not discuss contrary practice.

The Dupuy and Kerbrat book (Fr.) relates that domestic tribunals (including French courts) differentiate between sovereign and commercial activities of foreign states and that, in the United States, the United Kingdom, and Canada, this distinction has been

---

[197] *Id.* at 347.

[198] *Id.*

[199] *Id.*

[200] David P. Stewart, *Introductory Note on the UN Convention on Jurisdictional Immunities of States and Their Property*, 44 I.L.M. 801 (2005).

[201] Evans, *supra* note 72, at 347–48.

[202] *Id.* at 348–49.

[203] Jean Combacau & Serge Sur, Droit international public [Public International Law] 248–51 (10th ed. 2012).

[204] *Id.* at 248–49.

concretized by legislation.[205] The book indicates that the work of the International Law Commission on immunities was subject to many criticisms but eventually led to the UN Convention. It sets forth in detail various problems with the Convention, which the authors believe might explain why the necessary threshold for the Convention to enter into force has not yet been reached.[206] Nevertheless, they note that states are not as hostile to the text as they used to be and that France ratified the Convention in 2011. They explain that this change is encouraged by international courts, which refer to the UN Convention as expressing customary international law, at least in part.[207] Their book does not discuss contrary practice.

The Daillier, Forteau, and Pellet book (Fr.) declares that states no longer assert the system of absolute immunity, pointing out that almost every state applies the restrictive approach set out by Belgian and Italian courts since the end of the nineteenth century.[208] The evolution in favor of restrictive immunity was enshrined in the 1972 European Convention, which led the United Kingdom to reverse its approach.[209] The UN Convention then endorsed the restrictive approach, and its provisions partly codified the solutions developed by national jurisdictions, even though many divergences in state practice remained.[210] These divergences are not enumerated.

The Western books accurately describe a shift in state practice from the adoption of the absolute approach to immunity by all states to the adoption of a restrictive approach by a majority. Yet by concentrating so much on states that have made this shift, they have tended to sideline the practice of states that still endorse the absolute approach. They also often call into question the veracity of the practice of some of these states, which creates the impression that any residual holdouts in favor of absolute immunity are likely to give in over time. That may be true, Russia being a case in point. But it is not necessarily the case, and some non-Western powers that are rising in importance, most notably China and India, are still proponents of the absolute approach, at least in some of their actions and statements. The conclusion once again is that by failing to take a diverse, comparative approach to a given practice, textbooks can create a false sense of the universality or uncontroversial nature of that practice, whether it is from the book's own state or from other like-minded states.

VI. Divisions Between the Western and Non-Western Books

The Western and non-Western books often emphasize different subjects and betray different ideological underpinnings about what the law is or should be. Some of these differences can be seen in the way these books treat the law of outer space and unilateral humanitarian intervention.

---

[205] Dupuy & Kerbrat, *supra* note 148, at 143.

[206] *Id.* at 145–46.

[207] *Id.* at 146.

[208] Patrick Daillier, Mathias Forteau, & Alain Pellet, Droit international public [Public International Law] 497 (8th ed. 2009).

[209] *Id.* at 498.

[210] *Id.* at 501.

A. DIFFERENCES IN EMPHASIS: THE LAW OF OUTER SPACE

One way to get a sense of the emphases of different international law textbooks is to compare their tables of contents to see which topics they focus on and how much room is given to each issue. Appendix C lists the chapters in each of the books studied, which are followed by a number in square brackets that represents the percentage of the book devoted to that chapter.

When viewed in this way, many differences immediately become apparent. In terms of emphasis, for instance, the use of force and international humanitarian law play a much more central role in the US books in comparison with the Chinese books. In terms of national experience, this difference makes sense: the United States has been involved in many international armed conflicts in the previous decades, whereas China has not. In terms of approach, an early chapter of the Russian books routinely sets out the "principles" of international law, which are largely drawn from Article 2 of the UN Charter. This scheme then sets up the typical Russian approach of arguing deductively from these principles rather than inductively from state practice and case law.[211]

In some ways, these differences are analogous to the variations one observes when watching the Olympics in different states. Television stations from diverse countries are all reporting on the same event, but divergences in their emphasis and narratives create diverse impressions of which sports are the most important and which actors are the heroes. Similarly, examining a case study can help to illustrate how books from different countries may highlight or obscure particular subject areas and, in the process, foster diverging impressions about which subjects are important and which states are proactive or recalcitrant on the international stage. The example chosen for the purposes of this study is outer space law, which usually receives its own chapter in the Russian and Chinese books but is barely mentioned in the US books and is somewhere in between in the UK and French books.

This discussion focuses primarily on the Russian books on the subject because they often devote as much or more space to the law of outer space as they do to international trade law. For example, the Kuznetsov and Tuzmukhamedov book (Rus.) contains a thirteen-page chapter on international space law, but international trade law and international investment law are largely subsumed within two- and three-page subsections, respectively, in a broader chapter on international economic law, which also includes a range of other topics, such as international financial law and international customs law.[212]

---

[211] According to one Russian international lawyer,

> A notable example [of a Russian approach to international law] is the (over-)emphasis on "basic principles of international law" in Russian scholarship: first, every textbook would have a chapter (in rare cases only a paragraph) dedicated to this topic, stressing the peremptory character and the fundamental role of a handful of basic principles for the international legal order (meaning that Russian international lawyers, in the spirit of nineteenth century European scholarship, still imagine international law as some kind of a pyramid—a hierarchical, coherent and complete system of rules); second, Russian international lawyers would discuss particular cases based solely on deduction from these general principles.

E-mail on file with author.

[212] Kuznetsov & Tuzmukhamedov, *supra* note 36, at 497–544.

This difference in emphasis might partly be explained by historical reasons. The law governing outer space and satellites was of major importance for the Soviet Union during the Cold War, whereas that governing international trade was not. Twenty years on, some of these historical legacies linger, with Russia joining the WTO only in 2012. This difference in emphasis may have also resulted, at least in part, from path dependence and inertia within the academy, as many textbooks are simply new editions of older Soviet works. The "Soviet legacy lives," one Russian international lawyer observed, because nobody has the time or resources to do a complete rewrite.[213]

It might be tempting to assume that the Russian books all focus on the history of outer space because of its importance to the Soviet Union. Certainly, the books typically mention the Soviet Union's creation of the field with the launch of Sputnik 1 in 1957,[214] and the Vylegzhanin book (Rus.) singles out the "pioneering" work of Soviet jurist Evgeny A. Korovin and Czech jurist Vladimir Mandl on the subject.[215] Actually, however, these chapters pay little attention to the past and the Soviet Union's history regarding space law. They hardly explain why this issue was of concern to the Soviet Union, such as anger at the US practice during the Cold War of flying U-2 planes over the Soviet Union. Nor do they mention specific disputes, such as the fallout over the shooting down of Francis Gary Powers's CIA U-2 while on a reconnaissance mission over Soviet airspace in the 1960s.

Instead, two points are typical. First, many of the Russian manuals demonstrate a fixation with definitions. For example, the Vylegzhanin book (Rus.) and the Kovalev and Chernichenko book (Rus.) discuss the problem of gaps in current international space law, such as that key concepts have not been formally defined, like "spacecraft," "outerspace," and "activities in space."[216] According to one Russian international lawyer, this fixation on definitions is a classic trait of Russian international law scholarship that also figures in other areas, like sanctions and countermeasures, and it was an important way for academics to play it safe during Soviet times.[217]

Second, the books often express a general concern that the regulation of outer space faces modern challenges of immediate relevance and that the current laws, which were

---

[213] According to this lawyer,

> Authors do not have the same time to devote to writing and adding proper citations, updating the text. They fall back on just summarizing their understanding of the subject or relying significantly on previous editions of the same textbook or other textbooks.... Textbooks are written by large groups of authors (perhaps entire departments of international law) and each author (despite being overworked) would vigorously defend the place of his or her research subject (think space law). Thus even though trade law may be much more practically important to students compared to space law, space law would get its 10–15 pages, because many universities have a space law professor.

E-mail on file with author.

[214] *See, e.g.*, Kovalev & Chernichenko, *supra* note 37, at 427; Kuznetsov & Tuzmukhamedov, *supra* note 36, at 500.

[215] Vylegzhanin, *supra* note 47, at 872.

[216] Kovalev & Chernichenko, *supra* note 37, at 428, 430; Vylegzhanin, *supra* note 47, at 875. By contrast, the Ignatenko & Tiunov book (Rus.) tended to find that definitions existed. Ignatenko & Tiunov, *supra* note 44, at 638, 640.

[217] E-mail on file with author.

largely drafted thirty years ago, are not fit to address these problems so that new treaties need to be drafted.[218] According to one Russian international lawyer:

> The sections of Russian textbooks on space law are a great example of Russian scholars' dogmatic preoccupation with definitions (how do we define "space"? Where is the boundary of space?), conceptual classifications (e.g. "functions" of space law) and their positivist outlook for treaty-making ("draft a convention") as the only way to solve an international law problem.[219]

To rehearse one example, the Vylegzhanin book (Rus.) divides the history of space law into four phases and argues that, since the last burst of lawmaking in the 1980s, two major changes have occurred that should be addressed: the rise of private actors and the development of new technologies. The first stage (1957–67) was characterized by early academic works, particularly that of Korovin and Mandl.[220] The second stage (1968–79) was a period of "rapid development" in which many treaties were adopted on a variety of topics, including the saving and returning of astronauts, the moon, and the registration of objects launched into space.[221] During the third stage (1980–96), important resolutions were passed by the UN General Assembly, such as the Principles Governing the Use by States of Artificial Earth Satellites for International Direct Television Broadcasting.[222] The fourth and current stage has seen an increase in scope of activities in space with the aim of commercialization and a slowdown of lawmaking in the field since the 1980s.[223]

The current stage differs from the previous stages as a result of the rise of private actors and public-private partnerships in the development of space technology.[224] In the near future, the Vylegzhanin book (Rus.) predicts, the commercial sector will displace the government sector to become the major actor in the space industry.[225] Laws must address how this development affects responsibility for any damage caused by spacecraft, when private companies, rather than governments, launch them.[226] It will also be difficult to square the demands of the private sector with the requirements of international law. For example, private companies that use Earth remote sensing to collect and analyze data will likely want to make the information proprietary, since gathering it is expensive. But privatization might contradict Principle V of the General Assembly resolution Principles Relating to Remote Sensing of the Earth from Space (1986), which calls on states carrying out such sensing to "make available to other States opportunities for participation therein."[227] According to the Vylegzhanin book, the private use of Earth remote sensing

---

[218] *See, e.g.*, Kovalev & Chernichenko, *supra* note 37, at 426; Vylegzhanin, *supra* note 47, at 879, 884.

[219] E-mail on file with author.

[220] Vylegzhanin, *supra* note 47, at 872.

[221] *Id.* at 874.

[222] *Id.* at 875.

[223] *Id.* at 876.

[224] *Id.* at 882.

[225] *Id.* at 881.

[226] *Id.*

[227] G.A. Res. 41/65, annex, Principles Relating to Remote Sensing of the Earth from Space, princ. V (Dec. 3, 1986).

also raises questions about intellectual property rights and respect for citizens' right to privacy.[228]

In addition to the rise of new actors, the development of new technologies poses its own challenges for current space law. The Vylegzhanin book (Rus.) draws special attention to the space plane, which might become the next step in the development of space technology and which will give rise to new legal problems, such as when air law ceases to apply and space law begins.[229] The book concludes that the current focus of international space law is misplaced. Whereas previously international space technology was primarily used for military purposes, such as discovery of rockets and warnings about rocket attacks, today military space systems are increasingly used for civilian purposes, such as monitoring industrial and natural disasters and aiding navigation through the use of global positioning systems.[230] On the whole, then, the current laws of space no longer reflect how space is actually used; both the development of civilian space technology and the rise of private actors pose challenges that must be regulated.[231] Addressing these developments is a "pressing task."[232]

By contrast, the law of space is not given much space in the US casebooks. Neither the Carter and Weiner book (US) nor the Dunoff book (US) mention space, outer space, or any related topic in their tables of content or indexes. According to its index, the Damrosch book (US) mentions outer space in passing in four chapters. It appears briefly under the chapter entitled "States" with respect to airspace over land territory and references further reading if the reader is interested in efforts to determine where airspace ends and outer space begins.[233] It is mentioned in "Bases of Jurisdiction," which cites a treaty concerning "jurisdiction over objects launched into outer space and over any personnel thereof while in outer space."[234] It appears under "Use of Force," where it is mentioned that the Convention on the Prohibition of Military or Any Other Hostile Use of Environmental Modification Techniques applies to the Earth and "outer space."[235] And it pops up under "The Law of the Sea," with a reference to the Treaty Banning Nuclear Weapon Tests in the Atmosphere, in Outer Space and Under Water.[236]

The UK textbooks carry a bit more, though none comes close to giving the law of space its own chapter. Crawford's book (UK) devotes five pages to outer space law and scatters a few other references here and there.[237] The book notes that the field began with the Soviet Union's launch of Sputnik 1 in 1957 but that much remains to be done, including in relation to controlling military uses of space.[238] States have agreed to apply the

---

[228] Vylegzhanin, *supra* note 47, at 884.

[229] *Id.* at 883.

[230] *Id.* at 883–85.

[231] *Id.* at 900.

[232] *Id.* at 885.

[233] DAMROSCH ET AL., *supra* note 164, at 303.

[234] *Id.* at 793.

[235] *Id.* at 1297.

[236] *Id.* at 1444.

[237] CRAWFORD, *supra* note 185, at 347–51.

[238] *Id.* at 347.

principles of *res communis* to outer space, which means that no portion of outer space may be appropriated to the sovereignty of individual states.[239] It relates that Article 4 of the Outer Space Treaty (1967) creates a regime for demilitarization and that Russia and China proposed a draft treaty in 2008 on the prevention of the placement of weapons in outer space and of the threat or use of force against outer space objects, which the United States opposed.[240] The book also mentions that an important feature of the use of outer space is the employment of satellites for telecommunications and broadcasting, which is overseen by international organizations.[241]

Shaw's book (UK) allocates fourteen pages to the topic, with other references sprinkled throughout.[242] On weaponization, the book records disagreement over the prohibition on militarization in Article 4 of the Outer Space Treaty.[243] This question became "controversial in the light of the US Strategic Defense Initiative ('Star Wars'), which aimed to develop anti-satellite and anti-missile weapons based in space."[244] Article 4 requires that the moon and other celestial bodies shall be used "exclusively for peaceful purposes," which is viewed by some as banning all military activity and by others as prohibiting only aggressive military activity.[245] Shaw observes that disagreements have arisen as well over the right of states to use aircraft and spacecraft to conduct remote sensing of the earth's resources.[246] The Soviet Union and France jointly proposed the concept of the inalienable right of states to information about their natural resources in the face of objections by the United States.[247] The book also notes that in 1976, Brazil, Colombia, the Democratic Republic of the Congo, Ecuador, Indonesia, Kenya, Uganda, and Zaire asserted sovereignty over the portion of the geostationary orbit above their territory, but that "[o]ther states have vigorously protested against this and it therefore cannot be taken as other than an assertion."[248]

The treatment of outer space law is not as overtly ideological as the debates detailed below. Yet some of the Russian books contrast Russia's embrace of a demilitarized outer space with a sense of US aggression and recalcitrance on this issue. For instance, the Vylegzhanin book (Rus.) calls on the United Nations to address the pressing issues identified above and cites with approval Secretary-General Kofi Annan's statement about ensuring that space does not become another battlefield and that the fruits of technological progress should serve people of all nations.[249] But he believes that this goal will not be easy to achieve because the United States adopted a new space program in 2006 aimed at "procuring unilateral privileges in space" and refused to bind

---

[239] *Id.* at 350.

[240] *Id.* at 349–50.

[241] *Id.* at 350.

[242] MALCOLM SHAW, INTERNATIONAL LAW 541–52, 881–82 (6th ed. 2008).

[243] *Id.* at 545.

[244] *Id.* at 545 n.314.

[245] *Id.* at 545.

[246] *Id.* at 551.

[247] *Id.*

[248] *Id.* at 552.

[249] Vylegzhanin, *supra* note 47, at 885.

itself to any international legal limitations in this area.[250] For instance, the United States terminated the Anti-Ballistic Missile Treaty in 2002, whereas Russia proposed a treaty that would ban weapons in space in 2001. In 2002, Russia also announced its intention of starting a new method to secure openness and trust: voluntarily providing information about impending launches of spacecraft, their destination, and their basic parameters.[251]

Outer space law is intriguing to consider not only because Russia was a first mover in the field but also because Russia and China have agitated for treaties and international regulation at the same time as many Western states, most notably the United States, have resisted formal regulation. Since the 1980s, the UN Conference on Disarmament has considered proposals for the "prevention of an arms race in outer space."[252] In 2008, Russia and China proposed the above-mentioned draft treaty at the Conference on the Prevention of the Placement of Weapons in Outer Space and the Threat or Use of Force against Outer Space Objects.[253] In 2010, the General Assembly adopted by consensus the Resolution on Transparency and Confidence-Building Measures in Outer Space Activities, drafted by Russia and China, which called on the Secretary-General to establish a group of governmental experts to conduct a study on the issue.[254] In 2014, China and Russia submitted a new version of their draft treaty against weaponizing outer space.[255] The United States rejected both versions as "fundamentally flawed" and said that they did not provide a good basis for negotiations.[256]

By focusing on this area, Russian textbooks are able to develop a narrative about how Russia is peace loving and a champion of international law and legal developments, whereas the United States is aggressive and recalcitrant and has refused to be bound by international regulations.[257] A similar dynamic occurs in some other areas, such as the Internet, where China and Russia are pushing for new international treaties regulating cybersecurity and information security, and the United States and the United Kingdom are resisting regulation, particularly through the form of a UN multilateral treaty.[258] This dynamic is the opposite of the one often featured in topics focused on in Western international law textbooks and casebooks, such as human rights law and unilateral humanitarian

---

[250] *Id.* at 876–77.

[251] *Id.* at 877.

[252] *See* U.N. Office for Disarmament Affairs, Outer Space, https://www.un.org/disarmament/topics/outerspace/ (last visited Dec. 24, 2016).

[253] *See* Conference on Disarmament, Treaty on Prevention of the Placement of Weapons in Outer Space and of the Threat or Use of Force Against Outer Space Objects, CD/1839 (Feb. 29, 2008).

[254] G.A. Res. 65/68, ¶ 2 (Dec. 8, 2010).

[255] *See* Conference on Disarmament, Treaty on Prevention of the Placement of Weapons in Outer Space and of the Threat or Use of Force against Outer Space Objects, CD/1985 (June 10, 2014).

[256] Jeff Foust, *U.S. Dismisses Space Weapons Treaty Proposal as "Fundamentally Flawed,"* SPACE NEWS, Sept. 11, 2014.

[257] For instance, Kuznetsov & Tuzmukhamedov (Rus.) recount the "peaceful initiatives" of Russia that were directed toward limiting the use of outer space for military purposes, such as the USSR's submission of draft treaties on these issues to the UN General Assembly in 1981 and 1983, and agitation by Russia for a new treaty again in 2006 during its chairmanship of the Conference for Disarmament. Kuznetsov & Tuzmukhamedov, *supra* note 36, at 505.

[258] *See* Chapter 6.II.B.

intervention, where Western states and scholars are typically viewed as pushing for the development of the law, and non-Western states, like Russia and China, are portrayed as resisting such development.

The point is not that certain issues should or should not form part of international lawyers' understanding of the field's core or that one set of states is right and the other is wrong. Russia may well be pushing for the demilitarization of outer space because it feels at a technical and financial disadvantage compared with the United States in weaponizing outer space, and thus would prefer to contain the US advantage through international regulations. Similarly, China and Russia may be introducing treaties on cybersecurity and information security because they want to contain the US technological advantage while also denying their own offensive cyber actions, and to use such measures as a cover for cracking down on freedom of speech and the free flow of information on the Internet within their own territories.[259] Without taking a stance on these issues, this section simply seeks to show that the books in different states emphasize different subject areas in ways that portray distinct understandings of the field and permit divergent narratives about which states are peaceful and proactive and which are aggressive and uncooperative.

B. DIFFERENCES IN IDEOLOGY: UNILATERAL HUMANITARIAN INTERVENTION

The conflict between state sovereignty and human rights is considered one of the fundamental ideological tensions between Western liberal democratic states and non-Western authoritarian powers. To illustrate how this tension plays out, the focus turns to what the books say about the right of unilateral humanitarian intervention in general, and NATO's use of force in Kosovo/Serbia in particular, for two reasons.

First, a general narrative in Western approaches to international law is that state sovereignty and the principle of nonintervention used to be cornerstone commitments of this law, but that these principles have increasingly fallen under pressure by the rise of human rights following World War II. Unilateral humanitarian intervention and responsibility to protect (R2P) are presented as further steps along that progression. By contrast, it is commonly asserted that some of the BRICS (Brazil, Russia, India, China, and South Africa) are reasserting the preeminence of the state in international law, leading to a gradual turning back toward the system's Westphalian origins.[260]

Second, the NATO case study involved divided state practice within the permanent five members of the Security Council. The threat of a veto by China and Russia prevented the United States, the United Kingdom, and France from seeking Security Council authorization prior to using force unilaterally in Kosovo and other parts of Serbia. After the NATO strikes began, Russia proposed a Security Council resolution condemning

---

[259] *Id.*
[260] *See, e.g.,* William W. Burke-White, *Power Shifts in International Law: Structural Realignment and Substantive Pluralism,* 56 HARV. INT'L L.J. 1 (2015).

the use of force that failed by a vote of twelve to three (China, Namibia, and Russia).[261] NATO also (accidentally) bombed China's embassy in Belgrade, killing three Chinese reporters and outraging the Chinese public.[262]

The Dunoff book (US) presents a fairly typical approach to this issue for a US casebook. Its subchapter "Humanitarian Intervention: Stopping Repression in Kosovo case" is part of a larger chapter, "Use of Force."[263] The book defines humanitarian intervention as a use of force based on "disinterested and humanitarian reasons."[264] It gives a few often-cited examples of such interventions, such as India in Bangladesh in 1971, Vietnam in Cambodia in 1978, and Tanzania in Uganda in 1979, but notes that the intervening states generally sought to justify their actions under the doctrine of self-defense. It then briefly summarizes a variety of legal theories used by scholars and human rights activists to justify humanitarian intervention, including that humanitarian intervention that is not directed against a state's territorial integrity or political independence should not be deemed contrary to the prohibition of the use of force under UN Charter Article 2(4); that states exist to further the rights of their citizens, and thus states that attack their own people, or fail to protect them, should forfeit the legal protections associated with statehood; that when the Security Council is deadlocked, a preexisting customary international law right of humanitarian intervention should revive; and that the theory of necessity permits the use of force to avert a humanitarian disaster as the lesser of two evils.[265]

In line with its problem-oriented approach, this book then turns to Kosovo to illustrate the controversy. After a brief history of the conflict, the NATO bombing is explained as a response to Milošević's refusal to accept the proposed Rambouillet peace agreement.[266] The book discusses the legality of the bombing through "international views" consisting of a NATO press statement, the UN Secretary-General's statement pointing out that the Security Council should be involved when force is used, a US State Department statement, the ICJ case *Federal Republic of Yugoslavia v. Belgium*, and two AJIL articles.[267] The US position is the only state's position to receive individualized treatment. A US Senate hearing reported that reactions to the air strikes outside the NATO member states were largely supportive, with some notable exceptions, such as Russia, Austria, Belarus, China, Cuba, India, and Ukraine.[268]

---

[261] *See* Press Release, Security Council, Security Council Rejects Demand for Cessation of Use of Force Against Federal Republic of Yugoslavia, U.N. Press Release SC/6659 (Mar. 26, 1999).

[262] NATO's Secretary General described the bombing as a "tragic mistake," whereas China's UN ambassador described it as a "barbaric activity," a "violation of the sovereignty of China, and of the basic norms of international relations." *See* Press Release, Security Council, China, at Security Council Meeting, Registers Strongest Possible Protest over Attack Against Its Embassy in Belgrade, U.N. Press Release SC/6674/Rev.1 (May 8, 1999); *Embassy Strike "A Mistake,"* BBC NEWS, May 8, 1999, http://news.bbc.co.uk/2/hi/europe/338557.stm.

[263] DUNOFF ET AL., *supra* note 183, at 887–906.

[264] *Id.* at 887.

[265] *Id.* at 887–88.

[266] *Id.* at 888–89.

[267] *Id.* at 890–901.

[268] *Id.* at 890–94.

The ICJ section outlines the arguments made by Brownlie (a UK international law professor representing the Federal Republic of Yugoslavia) and Rusen Ergec (a Luxembourg international law professor representing Belgium). Brownlie, who relied on a 1986 British Foreign Office memorandum, argued against humanitarian intervention on the basis that the UN Charter did not incorporate it as an exception to the use of force, state practice post-1945 did not support such a right, and it posed a large potential for abuse. Ergec focused on an obligation to stop humanitarian catastrophes and violations of jus cogens norms and pointed to the rejection of the Russian resolution condemning the intervention as a sign of support for it. Belgium argued that the intervention was justified under the international law notion of necessity, but Yugoslavia argued that the criteria for necessity had not been met.[269]

The main section on scholarly reactions depicts a divide among those who condemned the intervention as an open breach of international law, those who praised it as "ushering in a new era in which the protection of human rights would take precedence over outmoded notions of state sovereignty," and those who offered a more "nuanced evaluation."[270] The book then excerpts some comments from the latter camp, including an AJIL article by Ruth Wedgwood (a US international lawyer) discussing the protection of human rights and the potential for humanitarian intervention to protect these UN Charter values without "any significant danger to stability"; and an AJIL article by Richard Falk (a US international lawyer) arguing that genocidal behavior cannot be shielded by claims of sovereignty, but neither can such claims be overridden by unauthorized uses of force delivered in an excessive and inappropriate manner.[271] In the notes, the book extracts an article from the *European Journal of International Law* by Bruno Simma (an Austrian/German international lawyer) on how damage to the UN Charter could be minimized by emphasizing the factors that made the Kosovo intervention singular and an exception, followed by an AJIL article by Christine Chinkin (a UK/Australian international lawyer) criticizing the intervention as evidence of the West's continuing to script international law while ignoring the constitutional safeguards of the system.[272]

The section ends with a discussion of R2P, including an address by Secretary-General Annan to the UN General Assembly and a report by the International Commission on Intervention and State Sovereignty, which suggested that states have a responsibility to protect their citizens but that, if they are unwilling or unable to do so, responsibility must be borne by the broader community of states.[273] A 2009 report by the UN Secretary-General is outlined in which a three-step process for R2P is set out (states have a duty to protect their citizens; the international community has a duty to assist in that protection; and the international community may step in when a state manifestly fails to fulfill this duty); a note mentions that the United States, Russia, and China joined the majority that supported this approach, though numerous developing countries expressed concerns.

---

[269] *Id.* at 894–98.
[270] *Id.* at 898.
[271] *Id.* at 898–901.
[272] *Id.* at 898–902.
[273] *Id.* at 902–05.

Additional notes explain that Russia sought to rely on humanitarian intervention to justify its actions in Georgia in 2008, but that this argument was criticized by the European Union's fact-finding mission. Finally, Jane Stromseth (a US international lawyer) argues that the norms for lawful unilateral humanitarian intervention cannot yet be determined because the precedent is ambiguous but that, over time, this exception will likely emerge as both lawful and legitimate.[274]

In summary, the above book devotes almost twenty pages to humanitarian intervention, the Kosovo conflict, and its legal aftermath. The issue is presented as a pressing matter of international law practice that is in a state of flux but moving toward greater protection of individual rights and more exceptions to sovereignty and noninterference.

A very different picture emerged from the Chinese international law textbooks, which typically assert the fundamental importance of the prohibitions on the use of force and intervention in internal affairs while failing to address R2P or NATO's intervention in Kosovo. The Liang, Wang, and Zeng book (China) suggests that the UN Charter Article 2(7) principle against intervention in matters that are essentially within the domestic jurisdiction of any state applies broadly, which leaves many matters that a state may deal with without being bound by international law; but the book notes that there was some debate about the precise meaning of "domestic affairs."[275] After referring to three General Assembly declarations endorsing the inadmissibility of intervention in internal affairs, the book explains that practice does not always match the theory. In particular, "[s]ome powerful states often use 'other state's violation of human rights' as an excuse to exercise 'humanitarian intervention.' In addition to directly intervening by use of force, they also manipulate these weaker states by economic intervention, diplomatic intervention and public opinions."[276]

The book then outlines the Article 2(4) prohibition on the use of force, emphasizing its inviolability by quoting passages from the Declaration on the Enhancement of the Effectiveness of the Principle of Refraining from the Threat or Use of Force in International Relations (1987).[277] As the quoted sentences illustrate, Chinese authors often refer to humanitarian intervention in quotation marks or with a dismissive qualification, such as "so-called humanitarian intervention," implying that it is not an accepted doctrine and that it is often invoked as a pretextual justification to use force.

---

[274] *Id.* at 905–06.

[275] LIANG, WANG, & ZENG, *supra* note 108, at 59 ("It is worth noting that 'matters which are essentially within the domestic jurisdiction' conveys a comprehensive meaning, it not only refers to domestic affairs, but also includes foreign affairs between one state and other subjects of international law. However . . . [i]nternational documents, including the UN Charter, do not provide how to define 'domestic affairs' or 'matters which are essentially within the domestic jurisdiction,' and therefore, states often have arguments on whether a certain matter can be viewed as a 'domestic affair.'").

[276] *Id.* at 59–60.

[277] *Id.* at 58 (including: "Every State has the duty to refrain in its international relations from the threat or use of force"; "The principle of refraining from the threat or use of force in international relations is universal in character and is binding, regardless of each State's political, economic, social or cultural system or relations of alliance"; and "No consideration of whatever nature may be invoked to warrant resorting to the threat or use of force in violation of the Charter.").

The Bai and Zhu book (China) states that the use of force is prohibited by the UN Charter, subject to the exceptions of Security Council authorization and self-defense.[278] The authors note that, owing to the deadlock in the Security Council during the Cold War, some scholars argued for a more flexible interpretation whereby uses of force would be allowed if (1) the Security Council was unable to function properly, or (2) they did not violate the objectives of the United Nations and did not affect the territorial integrity and political independence of another state (for example, by using force in another state to rescue a hostage).[279] The authors respond that the Charter contains no indication that a well-functioning Security Council is a prerequisite for complying with Article 2(4) and, in any event, Article 2(3) (the obligation to settle disputes through peaceful means) should always be kept in mind when interpreting Article 2(4) so that the exceptions to use force should not be overly broadened.[280] The book mentions the concepts of legality and legitimacy briefly and elliptically under its discussion of the Article 2(7) prohibition on interference in domestic affairs, stating:

> It is worth noting that, even though the principle of non-intervention has long been accepted by countries all over the world, it is sometimes difficult to identify the boundary between what is legal and just and what is illegal and unjust, because the non-intervention issue involves many complicated political factors under certain circumstances. No matter in the past or at present, the violation of the obligation of non-intervention happens all the time, and many intervening conducts are coated with claims about legality and justice.[281]

The Chinese international law textbooks barely touch on the subject of unilateral humanitarian intervention and never mention R2P or Kosovo. By contrast, Chinese ICJ judge Xue Hanqin makes clear in her book, *Chinese Contemporary Perspectives on International Law*, that China rejects the legality of unilateral humanitarian intervention and considered NATO's use of force in Kosovo to be clearly illegal.[282] She argues that an exception to the use of force for humanitarian intervention has never been established under international law and that such interventions are often tainted in practice by "imperialism and hegemonism."[283] In terms of state practice, she acknowledges that NATO's bombing of Kosovo was carried out in the name of unilateral humanitarian intervention, but concludes that it was a violation of international law that was criticized in many parts of the world, even though it met with little criticism in Western societies. She also notes that the possibility of institutionalizing this practice was met with opposition by non-Western states.

---

[278] BAI & ZHU, *supra* note 104, at 20.

[279] *Id.* at 21.

[280] *Id.*

[281] *Id.* at 22.

[282] XUE HANQIN, *supra* note 26, at 91–93.

[283] *Id.* at 91.

As Xue explains, China has been sharply critical of unilateral humanitarian intervention: "China invokes sovereignty often as a defense against external interference in its domestic affairs. In principle it does not accept the same intrusive practice applied against other States."[284] China views Western states as often relying on human rights rhetoric to justify intervening or using force in "failed" or "failing" states. China has been cautious about categorizing states in this way because, without a defined content of the notion, such convenient labeling may easily lead to undue interference in their internal affairs. In China's view, "[e]xcept for rare situations, outsiders' judgments on a state's capacity or willingness to carry out its responsibility to protect its people may not always be objective or justified."[285] Moreover, "[h]uman rights rhetoric is often used to establish a new regime of control and is sometimes more a reflection of the power politics of the Western world than a signal of global responsibility."[286]

As for the Russian books, the Kuznetsov and Tuzmukhamedov work (Rus.), like many of the Russian manuals, contains a foundational chapter, "Principles of International Law."[287] These principles, which are primarily drawn from Article 2 of the UN Charter, include the principles of the sovereign equality of states, noninterference in internal affairs, and nonuse or threat of force. The principle of noninterference and the principle of sovereign equality are "two sides of the same coin: the equality of sovereign States does not allow legal hegemony or pressure and interference in one another's affairs, and vice versa—interference reduces equality and independence to nil."[288] On the principle of the nonuse of force, the authors briefly describe Article 2(4) of the UN Charter and the two exceptions of collective security and self-defense, and then explain that

> [s]erious international problems in recent years have arisen in connection with the emergence of the doctrine and practice of "humanitarian intervention," when the military force of States or international organizations is used against another State on the pretext of the defense of human rights being massively violated. When carrying out such "humanitarian interventions" the situation may be politicized and priority given to policy not to law, disproportionate force being used, and so on. The clearest example of this was the military action of NATO against Yugoslavia in 1998.[289]

The Kolosov and Krivchikova book (Rus.) likewise unequivocally states that the use of force by the United States and its allies against Yugoslavia in 1999 was illegal: "there is no right to intervention as argued by some foreign international law scholars, especially no 'humanitarian intervention.'"[290] The Kovalev & Chernichenko book (Rus.) takes the

---

[284] *Id.* at 103–05.

[285] *Id.* at 92–93.

[286] *Id.* at 105.

[287] Kuznetsov & Tuzmukhamedov, *supra* note 36, at 129–62.

[288] *Id.* at 155.

[289] *Id.*

[290] Kolosov & Krivchikova, *supra* note 37, at 177.

same approach, explaining that the principle of respect for human rights is one of the fundamental principles of contemporary international law but that it complements, rather than contradicts, the other principles of international law. As a result, "no calls for the necessity to protect human rights can justify attempts to violate such norms as the sovereign equality of nations, non-intervention in other governments' domestic affairs, the prohibition on the threat or use of force, etc."[291] Human rights and freedoms cannot be used as a rationale for challenging peace and security, and the independence and equality of states. Instead, the realm of international cooperation on humanitarian questions and human rights must be "de-ideologized and de-politicized."[292]

The Kovalev and Chernichenko book (Rus.) goes further than the others and criticizes the United States for its unlawful and aggressive uses of force, asserting that, in response to criticism by other states, the "American administration strives to justify its actions, arbitrarily promoting international norms, and sometimes misinterpreting them (they cite preventive self-defense and so-called humanitarian interventions, meant to 'introduce' democracy into other countries)."[293] There is no discussion of whether a right of unilateral humanitarian intervention is emerging or whether such uses of force might be understood as illegal but legitimate. Rather, the authors contrast the "widespread point of view" in Western doctrine that only "intervention in the narrow sense" (that is, "dictatorial" intervention) is illegal, with Russian doctrine and practice that holds that "any intervention is forbidden," including attempts to interfere in the internal affairs of a state.[294]

With respect to Kosovo, the Kovalev and Chernichenko book (Rus.) describes NATO's intervention as an "aggressive" act perpetrated by "NATO's war criminals" that violated numerous international laws. The NATO use of force led to "massacres of civilians and the destruction of civilian buildings," and the "main targets of NATO's strikes "were civilian structures."[295] The book claims that, in his trial before the International Criminal Tribunal for the former Yugoslavia, "Milošević was held responsible for actions carried out by NATO's troops."[296] For example, "the defense in the trial against Milošević convincingly showed that the mass exodus of people from Kosovo (one of the main charges against Milošević) was not the result of orders from the Yugoslav government, but rather of NATO's bombing."[297] The book explains that the ICTY's refusal to bring charges against those involved in the NATO use of force revealed the tribunal's anti-Serbian bias.

Apart from the NATO-led strikes, the book claims that the very establishment of the ICTY violated the principle of nonintervention.[298] It criticizes multiple aspects of the ICTY's approach, from rethinking the decision in *Nicaragua v. United States*, to

---

[291] Kovalev & Chernichenko, *supra* note 37, at 277.

[292] *Id.* at 279.

[293] *Id.* at 20.

[294] *Id.* at 52.

[295] *Id.* at 578–79.

[296] *Id.* at 579.

[297] *Id.* at 579–80.

[298] *Id.* at 577.

eliminating the distinction between deportation and forcible relocation, to failing to apply the 1949 Geneva Conventions and instead creating its own norms.[299] The book also criticizes the ICTY for violating fundamental principles of law, including the presumption of innocence and the prohibition on retroactive application of criminal law. The ICTY's prosecution of Milošević is described as a sham and referred to as a "trial" in quotation marks. "In that trial practically all norms of international law were violated, including the provision of basic human rights."[300] For example:

> Milošević was kidnapped in Belgrade and transmitted (the term "extradition" does not apply here, since it refers to a legal method of transferring people from one state to the next). During the trial, the right of the accused to be on an equal footing with the plaintiff was repeatedly violated; access to crucial information was denied; rights guaranteed by the [International Covenant on Civil and Political Rights] and the European Convention on Human Rights were refused . . . and information was outright falsified.[301]

The book even claims that "Milošević died because of a conscious refusal to get him emergency medical help."[302]

As these examples demonstrate, the Western and non-Western books often plainly differ in emphasis and underlying ideology. Students learning international law from these books would be likely to receive very different accounts about which issues were important, what the law was, which actions were legitimate, which actors were peace loving and progressive, and how international law might develop.

VII. Divisions Between Western Books

Not all of the substantive divisions in the books occurred along Western/non-Western lines, as is illustrated by two differences in the content and approach of the Western textbooks: one from the realm of high politics (the US and UK invasion of Iraq in 2003), and the other from the realm of low politics (how to categorize types of jurisdiction). The differences that arise are not limited to matters of obvious political disagreement between states, but can include issues that are much less politicized.

A. DIFFERENCES IN HIGH POLITICS: 2003 IRAQ WAR

The French textbooks deal with the 2003 invasion as a clear violation of international law, typically meriting little in-depth analysis. This response is interesting because, on most issues, France comes out in proximity to its Western allies, the United States and

---

[299] *Id.* at 578.
[300] *Id.* at 579.
[301] *Id.*
[302] *Id.* at 580.

the United Kingdom, but, on this issue, it publicly split with them and sided with China, Russia, and Germany.

The Combacau and Sur book (Fr.) devotes barely 1 page out of 745 to the invasion of Iraq, discussing it under the heading "Unauthorized Coalitions."[303] The authors quickly summarize the legal arguments of the United States and the United Kingdom as justification for their intervention before deeming it unlawful because it violated the inspections regime laid down in Security Council Resolution 1441 and no evidence of weapons of mass destruction had been found.[304] The authors make no specific mention of French opposition to the 2003 invasion, writing instead that the intervention faced open opposition.[305]

The Daillier, Forteau, and Pellet book (Fr.) also devotes no more than 1 page out of 1,450 to the 2003 invasion of Iraq.[306] The authors treat it under the heading "Controversial legality of certain interventions and armed retaliation," and use it to illustrate the danger that unilateralism will lead to a violation of international law.[307] Although the United States and the United Kingdom asserted that they could rely on their own assessment of whether Iraq had violated Resolution 1441 in deciding whether to invade, the authors claim that the Security Council never authorized what appeared to be an armed aggression.[308] In any case, the reason given to justify the unilateral intervention, the possession and potential use of weapons of mass destruction, turned out to be false.[309] Although the Security Council indirectly approved the effects of the intervention after the conflict, the authors conclude that widespread opposition to the intervention made it unlikely to create a precedent.[310]

The Dupuy and Kerbrat book (Fr.) gives the issue the longest treatment (five pages), and its conclusion is clear: the US and UK intervention violated international law.[311] The authors explain that the two countries attempted to justify their use of force on the basis of previous Security Council resolutions arising out of the 1991 Gulf war, but that this attempt lacked any foundation. The section appears under the heading: "The US-UK intervention in Iraq: The deepening of the collective security crisis and the paradoxical finding that the UN is indispensable."[312] According to the authors, the UN inspectors, with Iraqi cooperation, were still trying to determine whether Saddam Hussein's regime possessed weapons of mass destruction. Unlike in Kosovo, where the collective security mechanism had broken down, in Iraq the United Nations was capable of carrying out the mandate laid out in Security Council Resolution 1441. Nevertheless, the Security Council was split over how to interpret this resolution. The United States and the United

---

[303] COMBACAU & SUR, *supra* note 203, at 669.

[304] *Id.* at 670.

[305] *Id.* at 669.

[306] DAILLIER, FORTEAU, & PELLET, *supra* note 208, at 1048–49.

[307] *Id.* at 1049.

[308] *Id.*

[309] *Id.*

[310] *Id.*

[311] DUPUY & KERBRAT, *supra* note 148, at 698–702.

[312] *Id.* at 698–99.

Kingdom argued that it justified their use of force without requiring a new resolution. By contrast, France, China, Russia, and Germany rightly did not interpret the resolution this way and a material breach of the previous cease-fire agreement justifying military intervention had never been established.[313]

The authors note that the United States and the United Kingdom were clearly uneasy about relying on previous Security Council resolutions since they also sought to rely on preventive self-defense, which is also unrecognized under international law, based on the threat of weapons of mass destruction. But less than a year after initiating the military intervention, both states had to confess that no weapons of mass destruction had been found.[314] Thus, the authors reason that the 2003 Iraq invasion did not result from institutionalized cooperation but rather from an action by powerful states that was beyond the wording and spirit of the UN Charter. Still, the authors conclude that, somewhat paradoxically, the episode actually reaffirmed the importance of the UN Charter system. From the beginning, the United States and the United Kingdom were at pains to explain how their actions were justified under the Charter. None of the subsequent Security Council resolutions legitimized the intervention after the fact. On the contrary, they affirmed the position of the other permanent members. It was also significant that the United States and the United Kingdom turned back to the Security Council for help in establishing a stable political regime in Iraq.[315]

How does this assessment compare with the US and UK books? These books take different approaches, which is best exemplified by comparing and contrasting two examples. The first is the Damrosch book (US), which deals with this issue under a section entitled "Collective Actions to Maintain or Restore International Peace and Security."[316] After setting out the general Security Council regime for using force under the UN Charter, this section turns to two examples of Security Council responses to threats to the peace: in Korea and in Iraq. Under Iraq, the Damrosch book (US) describes the history of Iraq's invasion of Kuwait, summarizes the sanctions adopted by the Security Council, and extracts key provisions of Resolution 678 that authorized the use of military force to eject Iraq from Kuwait.[317] It indicates that Iraq was expelled from Kuwait, after which Iraq accepted the terms of a comprehensive settlement of the conflict that was embodied in Resolution 687, from which the book extracts over two pages of text.[318]

The Damrosch book (US) then considers the issue of Iraq's attacks on the Kurds and Shiites, which led to Security Council Resolution 688, a resolution that recalled Article 2(7) and reaffirmed commitment to the sovereignty, territorial integrity, and political independence of Iraq, but condemned Iraq's repression of the Iraqi civilian population.[319] The book relates that France, the United Kingdom, and the United States set up safe

---

[313] *Id.* at 699–700.
[314] *Id.* at 701.
[315] *Id.* at 701–02.
[316] DAMROSCH ET AL., *supra* note 164, at 1227–44.
[317] *Id.* at 1229–31.
[318] *Id.* at 1231–35.
[319] *Id.* at 1235.

havens to protect Iraqi Kurdish refugees, noting that the United States declared that adequate security would be provided to those sites by these three states "consistent with United Nations Resolution 688."[320] These three states unilaterally declared no-fly zones in northern Iraq to protect Shiites, but, the book states, "No U.N. Security Council resolution specifically refers to such no-fly zones or explicitly confers authority to enforce them with military force."[321] It then poses the question, "Does Resolution 688 support these measures taken inside Iraq?"[322]

The Damrosch book (US) describes the military actions taken by France, the United Kingdom, and the United States during the 1990s and early 2000s to police the cease-fire and no-fly zones. These actions included air strikes in response to cease-fire violations, though the book notes that "by the late 1990s, France had dissociated itself from the military enforcement of the no-fly zones."[323] Iraq's refusal to allow UN inspectors to inspect and verify the destruction of weapons of mass destruction led to escalating tensions, culminating in the departure of UN inspectors and the launching by the United States and the United Kingdom of air strikes in 1998–99, which included more than ten thousand sorties that directed one thousand bombs and missiles against more than four hundred Iraqi targets.[324] According to the book, "[l]egal authority for the use of military force in the post-cease-fire phase was disputed," but the United States and its allies had relied on the argument that, if Iraq had breached the cease-fire agreement in Resolution 687, the earlier authorization to use force in Resolution 678 would have been revived.[325] It then references two AJIL articles taking opposite positions on this argument and points out that one set of authors argues that a valid claim of Security Council authorization to use force must be based on an explicit resolution.[326]

This nine-page background sets the stage for a seven-page consideration of the 2003 Iraq war. The Damrosch book (US) extracts two pages of text from Security Council Resolution 1441, followed by three pages from an AJIL article delineating the US argument as to why it was justified in using force under Resolution 1441 in light of material breaches by Iraq and why this preventive use of force was legal and did not evince disregard for international law.[327] Next, in a paragraph entitled "Divergent Legal Views," the book explains that the authors of the extracted article were the legal adviser and assistant legal adviser of the US State Department at the time of the 2003 operation and that they wrote the article in an official capacity.[328] It then avers that the US legal position was "sharply contested and indeed rejected in many quarters," but gives no further details.[329] "For a range of differing perspectives on the legality of the 2003 resumption of conflict

---

[320] *Id.*
[321] *Id.* at 1235–36.
[322] *Id.* at 1236.
[323] *Id.*
[324] *Id.*
[325] *Id.* at 1236–37.
[326] *Id.* at 1237.
[327] *Id.* at 1239–42.
[328] *Id.* at 1242.
[329] *Id.*

(some supportive, some strongly critical)," the book points to an AJIL Agora and an article by Sean Murphy, one of the casebook authors, in the *Georgetown Law Journal*, but does not detail their contents.[330] It also refers the reader back to an earlier section on the US doctrine of preemptive self-defense.[331] The book then poses a series of questions:

> Do you think that the US action in Iraq was an application of [the doctrine of preventive self-defense]? How do you evaluate the self-defense arguments (individual or collective, as the case may be)? Are you persuaded by the legal views adopted by the United States? If you had been asked to prepare a legal memorandum on the question at the time, what position would you have taken? What significance (if any) do you attribute to the subsequent inability of the United States and its coalition partners to locate any active programs for weapons of mass destruction in Iraq in 2003?[332]

The section is rounded out by an examination of the relationship between international and domestic authorizations of the use of force, and excerpts of part of Security Council Resolution 1483 (2003), which addressed the situation in Iraq after the invasion but "took no position on the lawfulness of the military operation up to that point."[333]

The Damrosch book (US) does not state that the invasion of Iraq was clearly legal. In fact, it notes on several occasions that the action was controversial and that the US position was sharply contested and rejected by some. Through two key choices, however, it creates a very different impression of the legality of the 2003 Iraq war from the French textbooks. First, it provides a detailed set of materials that permit the reader to understand the US and UK position and trace the involved revival argument, as well as the previous practice on enforcing no-fly zones. Second, it includes extracts from writings of key US government lawyers justifying the revival and anticipatory self-defense arguments, but does not include any explanation, let alone extracts of, the counterpositions adopted by states such as China, France, and Russia. For instance, it fully sets forth the US argument on how to interpret Resolution 1441, but not the reasons for the refusal of China, France, and Russia to pass a second resolution clearly authorizing the use of force or the way their interpretation of Resolution 1441 differed from that of the United States.

As a result, the book creates the impression that the legality of the second Iraq war was not a clearly lawful use of force or an obviously aggressive violation of the UN Charter. Instead, it was an arguable case on which reasonable minds could differ, and it puts the US argument forward and invites students to evaluate it. But a student's ability to evaluate the US position is hampered by a lack of information about its flaws or the positions taken by other key states. This lack does not necessarily mean that the book's authors agreed with the US government's position. In fact, one of the articles referred to was

---

[330] *Id.*
[331] *Id.*
[332] *Id.* at 1242–43.
[333] *Id.* at 1243–44.

written by one of the authors (Sean Murphy), and it describes the flaws of the revival argument in detail. But this article is not extracted, nor are the positions of China, Russia, and France, which makes it hard to get a real sense of the strength or weakness of the US and UK position. Also missing is a detailed account of the widespread criticism of the US and UK use of force by many states throughout the world.

A much different account is given in the Evans book (UK). Under a heading entitled "Implied or Revived Authorization of Force?," the book examines examples of states' attempts to rely on such authorization when they were unwilling or unable to obtain a Chapter VII resolution authorizing the use of force, a practice that the book deems "controversial."[334] On the 2003 Iraq war, the book points to "deep divisions" about the use of force between, on the one hand, the United States, the United Kingdom, and Australia (with the support of a coalition of forty-five other states), which undertook Operation Iraqi Freedom to secure the disarmament of Iraq of weapons of mass destruction, and, on the other hand, other states including Russia, China, France, and Germany, which argued for the continuation of UN weapons inspection instead of immediate military action. Only the United States invoked preemptive self-defense as a possible basis for the military action. Instead, the other states, together with the United States, relied on the interpretation of Security Council Resolutions 678, 687, and 1441.

The Evans book (UK) analyzes the three resolutions and the revival argument. On Resolution 1441, the book states that it "clearly did not expressly authorize force against Iraq" because "several permanent members of the Security Council were not willing to agree to such authorization."[335] After this resolution, the Evans account continues, Iraq allowed UN inspectors to return and, although it was slow to cooperate with them at first, in time that behavior improved. The United States and the United Kingdom argued that Iraq was in material breach, but there was "no such formal determination by the Security Council itself."[336] The book notes that the United States and the United Kingdom proposed a second resolution "expressly authorizing force" but "failed to convince other member States that military action was justified."[337] They then advanced the rationale that a second resolution was not necessary based on the revival argument, which the book briefly outlines.

The Evans book (UK) finds two main problems with the revival argument. First, it relied on a revival of the use of force authorized in Resolution 678, more than ten years earlier, although the book notes that the original resolution did not provide for a time limit on the use of force. Second, the coalition states assumed that they could unilaterally determine that there had been a material breach by Iraq and that the use of force was justified. But "States opposed to the use of force, such as Russia, China, France, and Germany, argued that such decisions were exclusively for the Security Council" and "this was also the view of the UN Secretary-General."[338] This conclusion is similar to that expressed in

---

[334] Evans, *supra* note 72, at 637–38.
[335] *Id.* at 637.
[336] *Id.* at 638.
[337] *Id.*
[338] *Id.*

the Crawford book (UK): "The better and certainly more widely held view rejects the doctrine of revival after more than a decade; and although the subsequent occupation of Iraq was covered by Chapter VII resolutions, this was done in terms which left the original illegality very much open."[339]

Part of the difference between the US books and the UK and French books is that the former are often casebooks that provide materials for the readers to evaluate, while the latter are frequently textbooks that present clear conclusions on the law. But in casebooks, much turns on what material is extracted or summarized so that readers are equipped to make a proper evaluation. In the Harris casebook (UK), for instance, the three UN Security Council resolutions are extracted and followed by a four-page excerpt from a document by the UK Foreign and Commonwealth Office stating its legal basis for the use of force in Iraq and a three-page argument by a UK scholar against the legality of the use of force, which relates in detail what happened in the UN Security Council and the positions taken by other relevant states, like Russia and Germany.[340] When the book then asks, "Whose arguments are more convincing?," readers have the benefit of two fleshed-out sides in order to make their own determination.[341] This is not always the case with the US books, which often leave the impression that the legality of the 2003 Iraq war was more arguable than the non-US books typically conclude.

B. DIFFERENCES IN LOW POLITICS: APPROACHES TO JURISDICTION

Differences between the books can also be found in important, though more routine, areas of the law such as jurisdiction, where the French and UK textbooks typically adopt a two-part approach to jurisdiction (jurisdiction to prescribe and to enforce) whereas the US casebooks usually embrace a three-part approach (jurisdiction to prescribe, to adjudicate, and to enforce).

Under the UK and French approach, jurisdiction to prescribe, also called prescriptive or legislative jurisdiction, concerns the authority of a state to make laws applicable to persons or activities. Jurisdiction to enforce, also called enforcement or executive jurisdiction, concerns the authority of a state to apply its laws with respect to persons or things. The UK books consistently take the view that international law divides jurisdiction into two parts.[342] The French textbooks uniformly take the same position, distinguishing between *compétence normative* and *compétence opératoire* or *d'exécution*.[343] This approach does not recognize a separate category of jurisdiction to adjudicate. Instead, it views

---

[339] CRAWFORD, *supra* note 185, at 766–67.

[340] HARRIS, *supra* note 172, at 814–23.

[341] *Id.* at 823.

[342] *See, e.g.,* CRAWFORD, *supra* note 185, at 456; Evans, *supra* note 72, at 314–37.

[343] *See, e.g.,* Combacau & Sur, *supra* note 203, at 357 (*compétence normative/législative* and *compétence opérationnelle*); DAILLIER, FORTEAU, & PELLET, *supra* note 208, at 561, 565 (or §§ 334, 336) (*compétence normative* and *compétence d'exécution*); DUPUY & KERBRAT, *supra* note 148, at 107 (*compétence normative* and *compétence opératoire/ d'exécution*); RAPHAËLE RIVIER, DROIT INTERNATIONAL PUBLIC [Public International Law], 351, 364 (2012) (*compétence normative* and *compétence opérationnelle*).

courts as potentially exercising either prescriptive or enforcement jurisdiction, depending on the activity in question, and limits their authority accordingly.

Under the US approach, jurisdiction is divided into three parts: jurisdiction to prescribe, the authority of a state to make law applicable to persons or activities; jurisdiction to adjudicate, the authority of a state to subject particular persons or things to its judicial process; and jurisdiction to enforce, the authority of a state to exercise its power to induce or compel compliance with law. The pedigree of the US approach lies in the history of the *Restatements* of US foreign relations law. There was no *First Restatement on the Foreign Relations Law of the United States* because the topic was not taken up until the second round of *Restatements*. The *Restatement (Second)* undertook to record the international law limits on a state's jurisdiction and, like the UK and French approach, adopted a two-part scheme distinguishing between jurisdiction to prescribe and to enforce.[344] It distinguished between jurisdictional rules of public international law, which it included, and jurisdictional rules under conflicts of law, which it excluded.[345] The *Restatement (Third)* departed from this approach by adopting the three-part scheme.[346] This approach draws on principles from international and national law, but the text does not always clearly and consistently indicate the origins or character of these principles. For instance, the Introductory Notes on jurisdiction in general and jurisdiction to adjudicate in particular reveal that the new three-part division reflects an unclear mix of US law and international law,[347] but the black-letter text of Section 401 (which is what people tend to read and cite) takes the position that "[i]nternational law recognizes limitations on a state's jurisdiction to [prescribe, adjudicate, and enforce]."[348]

All three US casebooks follow the three-part approach to jurisdiction.[349] The Dunoff book (US) does not advert to the possibility that this scheme might be a matter of US foreign relations law rather than international law or that other states might take a different approach.[350] The Carter and Weiner book (US) affirms the three-part scheme as a matter of international law but then hedges and qualifies. For instance, it states that "public international law distinguishes between three different types of authority" but then notes in brackets that "[t]he 1987 Restatement of Foreign Relations Law added the third

---

[344] Restatement (Second) of the Foreign Relations Law of the United States pt. I, intro. note, § 6 cmt. a (Am. Law Inst. 1965).

[345] *Id.* pt. I, intro. note.

[346] Restatement (Third) of the Foreign Relations Law of the United States § 401 (Am. Law Inst. 1987).

[347] *See id.* pt. IV, intro. note ("The rules in this Restatement governing jurisdiction to prescribe, as well as those governing jurisdiction to adjudicate and to enforce, reflect development in the law as given effect by United States courts. The courts appear to have considered these rules as a blend of international law and domestic law. . . ."); *id.* pt. IV, ch. 2, intro. note ("[I]t is not always clear whether the principles governing jurisdiction to adjudicate are applied as requirements of public international law or as principles of national law. This [Third] Restatement sets forth some international rules and guidelines for the exercise of jurisdiction to adjudicate in cases having international implications.").

[348] *Id.* § 401.

[349] Carter & Weiner, *supra* note 71, at 638–39; DAMROSCH ET AL., *supra* note 164, at 755; DUNOFF ET AL., *supra* note 183, at 325–26.

[350] DUNOFF ET AL., *supra* note 183, at 325–26.

category."[351] It later indicates that the *Restatement* "asserts" that there are limits on jurisdiction to adjudicate but then observes that the stated limits were "largely drawn from the due process jurisprudence of US constitutional law."[352] The Damrosch book (US) adopts the three-part approach but does not portray it as a matter of international law.[353]

One possible explanation for this divergence may lie in underlying differences of view about whether it is possible to distinguish between public and private law, and whether the public international law rules on jurisdiction apply only to exercises of public law or also to exercises of private law. Some legal systems, like the UK and French systems, make a strong distinction between public law cases (like criminal and regulatory cases) and private law cases (like tort and contract cases). The public international law textbooks of these states typically work from the assumption that the customary international law rules on jurisdiction apply to public law cases only, whereas private law cases are regulated by private international law or conflicts of law. Despite its name, private international law is considered to be a matter of domestic law or an area governed by international agreements, such as the Brussels Regulation, rather than by customary international law.

In other legal systems, like the US system, the public/private distinction is rejected as conceptually problematic, and the law commonly permits civil law claims to enforce public law values. For instance, private parties may bring civil damages claims before US courts to enforce what many would view as public laws, such as damages actions for antitrust violations and securities fraud. If it is not possible to distinguish between public and private law meaningfully, then it is not possible to assume that public international law regulates the former but not the latter. This concept is important because, whereas prescriptive and adjudicatory jurisdiction tend to go hand in hand when dealing with public law, the two are often separated when dealing with private law.

In public law cases, like criminal and regulatory prosecutions, courts usually apply the law of their own state, so that adjudicatory jurisdiction hardly needs to be considered separately from prescriptive jurisdiction. A court in State A is not likely to decide to hear a case (adjudicatory jurisdiction) but to apply the criminal or public law of State B (prescriptive jurisdiction). Because courts tend to apply their own state's criminal and public law, the main question becomes whether that state had jurisdiction to apply its law to that person or conduct in the first place. Thus, if one thinks that there is a real distinction between public and private law, and that public international law has developed a jurisdictional scheme to cover the former rather than the latter, there is little need to consider prescriptive and adjudicatory jurisdiction separately, as the two tend to go together.

By contrast, in private law cases, courts in State A often find that they have jurisdiction to adjudicate but apply the law of State B because, for instance, that is the law governing the contract or the injury on which a tortious claim is based occurred there. Prescription and adjudication are frequently disconnected in civil and private law cases, as states often exercise jurisdiction to adjudicate without exercising jurisdiction to prescribe. Thus, if

---

[351] Carter & Weiner, *supra* note 71, at 638.

[352] *Id.* at 705–06.

[353] DAMROSCH ET AL., *supra* note 164, at 755–57, 815–18.

one thinks that public international law applies to both public and private law cases because it is not possible to distinguish between the two, one is more likely to adopt a three-part approach to jurisdiction because it would be possible for the courts to exercise adjudicatory jurisdiction without exercising prescriptive jurisdiction.

Whether public international law regulates adjudicatory jurisdiction is also distinct from what the content of such regulation might be. It may be that international law regulates jurisdiction to adjudicate but that many of the rules set forth by the *Restatement (Third) of the Foreign Relations Law of the United States* and the US international law casebooks on jurisdiction to adjudicate are derived from US law rather than international law. For instance, the *Restatement* provides that US courts cannot generally take jurisdiction over criminal defendants in absentia, which is true as a matter of US law but is not required as a matter of international law given that many civil law states permit trials in absentia. It may also be that international law regulates jurisdiction to adjudicate but under different nomenclature. For instance, in French and UK international law textbooks, it is common to find discussion of jurisdiction and immunity. Perhaps these two subjects could be reconceptualized as one subject (jurisdiction) on the basis that the international law rules on immunity should be understood as limits on the right of a state to exercise jurisdiction to adjudicate.

Several important points can be taken from this case study. First, cross-country differences between the approaches adopted in textbooks and casebooks are not limited to areas involving clashes of ideology or high politics. They also occur in important, though much less politicized, areas, such as approaches to jurisdiction. Second, these divergences often betray deeper differences in the approaches and cultures of different legal systems regarding such issues as whether it is possible to distinguish between public and private law. Third, the books in different states often adopt one approach without describing the competing approaches or attempting to reconcile them. By way of exception, the Evans book (UK) refers to the three-part approach but quickly dispatches with the possibility of a separate category of jurisdiction to adjudicate as "unnecessary."[354] Only the Crawford book (UK) attempts to sort through how these two approaches connect or fail to connect, though it still embraces the UK approach.[355] As a result, divergent approaches are often accepted by distinct communities of international lawyers, and passed down to their students, without much reflection or dialogue.

The question then becomes, what does this mean for the wider field? This question is picked up in the next chapter.

---

[354] Evans, *supra* note 72, at 315–17.
[355] CRAWFORD, *supra* note 185, at 456 n.2, 471–76.

5

Patterns of Difference and Dominance

THIS CHAPTER EXAMINES three implications for the wider field of international law that follow from some of the patterns of difference and dominance observed in the profiles of international legal academics, as well as the content and structure of their textbooks.

First, a comparative international law approach can be used to draw out important lessons about the international legal academy. Although most legal academies and law schools remain relatively nationalized, there are outliers that are significantly more internationalized than their counterparts. If legal academies want to globalize, they can learn from these outliers. Further, although individual international lawyers may have strengths in different areas, certain areas of collective strength across academies have resulted from the educational influences on them, together with the socializing factors and incentive structures of those academies. Identification of these areas can be used to determine both comparative advantages and areas that are ripe for development within particular academies.

Second, since distinct national or regional communities of international lawyers may adopt similar assumptions and approaches within, but not necessarily across, groups, substantial disconnects can develop within the field. A good example of the silos that can result from these divisions were the parallel debates conducted by Western and Russian international lawyers over the Crimean turmoil in 2014. In other cases, international lawyers from different backgrounds evidence divergent approaches but actively seek to traverse these divides. An illustrative case is the steps taken by Chinese international lawyers to publish their views on the *South China Sea* arbitration and disputes in English.

Is International Law International? Anthea Roberts.
© Anthea Roberts 2017. Published 2017 by Oxford University Press.

Third, some of the patterns of dominance that emerge in the academies and textbooks are replicated elsewhere in the field. These include privileging sources and actors from Western states in general, and from the United States, the United Kingdom, and France in particular. Choice of language plays a particularly important role in reflecting and reinforcing patterns of dominance. In many institutions, the use of English and French as official languages leads to a predilection for Anglophone and Francophone lawyers and, although this tendency is harder to prove, probably their concepts and sources as well. Outside these institutional settings, English is increasingly being used as the field's lingua franca in ways that privilege Anglo-American sources and common law approaches in defining the "international."

I. Comparing International Legal Academies

Law has traditionally been understood as a local or national discipline. The vast majority of lawyers study state or national law and then practice in a specific domestic jurisdiction. Globalization, however, is changing the way lawyers think about legal fields and many areas of the law are becoming increasingly international and transnational in their content and application. University education is also being globalized, at least to some extent, though particularly at the elite level, with more and more students crossing borders to study in exchange or degree programs.[1] Globalization has become a buzzword for the marketing of law schools, as many now claim the mantle of "Global Law School,"[2] adopting a "global curriculum," hiring "global faculty," establishing research centers on "global law," and entering "global partnerships."[3]

Notwithstanding this apparent enthusiasm for all things global, legal academies and legal scholarship often remain steeped in national conventions that prevent or significantly limit international integration, even when inherently transnational fields like international law are concerned.[4] Hélène Ruiz Fabri, a French international lawyer, has claimed that partitioning along national lines remains much more pronounced in academia than practice.[5] Likewise, Nico Krisch, a German international lawyer, has noted that even though universality is a typically voiced ambition of international legal studies,

---

[1] See Chapter 3.I.

[2] See, e.g., Norman Dorsen, *Achieving International Cooperation: NYU's Global Law School Program*, 51 J. LEGAL EDUC. 332 (2001); *About NUS Law*, NAT'L UNIV. SING. L. SCH., https://law.nus.edu.sg/about_us/index.html (marketing itself as "Asia's Global Law School"); *About JGU*, Jindal Glob. L. Sch., http://jgu.edu.in/aboutjgls (India); *Global Opportunities*, N.Y.U. L. Sch., http://www.law.nyu.edu/global (all last visited Mar. 1, 2017).

[3] Harry W. Arthurs, *Law and Learning in an Era of Globalization*, 10 GERMAN L.J. 629, 630–31 (2009).

[4] This is also true of a lot of legal education. *See, e.g.*, NEIL WALKER, INTIMATIONS OF GLOBAL LAW 39–40 (2014); Susan L. DeJarnatt & Mark C. Rahdert, *Preparing for Globalized Law Practice: The Need to Include International and Comparative Law in the Legal Writing Curriculum*, 17 J. LEGAL WRITING INST. 3, 15–18 (2011); Carole Silver, *Getting Real About Globalization and Legal Education: Potential and Perspectives for the U.S.*, 24 STAN. L. & POL'Y REV. 457, 462–63 (2013); Carole Silver et al., *Globalization and the Business of Law: Lessons for Legal Education*, 28 NW. J. INT'L L. & BUS. 399, 402 (2008).

[5] Hélène Ruiz Fabri, *Reflections on the Necessity of Regional Approaches to International Law Through the Prism of the European Example: Neither Yes nor No, Neither Black nor White*, 1 ASIAN J. INT'L L. 83, 86 (2011).

academies are often organized along national and linguistic lines, partly because they are structured through national fields of higher education that are not overly permeable.[6] "Under the bell jar of the nation state, national academic systems developed their own distinctive traits," Armin von Bogdandy observes, a factor that "particularly applies to legal scholarship," which typically "focuses on 'its own' state and 'its own' legal system" even in the area of international law.[7]

So what can be learned from taking a comparative look at different national academies? This section identifies two lessons that one can draw from such a comparative survey.

A. IDENTIFYING OUTLIER ACADEMIES AND INSTITUTIONS

Academies differ considerably on how open they are to hiring foreign trained lawyers and some outlier academies and institutions are markedly more internationalized than their counterparts. International law academics should be the easy case for demonstrating the globalization of legal education because, in theory, their courses should be largely the same everywhere in the world, and they should be readily transportable between academies. The reality, however, is very different. Comparing the profiles of international lawyers across states provides insight into the degree of openness of national legal academies to foreign-trained academics, which in turn yields information about the slow and uneven globalization of legal education. Some legal academies, like the UK one, are filled with foreigners, whereas others, such as the French academy, are not.[8]

Germany constitutes a good case in point. Foreign nationals make up 6 percent of German academies across all disciplines, but this figure is lower than 2 percent for German law schools.[9] This lack of diversity may be caused by the criteria that legal scholars must fulfill to gain employment: foreign-trained lawyers are unlikely to have passed the first examination in Germany and rarely specialize in German law, which makes up the largest share of the curriculum. As a result, German law schools remain largely closed to foreign academics. A report on the state of the German legal academy thus recommends that the academy broaden its perspectives by creating long-term exchange opportunities for foreign scholars and altering some of its recruitment criteria to open up full-time positions to foreigners.[10]

---

[6] Nico Krisch, *The Many Fields of International Law: A Conceptual Framework with a Case Study of German International Law*, *in* COMPARATIVE INTERNATIONAL LAW (Anthea Roberts et al. eds., forthcoming 2017).

[7] Armin von Bogdandy, *National Legal Scholarship in the European Legal Area—A Manifesto*, 10 INT'L J. CONST. L. 614, 617 (2012).

[8] There is a question as to what extent this is a supply- or demand-side issue. In discussions, one French legal academic suggested that it was more of a supply-side issue as foreign applicants rarely apply for French positions. However, the fact that the French academy typically requires applicants to be fluent in French, even if they are teaching international subjects, and to have completed their PhDs in France, means that there are limits on the demand side that will, in turn, affect the supply of candidates applying.

[9] German Council Sci. and Humanities, Prospects of Legal Scholarship in Germany: Current Situation, Analyses, Recommendations 17, 91, chart 6 (2013).

[10] *Id.* at 45–46.

Taking a comparative approach reveals that some legal academies, like those in France and Germany, are highly nationalized in terms of their hiring and faculty composition, whereas others are much more internationalized, including those in the United Kingdom, the Netherlands, and Switzerland. Within legal academies that are very nationalized, such as those in France, Russia, and to some extent the United States, it is often possible to identify one or more institutions that are much more internationalized than their counterparts, including the Paris Institute of Political Studies (Sciences Po), New York University Law School (NYU), and Peoples' Friendship University of Russia.[11]

In terms of outlier academies, the UK academy is by far the most open and diverse of the academies studied. Although it is not easy to code for nationality, there is typically a relatively high correlation between an international lawyer's nationality and the state in which that lawyer obtained his or her first law degree, at least at this point in time.[12] Around 74 percent of UK international law academics at the elite schools received their first law degree from another country, compared with those in the United States (32 percent), Australia (20 percent), France (5 percent), China (4 percent), and Russia (0 percent).[13] These figures suggest that many non-nationals teach international law in the United Kingdom, which makes it more likely to result in a relatively denationalized and cosmopolitan experience for those academics and their students. It is also apt to result in conversations about international law per se, rather than the foreign relations law of the United Kingdom, because international law reflects the common language and comparative advantage of these academics.

Others have recognized the internationalized nature of the UK legal academy, which goes well beyond academics teaching transnational subjects like international, European, and comparative law. Christopher McCrudden noted that UK law schools have generally favored opening full-time, regular academic positions to those trained outside the United Kingdom.[14] For instance, the Oxford Law Faculty included full-time faculty members from Australia, Austria, Canada, the Czech Republic, France, Germany, Greece, Ireland, Israel, Italy, the Netherlands, South Africa, and Sweden. McCrudden contrasted this openness with the approach of Germany and the United States, where the criteria used as the basis for recruiting full-time legal academics have erected barriers to the recruitment of permanent, full-time foreign legal academics.

Some US law schools have sought to diversify by relying on foreign-trained visitors. By the 1990s, many of the foreign legal scholars who had come to the United States from Europe to escape the Holocaust, and who had done so much to enrich the study of international and comparative law in the United States, had died or were retiring. At the same

---

[11] The Peoples' Friendship University of Russia appears to be more internationalized in terms of its student body than the background of its academics.

[12] This may change over time. For instance, the percentage of foreign students who undertake JD degrees in the United States has been increasing in recent years. *See* David S. Clark, *American Law Schools in the Age of Globalization: A Comparative Perspective*, 61 RUTGERS L. REV. 1037, 1051 (2009).

[13] *See* Chapter 3.III.

[14] Christopher McCrudden, *A Comment on the Use of Foreign Professors in the German Council of Science and Humanities Report*, VERFASSUNGSBLOG, Feb. 20, 2014.

time, US law schools were evidencing increased interest in globalization, which led many to want to expand their international and transnational course offerings and some to make one such course compulsory.[15] In many cases, this need has been met by creating long- or short-term visiting relationships with foreign professors, as illustrated by the University of Michigan Law School and NYU. These visits are an important step toward internationalizing the legal academy and legal education, though they typically lead to less integration than the UK model.

If academies want to internationalize, much comes down to the incentives they create for the next generation of legal scholars. Encouraging transnational engagement means making speaking to international audiences, publishing in foreign and transnational journals and/or in multiple languages, and cooperating in cross-border research initiatives either requirements or significant pluses for hiring internationalists.[16] If such encouragement is not forthcoming, internationalists will largely follow the dominant domestic mold, which may create incentives for them to turn away from, rather than toward, transnational engagement, depending on the state in question. But academies should take care not to go too far in creating incentives to internationalize. For instance, the premium placed in Israel on studying in the United States and publishing in US journals has led to concern that Israeli scholars often focus on universal and theoretical issues at the expense of local and practical ones, leading to a decline in doctrinal scholarship on Israeli law and a disconnect between the academy and local practice.[17]

In terms of outlier institutions within given academies, NYU is an outlier in the US academy on every measure studied, being strikingly more denationalized than its sister schools. This difference can be seen by comparing the statistics for NYU's international law faculty with those for the international law faculties at the other elite US law schools.[18] For the NYU international law faculty, 78 percent completed their first law degree outside the United States, compared with 32 percent for the other elite US law schools. Moreover, 67 percent of the NYU international lawyers exhibited educational diversity in their law degrees, compared with 32 percent for the other elite US law schools. NYU international law academics were much less likely to have worked for the US government or clerked for a US court. They also published a substantially higher percentage of their articles in foreign or transnational journals than their peers at the other elite US law schools.

---

[15] *See, e.g., Internationalism: Engagement on a Global Scale*, UNIV. MICH. L. SCH. http://www.law.umich.edu/prospectivestudents/internationalism/Pages/default.aspx (compulsory course on Transnational Law); Jeri Zeder, *At Home in the World*, HARV. L. TODAY, July 29, 2008 (Harvard offers international legal studies courses as part of its required first-year curriculum) (both last visited Nov. 15, 2016).

[16] Von Bogdandy, *supra* note 7, at 625.

[17] Haim Sandberg, *Legal Colonialism—Americanization of Legal Education in Israel*, 10 GLOB. JURIST, art. 6, at 1, 7–11 (2010).

[18] NYU's figures were based on the profiles of Philip Alston, José Alvarez, Gráinne de Bárca, Ryan Goodman, Rob Howse, Benedict Kingsbury, Matthias Kumm, Alan Sykes, and Joseph Weiler. These academics were identified and coded in the same way as those who appear in the study in Appendix A.

These figures represent the regular NYU international law faculty, not the more diverse visiting faculty that forms part of the Hauser Global Law School Program. The Hauser Program, initiated in 1994:

> incorporates non-US and transnational legal perspectives throughout the law school's curriculum, promotes scholarship on comparative and global law, and brings the world's leading faculty, postdoctoral scholars, and graduate law students to NYU to teach, conduct research and study side by side with their American counterparts.
>
> By exchanging ideas and developing lasting relationships that transcend national boundaries, the Hauser Program has allowed for the creation of a broad and dynamic network of scholars throughout the world, one that can influence the future of legal education.[19]

NYU is the top-ranked law school in the United States for international law.[20] It is home to the editors in chief of the *American Journal of International Law*, the *European Journal of International Law* (EJIL), and the *International Journal of Constitutional Law*. Departing from US law review norms, NYU has now become home to the first US student-run international law journal to become peer reviewed.[21] Other outliers, like Sciences Po, invoke NYU as an example of a leader in responding to legal globalization.[22]

The international law group at NYU is atypical in the US law academy. Some of the academics have backgrounds that would look more at home in the UK academy. Others are US-trained, though have often done much of their publishing in peer-reviewed journals, which is more common in Europe than the United States. Indeed, writing for the twenty-year celebration of the first edition of EJIL, Martti Koskenniemi noted ironically that "[t]he European Journal has since then become one of the more interesting publications in the field and New York University has come to be regarded as the home of the world's most prestigious European law school."[23] Even though NYU is more internationalized than its counterparts, the diversity of its regular faculty nonetheless largely derives from its inclusion of international law academics trained in other Western states, including Australia, New Zealand, the United Kingdom, and Israel.

Michigan Law School also occupies an important place in the internationalization of the US legal academy.[24] Michigan was the first top law school to require students to take

[19] *About the Hauser Global Law School*, N.Y.U. L. Sch., http://www.law.nyu.edu/global/abouthauser (last visited Feb. 5, 2017).

[20] *International Law: Best Law Schools*, U.S. News & World Rep. (2016).

[21] Not one for understatement, the journal declared: "Given NYU's acknowledged leadership position in all aspects of international law, we believe that this is a natural development." Leah Trzcinski, *NYU's Journal of International Law and Politics Announces Inaugural Peer Reviewed Issue*, JILP Online F., Aug. 17, 2012.

[22] Christophe Jamin, La Cuisine du Droit 227–28 (2012).

[23] Martti Koskenniemi, *The Politics of International Law—20 Years Later*, 20 Eur. J. Int'l L. 7, 18 (2009).

[24] One explanation given for the historic strength of Michigan Law School is the key role of core faculty members, like Eric Stein, William Bishop, and John Jackson, in supporting international law. Another is Michigan Law School's historic strength in comparative law, with key comparative law faculty members and repeat visitors, such as Mathias Reimann and Christopher McCrudden, and its founding of the *American Journal of Comparative Law*. See *American Journal of Comparative Law*, Univ. Mich. L. Sch., http://www.law.umich.edu/mlawglobal/Pages/americanjournalofcomparativelaw.aspx (last visited Feb. 5, 2017).

a course in transnational law, though others, such as Harvard Law School, have since followed suit. Many of the leading international law academics, some of whom originally studied law outside the United States, spent time early in their academic careers at Michigan, including José Alvarez, Robert Howse, and Joseph Weiler. Michigan maintains a long-term, repeat visitor program of international law academics from other states, which counts among them such notable scholars as Bruno Simma (Austria/Germany) and Christine Chinkin (United Kingdom). In some cases, such as Simma's, these academics have become regular faculty members.

Reflecting core/periphery dynamics, leading US universities commonly lay claim to being "global" or "international" on the basis of the diversity of the students who undertake their Master in Laws (LLM) degrees and the presence of visiting faculty and researchers from around the world. But they typically cannot claim to be international in terms of having a high proportion of faculty that comes from around the world or has completed law degrees around the world. This absence is conspicuous in their marketing. For instance, Harvard's website used to state:

> At Harvard Law School, "international" is not just something we teach. It is something we are. The HLS community includes students from more than 85 countries. In 2013–14, hundreds of students worked, studied, and conducted research in 52 countries. . . . The scores of visitors and scholars from abroad, and over 4,500 alumni who live outside the United States, help make HLS truly international.[25]

Similarly, Yale Law School's website declares:

> Globalization has long been a priority at Yale Law School. . . . Leading foreign legal thinkers arrive at Yale every year to instruct students in international and foreign law. Students who hold foreign law degrees come to the Law School for a graduate education that will help them become leading intellectuals in their home countries.[26]

As these statements make clear from what they say and fail to say, internationalization is a feature of these law schools' students and visitors much more than their faculties.

By contrast, the National University of Singapore (NUS) markets itself as "Asia's Global Law School" and boasts that it is "[s]taffed by an outstanding permanent faculty diverse in origin and qualifications."[27] The dean, an international lawyer, holds law degrees from the Universities of Melbourne and Oxford, has taught international law at NYU and NUS, and is currently editor of the *Asian Journal of International Law* and secretary-general of the Asian Society of International Law.[28] One need not confine one's

---

[25] *About International Legal Studies*, HARV. L. SCH., http://www.law.harvard.edu/news/spotlight/ils/about/index.html (last visited Oct 10, 2014).
[26] *About International Law*, YALE L. SCH., https://www.law.yale.edu/studying-law-yale/areas-interest/international-law/about-international-law (last visited Feb. 5, 2017).
[27] *About NUS Law, supra* note 2.
[28] *Simon Chesterman*, NAT'L UNIV. SING. L. SCH., http://law.nus.edu.sg/about_us/faculty/staff/profileview.asp?UserID=lawsac (last visited Feb. 5, 2017).

attention to the international lawyers at NUS to see evidence of internationalization. Indeed, the internationalization of the entire faculty is palpable and far exceeds that of NYU. Of the sixty-four professors, associate professors, and assistant professors listed on the website, fifty-three received degrees from at least two states.[29] Of the remaining eleven who were educated in a single state, none was educated in Singapore. Eight were trained in the United Kingdom, two in the United States, and one in Australia.

The Western orientation of these educational patterns, particularly for the locations of second and third law degrees, is also clear. Twenty-six hold degrees from NUS, but these are overwhelmingly first law degrees. Fifteen faculty members hold degrees from Oxford, sixteen from Harvard, fourteen from the University of London schools, ten from Cambridge University, five from Yale, five from NYU, and three from Columbia Law School. Many of these are graduate degrees. Other law degrees were earned in Australia, Canada, China, France, Germany, India, Israel, Italy, Malaysia, New Zealand, South Africa, Sri Lanka, and Taiwan. In no sense is this law school likely to produce a nationalized perspective on law. Most of the NUS legal academics are themselves products of the globalization of legal education, so that international and comparative perspectives are apt to infuse their courses and scholarship. Examples like NUS are found in other states too, such as Jindal Global University in India.[30]

This internationalization can come at a cost. The more internationalized a faculty, the more detached it may be from its national environment. For example, more than half of the NUS professors have no degree from Singapore. Some law students will go on to international and transnational law careers, but many will want to practice in their home state, for which knowing domestic law and developing local connections will be necessary. It may be that in a small state like Singapore that engages in high levels of foreign trade, a much greater level of internationalization is appropriate than in states with large domestic markets and lower levels of foreign trade. We should not expect a one-size-fits-all approach between states.

Nor should there be a universal, cookie-cutter approach within states. NYU, NUS, and Sciences Po, which are all based in global cities,[31] have responded to an increasingly globalized legal market and developed prominent niches within their states.[32] But that

---

[29] For a list of faculty with their degrees, *see Academic Profiles*, NAT'L UNIV. SING. L. SCH., http://law.nus.edu. sg/about_us/faculty/staff/staffdiv.asp (last visited on Oct 10, 2014). After consultation with NUS to ensure the accuracy of this list, I excluded six academics on the basis that they were fractional appointments or on extended leave. Data on file with author.

[30] Jindal Global University describes it as having a vision of promoting "global courses, global programmes, global curriculum, global research, global collaborations, and global interaction through a global faculty." *See About JGU, supra* note 2. It also boasts that its "expert faculty comes from across the globe" and that its faculty members have "international educational background[s], scholarship, experience and orientation." *Id.* This is supported when one looks at the educational backgrounds of its faculty. *See Faculty*, JINDAL GLOB. L. SCH., http://jgu.edu. in/public/JGLS/faculty (last visited Feb. 5, 2017).

[31] New York is defined as an alpha++ city, and Paris and Singapore are defined as alpha+ cities in studies conducted by Jon Beaverstock, Richard G. Smith, and Peter J. Taylor as part of the Globalization and World Cities Research Network (GaWC). *See Global City*, WIKIPEDIA, http://en.wikipedia.org/wiki/Global_city (last modified Feb. 5, 2017, 3:43 PM).

[32] Christophe Jamin & William van Caenegem, *The Internationalisation of Legal Education: General Report for the Vienna Congress of the International Academy of Comparative Law, 20–26 July 2014, in* THE

does not mean that all of the other players in those states can or should replicate their approach. Some schools, such as Harvard, Yale, and the University of Paris I and II, may not need to internationalize to an appreciable degree to maintain their premier domestic and international reputations. Because a lower percentage of students in regional schools go on to international careers, a domestic focus of their teaching may be more appropriate. Legal education requires a mix of offerings that are more nationalized and more denationalized, leading some individuals and institutions to concentrate more on the domestic, and others more on the transnational and international.

Some of the outlier institutions provoke hostility from other domestic players. For instance, French law schools were outraged when Sciences Po obtained an *arrêté ministériel* from the Ministry of Justice authorizing it to train law students for the French bar exam.[33] Some law professors wrote scathingly about the development in popular newspapers, and others organized a petition against it.[34] Among other points, the law school was criticized for failing to compete on a level playing field, given that the French universities must open their doors to anyone with a high school degree and may not charge high fees, whereas Sciences Po is highly selective in its admissions and not only charges much higher fees but also receives supplemental government funding.[35]

Although some of the charges against Sciences Po probably stem from defensiveness by the old guard, the charge of elitism links more broadly to a darker side of legal globalization. Often becoming more diverse in terms of national origin equates with becoming less diverse socio-economically.[36] The students who are able to pursue foreign legal education, usually at a high cost, disproportionately represent the elite of their states. As Dezalay and Garth concluded from their studies on elites in Latin America, international strategies tend to be largely class determined, yet "those who study changes associated with 'globalization' tend to neglect this aspect."[37] Legal sociologists Bruce Carruthers and Terence Halliday make a similar point with respect to elites in Asia.[38]

One lesson to draw from this observation is that globalization may lead to greater transnational opportunities (horizontal or national diversity), but it may also foster greater inequality within states (lack of vertical or class diversity). To the extent that the advantages of globalization and legal education are class determined, they may result in

INTERNATIONALISATION OF LEGAL EDUCATION 3, 8–9 (Christophe Jamin & William van Caenegem eds., 2016) (although practitioners often stress the importance of domestic law, knowledge of international and foreign laws is considered more important in large global city law firms).

[33] JAMIN, *supra* note 22, at 12–13. Sciences Po had been offering master's degrees in law for some time before this, but graduates of these programs were not permitted to pass the bar exam unless they obtained a degree from a French law faculty.

[34] *Id.*

[35] *Id.* at 13–14.

[36] *See* David Leonhardt, *Getting into the Ivies*, N.Y. TIMES, Apr. 26, 2014; Paul Stephens, *International Students: Separate But Profitable*, WASH. MONTHLY, Sept./Oct. 2013.

[37] YVES DEZALAY & BRYANT G. GARTH, THE INTERNATIONALIZATION OF PALACE WARS: LAWYERS, ECONOMISTS, AND THE CONTEST TO TRANSFORM LATIN AMERICAN STATES 9 (2002).

[38] Bruce G. Carruthers & Terence C. Halliday, *Negotiating Globalization: Global Scripts and Intermediation in the Construction of Asian Insolvency Regimes*, 31 L. & SOC. INQUIRY 521, 546 (2006).

increased connections between individuals from different states while also leading to greater cleavages between different classes from within particular states. This lesson is relevant in thinking through some of the issues that are currently arising in the backlash against globalization in some states, like the United States.

B. IDENTIFYING DIFFERENT COMPARATIVE ADVANTAGES

Adopting a comparative international law approach allows one to identify the comparative advantages of different legal academies, as well as to develop a sense about areas that may be ripe for future development. For instance, the German legal academy excels at doctrinalism, the US legal academy outshines others in zeroing in on foreign relations law and fostering interdisciplinarity, the UK legal academy boasts unusual internationalization in its composition and orientation, and the Chinese legal academy has focused on developing special capacity in international economic law and the law of the sea.

1. German Excellence in Doctrinalism

Owing to their training and incentive structures, German and German-speaking international law scholars evidence noteworthy strength in doctrinal analysis, which they have parlayed into the international realm by writing commentaries.

A traditional specialty of German legal analysis lies in *Rechtsdogmatik*, which translates somewhat awkwardly into English as "legal dogmatics."[39] This form of "legal science" treats the materials of law (legislative practice, executive actions, court decisions, and so forth) as though they were naturally occurring phenomena, and it looks upon the role of the legal scientist (academic) as being to use inductive reasoning to determine the natural laws that explain these phenomena.[40] Technical mastery of the substance of the law and the ability to systematize large amounts of positive law and jurisprudence are thus key attributes of a successful legal scientist.[41] As legal science attempts to be "pure," legal scientists also focus their attention on legal phenomena and seek to exclude non-legal data, insights, and theories from social science and moral philosophy.[42]

---

[39] Anne Peters, *Die Zukunft der Völkerrechtswissenschaft: Wider den epistemischen Nationalismus* [The Future of Public International Law Scholarship: Against Epistemic Nationalism], 67 ZEITSCHRIFT FÜR AUSLÄNDISCHES ÖFFENTLICHES RECHT UND VOLKERRECHT (ZAÖRV) [Heidelberg J. Int'l L.] 721, 748, 771 (2007).

[40] JOHN HENRY MERRYMAN & ROGELIO PÉREZ-PERDOMO, THE CIVIL LAW TRADITION: AN INTRODUCTION TO THE LEGAL SYSTEMS OF EUROPE AND LATIN AMERICA 61–63 (3d ed. 2007).

[41] Krisch, *supra* note 6.

[42] MERRYMAN & PÉREZ-PERDOMO, *supra* note 40, at 62–67. Although the term apparently originates from the continental law tradition, it came to be particularly emphasized in Germany as a way to systematize the unstructured complexity of legal rules that existed at the end of the eighteenth century. French and English law, by contrast, relied more heavily on legislative and judge-made law, respectively. *See generally* Nils Jansen, *Rechtsdogmatik im Zivilrecht* [Legal Dogmatics in Civil Law], ENZYKLOPÄDIE ZUR RECHTSPHILOSOPHIE [Encyclopedia of Legal Philosophy], Apr. 8, 2011, paras. 1, 4; Aleksander Peczenik, *Scientia Juris: Legal Doctrine as Knowledge of Law and as a Source of Law*, *in* 4 TREATISE OF LEGAL PHILOSOPHY AND GENERAL JURISPRUDENCE 2 (Enrico Pattaro ed., 2005).

This approach has engendered in German legal scholarship a strong tradition of commentary writing, a form of scholarship that is closely connected to legal dogmatism, but it has resulted in a much weaker tradition of interdisciplinarity. Ralf Michaels, a German-trained international lawyer who works in the United States, contrasts Germany and the United States for their skill in doctrinal analysis and interdisciplinarity, respectively, on the basis of their corresponding traditions of positivism and legal realism:

> Globally, German law faculties will have a hard time achieving the same quality of interdisciplinarity as US law schools with their faculty who have PhDs in other subjects than law, at least in the social sciences. By contrast, German doctrinal scholarship will always be superior to that of other countries.... German law schools should not downplay the historic advantage they have in excelling at legal doctrine.[43]

Many German international law scholars have leveraged their training in legal dogmatics by writing commentaries that are prized in their home academy.[44] Commentaries on international treaties, like the UN Charter, the Statute of the International Court of Justice, and the Vienna Convention on the Law of Treaties, are becoming increasingly common and are proving influential within the field. Projects like the *Max Planck Encyclopedia of International Law*, which is published in English and online, are also increasingly prominent. A look at the editors and institutions that put these projects together, as well as the list of contributors, frequently reveals a high proportion of German institutions and German or German-speaking international lawyers.

There are many other examples. The *Commentary* on the UN Charter is edited by Bruno Simma, Daniel Erasmus-Kahn, Georg Nolte, and Andreas Paulus—all German nationals or dual nationals.[45] Out of a total of seventy-four contributing authors, sixty-three appear to be German (85 percent), and seven others are Austrian or Swiss.[46] This preponderance may be explained by the publication in 1991 of the original version in German at the initiative of the German Ministry of Foreign Affairs, and the German government funded its translation into English.[47] The *Commentary* on the Statute of

---

[43] Ralph Michaels, *"Law as the Study of Norms"—Foundational Subjects and Interdisciplinarity in Germany and the United States*, VERFASSUNGSBLOG, Feb. 19, 2014. For objections to his characterization, see Robert Howse, *Will Germany Always Really Best the US (and the World) in Doctrinal Legal Scholarship?*, *id.*

[44] Krisch, *supra* note 6; Peters, *supra* note 39, at 771. According to one German international lawyer, the German doctrinal tradition sees all topics as amenable to one of three types of book: a *Deskbook*, which is what the English call a treatise; a *Kommentar*, which is a commentary on a whole treaty; and a *Grand Kommentar*, which is a whole book about just one treaty provision.

[45] THE CHARTER OF THE UNITED NATIONS: A COMMENTARY (Bruno Simma, Daniel Erasmus-Kahn, Georg Nolte, & Andreas Paulus eds., 3d ed. 2012). Simma is a dual Austrian/German national.

[46] These statistics were compiled by looking at the respective author list for each commentary and making a determination based on the scholar's name, current institutional affiliation, and, when in doubt, his or her legal education. I did not undertake a detailed biography of each author, so there may be some errors in the sample.

[47] On the original initiative, see CHARTA DER VEREINTEN NATIONEN: KOMMENTAR at ix (Bruno Simma et al. eds., 1991). On the funding of the subsequent translation, see e-mail on file with author from the book's editor.

the International Court of Justice is edited by Andreas Zimmermann, Karin Oellers-Frahm, Christian Tomuschat, and Christian Tams, who again are all German.[48] Twenty-one of the forty-two authors (50 percent) are German. The *Commentary* on the Vienna Convention on the Law of Treaties is edited by two Germans: Kirsten Schmalenbach and Oliver Dörr.[49] Nine of the twelve contributing authors are German (75 percent) and the other three are Austrian. A team of German scholars is also responsible for editing the seven volumes of commentaries on aspects of the World Trade Organization. All of the editors are German, although the statistics for German authors vary by volume: volume 1 (100 percent),[50] volume 2 (89 percent),[51] volume 3 (75 percent),[52] volume 4 (11 percent),[53] volume 5 (36 percent),[54] volume 6 (48 percent),[55] and volume 7 (100 percent).[56] Volumes 1 and 7 are based on a German textbook and commentary, respectively.[57]

One point of contrast is the *Max Planck Encyclopedia*. Just as the Max Planck Institutes are outliers within the German academy on account of the great extent of their internationalization, so is the *Encyclopedia* an outlier in terms of its internationalization. As of December 2014, the *Max Planck Encyclopedia* had been written by 910 authors from ninety-two countries, including 30 percent from non-European countries. Although not dominant, Germans were still overrepresented with 285 authors (31 percent), and a fair proportion of other authors came from other German-speaking countries (33 from Austria (4 percent) and 39 from Switzerland (4 percent)). These totals compared with 111 from the United States (12 percent), 61 from the United Kingdom (7 percent), 23 from France (2.5 percent), 4 from Russia (0.5 percent), and 1 from China (0.1 percent).[58] The *Max Planck Encyclopedia* has evolved over time from several precursors. It began as Karl Strupp's *Wörterbuch des Völkerrechts und der Diplomatie* and was succeeded by Hans Jürgen Schlochauer's *Wörterbuch des Völkerrechts*, both of which were written in German. It was later published as the *Encyclopedia of Public International Law* under the auspices of the Max Planck Institute and the direction of Rudolf Bernhardt. The majority of authors were still native German speakers, but

---

[48] The Statute of the International Court of Justice: A Commentary (Andreas Zimmermann, Karin Oellers-Frahm, Christian Tomuschat, & Christian Tams eds., 2d ed. 2012).

[49] Vienna Convention on the Law of Treaties: A Commentary (Kirsten Schmalenbach & Oliver Dörr eds., 2d ed. 2011).

[50] Peter-Tobias Stoll & Frank Schorkopf, *WTO—World Economic Order, World Trade Law*, 1 Max Planck Commentaries on World Trade Law 1 (2006).

[51] *WTO—Institutions and Dispute Settlement*, 2 *id.* at 1 (Rüdiger Wolfrum et al. eds., 2006).

[52] *WTO—Technical Barriers and SPS Measures*, 3 *id.* at 1 (2007).

[53] *WTO—Trade Remedies*, 4 *id.* at 1 (2008).

[54] *WTO—Trade in Goods*, 5 *id.* at 1 (2011).

[55] *WTO—Trade in Services*, 6 *id.* at 1 (2008).

[56] *WTO—Trade-Related Aspects of Intellectual Property Rights*, 7 *id.* at 1 (Peter-Tobias Stoll et al. eds., 2008).

[57] Frank Schorkopf & Peter-Tobias Stoll, WTO—Welthandelsordnung und Welthandelsrecht (2002); TRIPS—Internationales und europäisches Recht des geistigen Eigentums (Peter Busche & Peter-Tobias Stoll eds., 2006), http://www.mpg.de/436582/forschungsSchwerpunkt?c=166410&force_lang=de (last visited Feb. 5, 2017) (summary of longer work).

[58] I am grateful to Frauke Lachenmann and Natalia Klein of the Max Planck Foundation for International Peace and the Rule of Law for providing me with these figures. Data on file with author.

it was written in English with the intention of addressing scholars everywhere. In its current incarnation, it is published by Oxford University Press in English and online and, though still directed by Germans, has consciously attempted to internationalize its authorship and readership.[59]

German-speaking international lawyers are not the only ones who write commentaries, nor are all commentaries written in English. For instance, there are three commentaries on the Vienna Conventions on the Law of Treaties: they were written or edited by Oliver Dörr and Kirsten Schmalenbach,[60] who are based in Germany and Austria; Mark Villiger,[61] who is a judge for Liechtenstein at the European Court of Human Rights; and Olivier Corten and Pierre Klein,[62] who are based in Brussels. The Corten and Klein *Commentary* was originally published in French by Bruylant and later issued in English by Oxford University Press.[63] Other commentaries have also been written in French,[64] though some projects that began in French were later completed in English.[65] Nevertheless, German and German-speaking international lawyers are widely recognized as holding a commanding position in this form of scholarship, particularly in the English language, which may be viewed as the offspring of their domestic legacy of commentary writing.[66]

2. US Interdisciplinarity vs. UK Internationalization

Despite the German academy's excellence in doctrinalism, two of the key recommendations in the report by the German Council of Science and Humanities on improving the German legal academy were that "the discipline should become more interdisciplinary" and "legal scholarship needs to become more international both on the level of research itself and in terms of its academic personnel."[67] Here, a comparison between the United States and the United Kingdom is instructive because, even though they are both core English-speaking states, they have different strengths when it comes to interdisciplinarity and internationalization as a result of divergences in the educational patterns and career incentives of their academics.

---

[59] *See infra* Part III.C.

[60] THE VIENNA CONVENTION ON THE LAW OF TREATIES: A COMMENTARY (Oliver Dörr & Kirsten Schmalenbach eds., 2012).

[61] MARK VILLIGER, COMMENTARY ON THE 1969 VIENNA CONVENTION ON THE LAW OF TREATIES (2009).

[62] THE VIENNA CONVENTIONS ON THE LAW OF TREATIES: A COMMENTARY (Olivier Corten & Pierre Klein eds., 2011).

[63] *Compare* LES CONVENTIONS DE VIENNE SUR LE DROIT DES TRAITÉS (Olivier Corten & Pierre Klein eds., 2006), *with* VIENNA CONVENTIONS ON THE LAW OF TREATIES, *supra* note 62.

[64] *See, e.g.*, LA CHARTE DES NATIONS UNIES: COMMENTAIRE ARTICLE PAR ARTICLE (Jean-Pierre Cot et al. eds., 3d ed. 2005); LE PACTE INTERNATIONAL RELATIF AUX DROITS CIVILS ET POLITIQUES: COMMENTAIRE ARTICLE PAR ARTICLE (Emmanuel Decaux ed., 2011); LA CONVENTION EUROPÉENNE DES DROITS DE L'HOMME: COMMENTAIRE ARTICLE PAR ARTICLE (Louis-Edmond Pettiti et al. eds., 2d ed. 1999).

[65] *See, e.g.*, THE LAW OF INTERNATIONAL RESPONSIBILITY (James Crawford et al. eds., 2010).

[66] *See, e.g.*, Christian Djeffal, *Commentaries on the Law of Treaties: A Review Essay Reflecting on the Genre of Commentaries*, 24 EUR. J. INT'L L. 1223, 1233–34 (2013).

[67] GERMAN COUNCIL SCI. AND HUMANITIES, *supra* note 9, at 14.

In the United States, legal academics generally earn a four-year college degree followed by a three-year graduate law degree. Many academics then also complete a master's degree and/or a doctorate, typically in a nonlegal subject such as history, economics, international relations, and sociology. Along with a broad acceptance of legal realism, this background has led to an increasing turn to interdisciplinary legal scholarship, including in international law. But the legal academy itself is quite nationalized in terms of the education of its professors. The vast majority of US law professors have received only one law degree in the United States; most had received their nonlaw degree in the United States as well, a minority of them from the United Kingdom.

Consider the educational profiles of all the tenured and tenure-track professors at the top ten law schools in the United States.[68] As regards first law degrees, 80 percent of full-time faculty received JDs in the United States. Only 1 percent received a JD as a second or third law degree after having received a legal degree abroad. Of those who did not hold a JD, roughly half had completed a first law degree from another country and the other half did not have a law degree. Around 8 percent received LLM degrees, 88 percent of them in the United States, and 6 percent had received a PhD, JSD, or SJD, 70 percent of them in the United States. While some academics had completed a first law degree outside the United States and then an LLM or JSD/SJD in the United States, it was almost unheard of for a US JD to acquire a further law degree abroad.

The lack of real internationalization clearly emerges when one looks at the nonlaw graduate degrees of these US academics. Forty-nine percent of all of the professors considered above had obtained nonlaw graduate degrees, including masters or PhDs or both. Of those, 73 percent received their nonlaw graduate degree from the United States and 20 percent from the United Kingdom; an additional 5 percent received nonlaw graduate degrees from both the United Kingdom and the United States, and a mere 2 percent received them from other countries. Internationalization hardly figures in the typical education pattern of US law professors, nor does foreign influence from states besides the United Kingdom. Given these numbers, it is little wonder that US legal scholarship is critiqued for "challenging disciplinary rather than jurisdictional boundaries."[69]

Whether the US legal system does not value foreign law sources because its legal elite does not undertake foreign law training, or whether the legal elite does not seek foreign legal training because the system does not value foreign law sources, is a chicken-and-egg question. In reviewing recent hiring trends, David Law and Wen-Chen Chan noted that law school hiring of teaching candidates who hold both a JD and a PhD is accelerating, but aspiring law professors who obtained their law degrees in the United States did not tend to go overseas for their PhDs, and there was scant evidence that teaching

---

[68] These figures are based on my own coding.

[69] Helge Dedek & Armand de Mestral, *Born to Be Wild: The "Trans-Systemic" Programme at McGill and the De-Nationalization of Legal Education*, 10 GERMAN L.J. 889, 890 (2009).

candidates were rewarded by the job market for having foreign legal training.[70] They concluded:

> The dearth of such training on the part of the nation's law professors . . . tends to ensure that little knowledge of foreign law will be imparted to the next generation of law clerks and judicial candidates. Thus, to the extent that the U.S. Supreme Court appears parochial in its choice of persuasive authorities, that parochialism can be traced back to the manner in which American law schools hire today's legal scholars and train tomorrow's law clerks and judges.[71]

By contrast, for those who begin their legal studies in the United Kingdom, it is common to receive a three-year degree (usually in law) followed by practical training and then an LLM and a PhD in law, often in the United Kingdom or the United States. Compared with US academics, far fewer UK beginning law academics have received undergraduate or graduate training in a nonlegal field. The UK academy also employs many law academics from a wide variety of other states (most frequently from Europe or the Commonwealth) who have received their first law degree in another state and then completed second and third law degrees in the United Kingdom or elsewhere, such as the United States. This reflects the greater rewards conferred by the UK academy for internationalization than interdisciplinarity.

UK legal academics are traditionally renowned for their black-letter-law approach, and they have embraced interdisciplinarity less than their US peers,[72] though a significant number of UK scholars are now adopting interdisciplinary approaches.[73] Socio-legal approaches are popular, as are interdisciplinary approaches based on the humanities, such as history, philosophy, and literature.[74] A study of the culture and identity of legal academics at English universities distinguished among academics engaged in black-letter law, socio-legal studies, critical legal studies, and legal feminism.[75] Social-science-based interdisciplinarity is not as widespread within the UK academy as within the US academy, though its presence appears to be increasing.[76]

In the United Kingdom, as elsewhere in Europe, international law, European law, and comparative law are central to the legal academic endeavor. As Helge Dedek and Armand de Mestral explain: "The internationalization and 'Europeanization' of law has been a

---

[70] David S. Law & Wen-Chen Chan, *The Limits of Global Judicial Dialogue*, 86 WASH. L. REV. 523, 574 (2011).

[71] *Id.*

[72] Although US legal scholarship is often hailed for its interdisciplinarity, some studies suggest that this claim is overrated and that doctrinal analysis remains an important mainstay of US scholarship, even in top-ranked journals. For instance, Robert C. Ellickson undertook a statistical analysis of US law review articles from 1982 to 1996, finding that there has been only a modest decline in doctrinal analysis, a modest rise in law and economics, and a boom and then bust in critical approaches. Robert C. Ellickson, *Trends in Legal Scholarship: A Statistical Study*, 29 J. LEGAL STUD. 517, 523–28 (2000). It is not clear whether the same findings would hold true today, more than fifteen years later.

[73] Mathias M. Siemsí Mac Síthigh, *Mapping Legal Research*, 71 CAMBRIDGE L.J. 651, 666–67, 670–71 (2012).

[74] *Id.*

[75] FIONA COWNIE, LEGAL ACADEMICS: CULTURE AND IDENTITIES 49–72 (2004).

[76] *Id.*

phenomenon that legal academia simply could not afford to ignore, and that was quickly recognized as a cornucopia of scholarly opportunity. . . ."[77] Similarly, von Bogdandy finds that, whereas the domestic legal system was "formerly conceived as creating a normative universe, it is now increasingly understood as being but a part of a normative pluriverse."[78] As a result, he concludes, "[g]ood contemporary scholarship comes with a comparative component and an international dimension."[79] From this perspective, a scholar who focuses only on domestic law becomes "increasingly old-fashioned, even outdated."[80]

In the United States, however, international law and comparative law occupy a relatively peripheral place in the legal academy. According to Koskenniemi, "[t]he international law professor is almost an extinct species at United States law schools."[81] Mathias Reimann observes that, in the United States, "comparative law does not play nearly as prominent a role in teaching, scholarship, and practice as one would expect in our allegedly cosmopolitan age. Perhaps the discipline is not in an outright crisis but it surely does not occupy a prominent place in the American legal universe either."[82] Although US scholars excel at interdisciplinarity with a social science bent, Dedek and Mestral explain that what remains "'legal' in American legal education has so far primarily focused on American law."[83] "Law and . . ." studies are most commonly "[American] law and . . ." studies.

One result of this difference is a much stronger focus on foreign relations law in the US than in the UK legal academies. That working for a US judge and the executive branch is a fairly common experience of US international law academics helps to reinforce the academy's emphasis on foreign relations law.[84] Many of the biggest names within the US international law academy concentrate primarily or substantially on questions of foreign relations,[85] or the way international law is received into the US legal system in particular or domestic legal systems in general.[86] This attention has led to influential work about the interaction between international and domestic law and theories about how one should understand the disaggregation of the state and the development of a transnational legal process. Part of the strength of this work lies in the prior exposure of these academics to

---

[77] Dedek & de Mestral, *supra* note 69, at 891.

[78] Armin von Bogdandy, *Positioning German Scholarship in the Global Arena: The Transformative Project of the German Law Journal*, *in* COMPARATIVE LAW AS TRANSNATIONAL LAW: A DECADE OF THE GERMAN LAW JOURNAL 19, 20 (Russell A. Miller & Peer C. Zumbansen eds., 2012).

[79] *Id.*

[80] Von Bogdandy, *supra* note 7, at 624.

[81] Martti Koskenniemi, *International Law in Europe: Between Tradition and Renewal*, 16 EUR. J. INT'L L. 113, 117 (2005).

[82] Mathias Reimann, *Stepping Out of the European Shadow: Why Comparative Law in the United States Must Develop Its Own Agenda*, 46 AM. J. COMP. L. 637, 637 (1998).

[83] Dedek & de Mestral, *supra* note 69, at 891.

[84] *See* Chapter 3.IV.

[85] *See, e.g.*, Curtis A. Bradley & Jack L. Goldsmith, *Congressional Authorization and the War on Terrorism*, 118 HARV. L. REV. 2047 (2005); Curtis A. Bradley & Jack L. Goldsmith, *Customary International Law as Federal Common Law: A Critique of the Modern Position*, 110 HARV. L. REV. 815 (1997).

[86] *See, e.g.*, Harold Hongju Koh, *International Law as Part of Our Law*, 98 AM. J. INT'L L. 43 (2004); Harold Hongju Koh, *The 1998 Frankel Lecture: Bringing International Law Home*, 35 HOUS. L. REV. 623 (1998); Harold Hongju Koh, *Transnational Legal Process*, 75 NEB. L. REV. 181 (1996); Anne-Marie Slaughter & William Burke-White, *The Future of International Law Is Domestic (or, the European Way of Law)*, 47 HARV. INT'L L.J. 327 (2006).

the inner workings of domestic courts and the executive branch. Since the September 11 terrorist attacks, there has also been a strong focus on national security law as evidenced by, for example, the framing and orientation of two of the main "international law" blogs in the United States (*Lawfare* and *Just Security*). Many of the contributors to these blogs have also held government positions, often with a national security angle as part of those jobs.

In the United Kingdom, by contrast, it is not common for international law academics to have worked for a domestic judge or as a UK government lawyer. Instead, some of the most prominent UK-based international law academics focus on appearing as counsel or arbitrator in cases before international courts and tribunals, though some also work on cases before domestic UK courts.[87] One can easily think of contributions that UK or UK-based international law academics have made to a host of issues concerning international dispute resolution and international legal doctrine. A prime case in point is James Crawford, who, as special rapporteur, shepherded a Draft Statute for the International Criminal Court and the Draft Articles on State Responsibility through the International Law Commission. But it is harder to think of the provision by UK academics of detailed accounts of the disaggregated state and how international law decisions are made within the UK government. A number of UK international law academics deal with questions such as the use of force and terrorism, but the specialty of national security law is not as prevalent in the UK academy as the US one. Blogs like *EJIL: Talk!* and the one for the *Cambridge Journal of International and Comparative Law* frame themselves very much as international law blogs, rather than national security or foreign relations law ones.

Another factor that may play into this difference is that many of these international lawyers have come to the United Kingdom from other countries and so may lack the interest or natural advantage that flows from having pursued a first law degree in the United Kingdom and being familiar with the domestic legal system. Only recently have books started to emerge that focus on international law in UK courts or the idea of foreign relations law of the United Kingdom or other Commonwealth states.[88] Indeed, Campbell McLachlan's 2014 book on foreign relations law,[89] which deals with Australia, Canada, New Zealand, and the United Kingdom, was the first such work since F. A. Mann's 1986 *Foreign Affairs in English Courts*.[90] Similar developments are afoot in Canada,[91] as is a large new project on comparative foreign relations.[92] This sort of scholarship was given

---

[87] *See* Chapter 3.IV.

[88] *See, e.g.*, SHAHEED FATIMA, INTERNATIONAL LAW AND FOREIGN AFFAIRS IN ENGLISH COURTS (2016); SHAHEED FATIMA, USING INTERNATIONAL LAW IN DOMESTIC COURTS (2005); CAMPBELL MCLACHLAN, FOREIGN RELATIONS LAW (2014); Campbell McLachlan, *The Allocative Function of Foreign Relations Law*, 2012 BRIT. Y.B. INT'L L. 349.

[89] MCLACHLAN, FOREIGN RELATIONS LAW (2014), *supra* note 88.

[90] F.A. MANN, FOREIGN AFFAIRS IN ENGLISH COURTS (1986).

[91] For instance, in 2014, Karen Knop introduced a new course at the University of Toronto called Foreign Affairs and the Canadian Constitution, which aimed at "help[ing] to inaugurate foreign affairs and the Canadian constitution as a field of legal inquiry in Canada." *See Foreign Affairs and Canadian Constitution*, UNIV. TORONTO L. SCH., http://www.law.utoronto.ca/course/foreign-affairs-and-canadian-constitution (last visited Oct. 2014, no longer on the website).

[92] This project is being headed by US international lawyer Curtis Bradley, who was awarded an Andrew Carnegie Fellowship to develop a global project on "Comparative Foreign Relations Law and Democratic Accountability."

impetus in part by a comparative assessment that this field was much better developed in the United States than in many other states.

3. Chinese Emphasis on International Economic Law and Law of the Sea

International lawyers in different states are often concentrated in particular subfields. For instance, international law academics in the top five US law schools commonly focus on foreign relations law, national security law, human rights, international economic law, or international law in domestic courts. Specialists in international environmental law or the law of the sea, despite the pressing importance of these issues for the next generation, are much harder to find. Yet if one looks at the elite Chinese law schools, many of their international law academics specialize in international economic law and law of the sea, whereas a much smaller number focus on human rights and the laws of war.

One factor that helps to explain the particular subject-matter focus of the Chinese international legal academy is the government's strategic use of research funding. There are three main sources of research funds for academic legal projects in China: the National Social Science Fund of China (NSSFC), the Ministry of Education Fund, and the Ministry of Justice Fund. The NSSFC is an accessible example because it puts out a call for proposals for academic funding every year and provides a list of recommended research topics.[93] According to Wang Xiaohui, deputy head of the Publicity Department of the Communist Party's Central Committee, the fund is "designed to support strategic research on China's overall economic and social development," and the results are "highly useful for the Party and the government in their decision-making processes."[94]

Using information that is available online, I compiled a list of the international law topics included in the NSSFC's Recommended Research Topics for 2009–14,[95] and in the list of Funded Research Proposals for 2007–14.[96] Appendix D lists these topics in full and describes how I selected and categorized them. Figure 17 shows which topics

---

See Bradley Receives Andrew Carnegie Fellowship, DUKE L. NEWS, Apr. 18, 2016. The project has held a number of conferences with the aim of producing an OXFORD HANDBOOK OF COMPARATIVE FOREIGN RELATIONS LAW. *See Duke-Japan Conference on Comparative Foreign Relations Law, id.*, June 29, 2016; *Duke University-Geneva Conference on Comparative Foreign Relations Law, id.*, Jan. 29, 2015.

[93] The fund was reportedly established in 1986 by the Communist Party of China (CPC) Central Committee and amounted to 1.746 billion yuan (about 269 million USD) between 2006 and 2010. *See China's Social Science Fund to Be Used More Efficiently: Official*, XINHUA, May 26, 2011. It used to be that proposals could be accepted only if they came within the recommended topics, though that is no longer the case.

[94] *See id.* According to Liu Yunshan, head of the Publicity Department of the Communist Party of China (CPC) Central Committee, the NPOPSS has used the fund to "study major issues surrounding China's reform and opening and the modernization, and supporting projects reflecting the national development strategies." *See Invigorating Social Science Study Urged*, XINHUA, Mar. 25, 2012.

[95] For official announcements of Recommended Research Projects from 2011 to 2014, see 项目申报 [Project Applications], NAT'L PLANNING OFFICE OF PHILOSOPHY AND SOCIAL SCI. [NPOPSS], http://www.npopss-cn.gov.cn/GB/219471/index.html. Unofficial announcements for Recommended Research Projects from 2009 to 2010, which have the same form and content as the official announcements, were located through Baidu searches and confirmed with Chinese academics for authenticity.

[96] For official announcements of Funded Research Projects from 2007 to 2014, see 立项名单 [List of Approved Projects], NPOPSS, http://www.npopss-cn.gov.cn/GB/219534/index1.html.

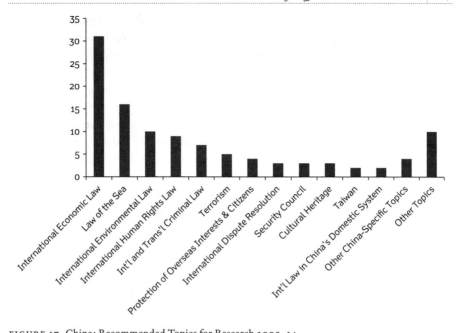

FIGURE 17   China: Recommended Topics for Research 2009–14

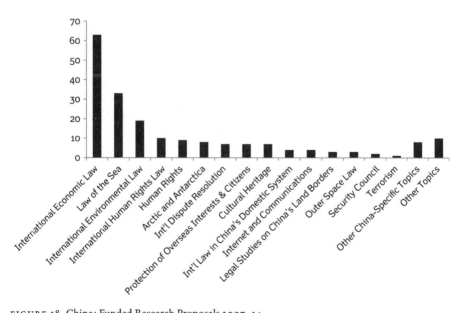

FIGURE 18   China: Funded Research Proposals 2007–14

were recommended, and Figure 18 shows which projects were actually funded. As these charts illustrate, the Chinese government creates incentives for Chinese international law academics to focus their research on areas of national interest, including international economic law and law of the sea.

International economic law forms the largest category in both Recommended Research Topics and Funded Research Proposals. As David Shambaugh observes, economic motivations are a distinguishing feature of Chinese foreign policy.[97] This focus should come as no surprise in view of China's 2001 accession to the World Trade Organization (WTO), its considerable involvement in WTO dispute resolution, and its deliberate efforts to build capacity in this area.[98] China is also the second highest signatory of investment treaties in the world, and claims by Chinese companies, including state-owned enterprises, and against the Chinese government are starting to be lodged. Although trade topics make up the bulk of this category, investment topics have increasingly gained attention in recent years.

Law of the sea is also a favorite subject, reflecting China's intense interest in the South and East China Sea disputes. Several of these topics show a particular pro-China, nationalist bent, strongly emphasizing protection of China's interests in the South China Sea. They include the Recommended Research Topic "Studies on the Protection of China's Interest in the South China Sea within China's Jurisdiction" and funded proposals such as "Legal Studies on the Protection of China's Interest in the South China Sea and the Cooperation Mechanism Between Mainland China and Taiwan," "Studies on the Strategies for the Protection of China's Core National Interests in the South China Sea," and "Studies on the Legal Strategies for Protecting China's Sovereignty over Nansha Islands Under New Circumstances." The newness of this focus is also noteworthy. As one Chinese academic explained, the Recommended Research Topics are sometimes "nearsighted" because they are designed to help with the immediate needs of China, rather than to plan ahead for future or potential problems.[99] The number of funded proposals relating to the South China Sea thus grew from zero in 2009 to six or seven in 2014 as the issue's salience increased after 2010, particularly with the initiation of the arbitration under the UN Convention on the Law of the Sea (UNCLOS) by the Philippines in 2013.

International environmental law also looms large in China, which reflects the acuteness of this problem for China as well as efforts it has made on this topic on the global stage. China argues that developed countries should bear the primary responsibility for global environmental protection since their higher level of industrialization means that they disproportionately contributed to climate change, and the greater resources at their disposal equip them to invest in technologies to reduce environmental harm.[100] While accepting nonbinding targets for emissions cuts, China has strongly supported a

[97] DAVID SHAMBAUGH, CHINA GOES GLOBAL: THE PARTIAL POWER 55 (2014) ("Economic motivations are thus a distinguishing feature of Chinese foreign policy.").

[98] See generally Gregory Shaffer & Henry Gao, From Paternalism to Partnership: The Development of WTO Law Capacity in China, in THE CHINESE LEGAL PROFESSION IN THE AGE OF GLOBALIZATION: THE RISE OF THE CORPORATE LEGAL SECTOR AND ITS IMPACT ON LAWYERS AND SOCIETY (David Wilkins & Sida Liu eds., forthcoming 2017). See also Chapter 4.III.B.

[99] E-mail on file with author.

[100] See, e.g., Zhu Lijiang, Chinese Practice in Public International Law: 2007, 7 CHINESE J. INT'L L. 735, 754–55 (2008); News Release, Nat'l Dev. and Reform Comm'n of the People's Republic of China, Implementation of the Bali Roadmap: China's Position on the Copenhagen Climate Change Conference (May 20, 2009), http://en.ndrc.gov.cn/newsrelease/200905/t20090521_280382.html (last visited Feb. 5, 2017).

"common but differentiated responsibilities" approach to dealing with climate change,[101] and thus has funded proposals on topics like "Fairness Issues in the Construction of New Order in International Climate Law." These subjects also evince an interest in mechanisms for reducing emissions, as well as understanding the link between trade and the environment.

The lack of focus on other subjects is also revealing. Topics that dominate international law research in some other states, like international law in domestic courts and the law of war, receive almost no attention. International human rights law was not absent from the lists, but neither was it of central importance. Roughly the same number of human rights proposals were funded as for proposals on China's interests in the Arctic and Antarctica, and just slightly more than on international dispute resolution, the protection of overseas interests and citizens, or cultural heritage.[102] Some of the funded proposals reflected concerns about China's interaction with international human rights bodies, like the Human Rights Council. No mention of democracy appeared in either list, though several topics and proposals dealt with the rule of law.

Through its strategic use of funding, among other measures, the Chinese government has sought to promote research on international law fields and issues of pressing national import.[103] According to one aspiring Chinese international law academic, from looking at these topics, "you will know where the money goes" and, from that, you will know "where the academy goes."[104] These incentives not only affect academics who receive funding but also all those who shape their research agendas with an eye to applying for funding, being promoted, or achieving certain markers of success. In many law schools, the grant of NSSFC or other government research funding is a precondition for applying for a professorship and a major factor in securing certain awards, such as the Ministry of Education's New Century Excellent Talents Supporting Plan.

China's strategic use of research funding may also have the effect of encouraging Chinese international law academics to analyze issues from the perspective of how best to protect China's interests. Take, for example, the following funded proposals on the Arctic

---

[101] *See generally* Christopher D. Stone, *Common But Differentiated Responsibilities in International Law*, 98 Am. J. Int'l L. 276, 276–79 (2004).

[102] One expert on China commented that this might partly be a result of the time period on which data were available: "The change in ratio on international human rights law occurred because, while the emphasis was very much on this from 1991, it tailed off once expertise was achieved and once China managed to contain and deflect international pressure on its human rights from about 1995. As one Chinese diplomat in Geneva told me in 1993: 'I know all about human rights, from A to Z' (and he pronounced it as an American zeeee!)." E-mail on file with author.

[103] Some Chinese academics have criticized this approach for encouraging research into pressing policy-oriented issues while neglecting more theoretical topics or subjects with a longer-term payoff. According to one scholar: "China pays more attention to settle urgent and practical issues by funding these researches, few basic and purely theoretical research topics are granted. If you apply for 'history of international law' or 'Islamic law,' then you are not likely to be granted, because to the application reviewers, these purely theoretical topics 'have nothing to do with China's concerns.'" According to another: "There is a serious negative effect of this strongly policy-oriented approach. That is, the theoretical, fundamental research has been paid far less emphasis, which . . . might not be helpful to improve the capability of 'knowledge-production' rather than 'knowledge-consumption' of Chinese international lawyers." E-mails on file with author.

[104] E-mail on file with author.

and Antarctic: "Studies on the Legal Issues in the Arctic Shipping Routes and China's National Interests," "International Legal Studies on China's Interests in the Arctic," "Studies on China's Arctic Shipping Routes and the Building of 'a Great Maritime Power,'" "Studies on the Construction of an International Legal Order in the Arctic and the Expansion of China's Interests," "Studies on China's Legal Path to Strengthen Presence in the Arctic," "Studies on the Legal Issues in Navigation in the Arctic from the Perspective of China's Interests," and "Studies on the Legal Protection of China's Interests in Antarctica." Both the theme and the perspective seem pretty clear.

One result of this strategic use of research funding is that China has been developing a strong cohort of international lawyers in fields like international economic law and law of the sea. China has also been giving its academics incentives to pursue graduate studies in Western states and to publish in foreign and transnational journals.[105] Thus, when issues of special concern to China arise, like the legality of the UNCLOS tribunal's assumption of jurisdiction in the *South China Sea* arbitration, China can draw on a stable of legal experts who are well positioned to write on these topics and can write in English in a way that reaches foreign audiences.[106] By contrast, the top US law schools have not recruited international lawyers with law of the sea expertise in the last generation, despite the importance of this topic to the US government.[107] Again, this appears to be a potential growth area for the next generation.

II. Identifying Scholarly Silos and Attempts to Connect

Because distinct communities of international lawyers often develop with similar assumptions and approaches within, but not necessarily between, groups, substantial disconnects can occur within the field. In some cases, substantial intragroup dialogue takes place, but intergroup dialogue is limited, which can result in the development by international lawyers in certain communities of self-referential and self-reinforcing approaches to international law. These silos may give their participants a false sense of reality and the universality of their positions while denying these lawyers the opportunity to understand and engage with others who hold diverse perspectives. An example can be found in the parallel debates over Crimea's annexation by, or reunification with, Russia in 2014 by Western and Russian international law scholars.

In other cases, international lawyers in different academies may evidence distinct perspectives but engage in conscious attempts to bridge the divide, often with the strategic aim of presenting their view to another audience. For example, in debates about the

[105] *See* Chapter 3.II and III.
[106] *See infra* Part II.B.
[107] There are some senior US law of the sea experts, such as Bernard Oxman (Miami) and John Norton Moore (Virginia), and some experts from the next generation, such as Craig Allen (University of Washington), James Kraska (Naval War College), and Raul Pedrozo (previously at the Naval War College). But, compared with China, law of the sea experts are few and far between in the US academy, particularly in the younger generation and at the elite schools.

validity of the *South China Sea* arbitration, many Chinese international lawyers have strongly supported China's position, whereas many Western international lawyers have taken a much more skeptical view of China's position. Instead of simply forming their own silo, Chinese officials and scholars have repeatedly sought to present China's perspective to foreign audiences, including by writing in English and citing Western international law scholars. This helped to enrich the English-language debates and allowed for greater consideration to be paid by Western scholars to the viewpoints of their Chinese counterparts. Yet, due to factors such as language barriers and explicit and implicit Chinese censorship, views critical of China's position were not generally available in Mandarin in Chinese outlets. In this way, the Chinese scholars facilitated outward, but not inward, diversity, strengthening the robustness and legitimacy of transnational debates but not necessarily domestic ones.

There are many possible causes for divergent viewpoints among different communities. Some might derive from different incentive structures, such as the level of academic freedom in different states and whether international lawyers feel able to dissent from their governments' positions without fearing costs or retribution. Others might reflect more subtle processes of socialization, such as divergent facts that are reported, or narratives that are developed, in different media sources. In these scenarios, one cannot prove that X causes Y. But, as international lawyers are shaped in different national environments, it is not unreasonable to surmise that differences in their national contexts might influence the way in which they understand and approach international law, so it is worth paying attention to these differences and possible contributing factors. In the end, engaging in a dialogue across communities does not guarantee that agreement will be reached or common ground found, but it at least permits awareness of diverse perspectives within a common debate.

The year 2016 has reminded many people of the dangers of living in bubbles of like-minded people domestically, but international lawyers are sometimes at risk of doing the same thing internationally. The surprising elections in the United States and the unexpected vote to Brexit have focused attention throughout the world on the problem of different communities creating their own silos in which shared views are reinforced in echo chambers. One of the lessons that many people have taken from this experience is the need to view more diverse media sources to understand how others with whom they disagree might be viewing a common problem or issue. This chapter suggests taking a parallel approach in international law. In doing so, it draws on two high profile disputes between Western states and Russia and China respectively and, given how recent these events were, it pays particular attention to how these issues were treated in the media and on blogs.

A. DEBATES ABOUT CRIMEA'S ANNEXATION BY, OR REUNIFICATION WITH, RUSSIA

A revolution in February 2014 ousted the pro-Russian Ukrainian president Viktor Yanukovych and sparked a political crisis in Crimea. Opposition parties and defectors from the old government put together a caretaker government to control Ukraine until new presidential and parliamentary elections could be held. This new government was recognized internationally but not by Russia, which viewed the revolution as a "coup d'état" and the caretaker government as illegitimate. A pro-Russian government formed in Crimea and held a referendum on reunifying Crimea with Russia, which passed overwhelmingly. Many states questioned the legitimacy of the referendum given the Russian presence within Crimea during the vote.

International law debates about the legality and legitimacy of what happened in Crimea were largely conducted in two parallel bodies of scholarship: one by Russian international lawyers, which was primarily written in Russian and published in Russia;[108]

---

[108] *See, e.g.*, С. Бабурин [S. Baburin], Ялтинские договоренности великих держав в 1945 г. и их уроки для международного права [1945 Yalta Agreement of the Great Powers and Their Lessons for International Law], 43 Вестник Омского университета, Серия "Право" [Rev. Omsk Univ., "Law" Series] 54 (2015); О.Г. Деревянко [O.G. Derevianko], Сравнительный конституционно-правовой анализ проведения АТО РФ на Северном Кавказе и Украиной в Луганской и Донецкой областях [Comparative Constitutional Analysis of Russia's Counter-Terrorism Operation in the North Caucasus and Ukraine's Counter-Terrorism Operation in Luhansk and Donetsk Regions], 51 Вестник Международного юридического института [Rev. Int'l Legal Inst.] 52 (2014); Инсур Фархутдинов [Insur Farkhutdinov], Евразийская интеграция и испытание украинской государственности в системе международного права [Eurasian Integration and a Test of Ukrainian Statehood in International Law], 79 Евразийский юридический журнал [Eurasian L.J.] (2014); А. Ибрагимов [A. Ibrahimov], Воссоединение Крыма и Севастополя с Российской Федерацией в призме международного права и мировой политики [Reunification of Crimea and Sevastopol with Russian Federation Through the Prism of International Law and World Politics], 4 Юридический вестник ДГУ [L. Rev. of Dagestan St. Univ.] 75 (2014); О.Н. Хлестов [O.N. Hlestov], Украина: право на восстание [Ukraine: The Right to Rebel], Международный правовой курьер [Int'l Legal Herald], http://www.inter-legal.ru/ukraina-pravo-navosstanie; А. Кудряшова [A. Kudriashova], Международно-правовые проблемы возвращения Крыма в состав России [International Legal Problems of Crimea's Return to Russia], Труды БрГУ. Серия: Гуманитарные и социальные проблемы развития регионов Сибири [Works of Fraternal State University, Series: Humanitarian and Social Problems of Siberia's Development] 26 (2014); В.А. Кряжков [V.A. Kriazhkov], Крымский прецедент: конституционно-правовое осмысление [Crimean Precedent: Reflections on Constitutional and Legal Aspects], 5 Сравнительное конституционное обозрение [Comp. Const. Rev.] (2014); Ю. Курилюк, И. Семеновский [Y. Kuriliuk & I. Semenovskiy], Правовой аспект вхождения Крыма и Севастополя в состав России [Legal Aspects of Crimean and Sevastopol's Joining Russia], 2 Научные записки молодых исследователей [Res. Notes Young Scholars] (2014); В. Самигуллин [V. Samigullin], Крым: историко-правовой аспект [Crimea: Historical and Legal Aspects], 3 Проблемы востоковедения [Problems Oriental Stud.] 13 (2014); К.П. Саврыга [K.P. Savryga], Украинский кризис и международное право: вооруженный конфликт на Востоке Украины и сецессия Крыма [Ukrainian Crisis and International Law: Armed Conflict in East of Ukraine and Crimean Secession], 187 Право и политика [Law & Pol.] 945 (2015); К. Сазонова [K. Sazonova], Международное право и украинский конфликт: что было, что будет, чем сердце успокоится [International Law and Ukrainian Conflict: What Has Happened, What Will Happen, How to Comfort the Heart], 1 NB: Международное право [NB: Int'l L.] 1 (2014); Н. Свечников, М. Богданова [N. Svechnikov & M. Bogdanova], Крымский референдум—некоторые аспекты политико-правового анализа [Crimean Referendum: Several Aspects of Political and Legal Analysis], Вестник Пензенского государственного университета [Rev. of Penza St. Univ.] 28 (2014); К. Б. Толкачев [K.B. Tolkachev], "Крымский вопрос" и современное право: к дискуссии о легитимности референдума ["Crimean Question" and Contemporary Law: re Discourse on Referendum's Legitimacy], 72 Евразийский юридический журнал [Eurasian L.J.] (2014); В.Л. Толстых [V.L. Tolstykh], Воссоединение Крыма с Россией: правовые квалификации [Reunification of Crimea and Russia: The Legal Qualifications], 72 Евразийский юридический журнал [Eurasian L.J.] 40 (2014); В.Л. Толстых [V.L. Tolstykh], Воссоединение Крыма и России: факты, квалификации, риторика [Reunification of Crimea and Russia: Facts, Qualification, and Rhetoric], 92–93 Новосибирский Юрист: газ. Новосиб. юрид. ин-та (фи-ла) ТГУ [Novosibirsk's L.: Mag. Novosibirsk L. Sch. (branch) Tomsk St. Univ.] 6 (2015); В.А. Томсинов [V.A. Tomsinov], "Крымское право" или Юридические основания воссоединения Крыма с Россией ["Crimean Law" or Legal Bases for the Reunification of the

and the other by Western international lawyers, which was primarily written in English and published in Western outlets.[109] These two scholarly communities engaged in very little interaction, subject to a handful of exceptions: a letter to the editors by Vladislav Tolstykh published in the *Chinese Journal of International Law*;[110] a letter written by Anatoly Kapustin, president of the Russian Association of International Law, to the Executive Council of the International Law Association;[111] and some blog posts on what Russian international lawyers were saying about the crisis.[112]

The recognition that the two scholarly debates were largely conducted in isolation from each other led Christian Marxsen, Anne Peters, and Matthias Hartwig to create a symposium in the *Heidelberg Journal of International Law* that brought together Russian

---

Crimea and Russia], Зерцало-М [Zertsalo-M] (2015); В.А. Томсинов [V.A. Tomsinov], Международное право с точки зрения воссоединения Крыма с Россией [International Law from the Perspective of Crimean Reunification with Russia], Законодательство Номер 6 [Leg., Vol. 6] (2014); Г. Цыкунов [G. Tsykunov], Историко-правовые основы вхождения Крыма в состав Российской Федерации [Historical and Legal Foundations for Crimean Reunification with Russia], 25 Известия Иркутской государственной экономической академии [News ST. Acad. Econ. Irkutsk] 550 (2015); Г.М. Вельяминов [G.M. Veliaminov], Воссоединение Крыма с Россией: правовой статус [Reunification of Crimea with Russia: A Legal Perspective], Институт Государства и права РАН [Inst. St. & L. Russian Acad. Sci.] 12 (2014); В.Д. Зорькин [V.D. Ziorkin], Право силы и сила права [The Law of Power and the Power of Law], Российская газета [Russian Gazette] (May 28, 2015); В.Д. Зорькин [V.D. Ziorkin], Право—и только право, О вопиющих правонарушениях, которые упорно не замечают [Law—And Only Law. On Egregious Violations that Go Unnoticed], Российская газета [Russian Gazette], Mar. 23, 2015.

[109] *See, e.g.*, THOMAS D. GRANT, AGGRESSION AGAINST UKRAINE: TERRITORY, RESPONSIBILITY, AND INTERNATIONAL LAW (2015); Veronica Bilkova, *The Use of Force by the Federation in Crimea*, 75 ZaöRV 27 (2015); Thomas D. Grant, *Current Developments: Annexation of Crimea*, 109 AM. J. INT'L L. 68 (2015); Christian Marxsen, *Territorial Integrity in International Law: Its Concept and Implications for Crimea*, 75 ZaöRV 7 (2015); Oleksandr Merezhko, *Crimea's Annexation by Russia: Contradictions of the New Russian Doctrine of International Law*, 75 ZaöRV 167 (2015); Ilya Nuzov, *National Ratification of an Internationally Wrongful Act: The Decision Validating Russia's Incorporation of Crimea*, 12 EUR. CON. L. REV. 353 (2016); Peter M. Olsen, *The Lawfulness of Russian Use of Force in Crimea*, 53 MIL. L. & L. WAR REV. 17 (2014); Alisa Gdalina, Note, *Crimea and the Right to Self-Determination: Questioning the Legality of Crimea's Secession from Ukraine*, 24 CARDOZO J. INT'L & COMP. L. 531 (2016); Trevor McDougal, Comment, *A New Imperialism? Evaluating Russia's Acquisition of Crimea in the Context of National and International Law*, 2015 BYU L. REV. 1947 (2015); Ashley Deeks, *Russian Forces in Ukraine: A Sketch of the International Law Issues*, LAWFARE, Mar. 2, 2014; Robert McCorquodale, *Ukraine Insta-Symposium: Crimea, Ukraine and Russia: Self-Determination, Intervention and International Law*, OPINIO JURIS, Mar. 10, 2014; Anne Peters, *Sense and Nonsense of Territorial Referendums in Ukraine, and Why the 16 March Referendum in Crimea Does Not Justify Crimea's Alteration of Territorial Status Under International Law*, EJIL: *TALK!*, Apr. 16, 2014; Ben Saul, *The Battle for Legal Legitimacy in Crimea*, THE DRUM, Mar. 3, 2014; Jure Vidmar, *Crimea's Referendum and Secession: Why It Resembles Northern Cyprus*, EJIL: *TALK!*, Mar. 20, 2014; Marc Weller, *Analysis: Why Russia's Crimea Move Fails Legal Test*, BBC NEWS, Mar. 7, 2014; Daniel Wisehart, *The Crisis in Ukraine and the Prohibition of the Use of Force: A Legal Basis for Russia's Intervention?*, EJIL: *TALK!*, Mar. 4, 2014.

[110] Vladislav Tolstykh, *Letter to the Editors: Reunification of Crimea with Russia: A Russian Perspective*, 13 CHINESE J. INT'L L. 879 (2014).

[111] Letter from Anatoly Kapustin, President of the Russ. Ass'n of Int'l Law, to Executive Council, Int'l Law Ass'n, June 5, 2014, http://www.ilarb.ru/html/news/2014/5062014.pdf (last visited Feb. 5, 2017) [hereinafter Kapustin Letter to ILA].

[112] *See, e.g.*, Anton Moiseienko, Guest Post: *What Do Russian Lawyers Say About Crimea?*, OPINIO JURIS, Sept. 24, 2014; Boris Mamlyuk, *Mapping Developments in Ukraine from the Perspective of International Law*, CAMBRIDGE INT'L L.J. BLOG, Mar. 12, 2014.

and Western scholars to debate Crimea.[113] They explained the impetus for the symposium as follows:

> Hardly any "Western" politician or scholar deems Russia's political course justifiable and justified under the precepts of international law. Inversely, from what we can perceive from the outside, Russian politicians and scholars seem confident to be able to properly justify the incorporation of Crimea within the framework of the existing international legal order. *The crisis is matched by the absence of a serious legal dialogue among international legal scholars of both camps.*[114]

The organizers emphasized the need to offer spaces for scholarly exchanges in which different academic universes could meet because, in their view, "the function and purpose of international law as a global order demands a genuinely transnational academic and practical legal discourse whose participants accept that arguments are sound only if they are fit for universal application."[115]

The Western and Russian international law scholars not only wrote in different languages, but often approached the topic in distinct ways. The Western scholars tended to treat the issue as one of Russia's illegal annexation of Crimea and unlawful use of force in, and violation of the territorial integrity of, Ukraine. This interpretation is obvious from the titles alone of these Western articles, which include "Territorial Integrity in International Law: Its Concept and Implications for Crimea," "The Use of Force by the Russian Federation in Crimea," "Crimea's Annexation by Russia: Contradictions of the New Russian Doctrine of International Law," "Analysis: Why Russia's Crimea Move Fails Legal Test," "Aggression against Ukraine: Territory, Responsibility, and International Law," and "Russia's Annexation of Crimea and International Law Governing the Use of Force." By contrast, the Russian international lawyers typically analyzed the situation as one of self-determination, focusing on Crimea's voluntary and lawful decision to reunite with its mother country, Russia with titles such as "'Crimean Law' or Legal Bases for the Reunification of the Crimea and Russia," "Reunification of Crimea and Russia: legal qualifications," "Legal Aspects of Crimean and Sevastopol's Entering into Russia," "Historical and Legal Foundations for Crimean Reunification as Part of Russia," "Reunification of Crimea and Sevastopol with Russian Federation Through the Prism of International Law and World Politics," "Reunification of Crimea and Russia: facts, qualification, and rhetoric," "International Law from the Perspective of Crimean Reunification with Russia," "Reunification of Crimea with Russia: A Legal Perspective," "Ukraine: The Right to Rebel," "Crimea's Self-Determination in the Light of Contemporary International Law,"

This symposium included articles in the first issue of *ZaöRV* in 2015 by authors Bilkova, Kapustin, Marxsen, Merezhko, Salenko, and Tolstykh, *supra* note 109.

[114] Christian Marxsen et al., *Introduction, Symposium: The Incorporation of Crimea by the Russian Federation in the Light of International Law*, 75 ZaöRV 3, 3 (2015) (emphasis added).

[115] *Id.* at 4.

and "Three Ideas of Self-Determination in International Law and the Reunification of Crimea with Russia."

Not all Russian scholars held identical views, nor did all Western scholars. But the commonalities within these groups were strong, whereas the divergence between them was palpable. The two groups of international lawyers generally evidenced divergent understandings of the facts. Russian international lawyers frequently asserted that there had been a "military," "unconstitutional" "coup d'état" in Kiev in which the legitimate head of state was overthrown; the United States and the European Union were guilty of intervening in the internal affairs of Ukraine to foment this coup and to support the installation of an illegitimate regime that then engaged in grave human rights violations, including "extrajudicial killings," "kidnappings," and "beatings" of Russians, Russian speakers, and those who opposed the new regime. The Western international lawyers tended not to characterize the conflict as a coup, did not lay the blame for it on the West, accepted the legitimacy of the interim government, and tended to dismiss claims that Russians and Russian speakers were being targeted as based on unsubstantiated propaganda spread by Russia and the Russian media.

Russian and Western international lawyers also mostly divided on their approach to key legal questions. According to the Russian international lawyers, the coup resulted in a dissolution of Ukraine into those who supported the coup and those who opposed it. The latter returned to their "natural state" and received the right to enter into a new social contract or to join an existing contract. Owing to the coup and the human rights violations, the Crimean people had a right to self-determination, and they exercised that right through a lawful referendum in which the people overwhelmingly voted to join Russia. By contrast, the Western scholars largely viewed Crimea as remaining a part of Ukraine, were unconvinced that the Crimean people's internal right to self-determination had been violated seriously enough to justify an external right to self-determination, and considered the referendum to have been illegitimately called and unsoundly conducted. Whereas the Russians portrayed the presence of Russian forces during the referendum as designed to safeguard the voting process, Western scholars viewed it as a threatening way of influencing the outcome and curtailing freedom of speech and assembly.

To the extent that the Russian international law scholars accepted that Russian forces were on Ukrainian territory, they attempted to justify their deployment as necessary to protect Russian citizens and "compatriots" (that is, ethnic Russians and Russian speakers), justified under the doctrine of humanitarian intervention, and based on consent because they were there at the invitation of the legitimate leaders of Ukraine and Crimea. By contrast, Western international lawyers debated whether international law permits a state to use force to defend its nationals abroad but generally found no legal basis for Russia to protect "compatriots" and no humanitarian catastrophe of the sort that would justify humanitarian intervention. Moreover, they typically viewed any argument based on invitation or consent as flawed because the ousted leader of Ukraine lacked effective control over the state, and the Crimean government, as a substate entity, lacked the right to issue such an invitation. Western scholars often worked hard to distinguish NATO's use of force in Kosovo and Kosovo's declaration of independence, whereas Russian scholars routinely cited the advisory opinion of the International Court of Justice (ICJ) on

Kosovo's declaration of independence and the positions taken by Western states with respect to Kosovo.

What points should be drawn from these parallel debates? First, one's understandings of how international law applies in a given case is inextricably enmeshed with one's understanding of the facts. But international lawyers in different states often rely on different media, which present different representations of reality. The Western scholars typically relied on Western news reports and statements by Western states and organizations to develop their understanding of the facts, whereas the Russian scholars embraced the facts that the Russian government and Russian news reports presented. Each tended to assume that the other was being swayed by misinformation spread by their state and media outlets. For instance, Russian international lawyer Kapustin detailed the deep connections between ethnic Russians in Ukraine and Russia based on their history, language, and culture, saying that one cannot "disregard these basic facts."[116] Nevertheless, he explained that the "US and the EU Mass Media, including reputable television broadcasting companies, ignore these facts and present the situation in such a manner that Ukraine has been allegedly invaded by 'pro-Russian separatists' that have set up authority over the local residents."[117] "Eventually," he concluded, "this fraud will be revealed."[118]

In reverse, German international lawyer Daniel Wisehart on the blog *EJIL: Talk!* gave the following account:

> Although there are divergent views between Western and Russian media on what is currently happening to Russian nationals in Crimea there seem to be no reports that would clearly establish that Russian nationals in Crimea or other parts of the Ukraine have been threatened. The Russian federation only generally asserts "a real threat to the lives and health of Russian citizens" but fails to establish in concreto how Russian citizens are endangered by the governmental transition that has occurred in the Ukraine on 23 February 2014.[119]

Similarly, US international lawyer Julian Ku on *Opinio Juris* concluded that much of the dispute was a factual one based on different media reports:

> Most scholars would accept the idea that self-determination is appropriate in certain exceptional circumstances, such as decolonization or when facing the threat of genocide or other mass killings. No one west of the Ukraine border seems to think Crimea qualifies (except the good folks at RT [the Russian government-funded television network]) because none of us think that the new Ukrainian government has threatened Crimea in any tangible way. But Russia could be understood to be

---

[116] Kapustin Letter to ILA, *supra* note 111, pt. 3.

[117] *Id.*

[118] *Id.*

[119] Daniel Wisehart, *The Crisis in Ukraine and the Prohibition of the Use of Force: A Legal Basis for Russia's Intervention?*, EJIL: *TALK!*, Mar. 4, 2014.

arguing the facts (see, Crimea really is threatened by the fascists in Kiev) rather than the law. I think it is a pretty ludicrous factual argument, but there it is.[120]

It would be easy for Western scholars to conclude that their media are free and unbiased, whereas Russian media are government sponsored and full of propaganda. Certainly, there is a huge gulf between the freedom of the press in the West and in states like Russia and China. But the Western media isn't perfect. For instance, the 2003 Iraq war led to doubts about the reliability of the media on questioning, rather than reinforcing, government views, and commentators have raised concerns about bias in the Western media's portrayal of Russia and Putin.[121] Discourse analysis of media reporting in different states about Kosovo suggested that different publics received very different pictures of what was going on and that these were often sympathetic to their own government's position.[122] Taking too black-and-white an approach would lead to discounting all views in these non-Western media sources and failing to apply any critical lens to the Western media, both of which are problematic. But while the situation is more gray, the shades of gray differ radically.

Second, the Western and Russian scholars' conclusions on the law tended to broadly align with the positions of their states or geopolitical regional groupings.[123] The unity of views expressed by the Russian international lawyers and the correlation between their positions and those of the Russian government were particularly striking. Russian international lawyer Maria Issaeva explained that the positions espoused by Russian academics "generally reflect—occasionally with some improvisation, but often word-for-word—the official Russian line expressed by the Russian President and Ministry of Foreign Affairs, including at the UN Security Council."[124] Whatever evidence there was for pluralism in the approaches of Russian international lawyers after the demise of the USSR, the case of Crimea had made it obvious, she concluded, that "Russian international legal doctrine continues to speak with unity of voice, and that voice continues to purport to be that of the Russian state."[125] But whether this unity of voice will extend to all areas of international law or whether it is a phenomenon that is reserved for areas of high politics, such as the use of force, remains unclear.

Although various Western scholars were critical of Europe's strategy toward Ukraine and the West's policies toward Kosovo, the Western scholars usually agreed that Russia's

---

[120] Julian Ku, *Is the Crimea Crisis a Factual or Legal Disagreement?*, OPINIO JURIS, Mar. 14, 2014.

[121] *See, e.g., Is Western Media Coverage of the Ukraine Crisis Anti-Russian?*, GUARDIAN, Aug. 4, 2014; Antony Loewenstein, *Ukraine: Western Media Coverage's Bias Should Be Held into Account*, GUARDIAN, Mar. 12, 2014; Piers Robinson, *Russian News May Be Biased—But So Is Much Western Media*, GUARDIAN, Aug. 2, 2016; *see also* PIERS ROBINSON ET AL., POCKETS OF RESISTANCE: BRITISH NEWS MEDIA, WAR AND THEORY IN THE 2003 INVASION OF IRAQ (2010).

[122] *See* Seth Ackerman & Jim Naureckas, *Following Washington's Script: The United States Media and Kosovo, in* DEGRADED CAPABILITY: THE MEDIA AND THE KOSOVO CRISIS 97 (Philip Hammond & Edward S. Herman eds., 2000); Philip Hammond, *Reporting "Humanitarian" Warfare: Propaganda, Moralism and NATO's Kosovo War*, 1 JOURNALISM STUDIES 365 (2000); Jin Yang, *Framing the NATO Air Strikes on Kosovo Across Countries Comparison of Chinese and US Newspaper Coverage*, 65 GAZETTE: INT'L J. FOR COMM. STUDIES 231 (2003).

[123] This point was also made by the editors of the Heidelberg Symposium. *See* Marxsen et al., *supra* note 114, at 4.

[124] MARIA ISSAEVA, QUARTER OF A CENTURY ON FROM THE SOVIET ERA: REFLECTIONS ON RUSSIAN DOCTRINAL RESPONSES TO THE ANNEXATION OF CRIMEA (forthcoming 2017).

[125] *Id.*

annexation of Crimea was manifestly illegal. There was room for criticism within these debates of the West's double standards and failure to adhere to international law in other circumstances, like NATO's use of force in Kosovo. Swiss-based international lawyer Nico Krisch noted that "it is ironical that these claims have come into the realm of the arguable because traditional constraints in the law on the use of force and self-determination have been blurred by instances of liberal interventionism over the last two decades."[126] Likewise, UK-based international lawyer Marko Milanovic complained of the "rampant hypocrisy" on the part of all the major players in the Crimean situation:

> Those same Western states that unlawfully invaded Iraq, and supported Kosovo's secession from Serbia while endlessly repeating that Kosovo was somehow a really super-special sui generis case, are now pontificating about the sanctity of the UN Charter and territorial integrity. On the other hand, that same Russia that fought two bloody wars in the 1990s to keep Chechnya within its fold, that same Russia that to this day refuses to accept the independence of Kosovo, has now rediscovered a principle of self-determination that apparently allows for the casual dismemberment of existing states.[127]

On the other hand, virtually no critical voices were raised in the Russian scholarly debates about Russia's approach to Crimea or Russia's own double standards with respect to Kosovo.[128] This lack is particularly noteworthy since the approaches taken by the Russian scholars on Crimea turned many of the approaches they had previously adopted on their head.[129] In their textbooks, the Russian scholars embraced the cardinal importance of the prohibition on the use of force and the principle of nonintervention, and rejected the notion of unilateral humanitarian intervention as a Western invention.[130] In Crimea, however, Russian scholars embraced the principles of self-determination and unilateral humanitarian intervention while remaining conspicuously silent about the importance of nonintervention and the nonuse of force. Instead of justifying their current positions by reference to their or Russia's previous statements, the Russian scholars—like the Russian government—relied on positions taken by Western states and scholars with respect to Kosovo. This posture allowed them to cite relevant precedents and criticize the West for hypocrisy and double standards without ever questioning Russia's or their own inconsistency.

---

[126] Nico Krisch, *Crimea and the Limits of International Law*, EJIL: *TALK!*, Mar. 10, 2014.

[127] Marko Milanovic, *Crimea, Kosovo, Hobgoblins and Hypocrisy*, EJIL: *TALK!*, Mar. 20, 2014.

[128] ISSAEVA, *supra* note 124 (noting that, among nearly two dozen international legal articles published by Russian scholars on the annexation of Crimea, only two firmly take a critical stance with respect to popular Russian justifications for state actions). For an exception from a PhD candidate from Moscow State University, who formerly studied at Harvard Law School, see Grigory Vaypan, *(Un)Invited Guests: The Validity of Russia's Argument on Intervention by Invitation*, CAMBRIDGE INT'L L.J. BLOG, Mar. 5, 2014.

[129] Lauri Mälksoo, *Crimea and (the Lack of) Continuity in Russian Approaches to International Law*, EJIL: *TALK!*, Mar. 28, 2014.

[130] *See* Chapter 4.VI.B.

Third, although most of the debates took place in their own echo chambers, some voices raised concern about the lack of engagement between these two scholarly communities and the way this divide might skew understandings of the debate. In discussing Oxford University Press's *Debate Map on Ukraine* and blogs like *Opinio Juris*, Boris Mamlyuk (a US international law professor who speaks Russian and specializes in Russia) lamented that they included little to no analysis of the international law arguments from the perspective of Russian jurists or policy makers even though the Russian blogosphere was brimming with international law coverage of Crimea.[131] "To start this dialogue across language barriers, professional jargon, and political commitments individual scholars will need space to collaborate," he explained, "lest we return to Cold War postures where international law occupies an uneasy place alongside ideology and propaganda."[132]

US international lawyer Ku acknowledged this deficiency on *Opinio Juris*, together with complaints about the blog's "pro-Western bias."[133] "Part of the problem," he explained, "is that there is a dearth of international law commentators writing in English in favor of the Russian legal position."[134] As this comment highlights, language barriers are real, and the language in which discussions are taking place and the content of those discussions are often linked. Plenty of Russian scholars wrote in support of the Russian position in Russian, but few such writings were available in English. Accordingly, "bridge" lawyers who speak both languages and follow both debates are instrumental in communicating information from one community to the other.[135]

Awareness of what different communities of international lawyers are saying is an important step in understanding international law as a transnational field. But one should not expect that fostering connections between such communities will necessarily lead to a shared understanding of the facts or a common approach to the law. As emerged from the Heidelberg symposium, the Russian and Western scholars remained very much divided, even when engaged in a common debate. The editors of that symposium noted that their aim was to document the exchange of arguments and, in doing so, bring into the Western debate the views of Russian and other Eastern European scholars. To serve this purpose, they clarified that they had not interfered substantively with the arguments made in the written contributions and the papers did not undergo peer review.[136] Instead, they chose to show the "authentic positions" of the authors, independently from what the symposium editors would have "preferred as a legal approach" and without "imply[ing] any substantive approval."[137]

---

[131] Boris Mamlyuk, *Crisis in Ukraine: A Cascade of Many International Law Violations*, HUFFINGTON POST, Mar. 13, 2014 (last updated May 13, 2014).

[132] *Id.*

[133] Ku, *supra* note 120.

[134] *Id.*

[135] Examples include Maria Issaeva, Lauri Mälksoo, and Boris Mamlyuk. A number of Ukrainian international lawyers emerged as bridges, though they were critical, rather than supportive, of Russian positions. *See, e.g.,* OLEKSANDR ZADOROZHNII, RUSSIAN DOCTRINE OF INTERNATIONAL LAW AFTER THE ANNEXATION OF CRIMEA (2016); OLEKSANDR ZADOROZHNII, Российская доктрина международного права после аннексии Крыма [The Russian International Legal Doctrine After the Annexation of Crimea] (2015).

[136] Marxsen et al., *supra* note 114, at 5.

[137] *Id.*

The implication of these qualifications was that, had the editors followed the normal peer review process, some or all of these Russian articles would have been rejected or modified. This admission links back to a point made earlier about who sits on editorial boards.[138] The editorial boards of many of the transnational international law journals are dominated by Western international law academics. These boards are likely to accept many of the claims and assumptions made by Western international law scholars, while being skeptical of many of the claims and assumptions made by the Russian international law scholars. This approach may well be justified as a matter of fact and law—I do not address that issue here. But these inclinations create a further disincentive for Russian international legal scholars seeking to publish in these journals. Imagine how the Western international law scholars would feel about publishing in Russian and submitting their pieces for review by all-Russian editorial boards. These realities encourage further divisions between these communities, reinforcing silos and disconnects.

B. DEBATES ABOUT THE *SOUTH CHINA SEA* ARBITRATION

In 2013, the Philippines launched an arbitration against China under UNCLOS.[139] Rather than seek a ruling on which state had sovereignty over certain maritime features, the Philippines requested a determination of the nature of those features (for example, which were islands, rocks, or neither) and which maritime rights they gave rise to (for example, an exclusive economic zone, a territorial sea, or neither). China objected to the tribunal's jurisdiction on various grounds, including that: the Philippines was de facto litigating issues of sovereignty, which are precluded under UNCLOS; the Philippine claims required delimitation of maritime boundaries, which China had excluded from its acceptance of UNCLOS dispute resolution; and the Philippines had failed to exhaust peaceful means of settling the dispute to which it had previously agreed.[140] China therefore refused to participate in the arbitration, and the tribunal adopted a broad ruling that was very favorable to the Philippines.[141]

Several points are noteworthy about the ensuing scholarly debates. First, as with their Russian counterparts in the debates about Crimea, Chinese international law scholars were almost uniform in supporting the Chinese government's view that the *South China Sea* tribunal lacked jurisdiction. A key example was the statement issued by the Chinese Society of International Law, entitled "The Tribunal's Award in the 'South China Sea Arbitration' Initiated by the Philippines Is Null and Void" (CSIL Statement), which was published on the website of the Chinese Ministry of Foreign Affairs.[142] After referring to the Chinese government's position paper setting

---

[138] *See* Chapter 3.III.C.

[139] *See* South China Sea (Phil. v. China), PCA Case No. 2013–19, Award, para. 4 (July 12, 2016), http://www.pcacases.com/web/view/7.

[140] *See id.*, para. 13.

[141] *Id.* paras., 13–14, 1203.

[142] CHINESE SOC'Y OF INT'L LAW, *The Tribunal's Award in the "South China Sea Arbitration" Initiated by the Philippines Is Null and Void*, June 10, 2016, http://www.fmprc.gov.cn/mfa_eng/zxxx_662805/t1371363.shtml (last visited Feb. 5, 2017) [hereinafter CSIL Statement].

out China's arguments as to why the tribunal lacked jurisdiction, the CSIL Statement declares: "The Chinese Society of International Law strongly supports the positions of the Chinese Government."[143]

The CSIL Statement and the positions taken by the Chinese government and Chinese officials are mutually reinforcing. For example, in a statement of the Ministry of Foreign Affairs, the Chinese government asserted that the tribunal's award on jurisdiction was "null and void" and had "no binding effect on China."[144] Likewise, the CSIL Statement explained that the jurisdictional award was groundless in both fact and law and thus was "null and void," which meant that any decision on the substantive issues would have "no legal effect."[145] The CSIL Statement concluded that "China's non-acceptance of and non-participation in the Arbitration and its non-recognition of any award" made by the tribunal have a "solid legal basis" and are "acts of justice to maintain and uphold international law."[146] Similarly, Liu Xiaoming, China's ambassador to the United Kingdom, argued that by "not accepting or recognizing the ruling, China is not violating but upholding the authority and dignity of international law."[147]

Perhaps the Chinese Society of International Law's support for the Chinese government should not come as a surprise. The Chinese Society is more closely associated with its government than, say, the American Society of International Law. The Chinese Society is a national academic group that has a Secretariat located in the China University of Foreign Affairs, which is governed by the Ministry of Foreign Affairs.[148] The Society receives "guidance" from the Ministry of Foreign Affairs,[149] and its current president (Li Shishi) is a top official with the National People's Congress and was formerly a top legal official of the State Council.[150] With this background, it would be hard to imagine the Society taking a view that was critical of or distinct from the Chinese government, particularly on a pressing issue of national importance. Of course, one cannot assume that the views of the Chinese Society of International Law reflect the views of all Chinese international lawyers.

---

[143] *Id.*

[144] Ministry of Foreign Affairs, Statement of the Ministry of Foreign Affairs of the People's Republic of China on the Award on Jurisdiction and Admissibility of the South China Sea Arbitration by the Arbitral Tribunal Established at the Request of the Republic of the Philippines, Oct. 30, 2015, http://www.fmprc.gov.cn/mfa_eng/zxxx_662805/t1310474.shtml (last visited Feb. 5, 2017).

[145] CSIL Statement, *supra* note 142.

[146] *Id.*

[147] Liu Xiaoming, *South China Sea Arbitration Is a Political Farce*, CHINA DAILY, July 25, 2016 (first published on the *Daily Telegraph* website on July 23, 2016).

[148] *See* 中国国际法学会 [Chinese Soc'y of Int'l Law], http://www.csil.cn/News/Detail.aspx?AId=16 (last visited Feb. 5, 2017).

[149] *See* 中国国际法学会 [Chinese Soc'y of Int'l Law], art. 4, http://www.csil.cn/News/Detail.aspx?AId=19 (last visited Feb. 5, 2017).

[150] 中国国际法学会会长致辞 [Speech by President of the Chinese Society of International Law], http://www.csil.cn/News/Detail.aspx?AId=17 (last visited Feb. 5, 2017). For biographical information on Li Shishi, see http://cn.chinagate.cn/politics/2008-03/14/content_12631668.htm (last visited Feb. 5, 2017) and http://www.npc.gov.cn/delegate/viewDelegate.action?dbid=121680 (last visited Feb. 5, 2017).

The CSIL Statement is not an isolated example, however. Similar statements have been issued by the Chinese Law Society,[151] the All China Lawyers Association,[152] and the Chinese Society of the Law of the Sea.[153] (Again, some of these groups are closely tied to the government, such as the All China Lawyers Association, which comes under the auspices of the Ministry of Justice.[154]) At a meeting in China, three hundred Chinese legal experts gathered to discuss the case and unanimously agreed that China was right to abstain from participating in the case because the tribunal lacked jurisdiction and that China had a legitimate right under international law to reject the arbitration.[155] Young Chinese PhD students in the Netherlands wrote an open letter endorsing China's legal position on the case that reportedly received more than twenty thousand signatures.[156] Prominent Chinese international lawyers who often write in foreign and transnational international law journals, such as Sienho Yee and Congyan Cai, have also criticized the tribunal's decision finding jurisdiction.[157]

Although Chinese international lawyers have been virtually unanimous as to the tribunal's lack of jurisdiction, at least publicly, they have disagreed somewhat over whether the government adopted the right strategy in failing to appear before the tribunal to argue the case. Some academics who did not agree with the government's approach to this issue remained silent on the matter, explaining privately that it was "not easy, actually impossible" for Chinese scholars located in China to publish this view in Chinese journals.[158] But this view was expressed by at least one prominent Chinese legal academic, Bing Ling, who was educated in both China and the United States and who holds an academic position in Australia rather than mainland China. Ling argued that China would have had a better chance of winning on jurisdiction if it had participated in the case, at least during the jurisdictional phase. He suggested that China should have learned from the US approach in the ICJ *Nicaragua* case where the

---

[151] *China Law Society Issues Statement on South China Sea Arbitration Initiated by the Philippines*, Xinhua, May 25, 2016.

[152] *All China Lawyers Association Issues Statement on South China Sea Arbitration Initiated by the Philippines*, Xinhua, June 7, 2016.

[153] *Chinese Society of the Law of the Sea Issues Statement on South China Sea Arbitration Initiated by the Philippines*, Xinhua, June 2, 2016.

[154] 中华全国律师协会 [All China Lawyers Association], art. 4, http://www.acla.org.cn/zhangchen.jhtml (last visited Feb. 5, 2017).

[155] *Chinese Legal Experts Refute Philippine Claim in South China Sea*, CCTV America, May 8, 2016.

[156] *Young Scholars to Launch Open Letter Against South China Sea Arbitration*, Xinhua, July 6, 2016; *An Open Letter on the South China Sea Arbitration*, China Daily, July 12, 2016; *20,000 Sign Open Letter on South China Sea Ruling*, Xinhua, July 13, 2016.

[157] *See, e.g., China Offers Philippines Talks if South China Sea Court Ignored: China Daily*, Reuters, July 5, 2016 (citing Sienho Yee: "Objectively the tribunal has no jurisdiction over the dispute" because "[n]egotiation has been agreed upon as the way to resolve the dispute"); *Interview: South China Sea Arbitration Abuses International Law: Chinese Scholar*, Xinhua, July 12, 2016 (citing Congyan Cai: "The Philippines' unilateral request for arbitration on the South China Sea could be deemed as abuse of international law, at least not in good faith" and "the arbitral tribunal did not conduct adequate review or a reasonable judgment on the legal role of negotiation in this case").

[158] E-mail on file with author.

United States appeared to contest jurisdiction and, when it lost on that point, refused to participate on the merits.[159]

Ling's argument generated significant controversy and debate within China.[160] Ku noted that, other than Ling, scholars within the Chinese legal establishment seem to have either expressed support for China's position or kept silent.[161] Ku attributes this "startling" unanimity of Chinese legal opinion to two potential factors. One, Chinese academics may be unwilling to dissent on an issue of importance to the government out of fear of censorship or soft retribution in the competitive domestic academic job market. Some newspapers have reported (anonymous) complaints by Chinese scholars of being shunned by the government if they express critical views on the case and of seldom having their dissenting views make the headlines in China's state-controlled media.[162] According to Jerome Cohen: "it requires an act of courage for any international law or foreign relations specialist within the government to contradict prevailing policy, although academic debate continues to be allowed."[163] Two, the unanimity may result from the genuine belief of most Chinese legal academics that the arbitral tribunal erred in asserting jurisdiction. Ku attributes this reaction to the Chinese international lawyers' mentality of not being "immune to the siren calls of nationalism."[164] But it may also be the result of a complex socialization process based on the way these scholars were educated, the reference materials that they commonly use, the media on which they rely, and the assumptions and boundaries that delimit mainstream academic debate within China.

For their part, Western international lawyers have split on the correctness of the tribunal's decision on jurisdiction. Before the jurisdictional award, Ku at *Opinio Juris* argued that there was "no basis for the ITLOS to assert jurisdiction over this dispute, without China's consent"[165] and that the Philippines would face a "huge challenge to get any

---

[159] 凌兵 [Ling Bing], 厘清南海仲裁案 "不参与不接受" 的几个问题 [Clarifying Several problems with Not Participating in the South China Sea arbitration],中国国际法促进中心 [Chinese Initiative on International Law], Dec. 28, 2015; 凌兵 [Ling Bing],为什么中国拒绝南海仲裁有损中国的权益 [Why China's Refusal to Participate in the South China Sea Arbitration Is Detrimental to China's Interests], *id.*, Dec. 18, 2015.

[160] For a rebuttal of Ling's argument, see, for example, 陆涛 [Lu Tao], 纸上谈兵维护不了中国的南海利益 [Empty Talk Is Not Likely to Protect China's Interest], 中国国际法促进中心 [Chinese Initiative on International Law], Dec. 23, 2015. For a discussion of the debate between Ling and Lu, see, for example, 孙莹 [Sun Ying], 南海仲裁案裁决在即! 中国要不要 "果断出击"？[South China Sea Arbitral Award Coming Soon! Should China "Decisively Go on the Offensive"?], 凤凰资讯 [Phoenix News], May 10, 2016, http://news.ifeng.com/a/20160510/48743954_0.shtml.

[161] Julian Ku, *China's Legal Scholars Are Less Credible After South China Sea Ruling*, FOREIGN POL'Y, July 14, 2016.

[162] Shi Jiangtao, *Is Beijing Courting Disaster by Shunning South China Sea Tribunal?*, S. CHINA MORNING POST, June 20, 2016 ("Speaking your mind at seminars organised by Beijing to discuss competing claims in the South China Sea won't see you invited back, something a leading mainland international law scholar discovered three months ago.").

[163] Jerome A. Cohen, *Forecasting the Aftermath of a Ruling on China's Nine-Dash Line*, FOREIGN POL'Y, Apr. 20, 2016.

[164] Ku, *supra* note 161.

[165] Julian Ku, *Why the Philippines Has No Chance of Making China Go to Court*, OPINIO JURIS, Apr. 17, 2012; *see also* Natalie Klein, *Some Lessons from Mauritius v. UK for Philippines v. China*, ILA REP., Apr. 16, 2015 ("it is, in my view, impossible to separate any consideration of entitlements from the question of who is so entitled" and the "territorial sovereignty dispute is the real heart of the problem in *Philippines v. China*").

arbitral tribunal to assert jurisdiction here."[166] By contrast, Diane Desierto at *EJIL: Talk!*
concluded that there were no persuasive reasons that would justify denying the tribunal
jurisdiction over the Philippines' narrowly framed Statement of Claim.[167] But the tribunal's decision to take jurisdiction in the case did not generate many blog posts and, by
the time the award on the merits was released, the focus of the blogs had largely shifted
to the award's substantive findings and to China's reaction to it.[168] Regardless of whether
the tribunal was correct in asserting jurisdiction, the Western scholars almost all viewed
China as bound by the decision.[169]

Second, as with the Crimean debates, news reports in China and the West tended to
present the story differently in terms of focus (which issues were important and required
explanation) and narrative (which states were aggressive and which were reactive, which
states were violating the international rule of law and which were upholding it). Each
set of media was also quick to discredit the other with accusations of censorship or bias.
For instance, *Foreign Affairs* reported on how the Chinese government used a combination of propaganda and censorship to discredit Western media as biased, especially in the
reporting of the South China Sea disputes.[170] Meanwhile, Wang Guan, the chief political
correspondent of CCTV America, explained that the West may boast a free press, but
that it was biased, as evidenced by the reporting on the South China Sea disputes.[171] One
cannot assume that international lawyers from a given state or geopolitical grouping rely
only on media from that state or grouping or that the views expressed in that media are
identical to those held by international lawyers. But understanding the different facts
that are reported, and the different narratives that are developed, in the media in different states can give some insights into the different doxas and opinions that exist in those
societies.

---

[166] Julian Ku, *Game Changer? Philippines Seeks UNCLOS Arbitration with China over the South China Sea*, Opinio Juris, Jan. 22, 2013.

[167] Diane Desierto, *The Jurisdictional Rubicon: Scrutinizing China's Position Paper on the South China Sea Arbitration—Part I*, EJIL: *TALK!*, Jan. 29, 2015; *see also* Diane Desierto, *The Jurisdictional Rubicon: Scrutinizing China's Position Paper on the South China Sea Arbitration—Part II*, EJIL: *TALK!*, Jan. 30, 2015.

[168] *See, e.g.,* Diane Desierto, *The Philippines v. China Arbitral Award on the Merits as a Subsidiary Source of International Law*, EJIL: *TALK!*, July 12, 2016; Julian Ku, *Short, Quick Take on the Philippines' Sweeping Victory in the South China Sea Arbitration*, Lawfare, July 12, 2016; Robert Williams, *Tribunal Issues Landmark Ruling in South China Sea Arbitration*, Lawfare, July 12, 2016. There were exceptions, like Douglas Guilfoyle on EJIL: *Talk!*, who concluded that the tribunal's jurisdictional finding was "not eccentric or bizarre" and argu-ments to the contrary ignore well known scholarship. *See* Douglas Guilfoyle, *Philippines v. China: First Thoughts on the Award in the South China Seas Case*, EJIL: *TALK!*, July 12, 2016; *see also* John E. Noyes, *In Re Arbitration Between the Philippines and China*, 110 Am. J. Int'l L. 102 (2016).

[169] *See, e.g.,* Julian Ku, *China's Ridiculously Weak Legal Argument Against Complying with the South China Sea Arbitration Award*, Lawfare, June 6, 2016; Ku, *supra* note 161. *But see* Stefan Talmon, Opinion, *Final Award in Sea Arbitration Will Be Flawed*, China Daily, July 9, 2016 (arguing that the problems with the tribunal's jurisdictional ruling "provide China with good legal arguments to reject the tribunal's final award").

[170] Bethany Allen-Ebrahimian, *How China Won the War Against Western Media*, Foreign Aff., Mar. 4, 2016. For an example of such reporting, see, for example, *Truth About South China Sea Should Not Be Misrepresented by Western Media*, Xinhua, July 8, 2016.

[171] *See South China Sea: CCTV Reporter Debates with American Expert on the Arbitration Case*, YouTube (July 22, 2016), https://www.youtube.com/watch?v=P510ELMTL1M (last visited Feb. 5, 2017).

In terms of focus, the Western media's perspective can be illustrated by the editorials and news reports on the South China Sea disputes and arbitration in the *New York Times*. In an early editorial on the case, the *Times* noted that China objected to the tribunal's jurisdiction but did not explain why.[172] After warning that China might ignore a negative decision, the Editorial Board concluded that China should participate in the tribunal proceedings if it "wants to be recognized as a leader in a world that values the resolution of disputes within a legal framework."[173] When the tribunal took jurisdiction, the paper reported that the Philippines had won an important ruling in the case but again did not explain China's objection.[174] Before the award on the merits, the Editorial Board explained that "China has been behaving in a bellicose fashion in the South China Sea for some time" and that this conduct was part of a "sustained and increasingly dangerous effort to assert sovereignty over a vital waterway in which other nations also have claims."[175] After noting that many experts expected the tribunal to rule against China, the board stated that the "right response would be for China to accept the court's decision," but noted that whether it would do so "remains to be seen."[176]

In terms of narrative, Western newspapers frequently situated the dispute in the context of China's rising global power, portrayed China as an aggressive bully in the region, and described China's reaction to the arbitration and award as a test case for whether China would comply with the international rule of law. For example, after the award was released, the Editorial Board of the *New York Times* framed the issue as follows: "How China reacts to the sweeping legal defeat over its claims to the South China Sea will tell the world a lot about its approach to international law, the use—measured or otherwise—of its enormous power, and its global ambitions."[177] The paper concluded that, so far, the signs were "troubling" because Beijing had "defiantly" rejected a court's jurisdiction over the case and insisted it would not accept the "path breaking" judgment.[178] The Editorial Board followed up with an article "China's Defiance in the South China Sea," which explained that "China's activities in the South China Sea have increasingly persuaded more and more people that it is determined to put into place the military facilities that will allow Beijing to bully and dominate its coastal neighbors."[179]

Concerns about China's aggressive posture were typically bolstered by articles about how China was building up and militarizing disputed islands in the South China Sea and chasing away foreign vessels and aircraft.[180] By contrast, the United States was presented

---

[172] Editorial, *The South China Sea, in Court*, N.Y. TIMES, July 17, 2015.

[173] *Id.*

[174] Jane Perlez, *In Victory for Philippines, Hague Court to Hear Dispute over South China Sea*, N.Y. TIMES, Oct. 30, 2015.

[175] Editorial, *Playing Chicken in the South China Sea*, N.Y. TIMES, May 20, 2016.

[176] *Id.*

[177] Editorial, *Testing the Rule of Law in the South China Sea*, N.Y. TIMES, July 12, 2016.

[178] *Id.*

[179] Editorial, *China's Defiance in the South China Sea*, N.Y. TIMES, Aug. 13, 2016.

[180] *See, e.g.*, Chris Buckley, *China, Denying Close Encounter with American Plane, Points Finger at U.S.*, N.Y. TIMES, May 19, 2016; Joe Cochrane, *China's Coast Guard Rams Fishing Boat to Free It from Indonesian Authorities, id.*, Mar. 21, 2016; Editorial, *China's Missile Provocation, id.*, Feb. 18, 2016; Michael Forsythe, *Possible Radar Suggests*

as a neutral state that was seeking to uphold freedom of navigation and to encourage the disputing parties to uphold the international rule of law. Thus, the Editorial Board of the *Times* stated:

> The United States, which is neutral on the various claims, can help ensure a peaceful, lawful path forward. The Obama administration has said that disputes should be resolved according to international law, a position it now reaffirms. It has built closer security relations with Asian nations and responded to China's assertiveness in the South China Sea with increased naval patrols. This combination of diplomacy and pressure is sound, but the hard part is getting the balance right.[181]

Likewise, the Editorial Board explained in another piece that "[t]he Obama administration has played an important restraining role. It has also demonstrated resolve in defending America's commitment to freedom of navigation by sending warships into the South China Sea."[182]

Unsurprisingly, the Chinese newspapers presented a far different picture of the arbitration and the United States' role in the region. Mirroring the language of Chinese government officials, many Chinese newspaper articles and editorials adopted emotive language that called into question the legitimacy and validity of the tribunal and its award. They often referred to the arbitration as "unlawful" or a "farce" and to the decision as a "so-called" award that was "illegal" and "invalid."[183] Many of the articles explained in detail why the tribunal lacked jurisdiction. For instance, an opinion editorial in the *China Daily* by China's ambassador to the United Kingdom argued that both the subject matter of the arbitration and the Philippines' intention in bringing the case involved determining issues related to territorial sovereignty and maritime delimitation, but that territorial sovereignty lay beyond the scope of UNCLOS and that China had excluded issues of maritime delimitation from its acceptance of dispute resolution under that treaty.[184]

Like the Chinese government, some of the news reports and opinion editorials questioned the impartiality, representativeness, and independence of the tribunal, noting,

---

Beijing Wants "Effective Control" in South China Sea, id., Feb. 23, 2016; Jane Perlez, China Building Airstrip on 3rd Artificial Island, Images Show, id., Sept. 15, 2015; Michael S. Schmidt, Chinese Aircraft Fly Within 50 Feet of U.S. Plane over South China Sea, Pentagon Says, id., May 18, 2016; Michael D. Shear, Obama Calls on Beijing to Stop Construction in South China Sea, id., Nov. 18, 2015; Derek Watkins, What China Has Been Building in the South China Sea, id., July 31, 2015.

[181] Editorial, *supra* note 177.

[182] Editorial, *supra* note 179.

[183] See, e.g., Liu Xiaoming, *supra* note 147; Op-ed, *Double Standards Applied in South China Sea Arbitration Profane International Law*, PEOPLE'S DAILY, July 16, 2016; Op-ed I on the Philippines' South China Sea Arbitration Farce: Grandstanding Cannot Cover up Illegal Moves, PEOPLE'S DAILY, Dec. 14, 2015; Op-ed II on the Philippines' South China Sea Arbitration Farce, China's Sovereignty over the South China Sea Islands Brooks No Denial, PEOPLE'S DAILY, Dec. 15, 2015; Shen Dingli, *Unlawful Arbitration Worsens Tensions in Disputed Fishing Waters*, GLOB. TIMES, July 13, 2016; Su Xiaohui, *It's Time to Stop Political Farce in the South China Sea*, CHINA US FOCUS, July 25, 2016; *Unlawful Arbitration Cannot Negate China's Sovereignty over South China Sea*, PEOPLE'S DAILY, July 12, 2016; Zhong Sheng, *Justice Is China's Best Ally in Sea Dispute*, CHINA DAILY USA, July 21, 2016.

[184] Liu Xiaoming, *supra* note 147.

for instance, that none of the five arbitrators came from Asia or had much knowledge of Asian history and culture.[185] Most of the arbitrators were picked by Shunji Yanai, then-president of the International Tribunal for the Law of the Sea and former Japanese ambassador to the United States (reference to which seemed designed to invoke concern about bias given tensions between China and Japan); four were Western and the other had pursued long-term study in the West (mention of which seemed intended to suggest the existence of Western bias).[186] The tribunal was dismissed as an ad hoc body rather than a standing court and as not being a UN body.[187] Some noted that the tribunal's fees were paid by the Philippines, suggesting that the decision had been bought, even though this is the norm for arbitration when one side fails to appear.[188]

Beyond attacking the tribunal's jurisdiction, the papers repeatedly stressed the double standards of the United States in calling for China to comply with UNCLOS and to abide by the tribunal's rulings so as to respect the international rule of law.[189] For instance, the *People's Daily* criticized the United States for gaining benefits under UNCLOS without ever having ratified it, and for refusing to accept the ICJ's jurisdiction and judgment in the *Nicaragua* case:

> Regarding the international rule of law, the US and some other countries can hardly qualify as a "teacher" to China. In addition, they should look back to their past mistakes, abandon their long-upheld hegemony, egoism, hypocrisy and double standard and implement the basic norms of the international law and international relations through practical actions.[190]

Similarly, an appraisal in the *People's Daily* written under the pen name "Guo Jiping," which is used for editorials that are meant to outline China's stance and viewpoints on major international issues, stated:

> The double standards adopted by the US have exposed its hypocrisy and deep-rooted "imperialistic mentality." That is to say, the US will only show strong support for

---

[185] *See, e.g., id.; Spotlight: Unmasking the Ragtag South China Sea Arbitral Tribunal*, XINHUA, July 18, 2016 [hereinafter *Ragtag South China Sea*].

[186] *Spotlight: South China Sea Arbitration Decided by Biased Arbitrators*, XINHUA, July 19, 2016.

[187] *See, e.g.,* Liu Xiaoming, *supra* note 147; *Ragtag South China Sea, supra* note 185; *Spotlight: Permanent Court of Arbitration Neither Permanent nor a Court*, XINHUA, July 16, 2016; *The Hague-based Permanent Court of Arbitration Not Related with UN*, XINHUA, July 13, 2016.

[188] *See, e.g.,* Fei Liena, Commentary, *Puppet Tribunal in S. China Sea Case Does Not Represent Int'l Law*, XINHUA, July 14, 2016; Liu Xiaoming, *supra* note 147; *Ragtag South China Sea, supra* note 185; Wang Hanling, *How Much Manila Spent for Favorable Ruling?*, CHINA DAILY USA, Aug. 2, 2016.

[189] *See, e.g.,* Chua Chin Leng, *The Hague's Theatrical Judgment on the South China Sea*, CHINA DAILY, June 29, 2016; Liu Xiaoming, *supra* note 147; *Spotlight: U.S. Refusal to Honor Court Ruling in Nicaragua Case Reflects Double Standards*, XINHUA, July 14, 2016; Zhang Junshe, *US Iraq Tricks Reused in Tribunal Award*, GLOB. TIMES, July 12, 2016.

[190] Op-Ed, *Double Standards Applied in South China Sea Arbitration Profane International Law*, PEOPLE'S DAILY, July 16, 2016.

international laws that are to its own benefit. Otherwise, no matter how legitimate a law may be, the US will pay it no attention. . . .[191]

The *South China Sea* arbitration plays into three world views that figure prominently in China's foreign policy: the "century of humiliation" (百年国耻), the view that cultural characteristics are inherent and unchanging, and the idea of history as destiny.[192] The Communist Party uses socializing mechanisms, including the media and the education system, to inculcate certain social and political messages into the Chinese people's everyday understanding of the world that can be employed to help explain or justify particular foreign policy actions. These narratives serve the function of creating the parameters within which the actions that other states take in response to China are likely to be interpreted by, and reacted to within, China.[193]

The century of humiliation continues to play an important role in shaping the approach of China and its people to the international legal system.[194] Far from admitting to China's being the aggressor or a bully, Chinese officials and media often invoke China's century of humiliation to cast the state as the victim of aggression by imperialist powers. China's century of humiliation lasted from the First Opium War in the 1840s to the Communist Party's takeover of power in 1949. As an opinion editorial in the *China Daily* indicated: "Unlike the US, whose history in the last 150 years has been seizing land and expanding territory, for China, it has been a bitter memory of that 'century of humiliation.'"[195] Chinese actors often draw on this narrative of humiliation as a starting point for discussions about how China should interact with other states. It also provides a helpful framework for understanding why Chinese people are particularly sensitive to what they perceive as Western bullying or attempts to infringe upon China's sovereignty.[196] An article in *Xinhua* elaborated:

Though China is growing into a strong country, the painful memory of history is not long gone. The Chinese people have not forgotten that the country stumbled into the 20th century with its capital under the occupation of the imperialists' armies, and for over a century before and after, China suffered the humiliation of foreign invasion and aggression. That is why the Chinese people and government are very

---

[191] *Unlawful Arbitration Cannot Negate China's Sovereignty over South China Sea*, PEOPLE'S DAILY, July 11, 2016.

[192] *See* MERRIDEN VARRALL, CHINESE WORLD VIEWS AND CHINA'S FOREIGN POLICY 1 (2015); *see also* KEVIN RUDD, BELFER CTR. FOR SCI. & INT'L AFFAIRS, U.S.-CHINA 21: THE FUTURE OF U.S.-CHINA RELATIONS UNDER XI JINPING 13 (2015).

[193] *See* VARRALL, *supra* note 192, at 3.

[194] PHIL C.W. CHAN, CHINA, STATE SOVEREIGNTY AND INTERNATIONAL LEGAL ORDER 63–107 (2015); Simon Chesterman, *Asia's Ambivalence About International Law and Institutions: Past, Present and Futures*, 27 EUR. J. INT'L L. 945, 953 (2016); Alison Kaufman, *The "Century of Humiliation," Then and Now: Chinese Perceptions of the International Order*, 25 PAC. FOCUS 1 (2010).

[195] Chen Weihua, *Century of Humiliation Still Cuts Deep into the Collective Psyche*, CHINA DAILY, Aug. 19, 2016.

[196] *See, e.g.*, WANG ZHENG, NEVER FORGET NATIONAL HUMILIATION: HISTORICAL MEMORY IN CHINESE POLITICS AND FOREIGN RELATIONS 102 (2012); Luo Xi, *The South China Sea Case and China's New Nationalism*, DIPLOMAT, July 19, 2016.

sensitive about anything that is related to territorial integrity and would never allow such recurrence even if it's just an inch of land.[197]

The narrative that cultural characteristics of states are inherent and unchanging is applied to both the United States and Japan. The United States is seen as a state with inherently hegemonic desires and a proven track record of interfering in the business of other states. Given China's experiences with Japan in World War II, Japan is viewed as inherently imperialistic and expansionist. Thus, the United States and Japan were portrayed as aggressive, trouble-making states trying to contain China's rise.[198] *Xinhua* asked, "Why does the United States want to poke its nose into the region?" before answering that "China's increasing say in the international rule-making process and growing influence on regional order establishment have made the United States uncomfortable, pricking its fragile ego as a hegemonic power."[199] According to the *China Daily*, the "strategic rebalancing [of the United States] to Asia is widely perceived as a policy shift that [was] intended to contain China's rise" and, to that end, it had encouraged countries such as the Philippines and Vietnam to "stir up trouble" in the South China Sea.[200] US freedom-of-navigation operations were described as "very dangerous" actions, a "muscle show," and an example of the US view that "might is right," and disparaged as "destabilizing regional peace and undermining coastal nations' security interests."[201]

The narrative of history as destiny comes through in the idea that China was a powerful, respected, and peaceful global actor in the past, and that its natural right is to fulfill the same role in the future. China is portrayed as an inherently peaceful state that has never been aggressively expansionist, so that its actions in the South China Sea should not be viewed as menacing. Instead, China is gradually resuming its rightful role prior to the First Opium War as a peaceful, though extremely powerful, actor within its region, in keeping with President Xi Jinping's idea of the "China dream" and of the current time as the period of "great renewal of the Chinese nation."[202]

---

[197] Fu Ying & Wu Shicun, *South China Sea: How We Got to This Stage*, XINHUA, May 14, 2016; *see also* Eric Fish, *How Historical "Humiliation" Drives China's Maritime Claims*, ASIA SOC'Y, June 16, 2016; Emily Rauhala, *China Believes It Is the Real Victim in the South China Sea Dispute*, WASH. POST, July 11, 2016; Merriden Varrall, *How China's Worldviews Are Manifested in the South China Sea*, NAT'L INT., Dec. 16, 2015.

[198] *See, e.g.*, Han Dongping, *Ruling of Arbitration Can't Challenge China's Territorial Integrity*, CHINA DAILY, July 1, 2016; *Japan Seeks to Contain China*, CHINA DAILY, Aug. 16, 2016; *Stay Vigilant to Japan's "China Threat*," XINHUA, Aug. 6, 2016; Wang Hui, *US' Actions Are Steadily Eroding Bilateral Trust*, CHINA DAILY, Aug. 3, 2016; Zhong Sheng, *U.S. Display of Military Power Act of Hegemony*, PEOPLE'S DAILY, June 22, 2016; Zhu Junqing, Commentary: *S. China Sea Arbitration Another Plot Hatched by U.S. to Reinforce Hegemony*, XINHUA, July 15, 2016.

[199] *China Voice: Behind South China Sea Tensions, U.S. Tries to Maintain Domination over World Issue*, XINHUA, May 25, 2016.

[200] Wang Hui, *supra* note 198.

[201] *See* Leslie Fong, *Freedom of Navigation Ops: US Exercising Right or Might?*, PEOPLE'S DAILY, June 4, 2016; *Freedom of Navigation in South China Sea Not U.S. Vessels' "Muscle Show*," PEOPLE'S DAILY, Feb. 23, 2016; *US Warships Abusing Freedom of Navigation Operations: PLA Newspaper*, XINHUA, May 12, 2016; *U.S. "Freedom of Navigation" Operations in South China Sea "Very Dangerous*," XINHUA, Apr. 28, 2016; Zhang Junshe, *It Is the US That Is Militarizing the South China Sea*, PEOPLE'S DAILY, Feb. 25, 2016.

[202] *China Focus: "A to Z" of China's Diplomacy Under Xi's Leadership*, XINHUA, June 29, 2016; *Xi Eyes More Enabling Int'l Environment for China's Peaceful Development*, XINHUA, Nov. 29, 2014.

Third, while the Crimean debates largely took place in parallel silos, those on the South China Sea demonstrate that Chinese officials and scholars frequently crossed the divide to make their case in English to foreign audiences through statements, position papers, speeches, letters to foreign newspapers, advertisements in foreign papers, and even videos played in New York City's Times Square.[203] The CSIL Statement and the Statement of the China Law Society were issued in English or with English translations. The open letter by the Chinese students in the Netherlands was written in English, Dutch, and Chinese in order to "spread it far and wide to gather as much support as possible."[204] Chinese scholars have published on the disputes in English-language books,[205] transnational journals,[206] and Western blogs.[207] Unlike their Russian counterparts, many of these Chinese academics have completed LLMs or PhDs in North America or Western Europe and have sufficient English-language skills for such writing.

The *Chinese Journal of International Law* was instrumental in facilitating exchange.[208] Founded in 2002, and published by Oxford University Press since 2005, the *Chinese Journal* describes itself as an "independent, peer-reviewed research journal edited primarily by scholars from mainland China" that is published in association with the Chinese Society of International Law and Wuhan University's Institute of International Law.[209] From the outset, this journal adopted an English-only language policy with the express aim of communicating viewpoints and materials from and about China to the rest of the world. As the opening issue explained:

China has been a major player in international affairs and international lawmaking. She has taken views on many issues that can be perceived as different from those of many States. In her management of international relations, she has travelled down the less-trodden path and exhibited an independent spirit. So it is only natural that the international community would need to have access to viewpoints and materials from and about China. Until now, however, there has been on the mainland

[203] In addition to the examples given above, see also Letters to the Editor, *The South China Sea Dispute: Beijing's View*, N.Y. TIMES, May 31, 2016; Letters to the Editor, *China-Philippines Dispute over South China Sea*, N.Y. TIMES, July 28, 2015; *South China Sea Video Displayed at NY Times Square*, XINHUA, July 27, 2016.
[204] *Young Scholars to Launch Open Letter Against South China Sea Arbitration*, XINHUA, July 7, 2016 (citing comments by Wang Zhili).
[205] See, e.g., ARBITRATION CONCERNING THE SOUTH CHINA SEA: PHILIPPINES VERSUS CHINA (Shicun Wu & Keyuan Zou eds., 2016) [hereinafter Wu & Zou]; UN CONVENTION ON THE LAW OF THE SEA AND THE SOUTH CHINA SEA (Shicun Wu, Mark Valencia, & Nong Hong eds., 2015).
[206] See, e.g., Jianjun Gao, *The Obligation to Negotiate in the Philippines v. China Case: A Critique of the Award on Jurisdiction*, 47 OCEAN DEV. & INT'L L. 272 (2016); Zhiguo Gao & Bing Bing Jia, *The Nine-Dash Line in the South China Sea: History, Status, and Implications*, 107 AM. J. INT'L L. 98 (2013).
[207] See, e.g., Liu Haiyang, *The Lawfare over South China Sea: Exceptional Rules vs. General Rules*, OPINIO JURIS, July 14, 2016.
[208] For another example of a Chinese journal that is published in English, see *China Legal Science*, which is sponsored by the China Law Society and published by China Legal Science Journals Press. For an explanation of the motivation behind founding this journal, see Chen Jiping, *Forward to the First Edition of China Legal Science*, 1 CHINA LEGAL SCI. 3 (2013).
[209] *About the Journal: Chinese Journal of International Law*, OXFORD JOURNALS, http://www.oxfordjournals.org/our_journals/cjilaw/about.html (last visited Feb. 26, 2017).

only a Chinese Yearbook of International Law published in Chinese and no journal of international law published in English.

We hope that the publication of the Chinese Journal of International Law . . . will fill the gap highlighted above, and will promote the mutual understanding, accommodation, co-existence, and mutual flourishing of the different civilizations in the world.[210]

The journal's editor in chief, Sienho Yee, embodies the internationalism of some of China's most prominent international law academics. Yee, a professor of international law at Wuhan University, received a JD from Columbia Law School, was formerly an associate professor of law at the University of Colorado School of Law, and has published numerous articles in foreign and transnational journals.[211] Many of the other members of the Editorial Board completed their first law degrees in China, but received LLMs and PhDs abroad before returning to teach in China. The Editorial Board also includes prominent non-Chinese international lawyers, among them some whose views have been associated with Third World or non-Western approaches to international law, such as Antony Anghie and Yuji Iwasawa.[212] The *Chinese Journal*'s pages contain contributions by Chinese and non-Chinese scholars and often feature articles and debates about issues on which China differs from other major powers, such as the rights of innocent passage and freedom of navigation.[213]

The *Chinese Journal of International Law* has published numerous articles on the South China Sea disputes, including by Chinese and non-Chinese scholars, which has allowed more Chinese voices to enter into English-speaking debates than was true of Russian voices in the Crimean debates. For example, Oxford University Press's website carries debate maps that link to English-language sources on specific topics, including "Ukraine Use of Force" and "Disputes in the South and East China Seas." For Crimea, the debate map includes only one Russian author and that author was critical of Russia.[214] For the South and East China Sea, the debate map includes multiple Chinese authors, who have generally supported China's stance.[215] The *Chinese Journal* has published multiple pieces by Chinese and non-Chinese authors questioning the tribunal's jurisdiction, including by

---

[210] Wang Tieya & Sienho Yee, *Foreword*, 1 CHINESE J. INT'L L. iii, iii (2002). The *Chinese Journal of Comparative Law*, founded in 2013, is also English only. *See About the Journal*, CHINESE J. COMP. LAW, http://cjcl.oxford-journals.org (last visited Feb. 26, 2017).

[211] *See Sienho Yee*, http://www.sienhoyee.org (last visited Feb. 26, 2017).

[212] *See Editorial Board*, CHINESE J. INT'L L., http://www.oxfordjournals.org/our_journals/cjilaw/editorial_board.html.

[213] *See, e.g.*, Erik Franckx, *American and Chinese Views on Navigational Rights of Warships*, 10 CHINESE J. INT'L L. 187 (2011); Raul Pedrozo, *Preserving Navigational Rights and Freedoms: The Right to Conduct Military Exercises in China's Exclusive Economic Zone, id.*, 9 (2010); Zhang Haiwen, *Is It Safeguarding the Freedom of Navigation or Maritime Hegemony of the United States?—Comments on Raul (Pete) Pedrozo's Article on Military Activities in the EEZ, id.* 31 (2010).

[214] *Debate Map: Ukraine Use of Force*, OXFORD PUB. INT'L L., http://opil.ouplaw.com/page/ukraine-use-of-force-debate-map (Vaypan) (last visited Feb. 5, 2017).

[215] *Debate Map: South China Sea*, OXFORD PUB. INT'L L., http://opil.ouplaw.com/page/222/debate-map-disputes-in-the-south-and-east-china-seas.

Chris Whomersley (former deputy legal adviser in the UK Foreign and Commonwealth Office), Stefan Talmon (University of Bonn), and Sreenivasa Rao Pemmaraju (former member and chairman of the International Law Commission from India).[216]

Another example of this sort of work is a book edited by German international lawyer Talmon and Chinese international lawyer Bing Bing Jia, who are both editors of the *Chinese Journal of International Law*, entitled *The South China Sea Arbitration: A Chinese Perspective*.[217] The book was aimed at offering a specifically Chinese perspective on some of the legal issues before the tribunal, to present the tribunal with a fuller picture of the facts underlying the Philippines' claims, and to assist the tribunal in reaching its decision given China's failure to appear in the case.[218] The editors endeavored to present a kind of "amicus curiae brief of interested academics acting in their capacity as independent experts of international law," while clearly supporting China's position on jurisdiction.[219] The book contains contributions by Chinese and non-Chinese authors, including a frequently downloaded chapter by Talmon setting out the case against the tribunal's jurisdiction.[220]

In addition to writing in English, Chinese officials and scholars often cite foreign international lawyers whose views are seen as supportive of China's position and whose Western origins are expressly referenced. For instance, Liu Xiaoming, China's ambassador to the United Kingdom, argued in a UK paper that the "recklessly partial tribunal" created more problems than it solved, and intensified rather than resolved disputes, before noting: "No wonder a former [Foreign and Commonwealth Office] legal advisor Chris Whomersley believes that the tribunal is potentially destabilizing the overall stability of international relations."[221] Similarly, Yang Yanyi, head of the Chinese Mission to the European Union, characterized the award as "illegal, illegitimate and invalid" before stating that "Chris Whomersley, former Deputy Legal Adviser of the UK's Foreign and Commonwealth Office, made a good point when he said there was 'no precedent for an international tribunal deciding upon the status of a maritime feature when the

---

[216] *See, e.g.*, Michael Sheng-ti Gau, *The Agreements and Disputes Crystalized by the 2009–2011 Sino-Philippine Exchange of Notes Verbales and Their Relevance to the Jurisdiction and Admissibility Phase of the South China Sea Arbitration*, 15 CHINESE J. INT'L L. 417 (2016); Sreenivasa Rao Pemmaraju, *The South China Sea Arbitration (The Philippines v. China): Assessment of the Award on Jurisdiction and Admissibility, id.* 265; Stefan A.G. Talmon, *The South China Sea Arbitration: Observations on the Award on Jurisdiction and Admissibility, id.* 309; Chris Whomersley, *The South China Sea: The Award of the Tribunal in the Case Brought by Philippines Against China—A Critique, id.* 239; Sienho Yee, *The South China Sea Arbitration (The Philippines v. China): Potential Jurisdictional Obstacles or Objections*, 13 *id.* 663.

[217] THE SOUTH CHINA SEA ARBITRATION: A CHINESE PERSPECTIVE (Stefan Talmon & Bing Bing Jia eds., 2014) [hereinafter SOUTH CHINA SEA ARBITRATION]. For another example of a book bringing together Chinese and non-Chinese authors, see Wu & Zou, *supra* note 205.

[218] *See* SOUTH CHINA SEA ARBITRATION, *supra* note 217, at v.

[219] *Id.* at vi.

[220] Stefan Talmon, *The South China Sea Arbitration: Is There a Case to Answer?, in* SOUTH CHINA SEA ARBITRATION, *supra* note 217, at 15. This is one of the top ten most downloaded articles of all time on SSRN on international arbitration. *See SSRN Top Downloads for LSN: International Arbitration*, SOCIAL SCI. RESEARCH NETWORK, http://papers.ssrn.com/sol3/topten/topTenResults.cfm?groupingId=990156&netorjrnl=jrnl (last visited Feb. 26, 2017).

[221] Liu Xiaoming, *supra* note 147.

sovereignty . . . is disputed.'"[222] Chinese newspapers have also cited Talmon's work and noted that he is an international law professor at the University of Bonn.[223]

Xinhua, the official press agency of China, hosts a website entitled "South China Sea Arbitration: the farce should come to an end."[224] Under a tab for "Int'l response," the website carefully curates articles in which experts from around the world have made critical comments about the tribunal's decision or supportive comments about some of China's positions.[225] In a slightly less pointed way, the CSIL Statement cites several Western law of the sea scholars in favor of some of its general points, while explicitly noting their origins, such as: "As written by Rothwell and Stephens, both Australian international lawyers, '[t]he Part XV dispute settlement mechanisms . . . do not have jurisdiction over disputes arising under general international law' . . ."; "Ted L. McDorman, a Canadian international lawyer, also wrote that, 'whether historic rights exist is not a matter regulated by UNCLOS' . . ."; and "As written by Klein, an Australian international lawyer, '[maritime entitlements] are rights of sovereignty' . . ."[226] The subtext of these references seems to be that Western international lawyers' authorship of these points makes them more credible and their legitimacy harder for Western states to deny.

These attempts to bridge the divide between Chinese and Western debates on the South China Sea involve two important asymmetries. First, in many more instances Chinese scholars chose to publish in English than foreign scholars chose to publish in Chinese. This asymmetry reflects and reinforces the increasing dominance of English as international law's lingua franca, discussed below.[227] In a few cases, Western international lawyers wrote articles for Chinese newspapers, but they were written in English and were generally critical of the tribunal's jurisdiction and did not present a view antithetical to China to a Chinese audience.[228] These differences likely result from language difficulties (few non-Chinese scholars are able to write in Mandarin), academic incentives (Western

---

[222] Daniela Vincenti, *South China Sea Arbitration: Illegal, Illegitimate and Invalid*, EurActiv.com, July 11, 2016 (quoting Yang Yanyi).

[223] *See, e.g., Arbitral Tribunal on South China Sea Illegal, Ridiculous*, Xinhua, July 8, 2016.

[224] *See South China Sea Arbitration: The Farce Should Come to an End*, Xinhua, http://www.xinhuanet.com/english/special/SouthChinaSea/index.htm (last visited Feb. 5, 2017).

[225] *Int'l Response, South China Sea Arbitration*, Xinhua, http://www.xinhuanet.com/english/special/SouthChinaSea/ir.htm (last visited Feb. 5, 2017); *see, e.g., South China Sea Issue Should Be Negotiated Between Claimant Countries: Cambodia Expert, id.*, July 18, 2016; *South China Sea Arbitral Tribunal Loses Its Own Face by Lack of Political Wisdom: Indian Expert, id.*, July 18, 2016; *Ad Hoc Tribunal on South China Sea Arbitration Has No Legal Relationship with PCA: Experts, id.*, July 17, 2016; *U.S. Stirs Up Tension in South China Sea, Sudanese Expert, id.*, July 16, 2016; *South China Sea Arbitration Award "Unfair": Ghanaian Analysts, id.*, July 16, 2016; *S. China Sea Arbitration Award Not Contribute to Peaceful Settlement of Dispute: Austrian Int'l Law Expert, id.*, July 16, 2016; *Arbitral Tribunal's Award on South China Sea Creates Bad Precedent, Says U.S. Expert, id.*, July 15, 2016; *UNCLOS Has No Jurisdiction over Territorial Issues: S. African Commentator, id.*, July 14, 2016; *PCA's Decision Is Extremely Dangerous: French Expert, id.*, July 14, 2016; *Arbitral Tribunal's Decision Against China Illegal: LatAm Experts*, Xinhua, July 13, 2016; *South China Sea Ruling "Biased and Legally Flawed": Sudan Experts, id.*, July 12, 2016.

[226] CSIL Statement, *supra* note 142.

[227] *See infra* Part III.B.

[228] *See, e.g.*, Stefan Talmon, *Final Award in Sea Arbitration Will Be Flawed*, China Daily, July 9, 2016; Stefan Talmon, *No Case to Answer for Beijing Before Arbitral Tribunal in South China Sea*, Glob. Times, May 20, 2013; Chris Whomersley, *Tribunal Proceedings on Manila's Claims Flawed*, China Daily, June 16, 2016.

scholars are more likely to be rewarded for publishing in Western outlets than non-Western ones), and China's press censorship (which would typically prevent dissenting views being expressed in the mainstream media).

Second, although Chinese scholars' publicly expressed opinions were virtually uniform, there were some splits within the Western camp. Chinese officials and scholars can point to Western scholars whose viewpoints support their own, but their Western counterparts generally cannot do the reverse. In many ways, this results from the greater freedom that exists within the Western international law academies. The uniformity of these Chinese opinions works to undermine their credibility. As Ku concluded: the "remarkably and suspiciously uniform" support of China's legal position has "injured the reputation of Chinese universities" and "damaged the credibility of Chinese legal scholars," undermining the persuasiveness of their scholarship on the issue outside China.[229] Similarly, Bing Ling, an international law expert at the University of Sydney, implored the Chinese government to "stop treating academics as its handmaids and surrounding itself with yes-men" because a "lack of diverse and dissenting voices may only lead to bad decisions."[230]

The attempts to bridge these scholarly communities and perspectives do not guarantee agreement, but reaching common ground is not necessarily the point. Western scholars need to understand the perspective of Chinese scholars on the arbitration and vice versa if they are to gain a full appreciation of how this case is seen in different communities. It may also encourage them to reconsider some of the assumptions, arguments and narratives that are often taken for granted in Western circles. Ultimately, this dialogue is likely to lead to more serious critical engagement with China's jurisdictional arguments than would have happened if Chinese officials and scholars had largely developed their objections in Chinese and directed them to a Chinese audience. And the need to justify their positions to foreign audiences should make Chinese scholars more aware of how their arguments are perceived outside China and the damage to their credibility if they are viewed as mere handmaidens of their government.

III. Identifying Patterns of Dominance

In focusing on differences that emerge among legal academies, the last section highlighted two points that are relevant for lessons about existing patterns of dominance within the field and how these patterns might change over time.

The first is the way lack of representation in international institutions fuels concerns and complaints about the inclusiveness, impartiality, and legitimacy of both those institutions and the international law they propound. This attitude was evident in China's criticisms of the international arbitral tribunal's composition of four Western arbitrators, one non-Western but Western-educated arbitrator, and no Asians.

---

[229] Ku, *supra* note 161.
[230] *See* Shi, *supra* note 162 (quoting Bing Ling).

The second is how choice of language shapes and limits transnational audiences and dialogue. Publication in English by Chinese scholars enabled them to engage in transnational debates in a way that Russian scholars who published in Russian could not reflects the increasing use of English as international law's lingua franca, which is marginalizing other languages within the field on the transnational plane.

Issues of representation and language are relevant to a key theme in this book: the dominance of certain actors and approaches in defining what counts as the "international." International law is partly constituted by people, materials, and ideas moving across borders. There are also various transnational sites, like international organizations, international tribunals, and international journals, where people from different national communities come together to produce, interpret, analyze, or apply international law. But how is the "international" constructed in and through these transnational sites and flows?

The ideal of international law suggests that it draws equally on people, materials, and ideas from all national and regional traditions. The notion of representation is thus often built into the fabric of international law sources and institutions. For instance, custom is meant to be based on the "general practice" of states,[231] which many international lawyers view as requiring both extensive and representative state practice.[232] Similarly, the Statute of the International Court of Justice provides that, in electing judges, states should bear in mind that in "the body as a whole the representation of the main forms of civilization and of the principal legal systems of the world should be assured."[233] Since people coming from different regions and trained in different legal traditions might hold different views on and approaches to international law, representation is meant to enable institutions to determine what is "international" across these groups and encourage diverse states to feel they have input regarding international norms and institutions.

Despite this emphasis on representation, it is clear that people, materials, and ideas from certain states and regions dominate particular transnational sites and flows in the international law. My studies of academics and textbooks revealed examples of such dominance, including in appearances as ICJ counsel by Western international law academics in general, and UK and French scholars in particular;[234] and in resort by the authors of textbooks from a wide variety of states primarily to the domestic case law of Western states, particularly the United States and the United Kingdom, when presenting foreign court decisions.[235] I suggest here that these patterns are indicative of broader patterns of dominance within the field rather than of academic profiles or textbook contents alone.

Adopting a comparative approach to international law encourages international lawyers to focus on whose norms are being globalized and how. Although the exact contours

---

[231] Statute of the International Court of Justice, art. 38, June 26, 1945, T.S. No. 993, 33 U.N.T.S. 993 [hereinafter ICJ Statute].

[232] Comm. on Formation of Customary Int'l Law, International Law Association, *Statement of Principles Applicable to the Formation of General Customary International Law*, 8, 20, 23 (2000).

[233] ICJ Statute, *supra* note 231, art. 9.

[234] *See* Chapter 3.IV.

[235] *See* Chapter 4.IV.

of dominance vary across subfields and among institutions, two patterns emerge relatively consistently: transnational sites are often dominated by Western actors in general, and by those from a handful of Western states in particular. In some forums, Anglophones and Francophones share this advantage; in others, the Anglophones take precedence. Importantly, to the extent that people, materials, and ideas from certain states and regions come to dominate certain transnational sites and flows, they may well be able to exert disproportionate influence in defining the "international." As I explore below, choice of language plays a critical role in this privileging process. My point is not to argue for or against monolingualism, bilingualism, or multilingualism, but to trace how different language choices work to privilege different actors and approaches within the system.

A. REPRESENTATION OF REGIONS AND NATIONALITIES

International courts and tribunals are often subject to a variety of formal and informal rules designed to achieve regional representation of judges. For example, the requirement for representation in the ICJ Statute is given effect by the informal allocation of a certain number of spots to each UN regional grouping. Similarly, the requirement in the Rome Statute of the International Criminal Court (ICC) that the selection of judges should take into account representation of the principal legal systems of the world and equitable geographical representation is achieved by requiring voting states to select a certain number of judges from each regional group.[236]

Although regional representation is often regulated at this most senior, visible level, it often remains unregulated or less regulated at other levels. Thus, the ICJ bench exhibits a significant degree of regional representation, but the ICJ bar is much less diverse. The staff of these international courts and tribunals also often come primarily from Anglophone and Francophone core Western states. Similar patterns emerge in investment treaty arbitration where arbitrators are selected by the disputing parties or arbitral institutions, which do not require regional representation.

Although most international courts and tribunals do not report on the regional representation of their staff, the ICC and the WTO do. According to the ICC's 2016 report, the court employs 320 professional personnel of eighty nationalities, excluding elected officials and linguistic staff who prepare translations.[237] The figure for nationalities seems very diverse, but specific regional groups are significantly over- and underrepresented. As shown in Table 8 on the next page, nationals from the Western Europe and Others Group (WEOG) are overrepresented, making up 61 percent of the ICC's professional staff, and their advantage increases as one moves up the professional grades.[238] Africa is reasonably well represented with 17 percent, perhaps partly reflecting the

---

[236] Rome Statute of the International Criminal Court, art. 36, July 17, 1998, 2187 U.N.T.S. 90.

[237] International Criminal Court, Assembly of States Parties, *Report of the Committee on Budget and Finance on the Work of Its Twenty-Sixth Session*, at 24, ICC-ASP/15/5 (July 12, 2016), https://asp.icc-cpi.int/iccdocs/asp_docs/ASP15/ICC-ASP-15-5-ENG.pdf.

[238] *Id.* at 26–30.

TABLE 8

ICC Professional Staff (Excluding Linguistic Staff) by Region

Region	Africa	Asia	Eastern Europe	GRULAC	WEOG
Number of Staff	55	19	25	26	195
Percentage of Total Staff	17%	5%	8%	8%	61%

Source: International Criminal Court, Assembly of States Parties, *Report of the Committee on Budget and Finance on the Work of Its Twenty-Sixth Session*, at 24, ICC-ASP/15/5 (July 12, 2016).

number of African cases and the court's language requirements, which favor staff from Anglophone and Francophone states. By contrast, the Group of Latin American and Caribbean Countries (GRULAC) and Asia are significantly underrepresented, with 8 percent and 5 percent, respectively.[239] And though the specific numbers shift somewhat from year to year, the diversity of ICC professional staff actually seems to have declined over time.[240]

Not all states have accepted the ICC's jurisdiction, and it would be reasonable for the court to draw its personnel predominantly from the states over which it has jurisdiction. The ICC thus sets recruitment targets for each regional group by reference to how many states parties are in that region and, on this measure, WEOG is still considerably overrepresented, and Asia and GRULAC are consistently underrepresented.[241] Only WEOG states count ten or more professional staff at the ICC. France and the United Kingdom lead the pack with forty-two and thirty nationals, respectively, followed by the Netherlands (eighteen), Spain (fourteen), Italy (thirteen), Germany (twelve), Canada (eleven), Australia (ten), Belgium (ten), and the United States (ten).[242] In terms of numerical targets for each state, France and the United Kingdom far exceed their target numbers of twenty, as do the Netherlands and the United States, whose targets are eight and zero, respectively. By contrast, Japan and South Korea have targets of forty-two and ten, yet actual numbers of zero and four. Neither China nor Russia has ratified the Rome Statute, resulting in targets of zero, but each accounts for one staff member.[243]

---

[239] *Id.* at 24–26.

[240] If one goes back to 2007, which is the first year for which figures are provided, WEOG states accounted for 57 percent of professional staff compared with 61 percent now. Africa and Eastern Europe have maintained a similar level from their initial figures of 18 percent and 8 percent, respectively. But GRULAC and Asian representation has gone down, from 11 percent and 6 percent, respectively, in 2007, to 8 percent and 5 percent, respectively, in 2015. In terms of weighted targets, the ICC was much closer to meeting its targets in 2007 than it was in 2015. *See* Int'l Crim. Court, Assembly of States Parties, *Report of the Committee on Budget and Finance on the Work of Its Eighth Session*, at 27–30, ICC-ASP/6/2 (May 29, 2007), https://asp.icc-cpi.int/iccdocs/asp_docs/library/asp/ICC-ASP-6-2_English.pdf.

[241] For graphs of targets and actual numbers of staff per regional group, see *supra* note 237 at 31–33.

[242] *Id.* at 34–38.

[243] *Id.*

The WTO also provides annual reports on the diversity of its professional staff, but it uses slightly different breakdowns to the UN regional groups. According to the 2016 report, Europe recorded the highest level of representation in its nonlinguistic professional staff (45 percent), followed by Asia (15 percent), North America (15 percent), Latin America (11 percent), Africa (10 percent), and Oceania (3 percent).[244] Individuals from Europe and North America dominate the WTO's professional staff, making up 60 percent of the total. But unlike that of the ICC, the WTO's staffing profile appears to be becoming more representative over time. As shown in Table 9, Europeans and North Americans comprised 54 percent and 19 percent of nonlinguistic professional staff, respectively, in 1995, which decreased to 45 percent and 15 percent in 2015, respectively. On the other hand, the figures for Africa, Asia, and Latin America grew from 2 percent, 12 percent, and 7 percent, respectively, in 1995, to 10 percent, 15 percent and 11 percent, respectively, in 2015.

Similar patterns characterize the number of professional staff from specific states: they are dominated by nationals of European and North American states, but other nationalities (particularly of some of the major emerging economies) are gaining ground. In 1995, the WTO nonlinguistic professional staff were drawn from twenty-four member states, and the following states counted ten or more staff members: France (eighteen), the United Kingdom (fifteen), the United States (fourteen), Canada (twelve), and Switzerland (eleven).[245] By 2015, these staff members were drawn from forty-nine member states and a more diverse group of states recorded ten or more staff members: France (thirty-six), the United States (twenty-six), the United Kingdom (twenty-two), Canada

TABLE 9

WTO Professional Staff (Excluding Linguistic Staff) by Region

Region	1995 No.	1995 %	2005 No.	2005 %	2010 No.	2010 %	2015 No.	2015 %
Africa	3	2.1	25	8.5	31	9. 8	38	10.4
Asia	18	12.4	37	12.6	45	14.2	56	15.4
Europe	78	53.8	146	49.7	150	47.3	165	45.3
Latin Am.	10	6.9	27	9.2	35	11.0	40	11.0
North Am.	27	18.6	48	16.3	44	13.9	54	14.8
Oceania	9	6.2	11	3.7	12	3.8	11	3.0
Total	145	100	294	100	317	100	364	100

Source: Comm. on Budget, Finance, and Admin., *2015 Annual Report on Diversity in the WTO Secretariat*, at 3, WTO Doc. BFA/W/287 (Apr. 4, 2016).

---

[244] Comm. on Budget, Finance, and Admin., *2015 Annual Report on Diversity in the WTO Secretariat*, at 3, WTO Doc. BFA/W/287 (Apr. 4, 2016).

[245] *Id.* at 15.

(twenty-one), Germany (twenty), Italy (nineteen), China (thirteen), Switzerland (thirteen), Brazil (eleven), India (eleven), Spain (eleven), and Australia (ten).[246]

Less-formalized forms of international dispute resolution, like investment treaty arbitration, are not typically subject to voting rules and practices designed to ensure a certain level of regional representation. In those areas, clear patterns of dominance are seen. According to statistics compiled by the International Centre for Settlement of Investment Disputes (ICSID) and updated to the end of 2015, 48 percent of its arbitrators, conciliators, and ad hoc committee members were from Western Europe, and 21 percent were from North America (Canada, Mexico, and the United States), amounting to 69 percent combined. South America and "South & East Asia and the Pacific" tied for a distant third with 10 percent of ICSID appointments each, followed by the Middle East and North Africa (4 percent), Central America and the Caribbean (3 percent), Sub-Saharan Africa (2 percent), and Eastern Europe and Central Asia (2 percent).[247]

Within the West, Sergio Puig's study of 1468 ICSID arbitral appointments spread across 396 individuals found that the United States, France, and the United Kingdom dominated the list of most frequently appointed arbitrators, exceeding any other nationalities by a large margin.[248] But most US nationals remained on the periphery of the network because, although many US nationals were appointed, not many were frequently reappointed.[249] In terms of the twenty-five most frequently appointed ICSID arbitrators, four came from Canada, three each including one dual national from France and the United Kingdom, two each from Argentina and Switzerland, and only one from the United States.[250]

These patterns are not uniform across all fields. For instance, in an analysis of 603 WTO panelist positions spread across 251 individuals, based on data through 2014, Joost Pauwelyn found only fourteen Americans, six Britons, and one French national, amounting to less than 3.5 percent of the total appointments.[251] US nationals made up only 2 percent of WTO panelist nominations, and European Union nationals made up only 12 percent.[252] The comparatively low level of EU and US panelists is mainly explained by the rule that WTO panelists may not be nationals of disputing parties or third parties to disputes, unless the disputing parties agree, which rules out EU and US nationals

---

[246] *Id.* at 16.

[247] World Bank, 1 The ICSID Caseload: Statistics 18 (2016).

[248] Sergio Puig, *Social Capital in the Arbitration Market*, 25 Eur. J. Int'l L. 387, 411–12 (2014); *see also* José E. Alvarez, The Public International Law Regime Governing International Investment 404 (2011) ("[T]he existing arbitration world is essentially too cozy and consists of a small number of repeat players dominated by prominent legal academics in Europe and the United States, along with a handful of law firms in London, Paris, New York and Washington, DC. . . .").

[249] Puig, *supra* note 248, at 410. One explanation for the more peripheral role of US arbitrators in Puig's analysis is that, while US companies may pick a US national as an arbitrator, ICSID cannot appoint a national from either disputing party as a chairperson. Another contributing factor is likely that fewer US academics have built up the symbolic capital associated with other forms of international dispute resolution, like practice as counsel before the International Court of Justice.

[250] *Id.* at 412.

[251] Joost Pauwelyn, *The Rule of Law Without the Rule of Lawyers? Why Investment Arbitrators Are from Mars, Trade Adjudicators from Venus*, 109 Am. J. Int'l L. 761, 770 (2015).

[252] *Id.*

in most cases.[253] But nationals of other Western states still top the list of the most frequently appointed panelists, led by New Zealand (fifty-five), Australia (forty-six), and Switzerland (forty-four).[254]

International lawyers from states or regions that are overrepresented in transnational forums have the opportunity to play a disproportionate role in constructing the "international," while states and regions that are underrepresented are likely to feel disenfranchised. The adoption of an English/French language policy often favors individuals from Anglophone and Francophone states, most notably the United States, the United Kingdom, and France. Yet, as the WTO example demonstrates, patterns of dominance are dynamic. The emerging economies Brazil, China, and India are now vital states within the international trading regime, and their level of representation within the WTO is growing. As their economic power and level of international participation increase, so will their calls for greater representation.

B. ENGLISH AS INTERNATIONAL LAW'S LINGUA FRANCA

Although multilingualism or bilingualism is built into the fabric of many international institutions, English is becoming increasingly dominant in a variety of transnational settings, including international meetings, education, and business.[255] It is hard to give a systematic account of this phenomenon, and variations are found across subfields, states, and regions, but numerous movements suggest that English is increasingly becoming the lingua franca for international law scholarship and practice, as it has done in other areas such as science.[256] If so, these shifts deserve attention because language choices are key in shaping and limiting transnational audiences and have clear distributional effects in terms of whom they privilege.

As regards scholarship, the movement toward English can be seen in the growing number of transnational journals that have chosen English as their sole language, such as the *Journal of International Criminal Justice*, the *Journal of International Economic Law*, the *Journal of International Dispute Resolution*, and the *ICSID Review*. All of these periodicals are "transnational" in the sense that their editorial boards comprise international lawyers from many states, rather than a single state primarily, and thus represent living examples of the globalization of legal scholarship. These English-only transnational

---

[253] Dispute Settlement Rules: Understanding on Rules and Procedures Governing the Settlement of Disputes, Art. 8.3, Apr. 15, 1994, Marrakesh Agreement Establishing the World Trade Organization, Annex 2, 1869 U.N.T.S. 401 (1994).

[254] Pauwelyn, *supra* note 251, at 772.

[255] *See, e.g.*, Ulrich Ammon & Grant McConnell, English as an Academic Language in Europe: A Survey of Its Use in Teaching (2003); David Crystal, English as a Global Language (2d ed. 2003); Nicholas Ostler, The Last Lingua Franca: The Rise and Fall of World Languages (2011); Barbara Seidlhofer, *English as a Lingua Franca*, 59 ELT J. 339 (2005).

[256] On English as the lingua franca in science, for example, The Dominance of English as the Language of Science: Effects on Other Languages and Language Communities (Ulrich Ammon ed., 2001); Rainer Enrique Hamel, *The Dominance of English in the International Scientific Periodical Literature and the Future of Language Use in Science*, 20 Association Internationale de Linguistique Appliquée Review 53 (2007); Augusto Carli & Ulrich Ammon, Introduction, 20 *id.* at 1 (2007).

international law publications do not appear to have many French- or Spanish-language counterparts.

The growth of English usage is also evident in the shift of some transnational international law journals toward being English only. The *European Journal of International Law*, for instance, permitted publication in English and French when it was founded in 1990, but it later changed to an English-only model. One scholar objected to the editor: "It is a shame that the EJIL forces all the authors to write in English—there is indeed in my eyes nothing European in such a stance. That is also the reason why I usually categorically refuse to write for your journal."[257] The editor responded by noting that the journal had received few French submissions and the two-language solution had alienated European scholars from other states, such as Germany and Italy. He also argued that, by publishing in English, "we are offering our non-native English authors the chance of having their work reach a vast audience which they otherwise might not have had if writing in their own language."[258]

The movement toward English can similarly be seen in decisions by international law journals and yearbooks in some non-English-speaking states either to start off as, or switch to, English-only publication. The *Japanese Annual of International Law*, which was refounded as the *Japanese Yearbook of International Law* for its fiftieth anniversary in 2008, has always been English only.[259] The *German Yearbook of International Law* was originally founded in 1948 as a German-language publication called *Jahrbuch für Internationales Recht* but changed its name and began publishing in English in 1976 to "reach the largest possible international audience."[260] The *Chinese Journal of International Law*, founded in 2002, adopted an English-only language policy, as did the *Asian Journal of International Law*, founded in 2011.[261] Exceptions exist,[262] but many journals from non-English-speaking states and regions are now solely in English.

The trend toward English has also taken hold at certain international law conferences. The official languages of the European Society of International Law are English and French, and the website notes that the society is "committed to promoting linguistic diversity while at the same time maximizing the ability of members to communicate effectively with one another."[263] At the founding conference, 85 percent of the papers presented were in English, and 15 percent were in French.[264] But by the society's Research

---

[257] Joseph Weiler, *From the Editor's Postbox: The Language Issue—Redux*, EJIL: *TALK!*, Apr. 2, 2012.
[258] *Id.*
[259] Shigeru Oda, *On Launching of the Japanese Yearbook of International Law*, 2008 JAPANESE Y.B. INT'L L. 1.
[260] GYIL, German Y.B. Int'l L., http://www.gyil.org (last visited Feb. 5, 2017).
[261] *Notes for Contributors and House Style*, ASIAN J. INT'L L., http://assets.cambridge.org/AJL/AJL_ifc.pdf.
[262] In terms of exceptions, see, for example, the *Revista Latinoamericana de Derecho Internacional*, founded in 2014, is a Spanish-only publication, while the Latin American *Journal of International Trade Law/Revista Latinoamericana de Derecho Comercial Internacional*, founded in 2012, is bilingual (English and Spanish). *See* Acerca de LADI, REVISTA LATINOAMERICANA DE DERECHO INTERNACIONAL, http://www.revistaladi.com.ar/acerca-de-ladi/ (last visited Dec. 27, 2016); Introduction, LATIN AM. J. INT'L TRADE LAW/REVISTA LATINOAMERICANA DE DERECHO COMMERCIAL INTERNACIONAL, http://derecho.posgrado.unam.mx/latam/04_production/#11 (last visited Feb. 5, 2017).
[263] *ESIL Goals*, EUR. SOC'Y INT'L L., http://www.esil-sedi.eu/node/177 (last visited Feb. 5, 2017).
[264] *Pre-2009 Conference Papers*, *id.*, http://www.esil-sedi.eu/node/239 (last visited Feb. 5, 2017).

Forum in 2013 and conference in 2014, the proportion of English papers had risen to 95 percent and 97 percent, respectively, even though neither event was held in an English-speaking state.[265] Despite some exceptions,[266] there are many conforming examples, such as the English-language meetings of the Asian Society of International Law.[267]

A similar point could be made about many of the international law blogs, which are typically published in English, including *EJIL: Talk!*, *International Economic Law and Policy Blog*, *International Law Reporter*, and *Opinio Juris*. Again, one can find exceptions, such as *SIDIBlog*, which is published in Italian, and *Sentinelle*, which is published in French. But, on the whole, English appears to have dominated the international law blogosphere.

As far as international law practice is concerned, it is often led by US and UK firms that operate out of major international cities like New York, London, and Paris. Of the top one hundred highest-grossing law firms in the world, ninety-one are headquartered in the United States and the United Kingdom.[268] The New York offices of US firms earn around $1.8 billion annually from international dispute resolution, and almost two-thirds of litigants in English commercial courts are foreign.[269] The legal sector accounts for 1.5 percent of UK gross domestic product (GDP), which is nearly double the percentage in other large European states.[270] At the same time, the domestic legal systems in some other states, such as Russia, have arguably been damaged by this outsourcing to UK and US courts and to Anglo-American law firms.[271]

The London bar plays a strikingly prominent role in supplying advocates and arbitrators for international dispute resolution, as evidenced by the "global" rankings of Chambers and Partners.[272] Although Paris and Geneva also rank highly as locations for international dispute resolution, English is the most common language of international arbitration. For instance, in a study of the language of investment treaty awards based on awards published on the website italaw.com, Wolfgang Aschner found that 82 percent of the awards were in English, whereas 8 percent were in French. Even though a vast number

---

[265] *See* Programme Overview: 5th Research Forum for International Law as a Profession, *id.*, http://www.esil2013.nl/conference-schedule/#2013-05-24 (last visited Feb. 5, 2017); Programme: ESIL 10th Anniversary Conference, *id.*, https://esil2014.univie.ac.at/programme (last visited Feb. 5, 2017).

[266] For instance, the Latin American Society of International Law Biennial Meetings has four working languages—Spanish, Portuguese, English, and French—though it is unclear from the programs which speakers use which languages.

[267] *Homepage*, Asian Soc'y Int'l L., http://asiansil.org (last visited Feb. 5, 2017).

[268] *International Commercial Law: Exorbitant Privilege*, Economist, May 10, 2014.

[269] *Id.*

[270] *Id.*

[271] *See* Delphine Nougayrède, *Outsourcing Law in Post-Soviet Russia*, 7 J. Eurasian L. 383 (2014). For a different view, see Paul Stephan, *International Investment Law and Municipal Law: Substitutes or Complements?*, 9 Capital Mkts. L.J. 354 (2014).

[272] *See Global Rankings for Public International Law*, Chambers and Partners, http://www.chambersandpartners.com/15649/96/editorial/2/1; *Global Rankings for Public International Arbitration*, Chambers and Partners, http://www.chambersandpartners.com/15649/57/editorial/2/1; *Global Rankings for International Arbitration in the UK Bar*, Chambers and Partners, http://www.chambersandpartners.com/15649/1985/editorial/2/2 (last visited Feb. 5, 2017).

of investment treaty disputes have arisen out of Latin America, only 7 percent of the awards were in Spanish.[273]

As noted above, language choices shape and limit national and transnational audiences. Editors of "international law" publications must confront difficult choices about the language policy they adopt. Should an international journal or yearbook be published in a world language to facilitate a transnational conversation? Or should it be published in the national language, and thereby facilitate the reception of international law ideas into the domestic setting? Both types of publication have their place, but they reach distinct audiences. The *German Law Journal* considered this dilemma at its inception, deciding to make itself an English-only online journal. As its co-founders explained, the *German Law Journal* was intended to be a forum for the "transnationalization" of legal cultures: its authors have written about transnational law but "have also performed or lived the engagement" through publishing online and in English about developments in German, European, and international law.[274]

Individual authors must also confront this choice. If international law academics want to engage in transnational conversations and develop spheres of influence outside their own states, they need to publish in world languages—like English, French, and Spanish—that are spoken in many states throughout the world. A French author writing in French may be read in many states in Francophone Africa, and an Argentine author writing in Spanish can reach other states in Latin America, as well as Spain. But to maximize their audiences, publishing in English is the most effective language choice. German-trained Michael Bohlander puts the point bluntly: "While still useful for a domestic debate, publications in languages other than English do not stand a serious chance of being noticed and cited on the international level. If authors from non-Anglophone countries want to influence the international discussion, they will have to use the common idiom."[275]

English speakers often accept the growing movement toward English as the lingua franca of international law practice and scholarship with a shrug of the shoulders ("it's just a reality") or a positive spin ("it enhances communication and consistency"). It is hard to imagine that they would take the same approach if English as the common language were supplanted by another language, such as Mandarin. Rarely do native English-speaking scholars acknowledge how much this movement privileges them and the concepts with which they are familiar. Some non-native English speakers may be unable to publish in transnational international law journals. Others may be able to write in English, but drafting will take them longer and will be more difficult; many report that the final product is less satisfactory because they are unable to express themselves

[273] E-mail on file with author. These numbers are merely indicative. Given that some disputes are not public, some awards remain confidential, and the selection of awards uploaded on italaw.com might be subject to certain selection biases, it is difficult to draw firm inferences from these numbers on the full population of awards.

[274] RUSSELL A. MILLER & PEER C. ZUMBANSEN, INTRODUCTION TO COMPARATIVE LAW AS TRANSNATIONAL LAW: A DECADE OF THE GERMAN LAW JOURNAL 3, 5 (Russell A. Miller & Peer C. Zumbansen eds., 2012).

[275] Michael Bohlander, *Language, Culture, Legal Traditions, and International Criminal Justice*, 12 J. INT'L CRIM. JUST. 491, 513 n.67 (2014).

as clearly or elegantly in their non-native tongue. As for practice, one Chinese official quipped: "just imagine if the USTR [Office of the US Trade Representative] had to defend itself in Chinese."[276]

By writing in English and citing English-language sources, non-native speakers may widen their audience and enhance perceptions of their "international" bona fides but may also simultaneously contribute to the marginalization of their own language and non-English language sources. Phil Chan, who completed the English-language book *China, State Sovereignty and International Legal Order*, writes explicitly about this dilemma, noting that the fact that:

> [M]any non-Western scholars must work in Western countries and publish in Western journals in order to obtain an audience and a semblance of respectability illustrates the marginalisation of both non-Western scholarship and non-Western scholars. It is, accordingly, with much regret that I need to use English-language research materials primarily, and not the abundance of Chinese-language research materials, in this book, lest this book be accused of Chinese biases or dismissed as lacking rigorous informed analysis. It is also hoped that my use of English-language research materials primarily will enable the book to reach a wider audience unfamiliar with Chinese language but whose understanding of the nexus between China's exercise of State sovereignty and international legal order is imperative to a proper understanding of China, the principle of State sovereignty, the state and legitimacy of international law, and the direction in which international legal order in its current form may and should proceed.[277]

Non-native English speakers sometimes bristle at what they consider to be the ignorance, arrogance, and imperialism of the native (often monolingual) English speakers. Thus, in an exchange at the American Society of International Law, Ian Brownlie, a UK international lawyer, approvingly stated:

> Generally speaking, the unity of international law has increased since 1945. The factors militating in favor of unity include, first, the fact that the literature is more and more truly international in content and tends to be published in the languages that are regarded as the leading languages of diplomacy. For example, the Italian and German Yearbooks of International Law are now published in English.[278]

In response, Japanese international lawyer Yasuaki Onuma lamented, "How can one expect such monolinguals to understand international law?"[279] While accepting that a common language is important from the viewpoint of utility or convenience, he urged

---

[276] Shaffer & Gao, *supra* note 98.
[277] PHIL C.W. CHAN, CHINA, STATE SOVEREIGNTY AND INTERNATIONAL LEGAL ORDER 20, n.1 (2015).
[278] Ian Brownlie, Remarks, *Comparative Approaches to the Theory of International Law*, 80 AM. SOC'Y INT'L L. PROC. 152, 154–55 (1986).
[279] *Id.* at 172–73.

international lawyers to accommodate different cultural expressions and concepts on the basis of equality among diverse cultures.[280]

The battle between domestic and international audiences, and monolingualism and multilingualism, is being played out explicitly in some non-English-speaking academies, like the German legal academy. A report by the German Council of Science and Humanities concluded that German is becoming less and less important as a legal research language, with the decline in the number of legal academics who can read and write German and the rise in the number that can read and write English.[281] The report concluded that, to be "appreciated internationally in proportion to its true academic weight, German legal scholarship should closely follow and actively participate in European and international academic debates."[282] This strategy requires German legal scholars to publish more frequently in foreign journals and integrate foreign literature into their own disciplinary discourses.[283] The report recommends a multilingual approach rather than an English-only or bilingual model.

This debate is ongoing. For instance, many faculties still require, or strongly encourage, students completing the Habilitation to write it in German, and to show significant engagement with the German literature, even when it would significantly limit the international audience for these works. Leading German international lawyers have objected to this approach, such as Krisch who wrote in the foreword to his doctorate: "Being written in German, [the text] follows the requirements of the Heidelberg law faculty, *even if this makes it unavailable to a broader readership.*"[284] At the time, Heidelberg had adopted a multilingual policy: PhDs could be written in, and only in, German . . . or Latin! (By contrast, Humboldt University in Berlin encourages its doctoral students to write in English to broaden their potential readership.[285]) These and other nationalist requirements are prompting some of the best and brightest German international lawyers to depart for other more internationalized academies, such as those of the United Kingdom, the Netherlands, and Switzerland.[286]

Some states stand as strong holdouts against treating English as the common language for international law scholarship, including Russia and France. Their opposition may partly reflect the international status of both Russian and French, which

---

[280] *Id.*

[281] German Council Sci. and Humanities, *supra* note 9, at 72.

[282] *Id.* at 15.

[283] *Id.*

[284] Nico Krisch, Selbstverteidigung und kollektive Sicherheit [Self-Defense and Collective Security] (2001) (PhD thesis, University of Heidelberg) (emphasis added).

[285] *See, e.g.,* Sergey Sayapin, The Crime of Aggression in International Criminal Law: Historical Development, Comparative Analysis and Present State (2014) (based on the author's PhD thesis at Humboldt University).

[286] Examples include Anne van Aaken (St. Gallen, Switzerland), Jutta Brunnée (Toronto, Canada), Bardo Fassbender (St. Gallen, Switzerland), Robin Geiss (Glasgow, the United Kingdom), Nico Krisch (Graduate Institute, Switzerland), Carsten Stahn (Leiden, the Netherlands), Stephan Schill (Amsterdam, the Netherlands), Christian Tams (Glasgow, United Kingdom), Ingo Venzke (Amsterdam, the Netherlands), and Katja Ziegler (Leicester, United Kingdom). Some such scholars return, such as Anne Peters (Max Planck, returning from Basel, Switzerland), and Stefan Talmon (Bonn, returning from Oxford, the United Kingdom).

are recognized as official languages of the United Nations and spoken in states other than Russia (primarily in the former Soviet sphere) and France (particularly in Francophone Africa). In the UN Audiovisual Library of International Law, Russian and French international lawyers typically deliver their lectures in their native tongue. By contrast, the German and Japanese scholars usually deliver their lectures in English. But here the strength of a state often correlates with its weakness and vice versa. Germany and Japan lost World War II and thus their languages were not accepted as UN languages, but now their international lawyers may enjoy a wider audience because they speak the lingua franca. The opposite pertains to Russia and France.[287]

In the case of Russia, the tendency of its international lawyers to publish primarily in Russian might partially result from ongoing effects of Cold War isolation, as well as Russia's abiding interest in promoting the Russian language. For instance, the 2013 Concept of the Foreign Policy of the Russian Federation lists "promoting the Russian language and strengthening its positions in the world" as a foreign policy goal.[288] It may also relate to the singularly political nature of international law since movement is afoot in other areas of the law in Russia. For instance, a few new Russian law journals are published in English with the aim of developing a foreign audience for Russian legal scholarship and allowing a two-way exchange between Russian and foreign legal ideas.[289] Even then, the editor in chief of the *Russian Law Journal*, an English-language journal established in 2013, felt obliged to aver that publishing abroad did not evidence a "lack of patriotism," or that Russian scholars had "cease[d] to love the homeland" but, rather, "promoted glorification of their homeland."[290]

France's stance reflects a clear policy of preserving the stature of the French language and protecting its status as one of the official languages of many international organizations and institutions. This approach helps to keep the French legal language alive internationally, along with the concepts that are native to it, and promotes the importance of multilingualism. As one French academic explained to me:

> It is not sufficient to ask for French-speaking academics to write in English; it is also necessary that English-speaking academics speak or at least understand French. We all know that we do not express the same ideas in French and in English. Since international law is international, it requires too a kind of reciprocity and French-speaking countries, organizations or universities have to set up mechanisms and programs to make French more attractive for non-French students and academics.[291]

---

[287] Lauri Mälksoo, Russian Approaches to International Law 92 (2015).

[288] Концепция внешней политики Российской Федерацииутверждена Президентом Российской Федерации В.В. Путиным 12 февраля 2013 г.) (утратила силу) [Concept of the Foreign Policy of the Russian Federation], para. 4(h) (Feb. 12, 2013).

[289] Examples include the *Russian Law Journal*, founded in 2013, and the *Kutafin University Law Review*, founded in 2014. *See* Russian L.J., http://www.russianlawjournal.org/ (last visited Oct. 17, 2016); *About Us*, Kutafin Univ. L. Rev. (KULawR), http://www.kulawr.ru/index/ (last visited Feb. 26, 2017).

[290] Dmitry Maleshin, *Chief Editor's Note on the Russian Legal Academia and Periodicals*, 3 Russian L.J., no. 2, 2015, at 5, 7.

[291] E-mail on file with author.

If French scholars started writing in English, they would undermine the French cause of supporting multilingualism and seeking to protect the privileged status of French in international organizations. But this approach also limits the audiences of these scholars. Jamin has argued that, somewhat paradoxically, the best way of protecting the Francophone may be to teach and publish in English because it enables non-Francophones to access French legal thinking.[292] Instead of seeking to imprison French law "in a citadel which we would have to defend," he encourages French law professors to be open to legal globalization, to seek to participate in and shape its forces.[293] When it comes to language, Russia and France are clearly concerned about winning the battle but losing the war, yet which fight should be understood as the battle and which as the war remains unclear—and both approaches give rise to serious casualties.

C. THE EFFECT OF CHOICE OF LANGUAGE ON THE FIELD

A lawyer's command of a language often goes hand in hand with socialization in a certain legal system.[294] Although it is difficult to determine what effect choice of language has on the field, it seems reasonable to assume that privileging certain languages results in privileging both native speakers of those languages, as well as the concepts, approaches, and sources with which they are familiar.[295]

The "linguistic design" of international courts (and other organizations) matters because it causes professionals with specific linguistic skills, cultural values, and expectations to work at and appear before those courts, which has far-reaching consequences on the court's composition, staffing, and internal culture, and possibly the substantive law produced.[296] Because many international courts and tribunals use two official languages, English and French, those who work there often come primarily from Anglophone and Francophone states.[297] This bilingual policy creates an opportunity for what French international lawyer Emmanuelle Jouannet has described as the "continuous 'selling' of each national legal model in order to influence the establishment of international norms and institutions."[298] Gleider Hernández concurs, describing privileged languages as enjoying a "vehicular" status:

> Where the laws, cases, and scholarly texts in international law are primarily in two languages, they employ the vocabulary and with it, the ideas channeled into

---

[292] JAMIN, *supra* note 22, at 236.

[293] *Id.* at 259, 265.

[294] Mathilde Cohen, *On the Linguistic Design of Multinational Courts: The French Capture*, 14 INT'L J. CONST. L. 498, 501 (2016).

[295] JACQUELINE MOWBRAY, LINGUISTIC JUSTICE: INTERNATIONAL LAW AND LANGUAGE POLICY 100–04 (2012).

[296] Cohen, *supra* note 294, at 498–99.

[297] Gleider I. Hernández, *On Multilingualism and the International Legal Process, in* 2 SELECT PROCEEDINGS OF THE EUROPEAN SOCIETY OF INTERNATIONAL LAW 441, 452 (Hélène Ruiz Fabri et al. eds., 2010).

[298] Emmanuelle Jouannet, *French and American Perspectives on International Law: Legal Cultures and International Law*, 58 ME. L. REV. 291, 300 (2006).

international law through those two languages. Thus, because of this "vehicular" status, the transfer of ideas from francophone and anglophone legal orders (especially, France, the United Kingdom and the United States) into international law is accelerated.[299]

Given the relatively low numbers of French speakers worldwide compared with those of other first and second languages, Mathilde Cohen has questioned whether "French capture" in international courts and tribunals remains appropriate in modern times.[300] Peter Laverack made a similar argument in an article published in the *Chinese Journal of International Law*.[301] Laverack contended that adopting a dual language policy, like French and English, can have the effect of disadvantaging international lawyers from large parts of the world where they are unlikely to speak both languages.[302] After analyzing the ICC's staffing patterns, which show a tendency for France and Francophone states to be especially overrepresented, he argued that French was "unfit for purpose" as a common working language because the bilingual policy had the effect of largely excluding participation of lawyers from Asia and Latin America. The only satisfactory solution, he concluded, was to abandon French in favor of a system that requires international lawyers to speak English plus another language, which would permit a common language but discourage monolingualism.[303]

Of course, many Russian and French international lawyers would object to this approach as solidifying and normalizing "English capture." When Laverack posted a similar analysis on *OUPblog*, one Francophone African international lawyer criticized the post for "dripping with Anglo-Saxon linguistic imperialism disguised under benevolent false concern for Asia and Latin America."[304] If one were really concerned about underrepresentation in Asia, she asked, why not add Chinese as an official language to the International Criminal Court since China is the most populous state in the world? Another Francophone objected that Western law is divided into two main categories: continental law, represented internationally by the French, and Anglo-Saxon law. If only English were retained, only Anglo-Saxon law, and the legal concepts associated with it, would be retained, the scholar concluded, which would militate against the aim of encouraging diversity.[305]

As these exchanges illustrate, what strikes some as an appeal to globalization and internationalization strikes others as a call to standardize legal thinking under an Anglo-Saxon, English-speaking common law model.[306] This point was amplified by

---

Hernández, *supra* note 297, at 452.

[300] Mathilde Cohen, *Continuing Impacts of French Legal Culture on the International Court of Justice*, in Comparative International Law (Anthea Roberts et al. eds., forthcoming 2017).

[301] Peter J. Laverack, *The Rise of Asia and the Status of the French Language in International Law*, 14 Chinese J. Int'l L. 567 (2015).

[302] *Id.* at 574.

[303] *Id.* at 583.

[304] Peter Laverack, *French Language in International Law*, OUPblog, July 25, 2016 (comment by Anna D) (author's translation).

[305] *Id.* (comment by Miart) (author's translation).

[306] *See, e.g.*, Blandine Mallet-Bricout, *Libres propos sur l'efficacité des systèmes de droit civil*, 56 Revue internationale de droit comparé 865 (2004) (opposing the standardization/Americanization of law and instead advocating pluralism and competition between different legal families, which might also result in hybrid

the authors of a study on the globalization of legal education who reasoned that the "common law's influence, perhaps predominance, has come about through the hegemony of the United States in international matters, and the expansion of English as the lingua franca of the law," noting that various national reporters expressed the resulting concern that "globalization is a different word for Americanisation, and that the latter is not necessarily desirable."[307]

Many international legal documents, from treaties to judgments, are drafted in multiple languages, and different versions can be used to clarify meanings or to open up room for new approaches or arguments.[308] After interviewing people who worked at various international courts and tribunals, Cohen reported that language diversity was praised for fostering the courts' legitimacy as international judicial bodies and for forcing all participants to remain constantly aware of the transnational, multicultural dimension of the project.[309] Hernández has likewise argued that maintaining multilingualism helps to ensure pluralism in legal discourse, which is essential in a truly multicultural environment.[310] People from different states have developed distinct legal concepts in their native languages, and not all concepts or modes of reasoning can necessarily be transported from one language to another.[311]

Yet the dominance of English, English-language sources, and common law approaches appears to be gaining ground, including within bilingual courts. In a study of the sources relied on in judgments of the International Tribunal for the former Yugoslavia (ICTY), Michael Bohlander and Mark Findlay reported that "the language of justice is mainly English, and to a somewhat lesser extent French," and that anything not written down in these two languages does not seem to be accorded great relevance for purposes of legal research.[312] Within the two languages, English-language common law sources were often privileged. For instance, they noted that the *Prosecutor v. Jelisic* ICTY judgment contains thirty-one footnotes referencing national legal systems, and the text includes many general expressions, like "national case law" or "any specific decided case, whether domestic or international," that make it appear that the citations will be global. But no civil law sources or sources written in a language other than English are cited, and most refer to US and UK law.[313]

---

approaches); Arlette Martin-Serf, *La modélisation des instruments juridiques, in* LA MONDIALISATION DU DROIT 179, 181 (Eric Loquin & Catherine Kessedjian eds., 2000) (noting complaints about "a new imperialism, of a juridical colonialism by the Anglo-Saxon world, of a tendency toward a hegemonic uniformity that could easily carry out the globalisation of American law").

[307] Jamin & van Caenegem, *supra* note 32, at 17.

[308] Vienna Convention on the Law of Treaties, art. 33, *opened for signature* May 23, 1969, 1155 U.N.T.S. 331.

[309] Cohen, *supra* note 300.

[310] *See* Hernández, *supra* note 297, at 457.

[311] French international lawyer Hélène Ruiz Fabri explains this dilemma, *supra* note 5, at 86 ("This linguistic aspect is the essence of a dilemma between the argument that to be read—and readable—by the largest possible public one needs to write in a common language, and the objection that all concepts or modes of reasoning cannot necessarily be transported from one language into another. This dilemma is more or less resolved depending on the countries, the advantage clearly going to the English language."). *See also* Hernández, *supra* note 297, at 453 ("That problem of translation goes well beyond linguistic concordance; it is rooted in a problem of vocabulary.").

[312] Michael Bohlander & Mark Findlay, *The Use of Domestic Sources as a Basis for International Criminal Law Principles,* 2 GLOB. CMTY. Y.B. INT'L L. & JURISPRUDENCE 3, 6 (2002).

[313] *Id.* at 8.

Citations to domestic case law often privilege Western states in general, and the United States and the United Kingdom in particular. No one has yet made a comprehensive study of the national sources that are relied on by all international courts and tribunals and the results will likely differ somewhat among institutions.[314] Damien Charlotin, however, has coded all of the case law referred to in judgments and awards by the ICJ, the ICTY, the International Criminal Tribunal for Rwanda, and investment treaty tribunals. He found that the highest number of references were to US case law (21.5 percent) and UK case law (17.5 percent), followed by French law (8 percent), Canadian law (7 percent), Australian law (6.5 percent), German law (6.5 percent), and Israeli law (5 percent).[315] These figures represent frequent recourse to the same "usual suspects" as appear in case citations in many international law textbooks (see Chapter 4).

In the international criminal law context, Bohlander concluded that, although the majority of the world's population lives in systems with a civil law origin, international criminal justice often (though not always) takes on a distinctly English-language common law feel.[316] The cost of this near-exclusiveness may seem low to international lawyers who are American, Australian, British, or Canadian because the concepts are familiar, but the "cost to your societal, historical and legal identity is high if you are none of these."[317] Bohlander warned that the rise of English brings with it the danger that international law will "see itself through the eyes of that language of law and all the cultural luggage that comes with it," and he urged that a jurisprudence is needed that "speaks English but which is not bound by the conceptual and traditional limits of the historical English-speaking culture."[318] It is not clear that this is possible, however.

Colin Picker similarly argued that, whereas international law was originally strongly civil law-like, it has shifted in the last sixty years to become more common law-like.[319] In studying this "common law drift" in the WTO, Picker identified one explanatory factor as the large number of officials, practitioners, and scholars in the field who pursued legal studies in common law states, including many civil-law-trained students who undertook postgraduate legal education in common law systems.[320] According to Picker, the

---

[314] For instance, German legal concepts have played a significant role in the International Criminal Court, particularly with respect to doctrines such as indirect co-perpetration. *See generally* NEHA JAIN, PERPETRATORS AND ACCESSORIES IN INTERNATIONAL CRIMINAL LAW: INDIVIDUAL MODES OF RESPONSIBILITY FOR COLLECTIVE CRIMES (2014); Neha Jain, *The Control Theory of Perpetration in International Criminal Law*, 12 CHI. J. INT'L L. 158 (2011); Jens David Ohlin, *Co-Perpetration: German Dogmatik or German Invasion?*, *in* THE LAW AND PRACTICE OF THE INTERNATIONAL CRIMINAL COURT: A CRITICAL ACCOUNT OF CHALLENGES AND ACHIEVEMENTS 517 (Carsten Stahn ed., 2015).

[315] On file with author (Damien Charlotin, PhD student at the University of Cambridge).

[316] Bohlander, *supra* note 275, at 491–92 ("English has become the *lingua franca* in international legal academic and practical dialogue, and there is a related concern that English—and its direct descendant, Anglo-American— intellectual and legal culture has drawn a thick veneer over the canvas of international criminal law as well.").

[317] Bohlander & Findlay, *supra* note 312, at 22.

[318] Bohlander, *supra* note 275, at 512–13.

[319] *See* Colin B. Picker, *International Law's Mixed Heritage: A Common/Civil Law Jurisdiction*, 41 VAND. J. TRANSNAT'L L. 1083, 1104–06 (2008); Colin B. Picker, *Beyond the Usual Suspects: Application of the Mixed Jurisdiction Jurisprudence to International Law and Beyond*, 3 J. COMP. L. 160, 162 (2008).

[320] Colin B. Picker, *A Framework for Comparative Analyses of International Law and Its Institutions: Using the Example of the World Trade Organization*, *in* COMPARATIVE LAW AND HYBRID LEGAL SYSTEMS 117, 133–34 (Eleanor Cashin Ritaine et al. eds., 2010).

ever-increasing role of English in international economic law suggests a continuing and potentially expanding influence of common law legal cultural characteristics,[321] which risks undermining the acceptability of these organizations and the implementation of their law in non-common-law states.[322]

Adopting a comparative international law approach helps to focus attention on "whose norms are being globalized and thus to recognize that any global norm may be one party's globalized localism."[323] "[N]owadays, a global lawyer is someone who speaks legal English and is aware of the common law's fundamentals," Antonios Platsas and David Marrani observed, which means that "every trained lawyer in the UK may be considered to be a de facto 'global lawyer.'"[324] US and UK law are particularly privileged in a range of other transnational legal fields, ranging from international commercial contracting[325] to the issuance of sovereign debt.[326] The *Economist* reported that, although emerging markets account for over half the world's GDP at purchasing-power parity, the United Kingdom and the United States "retain a stranglehold on cross-border finance, investment, mergers and acquisitions," partly because of the dominance of their law and law firms in structuring commercial contracts and dispute resolution.[327]

Globalization often produces distinct winners and losers. Just as America benefits from issuing the world's reserve currency, so the United States and the United Kingdom often enjoy the "exorbitant privilege" of issuing the world's "reserve law."[328] This capture marginalizes major civil law traditions, like the French and German systems. It is thus not uncommon to find civil-law-trained academics expressing concern that internationalization means "common-lawization," whereas it is rare to find common-law-trained academics warning of the reverse.[329] The US and UK capture also explains why states like China strongly support their lawyers in studying abroad in Western states, above all the English-speaking United States and United Kingdom, to enable them to become fluent in the

---

[321] Colin Picker, The Value of Comparative and Legal Cultural Analyses of International Economic Law 43–44 (May 13, 2012) (unpublished PhD thesis, University of New South Wales) (on file with UNSW Library).

[322] Colin B. Picker, *Comparative Legal Cultural Analyses of International Economic Law: A New Methodological Approach*, 1 CHINESE J. COMP. L. 21, 47 (2013).

[323] Terence C. Halliday & Pavel Osinsk, *Globalization of Law*, 32 ANN. REV. SOC. 447, 451 (2006).

[324] Antonios E. Platsas & David Marrani, On the Evolving and Dynamic Nature of UK Legal Education, in LEGAL EDUCATION, *supra* note 32, at 299, 299.

[325] For example, a global survey of general counsels and legal-department heads found that, when contracting parties came from different states and were relatively equally matched in terms of negotiating power, the law of each home state would be rejected in favor of a "neutral" third option, the most frequent choices being English law (40 percent) and US law (22 percent, including New York law (17 percent)). SCHOOL OF INTERNATIONAL ARBITRATION AT QUEEN MARY UNIVERSITY OF LONDON, 2010 INTERNATIONAL ARBITRATION SURVEY: CHOICES IN INTERNATIONAL ARBITRATION 11 (2010).

[326] For instance, in a study of the roughly fifteen hundred sovereign debt offerings in the post-World War II era, 82.4 percent of bonds issued were issued under either New York or English law with a roughly even split between the two. Michael Bradley, Irving De Lira Salvatierra, & Mitu Gulati, *Lawyers: Gatekeepers of the Sovereign Debt Market?*, 38 INT'L REV. L. & ECON. 150, 154, 156 (2014).

[327] ECONOMIST, *supra* note 268.

[328] *Id.*

[329] Jamin & van Caenegem, *supra* note 32, at 19. The dominance of English and New York law in international and transnational legal fields is also one reason why Sciences Po teaches these subjects in English and seeks to introduce its students to common law ways of thinking. JAMIN, *supra* note 22, at 212–16.

language of international law. With the rise of the Asian states, as well as the BRICS group of Brazil, Russia, India, China, and South Africa, we are likely to see an increasing turn to English as the common language of international law since these states are not French speaking and do not share a language. A turn to English may be more inclusive of lawyers from these states than a dual French/English policy, but such a turn will also further entrench the advantages enjoyed by international lawyers from English-speaking common law states.

D. THE EXAMPLE OF THE JESSUP MOOT COMPETITION

One arena in which some of these dynamics play out is international mooting competitions, such as the Jessup Moot Court Competition. According to the Jessup's website: "The Competition is a simulation of a fictional dispute between countries before the International Court of Justice, the judicial organ of the United Nations."[330] National rounds are held in states throughout the world, but the international round is held each year in Washington, D.C. Unlike the bilingual policy of the real ICJ, the Jessup's official language is English. Some of the national rounds may be held in other languages, but the memorials must be translated into English for the international rounds. Non-English-speaking teams may participate in the international rounds in their native language provided that they pay for an interpreter.[331] In practice, however, the vast majority of the teams plead in English, and most national rounds are held in English as well, even in non-English-speaking states.

Although teams are free to rely on sources from any states or in any languages, English-language common law sources are often privileged. I have not undertaken a statistical analysis of Jessup memorials, but instructive advice is given by a resource entitled "A Guide to the Philip C. Jessup International Law Moot Court Competition," which was published by the China Initiative on International Criminal Justice and written by former mooting students: one from mainland China, one from Hong Kong, and one from the United States.[332] This guide was initially distributed to participants of the Jessup China Regional Rounds in 2014, and was thereafter revised and updated for an international audience.[333] It contains a great deal of helpful information about how to research and present an effective argument at the Jessup. It also opens a useful window on some of the denationalizing and westernizing socialization processes that Jessup participants undergo.

For a student who had studied international law in China, in the Chinese language and using Chinese international law textbooks, this guide represents a crash course in how to appeal to an "international" audience. The guide suggests that students begin by choosing a comprehensive public international law textbook, noting that Shaw's *International*

---

[330] *See Philip C. Jessup International Law Moot Court Competition*, INT'L L. STUDENTS ASS'N, https://www.ilsa.org/jessuphome (last visited Nov. 4, 2016).

[331] *See Frequently Asked Questions*, INT'L L. STUDENTS ASS'N, https://www.ilsa.org/jessuphome/2014-08-15-09-28-07/faqs#V2 (last visited Nov. 4, 2016).

[332] CHINESE INITIATIVE ON INT'L CRIM. JUST., A GUIDE TO THE PHILIP C. JESSUP INTERNATIONAL LAW MOOT COURT COMPETITION (2014).

[333] *Id.* (preface).

Law (UK) is "highly recommended," as are "leading treatises" like Crawford's new edition of Brownlie's *Principles of Public International Law* (UK).[334] When it comes to non-ICJ cases, the guide recommends that students refer to domestic court decisions, such as by the US Supreme Court, the UK Supreme Court, the Canadian Supreme Court, and the Australian High Court.[335] For publicists, it shepherds students toward articles published in "key peer-reviewed international law journals," including but not limited to the *American Journal of International Law*, the *British Yearbook of International Law*, and the *European Journal of International Law*.[336] The guide mentions nothing about French sources, or Chinese, Russian, German, or Spanish ones, nor does it discuss translations. Different national textbooks and approaches seem to be largely left behind and, in their place, English-speaking common law sources in general, and US and UK ones in particular, become international standard bearers.

Competing in the Jessup is likely to have a denationalizing effect on many participants. One Australian international lawyer spoke of her exhilaration at discovering that, in her argument against the Argentine team, both teams used the same ICJ case. The teams had trained on different sides of the world yet were competing on the basis of a shared language. A Chinese international lawyer noted that the experience of "competing with as well as communicating with their peers from all over the world" was highly significant for many Chinese international law students, as it was often the first time they were able to step out of the "bubble" in which they learned international law at home.[337]

It is also one of the first times that teams from different states gain an impression of how teams from other states approach international law. For instance, numerous international lawyers from different states—developed and developing, Western and non-Western, English speaking and non-English speaking—have remarked to me how amazing and amusing they found the heavy reliance by US teams on domestic US case law. "I couldn't believe it," a Mexican international lawyer exclaimed, "they were relying on obscure US cases from lower level US courts as though what those courts said was international law!" "I wanted to tell them," she continued, "that is not international law. What would they think if I tried to prove something was international law by relying largely on Mexican cases?"[338]

The international Jessup experience made students from some states acutely aware of the existence of two different international law dialects—one national and the other transnational. In some cases, the chasm between these approaches led to or reinforced a disconnect between the younger, more denationalized student mooters and their older, more nationalized professors. As one young Russian international lawyer who had participated in the Jessup explained:

Everyone who wants to know "actual" international law (either as a practitioner or as a moot court participant) would use Western textbooks (European ones like

---

[334] *Id.* at 3–4.
[335] *Id.* at 7.
[336] *Id.* at 8.
[337] E-mail on file with author.
[338] E-mail on file with author.

Brownlie or Shaw are more familiar for a Russian eye than US casebooks) and other sources in English. And when you study international law like this, you completely distance yourself from traditional "old guard" law. "Our" international law is pretty much denationalized, and as a result we feel comfortable with it abroad but not at home.[339]

Meanwhile, the proficiency with which some of these non-native English speakers compete on the international stage may also engender a false sense of universality for those who trained in English-speaking common law states. For instance, one US international lawyer objected to the idea that there might be different traditions of international law in different states, or that differences between textbooks in different states or languages might matter, on the basis that he had judged mooting teams from Russia in the Jessup and they had all referred to the English-language textbooks and sources with which he was familiar. That may be true, but this observation papers over how and why that occurs, and with what effect.

The Jessup prides itself on being "the world's largest moot court competition, with participants from over 550 law schools in more than 87 countries."[340] But not everyone sees it that way. According to one French international lawyer, in France the Jessup is generally viewed as an "English-speaking" exercise.[341] This lawyer, who had considerable ICJ advocacy experience, also protested that "the Jessup is not at all 'ICJ-oriented'" but, rather, is conducted as a "trial before a common law court."[342] The judges constantly interrupt the parties' pleadings, which is "a universe away from the ICJ where questions are submitted after the hearings, with answers to be given in writing."[343] He felt that giving recommendations based on his ICJ practice seemed to be completely unhelpful to the Jessup participants, at least with respect to their oral pleadings, because they were not sufficiently common-law in style.

Although some French teams participate in the Jessup, many also compete in Le Concours Charles-Rousseau, which the website explains is the "French equivalent of the Jessup Moot Court Competition" and whose organizing committee is part of the Réseau francophone de droit international (Francophone Network of International Law.)[344] More than one hundred institutions from thirty-five countries have participated in the Rousseau moot, making it a noteworthy parallel to the Jessup, but on a significantly smaller scale.[345] And, whereas it draws teams from around the world, it exerts primary traction in France and other Francophone states like Belgium, Canada, Cameroon, and

---

[339] E-mail on file with author.

[340] *See* INT'L L. STUDENTS ASS'N, *supra* note 330.

[341] E-mail on file with author.

[342] *Id.*

[343] *Id.*

[344] *See Concours de procès simulé en droit international Charles-Rousseau-Présentation*, RÉSEAU FRANCOPHONE DE DROIT INTERNATIONAL, http://www.rfdi.net/rousseau.html (last visited Feb. 5, 2017).

[345] *See Carte des Participants*, RÉSEAU FRANCOPHONE DE DROIT INTERNATIONAL, http://www.rfdi.net/rousseau-part.html (last visited Feb. 5, 2017).

the Democratic Republic of the Congo.[346] The Rousseau is conducted in French, but the same French international lawyer explained with pride that "[i]n this moot, students are acting like real international lawyers, because we oblige them in particular to use English and French resources as well as any other relevant resources in a language that they can speak (Spanish, Italian, German, in particular)."[347]

The Jessup does not describe itself as the "English equivalent of the Rousseau moot." It is organized by a group that calls itself the International Law Students Association, not the Anglophone International Law Students Association. It assumes the mantle of the "international," but it also involves the greatest number and spread of participants in order to justify that title. The Jessup represents a lived example of how transnational engagement is often facilitated by the use of English as a common language, though in ways that may privilege Anglo-American sources and approaches in defining what counts as "international." Although the early years of the international competition were dominated by English-speaking states, most notably the United States and Australia, in recent years teams from many other states, including Argentina, Colombia, France, Mexico, the Philippines, South Africa, Singapore, and India, have also won the international title. Greater diversity marks the national backgrounds of the Jessup winners than those of the real ICJ bar, and it seems likely that the use of English plays a role in both promoting diversity on this level (representation) and truncating it on others (sources and approaches).

These patterns of difference and dominance in the lives of students of international law mirror larger patterns in the world at large, but new stresses are disrupting this traditional balance. Chapter 6 turns to these challenges for the future.

---

[346] *Id.*
[347] E-mail on file with author.

6

Disruptions Leading to a Competitive World Order

IDENTIFYING EXISTING PATTERNS of difference and dominance raises the question of how these patterns might be disrupted by various forces, including technological innovation, changes in domestic political preferences, and shifts in geopolitical power. As these patterns shift, so too will movement occur in the way in which communities of international lawyers are constructed and interact, and how they conceive of the field.

One disruptive force that may affect the nature of international law as a transnational legal field is technology. The Internet has enabled people representing diverse backgrounds, languages, and parts of the world to intercommunicate better, though it has also reinforced the formation of echo chambers by like-minded individuals. The surprise that many liberal elites felt in 2016 over the outcomes of the US presidential elections and the Brexit vote reflect some of the problems that can occur when people use the internet to surround themselves with confirming opinions instead of being aware of, and trying to understand, diverse perspectives. One of the lessons of this study is that this issue occurs across borders as well as within borders. The movement of sources online has also made it easier for international lawyers to access foreign documents, and improving translation software permits more lawyers to understand foreign language materials. Still, even though technology may enable greater access to diverse sources, it may also form a conduit for already-privileged sources to acquire even greater reach and influence. That is one of the effects of globalization.

On a domestic political level, debates are taking place in many states over the relative merits of globalization and nationalism, and recalibrations of the balance struck between the two have the potential to affect some of the dynamics studied in this book. The

Is International Law International? Anthea Roberts.
© Anthea Roberts 2017. Published 2017 by Oxford University Press.

makeup of UK law schools is a case in point. When this study was conducted, elite UK law schools evidenced radical double internationalization because they were made up of a high percentage of foreign students and academics.[1] This unique character partly resulted from the United Kingdom's position within the European Union and its embrace of globalization, both of which were subjected to strong pushback in the vote to withdraw from the Union. Although it is too early to tell what effect Brexit will have on UK universities, early reports suggest that it has already caused falling foreign student applications and fears that foreign academics will leave, or fail to apply to, the UK academy.[2] Similarly, the United States may see falling foreign student applications if Donald J. Trump is able to translate some of the anti-immigration sentiments he expressed in his US presidential campaign into executive policies or legislative enactments.

Although some states, like the United Kingdom and the United States, appear to be stepping back from their embrace of globalism, others, like China, seem to be stepping forward. China's government is increasing its funding to elite universities with the aim of moving up the global rankings and attracting five hundred thousand foreign students per year by 2020.[3] Top Chinese law schools are beginning to offer LLM programs in English designed to attract students from around the world.[4] The Chinese government is offering tens of thousands of scholarships to Chinese universities to foreign students, scholars, and diplomats,[5] including a significant number to individuals coming from Africa.[6] These efforts represent an attempt by China to build up its soft power by sensitizing foreign students to Chinese views, customs, and preferences, and to cultivate professional and personal networks that will carry on into the future.[7]

---

[1] *See* Chapter 3.I and II.

[2] *See, e.g.*, Jessica Elgot, *Universities Fear UK's Global Reputation in Jeopardy Due to Brexit*, GUARDIAN, Sept. 19, 2016; Jon Henley, Stephanie Kirchgaessner, & Philip Oltermann, *Brexit Fears May See 15% of UK University Staff Leave, Group Warns*, GUARDIAN, Sept. 25, 2016; Robert McCrum, *What Will Brexit Mean for Britain's World-Class Universities?*, GUARDIAN, Nov. 13, 2016; Sally Weale, *UK University Applications from EU Down by 9%, Says UCAS*, GUARDIAN, Oct. 27, 2016.

[3] Liu Dong, *Universities to Rival West's in 25 Yrs: Report*, GLOBAL TIMES, Feb. 4, 2010; Li Xing & Tan Yingzi, *China Offers Scholarships*, CHINA DAILY, July 22, 2011.

[4] For instance, China University of Political Science and Law, Wuhan University, Xiamen University, and Law School of Shanghai Jiao Tong University have all introduced English-language LLM and/or PhD programs, often with a focus on international or Chinese law, which are designed to attract international students. *See, e.g., Curriculum of LLM Program 2016–2017 Autumn Semester*, SCH. L., XIAMEN UNIV. (Sept. 8, 2016), http://enlaw. xmu.edu.cn/Home/Detail/13663?topic=9; *LLM in International Law*, CHINA UNIV. POL. SCI. & L., http:// www.lawschoolchina.com/llm (last visited Dec. 28, 2016); *L.L.M. Program*, KOGUAN L. SCH. SHANGHAI JIAO TONG UNIV., http://law.sjtu.edu.cn/International/Article120102.aspx (last updated Nov. 21, 2013); *Popular Programs*, WUHAN UNIV., http://admission.whu.edu.cn/courses_rec.html (last visited Dec. 28, 2016).

[5] *See Introduction to Chinese Government Scholarships*, CHINA SCHOLARSHIP COUNCIL (Dec. 8, 2015), http:// www.csc.edu.cn/laihua/scholarshipdetailen.aspx?cid=97&id=2070.

[6] DAVID SHAMBAUGH, CHINA GOES GLOBAL: THE PARTIAL POWER 110 (2014); STEPHEN MARKS, INTRODUCTION, IN AFRICAN PERSPECTIVES ON CHINA IN AFRICA 2 (Firoze Manji & Stephen Marks eds., 2007).

[7] SHAMBAUGH, *supra* note 6, at 241–45; Chen Jia, *Class Act Promotes Global "Soft Power,"* CHINA DAILY, Nov. 11, 2010. Other attempts by China to build its soft power include support for Confucius Institutes in many universities throughout the world. *See* Peter Mattis, *Reexamining the Confucian Institutes*, DIPLOMAT, Aug. 2, 2012.

These two movements reflect broader shifts in geopolitical power, which are the focus of this chapter. The substantive writing of this book was completed in late 2016, shortly after Trump was elected president of the United States but before he took office. During his campaign, Trump promised to upend many of the trademark US approaches to international law, such as support for free trade and strong defense alliances in Europe and the Pacific, so that his election has considerable capability to disrupt some of the current patterns in the field. At the time of writing, it remained too early to tell how Trump would govern, so this book does not focus on the changes in domestic political preferences of the United States (or the United Kingdom) or what impact these might have on the international legal order. Suffice to say that if Trump ends up governing according to the promises he made during his election campaign, 2016 will mark the start of a new, more nationalist, era that ends the period of high globalization that has occurred since the 1990s. Perceptions of America and its role in global leadership are also likely to shift, and significant divisions could well appear among various Western powers.

Whereas that remains to play out in the future, what appears to be clear for now is that the United Kingdom and the United States are pulling back from the project of globalization that they had previously spearheaded, while other states, including China and Russia, appear to be becoming more assertive about their place on the world stage. Global power is thus shifting from the unipolarity that marked the post-Cold War period to greater multipolarity, and from an era of a Western-led international order to one marked by greater competition, and increased need for cooperation, between Western and non-Western states. As a result, the world is entering into a new competitive world order in which Western states are likely to face more checks and balances in advancing their strategic and normative agendas, and various non-Western states will have greater ability to promote their interests, either singly or collectively. In adapting to this shift, international lawyers will need to develop an understanding of the international law approaches of a variety of "unlike-minded" states, as power will be disaggregated among a more diverse group of states than previously.

Accordingly, this chapter examines the way China and Russia are challenging certain Western approaches to international law, both individually and collectively. In doing so, I am not suggesting that China and Russia are the only or most important challengers to the existing world order. Indeed, with the election of Trump, the United States may well end up assuming that mantle. Nor should I be understood as suggesting that China and Russia do not support the existing system in important ways. For instance, studies of China suggest that its engagement with and support for the international system have increased significantly over time,[8] as evidenced by its active participation in dispute resolution at the World Trade Organization (WTO)[9] and its growing contributions to UN peacekeeping missions.[10] Nor am I assuming that China and Russia represent all

[8] Rosemary Foot & Andrew Walter, China, the United States, and Global Order 275 (2011).
[9] *See* Henry Gao, *China's Ascent in Global Trade Governance: From Rule Taker to Rule Shaker, and Maybe Rule Maker?*, *in* Making Global Trade Governance Work for Development 153 (Carolyn Deere-Birkbeck ed., 2011); *id., China's Participation in the WTO: A Lawyer's Perspective*, 2007 Sing. Y.B. Int'l L. 1.
[10] Courtney J. Fung, China's Troop Contributions to UN Peacekeeping (U.S. Inst. for Peace, Peace Brief No. 212, 2016); *id., What Explains China's Deployment to UN Peacekeeping Operations?*, 16

non-Western states (for instance, Brazil, India, and South Africa—the other states that make up the BRICS—are not authoritarian) or that the areas in which they pose challenges are the most important (other challenges, including climate change, terrorism, and nuclear nonproliferation, are of potentially existential importance). China and Russia also do not align on all issues, as evidenced by their divergent paths in international economic law and international environmental law.

Nevertheless, it is worth focusing on China and Russia because these two non-Western authoritarian states constitute the vanguard of challenging the dominance of Western liberal democratic states in crafting the structure and substance of international law. Even if the two states are not united in what they stand for, they are united to some extent by what they stand against. How their challenge to Western hegemony plays out will depend largely on the power and internal unity of the two groups and their ability to win other states over to their respective sides. This question only serves to emphasize the extent to which our understanding of international law will shift as geopolitical power shifts and why so much will depend on the ability of states to coexist and cooperate to achieve their goals. In this new competitive world order, international lawyers will find it increasingly important to be proficient in a comparative international law methodology to enable them to ascertain how issues are viewed and approached from different perspectives and therefore to see where new alliances may be formed and divisions overcome.

I. Shifting to a Competitive World Order

Western states have played a critical, and disproportionate, role in the creation of international law to date. Although there have been credible attempts to tell other stories,[11] traditional history writing in international law has often taken for granted that international law was originally created by Europeans and transported throughout the world through the colonial encounter.[12] In effect, what might have been understood initially as "European" international law was recast as "universal" international law.[13] In the wake of World War II, the United States, another Western state, played a pivotal role in shaping international law through its position as one of the two superpowers during the Cold War, and then as the unipolar power afterward.

INT'L REL. ASIA-PACIFIC 409 (2016); M. Taylor Fravel, *Economic Growth, Regime Insecurity, and Military Strategy: Explaining the Rise of Noncombat Operations in China*, 7 ASIAN SECURITY 177 (2011).

[11] *See, e.g.*, RAM PRAKASH ANAND, STUDIES IN INTERNATIONAL LAW AND HISTORY: AN ASIAN PERSPECTIVE (2004); TASLIM OLAWALE ELIAS, AFRICA AND THE DEVELOPMENT OF INTERNATIONAL LAW (1988); YASUAKI ONUMA, A TRANSCIVILIZATIONAL PERSPECTIVE ON INTERNATIONAL LAW (2010); *id.*, *When Was the Law of International Society Born? An Inquiry of the History of International Law from an Intercivilizational Perspective*, 2 J. HIST. INT'L L. 1 (2000).

[12] On this tendency, see BARDO FASSBENDER & ANNE PETERS, INTRODUCTION: TOWARDS A GLOBAL HISTORY OF INTERNATIONAL LAW 1, 4 (2012).

[13] *See* Antony Anghie, *Finding the Peripheries: Sovereignty and Colonialism in Nineteenth-Century International Law*, 40 HARV. INT'L L.J. 1, 3 nn.6–7 (1999).

During this time, states made two significant attempts to push back against the Western-led international law project. First, after many former colonies gained independence following World War II, they attempted to challenge some elements of the Western-led international order, especially in the UN General Assembly where they formed a majority. But, as these debates largely transpired between developed states that were powerful "haves" and developing states that were less powerful "have-nots," Western dominance remained intact to a large extent.[14] Second, in the Cold War period, geopolitics was structured around the bipolar division of power between the United States and the Soviet Union, which pitted Western, democratic capitalist states against non-Western, nondemocratic Communist states.

The bipolarity of the Cold War meant that some international institutions, most notably the UN Security Council, often experienced gridlock due to disagreements between the two camps. But after the fall of the Berlin Wall in 1989 and the collapse of the Soviet Union (USSR) in 1991, the United States emerged as the world's unipolar power,[15] and the End of History thesis suggested that all states were progressing toward the ultimate goal of democratic liberalism.[16] The 1990s were a time for renewed optimism in the West about the universality of international law; the transformative potential of international organizations, such as the UN Security Council and international courts; and the relative advantages of liberal values, such as human rights and democracy, compared with traditional international law notions, such as state sovereignty and noninterference. During this time, Western states and international lawyers seized on the opportunity to pursue liberal democratic agendas.

Yet the distribution of power shifted again. Even before Brexit and Trump's election, commentators were clearly predicting a transition from the unipolarity of the post-Cold War period into an era of greater multipolarity. In terms of economics and political power, the international system is moving past the era of dominance by Europe and the United States with the rise of the BRICS, as well as other states (sometimes referred to as the "rise of the rest").[17] As previous have-nots move to becoming haves, their ability to challenge the status quo increases. In terms of security, some commentators have argued that the "end of history has ended" and "geopolitics is back," focusing in particular on increased regional assertiveness by Russia in Crimea and China in the South and East China Seas.[18] The sense has been growing that Western states in general, and the United

[14] *See* Marc Galanter, *Why the "Haves" Come Out Ahead: Speculations on the Limits of Legal Change*, 9 Law & Soc'y Rev. 95 (1974).

[15] *See* Charles Krauthammer, *The Unipolar Moment*, 70 Foreign Aff., no. 1, 1990, at 23.

[16] *See* Francis Fukuyama, The End of History and the Last Man (1992); *id.*, *The End of History?*, Nat'l Int., Summer 1989, at 3.

[17] *See, e.g.*, Charles A. Kupchan, No One's World: The West, the Rising Rest, and the Coming Global Turn (2012); William W. Burke-White, *Power Shifts in International Law: Structural Realignment and Substantive Pluralism*, 56 Harv. Int'l L.J. 1 (2015); Congyan Cai, *New Great Powers and International Law in the 21st Century*, 24 Eur. J. Int'l L. 755 (2013).

[18] *See, e.g.*, John McLaughlin, *The Geopolitical Rules You Didn't Know About Are Under Siege*, OZY, Nov. 11, 2015; Walter Russell Mead, *The End of History Ends*, Am. Int., Dec. 2, 2013; *id.*, *The Return of Geopolitics: The Revenge of the Revisionist Powers*, 93 Foreign Aff., May–June 2014, at 69; Stewart Patrick & Isabella Bennett, *Geopolitics*

States in particular, can no longer sustain the leadership of the international system as they once did, and this sense only became more acute late in 2016.

A. THE SIGNIFICANCE OF CHANGING GEOPOLITICAL POWER

Several factors from the post-Cold War period can be identified that set the stage for this competitive world order, and these changes are likely to increase attention on comparative approaches to international law. Among these propelling factors was that despite the propensity of Western states, especially the United States, to present themselves as upholders of the international system and the international rule of law, the credibility of Western states as international law abiders came under serious attack in response to two uses of force without Security Council authorization after the Cold War. In 1998–99, in the face of a potential veto by China and Russia, the NATO states used force in Kosovo without Security Council authorization, re-enlivening debates about whether international law did or should permit states to engage in unilateral humanitarian intervention. In 2003, the United Kingdom and the United States used force in Iraq without gaining express Security Council authorization. These events fueled concern outside the West that the United States and its allies were guilty of double standards, sanctimoniously preaching the importance of abiding by international law and working within international institutions, but jettisoning both when it suited their interests.[19]

Some Western uses of force in non-Western states with the aim or effect of removing nondemocratic regimes also led to terrible results, including in both full-scale and lighter interventions. For instance, in 2003, after the United States and the United Kingdom toppled Saddam Hussein's military dictatorship, Iraq descended into sectarian politics and violence before becoming a staging ground for Al Qaeda and later the Islamic State of Iraq and Syria (ISIS).[20] During eight years of occupation, many US soldiers lost their lives, and the civilian death toll was staggering.[21] And in 2011, NATO forces engaged in an aerial campaign to protect civilians in the first Libyan civil war, which erupted as the Arab Spring spread across many states in the Middle East.[22] After Muammar al-Qaddafi's military regime was overturned, no one was able to form a stable government

---

Is Back—And Global Governance Is Out, NAT'L INT.: BUZZ (May 12, 2015), http://nationalinterest.org/blog/the-buzz/geopolitics-back%E2%80%94-global-governance-out-12868.

[19] For examples of these perceptions, see the discussions of newspaper reports and academic articles in China and Russia about the South China Sea and Crimea, respectively. *See* Chapter 5.II.

[20] Lizzie Dearden, *Former US Military Adviser David Kilcullen Says There Would Be No ISIS Without Iraq Invasion*, INDEP., Mar. 4, 2016; Patrick Wintour, *Intelligence Files Support Claims Iraq Invasion Helped Spawn ISIS*, GUARDIAN, July 6, 2016. *See generally* GEORGE PACKER, THE ASSASSINS' GATE: AMERICA IN IRAQ (2006).

[21] Sabrina Tavernise & Andrew W. Lehren, *A Grim Portrait of Civilian Deaths in Iraq*, N.Y. TIMES, Oct. 22, 2010; Chris Woods, *Does the U.S. Ignore Its Civilian Casualties in Iraq and Syria?*, N.Y. TIMES, Aug. 17, 2016.

[22] Press Release, Security Council, Security Council Approves "No-Fly Zone" over Libya, Authorizing "All Necessary Measures" to Protect Civilians, by Vote of 10 in Favour with 5 Abstentions, U.N. Press Release SC/10200 (Mar. 17, 2011); *see also* David D. Kirkpatrick, Steven Erlanger, & Elisabeth Bumiller, *Allies Open Air Assault on Qaddafi's Forces in Libya*, N.Y. TIMES, Mar. 19, 2011; *Libya: US, UK and France Attack Gaddafi Forces*, BBC NEWS, Mar. 20, 2011.

and violence and corruption continued until a second civil war erupted in 2014.[23] The costs and casualties involved, coupled with the negative outcomes, led to war weariness in the West and fanned serious anti-Western sentiments elsewhere.[24]

During the same period, Western economic power began to decline, while that of several non-Western economies significantly increased. The global financial crisis in 2008 saw a sharp decline in the economic stability and growth of the United States and Western Europe, and also led to serious concerns about the reliability of the Western capitalist model and the US-led global financial system.[25] These concerns came on top of a series of financial crises, such as in Argentina in 2001–02 and Asia in 1997, which were precipitated or exacerbated by some of the neoliberal policy prescriptions of Western-led international institutions, such as the International Monetary Fund.[26] Austerity policies and sovereign debt crises fed problems in developed states and regions, like the Greek debt crisis that threatened the Eurozone.[27] Meanwhile, after several decades of stunning double-digit growth, China emerged as the world's second-largest economy, while Brazil and India also entered the world's top ten largest economies.[28]

As the economic power of the BRICS increased, so have their calls for greater representation in international institutions. Recognizing the essentiality of emerging economies to managing the world economy, the Western-dominated Group of Seven (later Eight) gave way to the much more diverse Group of Twenty in 2009,[29] which was also the year of the first BRICS global summit.[30] In some cases, the group's calls for greater representation were stymied or delayed, such as by the failure of the US Congress to approve changes aimed at giving the BRICS greater voting rights in the International Monetary Fund. Partly in response to these delays, the group set up alternative multilateral regimes, such as the BRICS-led New Development Bank and the China-led Asia Infrastructure Investment Bank, both established in 2013.[31] The fact that many Western states, including close allies of the United States like Australia and the United Kingdom, joined the bank

---

[23] Kareem Fahim, *Still Torn by Factional Fighting, Post-Revolt Libya Is Coming Undone*, N.Y. TIMES, July 27, 2014; David D. Kirkpatrick, *Strife in Libya Could Presage Long Civil War*, N.Y. TIMES, Aug. 24, 2014; *Libya Profile— Timeline*, BBC NEWS, Nov. 21, 2016.

[24] *See* Eliot Cohen, *Lessons from 15 Years of War*, in US FOREIGN POLICY AND GLOBAL STANDING IN THE 21ST CENTURY: REALITIES AND PERCEPTIONS 15 (Efraim Inbar & Jonathan Rynhold eds., 2016); Dominic Tierney, *The Legacy of Obama's "Worst Mistake,"* ATLANTIC, Apr. 15, 2016.

[25] Jonathan Kirshner, *Geopolitics After the Global Financial Crisis*, INT'L REL. & SECURITY NETWORK, Sept. 3, 2014; Philip Stephens, *Crisis Marks Out a New Geopolitical Order*, FIN. TIMES, Oct. 10, 2008. *See generally* JONATHAN KIRSHNER, AMERICAN POWER AFTER THE FINANCIAL CRISIS (2014).

[26] *See, e.g.*, JOSEPH E. STIGLITZ, GLOBALIZATION AND ITS DISCONTENTS 89–132 (2002); *IMF Owns Up to Argentina Errors*, BBC NEWS, Mar. 25, 2004.

[27] *See Explaining Greece's Debt Crisis*, N.Y. TIMES, June 17, 2016.

[28] *See List of Countries by GDP (Nominal)*, WIKIPEDIA, https://en.wikipedia.org/wiki/List_of_countries_by_ GDP_(nominal) (last modified Dec. 25, 2016 08:28 PM); *List of Countries by GDP (PPP)*, WIKIPEDIA, https:// en.wikipedia.org/wiki/List_of_countries_by_GDP_(PPP) (last modified Dec. 26, 2016 07:28 AM).

[29] *Officials: G-20 to Supplant G-8 as International Economic Council*, CNN, Sept. 25, 2009.

[30] *See* ABOUT BRICS, BRICS INDIA: 2016, http://brics2016.gov.in/content/innerpage/about-usphp.php (last visited Nov. 26, 2016).

[31] Hong Yelin, *The AIIB Is Seen Very Differently in the US, Europe, and China*, DIPLOMAT, May 8, 2015; *IMF Delays Voting Reforms as BRICS Set Up Rivals*, BRICS POST, June 13, 2015.

as founding members despite Washington's objections was taken by many as a signal of America's waning diplomatic influence.[32]

Over a similar period, the world has seen a shift away from multilateralism and multilateral forums, partly because of differences of opinion between developed and developing states, resulting in an increased focus on regional agreements. A key example has been the failure to reach new agreements under the auspices of the WTO. The Doha Development Round, which commenced in November 2001, was the latest WTO trade negotiation round. The talks stalled in 2008 after the breakdown of negotiations over disagreements between major developed states, led by the European Union, Japan, and the United States, and major developing countries, led mainly by Brazil, China, India, and South Africa.[33] Since then, bilateral and regional free trade agreements have proliferated. Under President Barack Obama, the United States sought trade and investment deals with Europe (Transatlantic Trade and Investment Partnership (TTIP)) and various Asian and Pacific states (Trans-Pacific Partnership Agreement (TPP)), both of which excluded the BRICS. The strategy appeared to be that the United States wanted to agree on appropriate rules with like-minded or less powerful states first before inviting unlikeminded states, like China and India, to sign on to these rules.[34] Meanwhile, China, India, and others began negotiating a competing deal: the Regional Comprehensive Economic Partnership (RCEP).

The international security environment also changed during this period.[35] The 1940s to the late 1980s were marked by the competition between two superpowers: the United States and the Soviet Union. This division of power manifested itself in rivalry, for instance, between the US-led NATO alliance and the Soviet-led Warsaw Pact. During the post-Cold War era, which began in the early 1990s and lasted for twenty to twenty-five years, the United States was the sole superpower and had no real competitors. The Warsaw Pact disbanded, and the Soviet Union dissolved into Russia and various other former Soviet states. China had not yet reached a stage of economic or military development to compete seriously with the United States. But a shift began in the late 2000s. In response to increasing concern about the expansion of NATO, Russia invaded and occupied part of Georgia in 2008 without provoking a military response from Western states.[36] Starting in around 2010, and accelerating from 2013, China became much more

---

[32] Philippe Le Corre, *Dividing the West: China's New Investment Bank and America's Diplomatic Failure*, BROOKINGS, Mar. 17, 2015; Jane Perlez, *China Creates a World Bank of Its Own, and the U.S. Balks*, N.Y. TIMES, Dec. 4, 2015; Simon Reich, *China's New Investment Bank Challenges US Influence on Global Economics*, CONVERSATION, Apr. 10, 2015; David R. Sands, *Diplomatic Disaster: Obama Humiliated by Allies' Rush to Join China's New Bank*, WASH. TIMES, Mar. 18, 2015.

[33] *See generally The Doha Round . . . and Round . . . and Round*, ECONOMIST, July 31, 2008.

[34] *See* Heribert Dieter, *The Return of Geopolitics: Trade Policy in the Era of TTIP and TPP*, DIALOGUE ON GLOBALISATION: INT'L POL'Y ANALYSIS, Dec. 2014, at 1; Melissa K. Griffith, Richard Steinberg, & John Zysman, Great Power Politics in a Global Economy: Origins and Consequences of the TPP and TTIP (Oct. 17, 2015) (unpublished draft for conference discussion), http://www.brie.berkeley.edu/wp-content/uploads/2015/02/Great-Power-Politics-in-a-Global-Economy-Origins-and-Consequences-of-the-TPP-and-TTIP.pdf.

[35] RONALD O'ROURKE, CONG. RES. SERV., R43838, A SHIFT IN THE INTERNATIONAL SECURITY ENVIRONMENT: POTENTIAL IMPLICATIONS FOR DEFENSE—ISSUES FOR CONGRESS (2016).

[36] *Id.* at 7.

assertive about its claims with respect to the East and South China Seas, building up some of the islands and more aggressively patrolling the seas.[37] In 2014, Russia annexed Crimea, again without provoking a military response from the West.[38]

Some commentators viewed these events as a turning point, transforming the post-Cold War world into one of renewed struggle between great powers, this time involving the United States and its Western allies against China and Russia, acting both individually and collectively.[39] Many Western commentators believe that China and Russia are seeking to develop spheres of influence and regional hegemony that would challenge the global hegemony of the West in general, and the United States in particular.[40] The Chinese and Russian efforts in Crimea, Georgia, and the East and South China Seas are sometimes characterized as involving a "salami-slicing" or "cabbage strategy" designed to extend the spheres of influence of China and Russia incrementally without any single action's being significant enough to precipitate a military response from the West.[41] Some view the lack of a military response to Russia's actions in Crimea as an acknowledgment of Russia's sphere of influence, as reflected in President Obama's statement that "[t]he fact is that Ukraine, which is a non-NATO country, is going to be vulnerable to military domination by Russia no matter what we do."[42]

China and Russia appear to be closer now than they have been for a long time.[43] Russia pursued stronger economic ties with China in reaction to Western sanctions against Russia over Crimea, and China announced its One Belt, One Road initiative to increase connectivity and cooperation across Eurasia. Politically, China and Russia have been

---

[37] *Id.* at 2, 7–8, 27–29.

[38] *Id.* at 2, 7.

[39] *See, e.g.*, NOAH FELDMAN, COOL WAR: THE FUTURE OF GLOBAL COMPETITION (2013); ROBERT KAGAN, THE RETURN OF HISTORY AND THE END OF DREAMS 53–80 (2008); Peter Baker, *If Not a Cold War, a Return to a Chilly Rivalry*, N.Y. TIMES, Mar. 18, 2014; Mathew Burrows & Robert A. Manning, *America's Worst Nightmare: Russia and China Are Getting Closer*, NAT'L INT., Aug. 24, 2015; Steven Erlanger, *NATO's Hopes for Russia Have Turned to Dismay*, N.Y. TIMES, Sept. 12, 2014; Azar Gat, *The Return of Authoritarian Great Powers*, 86 FOREIGN AFF., July–Aug. 2007, at 59; James Kitfield, *The New Great Power Triangle Tilt: China, Russia vs. U.S.*, BREAKING DEF., June 19, 2014; Paul David Miller, *Crimea Proves That Great Power Rivalry Never Left Us*, FOREIGN POL'Y, Mar. 21, 2014; David E. Sanger, *Commitments on Three Fronts Test Obama's Foreign Policy*, N.Y. TIMES, Sept. 3, 2014; Lilia Shevtsova, *Putin Ends the Interregnum*, AM. INT., Aug. 28, 2014; Yasmin Tadjdch, *Work: "Great Power Competition" Has Returned*, NAT'L DEF.:BLOG (Nov. 22, 2015, 03:05 PM), http://www.nationaldefensemagazine.org/blog/Lists/Posts/Post.aspx?ID=2026; *see also* Andrew Clevenger, *Work: Future Includes Competition Between US, Great Powers*, DEF. NEWS, Nov. 20, 2015.

[40] *See, e.g.*, Robert Kagan, *The United States Must Resist a Return to Spheres of Interest in the International System*, BROOKINGS, Feb. 19, 2015; Tadjdeh, *supra* note 39; Clevenger, *supra* note 39.

[41] *See, e.g.*, RONALD O'ROURKE, CONG. RES. SERV., R42784, MARITIME TERRITORIAL AND EXCLUSIVE ECONOMIC ZONE (EEZ) DISPUTES INVOLVING CHINA: ISSUES FOR CONGRESS 23–24 (2016); Robert Haddick, *Salami Slicing in the South China Sea: China's Slow, Patient Approach to Dominating Asia*, FOREIGN POL'Y, Aug. 3, 2012; Harry Kazianis, *China's Expanding Cabbage Strategy*, DIPLOMAT, Oct. 29, 2013.

[42] Jeffrey Goldberg, *The Obama Doctrine*, ATLANTIC, Apr. 2016, at 70, 87.

[43] Dmitry Babich, Opinion, *Unwise Obama Policy Pushes China and Russia Closer Together*, RT, June 24, 2016; *China, Russia Eye Closer Friendship Amid Tensions with West*, STRAITS TIMES, June 26, 2016; *"Friends Forever": Xi Talks Up China's Ties with Russia During Putin Trade Trip*, GUARDIAN, June 26, 2016; Emma Graham-Harrison, Alec Luhn, Shaun Walker, Ami Sedghi, & Mark Rice-Oxley, *China and Russia: The World's New Superpower Axis?*, GUARDIAN, July 7, 2015.

working together increasingly on the world stage.[44] As non-Western states, both China and Russia have an interest in resisting some aspects of the Western-led international order, including Western dominance in international institutions and decision-making. As authoritarian states, they also have an interest in thwarting the spread of human rights and democracy through outside interventions and internal revolutions, which plays out in their positions on responsibility to protect and cybersecurity and information security.[45] According to Sino-Russian expert Bobo Lo:

> Russia and China have reached a broad consensus on core principles of international relations. They assert the primacy of national sovereignty and oppose humanitarian intervention by outside states and supranational bodies. They defend each other against western charges of human rights abuses and authoritarian rule. They talk up the United Nations, but conduct their foreign relations on the elitist basis of "the big players managing the big issues." Finally, they challenge American "unipolarity," and call instead for the "democratisation of international relations" and a "global multipolar order."[46]

One should not overstate the Sino-Russian alliance, which some aptly characterize as an "axis of convenience" that is more defined by what the two nations are against than what they are for.[47] The two states have a complicated history of forming and breaking alliances with each other.[48] In modern times, their economic trajectories are diverging since Russia is best understood as a declining great power, whereas China is an emerging superpower.[49] Russia is much more isolated from the United States, whereas China is heavily integrated with the United States through trade and investment. Although Russia in particular is keen to talk up the alliance,[50] and some Chinese scholars have advocated closer ties,[51] the depth and durability of China and Russia's current cooperation cannot yet be foreseen.[52] In particular, Russia may come to fear China's expansion to its east in

---

[44] Bobo Lo, *Sino-Russian Relations*, EUR. CHINA RES. & ADVICE NETWORK: SHORT TERM POL'Y BRIEF 87, May 2014, at 1.

[45] *See* Chester A. Crocker, *The Strategic Dilemma of a World Adrift*, SURVIVAL, Feb.–Mar. 2015, at 7; Michael Ignatieff, *Are the Authoritarians Winning?*, N.Y. REV. BOOKS, July 10, 2014; *id.*, *The New World Disorder*, N.Y. REV. BOOKS, Sept. 25, 2014; Christopher Walker, *The New Containment: Undermining Democracy*, WORLD AFF. J., May–June 2015; Ellen Bork, *Democracy in Retreat*, WORLD AFF. J.: DEMOCRACY RD. (May 11, 2015), http://www.worldaffairsjournal.org/blog/ellen-bork/democracy-retreat.

[46] Bobo Lo, *Ten Things Everyone Should Know About the Sino-Russian Relationship*, CER POLICY PAPER, Dec. 1, 2008, at 1, 2.

[47] BOBO LO, AXIS OF CONVENIENCE: MOSCOW, BEIJING, AND THE NEW GEOPOLITICS 3–5 (2008).

[48] *See generally* ALEXEI D. VOSKRESSENSKI, RUSSIA AND CHINA: A THEORY OF INTER-STATE RELATIONS (2003).

[49] *See generally* U.S. NAT'L INTELLIGENCE COUNCIL, GLOBAL TRENDS 2030: ALTERNATIVE WORLDS (2012).

[50] *See, e.g., "Our Views Are Either Similar or Coincide": Putin on Comprehensive Strategic China-Russia Alliance*, RT, June 23, 2016; *Putin Confident in Russia-China All-Round Cooperation*, XINHUA, June 23, 2016.

[51] *See, e.g.,* Yan Xuetong, *The Weakening of the Unipolar Configuration, in* CHINA 3.0 (Mark Leonard ed., 2012), 112–118; *id., Sino-Russian Strategic Relations Have the Most Substantial Meaning*, INT'L HERALD LEADER, Mar. 26, 2013.

[52] *See* ALEXANDER GABUEV, FRIENDS WITH BENEFITS? RUSSIAN-CHINESE RELATIONS AFTER THE UKRAINE CRISIS (2016), http://carnegieendowment.org/files/CEIP_CP278_Gabuev_revised_FINAL.pdf; Alexander

a similar way as it has viewed NATO's expansion to its west. And China appears to be much more concerned than Russia with the need to project the image of being a good international citizen, particularly with respect to issues such as international economic law and international environmental law.

Nevertheless, whether it is China acting individually, or China and Russia acting collectively, the new assertiveness of these states is highly unsettling to the United States because one of its central foreign policy goals has traditionally been to stop a regional hegemon from developing in Eurasia that might threaten its global hegemony. According to Ronald O'Rourke, writing for the US Congressional Research Service:

> From a U.S. perspective on grand strategy and geopolitics, it can be noted that most of the world's people, resources, and economic activity are located not in the Western Hemisphere, but in the other hemisphere, particularly Eurasia. In response to this basic feature of world geography, U.S. policymakers for the last several decades have chosen to pursue, as a key element of U.S. national strategy, a goal of preventing the emergence of a regional hegemon in one part of Eurasia or another, on the grounds that such a hegemon could represent a concentration of power strong enough to threaten core U.S. interests by, for example, denying the United States access to some of the other hemisphere's resources and economic activity.[53]

In 2011, under Obama, the United States announced its "Pivot to Asia" or "Rebalancing," which reflected this foreign policy goal[54] and was seen by many as an effort to contain rising Chinese power.[55] On the military level, the United States stepped up its efforts to challenge Chinese actions in the East and South China Seas that could give China a military advantage or infringe upon the United States' freedom of navigation in those seas. On the economic level, Obama and some US commentators began citing national security and geopolitics as a justification for passing the TPP on the basis that if the United States did not write the rules for global trade and investment, China would,

Korolev, *The Strategic Alignment Between Russia and China: Myths and Reality*, ASAN F., Apr. 30, 2015; Stephen Kotkin, *The Unbalanced Triangle*, 88 FOREIGN AFF., Sept.–Oct. 2009, at 130 (reviewing BOBO LO, *supra* note 47); Fu Ying, *How China Sees Russia: Beijing and Moscow Are Close, But Not Allies*, 95 FOREIGN AFF., Jan.–Feb. 2016, at 96.

[53] O'ROURKE, *supra* note 35, at 12.

[54] Hillary Rodham Clinton, *America's Pacific Century*, Remarks Delivered at the East-West Center, Honolulu (Nov. 10, 2011); Hillary Clinton, *America's Pacific Century*, FOREIGN POL'Y, Nov. 11, 2011; President Barack Obama, Speech Delivered at the Australian Parliament House, Canberra, Australia (Nov. 17, 2011); Press Release, Office of the White House Press Sec'y, Fact Sheet: The East Asia Summit (Nov. 19, 2011).

[55] *See, e.g.,* Luo Yuan, *One Should Be Alert But Also Calm When Facing U.S. Readjustment to Its Defense Strategy*, LIBERATION ARMY DAILY, Jan. 10, 2012; Ruan Zongze, *To Whom Does Pacific Century Belong?*, PEOPLE'S DAILY, Dec. 20, 2011; *id., What Does the U.S. Want on "Rebalancing,"* PEOPLE'S DAILY, June. 4, 2012; Tian Wang, *U.S. Uses "Hedging" Strategy to Deal with China's Rise*, PEOPLE'S DAILY, Dec. 26, 2011; Yuan Tian & Zhang Xin, *What Is Behind U.S. "Return to Asia" Strategy?*, LIBERATION ARMY DAILY, Dec. 26, 2011; Zhong Sheng, *Goals of U.S. "Return to Asia" Strategy Questioned*, PEOPLE'S DAILY, Oct. 18, 2011; *see generally* Michael D. Swaine, *Chinese Leadership & Elite Responses to the U.S. Pacific Pivot*, CHINA LEADERSHIP MONITOR, Summer 2012, at 1.

through competing trade deals like the RCEP and the Free Trade Area of the Asia-Pacific (FTAAP).[56]

But 2016 saw a backlash against globalization and the rise of nationalism in many Western states.[57] In the United Kingdom, the public voted to leave the European Union owing to concerns about rising economic inequality and increased immigration, as well as a desire to reassert national sovereignty.[58] In the United States, Trump was elected on a platform that rejected multilateral trade deals like the TPP, embraced harsher immigration policies, and questioned the status of US defense alliances in Europe and the Pacific.[59] The division between globalists and nationalists has become stark in these two states, as well as elsewhere across Europe. Compounding problems like the Greek Eurozone crisis, Brexit has exacerbated fears that the United Kingdom might break up, and the European Union as well, though the latter may rally in response to the former.[60] Focused on their own state's or region's internal problems, many commentators view these Western states and groupings as no longer willing and able to lead the international system in the way they once did.[61]

In their place, many now expect China, together with other non-Western states, to take a more active part in shaping international legal regimes, especially at the regional level. We should not expect China to replace the United States as a global hegemon or the BRICS to emerge as a cohesive force. In many ways, the rise of these states is more about breaking an existing hegemony than the forging of a new one. The forefront of this activity may well be in the international economic sphere where Trump has threatened to withdraw from the TPP after he takes office and negotiations over the TTIP are expected to languish,[62] whereas China has responded by raising ambitions with respect to Asian economic integration through the RCEP and the FTAAP.[63] Trump's policies

---

[56] See, e.g., Robert D. Blackwill, *America Must Play the Geoeconomics Game*, NAT'L INT., June 20, 2016; Roger Cohen, *If the Trans-Pacific Partnership Crumbles, China Wins*, N.Y. TIMES, June 2, 2016; Graeme Dobell, *The Trans-Pacific Partnership: An Economic Hard-Power Weapon?*, NAT'L INT.: BUZZ, June 5, 2015, http://nationalinterest.org/blog/the-buzz/the-trans-pacific-partnership-economic-hard-power-weapon-13050; Gerald F. Seib, *Obama Presses Case for Asia Trade Deal, Warns Failure Would Benefit China*, WALL ST. J., Apr. 27, 2015; Philip Stephens, *Trade Trumps Missiles in Today's Global Power Plays*, FIN. TIMES, Nov. 21, 2013.

[57] Jonathan Haidt, *When and Why Nationalism Beats Globalism*, AM. INT., July 10, 2016.

[58] George Friedman, *3 Reasons Brits Voted for Brexit*, FORBES, July 5, 2016; *Eight Reasons Leave Won the UK's Referendum on the EU*, BBC NEWS, June 24, 2016.

[59] John Harris, *The Reasons for Trump Were Also the Reasons for Brexit*, GUARDIAN, Nov. 11, 2016; Bethan McKernan, *The Real Reason People Voted for Donald Trump*, INDEPENDENT, Nov. 10, 2016; Sarah Butcher, *Blame an Economic Cycle That Began in the 1970s for Trump and Brexit, Says Deutsche Bank*, EFINANCIALCAREERS, Nov. 18, 2016.

[60] Ian Bremmer, *These 5 Facts Explain Why Brexit Could Lead to a U.K. Breakup*, TIMES, July 1, 2016; Kathy Gilsinan, *Could Britain Break Up?*, ATLANTIC, June 25, 2016; Pavel Seifter, Opinion, *The Real Danger Isn't Brexit. It's EU Break-Up*, GUARDIAN, May 26, 2016; *The Start of the Break-Up*, ECONOMIST, Aug. 6, 2016.

[61] Anne Applebaum, Opinion, *Is America Still the Leader of the Free World?*, WASH. POST, Nov. 9, 2016; Noam Chomsky, *Who Rules the World? America Is No Longer the Obvious Answer*, GUARDIAN, May 10, 2016.

[62] Julian Borger, *Transatlantic Trade Deal "Not Realistic" Under Trump, German Official Says*, GUARDIAN, Nov. 15, 2016; Stephen Dinan, *Donald Trump to Withdraw U.S. from Asian Trade Pact on His First Day in Office*, WASH. TIMES, Nov. 21, 2016; Nicky Woolf, Justin McCurry, & Benjamin Haas, *Trump to Withdraw from Trans-Pacific Partnership on First Day in Office*, GUARDIAN, Nov. 22, 2016; Tim Worstall, *With Trump's Election the TPP Probably Is Dead, Yes—As Is the TTIP*, FORBES, Nov. 11, 2016.

[63] Chris Dalby, *Spotlight: As TPP Withers, RCEP Takes Center Stage at APEC Economic Leaders' Meeting*, XINHUA, Nov. 21, 2016; Donald J. Lewis, Opinion, *China Ushers in New FTAAP Era*, CHINA DAILY EUR., Nov. 22, 2016;

denying climate change may also divert the focus to China and Europe for leadership on international environmental law.[64] And, depending on Trump's policies, various states throughout the world may be prompted to rethink the value of their defense alliances with the United States.[65]

Although it is too early to tell how these dynamics will play out, these shifts in geopolitical power are likely to fuel renewed interest in comparative international law. International law reflects international power. If international power becomes more competitive and fragmented, one can expect increased pressure to be placed on notions of universal international law. There is precedent for this sequence of events. A generation ago, conferences were organized around Western and Soviet approaches to international law.[66] It made sense for international lawyers to concentrate on this subject during the Cold War because the two superpowers maintained radically different understandings of and approaches to international law. Courses on topics like Comparative Approaches to International Law and Soviet, Chinese, and Western Approaches to International Law were taught at Harvard Law School, Columbia Law School, and University College London.[67] Some academics published on comparative international law in general,[68] and others on specific national systems, such as China's or Russia's approach to international law.[69]

Dan Steinbock, Opinion, *China Is Redefining the Free Trade in Asia Pacific*, CHINA DAILY, Nov. 22, 2016; Zhang Zhengfu, Commentary: *Fast-Forwarding the FTAAP*, XINHUA, Nov. 21, 2016.

[64] Matthew Carney, *Trump and China: Beijing Leadership Sees "Huge Chance" as President-Elect Flags Isolationist Approach*, ABC, Nov. 10, 2016; Zeng Jinghan, *With Trump's Election, Time for China to Save the World*, DIPLOMAT, Nov. 18, 2016; Anne Peters, *After Trump: China and Russia Move from Norm-Takers to Shapers of the International Legal Order*, EJIL: *TALK!*, Nov. 10, 2016, http://www.ejiltalk.org/after-trump-china-and-russia-move-from-norm-takers-to-shapers-of-the-international-legal-order.

[65] *See, e.g.*, Peter Apps, Commentary: *Trump, Putin and a Nervous NATO*, REUTERS, Nov. 15, 2016; Julian E. Barnes, *In Trump, NATO Faces a Challenge*, WALL ST. J., Nov. 9, 2016; Joe Kelly, *Labor at Odds over US Alliance After Trump Victory*, AUSTRALIAN, Nov. 17, 2016; Ramesh Thakur, *Trump's Effect on U.S. Allies*, JAPAN TIMES, Dec. 1, 2016.

[66] *See* LORI FISLER DAMROSCH, GENNADY M. DANILENKO, & REIN MULLERSON, BEYOND CONFRONTATION: INTERNATIONAL LAW FOR THE POST-COLD WAR ERA (1995); PAUL B. STEPHAN & BORIS M. KLIMENKO, INTERNATIONAL LAW AND INTERNATIONAL SECURITY—A U.S.-SOVIET DIALOGUE ON THE MILITARY AND POLITICAL DIMENSIONS (1991); INTERNATIONAL LAW AND THE INTERNATIONAL SYSTEM (William E. Butler ed., 1987); PERESTROIKA AND INTERNATIONAL LAW: CURRENT ANGLO-SOVIET APPROACHES TO INTERNATIONAL LAW (Anthony Carty & Gennady Danilenko eds., 1990) (essays by British and Soviet international lawyers); WILLIAM E. BUTLER, INTRODUCTION TO PERESTROIKA AND INTERNATIONAL LAW 1, 4 (William E. Butler ed., 1990) (essays by British and Soviet international lawyers arising from the Anglo-Soviet Symposium on Public International Law).

[67] *See* WILLIAM E. BUTLER, INTERNATIONAL LAW IN COMPARATIVE PERSPECTIVE vii (William E. Butler ed., 1980); *id.*, *International Law and the Comparative Method, in id.*, at 25, 29, 38 n.17; *id.*, *Anglo-American Research on Soviet Approaches to Public International Law, in id.* at 169, 173; *id.*, *American Research on Soviet Approaches to Public International Law*, 70 COLUM. L. REV. 218, 223–24 (1970).

[68] *See, e.g.*, BUTLER, INTERNATIONAL LAW AND THE COMPARATIVE METHOD, *supra* note 67, at 25, 29 n.17; *id.*, *Comparative Approaches to International Law*, 190 RECUEIL DES COURS 9, 58–61 (1985).

[69] *See, e.g.*, JEROME A. COHEN & HUNGDAH CHIU, PEOPLE'S CHINA AND INTERNATIONAL LAW (1974); KAZIMIERZ GRZYBOWSKY, SOVIET PUBLIC INTERNATIONAL LAW: DOCTRINES AND DIPLOMATIC PRACTICE (1970); PERESTROIKA AND INTERNATIONAL LAW, *supra* note 66; Hungdah Chiu, *The Development of Chinese International Law Terms and the Problem of Their Translation into English*, 27 J. ASIAN STUD. 485, 485–86 (1968).

By contrast, scholars often paid little attention in the 1990s and early 2000s to distinct national approaches to international law, let alone to the idea of comparative international law more generally. As the United States emerged as the world's only superpower after the collapse of the Soviet Union, the sense that the Western approach had won out took hold. Western scholars had demonstrated significant interest in Soviet approaches to international law during the Cold War under the theory of "know thy enemy,"[70] but Western interest in post-Soviet studies declined precipitously after the dissolution of the USSR.[71] This could be seen in university course catalogues, which typically showed markedly fewer offerings in post-Soviet international law studies than they had in Soviet studies, and in university library collections, which often included Soviet international law textbooks but not Russian post-Soviet ones.

As the international system moves to an increasingly multipolar world, however, international lawyers will increasingly need to understand different approaches to international law by unlike-minded powerful states. In their global history of international law, Bardo Fassbender and Anne Peters reflect that, if the history of international law since the sixteenth century was characterized as a global expansion of Western domination and ideas, many signs today suggest that this history is drawing to a close.[72] Powerful states often seek to impose their own version of international law so that, if the international system consists of multiple great powers, each may offer a distinct and competing version of the subject.[73] Under the circumstances, it is not surprising to see articles and books appearing on Russian, Chinese, and Asian approaches to international law.[74] How, one may ask, are these changing power dynamics likely to affect the content and structure of international law? One way to begin to answer this question is to look at how China and Russia characterize their approaches to international law.

B. CHINA AND RUSSIA'S JOINT DECLARATION ON INTERNATIONAL LAW

In June 2016, China and Russia issued joint statements on strengthening global strategic stability, developing legal regulation of information security and cybersecurity,

---

[70] See BUTLER, INTERNATIONAL LAW AND THE COMPARATIVE METHOD, *supra* note 67, at 31.

[71] See LAURI MÄLKSOO, RUSSIAN APPROACHES TO INTERNATIONAL LAW 7–8 (2015).

[72] FASSBENDER & PETERS, *supra* note 12, at 24.

[73] See HANQIN XUE, CHINESE CONTEMPORARY PERSPECTIVES ON INTERNATIONAL LAW: HISTORY, CULTURE AND INTERNATIONAL LAW 16 (2012); Anu Bradford & Eric A. Posner, *Universal Exceptionalism in International Law*, 52 HARV. INT'L L.J. 1 (2011); Paul B. Stephan, *Symmetry and Selectivity: What Happens in International Law When the World Changes*, 10 CHINESE J. INT'L L. 91, 107 (2009).

[74] See, e.g., MÄLKSOO, *supra* note 71, at 87; Simon Chesterman, *Asia's Ambivalence About International Law and Institutions: Past, Present and Futures*, 27 EUR. J. INT'L L. 945 (2016); Jacques deLisle, *China's Approach to International Law: A Historical Perspective*, 94 AM. SOC'Y INT'L L. PROC. 267 (2000); David P. Fidler, *The Asian Century: Implications for International Law*, 2005 SING. Y.B. INT'L L. 19; Lo Chang-fa, *Values to Be Added to an "Eastphalia Order" by the Emerging China*, 17 IND. J. GLOBAL LEGAL STUD. 13 (2010); Yasuaki Onuma, *A Transcivilizational Perspective on International Law: Questioning Prevalent Cognitive Frameworks in the Emerging Multi-Polar and Multi-Civilizational World of the Twenty-First Century*, 342 RECUEIL DES COURS 1 (2009); Eric Posner & John C. Yoo, *International Law and the Rise of China*, 7 CHINESE J. INT'L L. 1 (2006).

and promoting international law.[75] The Declaration of the Russian Federation and the People's Republic of China on the Promotion of International Law (Joint Declaration) sets out the principles that guide these two states in their approach to international law. Almost no information is publicly available about what led to the drafting of this declaration. But in adopting it, China and Russia appeared to be seeking to present a united challenge to Western hegemony in international law. The principles in the Joint Declaration also reflect many of the approaches to international law in the Chinese and Russian textbooks and conform with multiple statements made by Chinese and Russian officials in other contexts.

First, the Joint Declaration states that China and Russia "reiterate their full commitment to the principles of international law as they are reflected in the United Nations Charter, [and] the 1970 Declaration on Principles of International Law concerning Friendly Relations and Cooperation among States in accordance with the Charter of the United Nations."[76] Chief among these principles are the sovereign equality of all states (Article 2(1)), the obligation to settle international disputes by peaceful means (Article 2(3)), the obligation to refrain from the threat or use of force against the territorial integrity or political independence of any state (Article 2(4)), and the obligation not to intervene in matters that are essentially within the domestic jurisdiction of any state (Article 2(7)).[77]

This approach is consistent with Russian international law textbooks, which often emphasize the "principles" of international law.[78] Affirming the principles of international law as enunciated in the UN Charter has the advantage of elevating state sovereignty and equality, and devaluing human rights, as the latter appears as only one of the "purposes" of the United Nations in Article 1 rather than as one of the "principles" that regulate relations between states in Article 2.[79] Affirming Charter principles is consistent as well with the Five Principles of Peaceful Coexistence (处五项原则) developed by China and India, also referred to in the Joint Declaration. These principles are mutual respect for sovereignty and territorial integrity, mutual nonaggression, noninterference in each other's internal affairs, equality and mutual benefit, and peaceful coexistence; they do not include any mention of human rights.[80]

This emphasis on state sovereignty over human rights is a hallmark of many Chinese, and some Russian, statements on international law.[81] For instance, President Xi Jinping's

---

[75] *The Declaration of the Russian Federation and the People's Republic of China on the Promotion of International Law*, MINISTRY OF FOREIGN AFFAIRS OF THE RUSS. FED'N, June 25, 2016, http://www.mid.ru/en/foreign_policy/position_word_order/-/asset_publisher/6S4RuXfeYlKr/content/id/2331698 [hereinafter *Joint Declaration*]; *China, Russia Sign Joint Statement on Strengthening Global Strategic Stability*, XINHUA, June 26, 2016; *Joint Statement Between the Presidents of China and Russia*, CHINA DAILY, June 26, 2016.

[76] *Joint Declaration, supra* note 75, ¶ 1.

[77] *Id.* ¶¶ 2, 4.

[78] *See* Chapter 4.VI.

[79] Lauri Mälksoo, *Russia and China Challenge the Western Hegemony in the Interpretation of International Law*, EJIL: *TALK!*, July 15, 2016, http://www.ejiltalk.org/russia-and-china-challenge-the-western-hegemony-in-the-interpretation-of-international-law/.

[80] *Joint Declaration, supra* note 75, ¶ 1.

[81] *See also Are Human Rights Higher Than Sovereignty?*, PEOPLE'S DAILY, Mar. 17, 2006.

2014 speech on promoting the international rule of law contained eight references to sovereignty and no references to human rights.[82] He adverted to states' rights and the rights of the developing world but not to human rights. By contrast, Russia often affirms its commitment to both.[83] But in the 2005 Joint Statement of the People's Republic of China and the Russian Federation Regarding the International Order of the 21st Century, the two states accepted that human rights were "universal," yet declared that international human rights protections should be based on the principles of "firmly safeguarding the sovereign equality of all countries and not interfering in each other's internal affairs."[84]

Although China and Russia treat state sovereignty as the defining principle of international law, they frequently take a more elastic approach to the sovereignty of some of their neighbors. Russia views itself as having a sphere of influence in its "near abroad," which encompasses the states that emerged from the dissolution of the Soviet Union. It considers itself entitled to take certain actions to protect its interests in this area, such as intervening in favor of Russian speakers and compatriots in these former Soviet states, including Georgia and Ukraine.[85] China does not appear to have conceived an analogous idea of its "near abroad," though many Western and non-Chinese Asian commentators would view China's approach in the South China Sea as evidencing a similar conception. Many Chinese international lawyers would vigorously dispute that in asserting its territorial claims in the South China Sea, China is infringing upon other states' sovereignty rather than exercising its own legitimate sovereign rights.

It may be that China and Russia ultimately favor an approach that protects the sovereignty of different regional hegemons with their own spheres of influence. Appeals to sovereignty might be used to guard against interference by states from outside the region, and appeals to linguistic, cultural, and historical connections might be used to justify overriding the sovereignty of smaller states within those regions. If so, this position would represent more of a civilizational approach to sovereignty where sovereignty protects the Chinese and Russian civilizations, not just China and Russia as nation-states. This approach may also be in keeping with China's evolving stance on responsibility to protect, where it has proved more likely to support interventions approved by all the relevant regional organizations.[86]

On the other hand, China's extensive investments abroad may point in a different— and more interventionist—future direction. As China develops investments in states

---

[82] President Xi Jinping, China, Speech at "Five Principles of Peaceful Coexistence" Anniversary: Carry Forward the Five Principles of Peaceful Coexistence to Build a Better World Through Win-Win Cooperation (June 28, 2014), http://www.china.org.cn/world/2014-07/07/content_32876905.htm.

[83] See, e.g., Concept of the Foreign Policy of the Russian Federation, Министерство иностранных дел Российской Федерации [Ministry Foreign Aff. Russ.] (Dec.1, 2016, 6:41 PM), http://www.mid.ru/en/web/guest/foreign_policy/official_documents/-/asset_publisher/CptICkB6BZ29/content/id/2542248.

[84] Joint Statement of the People's Republic of China and the Russian Federation Regarding the International Order of the 21st Century, POL. AFF. ¶ 6 (July 12, 2005), http://www.politicalaffairs.net/china-russia-joint-statement-on-21st-century-world-order/.

[85] See, e.g., Transcript: Putin Says Russia Will Protect the Rights of Russians Abroad, WASH. POST, Mar. 18, 2014.

[86] Courtney J. Fung, Global South Solidarity? China, Regional Organisations and Intervention in the Libyan and Syrian Civil Wars, 37 THIRD WORLD Q. 33 (2016).

throughout the world, including many unstable states, one could expect the Chinese government to argue for the right to intervene to protect its citizens and interests, as it did in Libya and Yemen.[87] Indeed, the white paper China's Military Strategy lists "China's overseas interests" as a priority of the government's national security policy,[88] and the topic of the legal regime for safeguarding Chinese overseas interests and citizens receives research funding by the Chinese government.[89] The aim of such interventions, however, would likely be to protect Chinese nationals abroad, rather than to protect foreign nationals or to encourage regime change.

Second, the Joint Declaration states that China and Russia "share the view that the principle of *sovereign equality* is crucial for the stability of international relations."[90] Sovereign equality means that states enjoy their rights "on the basis of independence and on an equal footing," and thus have the right to "participate in the making of, interpreting and applying international law on an equal footing."[91] This statement stands against Western hegemonism in lawmaking and seems intended to emphasize that some ideas, such as human rights, the right to democracy, and the responsibility to protect, are promoted by Western states and scholars but have not been agreed to by other states. China and Russia view international law as often having been used as a tool of Western imperialism, and they embrace state sovereignty and sovereign equality as bulwarks against the subjection of states to supposedly "international" norms that they have not accepted.[92]

China's emphasis on sovereign equality, including equality in lawmaking, is sometimes characterized as a belief in "democracy between states" as opposed to "democracy within states."[93] It is not uncommon to hear references to democracy in statements about the international rule of law by Chinese officials. For instance, according to President Xi, the Five Principles of Peaceful Coexistence "embody the values of sovereignty, justice, democracy and rule of law,"[94] but that democracy is of an interstate, not intrastate, variety. In Xi's words: "We should jointly promote greater democracy in international relations. . . . The notion of dominating international affairs belongs to a different age, and

---

[87] Jonas Parello-Plesner & Mathieu Duchâtel, *How Chinese Nationals Abroad Are Transforming Beijing's Foreign Policy*, E. Asia F., June 16, 2015, http://www.eastasiaforum.org/2015/06/16/how-chinese-nationals-abroad-are-transforming-beijings-foreign-policy/.

[88] *Id.*

[89] *See infra* Appendix D (funded topics include Studies on the Chinese Model of Legal Protection of Overseas Security Interests (2013), Studies on the Chinese Model of Legal Protection of Overseas Interests (2013), Studies on Legal Regulation of the Risks in China's Overseas Contracting of Projects (2012); Studies on the Legal Protection of Armies Protecting State's Overseas Interest (2010), Studies on the Legal Regime for Promotion and Protection of China's Overseas Investments (2009)).

[90] *Joint Declaration, supra* note 75, ¶ 2 (emphasis added).

[91] *Id.*

[92] Ingrid Wuerth, *China, Russia, and International Law*, Lawfare, July 11, 2016, https://www.lawfareblog.com/china-russia-and-international-law.

[93] Julian Ku, *What Does China Mean When It Celebrates the "International Rule of Law"?*, Opinio Juris, Oct. 29, 2014, http://opiniojuris.org/2014/10/29/china-mean-celebrates-international-rule-law.

[94] Xi Jinping, *supra* note 82.

294 Is International Law International?

such an attempt is doomed to failure."[95] Chinese Foreign Minister Wang Yi made a similar point in his 2014 speech on the international rule of law:

> [W]e must ensure an equal and democratic participation in the making of international rules, so as to highlight the nature of international rule of law. Promoting greater democracy in international relations is the aspiration of all countries and represents the historical trend of development. We must work hard to bring all countries, particularly the developing countries, into the rule-making process as equals.[96]

This effort, Wang explained, is an important way to "resist the attempt to make the rules of certain countries as 'international rules,' and their standards 'international standards.'"[97]

All the same, the idea of promoting democracy between states is not taken as negating the significance of relations between great powers. In Xi's first major foreign policy speech, he stressed China's goal of promoting "democracy in international relations" but also outlined the importance of "build[ing] a sound and stable framework of major-country relations."[98] According to Kevin Rudd's summary of the speech, Xi spoke for the first time of China's "grand strategy" of embracing "a new great power diplomacy with Chinese characteristics" so as to craft a "new type of great power relations" with the United States.[99] This Group of Two approach could be seen, for example, in agreements between Xi and Obama on climate change.[100]

At times, Russia's emphasis on sovereign equality bears the hallmark more of trying to create equality between the five permanent members of the Security Council as great powers than of recognizing their sovereign equality with all other states. For instance, the 2013 Concept of the Foreign Policy of the Russian Federation noted that Russia's top foreign policy goal is "ensuring the security of the country, protecting and strengthening its sovereignty and territorial integrity, and securing its high standing in the international community as one of the influential and competitive poles of the modern world."[101] Likewise, it endorses active promotion of international peace and security "for the purpose of establishing a *just and democratic* system of international relations," while also insisting on an "equal[] partnership" with other states that embrace the "central coordinating role" of the United Nations.[102] This approach was consistent

---

[95] *Id.*

[96] Wang Yi, *China: A Staunch Defender and Builder of International Rule of Law*, 13 CHINESE J. INT'L L. 635, 638 (2014).

[97] *Id.*

[98] *Xi Eyes More Enabling Int'l Environment for China's Peaceful Development*, XINHUA, Nov. 29, 2014.

[99] KEVIN RUDD, BELFER CTR. FOR SCI. & INT'L AFFAIRS, U.S.-CHINA 21: THE FUTURE OF U.S.-CHINA RELATIONS UNDER XI JINPING 11 (2015); *see also* Suisheng Zhao, *A New Model of Big Power Relations? China–US Strategic Rivalry and Balance of Power in the Asia–Pacific*, 24 J. CONTEMP. CHINA 377 (2015).

[100] Mark Landler & Jane Perlez, *Rare Harmony as China and U.S. Commit to Climate Deal*, N.Y. TIMES, Sept. 3, 2016.

[101] *Concept of the Foreign Policy of the Russian Federation*, Министерство иностранных дел Российской Федерации [Ministry Foreign Aff. Russ.] ¶ 4(a) (Feb. 18, 2013, 8:15 PM), http://www.mid.ru/en/foreign_policy/official_documents/-/asset_publisher/CptICkB6BZ29/content/id/122186.

[102] *Id.* ¶ 4(c) (emphasis added).

with the message of President Vladimir Putin to President-elect Trump in his first call after the 2016 US election in which he called for a "collaborative dialogue" between the two states based on "equality, mutual respect and noninterference in the other's internal affairs."[103]

Third, in their Joint Declaration the two states "reaffirm the principle that States shall refrain from the threat or use of force in violation of the United Nations Charter" and fully support the principle of nonintervention in the internal affairs of states.[104] Accordingly, they "condemn unilateral military interventions,"[105] which seems to be a criticism of NATO's use of force in Kosovo and the UK and US use of force in Iraq in 2003. They also "condemn . . . any interference by States in the internal affairs of other States with the aim of forging change of legitimate governments,"[106] which seems aimed at the decision by the United States and others to seek regime change in Iraq in 2003 and in Libya in 2011. But the qualification of "legitimate" governments, rather than all governments, might reflect the evolution of Chinese and Russian practice with respect to humanitarian intervention in recent years.

These statements against interventionism in the Joint Declaration are consistent with Wang's concern that "promoting international rule of law is still faced with many difficulties and challenges. Hegemonism, power politics and all forms of 'new interventionism' pose a direct challenge to basic principles of international law including respect for sovereignty and territorial integrity and non-interference in other countries' internal affairs."[107] Similar language appeared in the white paper entitled "China's National Defence in 2000":

> Hegemonism and power politics still exist and are developing further in the international political, economic and security spheres. Certain big powers are pursuing "neo-interventionism," "neo-gunboat policy" and neo-economic colonialism. . . . Under the pretexts of "humanitarianism" and "human rights," some countries have frequently resorted to the use or threat of force, in flagrant violation of the UN Charter and other universally recognized principles governing international relations. In particular, the NATO, by-passing the UN Security Council, launched military attacks against the Federal Republic of Yugoslavia, producing an extremely negative impact on the international situation and relations between countries.[108]

---

[103] Neil MacFarquhar, *Putin and Trump Talk on Phone and Agree to Improve Ties, Kremlin Says*, N.Y. Times, Nov. 14, 2016; *Putin on Trump Victory: Russia Is Ready to Restore Relations with US*, RT, Nov. 9, 2016.

[104] *Joint Declaration, supra* note 75, ¶¶ 3–4.

[105] *Id.* ¶ 3.

[106] *Id.* ¶ 4.

[107] Wang Yi, *supra* note 96, at 637.

[108] *See* Info. Office of State Council, China's National Defence in 2000 (2000), http://china.org.cn/ e-white/2000/20-2.htm.

Many official Russian documents express much the same sentiment. For instance, the 2013 Concept of the Foreign Policy of the Russian Federation observes:

> Another risk to world peace and stability is presented by attempts to manage crises through unilateral sanctions and other coercive measures, including armed aggression, outside the framework of the UN Security Council. There are instances of blatant neglect of fundamental principles of international law, such as the non-use of force, and of the prerogatives of the UN Security Council when arbitrary interpretation of its resolutions is allowed. Some concepts that are being implemented are aimed at overthrowing legitimate authorities in sovereign states under the pretext of protecting civilian population.[109]

In addition to being used offensively as criticism, the principles of sovereignty and noninterference serve an important defensive function as justifications for limiting intervention in China's and Russia's domestic affairs. In Western states, international law students are often taught to view sovereignty as something of a dirty word, the S word, according to Louis Henkin.[110] But China has an altogether different view of the concept, which relates to its historical experiences during its century of humiliation.[111] Wang linked China's past experiences and its present approaches in his 2014 speech:

> Upholding international rule of law is a momentous choice China has made based on its own experience. In the more than 100 years after the Opium War, colonialism and imperialism inflicted untold sufferings on China. For many years, China was unjustly deprived of the right by imperialist powers to equal application of international law. The Chinese people fought indomitably and tenaciously to uphold China's sovereignty, independence and territorial integrity and founded New China. China strove to build a new type of relations with other countries in accordance with the Five Principles of Peaceful Coexistence on the basis of international law. It broke isolation, blockade and military threat imposed by imperialism and hegemonism, regained its lawful seat in the United Nations, started reform and opening-up program, became fully integrated into the international system, and made remarkable achievements in development. Seeing the contrast between China's past and present, the Chinese people fully recognize how valuable sovereignty, independence and peace are. China ardently hopes for the rule of law in international relations against hegemony and power politics, and rules-based equity and justice, and hopes that the humiliation and sufferings it was subjected to will not happen to others.[112]

---

[109] Ministry Foreign Aff. Russ., *supra* note 101, ¶ 31.

[110] Louis Henkin, Lecture, *That "S" Word: Sovereignty, and Globalization, and Human Rights, Et Cetera*, 68 Fordham L. Rev. 1 (1999).

[111] *See generally* Phil C. W. Chan, China, State Sovereignty and International Legal Order (2015).

[112] Wang Yi, *supra* note 96, at 635–36.

Thus, China and Russia "condemn extraterritorial application of national law by States not in conformity with international law as another example of violation of the principle of non-intervention in the internal affairs of States."[113] This statement seems to refer to the unequal treaties that were forced upon China by certain Western states following the Opium Wars, which have often been invoked to explain China's slowness to embrace international law,[114] but it may also apply to more contemporary actions of the United States and Europe in extending the extraterritorial reach of some of their laws.

Fourth, China and Russia explain that they "share the view that good faith implementation of generally recognized principles and rules of international law excludes the practice of double standards or imposition by some States of their will on other States."[115] This condemnation of double standards is aimed at Western states in general, and the United States in particular. It echoes complaints in the textbooks of both states about the imposition by Western states of double standards in many areas of international law, including human rights law, and ignoring international law rules when they do not serve their purposes, such as in the use of force. Chinese and Russian officials frequently make similar charges. For instance, Putin mocked Western accusations that Russia had violated international law in Crimea, stating that "it's a good thing that they at least remember that there exists such a thing as international law—better late than never," and railed against the West's double standards with respect to Kosovo and Crimea:

> Our western partners, led by the United States of America, prefer not to be guided by international law in their practical policies, but by the rule of the gun. They have come to believe in their exclusivity and exceptionalism, that they can decide the destinies of the world, that only they can ever be right. They act as they please: here and there, they use force against sovereign states, building coalitions based on the principle "If you are not with us, you are against us." To make this aggression look legitimate, they force the necessary resolutions from international organisations, and if for some reason this does not work, they simply ignore the UN Security Council and the UN overall.[116]

In the Joint Declaration, China and Russia point to the "imposition of unilateral coercive measures not based on international law, also known as 'unilateral sanctions,'" as an example of such double standards, apparently a reference to the unilateral sanctions imposed on Russia by many Western states in response to its annexation of Crimea.[117]

---

[113] *Joint Declaration, supra* note 75, ¶ 4.

[114] Simon Chesterman, *Asia's Ambivalence About International Law and Institutions: Past, Present and Futures*, 27 Eur. J. Int'l L. 945, 951 (2016).

[115] *Id.* ¶ 6.

[116] President Vladimir Putin, Address Before the State Duma Deputies, Federation Council Members, Heads of Russian Regions and Civil Society Representatives in the Kremlin (Mar. 18, 2014), *in Address by President of the Russian Federation*, President Russ. (Mar. 18, 2014, 3:50 PM), http://en.kremlin.ru/events/president/news/20603.

[117] *Joint Declaration, supra* note 75, ¶ 6.

Chinese officials likewise express concern about double standards in international relations, though their criticisms of the West are often slightly more veiled. Xi has stated: "In the international society, there should be just one law that applies to all. There is no such law that applies to others but not oneself, or vice versa. There should not be double standards when applying the law."[118] Similarly, Wang has complained that "[s]ome countries follow a pragmatist or a double-standard approach to international law, using whatever that suits their interests and abandoning whatever that does not."[119]

Fifth, both states "reaffirm the principle of peaceful settlement of disputes and express their firm conviction that States shall resolve their disputes through dispute settlement means and mechanisms that they have agreed upon."[120] This pronouncement seems intended to support the objection of China that it did not consent to the jurisdiction of the UNCLOS tribunal in the *South China Sea* arbitration with the Philippines and the objection of Russia that it was not provisionally bound to apply the Energy Charter Treaty in the *Yukos* arbitration. This concern is consistent with Wang's statement that "[n]ational and international judicial institutions should avoid overstepping their authority in interpreting and applying international law. Still less should they encroach on the rights and interests of other countries under the pretext of 'the rule of law' in total disregard of objectivity and fairness."[121]

The Joint Declaration affirms that the fundamental principle of resolving disputes peacefully and through agreed-upon mechanisms "applies equally to all types and stages of dispute settlement, including political and diplomatic means when they serve as a prerequisite to the use of other mechanisms of dispute settlement" and that it is "crucial for the maintenance of international legal order that all dispute settlement means and mechanisms are based on consent and used in good faith and in the spirit of cooperation, and their purposes shall not be undermined by abusive practices."[122] This language mirrors criticisms made by Chinese officials that the Philippines did not adequately exhaust diplomatic means of resolving the South China Sea disputes before unilaterally and abusively instigating arbitration.[123]

Finally, the Joint Declaration asserts that "international obligations regarding immunity of States, their property and officials must be honored by States at all times" and that "[v]iolations of these obligations are not in conformity with the principle of sovereign equality of States and may contribute to the escalation of tensions."[124] According to Ingrid Wuerth, one of the reporters on immunity for the *Restatement*

---

[118] Xi Jinping, *supra* note 82.

[119] Wang Yi, *supra* note 96, at 637.

[120] *Joint Declaration, supra* note 75, ¶ 5.

[121] Wang Yi, *supra* note 96, at 638.

[122] *Joint Declaration, supra* note 75, ¶ 5.

[123] *See, e.g., Statement of the Ministry of Foreign Affairs of the People's Republic of China on the Award on Jurisdiction and Admissibility of the South China Sea Arbitration by the Arbitral Tribunal Established at the Request of the Republic of the Philippines*, MINISTRY FOREIGN AFF. CHINA (Oct. 30, 2015), http://www.fmprc.gov.cn/mfa_eng/zxxx_662805/t1310474.shtml.

[124] *Joint Declaration, supra* note 75, ¶ 8.

(Fourth) of the Foreign Relations Law of the United States, this statement "suggests that state immunity is alive and well—maybe including the absolute rather than the restrictive view of foreign state immunity."[125] China and Russia also condemn "terrorism in all its forms and manifestations as a global threat that undermines the international order based on international law" and maintain that countering this threat requires "collective action in full accordance with international law, including the United Nations Charter."[126]

II. Disagreements in Practice, Not Just Words

It would be one thing if China and Russia's Joint Declaration were just a piece of paper. But these two states, both individually and collectively, have been acting on their interests and approaches to international law in ways that have constrained Western agendas, promoted their own agendas, and challenged certain interpretations of international law. This behavior is illustrated by the examples of Syria and the doctrine of responsibility to protect, proposals for a multilateral treaty on cybersecurity and information security, and debates about the permissible scope of freedom of navigation. In each case, China and Russia support a vision of international law that is much more protective of sovereignty, sovereign equality, and territorial integrity than the apparently more human-rights-friendly and access-oriented approach embraced by many Western states.[127]

A. CONSTRAINING WESTERN AGENDAS:
  UNILATERAL HUMANITARIAN INTERVENTION

A key narrative in many of the Western international law textbooks is the idea that international law used to be a system based primarily on state sovereignty but that, since the end of World War II, the inviolability of this principle has declined while the relative importance of human rights has risen.[128] One of the main battlegrounds in which this contestation crystallized involved the doctrines of unilateral humanitarian intervention and the responsibility to protect. Unsurprisingly, then, this area was among those that led the way in China and Russia's efforts to constrain Western agendas by reasserting the superiority of state sovereignty and nonintervention, and refusing to authorize Security Council-approved intervention in Syria.

Following NATO's use of force in Kosovo, some Western states and many Western scholars began championing the idea of recognizing a right to unilateral humanitarian

---

[125] Wuerth, *supra* note 92.
[126] *Joint Declaration, supra* note 75, ¶ 7.
[127] CHAN, *supra* note 111, at 17 ("The most fundamental disagreements between China (and many non-Western States) and Western powers inhere in the conceptions, protection, implementation and violations of human rights, democracy and self-determination, and how international peace and security ought to be maintained.").
[128] *See* Chapter 4.VI.B.

intervention or the responsibility to protect.[129] The latter took its name from a 2001 report by the International Commission on Intervention and State Sovereignty,[130] which worked from the premise that "(1) [s]tate sovereignty implies responsibility, and the primary responsibility for the protection of its people lies with the state itself," but that "(2) [w]here a population is suffering serious harm . . . and the state in question is unwilling or unable to halt or avert it, the principle of non-intervention yields to the international responsibility to protect."[131] Instead of being a right, state sovereignty was recast as a responsibility, such that when a state failed in its duties, it might forfeit its right to invoke sovereignty as a shield.

Responsibility to protect gave rise to extensive debate over whether a decision on intervention had to be made by the existing collective security institutions, like the UN Security Council, or whether individual states could lawfully take matters into their own hands if those institutions were unable or unwilling to act. The original International Commission on Intervention and State Sovereignty favored Security Council authorization but considered that, if the Council failed to discharge its responsibility to protect in conscience-shocking situations, concerned states might act unilaterally.[132] By contrast, the version of responsibility to protect that the 2005 World Summit and the UN Secretary-General adopted eschewed unilateral action and rather required humanitarian intervention to take place through the Security Council, in accordance with the UN Charter.[133]

In March 2011, the Security Council adopted Resolution 1973 authorizing the establishment of a no-fly zone and the taking of "all necessary measures . . . to protect civilians and civilian populated areas under threat of attack" in Libya.[134] To many, the resulting UN-mandated NATO use of force represented the "coming of age" moment for the doctrine of responsibility to protect. China and Russia abstained on Resolution 1973 instead of vetoing it, but disagreements soon emerged about the permissible scope of military activity. In particular, China and Russia criticized NATO for exceeding the resolution's mandate by arming rebels and attacking a broad range of targets beyond those necessary for the protection of civilians.[135] They also accused NATO of using the resolution as a pretext for regime change by ousting the Qaddafi regime.[136]

---

[129] See, e.g., FERNANDO R. TESÓN, HUMANITARIAN INTERVENTION: AN INQUIRY INTO LAW AND MORALITY (3d ed. 2005); Monica Hakimi, Toward a Legal Theory on the Responsibility to Protect, 39 YALE J. INT'L L. 247 (2014); Harold Hongju Koh, The War Powers and Humanitarian Intervention, 53 HOUS. L. REV. 971 (2016).

[130] INT'L COMM'N ON INTERVENTION AND STATE SOVEREIGNTY, THE RESPONSIBILITY TO PROTECT (2001), http://responsibilitytoprotect.org/ICISS%20Report.pdf.

[131] Id. at XI.

[132] Id. at XII–XIII.

[133] G.A. Res. 60/1, World Summit Outcome, ¶¶ 138–40 (Oct. 24, 2005); U.N. Secretary-General, Implementing the Responsibility to Protect, U.N. Doc A/63/677 (Jan. 12, 2009).

[134] S.C. Res. 1973, ¶ 4 (Mar. 17, 2011).

[135] Andrew Jacobs, China Urges Quick End to Airstrikes in Libya, N.Y. TIMES, Mar. 22, 2011; Russia Accuses NATO of Going Beyond UN Resolution on Libya, RT, Apr. 17, 2011; Patrick Goodenough, Russia, China Accuse West of Exceeding UN Resolution, Making Libyan Crisis Worse, CNS NEWS, Mar. 29, 2011.

[136] Andrew Garwood-Gowers, The Responsibility to Protect and the Arab Spring: Libya as the Exception, Syria as the Norm?, 36 UNSW L.J. 594, 609 (2013); Roy Allison, Russia and Syria: Explaining Alignment with a Regime in Crisis, 89 INT'L AFF. 795, 797–98 (2013); NATO to End Libya Campaign on 31 October, GUARDIAN, Oct. 22, 2011.

Against this background, the question arose about the Security Council's authorizing force to intervene in Syria's civil war. On three occasions, China and Russia vetoed Western-sponsored Security Council draft resolutions proposing measures against the regime of Bashar al-Assad.[137] Whereas the Western states wanted to pressure President Assad to step aside, China and Russia opposed external attempts at regime change. The Western states accused the Assad regime of brutally cracking down on pro-democracy demonstrators, but China and Russia characterized the situation as an armed conflict between a government and an opposition. Instead of embracing Libya as an example of responsibility to protect, China and Russia viewed it as a dangerous precedent for pretextual intervention, recalling that the Western states had transgressed the agreed-upon consensus on protecting civilians to effect regime change.[138]

This event illustrates how some of the themes espoused in China and Russia's Joint Declaration operate in practice. First, doctrines like unilateral humanitarian intervention and the responsibility to protect are premised on a fundamental recalibration between state sovereignty and human rights. China and Russia resisted efforts to rely on values such as human rights and democracy to justify intervention and instead reasserted the fundamental importance of state sovereignty and nonintervention, but with some nuances. For instance, the 2013 Concept of the Foreign Policy of the Russian Federation states: "It is unacceptable that military interventions and other forms of interference from without which undermine the foundations of international law based on the principle of sovereign equality of states, be carried out on the pretext of implementing the concept of 'responsibility to protect.'"[139] Similarly, in the explanation of one of China's vetoes, Ambassador Li Baodong declared:

> [S]overeign equality and non-interference in other countries' internal affairs are basic norms governing state-to-state relations enshrined in the UN Charter. . . . We have consistently maintained that the future and fate of Syria should be independently decided by the Syrian people, rather than imposed by outside forces. . . . Our purpose is to safeguard the interests of the Syrian people and Arab countries, the interests of all countries—small and medium-sized countries in particular—and to protect the role and authority of the United Nations and the Security Council, as well as the basic standards that govern international relations.[140]

---

[137] U.N. SCOR, 66th Sess., 6627th mtg. at 2, U.N. Doc. S/PV.6627 (Oct. 4, 2011); U.N. SCOR, 67th Sess., 6711th mtg. at 2, U.N. Doc. S/PV.6711 (Feb. 4, 2012); U.N. SCOR, 67th Sess., 6810th mtg. at 2, U.N. Doc. S/PV.6810 (July 19, 2012).

[138] Chris Buckley, *China Defends Syria Veto, Doubts West's Intentions*, Reuters, Feb. 5, 2012; *West Pushes for "Regime Change" in Syria, Further Complicates Crisis*, Xinhua, Feb. 8, 2012; Yang Liming, *Syria Becomes Focus of Struggle Among Great Powers*, China Youth Daily, Feb. 8, 2012; Zhong Sheng, *Why China Vetoes UN Draft Resolution for Syria Issue*, People's Daily, Feb. 8, 2012; *see also* Zhu Wenqi, *Responsibility to Protect: A Challenge to Chinese Traditional Diplomacy*, 1 China Legal Sci. 97 (2013).

[139] Ministry Foreign Aff. Russ., *supra* note 101, ¶ 31(b).

[140] U.N. SCOR, 67th Sess., 6810th mtg., *supra* note 137, at 13–14.

302 | Is International Law International?

That does not mean the two states always oppose intervention. China's position on responsibility to protect has evolved considerably. Initially, it strongly opposed unilateral humanitarian intervention and any version of responsibility to protect that would permit states to intervene unilaterally in other states. It is now prepared, however, to accept the latter provided that the principle is invoked strictly within the confines of the 2005 World Summit Outcome and the intervention does not have the aim or effect of regime change.[141] Russia formerly opposed unilateral humanitarian intervention but invoked the doctrine in support of its actions in Crimea.[142] On balance, even though these two states tend to rate state sovereignty and nonintervention more highly than their Western counterparts, their positions have become more qualified over time.

Second, many of the advocates of unilateral humanitarian intervention and the responsibility to protect supported the notion of bypassing the UN Security Council if it was unwilling or unable to protect against egregious violations of human rights. The possibility that the United States and its allies might launch unilateral strikes against Syria allowed China and Russia to claim that they were acting as the guardians of international law, whereas the West was undermining international law and international institutions. For instance, according to Putin:

> We are not protecting the Syrian government, but international law. We need to use the United Nations Security Council and believe that preserving law and order in today's complex and turbulent world is one of the few ways to keep international relations from sliding into chaos. The law is still the law, and we must follow it whether we like it or not. Under current international law, force is permitted only in self-defense or by the decision of the Security Council. Anything else is unacceptable under the United Nations Charter and would constitute an act of aggression.[143]

Similarly, an editorial by "Zhong Sheng," a pen name for the "Voice of China" that is used in the *People's Daily* to issue explanations of the government's position, stated:

> Certain countries only show superficial respect for the United Nations, but have no real respect for it. They merely want to use the Security Council as a rubber stamp. If their resolution passes, they will gain legitimacy for their actions. However, if their resolution is blocked, they will condemn those who vote against the resolution, and do whatever they want regardless.[144]

---

[141] FOOT & WALTER, *supra* note 8, at 50–51; COURTNEY J. FUNG, CHINA AND THE RESPONSIBILITY TO PROTECT: FROM OPPOSITION TO ADVOCACY 2 (U.S. Inst. for Peace, Peace Brief No. 205, 2016); Allen Carlson, *More Than Just Saying No: China's Evolving Approach to Sovereignty and Intervention Since Tiananmen, in* NEW DIRECTIONS IN THE STUDY OF CHINESE FOREIGN POLICY 217 (Alastair Iain Johnston & Robert Ross eds., 2006); Jonathan E. Davis, *From Ideology to Pragmatism: China's Position on Humanitarian Intervention in the Post-Cold War Era*, 44 VAND. J. TRANSNAT'L L. 217 (2011).

[142] *See* Chapter 5.II.A.

[143] Vladimir V. Putin, Opinion, *A Plea for Caution from Russia*, N.Y. TIMES, Sept. 11, 2013.

[144] Zhong Sheng, *Preventing UN Security Council from Becoming a Rubber Stamp*, PEOPLE'S DAILY, Feb. 8, 2012.

Third, Western states and the Western media often presented the vetoes as unconscionable acts designed to shield Assad, a Russian ally, despite his brutal actions in cracking down on pro-democracy demonstrators.[145] For their part, China and Russia pointed to the ongoing casualties and conflict in Iraq and Afghanistan as a warning of the potentially disastrous outcomes that occur when powerful states intervene in the domestic affairs of other states. For instance, in an opinion editorial in the *New York Times*, Putin declared:

[F]orce has proved ineffective and pointless. Afghanistan is reeling, and no one can say what will happen after international forces withdraw. Libya is divided into tribes and clans. In Iraq the civil war continues, with dozens killed each day. In the United States, many draw an analogy between Iraq and Syria, and ask why their government would want to repeat recent mistakes.[146]

Likewise, Zhong Sheng of the *People's Daily* argued "using violence to restrain violence will not bring long-term peace" on the basis that:

It is not hard for the most powerful military alliance to overthrow a small country's administration through war. The problem is that the military giant will withdraw after the war. Even if it stays for a while, it will not tak[e] protecting lives of local civilians as its primary task. The tragedies that have occurred in Iraq and Afghanistan have proved it.[147]

Far from endorsing the principle of responsibility to protect, authoritative and quasi-authoritative Chinese statements have scrupulously avoided any mention of the possible application of responsibility to protect as a justification for intervention in Syria.[148] These themes were articulated more explicitly in the *Global Times*, a fervently nationalist Chinese newspaper, in an article entitled "Values Are Thin Excuses to Start New Wars."[149] It accused Western states of intervening in the domestic affairs of other states by fomenting or encouraging revolutions, like those in the Arab Spring, especially through use of the Internet. The paper reported that the United States and Europe were adopting

[145] *See, e.g.*, David M. Herszenhorn, *For Syria, Reliant on Russia for Weapons and Food, Old Bonds Run Deep*, N.Y. TIMES, Feb. 18, 2012; Neil MacFarquhar, *With Rare Double U.N. Veto on Syria, Russia and China Try to Shield Friend*, N.Y. TIMES, Oct. 5, 2011.

[146] Putin, *supra* note 143.

[147] Zhong Sheng, *supra* note 138; accord, Tian Wenlin, *"Humanitarian Intervention" May Cause Bigger Disaster*, PEOPLE'S DAILY, June 1, 2012; *see also id.*, *Be Wary of Attempt to Resolve Syrian Crisis Outside UN Framework*, PEOPLE'S DAILY, Aug. 15, 2012; *id.*, *Regime Change Should Not Be Determined by External Forces*, PEOPLE'S DAILY, July 18, 2012.

[148] Michael D. Swaine, *Chinese Views of the Syrian Conflict*, CHINA LEADERSHIP MONITOR, Fall 2012, at 1 n.17 (explaining the absence of reference to English or Chinese words associated with "Responsibility to Protect" in relation to Syria, including in the official website of the Ministry of Foreign Affairs of the People's Republic of China, the archives of *People's Daily*, the archives of *Liberation Army Daily*, and the databases of the Chinese Government and the Communist Party of China).

[149] *Values Are Thin Excuses to Start New Wars*, GLOBAL TIMES, Feb. 7, 2012.

"value diplomacy as a powerful tool in the current global competition" to compensate for their declining economic and technological power.[150] It also noted that Western states had the power to topple regimes of small states, but that they no longer had the finances or staying power to rebuild them, which meant that interventions usually ended in a complete mess.

It is too early to tell whether and how the doctrine of responsibility to protect will live on. Other proposals have emerged, such as Brazil's idea of responsibility while protecting.[151] But the terrible consequences that befell both Libya, where it was used, and Syria, where it was not, have cast doubt on the ongoing vitality and usefulness of this doctrine.[152] Either way, this case study shows China and Russia working to constrain Western agendas that seek to recalibrate the balance between state sovereignty and human rights.[153] They helped to deflect the global debate from unilateral humanitarian intervention and toward responsibility to protect, and they policed the application of the latter to ensure that it was not used to effect regime change. Their own positions on the issue have evolved and are likely to further evolve, but they are asserting their right to be at the decision-making table.

The Syrian crisis also represents an example of the importance of cooperation between Western and non-Western states in this new competitive world order. After reports of the Assad regime's use of chemical weapons in Ghouta in 2013, a coalition of Western states, led by France and the United States, threatened unilateral airstrikes on Syria.[154] When the US secretary of state said that airstrikes could be averted if Syria turned over all of its chemical weapons within one week, Russia suggested that Syria relinquish its weapons and Syria welcomed the proposal.[155] Following a jointly negotiated proposal from

---

[150] *Id.*

[151] Permanent Rep. of Brazil to the U.N., Letter dated Nov. 9, 2011 from the Permanent Rep. of Brazil to the United Nations addressed to the Secretary-General, U.N. Doc. A/66/551 (Nov. 11, 2011); *see also* Oliver Stuenkel, *Brazil as Norm Entrepreneur: The Responsibility While Protecting, in* IMPLEMENTING THE RESPONSIBILITY TO PROTECT: NEW DIRECTIONS FOR INTERNATIONAL PEACE AND SECURITY? 59 (Eduarda Passarelli Hamann & Robert Muggah eds., 2013).

[152] Martha Hall Findlay, *Can R2P Survive Libya and Syria?*, STRATEGIC STUD. WORKING GROUP PAPERS, Nov. 2011, at 1; David Rieff, Opinion, *R2P, R.I.P.*, N.Y. TIMES, Nov. 7, 2011; Mohammed Nuruzzaman, *Revisiting "Responsibility to Protect" After Libya and Syria*, E-INT'L REL., Mar. 8, 2014.

[153] For commentary on China's evolving approach to responsibility to protect, see, for example, Jochen Prantl & Ryoko Nakano, *Global Norm Diffusion in East Asia: How China and Japan Implement the Responsibility to Protect*, 25 INT'L REL. 204 (2011); Sarah Teitt, *Assessing Polemics, Principles and Practices: China and the Responsibility to Protect*, 1 GLOBAL RESP. TO PROTECT 208 (2009); *id., China and the Responsibility to Protect*, 6 ASIA-PAC. CTR. FOR RESP. TO PROTECT: POLICY BRIEF 1 (2016); Liu Tiewa, *China and Responsibility to Protect: Maintenance and Change of Its Policy for Intervention*, 25 PAC. REV. 153 (2012); Liu Tiewa & Zhang Haibin, *Debates in China About the Responsibility to Protect as a Developing International Norm: A General Assessment*, 14 CONFLICT, SECURITY & DEV. 403 (2014).

[154] Richard Spencer, *Syria: France Threatens Military Force in Wake of Chemical Weapons Claims*, TELEGRAPH, Aug. 22, 2013; Frederik Pleitgen & Tom Cohen, *"War-Weary" Obama Says Syria Chemical Attack Requires Response*, CNN, Aug. 30, 2013.

[155] Anne Gearan, Karen DeYoung, & Will Englund, *Syria Says It "Welcomes" Russia Proposal on Chemical Weapons*, WASH. POST, Sept. 9, 2013; Michael R. Gordon & Steven Lee Myers, *Obama Calls Russia Offer on Syria Possible "Breakthrough,"* N.Y. TIMES, Sept. 9, 2013; *Russian Offers Troops to Help Remove Syria Chemical Arms*, BBC NEWS, Sept. 22, 2013.

Russia and the United States, Syria agreed to join the Organisation for the Prohibition of Chemical Weapons and handed over information about its chemical weapons, and a time line was agreed on for the verification, removal, and destruction of these weapons.[156]

These developments culminated in the Security Council's passage of Resolution 2118 in 2013, which (1) found that the use of chemical weapons in Syria, and anywhere else, "constitutes a threat to international peace and security," (2) imposed binding obligations on Syria through the use of terms such as "decides" and by referencing Article 25 of the UN Charter, but (3) did not authorize the use of force under Chapter VII.[157] Formerly, there had been debate about whether only Chapter VII resolutions were binding.[158] In this case, the United States hoped for a binding resolution, but China and Russia would not include a reference to Chapter VII because they did not want any suggestion that they had impliedly agreed to the use of force after what had happened in Libya. The consequence was a compromise in which the Security Council agreed upon binding measures without invoking Chapter VII.[159]

The end result allowed both sides to claim victory and initiated a process for removing chemical weapons from Syria. The United States was able to claim that "[w]e sought a legally binding resolution, and that is what the Security Council has adopted" and that "in the event of non-compliance, the Council will impose measures under Chapter VII of the Charter of the United Nations."[160] At the same time, Russia was able to claim that "[t]he resolution does not fall under Chapter VII of the Charter of the United Nations and does not allow for any automatic use of coercive measures of enforcement."[161] The resolution also reaffirmed a "strong commitment to . . . sovereignty, independence and territorial integrity" and was based on Syria's sovereign decision to join the Organisation for the Prohibition of Chemical Weapons.[162] In this way, it accorded with China and Russia's aim of protecting state sovereignty against outside intervention.

Meanwhile, after failing to achieve Security Council authorization to use force, the United States began arming and training the Syrian rebels who were fighting the Assad regime and ISIS, and later, the United States and some of its Western allies began a

---

[156] *Q&A: Syria Chemical Weapons Disarmament Deal*, BBC News, Jan. 30, 2014.

[157] S.C. Res. 2118 (Sept. 27, 2013).

[158] Article 25 of the UN Charter provides that "The Members of the United Nations agree to accept and carry out the decisions of the Security Council in accordance with the present Charter." Only "decisions" of the Security Council are binding and some commentators thought that only Chapter VII resolutions could include binding decisions. This resolution made clear that such decisions could be taken outside of the Chapter VII framework, creating binding obligations on states without giving rise to the argument that the Security Council had impliedly authorized the use of force.

[159] For discussion, see John Bellinger, *The Security Council Resolution on Syria: Is It Legally Binding?*, Lawfare, Sept. 28, 2013, https://www.lawfareblog.com/security-council-resolution-syria-it-legally-binding; Ryan Goodman, *Are the Press Reports of the Security Council's Draft Syria Resolution Accurate? How Weak or Strong Is It?*, Just Security, Sept. 27, 2013, https://www.justsecurity.org/1245/securitycouncilsyriaresolution; Marko Milanovic, *A Few Thoughts on Resolution 2118*, EJIL: Talk!, Oct. 1, 2013, http://www.ejiltalk.org/a-few-thoughts-on-resolution-2118.

[160] U.N. SCOR, 68th Sess., 7038th mtg. at 5, U.N. Doc. S/PV.7038 (Sept. 27, 2013).

[161] *Id.* at 4.

[162] S.C. Res. 2118, *supra* note 157.

bombing campaign targeting ISIS.[163] Russia also intervened in the Syrian war, but with the consent of the Assad regime, fighting ISIS and "other terrorists," which includes some of the Syrian rebels.[164] This difference plays into Russia's narrative that it is working to defend state sovereignty and uphold international law because it intervened by invitation, whereas the United States is violating international law and territorial integrity because it is intervening without consent.[165] Whether Western international lawyers agree with this critique or not, they need to be cognizant of it.

B. PURSUING NON-WESTERN AGENDAS:
CYBERSECURITY AND INFORMATION SECURITY

In addition to constraining Western agendas, China and Russia have also been active in advancing their own agendas in fields such as cybersecurity and information security. This field is characterized by a split between two competing approaches. China and Russia define the problem as one of "information security" and advocate for a sovereignty-based model of governance through an international treaty negotiated and signed by states. The United States, the United Kingdom, and several other Western states frame the problem as one of "cybersecurity" and seek a multistakeholder model of governance that includes state and nonstate actors in the formulation of soft law cyber norms.[166] The clash between these camps brings to the fore many of the disagreements identified in this study, five elements of which are particularly noteworthy.

First, Russia was the first mover in seeking legal regulation of this field followed by China, whereas the United States and the United Kingdom have attempted to limit legal regulation.[167] According to Richard Clarke and Robert Knake, "The United States, almost single-handedly, is blocking arms control in cyberspace," and "Russia, somewhat ironically, is the leading advocate."[168] This dynamic in which non-Western states are acting as norm entrepreneurs resembles what occurs in some other fields, like outer space law, but it is the opposite of the dynamic on Western-led agendas like unilateral humanitarian intervention and responsibility to protect.

Russia took the lead in establishing an international debate on the global governance of information security and cybersecurity. In 1998, the Russian Federation submitted a draft resolution on cybersecurity to the UN Secretary-General called "Developments

---

[163] Tara McKelvey, *Arming Syrian Rebels: Where the US Went Wrong*, BBC NEWS, Oct. 10, 2015.
[164] *Lawmakers Authorize Use of Russian Military Force for Anti-IS Airstrikes in Syria*, TASS RUSSIAN NEWS AGENCY, Sept. 30, 2015; *Russia Joins War in Syria: Five Key Points*, BBC NEWS, Oct. 1, 2015.
[165] Sharmine Narwani, *Breaking International Law in Syria: US-NATO's "Humanitarian Air Strikes,"* RT, Nov. 25, 2015; Scott Stearns, *Russia: US Airstrikes in Syria Violate International Law*, VOA NEWS, Sept. 26, 2014. *See generally* Laura Visser, *Russia's Intervention in Syria*, EJIL: TALK!, Nov. 25, 2015, http://www.ejiltalk.org/russias-intervention-in-syria.
[166] Kristen E. Eichensehr, *The Cyber-Law of Nations*, 103 GEO. L.J. 317, 330–31 (2015).
[167] *See generally* TIM MAURER, CYBER NORM EMERGENCE AT THE UN: AN ANALYSIS OF THE ACTIVITIES AT THE UN REGARDING CYBER SECURITY (Belfer Ctr. for Sci. & Int'l Aff., Discussion Paper 2011-11, 2012).
[168] RICHARD A. CLARKE & ROBERT KNAKE, CYBER WAR: THE NEXT THREAT TO NATIONAL SECURITY AND WHAT TO DO ABOUT IT 218 (2010).

in the field of information and telecommunications in the context of international security."[169] Russia explained its concern about the use of "information weapons" for purposes "incompatible with the objectives of maintaining international stability and security, the observance of the principles of non-use of force, non-interference in internal affairs and respect for human rights and freedoms."[170] Russia's goal in introducing this resolution was ultimately to work toward the negotiation of a treaty regulating "information weapons."[171] Russia cited the problem of the increasing militarization of the Internet by Western states and the need to prevent "escalation of the arms race based on the latest developments of the scientific and technological revolution."[172]

Strong differences of view emerged between major Western and non-Western powers. The United States and the United Kingdom in particular were skeptical about Russia's movements toward an international treaty regulating cybersecurity. If Russia's actions were partially motivated by fear of being outdone in a cyber arms race, the more technologically advanced United States had little reason to want to limit its own cyber capabilities.[173] Some Western states viewed an international treaty as something that might ultimately limit themselves, while doing little to curb the actions of Russia and other unfriendly states and nonstate actors.[174] The United States and the United Kingdom evidenced discomfort about how broadly Russia was seeking to characterize the issue of "information security." They were concerned that Russia was trying to create a treaty that would justify limiting the free flow of information and increasing government control over the Internet so as to protect against political instability and civil unrest.[175] This concern intensified after the significant use of the Internet and social media in the Arab Spring.

Despite skepticism by Western states, a slightly amended version of Russia's draft resolution was ultimately adopted,[176] and a resolution under the same name continued to be adopted each year until 2005. But in 2005, the United States voted against the Russian-sponsored General Assembly resolution for the first time. The resolution was then not adopted by consensus in each of the next three years.[177] Meanwhile, also in 2005,

---

[169] Permanent Rep. of Russ. to the U.N., Letter dated Sept. 23, 1998 from the Permanent Rep. of Russ. addressed to the Secretary-General, U.N. Doc. A/C.1/53/3 (Sept. 30, 1998).

[170] *Id.*, app.

[171] U.N. Secretary-General, *Developments in the Field of Information and Telecommunications in the Context of International Security*, at 9, U.N. Doc. A/54/213 (Aug. 10, 1999).

[172] Permanent Rep. of Russ. to the U.N., *supra* note 169, app.

[173] *See* MAURER, *supra* note 167, at 21.

[174] *See id.* at 17; Siobhan Gorman, *U.S. Backs Talks on Cyber Warfare*, WALL ST. J., June 4, 2010.

[175] *See* U.N. Secretary-General, *supra* note 171, at 9–10; *id., Developments in the Field of Information and Telecommunications in the Context of International Security*, at 11, U.N. Doc. A/59/116 (June 23, 2004); Christopher A. Ford, *The Trouble with Cyber Arms Control*, NEW ATLANTIS: J. TECH. & SOC'Y, Fall 2010, at 52, 62.

[176] Compare draft resolutions Russ., Developments in the Field of Information and Telecommunications in the Context of International Security, U.N. Doc. A/C.1/53/L.17 (Oct. 26, 1998) and *id.*, Developments in the Field of Information and Telecommunications in the Context of International Security, U.N. Doc. A/C.1/53/L.17/Rev.1 (Nov. 2, 1998), with the final UN General Assembly Resolution G.A. Res. 53/70 (Jan. 4, 1999).

[177] ENEKEN TIKK-RINGAS, DEVELOPMENTS IN THE FIELD OF INFORMATION AND TELECOMMUNICATION IN THE CONTEXT OF INTERNATIONAL SECURITY: WORK OF THE UN FIRST COMMITTEE 1998–2012, at 7 (2012).

the Group of Governmental Experts had been supposed to report to the UN General Assembly on "existing and potential threats in the sphere of information security and possible cooperative measures to address them." The group, which consisted of fifteen states including the permanent members of the Security Council, was unable to reach a common position and failed to produce a report.[178] Following the US veto in 2005, the issue became more multilateral. In 2006, the resolution was cosponsored by Russia and eight other non-Western states (Armenia, Belarus, China, Kazakhstan, Kyrgyzstan, Myanmar, Tajikistan, and Uzbekistan), and Chile, Cuba, Japan, Serbia, and Brazil joined the resolution in later years at different points.[179] By 2009, the resolution had gained thirty cosponsors.[180]

The second noteworthy element of the proposals on cybersecurity is that different groupings of states sought to utilize different forums to advance their agenda. Russia had initially brought its resolution to the UN General Assembly's First Committee on Disarmament and International Security, styling the issue as a politico-military one about cyberwarfare. The United States and the United Kingdom tried to redefine the issue more narrowly, shifting the focus to the economic stream on cybercrime by emphasizing that the real problem was the need to protect against cyber offenses by criminals and terrorists.[181] These two states thus promoted the Council of Europe's Convention on Cybercrime, and the United States introduced resolutions entitled "Combating the criminal misuse of information technologies" in the UN General Assembly's Third Committee, and "Creation of a global culture of cybersecurity" in the Assembly's Second Committee.[182] These attempts to shift the forum within the United Nations were ultimately unsuccessful, but Russia's agenda in the First Committee was also stalled from 2005 to 2009.

In view of differences of opinion at the multilateral level, both camps took the issue to their own groupings of like-minded states to develop favorable norms. In June 2009, Russia pursued its proposal in the Shanghai Cooperation Organization, an international organization comprising six non-Western states (China, Kazakhstan, Kyrgyzstan, Russia, Tajikistan, and Uzbekistan) that was established in 2001 for the purposes of political, military, and economic cooperation. These states concluded an agreement on cooperation in the field of international information security (SCO Agreement), which expanded upon Russia's annual First Committee resolution.[183] In 2011, four members of the Shanghai Cooperation Organization, including China and Russia, submitted a Draft

---

[178] U.N. Secretary-General, *Group of Governmental Experts on Developments in the Field of Information and Telecommunications in the Context of International Security*, ¶ 5, U.N. Doc. A/60/202, 2 (Aug. 5, 2005).

[179] *See* Disarmament Resols. & Decisions Database, View by GA Resolution Number, https://gafc-vote.un.org (last visited Nov. 26, 2016).

[180] MAURER, *supra* note 167, at 26.

[181] *Id.* at 15–45.

[182] G.A. Res. 55/63 (Jan. 22, 2001); G.A. Res. 57/239 (Jan. 31, 2003).

[183] Agreement Between the Governments of the Member States of the Shanghai Cooperation Organization on Cooperation in the Field of International Information Security, June 16, 2009, https://ccdcoe.org/sites/default/files/documents/SCO-090616-IISAgreementRussian.pdf (unofficial English translation at https://ccdcoe.org/sites/default/files/documents/SCO-090616-IISAgreement.pdf) [hereinafter SCO Agreement].

International Code of Conduct for Information Security to the General Assembly.[184] A week later, Russia released a concept for a Convention on International Information Security.[185] In 2015, all six members of the Shanghai Cooperation Organization submitted a new Draft International Code of Conduct for Information Security to the General Assembly.[186]

At the same time, in the Western camp NATO held its first meeting on cybersecurity in 2008 in Bucharest, which prompted it to create two new NATO divisions focused on cyber-attacks: the Cyber Defence Management Authority and the Cooperative Cyber Defence Centre of Excellence.[187] In 2009, the NATO Centre of Excellence invited a group of independent experts on the law of armed conflict—the International Group of Experts—to produce a manual on cyber warfare called the *Tallinn Manual on the International Law Applicable to Cyber Warfare* (often referred to as the *Tallinn Manual* or *Tallinn 1.0*), which is discussed below. In 2011, the United Kingdom hosted the first International Conference on Cyberspace in London, which seemed intended to develop a Western consensus to counterbalance the Chinese and Russian approach and lead to subsequent annual conferences. The "London Conference" has in fact continued, having been hosted in Budapest (2012), Seoul (2013), and The Hague (2015).[188] The Estonian government has been active in this field since it was the victim of cyber attacks in 2007,[189] as has the Netherlands, a strong proponent of the idea that states should not interfere with the "public core" of the Internet.[190]

In addition to the UN Group of Governmental Experts, the Shanghai Cooperation Organization, the London Process, and the *Tallinn Manual*, many other actors and forums are addressing different aspects of this issue. These include the Internet Governance Forum; the Wassenaar Arrangement on Export Controls; the NetMundial Meeting in Brazil; the International Telecommunication Union; and the Group of Twenty, which adopted the no-commercial-cyber-espionage commitment that Obama

---

[184] Permanent Rep. of China, Russ., Tajikstan and Uzbekistan, Letter dated Sept. 12, 2011 from the Permanent Rep. of China, Russ., Tajikistan and Uzbekistan to the United Nations addressed to the Secretary-General, annex, U.N. Doc. A/66/359 (Sept. 14, 2011).

[185] Convention on International Information Security (Concept), published Sept. 22, 2011, http://www.mid.ru/en/foreign_policy/official_documents/-/asset_publisher/CptICkB6BZ29/content/id/191666.

[186] Permanent Rep. of China, Kazakhstan, Kyrgyzstan, Russ., Tajikistan and Uzbekistan, Letter dated Jan. 9, 2015 from the Permanent Rep. of China, Kazakhstan, Kyrgyzstan, Russ., Tajikistan and Uzbekistan to the United Nations addressed to the Secretary-General, annex, U.N. Doc. A/69/723 (Jan. 13, 2015).

[187] *See* N. Atlantic Treaty Org. [NATO], Cyber Defence, http://www.nato.int/cps/en/natohq/topics_78170.htm (last updated Jan. 17, 2017, 10:54 AM); NATO Cooperative Cyber Def. Ctr. Excellence [CCDCOE], https://ccdcoe.org/ (last visited Nov. 26, 2016).

[188] *See Global Conference on Cyber Space*, Global F. on Cyber Expertise, https://www.thegfce.com/about/contents/gccs (last visited Nov. 26, 2016).

[189] *See, e.g., The Conference on State Practice and the Future of International Law in Cyberspace*, Cyber Norms Platform, http://www.cybernormsplatform.org/ (last visited Nov. 26, 2016) (The conference is organized by the Ministry of Foreign Affairs of the Republic of Estonia and the Cyber Policy Institute.).

[190] *See* Dennis Broeders, The Public Core of the Internet (2015) (translation of the Dutch report "De publieke kern van het Internet" that the Netherlands Scientific Council for Government Policy presented to the Dutch Minster for Foreign Affairs on Mar. 31, 2015).

and Xi agreed to in September 2015.[191] Thus, multiple forums are involved and the camps have devolved into more decentralized and variegated groupings than a simple China/Russia and United States/United Kingdom split.

Third, the two camps have expressed distinct understandings on a range of substantive international law issues, including the applicability and appropriateness of applying existing laws to this new domain. China and Russia argued for the negotiation of a new treaty on information security on the basis that current laws either did not apply to cyber activities or were not suited to the task of regulating this new technology. By contrast, the United Kingdom took the position that a new multilateral treaty governing cybersecurity was unnecessary because the existing law of armed conflict, specifically the principles of necessity and proportionality, governed the use of such technologies.[192] Likewise, the United States claimed that "[t]he same laws that apply to the use of kinetic weapons should apply to state behavior in cyberspace."[193] Neither the first nor the second Group of Governmental Experts was able to reach agreement on this issue.[194]

It was only when the 2013 report of the third Group of Governmental Experts was submitted that the parties agreed that "[i]nternational law, and in particular the Charter of the United Nations, is applicable" to information security and cybersecurity,[195] which was viewed as a win for the Western camp. But the report also recognized the principles of "[s]tate sovereignty and international norms and principles that flow from sovereignty," including that states have jurisdiction over information and communications technology infrastructure within their territory,[196] which was viewed as a win for China and Russia. The report also noted that "[c]ommon understandings on how such norms shall apply . . . requires further study" and that, given the unique attributes of cyber technologies, "additional norms could be developed over time."[197] The failure to develop such norms in more detail in the 2015 report of the fourth Group

---

[191] The President's News Conference with President Xi Jinping of China, 2015 Daily Comp. Pres. Doc. 647 (Sept. 25, 2015); *see also* Ellen Nakashima & Steven Mufson, *U.S., China Vow Not to Engage in Economic Cyberespionage*, WASH. POST, Sept. 25, 2015.

[192] U.N. Secretary-General, *Developments in the Field of Information and Telecommunications in the Context of International Security, supra* note 171, at 11; *id., Developments in the Field of Information and Telecommunications in the Context of International Security*, at 15, U.N. Doc. A/65/154 (July 20, 2010).

[193] Ford, *supra* note 175, at 66–67; John Markoff, *Step Taken to End Impasse over Cybersecurity Talks*, N.Y. TIMES, July 17, 2010; Harold Hongju Koh, *International Law in Cyberspace*, 54 HARV. INT'L L.J. ONLINE 1, 3–4 (2012).

[194] U.N. Secretary-General, *Group of Governmental Experts on Developments in the Field of Information and Telecommunications in the Context of International Security*, at 2, U.N. Doc. A/60/202 (Aug. 5, 2005); Rep. of the Group of Governmental Experts on Developments in the Field of Information and Telecommunications in the Context of International Security (2010), transmitted by Note from the U.N. Secretary-General titled Group of Governmental Experts on Developments in the Field of Information and Telecommunications in the Context of International Security, U.N. Doc. A/65/201 (July 30, 2010).

[195] Rep. of the Group of Governmental Experts on Developments in the Field of Information and Telecommunications in the Context of International Security (2013), transmitted by Note from the U.N. Secretary-General titled Group of Governmental Experts on Developments in the Field of Information and Telecommunications in the Context of International Security, ¶ 19, U.N. Doc. A/68/98 (June 4, 2013).

[196] *Id.* ¶ 20.

[197] *Id.* ¶ 16.

of Governmental Experts indicates that substantial differences remain between the camps.[198]

The two groups of states frame the nature and extent of the problem in distinct ways, as captured by the different nomenclature of "information security" and "cybersecurity."[199] Russia has defined an "information weapon" to include "mass manipulation of a State's population with a view to destabilizing society and the State" and listed such potential threats posed by information weapons as "[u]se of information with a view to undermining other State's economic and social systems and psychological manipulation of a population for the purpose of destabilizing society."[200] In keeping with the Russian approach, the 2009 SCO Agreement defines an "information war" as a

> confrontation between two or more states in the information space aimed at damaging information systems, processes and resources, critical and other structures, undermining political, economic and social systems, [and] mass psychologic[al] brainwashing to destabilize society and state, as well as to force the state to tak[e] decisions in the interests of the opposing party.[201]

The SCO Agreement lists the major threats to information security, among them "[d]issemination of information harmful to the socio-political and socio-economic systems, spiritual, moral and cultural environment of other States."[202] By contrast, the United Kingdom and the United States have adopted a narrower approach that focuses on cybersecurity rather than information security, as their goal has been to focus on cybercrimes rather than more general Internet controls.[203]

Fourth, another element of the cyber debates has been the development of a geopolitical division between Western liberal democratic states and authoritarian states about how to regulate the Internet.[204] The former liken the Internet to a "global commons" and see it as connected to "a bottom-up, multi-stakeholder approach to . . . governance" advanced by governments and the private sector and civil society, and "underpinned by principles of . . . democratic governance and respect for human rights," including freedom of speech

---

[198] Rep. of the Group of Governmental Experts on Developments in the Field of Information and Telecommunications in the Context of International Security (2015), transmitted by Note from the U.N. Secretary-General titled Group of Governmental Experts on Developments in the Field of Information and Telecommunications in the Context of International Security, U.N. Doc. A/70/174 (July 22, 2015).

[199] *See* CAMINO KAVANAGH, TIM MAURER, & ENEKEN TIKK-RINGAS, BASELINE REVIEW: ICT-RELATED PROCESSES & EVENTS: IMPLICATIONS FOR INTERNATIONAL AND REGIONAL SECURITY (2011–2013) (2014); Keir Giles & William Hagestad, *Divided by a Common Language: Cyber Definitions in Chinese, Russian and English*, 5 INT'L CONF. CYBER CONFLICT PROC. 413 (2013).

[200] U.N. Secretary-General, *Developments in the Field of Information and Telecommunications in the Context of International Security*, addendum, U.N. Doc. A/56/164/Add.1 (Oct. 3, 2001). On the sources and content of different definitions, see Oona Hathaway et al., *The Law of Cyber-Attack*, 100 CAL. L. REV. 817, 824–25 (2012).

[201] SCO Agreement, *supra* note 183, annex 1.

[202] *Id.* annex 2.

[203] John Markoff & Andrew E. Kramer, *In Shift, U.S. Talks to Russia on Internet Security*, N.Y. TIMES, Dec. 12, 2009.

[204] KAVANAGH, MAURER, & TIKK-RINGAS, *supra* note 199, at 34. *See generally* TIM WU & JACK GOLDSMITH, WHO CONTROLS THE INTERNET? (2008).

and free movement of information.[205] The latter view the Internet as used within states and thus as subject to national regulation (the "bordered Internet"). This position permits "a more top-down, territorial vision of how cyberspace should be governed" and "is underpinned by the principles of state sovereignty and non-interference."[206] According to this view, freedom of speech and the free flow of information should be controlled, as they can threaten state stability and governmental control.

On the substantive level, because the United States and the United Kingdom regard the Internet as a global commons, the US International Strategy for Cyberspace, for instance, prizes "openness and innovation on the Internet" and opposes "arbitrary restrictions on the free flow of information or [its use] to suppress dissent or opposition activities."[207] The United Kingdom has warned that regulating information security might "impinge on the free flow of information, which [is] recognized . . . as a key principle of the information society."[208] China, however, sees these cyber debates as another example of US double standards, perpetrated by attempts to defend hegemony under the mantle of defending freedom.[209] China has maintained that "the free flow of information should be guaranteed under the premises that national sovereignty and security must be safeguarded" and that "each country has the right to manage its own cyberspace in accordance with its domestic legislation."[210] China and Russia's 2011 International Code of Conduct for Information Security would also require states "[t]o reaffirm all the rights and responsibilities of States to protect, in accordance with relevant laws and regulations, their information space and critical information infrastructure from threats, disturbance, attack and sabotage."[211] This approach is consistent with the Chinese approach of balkanizing the Internet, such as by adopting strict national legislation and establishing the "Great Firewall of China." It is thus common to find references to the need to protect China's "virtual territory" and "cyber sovereignty."[212]

---

[205] KAVANAGH, MAURER, & TIKK-RINGAS, *supra* note 199, at 34.

[206] *Id.*

[207] NAT'L SECURITY COUNCIL, INTERNATIONAL STRATEGY FOR CYBERSPACE: PROSPERITY, SECURITY, AND OPENNESS IN A NETWORKED WORLD 22 (2011), http://www.whitehouse.gov/sites/default/files/rss_viewer/international_strategy_for_cyberspace.pdf.

[208] U.N. Secretary-General, *Developments in the Field of Information and Telecommunications in the Context of International Security, supra* note 175, at 11.

[209] *See, e.g.,* Jing Nanxiang (荆南翔), 网络自由与网络自律 [Cyber Freedom and Cyber Self-Discipline], LIBERATION ARMY DAILY, Dec. 20, 2011 ("We must take a clear-cut stand against the 'double standards' of Western countries and prevent certain countries from turning the Internet into a tool for interfering in the internal affairs of other countries in the name of 'freedom.'"); Zhong Sheng, *Joint Efforts Needed to Improve Cyber Space Rule*, PEOPLE'S DAILY, July 12, 2013; *id., To Defend "Freedom," or to Defend Hegemony?*, PEOPLE'S DAILY, Jan. 26, 2010.

[210] U.N. Secretary-General, *Developments in the Field of Information and Telecommunications in the Context of International Security*, at 7, U.N. Doc. A/62/98 (July 2, 2007); *id., Developments in the Field of Information and Telecommunications in the Context of International Security*, at 4, U.N. Doc. A/61/161 (July 18, 2006).

[211] Permanent Rep. of China, Russ., Tajikstan and Uzbekistan, *supra* note 184, annex.

[212] *See, e.g.,* Wu Jianguo, *Defending the Cyber Territory*, LIBERATION ARMY DAILY, Mar. 1, 2000, *cited in* Michael D. Swaine, *Chinese Views on Cybersecurity in Foreign Relations*, CHINA LEADERSHIP MONITOR, Fall 2013, at 1 n.15 (2013); Zhong Sheng (钟声), 填补网络空间 "规则空白" [Fill in "Regulation Blank" in Cyberspace], PEOPLE'S DAILY, July 9, 2013.

On the procedural level, the United States and the United Kingdom are resistant to treaty-based models and prefer to develop soft law norms through a multistakeholder process that includes nongovernmental organizations, the private sector, civil society, academia, and individuals.[213] The US International Strategy for Cyberspace endorses "multi-stakeholder venues for the discussion of Internet governance issues,"[214] and the European Parliament has stated that a "single, centralised international institution, is not the appropriate body to assert regulatory authority over either internet governance or internet traffic flows" and that "internet governance and related regulatory issues should continue to be defined at a comprehensive and multi-stakeholder level."[215] For their part, China and Russia seek to develop international regulation through a multilateral model with the goal of a binding treaty that is negotiated and signed by states. China and Russia's 2011 International Code of Conduct for Information Security seeks "the establishment of a multilateral, transparent and democratic international management of the Internet."[216] The two states tend to be skeptical about many of the nonstate actors in the multistakeholder process because they consider them more likely to sympathize with the views of Western states. Russian international lawyers are also skeptical about recognizing nonstate actors as subjects of international law, particularly any which might be capable of contributing to the formation of international law.[217]

Fifth, as with other examples explored in this book, the media and academy in different states often present disparate narratives of the facts and analyses of the law. For example, in US media, cybersecurity is depicted as a pressing concern, given Chinese and Russian hackers, among others.[218] In Chinese media, by contrast, China is portrayed as the victim of hackers rather than as an aggressor.[219] Typically, Chinese officials and media vehemently deny that China engages in cyber attacks against Western states and often avow that China has only "defensive" and not "offensive" cyber capabilities.[220]

International legal academics frequently adopt approaches that are broadly sympathetic to the position of their state or geopolitical alliance.[221] The most obvious example is the *Tallinn Manual*, which was produced by the International Group of Experts.[222] The

---

[213] Eichensehr, *supra* note 166, at 352–64.

[214] Nat'l Security Council, *supra* note 207.

[215] European Parliament Resolution of Nov. 22, 2012 on the Forthcoming World Conference on International Telecommunications (WCIT-12) of the International Telecommunications Union, and the Possible Expansion of the Scope of International Telecommunication Regulations, 2015 O.J. (C 419) 101, 102–03.

[216] Permanent Rep. of China, Russ., Tajikistan and Uzbekistan, *supra* note 184, annex, subpara. (g).

[217] *See* Chapter 4.I.C.

[218] Alexander Abad-Santos, *China Is Winning the Cyber War Because They Hacked U.S. Plans for Real War*, Atlantic, May 28, 2013; Ian Bremmer, *These 5 Facts Explain the Threat of Cyber Warfare*, Time, June 20, 2015; Adrian Chen, *The Agency*, N.Y. Times, June 2, 2015.

[219] *See, e.g., China Defense Ministry Refutes Cyber Attack Allegations*, Xinhua, Feb. 20, 2013; Zhong Sheng, *Groundless Accusation Harmful to Cyber Security Cooperation*, People's Daily, Nov. 16, 2012. *See generally* Swaine, *supra* note 212.

[220] *See, e.g.,* Jing Nanxiang, *supra* note 209; Swaine, *supra* note 212, at 9.

[221] *Compare, e.g.,* Andrey Krutskikh & Anatoly Streltsov, *International Law and the Problem of International Information Security*, 60 Int'l Aff. 64 (2014), *with, e.g.,* Eichensehr, *supra* note 166.

[222] Tallinn Manual on the International Law Applicable to Cyber Warfare (Michael N. Schmitt ed., 2013) [hereinafter Tallinn Manual].

Tallinn Manual process was funded, hosted, and facilitated by the NATO Cooperative Cyber Defence Centre of Excellence.[223] But the introduction stresses that it is an expert-driven product, rather than a NATO or NATO-endorsed document:

> It is essential to understand that the Tallinn Manual is not an official document, but is only the product of a group of independent experts acting solely in their personal capacity. The Manual does not represent the views of the NATO CCD COE, its sponsoring nations, or NATO. In particular, it is not meant to reflect NATO doctrine. Nor does it reflect the position of any organization or State represented by observers.[224]

Yet the resulting document was criticized by commentators from some non-Western states, like Russia, for adopting positions that largely accorded with those of major NATO states, such as the United States.[225] To discredit the effort as one-sided and political, leading Russian commentators took to referring to the group as the "NATO experts" instead of "independent experts."[226]

According to the *Manual*, the members of the International Group of Experts were "carefully selected to include legal practitioners, academics, and technical experts" who were knowledgeable about cyber issues.[227] But the group was far from diverse, geographically or geopolitically.[228] One commentator described the legal experts involved as having "distinctly American and Old European backgrounds,"[229] and another noted the complete absence of experts from former Warsaw Pact states, even though the project was based in Tallinn.[230] Not only did all of the *Tallinn Manual*'s drafters, technical experts, observers, and peer reviewers hail from the United States, Western Europe, or Australia, but also the *Manual* relied extensively on national military manuals from a handful of Western states (most notably Canada, Germany, the United Kingdom, and the United

---

[223] *See Tallinn Manual 2.0 to Be Completed in 2016*, NATO COOPERATIVE CYBER DEFENCE CTR. EXCELLENCE, Oct. 9, 2015, https://ccdcoe.org/tallinn-manual-20-be-completed-2016.html.

[224] TALLINN MANUAL, *supra* note 222, at 23.

[225] Elena Chernenko, *Russia Warns Against NATO Document Legitimizing Cyberwars*, RUSS. BEYOND HEADLINES, May 29, 2013 ("The Tallinn Manual met with a highly positive reaction in the West, with many American experts noting that its key ideas reflect Washington's view that no new laws need to be created for cyberspace. The Russian authorities—especially the military—have taken a very guarded view of the Tallinn Manual. Moscow thinks its publication marks a step toward legitimizing the concept of cyberwars.").

[226] Elena Chernenko (Елена Черненко), Виртуальный фронт [Virtual Front], 20 KOMMERSANT-VLAST 11 (May 27, 2013), http://www.kommersant.ru/doc/2193838; Krutskikh & Streltsov, *supra* note 221, at 75.

[227] TALLINN MANUAL, *supra* note 222, at 9.

[228] Chernenko, *supra* note 226 (referring to the criticism that the essential flaw in the drafting of the *Tallinn Manual* was that it did not include representatives of a number of key non-NATO states and therefore it cannot claim to be universal); Ashley Deeks, *Tallinn 2.0 and a Chinese View on the Tallinn Process*, LAWFARE, May 31, 2015, https://www.lawfareblog.com/tallinn-20-and-chinese-view-tallinn-process (summarizing the position of Huang ZhiXiong, a professor at Wuhan University, who "bemoaned the purely Western perspective brought to the drafting of Tallinn 1.0, which failed to include non-Western states such as China or Russia").

[229] Lauri Mälksoo, *The Tallinn Manual as an International Event*, DIPLOMAATIA, Aug. 2013 (book review).

[230] Robert Clark, *The Cybersecurity Canon: Tallinn Manual on the International Law Applicable to Cyber Warfare*, PALO ALTO NETWORKS, July 9, 2015 (book review).

States).[231] Consequently, the views expressed did not always clearly reflect an international consensus, such as the *Tallinn Manual*'s conclusion that the current laws on the use of force and international humanitarian law applied to cyber acts, despite China and Russia's lack of agreement with this position at the time.[232]

One reason for the lack of diversity in the composition of *Tallinn 1.0* was that the organizers originally viewed themselves as producing an academic product and did not expect the level of influence, and concomitant level of scrutiny, that the work received. Still, in light of these developments, the organizers of *Tallinn 2.0* ensured that the group was more diverse the second time around by including representatives from China, Thailand, and Belarus, among others.[233] The drafters of *Tallinn 2.0* have presented multiple versions to meetings of states in which their feedback was sought.[234] By adopting this process, the group is attempting to be both more representative and more responsive to feedback from a wide array of states. Nonetheless, the divisions that have surfaced between Western and non-Western states on cybersecurity in general, and on the *Tallinn Manual* in particular, are emblematic of some of the differences that occur more generally in the divisible college of international lawyers.

At the time of writing, *Tallinn 2.0* was yet to be launched. But a furor had developed in the United States about Russia's use of cyber technology to procure and spread materials from the Democratic National Committee in an effort to influence the US election.[235] These developments only reinforce how important cybersecurity is and how divided and adversarial some of the key states in this area have become. How this issue will move forward once Trump assumes the presidency is anyone's guess. But in seeking to understand and make progress on this issue, it will be important for international lawyers to be fully cognizant of the approaches of multiple, unlike-minded states, whether they agree with their approaches or not.

C. CHALLENGING INTERPRETATIONS: FREEDOM OF THE SEAS

In addition to constraining Western agendas and pursuing their own agendas, China and Russia sometimes work separately to challenge specific interpretations of international law rules. The debate between China and the United States over the principle of freedom of navigation serves as a good example. The United States, as the preeminent maritime power, has long supported an expansive approach to the principle of freedom of the seas, which refers to the rights, freedoms, and uses of the sea and airspace that are guaranteed to all nations under international law. As China has grown in power, it has become a forceful proponent of the right of the coastal state to regulate the activities of foreign

[231] *See* Kristen E. Eichensehr, Book Review, 108 AM. J. INT'L L. 585, 585 (2014) (reviewing the *Tallinn Manual*).
[232] *See id.* at 588.
[233] E-mails on file from organizers of *Tallinn 1.0* and *Tallinn 2.0*.
[234] *Id.*
[235] Eric Lipton, David E. Sanger, & Scott Shane, *The Perfect Weapon: How Russian Cyberpower Invaded the U.S.*, N.Y. TIMES, Dec. 13, 2016; Sam Thielman, *FBI and Homeland Security Detail Russian Hacking Campaign in New Report*, GUARDIAN, Dec. 29, 2016.

military forces operating within its exclusive economic zone (EEZ) and territorial sea. Both sides view their interpretation as essential to protecting their national security interests and, in China's case, its territorial integrity. This dispute has also stood at the center of a series of high-profile incidents between Chinese and US ships and aircraft in these zones.[236]

A state's territory includes its territorial sea, which extends twelve nautical miles from its land territory, and a state enjoys wide powers to regulate activities in this zone.[237] The state also has certain rights to regulate activities in its EEZ, which extends up to two hundred nautical miles from its land territory.[238] EEZs were established under the UN Convention on the Law of the Sea (UNCLOS), to which China is a party but which the United States has signed but failed to ratify.[239] The United States has long promoted a broad understanding of freedom of the seas, arguing that the world's seas should be understood as a global commons in which ships from all states may sail. China, by contrast, views the operation of military ships and aircraft within a coastal state's EEZ and territorial sea as involving an unjustified infringement on state sovereignty and a risk to national security. This dispute has become stark in the two states' approach to freedom of navigation in China's nearby seas.

The United States argues that UNCLOS gives coastal states the right to regulate economic activities in their EEZ, such as fishing, exploring for oil, and conducting "marine scientific research," but that it does not give them the right to regulate foreign military ships and aircraft in the EEZ beyond the state's territorial waters. This argument applies to all military uses, as well as military and hydrographic surveying. On this view, the EEZ was established for the sole purpose of giving coastal states greater control over resources, not to confer any additional right to assert national security interests. China, however, contends that UNCLOS entitles coastal states to regulate economic activities and foreign military activities in their EEZs. China focuses on the requirement in UNCLOS that activities be conducted for "peaceful purposes," which it says military uses offend, and the need for activities in the EEZ to take place with "due regard" for the rights of coastal states, which include protecting their security interests. Moreover, China interprets "marine scientific research," which is not defined by UNCLOS, as not being limited to regulating resource-related research.[240]

Although these debates are styled as concerning international law, they reflect much deeper national and security interests of both states.[241] The United States aims at ensuring

---

[236] For background, see Peter Dutton, *Introduction* to MILITARY ACTIVITIES IN THE EEZ: A U.S.-CHINA DIALOGUE ON SECURITY AND INTERNATIONAL LAW IN THE MARITIME COMMONS 1, 3 (Peter Dutton ed., 2010).

[237] United Nations Convention on the Law of the Sea, art. 2, Dec. 10, 1982, 1833 U.N.T.S. 397.

[238] *Id.*, arts. 55–75.

[239] *See* Division for Ocean Aff. & L. Sea, Chronological Lists of Ratifications of, Accessions and Successions to the Convention and the Related Agreements, http://www.un.org/depts/los/reference_files/chronological_lists_of_ratifications.htm (last updated Feb. 3, 2017).

[240] For examples of these arguments, see sources cited *infra* note 250.

[241] *See* Ramses Amer & Li Jianwei, *China and US Views on Military Vessel Rights in the EEZ Is More Than a Legal Matter?*, CHINA US FOCUS, Aug. 10, 2011.

that its military ships and aircraft can operate freely in the EEZ, which enables it to exercise its military strength more effectively than if it had to project its military power from more than two hundred miles offshore. Freedom of navigation also permits it to ensure that commercial vessels can travel freely through these waters, which is a vital concern given the volume of trade that passes through these seas. The United States is particularly concerned to guarantee these freedoms in China's near seas to keep China's rising military power in check. But it also worries about admitting a precedent that might affect its ability to operate freely in the EEZ in other areas of the world, including the western Pacific, the Persian Gulf, and the Mediterranean Sea. By contrast, as a weaker maritime power than the United States, and with security interests in fewer places around the globe, at least to date, China is less concerned about ensuring freedom of the seas in other states' EEZs. Instead, China focuses primarily on outside interference in its own EEZ, which it views as an unwelcome intrusion into its domestic security. Consistently with its aim to become the dominant regional power, China views its EEZ as areas in which national maritime power, rather than international maritime power, should dominate.[242] The ultimate fate of Taiwan also hovers in the background of these debates.

These opposing perspectives have led to a series of clashes between Chinese and US ships and aircraft in China's EEZ and adjacent airspace. These include incidents in 2001, 2002, and 2009, in which Chinese ships and aircraft confronted the US naval ships Bowditch, Impeccable, and Victorious, which were conducting survey and surveillance operations in China's EEZ; a collision in 2001 between a Chinese fighter and a US Navy EP-3 electronic surveillance aircraft, which led to the death of the Chinese pilot; a confrontation in 2013 between a Chinese Navy ship and the US naval ship Cowpens; the interception in 2014 by a Chinese fighter of a US Navy P-8 maritime patrol aircraft; and the approach in 2016 by Chinese fighters within fifty feet of a US Navy EP-3 electronic surveillance aircraft.[243] The United States routinely complains about China's illegal actions, aggressive approach, and unsafe maneuvers. China meanwhile objects that US ships and aircraft are violating international law by infringing upon its sovereign rights and national security interests.[244] These interactions are dangerous in themselves and are considered a potential flashpoint for violent confrontation between these two great powers.

Although this matter is commonly discussed as a debate between the United States and China, other states have lined up on either side of the divide. The US position can generally be summed up as "[t]he United States, *like most other countries*, believes that coastal states under UNCLOS have the right to regulate economic activities in their EEZs, but do not have the right to regulate foreign military activities in their EEZs."[245] But it is rare to find a list of these states or an explanation of the basis for determining their support.

---

[242] Robert E. Kelly, *What Would Chinese Hegemony Look Like?*, DIPLOMAT, Feb. 10, 2014; Jim Talent, *The Equilibrium of East Asia*, NAT'L REV., Dec. 5, 2013.

[243] O'ROURKE, *supra* note 41, at 12.

[244] For a discussion of the different narratives, see Alex G. Oude Elferink, *Arguing International Law in the South China Sea Disputes: The Haiyang Shiyou 981 and USS Lassen Incidents and the* Philippines v. China *Arbitration*, 31 INT'L J. MARINE & COASTAL L. 205 (2016).

[245] O'ROURKE, *supra* note 41, at 30 (emphasis added).

At the time of ratifying UNCLOS, Brazil, Bangladesh, Cape Verde, Malaysia, India, and Pakistan made declarations that coastal state consent was required before a foreign ship could conduct military activities in its EEZ, whereas Italy, Germany, the Netherlands, and the United Kingdom disputed these interpretations.[246] Since then, the US Navy has acknowledged that at least twenty-seven states have imposed restrictions on foreign navies' operations in their EEZs that do not conform with America's approach, including many states from the Asia-Pacific region: Bangladesh, Brazil, Burma, Cambodia, Cape Verde, China, Egypt, Haiti, India, Iran, Kenya, Malaysia, the Maldives, Mauritius, North Korea, Pakistan, Portugal, Saudi Arabia, Somalia, Sri Lanka, Sudan, Syria, Thailand, the United Arab Emirates, Uruguay, Venezuela, and Vietnam.[247]

US and Chinese international lawyers and academics often line up with the positions of their respective governments.[248] Recognizing that this divide resulted in two separate debates, as two communities of international lawyers worked from distinct assumptions and reached diverse conclusions, the US Naval War College hosted a group of international lawyers and academics from both states to explore these divergent approaches.[249] The collection of essays arising from the meeting manifested this divide. On the substantive issue, the US international lawyers all supported the United States interpretation of permissible activities in the EEZ, whereas the Chinese international lawyers all advanced the Chinese view.[250] As the author of the concluding chapter, international politics professor Alan Wachman, noted:

[E]fforts by American and Chinese commentators to convince each other of views they proffer as unassailable have, thus far, failed. Indeed, Americans and Chinese advocates frequently "talk past" one another. Where the EEZ is concerned, statesmen, scholars, soldiers, and other commentators advance assertions that flow from premises that are simply not shared by nationals in the other state.[251]

---

[246] *See* Division for Ocean Aff. & L. Sea, Declarations and Statements, http://www.un.org/depts/los/convention_ agreements/convention_declarations.htm (last updated Oct. 29, 2013).

[247] O'ROURKE, *supra* note 41, at 11; *see also* Tim Stephens & Donald R. Rothwell, *Marine Scientific Research, in* THE OXFORD HANDBOOK OF THE LAW OF THE SEA 559, 571 (Donald R. Rothwell, Alex G. Oude Elferink, Tim Stephens, & Karen N. Scott eds., 2015).

[248] For a striking example, see, for example, Raul Pedrozo, *Preserving Navigational Rights and Freedoms: The Right to Conduct Military Exercises in China's Exclusive Economic Zone,* 9 CHINESE J. INT'L L. 9 (2010); Zhang Haiwen, *Is It Safeguarding the Freedom of Navigation or Maritime Hegemony of the United States?—Comments on Raul Pedrozo's Article on Military Activities in the EEZ, id.* 31.

[249] *See* MILITARY ACTIVITIES IN THE EEZ, *supra* note 236.

[250] For examples of these conflicting approaches, see Peng Guangqian, *China's Maritime Rights and Interests, in* MILITARY ACTIVITIES IN THE EEZ, *supra* note 236, at 15; Xue Guifang (Julia), *Surveys and Research Activities in the EEZ: Issues and Prospects, in id.* at 89; Wu Jilu, *The Concept of Marine Scientific Research, in id.* at 65; James S. Kraska, *Resources Rights and Environmental Protection in the Exclusive Economic Zone: The Functional Approach to Naval Operations, in id.* at 75; Raul (Pete) Pedrozo, *Coastal State Jurisdiction over Marine Data Collection in the Exclusive Economic Zone: U.S. Views, in id.* at 23; Andrew S. Williams, *Aerial Reconnaissance by Military Aircraft in the Exclusive Economic Zone, in id.* at 49; Yu Zhirong, *Jurisprudential Analysis of the U.S. Navy's Military Surveys in the Exclusive Economic Zones of Coastal Countries, in id.* at 37.

[251] Alan M. Wachman, *Playing by or Playing with the Rules of UNCLOS?, in* MILITARY ACTIVITIES IN THE EEZ, *supra* note 236, at 107, 111.

Both states and sets of lawyers have worked from the assumption that there is one global system of international law, but each has struggled to ensure that the international norms reflect their preferred values.[252]

In keeping with earlier observations about how strongly Chinese international lawyers have propounded China's interests in the *South China Sea* arbitration, Peter Dutton noted that in the EEZ context "China has also mobilized its lawyers" and its "international-law specialists have become adjunct soldiers in China's legal campaign to challenge the dominant, access-oriented norms at sea, especially for military freedoms of navigation in the exclusive economic zone."[253] Albeit an insightful observation about the Chinese, and one that has played out in other disputes like the *South China Sea* arbitration considered in Chapter 5, the comment betrays a lack of insight into how the Chinese might view the US international lawyers. Indeed, three of the US international lawyers who write most often on disputes about this issue are Dutton, Raul (Pete) Pedrozo, and James Kraska, who all contributed to the collection.[254] Each of these academics holds a position at the US Naval War College, two of them formerly worked for the US Navy, and one was the formerly the legal adviser to the US Joint Chiefs of Staff.[255] One could well imagine China's viewing these US international lawyers as "adjunct soldiers" in America's legal campaign to maintain the access-oriented norms at sea, especially for military freedom of navigation in the exclusive economic zone.

Even if Chinese and US international lawyers cannot agree on how to approach the right of foreign military forces to operate in the EEZ, it behooves them to understand each other's perspectives and to see how the same actions might be viewed through other eyes. This was the point made by the concluding author of the study, Professor Wachman of the Fletcher School of Law and Diplomacy, Tufts University, who specialized in East Asian politics and Sino-American relations and had formerly been the co-director of the Johns Hopkins University–Nanjing University Center for Chinese and American Studies in China and president of the China Institute in America.[256] As he explained:

> Americans have become so habituated to unfettered operation in the Pacific that few question the legitimacy or ethical propriety of doing so. Americans on both sides of the ideological divide seem to support, without reflection, the notion of this entitlement. Americans may assume that such dominance is self-evidently in the interests

---

[252] *Id.* at 115.
[253] Dutton, *Introduction, supra* note 236, at 1, 3.
[254] *See, e.g.,* Peter A. Dutton, *Caelum Liberam: Air Defense Identification Zones Outside Sovereign Airspace,* 103 Am. J. Int'l L. 9 (2009); Peter Dutton & John Garofano, *China Undermines Maritime Laws,* Far E. Econ. Rev. 44 (2009); Kraska, *supra* note 250, at 75; Pedrozo, *supra* note 250, at 23; Raul Pedrozo, *Military Activities in and over the Exclusive Economic Zone, in* Freedom of Seas, Passage Rights and the 1982 Law of the Sea Convention 241 (M.H. Nordquist, Tommy Koh, & John Norton Moore eds., 2009); Raul Pedrozo, *Close Encounters at Sea, The USNS Impeccable Incident,* 62 Naval War C. Rev. 101 (2009); Pedrozo, *supra* note 248; James Kraska, *Commentary: Defend Freedom of Navigation,* Def. News, June 8, 2015.
[255] *About the Contributors, in* Military Activities in the EEZ, *supra* note 236, at 123–24.
[256] *Alan M. Wachman,* Wikipedia, https://en.wikipedia.org/wiki/Alan_M._Wachman (last modified Jan. 26, 2017 3:39 AM).

of other states because the United States defends the "global commons." One consequence is that Americans may refrain from reflecting on how the U.S. naval presence
appears in the eyes of the PRC.[257]

From China's perspective, the US naval presence in the western Pacific is a threat to
Chinese national security and an example of Western hegemony. Claims to the importance of ensuring freedom of navigation are likely to be perceived by Chinese readers as
"self-serving justifications for the sustenance of American primacy."[258]

An important element in finding out if agreement can be reached, or a compromise
effected, is for each side to put itself in the shoes of the other so that it can appreciate its
particular perspective and interests. Thus, as Dutton explained, one of the key advantages
of the workshop was that it gave the lawyers from each side an extraordinary level of
insight into the perspective of the other and, in seeing the "nature and source of friction
more clearly—even military activities in the EEZ through the lenses of the other's eyes—
perhaps wise minds on both sides will be able to divine cooperative paths to peace and
security" in the Asia-Pacific region going forward.[259] Taking this sort of a comparative
approach not only enhances knowledge of the other, but also enables international lawyers to look more critically at their state's own position and to become more aware of how
some arguments and actions might be viewed differently by those with other perspectives.[260] It is to this issue—the importance of seeing international law and international
issues through the eyes of others—to which the conclusion now turns.

---

[257] Wachman, *supra* note 251, at 114.

[258] *Id.*

[259] DUTTON, *supra* note 236, at 1, 3, 12–13.

[260] *See* Max Fisher, *Obama, Acknowledging U.S. Misdeeds Abroad, Quietly Reframes American Power*, N.Y. TIMES,
Sept. 7, 2016 (discussing the way that US foreign policy is viewed very differently by Americans and non-
Americans, including US allies).

Conclusion

I BEGAN THIS project by seeking to change the question from the commonly asked, Is international law law?, to the less frequently analyzed, Is international law international? At times, however, this project made me wonder whether the two questions are inextricably linked. If international lawyers in diverse places view and deal with international law differently, and these differences subsist either consciously or unconsciously, does that mean that international law is not law? If one lays bare some of the patterns of dominance within the field and analyzes how shifting geopolitical power might disrupt these dynamics, how can one separate international law from international politics? I do not have good answers to these questions.

What I do have is a different understanding of my field and my relationship to it. International law aspires to be a universal field, but it is also, and inevitably, a deeply human product. No international lawyer can understand all aspects of the field from all viewpoints, myself included. We are all shaped by our experiences, interests, and vantage points. The best that international lawyers can do is to attempt to become conscious of some of the frames that shape their understandings of and approaches to the field and be aware of how these might be similar to and different from those of others. Consciously assuming a comparative international law approach may help international lawyers to look at their field through different eyes and from different perspectives, enabling them to understand others more fully and to critique themselves and their own state more perceptively.[1]

---

[1] Anne van Aaken, *Emerging from Our Frames and Narratives: Understanding the World Through Altered Eyes*, EJIL: *TALK!* (Dec. 23, 2014).

Is International Law International? Anthea Roberts.
© Anthea Roberts 2017. Published 2017 by Oxford University Press.

This study has examined some of the problems facing the world today through the lens of international law and those who practice, study, and teach it. It is unclear where the global condition is heading and many questions remain. Will the United States under President Trump seek to undermine the international liberal world order that it helped to construct? Will the European Union and the United Kingdom survive rising nationalist sentiments and economic strains without changing their political form? Will China step up to play a more significant role on the international stage, particularly in relation to areas like international economic law and interational environmental law? How will relations between Russia and the United States and Europe develop, or between Western states and Iran and North Korea? What role will other emerging powers play in this story, such as Brazil and India? What will the future hold for the Middle East? And will potential existential threats, like climate change and nuclear proliferation, be managed effectively?

No one can be certain of the answers to these questions. What is clear, however, is that some of the patterns of difference and dominance that have defined the international legal field to date are experiencing significant disruptions. If international law is no longer simply decided by the West and exported to the rest, its content and structure will change, making it more incumbent on international lawyers to understand the approaches and interests of a broader set of unlike-minded states. To do so, international lawyers will need to expand their networks and sources to encompass a more diverse range of perspectives and materials than has often taken place within the divisible college to date.

Yet domestic sentiment in many states is moving in the opposite direction. In a growing number of Western states, populism has challenged globalism and nationalist and anti-immigration rhetoric is on the rise. Part of the explanation lies in economics. Globalization has raised prosperity throughout much of the world, but the poor and working classes in the United States and some other Western states have been, or have felt, left behind in comparative terms.[2] Some politicians blame other countries, like President Trump who claimed that China and Mexico had been "raping" and "killing" the United States with unfair trade deals.[3] Others blame the top one percent for disproportionately reaping the rewards of an increasingly globalized economy.[4]

Psychological and cultural factors also play a role in the antiglobalization revolt. Some commentators point to the appeal of authoritarianism to help explain Trump's rise.[5] Individuals with authoritarian tendencies tend to feel unsettled by social change and to draw firm lines between their ingroup (to whom they express loyalty) and outsiders (whom they view as a threat). When events occur that trigger their fears, like the rapid

[2] *Shooting an Elephant*, ECONOMIST, Sept. 17, 2016; Luke Kawa, *Get Ready to See This Globalization "Elephant Chart" Over and Over Again*, BLOOMBERG MARKETS, June 27, 2016; Andrew Walker, *Globalisation: Where on the Elephant Are You?*, BBC NEWS, Oct. 5, 2016.

[3] Dan Primack, *Is Donald Trump Right That Mexico Is "Killing Us" on Trade?*, FORTUNE, Aug. 10, 2015; Jeremy Diamond, *Trump: "We Can't Continue to Allow China to Rape Our Country,"* CNN, May 2, 2016.

[4] Bernie Sanders, *Democrats Need to Wake Up*, N.Y. TIMES, June 28, 2016.

[5] Jonathan Haidt, *When and Why Nationalism Beats Globalism*, AM. INT., July 10, 2016.

social and economic changes that accompanied the rise of high globalization in the 1990s and 2000s, they are likely to react by electing strongman leaders who promise to be tough on immigration and national security. Other commentators point to cultural factors in explaining the pushback, particularly as the votes in favor of Trump and Brexit were disproportionately cast by older, less-educated, white, male voters who likely felt that the changes that had occurred in the last generation had challenged and degraded their economic and social status relative to other groups.[6]

The resulting struggle between "globalists" and "nationalists" has led social psychologist Jonathan Haidt to suggest that the thorniest question for states after 2016 may be:

> How do we reap the gains of global cooperation in trade, culture, education, human rights, and environmental protection while respecting—rather than diluting or crushing—the world's many local, national, and other "parochial" identities, each with its own traditions and moral order? In what kind of world can globalists and nationalists live together in peace?[7]

International lawyers need to be sensitive to these dynamics. By their nature, international lawyers are part of two communities: a transnational community and a national one. If international lawyers spend too much time connecting with their transnational colleagues, they risk becoming disconnected from the concerns and perspectives of their fellow citizens, including those who are apathetic about or hostile to international law and globalization. But if they spend too much time focusing on their national context and catering to parochial sentiments, they risk forgoing the benefits of connecting with citizens of other states and seeing the world and international law through others' eyes.

International lawyers are not "abstract universals" but, instead, are both "universal and particular at the same time, speaking a shared language but doing that from their own, localizable standpoint."[8] Rather than seek to find some Archimedian "international" midpoint, international lawyers might imagine their role as being to pass back and forth between the national and the transnational to facilitate interaction and understanding between the two.[9] What the year 2016 has demonstrated is that stark divisions operate not only between states but also within states, and it behooves international lawyers to be conscious of both. If international lawyers operate in silos, either domestically or transnationally, they risk failing to connect with, and understand the perspectives of, those coming from diverse backgrounds and holding diverse perspectives.

In seeking to fathom and move between the national and the transnational, international lawyers must also be mindful of the way that states' identities and interests change over time. If there are two macro stories that can be told about changes in the

---

[6] Ronald F. Inglehart and Pippa Norris, *Trump, Brexit, and the Rise of Populism: Economic Have-Nots and Cultural Backlash*, Faculty Research Working Paper Series, Harvard Kennedy School, August 2016, https://papers.ssrn.com/sol3/papers.cfm?abstract_id=2818659.

[7] *Id.*

[8] Martti Koskenniemi, *The Case for Comparative International Law*, 2009 FINNISH Y.B. INT'L L. 1, 4.

[9] *Id.*

international system in the last few decades, they would be stories of rising economic inequality within states and rising economic equality among states.[10] Both stories are likely to lead to changes in domestic political preferences and shifts in geopolitical power. In terms of rising domestic inequality, the United States has long heralded itself as a bastion of democracy and as a place of strong social mobility in line with the American dream. However, growing economic inequality within the United States has resulted in a hollowing out of its middle class and lower levels of social mobility than in Europe.[11] Concerns are also increasingly expressed that the United States is more democratic in form than in substance given that growing role of money in US politics and the vastly greater responsiveness of political representatives to the interests of wealthy voters compared to lower and middle class ones.[12]

In terms of rising equality among states, China has undergone enormous transitions in the last few centuries and decades, from its time as the most powerful state in its region during the Middle Kingdom period, to its fall and subordination through its century of humiliation, to its return to great-power status following its entry into the globalized economy. Under the leadership of President Xi Jinping, China appears to be both stepping up its engagement on the international stage, at least with respect to some issues like international economic law, international environmental law, and peacekeeping, and becoming more repressive at home.[13] The United States has enjoyed unprecedented power since World War II and has long advocated a Western, liberal conception of the world order but is now having to contend with a loss of heft and prestige internationally and the rise of nonliberal, more nationalist sentiments domestically.[14]

As the power balance between these states changes, and as their internal identities shift, international lawyers may find that the visions of the law they articulate will come closer together in some respects (for example, on the significance of state sovereignty and on the diminished importance of promoting liberalism abroad) and veer further apart in others (for example, on the benefits of international trade and how best to respond to climate change).[15] We have already seen in some fields, like the investment treaty sphere, that the interests of the United States (formerly, primarily a capital exporter) and China (formerly, primarily a capital importer) shifted considerably over time as their identities changed to become dual capital-importers and capital-exporters. As a result, the investment treaty policies of these two states have moved markedly closer in the 2000s. One might expect similar developments with respect to other issues, such as extraterritorial jurisdiction and state sovereignty, when the realization by rising and falling great powers that they have significant interests on both sides of an issue may temper their tendency to embrace extreme positions.

---

[10] Branko Milanovic, Global Inequality: A New Approach for the Age of Globalization (2016).
[11] James Surowiecki, *The Mobility Myth*, New Yorker, Mar. 3, 2016.
[12] Martin Gilens & Benjamin I. Page, *Testing Theories of American Politics: Elites, Interest Groups, and Average Citizens*, 12 Persp. on Pol. 564 (2014).
[13] James Fallows, *China's Great Leap Backwards*, Atlantic, Dec. 2016.
[14] Matthew Keating, *The Fall of Liberalism?*, Harv. Pol. Rev., Dec. 31, 2016.
[15] Stephen L. Carter, *Trump and the Fall of Liberalism*, Bloomberg View, Nov. 11, 2016; Roger Cohen, *The Death of Liberalism*, N.Y. Times, Apr. 14, 2016; Stephen M. Walt, *The Collapse of the Liberal World Order*, Foreign Pol'y, June 26, 2016.

As states' identities, interests and relative power change, so too will international law. International law is unlikely ever to be fully "international." For the foreseeable future, it will be caught between the ideal of Esperanto and the reality of both multilingualism and English as the lingua franca. My hope is that, by taking a comparative international law approach, international lawyers will become more humble, open, and reflexive in their engagement with international law and more conscious of the field's contingency and capacity to change. Comparativism challenges international lawyers to see the world through the eyes of others instead of just accepting their own self-reinforcing version of the truth. It also encourages international lawyers to build bridges between different communities through civil and respectful dialogue and exchange—something that is crucial in this age of growing political polarization and increasingly hostile political debate. If 2016 has taught international lawyers any lessons, it is the importance of recognizing and seeking to understand the perspectives and experiences of those coming from diverse backgrounds. One might not always like what those in other communities have to say and one may view their values as a threat to one's own. But failing to listen and engage is dangerous in its own right and may lead to a stronger backlash in the longer term. This lesson is an important one to employ both within, and among, different states.

Academics Included in the Study

After identifying the five elite law schools in China, France, Russia, the United Kingdom, and the United States in accordance with the method described in Chapter 2, I added five elite law schools from Australia in order to look for certain core-periphery dynamics between the United Kingdom and its ex-colony, Australia. I then had to identify which "international law" academics to include in the study from these universities.

I included only regular faculty members who were tenured or on a tenure track. In some states, this meant including lecturers, senior lecturers, readers, and professors. In others, it meant assistant professors, associate professors, and professors. I did not include clinical, adjunct, or visiting faculty members. Some legal academies internationalize themselves by relying on adjuncts or foreign visitors, but I wanted to determine the level of internationalization of the core faculty members because adjuncts and visitors are often much less integrated into the general faculty than regular appointees.

Out of these faculty members, I created a panel selection that awarded points based on various indicia that might indicate whether someone was an international law academic. I wanted to rely on publicly available information only, with a cutoff date of the end of 2013 as I began the study in 2014. I needed to identify a range of criteria that would work, in the aggregate, across a variety of legal academies accounting for differences such as publishing preferences and how much information is available on university websites. The criteria I adopted were:

1. Did the academic identify himself or herself in his or her university profile as having a specialty or research interest in international law or public international law?
2. Did the academic identify as having a specialty or research interest in a sub-field of international law, e.g., international human rights, international trade,

Is International Law International? Anthea Roberts.
© Anthea Roberts 2017. Published 2017 by Oxford University Press.

international investment, international environment, international criminal law, foreign relations law, and national security?

3. Was the academic listed as teaching international law or public international law?
4. Was the academic listed as teaching a subfield of international law, e.g., international human rights, international trade, international investment, international environment, international criminal law, foreign relations law, and national security?
5. Had the academic published one or more books on international law, foreign relations law, or a subfield of international law?
6. Were more than 25 percent of the academic's articles in journals with the word "international," "transnational," "global," or "world" in the journal name?
7. Were more than 50 percent of the academic's articles in journals with the word "international," "transnational," "global," or "world" in the journal name?

Two people coded every academic separately. I included academics in the study when they scored an average of 3.5 points or higher based on an average of the two coders' results. Again, I do not claim to have included or excluded all of the right academics, but I have no reason to believe that the selection was systematically biased in one direction or another. On the basis of this measure, the data set included between twenty and sixty international law academics from each of the six states studied, totaling 208 academics overall. The full list is reproduced in Table 10 below.

TABLE 10

List of Academics Included in the Study

Country	Institution	Academic
Australia	Australian National University	Anton, Don
Australia	Australian National University	Boreham, Kevin
Australia	Australian National University	Charlesworth, Hilary
Australia	Australian National University	Heathcote, Sarah
Australia	Australian National University	Nasu, Hitoshi
Australia	Australian National University	Rothwell, Don
Australia	Monash University	Boas, Gideon
Australia	Monash University	Castan, Melissa
Australia	Monash University	Debeljak, Julie
Australia	Monash University	Kyriakiakis, Joanna
Australia	Monash University	McBeth, Adam
Australia	Monash University	O'Sullivan, Maria
Australia	Monash University	Waincymer, Jeffrey
Australia	University of New South Wales	Byrnes, Andrew
Australia	University of New South Wales	Davis, Megan
Australia	University of New South Wales	Lixinski, Lucas
Australia	University of New South Wales	McAdam, Jane

Country	Institution	Academic
Australia	University of New South Wales	Michaelsen, Christopher
Australia	University of New South Wales	Rayfuse, Rosemary
Australia	University of New South Wales	Williams, Sarah
Australia	University of Sydney	Baghmooians, Irene
Australia	University of Sydney	Brown, Chester
Australia	University of Sydney	Crawford, Emily
Australia	University of Sydney	Crock, Mary
Australia	University of Sydney	Johns, Fleur
Australia	University of Sydney	Mowbray, Jacqueline
Australia	University of Sydney	Pert, Alison
Australia	University of Sydney	Saul, Ben
Australia	University of Sydney	Stephens, Tim
Australia	University of Melbourne	Duxbury, Alison
Australia	University of Melbourne	Evans, Carolyn
Australia	University of Melbourne	Foster, Michelle
Australia	University of Melbourne	Gover, Kirsty
Australia	University of Melbourne	Heller, Kevin Jon
Australia	University of Melbourne	Kurtz, Jurgen
Australia	University of Melbourne	McCormack, Tim
Australia	University of Melbourne	Mitchell, Andrew
Australia	University of Melbourne	Orford, Anne
Australia	University of Melbourne	Oswald, Bruce
Australia	University of Melbourne	Otto, Dianne
Australia	University of Melbourne	Pahuja, Sundhya
Australia	University of Melbourne	Peel, Jacqueline
Australia	University of Melbourne	Simpson, Gerry
Australia	University of Melbourne	Voon, Tania
Australia	University of Melbourne	Young, Margaret
China	Chinese University of Political Science and Law	Gao Jianjun (高健军)
China	Chinese University of Political Science and Law	Guo Hongyan (郭红岩)
China	Chinese University of Political Science and Law	Jin Zhe (金哲)
China	Chinese University of Political Science and Law	Kong Qingjiang (孔庆江)

(*Continued*)

TABLE 10 (Continued)

Country	Institution	Academic
China	Chinese University of Political Science and Law	Li Juqian (李居迁)
China	Chinese University of Political Science and Law	Liao Minwen (廖敏文)
China	Chinese University of Political Science and Law	Lin Canling (林灿铃)
China	Chinese University of Political Science and Law	Ma Chengyuan (马呈元)
China	Chinese University of Political Science and Law	Mo Shijian (莫世健)
China	Chinese University of Political Science and Law	Shi Xiaoli (史晓丽)
China	Chinese University of Political Science and Law	Zhou Jianhai (周建海)
China	Chinese University of Political Science and Law	Zhu Jiangeng (朱建庚)
China	Chinese University of Political Science and Law	Lan Hua (兰花)
China	Chinese University of Political Science and Law	Jiao Jie (焦杰)
China	Chinese University of Political Science and Law	Cheng Xiaoxia (成晓霞)
China	Chinese University of Political Science and Law	Lan Lan (兰兰)
China	Chinese University of Political Science and Law	Li Qiang (李强)
China	Chinese University of Political Science and Law	Wang Chuanli (王传丽)
China	Chinese University of Political Science and Law	Yang Fan (杨帆)
China	Chinese University of Political Science and Law	Xin Chongyang (辛崇阳)
China	Chinese University of Political Science and Law	Zhang Li (张力)
China	Chinese University of Political Science and Law	Zhang, Liying (张丽英)
China	Chinese University of Political Science and Law	Zhu Lijiang (朱利江)
China	Peking University	Bai Guimei (白桂梅)

Country	Institution	Academic
China	Peking University	Chen Yifeng (陈一峰)
China	Peking University	Gong Renren (龚刃韧)
China	Peking University	Li Ming (李鸣)
China	Peking University	Rao Geping (饶戈平)
China	Peking University	Shao Jingchun (邵景春)
China	Peking University	Song Ying (宋英)
China	Peking University	Wu Zhipan (吴志攀)
China	Peking University	Yi Ping (易平)
China	Peking University	Zhang Xiaojian (张潇剑)
China	Renmin University	Han Liyu (韩立余)
China	Renmin University	Shao Shaping (邵沙平)
China	Renmin University	Yu Jinsong (余劲松)
China	Renmin University	Yu Mincai (余民才)
China	Renmin University	Zhu Wenqi (朱文奇)
China	Tsinghua University	Che Pizhao (车丕照)
China	Tsinghua University	Jia Bing Bing (贾兵兵)
China	Tsinghua University	Li Zhaojie (李兆杰)
China	Tsinghua University	Lv Xiaojie (吕晓杰)
China	Tsinghua University	Yang Guohua (杨国华)
China	Tsinghua University	Zhang Xinjun (张新军)
China	Wuhan University	Feng Jiehan (冯洁菡)
China	Wuhan University	Huang Deming (黄德明)
China	Wuhan University	Huang Zhixiong (黄志雄)
China	Wuhan University	Luo Guoqiang (罗国强)
China	Wuhan University	Qi Tong (漆彤)
China	Wuhan University	Shi Lei (石磊)
China	Wuhan University	Xiao Jun (肖军)
China	Wuhan University	Yang Zewei (杨泽伟)
China	Wuhan University	Yee Sienho (易显河)
China	Wuhan University	Yu Minyou (余敏友)
China	Wuhan University	Zeng Lingliang (曾令良)
China	Wuhan University	Zhang Xianglan (张湘兰)
France	Aix-Marseilles Paul Cézanne	Dubois, Sandrine Maljean
France	Aix-Marseilles Paul Cézanne	Gherari, Habib
France	Aix-Marseilles Paul Cézanne	Kerbrat, Yann
France	Aix-Marseilles Paul Cézanne	Lanfranchi, Marie Pierre
France	Aix-Marseilles Paul Cézanne	Marchi, Jean François

(Continued)

TABLE 10 (Continued)

Country	Institution	Academic
France	Paris I Panthéon Sorbonne	Ascensio, Hervé
France	Paris I Panthéon Sorbonne	Burdeau, Geneviève
France	Paris I Panthéon Sorbonne	Eisemann, P.M.
France	Paris I Panthéon Sorbonne	Fabri, Hélène Ruiz
France	Paris I Panthéon Sorbonne	Jouannet, Emmanuelle
France	Paris I Panthéon Sorbonne	Maddalon, Philippe
France	Paris I Panthéon Sorbonne	Pingel, Isabelle
France	Paris I Panthéon Sorbonne	Sorel, Jean-Marc
France	Paris II Assas	Alland, Denis
France	Paris II Assas	Cahin, Gérard
France	Paris II Assas	Decaux, Emmanuel
France	Paris II Assas	de Frouville, Oliver
France	Paris II Assas	El Boudouhi, Saïda
France	Paris II Assas	Martin-Bidou, Pascale
France	Paris Ouest Nanterre La Défense	Chaumette Vaurs, Anne-Laure
France	Paris Ouest Nanterre La Défense	Chemain, Regis
France	Paris Ouest Nanterre La Défense	Forteau, Mathais
France	Paris Ouest Nanterre La Défense	Pellet, Alain
France	Paris Ouest Nanterre La Défense	Thouvenin, Jean Marc
France	Sciences Po Paris Law School	Perelman, Jeremy
Russia	Higher School of Economic National Research University (primarily at the Diplomatic Academy)	Chernichenko, Stanislav
Russia	Higher School of Economic National Research University	Ganyushkina, Yelena
Russia	Higher School of Economic National Research University	Ivanov, Eduard
Russia	Higher School of Economic National Research University	Romashev, Yuriy
Russia	Higher School of Economic National Research University	Rusinova, Vera
Russia	Kutafin Moscow State University of Law	Anufrieva, Lyudmila
Russia	Kutafin Moscow State University of Law	Bekyashev, Kamil

Country	Institution	Academic
Russia	Kutafin Moscow State University of Law	Sokolova, Natalya
Russia	Kutafin Moscow State University of Law	Volosov, Marlen
Russia	Lomonosov Moscow State University	Glotova, Svetlana
Russia	Lomonosov Moscow State University	Kremnev, Petr
Russia	Moscow State Institute of International Relations	Bekyashev, Damir
Russia	Moscow State Institute of International Relations	Bobylyov, Gennadiy
Russia	Moscow State Institute of International Relations	Glikman, Olga
Russia	Moscow State Institute of International Relations	Ivanov, Dmitriy
Russia	Moscow State Institute of International Relations	Kolosov, Yuriy
Russia	Moscow State Institute of International Relations	Kukushkina, Anna
Russia	Moscow State Institute of International Relations	Maleyev, Yuriy
Russia	Moscow State Institute of International Relations	Robinov, Aleksey
Russia	Moscow State Institute of International Relations	Savaskov, Pavel
Russia	Moscow State Institute of International Relations	Vereina, Larisa
Russia	Moscow State Institute of International Relations	Vylegzhanin, Aleksandr
Russia	Saint-Petersburg State University	Bakhin, Sergey
Russia	Saint-Petersburg State University	Galenskaya, Lyudmila
Russia	Saint-Petersburg State University	Sidorchenko, Viktor
Russia	Saint-Petersburg State University	Talimonchik, Valentina
United Kingdom	London School of Economics	Beyani, Chaloka
United Kingdom	London School of Economics	Chinkin, Christine
United Kingdom	London School of Economics	Hovell, Devika
United Kingdom	London School of Economics	Humphreys, Stephen

(*Continued*)

TABLE 10 (Continued)

Country	Institution	Academic
United Kingdom	London School of Economics	Lang, Andrew
United Kingdom	London School of Economics	Marks, Susan
United Kingdom	London School of Economics/ Columbia University	Roberts, Anthea
United Kingdom	London School of Economics	Salomon, Margot
United Kingdom	University College of London	Guilfoyle, Douglas
United Kingdom	University College of London	Mills, Alex
United Kingdom	University College of London	Paparinskis, Martins
United Kingdom	University College of London	Sands, Philippe
United Kingdom	University College of London	Trapp, Kimberley
United Kingdom	University College of London	Wilde, Ralph
United Kingdom	University of Cambridge	Bartels, Lorand
United Kingdom	University of Cambridge	Crawford, James
United Kingdom	University of Cambridge	Gray, Christine
United Kingdom	University of Cambridge	MacKenzie, Catherine
United Kingdom	University of Cambridge	Nouwen, Sarah
United Kingdom	University of Cambridge	O'Keefe, Roger
United Kingdom	University of Cambridge	Vinuales, Jorge
United Kingdom	University of Cambridge	Waibel, Michael
United Kingdom	University of Cambridge	Weller, Marc
United Kingdom	University of Oxford	Akande, Dapo
United Kingdom	University of Oxford	Ghanea, Nazila
United Kingdom	University of Oxford	Goodwin-Gill, Guy
United Kingdom	University of Oxford	Redgwell, Catherine
United Kingdom	University of Oxford	Sarooshi, Dan
United Kingdom	University of Oxford	Shacknove, Andrew
United Kingdom	University of Oxford	Tzanakopoulos, Antonious
United Kingdom	Kings College London	Hestermeyer, Holger
United Kingdom	Kings College London	Murphy, Cian
United Kingdom	Kings College London	Ortino, Federico
United Kingdom	Kings College London	Schultz, Thomas
United Kingdom	Kings College London	Webb, Philippa
United States	University of Chicago	Ginsburg, Tom
United States	University of Chicago	Posner, Eric
United States	Columbia University	Bradford, Anu
United States	Columbia University	Cleveland, Sarah
United States	Columbia University	Damrosh, Lori
United States	Columbia University	Doyle, Michael

Country	Institution	Academic
United States	Columbia University/European Union Institute	Mavroidis, Petros
United States	Columbia University/London School of Economics	Roberts, Anthea
United States	Columbia University	Waxman, Matthew
United States	Harvard University	Alford, Bill
United States	Harvard University	Blum, Gabriella
United States	Harvard University	Goldsmith, Jack
United States	Harvard University	Kennedy, David
United States	Harvard University	Neuman, Gerald
United States	Harvard University	Wu, Mark
United States	Stanford University	Martinez, Jenny
United States	Yale University	Brilmayer, Lea
United States	Yale University	Hathaway, Oona
United States	Yale University	Koh, Harold
United States	Yale University	Reisman, Michael
United States	Yale University	Stone Sweet, Alec

Scholars Referred to in Select Chinese and Russian International Law Textbooks

TABLE II

List of Scholars Referred to in Three Chinese International Law Textbooks

LIU & CHEN (1998)

Page	Author	Nationality
38	Zhou	China
39	William W. Bishop	US
46	David Harris	UK
50	J. M. Sweeney	US
54	William W. Bishop	US
57	Holborn Law Tutors (a college casebook)	UK
59	Hersch Lauterpacht	UK
63	David Harris	UK
67	J. M. Sweeney	US
71	Max Planck Encyclopedia (no author given)	German publication
74	Max Planck Encyclopedia (no author given)	German publication
77	Max Planck Encyclopedia (no author given)	German publication
80	Hersch Lauterpacht (Wang trans.)	UK (Chinese translation)
84	Max Planck Encyclopedia (no author given)	German publication
87	David Harris	UK

(Continued)

TABLE 11 (Continued)

LIU & CHEN (1998)

Page	Author	Nationality
90	Max Planck Encyclopedia (no author given)	German publication
94	Max Planck Encyclopedia (no author given)	German publication
118	William W. Bishop	US
126	Hersch Lauterpacht (Wang trans.)	UK (Chinese translation)
	Max Planck Encyclopedia (no author given)	German publication
129	Holborn Law Tutors	UK
138	Max Planck Encyclopedia (no author given)	German publication
147	Hersch Lauterpacht	UK
155	Zhou	China
167, 286	James Brown Scott	UK
180	William W. Bishop	US
183	Max Planck Encyclopedia (no author given)	German publication
190	Hersch Lauterpacht (Wang trans.)	UK (Chinese translation)
197	Moira L. McConnell	Canada
206	Max Planck Encyclopedia (no author given)	German publication
210	Gary Knight	US
216	D. M. Johnson	Canada
254	Max Planck Encyclopedia (no author given)	German publication
257	Max Planck Encyclopedia (no author given)	German publication
260	Max Planck Encyclopedia (no author given)	German publication
263	Peter W. Martin	US
272	David Harris	UK
278	Max Planck Encyclopedia (no author given)	German publication
281	Max Planck Encyclopedia (no author given)	German publication
289	Max Planck Encyclopedia (no author given)	German publication
293	Holborn Law Tutors	UK
297	Max Planck Encyclopedia (no author given)	German publication
304	Max Planck Encyclopedia (no author given)	German publication
311	Holborn Law Tutors	UK
348	Louis Henkin	US
350	Max Planck Encyclopedia (no author given)	German publication
357	Lee (Treaties)	China
379	Max Planck Encyclopedia (no author given)	German publication
383	Max Planck Encyclopedia (no author given)	German publication
385	Max Planck Encyclopedia (no author given)	German publication
390	Max Planck Encyclopedia (no author given)	German publication

LIU & CHEN (1998)

Page	Author	Nationality
394	Max Planck Encyclopedia (no author given)	German publication
399	Hersch Lauterpacht	UK
425	Wang (Law Dictionary)	China
447	David Harris	UK
479	William W. Bishop	US
483	Max Planck Encyclopedia (no author given)	German publication
List of References	James Brown Scott	UK
	Manley Ottmer Hudson	US
	Herbert W. Briggs	US
	William W. Bishop	US
	Louis Henkin	US
	David Harris	UK
	Holborn Law Tutors	UK
	Martin Dixon	UK
	J. M. Sweeney	US
	Max Planck Encyclopedia (no author given)	German publication
	Hersch Lauterpacht	UK

BAI & ZHU (2007)

Page	Author	Nationality
4	John Austin	UK
5	Louis Henkin	US
6	Wang	China
7	R. Jennis & A. Watts (Wang trans.)	UK (Chinese translation)
	Ian Brownlie	UK
8, 9	Li (Treaties)	China
10	Wang	China
	Li (Treaties)	China
11	Peter Malanczuk	Canadian/German author who took over a prominent UK international law textbook by Akehurst
13	Chen (Casebook)	China
	Wang	China
	Peter Malanczuk	Canadian/German

(*Continued*)

TABLE 11 (Continued)

BAI & ZHU (2007)

Page	Author	Nationality
27	Wang	China
	Peter Malanczuk	Canadian/German
	Eric Stein	US
45	Chen (Casebook)	China
61	Chen (Casebook)	China
169	Zhou	China
203	Zhu	China
237	Zhu	China
252	Gong	China
283	Li (Treaties)	China
300	C. F. Amerasinghe (Zhu trans.)	UK (Chinese translation)
List of reference sources	R. Jennings & A. Watts (Wang trans.)	UK (Chinese translation)
	Wang	China
	Cheng	China
	Duan	China
	Shao	China
	H. S. Wang	China
	Wang (Introduction of International Law)	China
	Li (Sources of International Law)	China
	S. Y. Liang	China
	Chao (International Aviation Law)	China
	Chen (International Maritime Law)	China
	Li (Treaties)	China
	Rao (The Law of International Institutions)	China
	B. Sen (Zhou trans.)	Indian (Chinese translation)
	Bei & Li (References of International Law)	China
	Ian Brownlie	UK
	Peter Malanczuk	Canadian/German
	J. G. Starke	UK
	Carl Q. Christol (Outer Space)	US
	D. W. Bowett (International Institution)	UK
	I. H. Ph. Diederiks-Verschoor (Air Law)	Netherlands
	Surya P. Sharma (Territorial Acquisition)	Indian
	D. P. O'Connell (The Law of the Sea)	New Zealand

Page	Author	Nationality
4	Hugo Grotius	Netherlands
	Jeremy Bentham	UK
5	Alfred Verdroß (Li trans.)	Austria (Chinese translation)
	Liang	China
8	S. Pufendorf	Germany
	J. Austin	UK
10	New Haven School	US
	Zhou	China
13	Georg Jellinek	Germany
	Georg Wilhelm Friedrich Hegel	Germany
14	H. Kelsen	Austria
	H. Triepel	Germany
20	American Journal of International Law (author unknown)	US
22	Hugo Grotius	Netherlands
24	Jennings & Watts (Wang trans.)	UK (Chinese translation)
	H. G. Schermers	Netherlands
25	Antonio Cassese	Italy
26	Liang	China
28	Antonio Cassese	Italy
29	Zeng	China
31	Zhang (History)	China
34	Liang	China
	Ian Brownlie (Zeng trans.)	UK (Chinese translation)
35	Hugh Thirlway	UK
	Malcolm D. Evans	UK
	Liang	China
36	Ian Brownlie (Zeng trans.)	UK (Chinese translation)
	Wang	China
	Zhou	China
39	Hersch Lauterpacht	UK
42	Bin Cheng	Chinese origin but UK national
47	Arthur Watts	UK
48	Arthur Watts	UK

(Continued)

TABLE 11 (Continued)

LIANG, WANG, & ZENG (2011)

Page	Author	Nationality
55	Vladimir Lenin	Russia
57	Zeng (Sovereignty)	China
64	Antonio Cassese	Italy
66	Those who argue that "states" are the main subject of international law	Various foreign countries (unnamed)
67	Those who argue that "individuals" are the main subject of international law	Various foreign countries (unnamed)
68	Li	China
69	J. G. Starke (Chao trans.)	UK (Chinese translation)
70	Chen	China
71	Chen	China
	Hersch Lauterpacht (Wang trans.)	UK (Chinese translation)
	J. G. Starke (Chao trans.)	UK (Chinese translation)
	Kozhevnikov (Liu trans.)	Russia (Chinese translation)
	Jennings & Watts (Wang trans.)	UK (Chinese translation)
74	Nikolaos Politis (Yuan trans.)	Greece (Chinese translation)
75	Jessup (excerpt from Zhou's textbook)	US (in Chinese)
	Hans Kelsen (Wang trans.)	Austria (Chinese translation)
	Hersch Lauterpacht (Wang trans.)	UK (Chinese translation)
	Jennings & Watts (Wang trans.)	UK (Chinese translation)
	Zhou	China
	Wang	China
	Li	China
78	Wang	China
	Hans Kelsen (Shen trans.)	Austria (Chinese translation)
84	J. G. Starke (Chao trans.)	UK (Chinese translation)
	Zhou	China
85	Zhou	China
	Wang	China
	Jennings & Watts (Wang trans.)	UK (Chinese translation)
	J. G. Starke (Chao trans.)	UK (Chinese translation)
89	Antonio Cassese (Tsai trans.)	Italy (Chinese translation)
102	Vladimir Lenin	Russia

Page	Author	Nationality
122	Tim Hiller (Qu trans.)	UK (Chinese translation)
125	Zhou	China
147	Wei	China
163	Gao, Zhang, & Jia	China
177	Nan	China
183	Henry McMahon	UK
	D. Goedhuis	Netherlands
184	Manfred Lachs	Poland
210	Wang (International Environment Law)	China
	Wang	China
213	Wang (International Environment Law)	China
215	Ved P. Nanda	India
220	Wang (International Environment Law)	China
226	Wang (International Environment Law)	China
237	Li (Nationality Law)	China
239	Li (Nationality Law)	China
242	Zhou	China
243	Zhou	China
249	Wang	China
255	Zhou	China
257	Zhou	China
	Chen	China
263	Wan	China
265	James W. Nickel	US
267	Zhang (Human Rights)	China
268	Paul Shutter	UK
288	Liang	China
293	Liang	China
	D. W. Bowett	UK
296	Liang	China
298	Liang	China
302	Liang	China
304	Liang	China
305	A. LeRoy Bennett	US
308	Liang (UN and China)	China
	Liang	China

(Continued)

TABLE II (Continued)

LIANG, WANG, & ZENG (2011)

Page	Author	Nationality
309	Liang	China
312	Liang	China
314	Liang	China
317	Zhou	China
319	Ludwick Dembinski	Netherlands
349	Li (Treaties)	China
351	Zhou	China
355	Li (Treaties)	China
356	Li (Treaties)	China
358	Li (Treaties)	China
360	Li (Treaties)	China
373	Zeng (WTO Law)	China
390	J. G. Starke (Chao trans.)	UK (Chinese translation)
391	Huang	China
392	J. G. Starke (Chao trans.)	UK (Chinese translation)
429	Charles Rousseau (N. Zhang trans.)	Canada (Chinese translation)
438	He	China

TABLE 12

List of Scholars Referred to in Three Russian International Law Textbooks

KOVALEV & CHERNICHENKO (2008)

Page	Author	Nationality
90	M. M. Boguslavskii	Russian
92	L. Oppenheim	UK
96	N. G. Vilkova	Russian
164	Vattel	Swiss
320	V. V. Komarova	Russian
321	A. F. Nikitin	Russian
321	V. V. Boitsova	Russian
322, 324, 326	N. Iu. Kameneva	Russian
322, 326	L. I. Zakharova	Russian
324	V. A. Tumanov	Russian

KOVALEV & CHERNICHENKO (2008)

Page	Author	Nationality
325	M. S. Bashimov	Kazakhstan/Russian
388	K. A. Bekiashev & M. E. Volosov	Russian
450	M. M. Lebedeva	Russian
	V. G. Baranovskii	Russian
452	R. Schuman	French
453	Iu. V. Shishkov	Russian
	N. N. Livetsev & V. N. Kharlamova	Russian
455	W. Molle	Dutch
457	N. Walter & W. Becker	German
713	A. Iu. Kapustin	Russian
817	F. F. Martens	Russian

IGNATENKO & TIUNOV (2013)

Page	Author	Nationality
26	I. A. Pokrovsky	Russian
33, 37	G. I. Tunkin	Russian
33, 115	V. S. Vereshchetin	Russian
69	V. D. Perevalov	Russian
70	S. B. Krylov	Russian
71	V. V. Durdenevsky	Russian
75, 536	F. F. Martens	Russian
89	Grotius	Dutch
	Bluntschli	Swiss
113	L. A. Modzhorian	Russian
	N. V. Zakharova	Russian
114	E. A. Korovin	Russian
	A. I. Kovler	Russian
	Malcolm Shaw	UK
116, 285	E. Jiménez de Aréchaga	Uruguayan
138, 282	I. I. Lukashuk	Russian
161	A. Y. Skuratova & I. I. Siniakin	Russian
259, 679	T. N. Neshataeva	Russian
403	L. A. Kamarovsky	Russian
	N. N. Poliansky	Russian
	Manley Hudson	US

(*Continued*)

TABLE 12 (Continued)

IGNATENKO & TIUNOV (2013)

Page	Author	Nationality
461	N. I. Marysheva	Russian
502, 503	V. E. Petrovsky	Russian
	Mark T. Clark	US
503	S. S. Park	Korean/US
675	P. E. Nedbailo	Ukrainian
677	E. A. Pushmina	Russian
679	V. V. Panov	Russian
	L. A. Lunts	Russian
700	V. A. Tumanov	Russian

KUZNETSOV & TUZMUKHAMEDOV (2009)

Page	Author	Nationality
1	Iu. A. Baskin	Russian
1	A. Mills	Australian/UK-based
1	L. Kh. Mingazov	Russian
1	V. I. Kuznetsov	Russian
2	J. Bentham	UK
5	T. Aquinas	Italian
5	J. Bodin	French
5	H. Bonet	French
5	G. de Legnano	Italian
5	J. Selden	UK
5	F. Suárez	Spanish
5	F. de Vitoria	Spanish
6	C. van Bynkershoek	Dutch
6	S. Pufendorf	German
6	R. Zouche	UK
9	P. P. Shafirov	Russian
9	E. David	Belgian
9	D. I. Kachenovskii	Russian
9	M. N. Kapustin	Russian
9	P. E. Kazanskii	Russian
9	N. M. Korkunov	Russian
9	M. N. Kapustin	Russian
17	A. Pellet	French
17	R. L. Bobrov	Russian
17	P. Dallier	French

Page	Author	Nationality
17	A. Cassese	Italian
25	V. S. Vereschetin	Russian
37	M. M. Avakov	Russian
37	G. M. Veliaminov	Russian
40	N. A. Ushakov	Russian
67	A. I. Kovler	Russian
67	L. Wildhaber	Swiss
69	R. Geiger	Austrian
69	N. B. Krylov	Russian
73	W. M. Reisman	US
75	G. Abi-Saab	Egyptian/Swiss-based
75	B. Simma	Austrian/German
76	W. Friedmann	US
76	M. I. Lazarev	Russian
76	I. de Lupis	Swedish/UK
77	V. A. Mazov	
77	Ch. Okeke	Nigerian
79	J. Hendry	US
85	G. I. Morozov	Russian
87	K. Wolfke	Polish
90	J. E. Alvarez	US
93	V. I. Margiev	Russian
125	S. Bastid	French
125	D. Bowett	UK
125	E. B. Haas	US
125	S. Rosenne	Israeli
125	A. Sereni	Italian
125	F. Seyersted	Norwegian
125	L. Valki	Hungarian
129	Iu. A. Reshetov	Russian
163	V. V. Gavrilov	Russian
163	B. L. Zimnenko	Russian
163	S. Iu. Marochkin	Russian
165	R. Ago	Italian
165	C. Bergbohm	Estonian
165	M. Gandji	Indian

(Continued)

TABLE 12 (Continued)

KUZNETSOV & TUZMUKHAMEDOV (2009)

Page	Author	Nationality
165	G. W. F. Hegel	German
165	J. Humphrey	Canadian
165	A. Lasson	German
165	M. Wenzel	German
165	P. Zorn	German
166	D. Anzilotti	Italian
166	L. Henkin	US
166	C. Rousseau	French
166	H. Zeidel [G. Seidel]	German
167	A. L. Makovskii	Russian
167	V. A. Vasilenko	Ukrainian
168	O. N. Khletsov	Russian
181	E. M. Ametistov	Russian
182	H. J. Berman	US
197	V. P. Basik	Russian
197	Iu. R. Boiars [Bojārs]	Latvian
197	L. N. Galenskaia	Russian
197	D. Ivanov	Russian
197	O. E. Kutafin	Russian
229	E. A. Lukasheva	Russian
229	G. E. Lukianstev	Russian
229	A. P. Movchan	Russian
229	Ia. A. Ostrovskii	Russian
229	V. A. Kartashkin	Russian
234	R. Cassin	French
235	J. F. Green	US
238	R. Higgins	UK
238	C. Tomuschat	German
239	D. Turk	Slovenian
255	V. P. Popov	Russian
287	R. A. Kalamkarian	Russian
287	Ch. Pinto	Sri Lankan
287	F. Orrego Vicuña	Chilean
305	F. I. Kozhevnikov	Russian
305	R. S. Lee	Chinese
305	C. Peck	Australian

Page	Author	Nationality
305	G. V. Sharmazanashvili	Russian
321	P. B. Stephan	US
339	Iu. G. Demin	Russian
339	B. V. Ganiushkin	Russian
339	S. A. Kuznetsov	Russian
339	Iu. M. Smirnov	Russian
345	A. M. Slaughter	US
365	A. A. Timarenko	Russian
365	D. A. Ursin	Russian
365	O. G. Zaitseva	Russian
399	Iu. G. Barsegov	Russian
399	V. V. Golitsyn	Russian
399	S. A. Gureev	Russian
399	M. L. Lopatin	Russian
399	I. M. Tarasova [I. N. Tarasova]	Russian
399	V. K. Zilanov	Russian
401	C. Campbell-Mohn	US
401	A. N. Vylegzhanin	Russian
404	V. A. Nezabitovskii	Russian
433	R. Barnes	UK
433	Iu. V. Bobrova	Russian
433	M. D. Evans	UK
433	D. Freestone	UK
433	V. N. Gutsuliak	Russian
433	A. A. Kovalev	Russian
433	D. Ong	UK
433	A. S. Skaridov	Russian
436	M. Hayashi	Japanese
451	R. R. Baxter	US
467	V. D. Bordunov	Russian
467	Iu. N. Maleev	Russian
467	A. N. Vereshchagin	Russian
497	A. V. Iakovenko	Russian
497	G. P. Zhukov	Russian
511	D. K. Labin	Russian
511	A. S. Smbatian	Russian

(Continued)

TABLE 12 (Continued)

KUZNETSOV & TUZMUKHAMEDOV (2009)

Page	Author	Nationality
511	V. M. Shumilov	Russian
518	V. M. Koretskii	Russian
519	I. S. Pereterskii	Russian
545	O. S. Kolbasov	Russian
545	E. Iu. Kuzmenko	Russian
545	D. B. Magro [Magraw]	US
545	E. S. Molodtsova	Russian
545	A. S. Timoshenko	Russian
545	S. V. Vinogradov	Russian
545	M. N. Kopylov	Russian
577	E. A. Ivanov	Russian
577	N. I. Kostenko	Russian
577	D. E. Liakhov	Russian
577	V. P. Panov	Russian
577	K. S. Rodionov	Russian
577	Iu. S. Romashev	Russian
607	I. I. Artsibasov	Russian
607	V. A. Batyr	Russian
607	I. I. Kotliarov	Russian
607	S. A. Egorov	Russian
610	L. Doswald-Beck	Swiss
610	J.-M. Henkaerts	Swiss
634	B. Tuzmukhamedov	Russian
657	Iu. Iu. Berestnev	Russian
657	M. M. Biriukov	Russian
657	S. Iu. Kashkin	Russian
657	Iu. B. Kashlev	Russian
657	P. V. Savaskov	Russian
657	V. A. Tumanov	Russian
1, 11	G. S. Starodubtsev	Russian
1, 12, 13, 17, 28, 37, 69, 85, 87, 92, 95, 166	G. I. Tunkin	Russian
1, 17, 166, 287	D. B. Levin	Russian

Page	Author	Nationality
1, 17, 37, 41, 69, 95, 163, 166, 168, 178, 181, 255	I. I. Lukashuk	Russian
1, 17, 66, 166	M. N. Shaw	UK
1, 4	R. Bernhardt	German
1, 9, 95	V. E. Grabar	Russian
125, 164	H. Kelsen	Austrian
125, 164, 229	H. Lauterpacht	UK
125, 166	A. Verdroß	Austrian
129, 287	E. A. Pushmin	Ukrainian
13, 17, 24, 28, 40, 41, 577	V. N. Kudriavtsev	Russian
13, 17, 39, 40, 305	S. B. Krylov	Russian
163, 166, 167, 176, 181, 229	R. A. Müllerson	Estonian
165, 166	H. Triepel	German
165, 229	R. Falk	US
166, 167, 168	E. T. Usenko	Russian
166, 167, 173, 181	N. M. Mironov	Russian
166, 167, 610	I. P. Blishchenko	Russian
17, 166	V. M. Shurshalov	Russian
17, 166, 167	V. G. Butkevich	Ukrainian
17, 37, 40	D. I. Feldman	Russian
17, 37, 41, 77, 129, 163, 166– 68, 197, 229, 255	S. V. Chernichenko	Russian

(*Continued*)

TABLE 12 (Continued)

Page	Author	Nationality
	KUZNETSOV & TUZMUKHAMEDOV (2009)	
17, 37, 46, 52, 129, 163, 165	I. Brownlie	UK
17, 40	V. N. Durdenevskii	Russian
17, 40, 399	N. A. Ushakov	Russian
17, 41, 230, 511	K. A. Bekiashev	Russian
17, 45, 125	L. Oppenheim	UK
17, 66, 87, 129	E. Jiménez de Aréchaga	Uruguayan
229, 287, 305, 657	L. M. Entin	Russian
25, 305	V. S. Vereshchetin	Russian
3, 166	C. C. Hyde	US
3, 17, 129	O. I. Tiunov	Russian
3, 17, 37, 163, 166, 167, 176, 577	G. V. Ignatenko	Russian
305, 399, 401, 433	A. N. Vylegzhanin	Russian
321, 399	B. M. Klimenko	Russian
321, 641	R. M. Timerbaev	Russian
339, 340, 511	K. K. Sandrovskii	Ukrainian
365, 610	A. Kh. Abashidze	Russian
37, 129, 163, 321, 577, 607, 610, 634	B. R. Tuzmukhamedov	Russian
37, 40, 167, 607	G. I. Kurdiukov	Russian
37, 41	N. V. Zakharova	Russian
4, 230, 365, 657	E. S. Krichikova	Russian
4, 85, 230, 255, 497, 657	Iu. M. Kolosov	Russian
40, 365	E. A. Shibaeva	Russian

Tables of Content for International Law Textbooks

TABLE 13

Tables of Content for International Law Textbooks, Casebooks, and Manuals

Name of Book	Title of Chapter [% of Book]
CHINESE BOOKS	
International Law (Bai & Zhu)	Introduction [7.4%]
	States Under International Law [11.1%]
	Individuals Under International Law [6.3%]
	Human Rights Under International Law [11.6%]
	Territories Under International Law [9%]
	International Maritime Law [7.7%]
	International Space Law [5.3%]
	Law of Foreign and Consular Relations [10.6%]
	Treaties [6.3%]
	Law of International Organizations [6.6%]
	Peaceful Settlement of International Disputes [5%]
	International Humanitarian Law [10.3%]
International Law (Liang, Wang, & Zeng)	Nature and Foundation of International Law [6.8%]
	Sources and Codification of International Law [3.4%]
	Basic Principles Under International Law [3.2%]
	Subject of International Law [2.7%]
	States Under International Law [5.9%]
	International Legal Responsibilities [4.1%]

(*Continued*)

TABLE 13 (Continued)

Name of Book	Title of Chapter [% of Book]
	Law of Territories [4.5%]
	Maritime Law [7.7%]
	Space Law [6.1%]
	International Environmental Law [5.4%]
	Individuals Under International Law [6.1%]
	International Human Rights Law [5.6%]
	Law of International Organizations [6.3%]
	Law of Foreign and Consular Relations [4.3%]
	Treaties [6.8%]
	International Economic Law [4.7%]
	Law of International Dispute Settlement [5.9%]
	Law of War [6.1%]
International Law Cases (Liu & Chen)	Introduction to International Law [24.1%]
	State Territories [11.8%]
	Maritime Law [15.9%]
	Aviation Law [3.5%]
	International Environmental Law [2.7%]
	Individuals Under International Law [12.6%]
	Treaties [6.2%]
	International Economic Law [12%]
	International Human Rights Law [5.4%]
	War and Neutrality [4.1%]
International Law (Wang)	Introduction [6.6%]
	Basic Principles Under International Law [2.5%]
	Subjects of International Law [5.2%]
	Rights and Obligations of a State Under International Law [5.2%]
	State Responsibilities [4.6%]
	Residents Under International Law [3.7%]
	International Protection of Human Rights [5.2%]
	Territories Under International Law [3.9%]
	Maritime Law [5.4%]
	Air Space and Aviation [4.8%]
	Outer Space Law [5.2%]
	Diplomatic and Consular Relations [6%]
	Treaties [6.2%]
	International Protection of Environment [5.8%]
	International Economic Law [5.2%]
	International Organizations [7.1%]
	International Dispute Settlement [6.8%]
	War and Armed Conflict Law [7.1%]

Name of Book	Title of Chapter [% of Book]
	FRENCH BOOKS
Droit International Public (Dallier, Forteau, & Pellet)	History of International Law [3%]
	Theory of International Law [3%]
	Conclusion of Treaties [4.7%]
	Validity of Treaties [2%]
	Application of Treaties [5.8%]
	End of Conventional Norms [2%]
	"Spontaneous" Modes of Formation [2.3%]
	Voluntary Modes of Formation [2.8%]
	Means of Determination of Rules of Law [1.1%]
	Definition of the State in International Law [4.4%]
	Competences of the State [4.1%]
	Formation and Transformation of the State [4.4%]
	International Organizations (General Theory) [5%]
	Private Persons [7.9%]
	Diplomatic and Consular Relations [1.7%]
	International Responsibility of the States and the International Organizations [5.2%]
	Non-Judicial Dispute Settlement [4.3%]
	Limitation to the Use of Constraint [4.4%]
	Peacekeeping and Maintaining of International Security [4.3%]
	General Characteristics of the Law of Economic Relations [2.4%]
	Monetary and Financial Relations [3.6%]
	International Flow of Goods and Services [2.2%]
	The Sea [5.9%]
	International Channels, Rivers, and Lakes [1.8%]
	Air and Outer Space [2.2%]
	General Characteristics of Environmental International Law [2.9%]
	Sectoral Approaches [1.9%]
Droit International Public (Combacau & Sur)	International Relations and Law [5.4%]
	Elements of Formation of International Law [8.9%]
	International Law of Treaties [7.2%]
	Techniques of Application of International Law [7.5%]
	The State in International Law [11.3%]
	Domestic Subjects in International Law [11.8%]
	Status and International Condition of Spaces [6.4%]
	International Regimes of the Use of Spaces [9.4%]
	The International Responsibility of the State [5%]

(*Continued*)

TABLE 13 (Continued)

Name of Book	Title of Chapter [% of Book]
	Law of International Litigation [8%]
	Law of Peace and International Security [12.1%]
	Law of International Organizations [5.1%]
Droit International Public (Dupuy & Kerbrat)	The International Society and Its Law [3%]
	The State [15.4%]
	International Organizations [7.3%]
	Private Persons [6.8%]
	Traditional Modes of Formation of International Law [12.3%]
	Constancies and Evolutions of Modes of Formation of Contemporary International Law [4.6%]
	Application of International Law in the Domestic Legal Order [5.5%]
	Application of International Law in the International Legal Order [11.8%]
	Pacific Dispute Resolution and Avoidance of the Use of Force [14.9%]
	Trade Regulation and the Promotion of Development [8%]
	The Use of International Areas and the Management of the Humanity's Resources, Including the Environment [7.9%]

RUSSIAN BOOKS

International Law (3d ed.) (Kovalev & Chernichenko)	Foundation and Development of International Law [0.98%]
	Notions, Peculiarities, and the System of International Law [1.7%]
	Norms and Principles of International Law [3.2%]
	Sources of International Law [1.7%]
	The Relationship between International and Domestic Law [2.8%]
	International Law in the National Legal System [6.7%]
	Subjects of International Law [3.4%]
	The Population and International Law [2.4%]
	Territory and International Law [2.2%]
	Use of Force and Responsibility in International Law [1.6%]
	The Law of International Treaties [3.5%]
	International Human Rights Law [6.2%]
	International Maritime Law [8.1%]
	International Airspace Law [3.1%]
	International Space Law [1.3%]
	International Economic Law [10.1%]
	International Environmental Law [2.2%]
	International Cooperation in the Fight against Crime and Terrorism [5.1%]
	Diplomatic Law [3.3%]

Name of Book	Title of Chapter [% of Book]
	International Summits [3.1%]
	The Law of the European Union [3.8%]
	Peaceful Resolution of International Disputes [2.8%]
	The Law of International Security [3.2%]
	The Law of Armed Conflict [3.8%]
	International Criminal Law [4.8%]
International Law (Shumilov)	The History of International Law [3.4%]
	The Theory of International Law [15.2%]
	The Relationship Between International and Domestic Law [8.2%]
	International Law in the International Armed-Political System [12.2%]
	International law in the International Economic System [34.5%]
	International Law in the International Socio-Cultural System [6.7%]
	International Law and Different Types of Territory [4.5%]
	International Courts[5.7%]
	Law of Treaties [1.3%]
International Law (Tolstykh)	Notions and Peculiarities of International Law [1.8%]
	History of International Law [2.9%]
	History of the Study of International Law [2.5%]
	Development of International Law in Russia [2.1%]
	Norms of International Law [4.9%]
	Sources of International Law [4.7%]
	International Law and Domestic Law [3.3%]
	Law of International Treaties [4.1%]
	Types of Subjects of International Law [6.2%]
	Jurisdiction and International Law [1.7%]
	Recognition and Succession [4.6%]
	International Organizations [3.1%]
	Resolving International Disputes [7.7%]
	International Legal Responsibility [4.7%]
	Law of International Security [4.7%]
	International Human Rights Law [3.3%]
	International Legal Questions About Citizenship [3.3%]
	International Humanitarian Law [5.5%]
	Foreign Relations Law [3.3%]
	Territory and International Law [3.3%]
	International Law of the Sea [4.5%]

(Continued)

TABLE 13 (Continued)

Name of Book	Title of Chapter [% of Book]
	International Airspace Law [1.2%]
	International Space Law [1.4%]
	International Environmental Law [2.7%]
	International Economic Law [2.6%]
International Law (Vylegzhanin)	Notions of International Law, Its Study, Subjects, and System [1.9%]
	History of International Law and Its Study [3.4%]
	Sources of International Law [1.8%]
	Principles of International Law [1.8%]
	The Subjects of International Law [1.4%]
	International Laws of Recognition and Succession of Governments [2.0%]
	Territories (General International Legal Questions) [1.2%]
	Legal Regime of the Arctic [2.6%]
	Legal Regime of Antarctica [2.1%]
	The International Legal Regime of the Caspian [1.3%]
	International Legal Questions of Citizenship, Human Rights Defense, and Freedoms [6.7%]
	The Law of International Treaties [3.3%]
	The Law of International Organizations [9.7%]
	International Summits (International Legal Questions) [1.1%]
	Peaceful Resolution of International Conflicts [3.3%]
	Responsibility in International Law [2.7%]
	Diplomatic Law [2.1%]
	Consular Law [3.1%]
	International Legal Bases for the Protection of the Environment [3.3%]
	International Humanitarian Law [4.7%]
	The Law of International Security [6.7%]
	The International Legal Bases for the Fight Against Crime [4.7%]
	International Law of Mass Information [1.9%]
	International Law of the Sea [4.5%]
	International Air Law [3.3%]
	International Space Law [3.1%]
	The Beginning of International Economic Law [10%]

Name of Book	Title of Chapter [% of Book]
International Law: A Russian Introduction (Kuznetsov & Tuzmukhamedov)	Concise Survey of Origin and Development of International Law, Russia and International Law [2.3%]
	Concept, Peculiarities, and System of International Law [2.7%]
	Subjects of International Law [4.8%]
	Sources of International Law [3.8%]
	Law of International Treaties [4.8%]
	Principles of International Law [5.1%]
	International Law and National Law: Correlation and Interaction [4.9%]
	Population and International Law [4.5%]
	International Protection of Human Rights [3.9%]
	International Legal Responsibility [4.5%]
	Peaceful Settlement of Disputes [2.7%]
	International Court of Justice [2.2%]
	International Security and International Law [2.6%]
	Foreign Relations Law [3.8%]
	International Organizations and International Law [5.0%]
	Territories and Boundaries in International Law [4.9%]
	International Law of the Sea [4.9%]
	International Air Law [4.2%]
	International Space Law [2.0%]
	International Economic Law [5.1%]
	International Ecological Law [4.6%]
	International Law Enforcement [4.3%]
	Law of Armed Conflicts: International Humanitarian Law [4.9%]
	Disarmament and Concomitant Measures in International Law [2.3%]
	European Law [5.1%]
UK BOOKS	
International Law (Evans)	A Short History of International Law [3.4%]
	What Is International Law For? [3.1%]
	Wicked Heresies or Legitimate Perspectives? Theory and International Law [4.4%]
	The Sources of International Law [3.2%]
	Soft Law in International Law-Making [2.2%]
	International Law and "Relative Normativity" [3.7%]
	The Practical Working of the Law of Treaties [3.7%]

(Continued)

TABLE 13 (Continued)

Name of Book	Title of Chapter [% of Book]
	Statehood, Self-Determination, and Recognition [5.8%]
	International Organizations [3.8%]
	The Individual and the International Legal System [3.4%]
	Jurisdiction [3.2%]
	International Law and Restraints on the Exercise of Jurisdiction by National Courts of States [4.7%]
	Immunities Enjoyed by Officials of States and International Organizations [3.7%]
	The Relationship Between International and National Law [3.5%]
	The Nature and Forms of International Responsibility [3.7%]
	Issues of Admissibility and the Law on International Responsibility [3.8%]
	The Responsibility to Protect [3.2%]
	Countermeasures and Sanctions [3.3%]
	The Means of Dispute Settlement [3.2%]
	The International Court of Justice [3.4%]
	The Use of Force and the International Legal Order [4.3%]
	The Law of the Sea [4.3%]
	International Environmental Law [4.1%]
	International Economic Law [3.5%]
	International Criminal Law [3.8%]
	International Protection of Human Rights [3.5%]
	The Law of Armed Conflict (International Humanitarian Law) [4.1%]
International Law (Shaw)	The Nature and Development of International Law [3.2%]
	International Law Today [2.0%]
	Sources [4.5%]
	International Law and Municipal Law [5.0%]
	The Subjects of International Law [5.3%]
	The International Protection of Human Rights [6.0%]
	The Regional Protection of Human Rights [3.9%]
	Individual Criminal Responsibility in International Law [3.5%]
	Recognition [3.2%]
	Territory [5.0%]
	The Law of the Sea [6.9%]
	Jurisdiction [3.9%]
	Immunities from Jurisdiction [6.1%]
	State Responsibility [5.0%]

Name of Book	Title of Chapter [% of Book]
	International Environmental Law [4.4%]
	The Law of Treaties [4.1%]
	State Succession [4.1%]
	The Settlement of Disputes by Peaceful Means [3.5%]
	The International Court of Justice [4.6%]
	International Law and the Use of Force by States [3.7%]
	International Humanitarian Law [2.7%]
	The United Nations [5.8%]
	International Institutions [3.6%]
Brownlie's Principles of Public International Law (Crawford)	Preliminary Topics [14.5%]
	Personality and Recognition [11.4%]
	Territorial Sovereignty [6.7%]
	Law of the Sea [10.1%]
	The Environment and Natural Resources [4.4%]
	International Transactions [10.3%]
	State Jurisdiction [8.0%]
	Nationality and Related Concepts [3.9%]
	The Law of Responsibility [8.9%]
	The Protection of Individuals and Groups [11.2%]
	Disputes [10.6%]
Cases and Materials on International Law (Harris)	Introduction [1.2%]
	The Sources of International Law [5.2%]
	International Law and Municipal Law [3.4%]
	Personality [8.2%]
	Territory [7.2%]
	State Jurisdiction [10.6%]
	The Law of the Sea [11.3%]
	State Responsibility [13.0%]
	Human Rights [11.7%]
	The Law of Treaties [9.6%]
	The Use of Force [12.8%]
	Arbitration and Judicial Settlement of Disputes [5.8%]

US BOOKS

International Law: Cases and Materials (Damrosch)	Nature of International Law [3.4%]
	Sources: Customary International Law [4.3%]
	The Law of Treaties [7.2%]
	Other Sources of Law [4.3%]
	States [6.7%]
	International and Non-Governmental Organizations [2.8%]

TABLE 13 (Continued)

Name of Book	Title of Chapter [% of Book]
	Individuals and Corporations [3.3%]
	Rules on State Responsibility [3.7%]
	Dispute Settlement [6.2%]
	International Law in National Law [6.7%]
	Bases of Jurisdiction [6.2%]
	Immunity from Jurisdiction [6.8%]
	Human Rights [6.1%]
	Injury to Aliens and Foreign Investors [5.0%]
	Use of Force [11.4%]
	International Criminal Law [4.3%]
	The Law of the Sea [7.4%]
	International Environmental Law [2.2%]
	State Succession [2.0%]
International Law (Carter)	What Is International Law? [7.3%]
	The Creation of International Norms—Treaties, Customary Law, International Organizations, and Private Norm-Creation [5.9%]
	International Law in the United States [11.3%]
	International Dispute Resolution [12.7%]
	States and Other Major International Entities [9.2%]
	Foreign Sovereign Immunity and the Act of State Doctrine [8.8%]
	Allocation of Legal Authority Among States [7.3%]
	International Human Rights and Responsibility for Injuries to Aliens [7.9%]
	Law of the Sea [5.7%]
	International Environmental Law [4.5%]
	Use of Force and Arms Control [13.2%]
	International Criminal Law [6.2%]
International Law: Norms, Actors, Process (Dunoff)	Tracing the Evolution of International Law Through Two Problems [3.1%]
	Making Law in a Decentralized System [7.0%]
	The Traditional Actors: States and International Organizations [8.0%]
	The Challenge of Non-State Actors [4.9%]
	International Law in the Domestic Arena [8.4%]
	The Reach of Domestic Law in the International Arena: Jurisdiction and Its Limits [7.2%]
	The Claims of Individuals on States: International Human Rights [8.8%]

Name of Book	Title of Chapter [% of Book]
	Mitigating the Harms of War: International Humanitarian Law [7.4%]
	Individual Accountability for Violations of Human Dignity: International Criminal Law and Beyond [8.0%]
	Responding to the First Global Commons Issue: The Law of the Sea [5.9%]
	Protecting the International Environment [6.7%]
	Managing the World Economy [5.0%]
	The Use of Force [8.1%]
	Conceptual Challenges to International Law: Legitimacy, Relevance, and Justice [11.5%]

Chinese Research Funding by Topic

The National Social Science Fund of China (NSSFC) puts out a call for proposals for academic funding every year and provides a list of "Recommended Research Topics." It is possible to locate online the NSSFC's Recommended Research Topics for 2009–14, as well as the list of Funded Research Proposals for 2007–14 (reproduced below). For references, see Chapter 5.I.B.

My Chinese research assistants and I went through the list of law topics and identified public international law subjects that were recommended for research or selected for funding. One research assistant made the initial selections and translated them, and they were then double-checked by a second research assistant. I narrowed these selections by removing topics that did not appear to form part of public international law, and these were checked by a third Chinese research assistant. Typically, only the titles of the projects were included, so it was not always possible to tell whether topics simply involved international issues or also implicated international law. This applied in particular to topics about the global economic order and international financial regulation. It is also possible that some topics had a significant international law dimension without its being obvious from the title.

After identifying these topics, I organized them into groupings, such as international economic law, law of the sea, and international human rights law. This process required some judgment calls: there was discretion about which headings to use; not everyone would agree on which topic should be placed under which heading; and some topics could conceivably have been listed under two or more headings. So that people can form their own views, a complete list is provided below with the original Chinese followed by English translations.

TABLE 14

List of Recommended Research Topics by the National Social Science Fund of China (2009–14)

Ref.	Topic	Year
INTERNATIONAL ECONOMIC LAW—TRADE, INVESTMENT, AND OTHER		
1.	跨太平洋伙伴关系协议 (TPP) 相关法律问题研究 [Studies on the Relevant Legal Issues on the Trans-Pacific Partnership Agreement (TPP)]	2014
2.	世界贸易组织中国涉诉案件的法律分析 [Legal Analysis on Lawsuits Involving China in the WTO]	2014
3.	上海合作组织能源俱乐部法律机制研究 [Studies on the Legal Framework of the Shanghai Cooperation Organization Energy Club]	2014
4.	上海合作组织框架下贸易投资便利化法律机制研究 [Studies on the Legal Instruments for Trade and Investment Facilitation Within the Shanghai Cooperation Organization]	2014
5.	《与贸易有关的知识产权协议》(TRIPS) 框架下中国药品试验数据保护制度研究 [Studies on Data Protection Mechanisms for Pharmaceutical Experiments in China Under the TRIPS Agreement]	2013
6.	WTO 体制下烟草控制与贸易争端问题研究 [Studies on Tobacco Control and Trade Disputes Under the WTO]	2013
7.	跨境经济合作区法律问题研究 [Studies on the Legal Issues on Cross-Border Economic Cooperation Zones]	2013
8.	双边投资协定发展趋势研究 [Studies on the Trends in the Making of Bilateral Investment Treaties]	2013
9.	建立国际经济新秩序重大法律问题研究 [Studies on the Major Legal Issues on the Construction of a New International Economic Order]	2013
10.	全球治理视野下的国际金融软法研究 [Studies on Soft Law in International Finance from the Perspective of Global Governance]	2013
11.	全球化背景下我国金融安全的法律保障研究 [Studies on the Legal Mechanisms for Protecting Financial Security in China in the Era of Globalization]	2013
12.	国际金融中心法律保障比较研究 [Comparative Studies on the Legal Institutions of Major International Financial Centers]	2013
13.	WTO 争端解决机制的申诉方利益取向与对策研究 [Studies on the Complainants' Interests and Strategies in the WTO Dispute Settlement Mechanism]	2012
14.	我国出口管理制度改革问题研究 [Studies on Reforming the Export Administration System in China]	2012

Ref.	Topic	Year
15.	应对西方国家贸易保护主义法律问题研究 [Studies on the Legal Issues in China's Response to Trade Protectionism in Western Countries]	2011
16.	对外投资法律保障机制研究 [Studies on the Legal Instruments for Protecting Overseas Investments]	2011
17.	推动国际经济体系改革的法律问题研究 [Studies on the Legal Issues in Promoting Reforms of the International Economic System]	2011
18.	经济全球化与中国法制改革问题研究 [Studies on Economic Globalization and the Reforms on China's Legal System]	2011
19.	WTO 多哈回合谈判未决议题的法律对策研究 [Studies on the Legal Strategies Regarding the Unresolved Issues from the WTO Doha Round Negotiations]	2010
20.	多边贸易体制发展趋势与对策研究 [Studies on the Trends in the Development of Plurilateral Trade Regimes and China's Corresponding Strategies]	2010
21.	国外文化产业促进法研究 [Studies on the Promotion of Cultural Industries in Foreign Legal Regimes]	2010
22.	跨国投资法律制度研究 [Studies on the Legal Regime Governing Cross-Border Investments]	2010
23.	双边投资协定核心条款研究 [Studies on the Core Clauses in Bilateral Investment Treaties]	2010
24.	国际区域经济合作法律机制研究 [Studies on the Legal Instruments for International Regional Economic Cooperation]	2010
25.	WTO 农业协议问题研究 [Studies on the Issues on the WTO Agreement on Agriculture]	2009
26.	WTO 贸易救济法律制度研究 [Studies on the WTO Legal Regime on Trade Remedies]	2009
27.	FDI 法律问题研究 [Studies on the Legal Issues in Foreign Direct Investment (FDI)]	2009
28.	经济全球化与法律 [Economic Globalization and Law]	2009
29.	区域经济合作具体法律制度研究 [Studies on the Legal Regimes for Regional Economic Cooperation]	2009
30.	防范金融风险与金融监管国际合作研究 [Studies on the Management of Financial Risks and International Cooperation in Financial Regulation]	2009
31.	全球化时代的国家经济安全维护研究 [Studies on the Protection of National Economic Security in the Age of Globalization]	2009

(Continued)

TABLE 14 (Continued)

Ref.	Topic	Year
	LAW OF THE SEA	
1.	建设海洋强国背景下的海法体系构建研究 [Studies on Building a System of Maritime Law Under the Context of "Becoming a Great Marine Power"]	2014
2.	中国南海管辖海域权益维护研究 [Studies on the Protection of the China's Interests in the Chinese-Administered Areas of the South China Sea]	2014
3.	海洋强国战略与东海争端冲突法律问题研究 [Studies on the Strategy of "Becoming a Great Marine Power" and the Legal Issues in the Disputes over the East China Sea]	2014
4.	北极航线与中国国家利益的法学研究 [Legal Studies on the Arctic Shipping Routes and China's National Interests]	2014
5.	国际海洋法在解决我国南海权益争端中的应用研究 [Studies on the Application of the Law of the Sea in Resolving China's Disputes in the South China Sea]	2013
6.	水下文化遗产的管辖与归属研究 [Studies on the Jurisdictional and Ownership Issues in Underwater Cultural Heritage]	2013
7.	东亚海洋环境合作机制研究 [Studies on the Mechanisms for Marine Environmental Cooperation in East Asia]	2013
8.	国际反避税合作法律问题研究 [Studies on the Legal Issues in International Cooperation Against Tax Avoidance]	2012
9.	中国拥有南沙群岛的法律制度研究 [Legal Studies on China's Sovereignty over the Nansha Islands]	2012
10.	国际海底区域矿产资源开发法律问题研究 [Studies on the Legal Issues in Mineral Exploration in the International Seabed Area]	2012
11.	中国东海和南海油气资源开发问题研究 [Studies on China's Exploitation of Oil and Gas Resources in the East China Sea and the South China Sea]	2011
12.	海洋矿产资源开发中的国际法问题研究 [Studies on the International Legal Issues in the Exploitation of Marine Mineral Resources]	2011
13.	国际海洋法的发展与完善研究 [Studies on the Evolution of the Law of the Sea]	2011
14.	我国管辖海域法律问题研究 [Studies on the Legal Issues on China's Jurisdictional Waters]	2010
15.	国际海洋法的发展和完善研究 [Studies on the Evolution of the Law of the Sea]	2009
16.	海上执法问题研究 [Studies on Maritime Law Enforcement]	2009

Ref.	Topic	Year
	INTERNATIONAL ENVIRONMENTAL LAW	
1.	跨界河流开发利用的国际环境法律问题研究 [Studies on the Issues in International Environmental Law on the Commercial Exploitation of Transboundary Rivers]	2014
2.	海洋生态损害国家索赔制度构建研究 [Studies on the Design of a Public Enforcement Regime for Damages to Marine Ecology]	2013
3.	碳关税法律问题研究 [Studies on the Legal Issues in a Carbon Tariff]	2012
4.	环境保护与国际贸易的关系研究 [Studies on the Relations Between Environmental Protection and International Trade]	2011
5.	淡水资源的国际保护研究 [Studies on the International Protection of Freshwater Resources]	2011
6.	跨界损害问题的归责与赔偿研究 [Studies on the Attribution and Compensation of Transboundary Harm]	2011
7.	气候变化与技术创新及转让问题研究 [Studies on Climate Change and Technological Innovation and Transfer]	2011
8.	气候变化背景下碳捕捉与储存利用法律问题研究 [Studies on the Legal Issues in Carbon Capture, Utilization, and Storage]	2011
9.	气候变化与国际贸易法律问题研究 [Studies on the Legal Issues in Climate Change and International Trade]	2010
10.	科学发展观与国际资源环境法研究 [Studies on the Scientific Outlook on Development and International Environmental Law]	2009
	INTERNATIONAL HUMAN RIGHTS LAW	
1.	国际人权对话与合作机制研究 [Studies on the Mechanisms for Engagement and Cooperation on International Human Rights]	2014
2.	国际人权法律制度的发展和完善研究 [Studies on the Evolution of International Human Rights Law]	2011
3.	国际人权公约的履约研究 [Studies on States' Compliance with International Human Rights Conventions]	2011
4.	少数人权利保护研究 [Studies on the Protection of the Human Rights of Minorities]	2011
5.	难民权利保护问题研究 [Studies on the Protection of Refugee Rights]	2011
6.	残疾人社会福利保障制度的国际比较研究 [Studies on Comparative Social Welfare Protection for the Disabled]	2010
7.	国际人权法新问题研究 [Studies on the Emerging Issues in International Human Rights Law]	2010
8.	人权法理论研究领域 [The Jurisprudence of Human Rights Law]	2009
9.	区域性人权保护制度研究 [Studies on the Regional Mechanisms for Human Rights Protection]	2009

(Continued)

TABLE 14 (Continued)

Ref.	Topic	Year
	INTERNATIONAL AND TRANSNATIONAL CRIMINAL LAW	
1.	和谐世界语境下刑事法治国际化研究 [Studies on the Internationalization of Criminal Law Under the Context of the "Harmonious World"]	2013
2.	《联合国反腐败公约》的适用研究 [Studies on the Application of the United Nations Convention Against Corruption]	2011
3.	国际刑法与国际刑事法院研究 [Studies on International Criminal Law and the International Criminal Court]	2011
4.	国际刑事公约在国内法中的贯彻研究 [Studies on the Incorporation of International Criminal Law Treaties in Domestic Law]	2010
5.	刑事司法协助法研究 [Studies on Judicial Assistance in Criminal Matters]	2010
6.	国际刑事诉讼法律制度研究 [Studies on International Criminal Procedures]	2010
7.	反腐败国际刑事合作机制研究 [Studies on International Criminal Anti-Corruption Cooperation]	2009
	TERRORISM	
1.	中外反恐立法比较研究 [Comparative Studies on Anti-Terrorism Legislation]	2014
2.	国际恐怖主义犯罪研究 [Studies on International Terrorism Crimes]	2011
3.	国际领域内打击恐怖主义的协作机制研究 [Studies on the Mechanisms for International Cooperation in Combating Terrorism]	2011
4.	惩治与防范恐怖主义犯罪研究 [Studies on Preventing and Punishing Terrorist Crimes]	2010
5.	恐怖犯罪惩治与防范研究 [Studies on the Punishment and Prevention of Crimes of Terror]	2009
	PROTECTION OF OVERSEAS INTERESTS AND CITIZENS	
1.	维护我国海外合法权益研究 [Studies on the Protection of China's Legitimate Overseas Interests]	2013
2.	海外利益法律保护的中国模式研究 [Studies on the Chinese Model on the Legal Protection of Overseas Interests]	2013
3.	海外利益保护法律问题研究 [Studies on the Legal Issues in the Protection of Overseas Interests]	2010
4.	中国公民境外保护问题研究 [Studies on the Overseas Protection of Chinese Citizens]	2009

Ref.	Topic	Year
	OTHER CHINA-SPECIFIC TOPICS	
1.	我国在国际法发展中的立场与话语权研究 [Studies on China's Position and Influence in the Evolution of International Law]	2014
2.	我国法律外交战略研究 [Studies on China's Strategies in Legal Diplomacy]	2014
3.	国际法治发展趋势及对我国和平发展的影响研究 [Studies on the Trends in the Evolution of International Rule of Law and Its Impact on China's Peaceful Development]	2011
4.	我国陆地边界法律问题研究 [Studies on the Legal Issues on China's Land Borders]	2010
	INTERNATIONAL DISPUTE RESOLUTION	
1.	当代国际争端解决的国际法新议题与中国对策研究 [Studies on the Emerging International Legal Issues in International Dispute Resolution and China's Response and Strategy]	2013
2.	国际争端解决机制的新发展与中国对策研究 [Studies on the Development of International Disputes Resolution and China's Response and Strategy]	2012
3.	国际裁判机构的兴起及其对国际法的影响研究 [Studies on the Rise of International Adjudication and Its Impact on International Law]	2010
	SECURITY COUNCIL	
1.	安理会决议在中国执行问题研究 [Studies on the Implementation of Security Council Resolutions in China]	2014
2.	联合国集体安全机制的改革与完善研究 [Studies on the Reform of the UN Collective Security System]	2011
3.	集体安全体制与国际法研究 [Studies on the UN Collective Security System and International Law]	2009
	CULTURAL HERITAGE	
1.	文化遗产的国际法保护研究 [Studies on the International Legal Protection of Cultural Heritage]	2011
2.	文化表现多样性的国际法律制度建设研究 [Studies on the Construction of the International Legal Regime on Cultural Diversity]	2009
3.	文化财产的跨国流转与返还法律问题研究 [Studies on the Legal Issues in the Cross-Border Transfer and Repatriation of Cultural Assets]	2009

(Continued)

TABLE 14 (Continued)

Ref.	Topic	Year
	TAIWAN	
1.	"一国两制"与台湾问题研究 [Studies on "One Country, Two Systems" and the Taiwan Issue]	2012
2.	推进两岸关系和平发展的法律问题研究 [Studies on the Legal Issues in Promoting the Peaceful Development of Cross-Strait Relations]	2011
	INTERNATIONAL LAW IN CHINA'S DOMESTIC SYSTEM	
1.	国内法治与国际法治的互动研究 [Studies on the Interaction Between Domestic Rule of Law and International Rule of Law]	2014
2.	国际条约对国内影响的评估机制研究 [Studies on the Appraisal Mechanisms for Assessing the Domestic Impact of International Treaties]	2010
	OTHER TOPICS	
1.	区域一体化法律问题研究 [Studies on the Legal Issues in Regional Integration]	2013
2.	时际法的理论与国际实践研究 [Studies on the Theory and International Practice of Intertemporal Law]	2013
3.	后冷战时期的国际法律秩序问题研究 [Studies on the International Legal Order in the Post-Cold War Era]	2012
4.	实施互利共赢开放战略的国际法律问题研究 [Studies on the International Legal Issues in Implementing the "Mutual Benefit and Opening-up" Strategy]	2011
5.	国家主权权利的发展与限制研究 [Studies on the Evolution of States' Sovereign Rights and Their Limits]	2011
6.	国际法体系化研究 [Studies on the Systematization of International Law]	2010
7.	全球治理法律问题研究 [Studies on the Legal Issues in Global Governance]	2010
8.	国际法基础理论 [Foundational Theories of International Law]	2009
9.	食品安全国际法律制度建设研究 [Studies on the Construction of the International Food Security Legal System]	2009
10.	国家及其财产豁免管辖制度研究 [Studies on the Jurisdictional Immunities of States and Their Property]	2009

TABLE 15

List of Research Topics Funded by the National Social Science Fund of China (2007–14)

Ref.	Topic	Year
	INTERNATIONAL ECONOMIC LAW—TRADE, INVESTMENT, AND OTHER	
1.	《跨太平洋伙伴关系协议》(TPP) 知识产权问题研究 [Studies on Intellectual Property Issues in the Trans-Pacific Partnership Agreement (TPP)]	2014
2.	TPP 投资协议中的争端解决机制研究 [Studies on the Dispute Resolution Mechanism in TPP Investment Treaties]	2014
3.	WTO 争端解决机制中国败诉的原因及对策分析 [Analysis on Explaining China's Losing Suits Under the WTO Dispute Settlement Mechanism and the Corresponding Strategies]	2014
4.	世界贸易组织中国涉诉案例的裁判生成与指导制度研究 [Studies on the Guiding Principles Informing the Judgments in WTO Cases Involving China]	2014
5.	世贸组织裁决的国内执行问题研究 [Studies on the Domestic Implementation of WTO Rulings]	2014
6.	国际投资协定发展趋势研究 [Studies on the Recent Trends in International Investment Treaties]	2014
7.	国际投资法的晚近变革及中美中欧投资条约谈判对策问题研究 [Studies on the Recent Developments in International Investment Law and the Strategies for Sino-US and Sino-European Investment Treaty Negotiations]	2014
8.	海外能源投资权利救济保障机制研究 [Studies on the Remedies for the Violation of Investors' Rights in Overseas Energy Investments]	2014
9.	WTO 补贴与反补贴谈判焦点问题研究 [Studies on the Key Issues in Negotiations on WTO Rules on Subsidies and Countervailing Measures]	2014
10.	国际投资仲裁视角下的海外中资利益保护研究 [Studies on the Protection of China's Overseas Interests from the Perspective of International Investment Arbitration]	2014
11.	上海合作组织能源俱乐部法律机制研究 [Studies on the Legal Framework of the Shanghai Cooperation Organization Energy Club]	2014
12.	美式与欧式跨区域贸易协定比较研究与我国对策研究 [Comparative Studies on American and European Trans-Regional Trade Treaties and China's Corresponding Strategies]	2014
13.	打造升级版背景下中国—东盟自由贸易区物流合作发展法律保障研究 [Studies on the Legal Protection for the Cooperation and Development of the Logistics Industry in the ASEAN-China Free Trade Area (ACFTA)]	2014

(Continued)

TABLE 15 (Continued)

Ref.	Topic	Year
14.	我国参与全球金融治理的法律问题研究 [Studies on China's Involvement in Global Financial Governance]	2014
15.	中非经贸投资纠纷解决机制研究 [Studies on the Dispute Resolution Mechanisms for Sino-African Investment Disputes]	2013
16.	转基因食品国际贸易中维护国家非传统安全的法律策略研究 [Studies on the Legal Strategies for Preventing Non-Traditional Security Threats in the International Trade of Genetically Modified Food]	2013
17.	《与贸易有关的知识产权协议》框架下中国药品试验数据保护制度研究 [Studies on Data Protection Mechanisms for Pharmaceutical Experiments in China Under the TRIPS Agreement]	2013
18.	美国新反补贴税法的违法性与中国对策研究 [Studies on the Illegality of the New US Countervailing Duties and China's Corresponding Strategies]	2013
19.	数字化信息产品交易的 WTO 法律问题研究 [Studies on the Transactions of Information Products Under the WTO]	2013
20.	国际贸易中的数字知识产权执法研究 [Studies on the Enforcement of Digital Intellectual Property Rights in International Trade]	2013
21.	中国 FTA 范式研究 [Studies on a Chinese Model of Free Trade Agreements (FTA)]	2013
22.	世界贸易组织与区域贸易协定间争端解决机制管辖权冲突与调和研究 [Studies on Jurisdictional Conflicts and Coordination Between the WTO and Regional Trade Treaties' Dispute Settlement Bodies]	2013
23.	WTO 法理框架中生态文明理念的建构及中国对策研究 [Studies on the Construction of an "Ecological Civilization" Theory and China's Strategies Under the WTO Jurisprudence]	2013
24.	联合国际法院与世界贸易组织上诉机构条约解释实践的比较研究 [Comparative Studies on the Treaty Interpretation Practices of the International Court of Justice and the WTO Appellate Body]	2013
25.	国际经济秩序的中国立场研究 [Studies on China's Position on the International Economic Order]	2013
26.	主权债务争端解决与中国对策研究 [Studies on the Resolution of Sovereign Debt Disputes and China's Strategies]	2013
27.	国际经济新秩序与主权信用评级制度研究 [Studies on the New International Economic Order and the Sovereign Credit Rating Systems]	2013
28.	国际投资争端解决中的补偿计算研究 [Studies on Calculating the Compensation in International Investment Dispute Resolution]	2012

Ref.	Topic	Year
29.	国际投资争端解决机制最新发展及中国对策研究 [Studies on the Latest Development in International Investment Dispute Resolution Mechanisms and China's Strategies]	2012
30.	WTO 补贴规则与我国产业补贴政策的变革研究 [Studies on the WTO Rules on Subsidies and the Reform of China's Subsidy Policies]	2012
31.	武装冲突环境下中国海外投资保护法律问题研究 [Studies on the Legal Issues in the Protection of China's Overseas Investment During Armed Conflicts]	2012
32.	WTO 体制中成员集团化法律问题研究 [Studies on the Legal Issues in the Rise of Collective Action Between Members of the WTO]	2012
33.	WTO 扩散效应研究 [Studies on the Diffusion Effect of the WTO]	2012
34.	WTO 争端解决机制的申诉方利益取向与对策研究 [Studies on the Complainants' Interests and Strategies in the WTO Dispute Settlement Mechanism]	2012
35.	区域贸易协定争端解决机制: 理论及其条约法实践 [Dispute Resolution Mechanisms in Regional Trade Agreements: Theories and Treaty Law Practice]	2011
36.	中日韩自贸区竞争与反倾销规则协调研究 [Studies on the Coordination of Anti-Dumping Policies Within the China–Japan–South Korea Free Trade Zone]	2011
37.	中国双边投资条约发展研究 [Studies on the Development of China's Bilateral Investment Treaties]	2011
38.	中国双边投资保护条约 (BIT) 的差别化缔约实践法律问题研究 [Studies on China's Differentiated Practice on Bilateral Investment Treaty Negotiations]	2011
39.	国外对华反补贴案例及对策研究 [Studies on the Cases on Foreign Countervailing Duties Against China and China's Corresponding Strategies]	2011
40.	反假冒贸易协定对我国的潜在影响及其对策研究 [Studies on the Prospective Impact of the Anti-Counterfeiting Trade Agreement and China's Strategies]	2011
41.	WTO 争端解决机制的证据规则研究 [Studies on the Evidentiary Rules in the WTO Dispute Settlement Mechanism]	2011
42.	对外投资保护视野下的国际投资仲裁管辖权冲突问题研究 [Studies on the Conflict of Jurisdictions in International Investment Arbitrations from the Perspective of the Protection of Outbound Investments]	2011

(Continued)

TABLE 15 (Continued)

Ref.	Topic	Year
43.	主权财富基金投资法律风险及监管模式研究 [Studies on the Legal Risks of Investing in Sovereign Wealth Funds and Possible Regulatory Regimes]	2011
44.	国际金融法视角下的金融业宏观审慎监管 [Macroprudential Regulation of the Financial Industry from the Perspective of International Financial Law]	2011
45.	推进布雷顿森林机构治理改革的法律问题研究 [Studies on the Legal Issues in Promoting Reforms in the Governance of Bretton Woods Institutions]	2011
46.	经济全球化背景下国际税收行政合作法律问题研究 [Studies on the Legal Issues in International Administrative Cooperation in Tax Matters in an Era of Economic Globalization]	2011
47.	世界贸易组织多哈回合谈判农业未决议题的法律对策研究 [Studies on the Legal Strategies Regarding Unresolved Agricultural Issues from the WTO Doha Round Negotiations]	2010
48.	世界贸易组织争端解决中的审查标准研究 [Studies on the Standards of Review in the WTO Dispute Settlement Process]	2010
49.	《双边投资协定》核心条款的法解释学研究 [Studies on the Legal Interpretation of Core Clauses in Bilateral Investment Treaties]	2010
50.	双边投资协议核心条款研究 [Studies on the Core Clauses in Bilateral Investment Treaties]	2010
51.	区域贸易安排中的所得税问题研究 [Studies on Income Tax Issues in Regional Trade Arrangements]	2010
52.	WTO《农业协定》与我国农业国内支持法律制度研究 [Studies on the WTO Agreement on Agriculture and China's Domestic Support for Agriculture]	2009
53.	多边贸易体制下碳税问题研究 [Studies on the Issue of a Carbon Tax Under the Multilateral Trade System]	2009
54.	自由贸易区的原产地规则问题研究 [Studies on the Rules of Origin in Free Trade Zone Arrangements]	2009
55.	《TRIPS 协定》执行程序刑事部分研究 [Studies on the Criminal Procedures for Enforcing the TRIPS]	2009
56.	自由贸易协定中的知识产权问题及我国的对策 [Studies on Intellectual Property Issues in Free Trade Agreements and China's Strategies]	2009
57.	中国-东盟知识产权保护与合作的法律协调研究 [Studies on the Coordination of Intellectual Property Protection Between China and ASEAN]	2009

Ref.	Topic	Year
58.	国际投资法制中的公共利益保护问题研究 [Studies on the Protection of the Public Interest in International Investment Law]	2009
59.	中国海外投资环境规制的对策研究 [Studies on China's Strategies Regarding the Limitation on Overseas Investment]	2009
60.	主权财富基金国际规制法律问题研究 [Studies on the Legal Issues in the International Regulation of Sovereign Wealth Funds]	2009
61.	WTO 贸易救济权研究 [Studies on Trade Remedies Under the WTO]	2008
62.	"和谐世界"理念下国际知识产权制度重构的若干法律问题研究 [Studies on the Restructuring of the International Intellectual Property System Under the Concept of a "Harmonious World"]	2008
63.	金融期货风险的国际法律控制研究 [Studies on the International Regulation on the Risks in Financial Futures]	2008

LAW OF THE SEA

Ref.	Topic	Year
1.	面向国际争端管控的南海资源共同开发的国际法问题研究 [Studies on the International Legal Issues in the Joint Development of Resources in the South China Sea in the Context of International Dispute Management]	2014
2.	南海无居民海岛开发与保护法律问题研究 [Legal Studies on the Development and Protection of Uninhabited Islands in the South China Sea]	2014
3.	中国东盟海洋生态环境合作与争端解决机制研究 [Studies on the Cooperation in the Protection of the Marine Ecological Environment and the Dispute Resolution Mechanisms Between China and ASEAN]	2014
4.	中国拥有南沙群岛主权证据问题研究 [Studies on the Evidence Supporting China's Sovereignty over the Nansha Islands]	2014
5.	中越南海主权争议的法理研究 [The Jurisprudence on the Sovereignty Disputes over the South China Sea Between China and Vietnam]	2014
6.	南海诸岛位置图的国际法效力研究 [Studies on the Legal Force of the Position Map of the South China Sea Islands in International Law]	2014
7.	海洋强国战略与中日东海争端冲突中的法律问题研究 [Studies on the Strategy of "Becoming a Great Marine Power" and the Dispute over the East China Sea Between China and Japan]	2014
8.	海上防空识别区理论与实践的法律研究 [Studies on the Theories and Practice of Air Defense Identification Zones]	2014

(Continued)

TABLE 15 (Continued)

Ref.	Topic	Year
9.	我国南海权益维护及其两岸合作机制的法律研究 [Studies on the Protection of China's Interests in the South China Sea and the Mechanisms for Cooperation Between Mainland China and Taiwan]	2013
10.	南海岛礁在海域争端中的划界作用研究 [Studies on the Demarcation Effects of Reefs in the Disputes over Waters in the South China Sea]	2013
11.	国际海洋法在南海争端中的适用及其局限问题研究 [Studies on the Application and the Limits of the International Law of the Sea in the Disputes over the South China Sea]	2013
12.	钓鱼岛争端视野下的琉球法律地位问题研究 [Studies on the Legal Status of Ryukyu Islands in the Context of the Diaoyudao Island Dispute]	2013
13.	海洋争端国际仲裁的新发展与中国对策研究 [Studies on the Recent Trends in International Arbitration of Maritime Disputes and China's Strategies]	2013
14.	国际海底区域生物资源商业勘探的法律问题研究 [Studies on the Legal Issues in the Commercial Exploration of Biological Resources in the International Seabed Area]	2013
15.	水霸权、安全秩序与制度构建-国际河流水政治复合体研究 [Hydro-Hegemony, Security Order and Institution Construction: On the International Hydro-Political Complex]	2013
16.	南海低敏感领域合作机制研究 [Studies on the Mechanisms for Cooperation on Less-Sensitive Areas in the South China Sea]	2012
17.	新形势下我国维护南沙群岛主权的法律对策研究 [Studies on the Legal Strategies for Protecting China's Sovereignty over the Nansha Islands Under the New Circumstances]	2012
18.	南沙群岛领海基线划定问题研究 [Studies on Drawing the Baselines for China's Territorial Waters Around the Nansha Islands]	2012
19.	中国拥有南沙群岛主权法律问题研究 [Studies on the Legal Issues in China's Sovereignty over the Nansha Islands]	2012
20.	无居民海岛使用权研究 [Studies on the Right to Use Uninhabited Islands]	2012
21.	中日东海大陆架划界国际法问题研究 [Studies on the International Legal Issues in the Demarcation of the Continental Shelf in the East China Sea Between China and Japan]	2012
22.	南海油气资源开发的法律困境及对策研究 [Studies on the Legal Dilemma in Oil and Gas Exploitation in the South China Sea and the Corresponding Strategies]	2012

Ref.	Topic	Year
23.	国际海底区域矿产资源开发法律问题研究 [Studies on the Legal Issues in the Commercial Exploration of Mineral Resources in the International Seabed Area]	2012
24.	海域使用权流转法律制度研究 [Studies on the Legal Instruments for the Transfer of the Right to Use the Sea Areas]	2012
25.	海洋发展战略中填海造地的法律规制研究 [Studies on the Regulation of Land Reclamation in China's Strategy for Marine Development]	2012
26.	海洋油气开发污染损害赔偿原理与机制研究 [Studies on the Principles and Mechanisms for the Compensation of Marine Pollution Damages from Oil and Gas Exploitation]	2012
27.	钓鱼岛问题与中日争端对策研究 [Studies on the Diaoyu Islands Dispute and China's Response and Strategy on the Sino-Japanese Disputes]	2011
28.	岛屿争端解决中的国际法问题研究 [Studies on the International Legal Issues in the Resolution of Island Disputes]	2011
29.	中国在南海U形线内的历史性权利研究 [Studies on China's Historical Rights Within the U-Shaped Line in the South China Sea]	2011
30.	南海地区国家核心利益的维护策略研究 [Studies on the Strategies for the Protection of China's Core National Interests in the South China Sea]	2010
31.	南海问题及其解决方案法律问题研究 [Legal Studies on the South China Sea Disputes and Possible Solutions]	2010
32.	国际海事法视阈下的索马里海盗问题研究 [Studies on the Somalia Pirates from the Perspective of the Law of the Sea]	2010
33.	海上恐怖主义犯罪及海盗犯罪的刑事规制对策研究 [Studies on the Criminal Rules on Crimes of Piracy and Terrorism on the Sea]	2009

INTERNATIONAL ENVIRONMENTAL LAW

1.	核能安全与环境保护的国际法问题研究 [Studies on the International Legal Issues in Nuclear Power Safety and Environmental Protection]	2014
2.	国际贸易法制视野下的气候公约外多边机制研究 [Studies on Multilateral Mechanisms Outside the Framework of United Nations Framework Convention on Climate Change from an International Trade Law Perspective]	2014
3.	应对气候变化资金机制的国际法问题及其新动向研究 [Studies on the International Legal Issues and the Recent Trends in the Funding Mechanisms for Actions on Climate Change]	2014

(Continued)

TABLE 15 (Continued)

Ref.	Topic	Year
4.	欧盟航空碳排放税的国际法规制和我国对策研究 [Studies on International Legal Issues in the European Airline Carbon Emissions Tax and China's Strategies]	2013
5.	国际法视野下二氧化碳海洋封存问题及规则研究 [Studies on the Issues in Carbon Sequestration in the Ocean from the Perspective of International Law]	2013
6.	国际气候法律新秩序构建中的公平性问题研究 [Studies on the Fairness Issues in the Construction of a New Order in International Climate Law]	2013
7.	欧盟航空碳关税法律研究 [Studies on the Law of the European Union on the Airline Carbon Emissions Tax]	2012
8.	国际气候法律新秩序构建中的公平性问题研究 [Studies on the Fairness Issues in the Construction of a New Order in International Climate Law]	2012
9.	应对气候变化的国际技术转让法律制度研究 [Studies on the Law on International Technology Transfer in the Context of Climate Change]	2012
10.	中国与周边国家水资源合作开发机制研究 [Studies on the Cooperative Development of Water Resources Between China and the Surrounding Nations]	2011
11.	西部国际河流开发与保护法律保障制度研究 [Studies on the Legal Safeguard for the Development and Protection of International Rivers in Western China]	2011
12.	国际河流法的理论与实践 [The Theory and Practice of International Water Law]	2011
13.	中国-东盟能源安全合作法律问题研究 [Studies on the Legal Issues in the Cooperation between China and ASEAN on Energy Security]	2011
14.	跨界损害问题的归责与赔偿研究 [Studies on the Attribution and Compensation of Transboundary Harm]	2011
15.	转基因生物跨界侵权损害赔偿研究 [Studies on the Compensation for Transboundary Harm Caused by Genetically Modified Organisms]	2011
16.	气候变化下中国海外能源投资法律保护研究 [Studies on the Legal Protection of China's Overseas Energy Investment Under the Context of Climate Change]	2010
17.	气候变化与国际粮食贸易中的法律问题研究 [Studies on the Legal Issues in Climate Change and International Grain Trade]	2010

Ref.	Topic	Year
18.	气候变化框架下国际贸易法的创新与我国应对策略研究 [Studies on the Innovations in International Trade Law and China's Corresponding Strategies Under the Context of Climate Change]	2010
19.	气候变化背景下以节能减排为目的的贸易措施与WTO规则的关系: 挑战与回应 [The Relation between the WTO Rules and Trade Measures Aimed at Energy Efficiency and Waste Reduction Under the Context of Climate Change: Challenges and Responses]	2009

INTERNATIONAL AND TRANSNATIONAL CRIMINAL LAW

1.	法治反腐背景下境外追逃问题研究 [Studies on Extraterritorial Pursuits in the Context of Anti-Corruption Under the Rule of Law]	2014
2.	构建中国与ICC刑事法治和谐关系的对策研究 [Studies on the Strategies for Building a Harmonious Relation Between China and the ICC Criminal Justice System]	2013
3.	中国与东盟国家刑事司法协助路径探究 [Studies on the Mechanisms of Judicial Assistance Between China and the ASEAN Countries in Criminal Cases]	2013
4.	国际国内洗钱刑事定罪立法与监管比较研究 [Comparative Studies on the Law and Regulation on International and Domestic Money Laundering]	2012
5.	国际刑事法院的理论与实践 [The Theory and Practice of the International Criminal Court]	2011
6.	联合国反腐败公约在中国适用问题研究 [Studies on the Application of the United Nations Convention Against Corruption in China]	2011
7.	国际刑事法治的发展趋势及对我国和平发展的影响研究 [Studies on the Recent Trends in International Criminal Justice and Their Impact on China's Peaceful Development]	2011
8.	中国刑法贯彻国际刑事公约研究 [Studies on China's Criminal Law's Implementation of International Criminal Conventions]	2010
9.	反跨国拐卖妇女儿童犯罪国际合作机制研究—以大湄公河次区域云南边境一线为例 [Studies on International Cooperation in Combating International Trafficking of Women and Children: The Example of the Yunan Border Areas in the Greater Mekong Subregion]	2010
10.	法人跨国犯罪的国际法问题研究 [Studies on the International Legal Issues on Transnational Crimes Committed by Legal Persons]	2008

(Continued)

TABLE 15 (Continued)

Ref.	Topic	Year
	HUMAN RIGHTS	
1.	人权的普遍性与主体性问题研究 [Studies on the Universality and Subjectivity of Human Rights]	2014
2.	中国参与人权国际合作的法律问题研究 [Studies on the Legal Issues in China's Participation in the International Cooperation on Human Rights]	2012
3.	国际人权民事诉讼中的国家豁免问题研究 [Studies on Sovereign Immunity in International Civil Litigations for Human Rights Violations]	2012
4.	中国接受人权条约个人申诉机制的挑战与机遇研究 [Studies on the Challenges and Opportunities in China's Acceptance of Individual Appeal Mechanisms Under International Human Rights Treaties]	2011
5.	联合国人权理事会普遍定期审议机制研究 [Studies on the Universal Periodic Review Process in the UN Human Rights Council]	2011
6.	人权法意义下的国家义务研究 [Studies on State Obligations Under the Context of Human Rights Law]	2010
7.	国际人权监督与缔约国报告制度发展趋势研究 [Studies on the Recent Trends in International Human Rights Supervisory Mechanisms and Contracting Parties Reporting Systems]	2010
8.	与经济、社会和文化权利相关的国际法实施机制研究 [Studies of the Implementation Mechanisms of International Law on Economic, Social, and Cultural Rights]	2010
9.	自然人流动国际规则研究 [Studies on the Movement of Natural Persons in International Law]	2008
	ARCTIC AND ANTARCTICA	
1.	北极航线与中国国家利益的法学研究 [Studies on the Legal Issues in the Arctic Shipping Routes and China's National Interests]	2014
2.	中国北极权益的国际法问题研究 [International Legal Studies on China's Interests in the Arctic]	2014
3.	中国北极航线战略与海洋强国建设研究 [Studies on China's Arctic Shipping Routes and the Building of "a Great Maritime Power"]	2013
4.	北极国际法律秩序的构建与中国权益拓展问题研究 [Studies on the Construction of an International Legal Order in the Arctic and the Expansion of China's Interests]	2013
5.	中国增强在北极实质性存在的法律路径研究 [Studies on China's Legal Path to Strengthen Presence in the Arctic]	2013

Ref.	Topic	Year
6.	我国权益视角下的北极航行法律问题研究 [Studies on the Legal Issues in Navigation in the Arctic from the Perspective of China's Interests]	2012
7.	中国南极权益维护的法律保障研究 [Studies on the Legal Protection of China's Interests in Antarctica]	2011
8.	海洋法视角下的北极法律问题研究 [Studies on the Legal Issues on the Arctic from the Perspective of the Law of the Sea]	2008

INTERNATIONAL DISPUTE RESOLUTION

Ref.	Topic	Year
1.	国际法上的司法干涉问题研究 [Studies on Interference with the Judiciary in International Law]	2013
2.	跨界含水层国际争端解决国际法机制研究 [Studies on International Dispute Resolution Mechanisms for Transboundary Aquifer Disputes]	2013
3.	国际经济争端解决机制新发展与中国对策研究 [Studies on the Development of International Economic Dispute Resolution Mechanisms and China's Strategies]	2012
4.	国际体育仲裁程序机制专题研究 [Studies on the International Sports Arbitration Procedures]	2011
5.	国际商事仲裁中的国家豁免问题研究 [Studies on State Immunity in International Commercial Arbitration]	2011
6.	国际能源合作开发中的争端解决机制研究 [Studies on the Dispute Resolution Mechanisms in International Cooperation on Energy Development]	2010
7.	体育争端解决中国际法与国内法协调研究 [Studies on the Coordination of International Law and Domestic Law in Sports Dispute Resolution]	2008

PROTECTION OF OVERSEAS INTERESTS AND CITIZENS

Ref.	Topic	Year
1.	海外安全利益法律保护的中国模式研究 [Studies on the Chinese Model for the Legal Protection of Overseas Security Interests]	2013
2.	海外利益法律保护的中国模式研究 [Studies on the Chinese Model for the Legal Protection of Overseas Interests]	2013
3.	境外务工人员权利保障研究 [Studies on the Protection of Overseas Workers' Rights]	2013
4.	海外投资中劳工权保障的法律问题研究 [Studies on the Legal Issues in the Protection of Workers' Rights in Overseas Investments]	2012
5.	中国海外工程承包风险的法律规制研究 [Studies on the Regulation of Risks in China's Overseas Construction Projects]	2012
6.	军队维护国家海外利益法律保障研究 [Studies on the Legal Protection of Troops Protecting a State's Overseas Interests]	2010

(Continued)

TABLE 15 (Continued)

Ref.	Topic	Year
7.	促进与保护我国海外投资的法律体制研究 [Studies on the Legal Regime for the Promotion and Protection of China's Overseas Investments]	2009

CULTURAL HERITAGE

Ref.	Topic	Year
1.	第二次世界大战期间被掠文物返还的法律问题研究 [Studies on the Legal Issues in the Return of Cultural Relics Stolen During the Second World War]	2014
2.	我国水下文化遗产管辖与权属争议问题研究 [Studies on the Disputes on the Jurisdiction and Ownership over China's Underwater Cultural Heritage]	2013
3.	全球化背景下的自由贸易和文化多样性的国际法研究 [Studies on International Law, Free Trade, and Cultural Diversity in an Era of Globalization]	2012
4.	贸易自由化背景下我国文化产业政策法规的发展与改革研究 [Studies on the Development and Reform of China's Policies on Cultural Industries in an Era of Trade Liberalization]	2012
5.	国际法视野下的非物质文化遗产保护问题研究 [Studies on the Protection of Intangible Cultural Heritage from the Perspective of International Law]	2011
6.	国际文化产品贸易公法研究 [Studies on Public International Law on the Trade of Cultural Products]	2011
7.	文物返还的国际法问题研究 [Studies on the International Legal Issues in the Return of Cultural Relics]	2011

INTERNATIONAL LAW IN CHINA'S DOMESTIC SYSTEM

Ref.	Topic	Year
1.	国际条约在中国法律体系中的地位分析与制度设计研究 [Studies on the Role of International Treaties in China's Legal System and the Design of the System]	2014
2.	国际法视域下中国转基因食品安全立法困境与出路研究 [Studies on the Problems and Solutions in China's Legislation on Food Security Regarding Genetically Modified Food from the Perspective of International Law]	2013
3.	中国近代条约执行问题研究 [Studies on the Implementation of Treaties in Modern China]	2011
4.	国际非政府组织在华运作的法律监管问题研究 [Studies on the Regulation on the Operation of International NGOs in China]	2010

INTERNET AND COMMUNICATIONS

Ref.	Topic	Year
1.	新国家安全观视角下的网络主权国际法问题研究 [Studies on Network Sovereignty Under International Law from the New National Security Perspective]	2014

Ref.	Topic	Year
2.	国际法和比较法视角下的互联网监管问题研究 [Studies on Internet Regulation from the Perspectives of International Law and Comparative Legal Studies]	2013
3.	互联网治理中的国际法问题研究 [Studies on the International Legal Issues in Internet Governance]	2011
4.	国际通信法律制度研究 [Studies on International Communications Law]	2008

LEGAL STUDIES ON CHINA'S LAND BORDERS

Ref.	Topic	Year
1.	构建我国周边区域维和机制法律问题研究 [Studies on the Legal Issues in the Construction of a Regional Peacekeeping Mechanism in Areas Surrounding China]	2013
2.	国际法学视角下整合式边境管理法律制度研究 [Studies on Integrated Border Management from the Perspective of International Law]	2013
3.	中印领土争议东段地区的治理机制与社会变迁研究 [Studies on the Governance and Social Changes in the Eastern Part of the Disputed Territories between China and India]	2011

OUTER SPACE LAW

Ref.	Topic	Year
1.	空间碎片造成损害责任制度研究 [Studies on the Liability for Space Debris]	2012
2.	外层空间商业化利用及其法律规制 [The Commercial Exploitation of the Outer Space and the Regulatory Regime]	2009
3.	外层空间非军事化法律机制的构建问题研究 [Studies on the Mechanism Design for Demilitarizing the Outer Space]	2008

SECURITY COUNCIL

Ref.	Topic	Year
1.	多法域环境下安理会制裁决议在我国的执行问题研究 [Studies on the Enforcement of Security Council Sanctions Across Jurisdictions]	2014
2.	中国执行安全会金融制裁决议法律问题研究 [Studies on China's Implementation of Security Council Resolutions on Financial Sanctions]	2011

TERRORISM

Ref.	Topic	Year
1.	全球化信息化社会环境中的新型恐怖活动及其整体法律对策研究 [Studies on New Forms of Terrorist Activities and Overall Legal Strategies in a Globalized Information Society]	2013

OTHER CHINA-SPECIFIC TOPICS

Ref.	Topic	Year
1.	中国国家安全战略的国际法研究 [Studies on International Law and China's National Security Strategies]	2014

(Continued)

TABLE 15 (Continued)

Ref.	Topic	Year
2.	边疆民族地区经济开发与周边国家经济合作法律环境研究 [Studies on the Legal Environment for Economic Development and Cooperation with China's Neighboring Countries]	2012
3.	完善我国的条约保留制度研究 [Studies on Improving the Chinese Approach to Treaty Reservations]	2012
4.	大国视野下中国国际法的若干基础理论问题研究 [Studies on Several Foundational Theories on International Law in China from the Perspective of a Regional Power]	2011
5.	当代国际核政治与我国国家安全研究 [Studies on Contemporary International Nuclear Politics and China's National Security]	2011
6.	近代中国与国际法 [Modern China and International Law]	2011
7.	国家利益视角下的国际法与中国应对策略研究 [Studies on International Law from the Perspective of National Interests and China's Responding Strategies]	2010
8.	我国政府参与全球性治理若干法律问题研究 [Studies on the Legal Issues in the Participation of the Chinese Government in Global Governance]	2010

OTHER TOPICS

Ref.	Topic	Year
1.	二战后世界范围内对日本战犯的首次庭审 [The First War Crimes Trials of Japanese War Criminals after World War II]	2014
2.	国际法治论 [Studies on the International Rule of Law]	2013
3.	条约解释的要素与结构 [The Elements and Structure of Treaty Interpretation]	2011
4.	国际视野下防止公职人员利益冲突法律问题研究 [Studies on Preventing Conflicts of Interest in Government from an International Perspective]	2011
5.	国际法视角下的中日战后历史遗留问题研究 [Studies on the Unresolved Issues of the Sino-Japanese War from the Perspective of International Law]	2010
6.	灾难国际救助的法律问题研究 [Studies on the Legal Issues in International Disaster Relief]	2009
7.	国际法视野下的粮食安全问题研究 [Studies on Food Safety from the Perspective of International Law]	2009
8.	国际法中普遍性法律利益的保护问题研究 [Studies on the Protection of Universal Legitimate Interests in International Law]	2008
9.	国际法上的类比 [Analogies in International Law]	2008
10.	国际法治与和谐世界构建研究 [Studies on Building a "Harmonious World" and the International Rule of Law]	2008

Index

Note: Page numbers followed by "*f*" and "*t*" refers to figures and tables.